WHAT TH
don't TELL YOU
BEING A MOTHER AND
LOOKING AFTER BABIES

1. This book may be kept three weeks.
   It is to be returned on / before the last date
   stamped below.
2. A fine of 20p will be charged for every week
   or part of week a book is overdue.

WHAT THEY *don't* TELL YOU ABOUT BEING A MOTHER AND LOOKING AFTER BABIES

The definitive guide to the first two years

———————————

Nikki Bradford and Jean Williams

HarperCollins*Publishers*

HarperCollins*Publishers*
77–85 Fulham Palace Road
Hammersmith, London W6 8JB

A Paperback Original 1997
1 3 5 7 9 8 6 4 2

A catalogue record for this book
is available from the British Library

ISBN 0 00 638398 X

Set in Stone Serif by
Rowland Phototypesetting Limited
Bury St Edmunds, Suffolk

Printed and bound in Great Britain by
Caledonian International Book Manufacturing Ltd, Glasgow

Contents

Acknowledgements

We are extremely grateful to the following people – all of whom are top experts in their field – for all their professional advice, the generosity with which they gave us their time when they were so busy, and their enthusiasm in helping us find the information we needed to compile this book:

Dr Ivan Benett, Manchester GP

Dr Michael Brush, Honorary Consultant in Biochemistry, St Thomas's Hospital, London

Mr P. Chakravanti, consultant in paediatric immunology at the Portland Hospital for Women & Children, London

Professor Geoffrey Chamberlain, past President of the Royal College of Obstetricians & Gynaecologists

Professor Emeritus of London University, and past President of the Royal College of Obstetricians and Gynaecologists

Professor Martin Curzon, Division of Child Dental Health, Leeds Dental Institute

Mark Evans, past President of the National Institute of Medical Herbalists

Gillian Fletcher, obstetric physiotherapist and postnatal exercise trainer for the National Childbirth Trust

Jackie Fletcher, founder of JABS (Justice, Awareness & Basic Support)

Fiona Ford and Charlotte Evans, University of Sheffield Centre for Pregnancy & Nutrition

Dr Robert Fraser, Senior Lecturer in Obstetrics & Gynaecology at the University of Sheffield

Ann Furedi, Director of the Birth Control Trust

Kevin Ganger, consultant obstetrician, Ashford Hospital, Kent

Gail Goldberg, Senior Research Fellow at the Dunn Nutrition Institute, Cambridge University

Sarah Harvey, health visitor and former midwife

Dr David Haslam, Chairman of the Examining Committee for the Royal College of General Practitioners, and patron of CRY-SIS

Dr Mary Jones, retired, former Head of Leicester Royal Infirmary's PMS clinic

Dr Rachel Joyce, Dept of Public Health Medicine, Merton, Sutton and
  Wandsworth Health Authority
Professor Channi Kumar, Institute of Psychiatry, The Maudsley Hospital,
  London
Alice Laidlaw, paediatric dietician at the Alder Hay Children's Hospital,
  Liverpool
Felicity Lee, vaccination policy co-ordinator for the Society of
  Homeopaths
Susan Lewis-Jones, Consultant Dermatologist at Wrexham Maelor
  Hospital, Wales
Kirstin Limb, Scientific Researcher, Dawbarns Solicitors, King's Lynn
Christine Norton, past Director of The Continence Foundation, now
  Research Nurse at St Mark's Hospital for the Colon & Rectum, London
Dr David Peters, past Director of the British Holistic Medical Society
Dr Andrew Prentice, Head of The Energy Group, Medical Research
  Council, Dunn Nutrition Institute, Cambridge University
Charlotte Preston, former health visitor
Gina Purrman, the Real Nappy Association
Dr Ian St James-Roberts, The Thomas Coram Centre (Institute of Child
  Health) University of London
Stephen Sandler, Director of the Expectant Mother's Clinic, the British
  School of Osteopathy, London
Dr Doria Schmidt, Lecturer in Sexual Therapy, Birkbeck College,
  University of London
Professor Michael Silverman, Head of Paediatric Respiratory Medicine,
  Leicester Royal Infirmary
Dr Alan Stewart, Consultant Clinical Nutritionist, and medical advisor to
  the Women's Nutritional Advisory Service
Andrew Wakefield, Consultant Gastroenterologist at the Royal Free
  Hospital, London
Dr Peter White, Senior Lecturer and Honorary Consultant Psychiatrist,
  St Bartholomew's Hospital, London
The National Eczema Society, The Foundation for the Study of Infant
  Deaths, The National Asthma Campaign and cartoonist Jackie Flemming

**This is the book that tells you all
the things which new mothers usually
have to find out the hard way.**

Complementary Medicine for Mothers and Babies

Complementary therapies such as aromatherapy, homeopathy, herbalism and the Bach Flower Remedies can be extremely helpful for treating and soothing many of the problems you or your baby might experience at some point during the first year. They are especially good for colic, teething, itchiness and sleeping difficulties in babies, and for helping to soothe some of the childhood illnesses. New mothers themselves might find them particularly helpful for tiredness, irritability, post-labour healing, breastfeeding problems and back discomfort, and to help you relax – when you have the time.

Once seen as something you tried as a last resort when ordinary medicine wasn't working, it is now becoming well recognized that these natural therapies have a vital place, either alongside orthodox medicine (as the term 'complementary' suggests), or as a gentle, natural option to try before seeking medical help for non-emergency conditions.

Several of the therapies are gaining considerable respect from doctors in orthodox medicine. Some, such as osteopathy and chiropractic, have been formally regulated by Acts of Parliament; others, including homeopathy, acupuncture and aromatherapy, have been validated by proper medical trials. Several NHS hospitals offer the therapies to patients and staff. These pioneering centres include the Hammersmith Hospital cancer unit in London, the famous Walton Hospital Pain Unit in Liverpool, the Chelsea & Westminster Hospital's HIV unit in London, Addenbrooke's Hospital in Cambridge, and the Royal Devon & Exeter Hospital.

GP support for complementary therapies is also growing fast. Some large practices are employing acupuncturists, osteopaths, massage therapists and healers at their own surgeries. A recent *Which?* survey showed that eight out of 10 GPs have referred patients to a complementary practitioner, and that 80 per cent of people were pleased with the results of therapies they have tried. Another report from the Royal College of General Practitioners in 1995 found that three-quarters of young trainee doctors are so interested in the field that they want to train in at least one complementary therapy themselves, as well as in orthodox medicine.

Complementary therapies work gently and naturally, but need to be treated with respect as they can be powerful. Just because something is natural does not mean you can't do any harm with it if you use it inappropri-

It is vital to ensure that you and your baby or child are treated by a therapist who has completed the appropriate professional training, and who is *fully qualified*.

The Institute of Complementary Medicine, PO Box 194, London SE16 1QZ (0171 237 5165) has a large (but not fully comprehensive) register of properly qualified professional complementary therapists in all the different disciplines, from acupuncture to reflexology. Practitioners' fees range from about £20 for a first session up to £50 (more for a top Harley Street medical homeopath). Many therapists offer fees on a sliding scale based on ability to pay if need be, and reduced rates for babies and children.

Otherwise, check with the therapies' own associations – addresses given below.

ately – you can. It is also important to know that in some circumstances the therapies simply aren't relevant. For instance, if your baby has a roaring bacterial ear infection causing them acute pain, they will need a course of antibiotics and painkilling medication – and quick – rather than some gentle herbal infusions or a rub with essential oils.

In case you haven't come across some of them before, here is a very brief explanation of each of the therapies that appear later in the book.

HOMEOPATHY

Based on the principle of 'like treats like', homeopathic remedies involve giving the person who is unwell minute quantities of the substance which would, in a healthy person, produce the very symptoms you are trying to cure. One example of this is tiny quantities of pollen grains being given to treat a child with hay fever, or traces of coffee (Coffea) to help promote sleep.

Homeopathy also has a very different way of looking at the symptoms of illness. Its practitioners believe that your body knows what it is doing, that symptoms of illness are indications that it is working to try to deal with the cause of the trouble; and that this process should be encouraged and the child or adult supported throughout it, rather than just having those symptoms suppressed, as Calpol would suppress a mild to moderate temperature. For example, conventional treatment for bronchitis would often involve a cough suppressant, whereas a homeopath would see the cough as a healing mechanism and prescribe a remedy which might initially aggravate the cough before helping it to dispel. Homeopathic treatments have been proven in many clinical trials, and are so safe that even tiny babies can benefit from them.

All the remedies suggested in the book, unless otherwise stated, come from top medical homeopath Dr Andrew Lockie, whose practice is in Guildford. His book, *The Family Guide to Homeopathy* (Hamish Hamilton), is a classic for explaining treatments for babies and toddlers in detail.

The British Homeopathic Association, 27a Devonshire Street, London W1N

1RJ (0171 935 2163) for homeopaths who are also medical doctors.

The Society of Homeopaths, 2 Artizan Road, Northampton, NN1 4HU (01604 21400) for non-medically trained homeopaths.

HERBAL MEDICINE

Herbal remedies are made from the *whole*, or part of the whole, of a plant (e.g., its roots, leaves, flowers, bark) rather than just its active ingredient, as in conventional medicine. Different herbs are prescribed for different symptoms, and remedies may be made in the form of an infusion (a mild tea) which is drunk – for a child often a teaspoon or two would be sufficient – a lotion, a tincture (the herbs suspended in alcohol), capsules, or a poultice applied to the affected parts. Common standardized herbal remedies, such as calendula (marigold) ointment or aloe vera gel for soreness and itching, can be bought ready made in health food shops. All remedy suggestions in this book come from Mark Evans, past President of the National Institute of Medical Herbalists. His practices are in Bath.

The National Institute of Medical Herbalists, 56 Longbrook Street, Exeter, Devon EX4 6AH (01392 426022).

CHINESE HERBAL MEDICINE

Though based on the underlying philosophy of ancient Chinese medicine – that for good health there must be a balance maintained within the body between the opposite but complementary forces of Yin and Yang, and that energy (Chi or Qi) imbalances may provoke illness – the method of treatment is similar to ordinary herbal medicine. However, the herbs and plants used – such as kudzurine or fritillaria – are either found in Taiwan or China itself. In adults this form of medicine is often used in conjunction with acupuncture. Chinese herbal medicine for children has recently gained considerable respect for treating severe eczema, even in young babies, but it is not without potential side effects.

The Register of Chinese Herbal Medicine, PO Box 400, Wembley, Middlesex HA9 9SZ (0181 904 1357) for professionally trained practitioners.

CRANIAL OSTEOPATHY

This therapy involves gentle manipulation of the bones of the skull. There are 28, which are not fixed but move slightly, especially in babies and young infants whose fontanelle is not yet closed. The touch used is so light that many people claim they can barely feel it, but most find it soothing and relaxing. The therapeutic movements affect the pulse and pressure of the cerebrospinal fluid which bathes both the brain and the spinal cord. If it is disturbed, for instance by excessive compression of the baby's head as it passes down the birth canal to be born (this can happen in problematic or prolonged labour) or by assisted delivery techniques such as ventouse suction or forceps, it can cause a wide range of difficulties such as colic and sleep disorders, extreme irritability and restlessness. Cranial osteopaths report considerable success with those problems.

The Osteopathic Information Service, PO Box 2074, Reading, Berkshire RG1 4YR (01734 51205).

AROMATHERAPY

Aromatic essential oils or essences are the concentrated, highly scented extracts of flowers, plants, trees and spices. Sometimes referred to as vegetable hormones, they can be diluted in plain carrier oil and massaged onto the body, after which it is thought that small amounts reach the bloodstream and affect the different systems of the body, including the neurological, circulatory and respiratory systems. Under a professionally qualified aromatherapist's advice, these oils can also be added to a warm bath, or mixed with water in a vaporizer or humidifier, turned into steam, and inhaled.

Different oils have different effects on the system – calming, revitalizing, decongestant, antispasmodic, antiinflammatory. They have a gentle action, and in addition to smelling wonderful, a single oil may have more than one property. Several clinical trials have shown, for instance, that Lavender essential oil is anti-infective, calming and sleep promoting. All remedy suggestions in this book have come from Dr Vivienne Lunny, former medical pathologist at the Mount Vernon and Harefield Hospitals, and former head of the Aromatherapy Organizations Council. Her practice is in Stevenage.

The Aromatherapy Organizations Council, 3 Latymer Close, Baybrook, Market Harborough, Leicester (01858 434242).

BACH FLOWER REMEDIES

This is a collection of 38 different remedies made from distillations of British wild flowers and plants, such as chicory, clematis, elm tree, honeysuckle, heather, white chestnut and wild rose. They are named after their creator, an English physician and bacteriologist called Dr Edward Bach. He believed that the dew on these plants and flowers was impregnated with their medicinal properties and began giving it successfully to his patients. When he couldn't collect enough, he made it himself by floating freshly picked flowers and plants in clear water, in bright sunlight.

The remedies are designed to treat the whole child or adult, and are especially helpful for the psychological and emotional aspects of illness which may be just as important as physical symptoms like itchy spots and diarrhoea – e.g., fear, whininess, clinginess, extreme irritability, shock and feeling exceptionally sorry for themselves.

There are many practitioners trained in the use of Bach Flower Remedies, but as they are straightforward to use at a basic level, parents can treat their own babies and children having consulted a book (see below) or attended an introductory seminar (see Useful Addresses for details). Mothers and fathers also have a head start in working out which remedies might help their babies or toddlers because they understand their own child's personality and constitution better than anyone else. The remedies are available in health food shops and independent chemists for about £3 each, as are the books which explain how to use them e.g., midwife Judy Howard's *The Bach Flower Remedies Step by Step*, or *A Guide to Bach Flower Remedies* by Julian Barnard, both published by C. W. Daniel.

The Bach Centre, Mount Vernon, Bakers Lane, Sotwell, Wallingford, Oxon OX10 0PZ (01491 834678); contact for courses and further information.

COLOUR THERAPY

Colour can affect our mood, and – as shown by recent research showing blue light can lower blood pressure, or red flashing lights can treat migraine – is also used to restore health and wellbeing. It can be used in the form of coloured light, clothing or environmental decor, and is based on the theory that each colour, as part of the light spectrum, vibrates at its own frequency. Human cells also vibrate at specific frequencies. It is thought that many types of illness are the result of cells vibrating at the 'wrong' frequency, and that they can be encouraged back into line by the therapeutic use of colour. Colour therapy is used to treat problems such as mood disorders and sleep difficulties as well as serious diseases like cancer and HIV. Babies and children are said to respond well to the gentle effect of colour therapy.

The Institute of Complementary Medicine, PO Box 194, London SE16 1Q2.

ACUPUNCTURE

Acupuncture is founded on the belief that our wellbeing depends on the balance of energy (Chi/Qi) which flows throughout our body along channels beneath our skin called meridians. Both mental and physical conditions such as illness, infection, poor diet, stress, anger and grief can impair the flow of Qi and make us more susceptible to disease and disorder.

Acupuncture should be carried out by a properly qualified practitioner. Contact the British Acupuncture Council to find one in your area (see below).

A course of acupuncture is expensive. Treatments cost from £30 for a first visit and from £15 for consultations thereafter. Normally around 15 treatments are recommended, and although some people feel dramatic benefits after only a few sessions, for others the process is more subtle and may take longer. Normally you should begin to feel some benefit after five treatments.

The British Acupuncture Council, Park House, 206 Latimer Road, London W10 6RE (0181 964 0222) for a qualified practitioner.

NUTRITIONISTS

Your GP should be able to refer your baby or toddler to a nutritionist on the NHS, but NHS dieticians are a dying breed thanks to local health authority resources cuts, and so the waiting list may be long.

A private consultation with a nutritionist ranges from about £20 for a fully qualified practitioner. Call the British Dietetic Association or the Society for Promotion of Nutritional Therapy (see below) for details of one near you with a special interest in infant nutritional problems.

Fees rise to £80 plus for a medically qualified doctor with specialist training in nutrition. These doctors are called clinical nutritionists and your GP needs to write to their professional association at The British Society of Environmental & Nutritional Medicine.

The British Dietetic Association, 7th Floor, Elizabeth House, 22 Suffolk Street, Queensway, Birmingham B1 1LS (0121 643 5483).

The Society for Promotion of Nutritional Therapy, PO Box 47, Heathfield, East Sussex TN21 8ZX (01435 867007).

The British Society of Environmental & Nutritional Medicine, Acorns, Romsey Road, Cadnam, Southampton. Ask you GP to write to them to obtain the name and address of one of their members working in your area. They will be a medical doctor with specialist training in nutrition, probably in private practice. The Society does not respond to letters/enquiries from the general public.

GETTING HOLD OF THE PRODUCTS

Aromatherapy oils
Neal's Yard Remedies, 15 Neal's Yard, London WC2 9DP.
Tel: 0171 379 0705.
Good quality aromatherapy oils and dried herbs by mail order, also available at several retail outlets. Also medicinal herbs. Prices vary considerably depending on what you are buying, but begin at around 50p for 3 oz of dried chamomile flowerheads.

Bodytreats International, 15 Approach Road, London SW20 8BA.
Tel: 0181 395 8696.
Mail order. Essential oils cost from around £3.99 per 15ml bottle of basic lavender, but for the more expensive ones, such as chamomile Blue, prices can be as high as £40.

Homeopathic remedies
The following are mail-order and over-the-counter suppliers of good quality homeopathic remedies, whose trained homeopathic pharmacists can also give basic advice over the phone:

Ainsworths Homeopathic Pharmacy, 36 New Cavendish Street,
London W1M 7LH.
Tel: 0171 935 5330.

Helios Homeopathic Pharmacy, 97 Camden Road, Tunbridge Wells,
Kent TN1 2QR.
Tel: 01892 537254, or 536393 for mail order.
Remedies cost from about £3 per phial of tiny pills or granules.

Medical herbalism
The National Institute of Medical Herbalists, 56 Longbrook Street,
Exeter, Devon EX4 6AH.
Tel: 01392 426022.
Information on your nearest qualified practitioner.

G. Baldwin & Co., Herbalist Health Foods, 173 Walworth Road,
London SE17 1RW.
Tel: 0171 703 5550.
Mail-order suppliers of good quality dried herbs for home use.

Bach Flower Remedies
The Bach Centre, Mount Vernon, Bakers Lane, Sotwell, Wallingford,
Oxon OX10 0PZ.
Tel: 01491 834678.
Information, advice and details of seminars and introductory day courses
on how to use the remedies. Remedies by mail order, starting from about
£2.99 per 15ml bottle.

The remedies are also available from independent chemists, Holland &
Barrett health food shops and Neal's Yard outlets.

Your Baby

Happy, Successful Breastfeeding

If you decide you are going to feed your new baby yourself, your own breastmilk and colostrum (the yellowish white early milk of the first few days after birth) are the perfect foods. This is especially true during the first five months when your baby grows faster than at any other time in their life.

Once you get the hang of it – which you may or may not do right away – breastfeeding is the easiest and most convenient way to feed a baby. You can do it anywhere, any time, with no bottles repeatedly to make up, sterilize, carry about, keep cool and heat up. Breastfeeding is one excellent way to deepen the powerful emotional and physical bond between you and your tiny baby. And, though few people will tell you this beforehand, it feels good – both the gentle action of suckling, plus the hormones and neurochemicals involved in the breastfeeding process, can produce deep calm, peace and a contentment which many women describe as blissful.

However, though breastfeeding may be the most natural thing in the world, it is not totally instinctive and there is no law saying you have to do it perfectly straight away. Feeding your baby yourself is something of a gentle

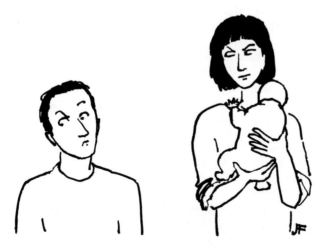

'If you think it's so bloody NATURAL then go and catch me a bison'

skill which new mothers and babies learn together. It is perfectly normal to have one or two problems initially, but virtually all of them can be sorted out easily and quickly.

So, it may take a couple of days or it may take a couple of weeks before you are completely confident, but when you are, you can, as one new mother put it, 'cheerfully feed anywhere in any position. I reckon we could do it hanging upside down from a chandelier if we had to. But for the first few days I was literally crying with frustration because I just couldn't seem to get Luke latched on right, whatever I did.'

You don't need to be a first-time mother to have a slightly rocky beginning to breastfeeding. Even mothers who have breastfed before may find they have to make one or two adjustments the second or third time around because every baby and each set of circumstances is different. Equally, if you had breastfeeding difficulties with your first baby, it does not follow that you will have any next time around.

Often, the secret of successful breastfeeding is the right help when you need it, as often as you need it. It can be that simple. So don't hesitate to ask for support from your midwife or breastfeeding counsellor early on. It does not make any difference whether your breasts are big or tiny, cucumber-shaped or conical, or whether you have inverted nipples, a double nipple, tiny nipples or large ones. Breasts and nipples come in all shapes and sizes and they are virtually all excellent for feeding your baby. According to the World Health Organization, there is hardly ever a physical reason why a woman cannot breastfeed if she wants to: 98 per cent of women can do so if they wish.

If breastfeeding is not for you

However, if you feel strongly that breastfeeding is not for you, or you are having such trouble with it that it is causing you distress – which you may well be communicating to your baby – do not be pressured by well-meaning health professionals or other breastfeeding mothers into carrying on against your better judgement.

'I just hated the sensation,' recalls one mother of three, who is also a health visitor and former midwife. 'It felt so animal-like.'

A new mother from Liverpool said, 'I tried and tried, but Katie just didn't seem to be getting much milk out, and it made my nipples so sore that each feed – and remember there are at least eight a day – was a total misery. I kept thinking *Why am I doing this when I have some perfectly good bottles in*

How many women breastfeed?

Around 65 per cent of mothers try to breastfeed at least once or twice. However, possibly because many do not get the support and help they need when they come up against any initial problems (most of which can be solved quite easily and quickly), this has dropped to 40 per cent by six weeks, and 25 per cent by four months.

the cupboard downstairs? When I finally packed it in after ten days, all I felt was relief.' This mother in fact went on to breastfeed her next child with no difficulties, thanks to some timely help from her community midwife, who somehow managed to drop in every day, for several days.

Many millions of babies have grown up happily and healthily on formula milk. There is no reason why yours should not make that many millions and one. If you feel it's for the best, let it go. Life's too short. Buy six bottles, a bumper tin of formula milk and enjoy your baby. You can feel close, and nurture them just as well when you are cuddling them for a bottle feed as when they are being breastfed. (See How to Stop Breastfeeding, p. 37.)

THE PLUSES OF BREASTFEEDING

The perfect food

Breastmilk provides the perfect nutritional balance for your baby and is the most easily digestible form of milk there is. Your milk and colostrum (pre-milk) are both rich in your own antibodies, so breastfed babies are less likely to catch a wide range of infections such as coughs, colds, bronchitis and gastroenteritis. It is now generally accepted that breastfed babies are also:

- less likely to develop allergies and allergy-related disorders such as asthma and eczema, both of which are becoming increasingly common in babies and infants under two years old,
- have a reduced risk of respiratory infection for the whole of the first year,

even if you stop breastfeeding after a few months. Breastfeeding may also help protect your baby from developing paediatric diabetes and coeliac disease.

Many vitamins and minerals (such as zinc and magnesium, which are important for neurological development) come in higher concentrations in breast milk than formula, and 100 per cent of the protein in breast milk is absorbed by the baby's gut, compared with 50 per cent of the protein in formula. Breast milk contains a fat-digesting enzyme to help the baby's fat absorption, which explains why bottle-fed babies' stools smell stronger – they contain undigested fat.

There is also some evidence that substances in breast milk called Long Chain Fatty Acids contribute to brain and eye development. However, there are no conclusions yet about whether formula manufacturers should add these substances to their milk. One particular study in 1994 by the University

---

If you possibly can, try to breastfeed your baby for at least the first few days, even if you do not carry on. They may only be getting small amounts of colostrum, but this is very rich in antibodies, which will help protect them from infection.

> Breast milk is perfect for babies – and *your* breast milk is perfect for *your* baby. 'No two mothers make the same milk, no two babies need the same milk. Your milk is custom-made to meet the needs of your baby,' says American paediatrician Professor William Sears of the University of South California School of Medicine.

of Tennessee found that when premature babies were given formula milk with LPCs added they had better eyesight and did better on mental development tests at a year old than premature babies who had just been given ordinary formula. And back in 1992 the British Nutrition Foundation published its own report recommending that baby milk manufacturers should add in one special fatty acid but in 1995 only one company, Milupa, had bothered to do so (to their Aptamil and Milupan brands).

There is also research (at the University of Tokyo, for instance) suggesting that breastfeeding is better for tooth and jaw development than bottle-feeding. Bottle-fed babies do not have to work as hard with their tongues as breastfed babies to get the milk flowing, and a bottle-fed baby will also push its tongue forward to prevent milk flowing into its mouth too fast. Some dentists believe this might in some cases contribute to the malpositioning of teeth.

Soothing and bonding

Breastfeeding is a gentle, rewarding way for you and your baby to get to know and love one another and can greatly help the bonding process between you. For some mothers it is instant infatuation on sight anyway, which breastfeeding deepens but does not necessarily initiate, but for others unconditional mother–baby love takes far longer to develop. If this is so for you and your baby, breastfeeding can be a great help. It is also one of the most effective ways to comfort and soothe a crying, discontented, unwell or sleepless baby. Anecdotally, breastfed babies appear less grizzly and more content, which may be explained partially by research carried out in Sweden in 1994 which found that, of the many substances in breastmilk, one closely resembled a very mild form of the tranquillizer benzodiazepine.

Easy and convenient

Breast milk is always available, at the right strength, the right temperature and as much as your baby needs – its make-up changes as your baby becomes bigger and hungrier. You can, social circumstances permitting, feed your baby wherever you are if you are out and about – in the park, on the bus, in the pub, on the beach, at a party, at the local lido (although you may find you are drawing up your own personal list of local pro- and anti-breastfeeding places. Other breastfeeding mothers living near you are good sources of information on this).

If you breastfeed, you do not need to spend time mixing infant feed, washing, sterilizing and storing bottles and teats, and heating up the milk to the right temperature. All this is pretty fiddly, *and* you have to get out of bed and heat up bottles in the middle of the night.

Sleeping better
You may well sleep better and fall back to sleep more quickly after breastfeeding because the let-down reflex hormone oxytocin affects the brain's receptors for a type of opiate-like chemical called dipamine produced naturally by the body. As sleep is so precious to new mothers, this is a major plus.

Makes you feel confident and good about yourself
Many women feel very empowered when they find their bodies can produce the food which nourishes their babies so perfectly and which enables them to grow well and healthily. As one new mother put it, 'I looked at my baby, who had been putting on a steady four to ten ounces a week with no more food than what she took from my breasts, and thought, *I did that, all on my own, for her. Isn't it wonderful?*'

It's physically pleasurable
It makes you feel sleepy, relaxed, peaceful and calm. Many women say it gives them real sensual satisfaction.

Helps the womb recover
Breastfeeding helps your stomach become flatter faster (though this is not the same as losing weight). The hormone oxytocin which is involved in the release of milk from your breasts when your baby suckles causes your womb to contract and tighten, encouraging it to shrink back to its former compact size. Some women experience this as afterpains; see page 23.

Can be a contraceptive
Breastfeeding can be a very effective natural form of contraception if you do it *fully*. Fully means *no* bottles of formula milk, and feeding your baby *on demand* day *and* night. It offers 98 per cent effective contraceptive protection, on a par with the IUD and the progesterone-only pill. But the contraceptive effect weakens *immediately* your baby starts going longer than three to four hours without a feed, day or night. If you especially do not want to

---

Does breastfeeding help weight loss?
Weight loss is often given as an excellent reason for breastfeeding, but there is no real proof that it helps after the first few months. Any encouraging research admits that the amounts lost are pretty small.

However, there is evidence that *longer-term* breastfeeding encourages you to shed a few extra pounds. Longer term means at least six months, according to a report in the prestigious medical magazine *The American Journal of Clinical Nutrition* in 1993.

become pregnant again right away, you may want to think about another form of birth control. (See Postnatal Contraception page 499, for full details.)

Costs less
The final consideration is that breastmilk is free – no small matter if you are on a tight budget, as formula milk costs in the region of £5.29 for a 900g tin, which would last a three-month-old baby drinking five feeds a day made up of 31.5g of formula milk each less than six days.

There might be harmful chemicals in formula milk
Breastmilk may also be best for your baby because of what it *doesn't* have in it.

In May 1996 an uproar developed over the discovery that leading brands of baby formula milk contained unacceptably high levels of certain chemicals which can, in animals at least, damage fertility. Called phthalates, they are widely used in industry to soften plastics such as PVC. Experimental work carried out by the Medical Research Council in 1995 had found that these chemicals damaged the developing testicles of baby rats. Phthalates are also one of the chemicals thought to be connected to the world-wide fall in sperm counts (which have halved over the last fifty years), with certain female fertility problems, and with some types of cancer.

At the time of writing, no one will reveal exactly which brands of baby milk contain these 'gender-bending' chemicals because the Infant & Dietetic Foods Association which represents the formula milk manufacturers is saying nothing: claiming this information is felt to be 'commercially sensitive'. You bet it is. The Ministry of Agriculture is also playing the problem down, claiming the chemicals' levels in baby milks are below the Tolerable Daily Intakes (TDIs). This is not in itself reassuring, as the TDIs were set before any evidence was found of the chemicals' potentially harmful effects. As most books take at least nine months from final writing to appearance in the shops, the issue will have progressed further by the time you read this. For an update contact the NCT, the Baby Milk Action Group or The London Food Commission (see Useful Addresses).

BREASTFEEDING: THE BASICS

How long should I do it for?
The answer you get depends on who you talk to. Some doctors claim six weeks is enough for a good start in life. Most would say six to nine months, meaning at least *some* breastmilk, plus formula, water and food as they get older. The American Academy of Paediatricians suggests a year, the World Health Organization two years.

Physiologically you can breastfeed your child for as long as you both want. Socially, most mothers seem to find the continued nursing of an 18-month-old or two-year-old for a bit of comfort and night soothing unremarkable and acceptable, but begin to feel uncomfortable about the same being offered to a three-year-old, especially if the child is a boy.

The issue of extended nursing can be very emotive and has even been successfully used in American courts of law as evidence that the mother is unfit and harming her child. If you would like to continue nursing your toddler but are having trouble with the reactions from other people, or would just like to talk to someone about it, call up the NCT or La Leche League for support and information. They will also be able to put you in touch with other mothers who have nursed their children for longer than most.

There are several theories about how long you should breastfeed for. One is that breastfeeding should continue until the baby has tripled its birthweight, which usually happens by around twelve months. Another is that all mammals, humans included, should nurse their young for as many weeks or months as they were growing in the womb, which means 40 weeks, or nearly ten months. American anthropologist Professor Kathrine Dettwyler recently published her own estimates based on monkeys, suggesting the optimum time is three years, and pointing out that, biologically speaking, it could be up to *seven* years – news that would make even the most pro-breastfeeding mother blanch. So just what are you supposed to do?

When all is said and done, the only when-to-stop-breastfeeding rule mothers should take notice of is *whenever it feels right for both you and your baby*. Anything between three and 12 months is regarded in Britain as average. With this question, as with so many that arise when you are raising a child, Dr Benjamin Spock's encouraging words ring as true now as when he first wrote them in 1945: 'Trust yourself. You know more than you think you do . . . Whatever good mothers and fathers instinctively feel they should do for their children is usually right.'

It's your baby, so it's up to you. Having read up on the subject and talked to any experts you can find whose suggestions strike a chord with you, take into account other factors such as returning to work, sleep difficulties or even another pregnancy, then make your own decision. And never mind what your mother, friend, doctor or local pro-breastfeeding group says.

How often?
Breastfeeding rigidly by the clock too early on is one very good way to reduce your milk supply. Your own mother was probably encouraged to feed strictly by the clock, which is one reason why our mothers and mothers-in-law are sometimes not as understanding about on-demand feeding as they might be. Very few babies are happy with a rigid feeding plan before they are about six weeks old, and demand-feeding is the easiest way to breastfeed up to this point. But after this it *is* possible, if they are feeding well and gaining weight, to coax them into a four-hourly routine, adjusting it as necessary if they seem particularly hungry, are unwell and need more comfort than usual, or want to be fed little and often for a while. At this stage, if they take a good, full feed each time, it is very unlikely to reduce your supply. Some babies fall naturally into their own four-hourly routine eventually anyway.

Just as four-hourly feeding suits some mothers and babies well, feeding on demand suits others. Neither approach is better or worse than the other. Follow your instincts.

Should I eat and drink more?

You may well feel hungrier and thirstier than usual during the time you are breastfeeding your baby. Drink as much milk, water or diluted fruit juice as you feel you need, but avoid more than one or two cups of tea or coffee a day as they are diuretic and will dehydrate you. You may wish to avoid coffee altogether, as small amounts of the caffeine pass into breast milk and can make your baby restless or irritable.

The Department of Health's figures suggest that if you are breastfeeding your baby fully (no other food, and no bottles) you'd be using up an extra 700 to 870 calories a day. Some women handle this by eating more than usual, others by rushing around less. Do not automatically try to fit in another 800 calories a day (one substantial meal's worth). You probably don't need all that. Be guided by your appetite. If you are really hungry, eat; but do not make yourself eat extra when you do not especially want it because you think you have to. You don't, and you will get back to your pre-pregnancy weight faster if you don't. Go for complex carbohydrate foods and quick snacks such as pasta, baked potatoes, bananas, wholemeal sandwiches or rice dishes as the energy is released slowly and steadily into your system and they keep you going longer (see Beating Exhaustion page 311 for more suggestions), and eat plenty of fresh fruit and veg.

HOW TO BREASTFEED COMFORTABLY AND EASILY

Latching on comfortably

Any new mothers who are finding breastfeeding a bit difficult might like to try the following suggestions. (Breastfeeding comfortably after a Caesarean requires a bit of special care because of the position of the stitches in your abdomen, though it can usually be done very successfully – see page 389.)

- First sit comfortably yourself. A low chair without arms is ideal if you have one. Or try an ordinary chair, making sure you sit straight, supported by a cushion in the small of your back. Put your feet on something – possibly a thick phone directory or another cushion. Some women like sitting cross-legged on the floor, against the bedhead, or on the sofa. Make sure your back is supported.
- Put a pillow on your lap so you do not have to hunch over. Bring your baby's mouth up to your breast, rather than take your breast down towards your baby.
- Turn their whole body towards you, not just their head. Position them so that their nose is on a level with your nipple.
- Brush their mouth with your nipple to encourage them to open wide, as if they are about to yawn. If they are not already turned towards you, try talking softly to them, or stroke their cheek with your finger.
- As soon as you see their mouth opening wide, bring it to your breast with a quick movement of your hand or forearm, whichever is supporting their head.

How to tell if your baby has latched on well

Your baby's cheeks should be rounded outwards with a good mouthful of nipple, areola, and possibly breast too. Their lower lip needs to be curved outwards and downwards, and there should be no audible sucking and slurping noises. If there are, it suggests that your baby is sucking their own tongue and not creating a tight enough seal around your areola.

Do not take too much notice of the standard advice which some health professionals are still giving mothers – that the entire areola should disappear into your baby's mouth. It is only relevant if your areolas are fairly small, about the size of a 2p piece. If they are larger, this is a physical impossibility. Try instead just to get the bottom part of the areola in, with your baby's bottom lip curled down and back.

Latched on well

- Get them to take a large mouthful of breast – as much of the nipple and lower part of the areola (the coloured area around the nipple) as possible. As you do so, draw your baby towards you welcomingly. The nipple should be quite far back towards the top of their mouth, and rather than sucking on the nipple like a straw, they should be almost stroking the milk out of the breast with their tongue. Even if the nipples are sore, if you possibly can, try not to wince or pull away as your baby latches on to you, or the messages you give will be a confusing mixture of welcome and recoil. (See page 34 for help with sore nipples.)
- When your baby has finished feeding they will usually let go of their own accord, but if they have fallen asleep with your nipple still firmly in their mouth, do not try to pull it away as this can make your nipples very sore. Instead, gently slide your (clean) little finger into the corner of their mouth to break the suction.

Conflicting advice

If you find you are getting a great deal of conflicting advice from everyone which is muddling you, try picking one person whom you like and trust, and whose advice rings a bell with you – your community midwife, your mother, a breastfeeding counsellor from La Leche or the NCT, or a close friend who has breastfed – and stick with whatever they suggest. Confusion can be the final straw that finishes off a new breastfeeding mother altogether.

One breast or both breasts?

It makes little difference whether you feed from one breast or both at any one feed. However, if you like to feed from one at one feed, then the other at the next, to remember which one's turn it is for sure, fasten a safety pin on the side the next feed will be from (though often the extra fullness there will tell you).

How do I know my baby is getting enough?

Breasts do not have fluid ounces marked on them, so unlike with bottle-feeding, you can never be sure how much your baby has taken in. It is highly likely that if you let them suckle from each breast at each feed for as long as they seem to want to, they will regulate this themselves. The following five signs all point to the fact that your breastfeeding is going well and your baby is getting all the milk they need:

- They are steadily putting on weight.
- They have pale yellow or clear urine.
- They have at least six wet (not just damp) nappies a day.
- They have regular, soft – but not liquefied – mustard-yellow stools, which look slightly curdled.
- They are breastfeeding well and happily.

Enough for twins?

Do not worry if you have twins and want to breastfeed but fear you will not make enough milk, because you probably will. Breasts make milk in response to being suckled upon because demand regulates supply. If you are the mother of twins and are breastfeeding, it is likely that you will be making twice as much milk as the mother of a single baby. If you are having difficulties or find feeding two babies seems to be tiring you, talk to TAMBA for advice and support.

EXPRESSING MILK AND MIXED FEEDING

Expressing is a very useful technique to learn because, first, it can be helpful to relieve pressure in your breasts if they are becoming overfull or engorged (see page 26 below), and, secondly, it gives breastfeeding mothers some freedom of movement as their partner or another carer can give their baby the expressed milk in a bottle. You may want to think about doing this if, for instance, you want an uninterrupted stretch of five or six hours' night sleep, or if you would like to go out for a while without feeling pressured to be back in time to feed your baby.

A bottle teat is not really that similar to a mother's nipple, no matter

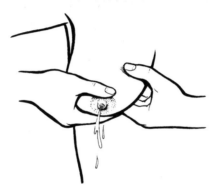

Expressing milk by hand

what bottle manufacturers say, but babies usually become happily used to both, especially if introduced to them early on. If you would like to get your baby used to both bottle and breastfeeding, wait until the latter has been firmly established, but not so long that they have developed an exclusive liking for your nipple – say a couple of weeks after birth, sooner if you feel confident.

Purists might say that introducing one bottle feed a day will encourage 'nipple confusion' and perhaps result in your baby refusing the breast altogether. In practice, this is not usual. The other argument used against 'mixed feeding' is that it may reduce your milk supply. Again, in practice, as long as you replace only one feed a day, this tends not to happen. If it does, stop the once-a-day bottle and restimulate your breast-milk production with breastfeeding only for a few days.

How to express milk
Like breastfeeding itself, mothers need to find what works best for them with a little trial and error, plus some practice in peace and quiet. There are many different methods of getting milk out of the breast and each mother finds her own.

By hand
Here is just one method of expressing by hand. You may find other variations for yourself as you become more confident.

Step 1. Cup your hand under your breast and place your thumb on the upper edge of your areola. You can use either hand on either breast, but most women seem to use their right hand for their right breast and their left hand for their left breast. The base of your forefinger (pointing finger) should rest against the lower edge of your areola or just below it, depending on how large your nipples are.

Make sure you have a generous handful of breast between your thumb and the rest of your hand, feeling the weight of your breast resting in your cupped hand.

Step 2. Begin gently 'milking' your breast, by pressing your entire hand backwards and inwards towards your chest while *at the same time* gently squeezing thumb and forefinger together.

Once you have the movement right, it will take your milk a minute or two to begin to flow, but when it does it will come through in a steady, pulsing stream. It may do so quite powerfully initially with a squirting action, or it may be more of a gentle dribble – it doesn't matter which.

What helps
- Warmth and relaxation. You will probably find that you cannot express your milk very well unless you have some privacy, and some unhurried peace and quiet. Warmth also helps stimulate your milk to flow. Try and combine both by doing some gentle expression practice sitting in a warm bath or under a hot shower the first few times until you really get the hang of it.
- Just concentrate on expressing the milk at first, never mind about trying to collect it as well. Use some clean tissues or a cloth to catch the milk if you are not in a bath or shower.
- Express before a feed rather than afterwards. There will be more milk in your breasts so it will be easier.
- Some women find that if they gently massage their breasts with their hands, stroking lightly downwards towards the nipple for a few minutes, their milk flows more easily.
- When you are confident with expressing and would like to start collecting the milk, just hold a wide-mouthed container, such as a cup, below the flow of milk.
- Some women find that if they think about their baby when they express milk, have their baby on their lap, or just look at a photograph of them, it helps.

Breast pumps
There are several different types of breast pump available, from electrical ones which your hospital or the NCT can hire to you (you can also buy them), to hand- and battery-operated ones. Some are useless (avoid the ones at the cheaper end of the market) and some are rather too vigorous for sensitive women, but you are likely to find one that works well for you. Ask your breastfeeding counsellor or community midwife for advice.

What to do with the milk
Your breastmilk will keep in the fridge for up to 24 hours. It does have some naturally occurring bacteria in it, so you shouldn't keep it for longer. The container you put it in must be sterilized, and must have a lid. You could use a feeding bottle with its top and cover in place.

Warm the milk up when you need it. If it separates out a little, just give it a few gentle shakes before use.

Expressing as you feed

Some mothers find they do not need to do any active milk expressing because as they feed their baby from one breast, the other leaks quite copiously. They simply collect this milk by placing a drip-catching device over the unused but leaking breast. A drip catcher is about five inches in diameter, made from plastic and looks like a lidded flying saucer with a small pouring spout on the side. It has a hole in the centre which fits over your nipple, and it is held in place against your breast by your bra. By using it at each feed you could easily collect enough milk for a single bottle feed without even trying. You can get them from the major branches of babycare shops, for instance Mothercare, from big branches of Boots, and in the baby departments of some department stores.

COMMON PROBLEMS AND WHAT TO DO ABOUT THEM

Afterpains

Afterpains are what you may feel as your womb contracts slowly back to its original size. They usually occur when you are breastfeeding, as the hormone stimulated by the baby's suckling to release milk from the ducts in your breasts also encourages your womb to contract. Afterpains range from slightly uncomfortable, like a mild period pain, to very strong – some women describe the latter as almost like labour pains themselves.

Though afterpains can be virtually unnoticeable, they are sometimes severe enough to make breastfeeding miserable. Fortunately they generally only last for up to seven days, fourteen at the worst, even though it can take up to six weeks for your womb to go completely back to its original size. They may not be noticeable after your first baby, but can become progressively sharper with subsequent babies, since the fibrous scar tissue laid down to mend the tears that occur during labour does not stretch as easily as muscle tissue second or third time round.

Afterpains may be especially uncomfortable if you have had your baby by Caesarean, because both your womb and the abdominal wall have healing stitches in them. Ask for strong painkillers, and try the suggestions below.

For advice on how to feed comfortably after a Caesarean, see page 389.

What helps

The only medical treatment is strong painkillers, which should preferably be paracetamol-based. Ask your midwife about these while you are in hospital, or if you are at home, ring your GP for a prescription your partner can collect on your behalf.

There are some things you can do to help yourself:

- Use the same breathing and relaxation techniques you learnt while you were pregnant in preparation for labour. If you are not familiar with these

techniques, just take a deep breath when you feel an afterpain coming, then gently but steadily empty your lungs as it starts to bite, as if you are blowing the pain away.
- If you have not been prescribed painkillers, take two paracetamol twenty to thirty minutes before you begin to breastfeed.
- Hold a warm (not too hot) hot-water bottle against your lower stomach, as heat has a comforting and mildly analgesic effect.

BITING

It is not unusual for babies to try biting their mothers' nipples once or twice when they are breastfeeding. Even toothless babies (who may have rock-hard gums) can hurt. Usually they are put off by the reaction it provokes, and do not try it again. However, a few continue to bite or chew painfully at each feed, leaving grazes and even drawing blood. Mothers whose babies are regular 'biters' report that even screaming each time they bite does not help. 'I thought this would effectively communicate to [my nine-month-old son] in no uncertain terms that I was not pleased and he would stop doing it, but he simply laughed. My counsellor explained that the whole thing had probably become a game to him, rather like an activity centre: bite this bit and out comes a funny loud noise. Works every time.'

Possible causes and solutions
- *Sore gums.* Try offering something cool to chew on before feeding (see Healthy Teeth – and Teething page 131 for suggestions).
- *Attention seeking.* An older baby may bite to seek attention – perhaps they do not want you to chat on the phone or feed their older sister while you are also feeding them. Try showing them they have your undivided attention, maintaining eye contact and talking softly to them, and try not to feed them while you are talking to someone else.
- *Does not want to feed.* If your baby is not really hungry they may turn their head away from your breast while still hanging on to your nipple. Do not try too hard to persuade them to feed, as biting may be their way of showing you they are not very interested at that moment.
- *Easily distracted.* If your baby is easily distracted by noises, voices and activity, and turns towards something while still hanging on to your nipple, feed them in a calm, quiet place whenever possible. Be ready to break their suction quickly with your little finger if you can see they are about to be distracted.
- *Problems with milk flow.* A baby might become frustrated and irritated by too much or too little milk flowing, and may bite to show their displeasure. Warmth and relaxation speed up a slower let-down reflex, while expressing a little milk before feeding may help an overfull breast.
- *Gone to sleep.* A baby who has fallen asleep at the breast may be tempted to bite if you try to move them off. Slide your little finger into the corner of their mouth so they bite your finger, not your breast.

Other things to try

- If your shout of pain and surprise does not deter them, try staying as calm as you can. They may be finding your strong reaction quite entertaining without understanding that they are causing you distress. Remember that your baby is not biting from spite as they do not realize it hurts you.
- Say 'no' firmly to your baby after they bite, slide your finger into their mouth if they are still feeding, and move them off the nipple. Some mothers further emphasize their displeasure by straightaway placing their baby gently on the floor for a short time. Most babies will not like this, and may begin to connect it with biting.
- If your nipples are sore from a bite or two, apply a little expressed milk at the end of each feed. If one nipple really hurts, feed from the other breast and express from the sore one until it has healed sufficiently to try again.
- Be positive when your baby does not bite during a feed. Give them a big hug and a kiss, tell them how good they have been and how pleased you are with them.

BLOCKED DUCTS

Milk ducts can become plugged with solidified milk. You may notice a small red lump on your breast or a white spot on the nipple. The pain, which is usually mild, may come on gradually and may also shift its position, and there may be some infection which gives you a slight temperature and causes you to feel slightly unwell. Blocked ducts are sometimes confused with mastitis, but this is a more severe problem (see page 30) which can cause considerable pain and a higher temperature.

Blocked ducts may be caused by stopping your baby feeding before they would naturally stop themselves, or by missed or hurried feeds, resulting in the breast or a segment of the breast not being emptied properly. Another common time to develop a blocked duct is when your baby begins to sleep longer at night or all night long.

What helps

- Feed from the affected breast first.
- Encourage unblocking by sitting in a warm bath, soaping your breasts to make them slippery, then using your fingers or a wide-toothed comb or Afro comb to gently smooth the lumps towards your nipple.
- A warm bath or shower before feeding helps milk flow strongly.
- Feed frequently.
- Change the baby's feeding position so they clear all your milk ducts.
- Express as much milk as is comfortable from the affected side, by hand or breast pump.
- Increase the blood supply to the breast by vigorous arm-swinging exercises.

> The La Leche League advises that you do not give up breastfeeding if you have a blocked duct, or it may well make the problem worse.

DRY VAGINA

No one usually tells mothers who are planning to breastfeed that the additional prolactin your body produces to help make your milk can also suppress your oestrogen production. Oestrogen is vital for vaginal lubrication, so if its output is reduced you may find your vagina feels drier than usual. Not only is this uncomfortable if you are having intercourse once again with your partner, but it leaves you more vulnerable to genital infections, such as thrush, which can produce itching and soreness.

Dryness only lasts for as long as you breastfeed. When you stop, your vaginal moisture levels will be back to normal within a matter of days. In the meantime, though, try using a bland lubricant like KY gel, not just for lovemaking but two or three times a day to keep the area moist and comfortable. The other option is oestrogen cream, which lasts longer than KY, and which your GP can prescribe for you on request.

ENGORGEMENT

If your breasts feel hot and painful and the skin is taut and stretched to near-bursting, they are probably engorged. Primary engorgement usually occurs in the first few days after birth as the milk is starting to come through. Most mothers find that their breasts swell uncomfortably at this stage, either just around the nipple area, or over the entire breast. Secondary engorgement can develop after you have been feeding your baby perfectly well for some time, and is probably caused by milk not being removed at the same rate as it is being made. This might be because of a change in routine, or because the baby isn't being left to feed for as long as they want to.

Causes
The most common reason for primary engorgement is that the baby is not latched on properly to your breast (see page 18 on latching on). This is often not immediately obvious and it may only need a very small adjustment of position to put it right. Ask your midwife or NCT or La Leche breastfeeding counsellor to come and see you feeding your baby and check if a little realignment might help.

> If left untreated, engorgement may lead to mastitis – an infection of the breast (see page 30) – so it is important to deal with it quite quickly.

The other very common reason is delay in putting the baby to the breast for the first time. This is why it is a good idea to let your baby suckle as soon as possible after they are born – within the first hour if you can. New mothers who have had a Caesarean are more likely to have engorgement problems as it may take time to find a comfortable way to feed. If the Caesarean is done under a general anaesthetic, both you and the baby may feel too groggy and sleepy to feed for several hours afterwards, possibly even a couple of days. (See Recovering Fast From a Caesarean page 383, if you've had a Caesarean.)

Engorgement can also be caused by a long list of other factors:

- Giving extra fluids to your baby, besides your own breastmilk, such as water, diluted juices or formula. This can reduce the amount of your own milk your baby drinks, which encourages it to build up in your breasts.
- Overusing a dummy, for the same reason. (See Healthy Teeth – and Teeth- ing page 137 for more about dummies.)
- Feeding less than eight to 12 times in 24 hours. This can happen if your baby is particularly sleepy, perhaps because you've had a strong pethidine injection during labour, or just because they happen to be dozy and you're reluctant to keep on waking them up.
- Feeding for very short periods only. It is almost impossible to make a tiny baby prolong their feed if they feel they have already drunk enough, so try to make the short feeds very frequent instead. However . . .
- Feeding frequently for very short periods can also cause engorgement. Whether you are doing it for the reason above, for comfort because your baby is unwell for a few days, or over a long car or plane trip, try to drop back to more widely spaced feeds as soon as you can.
- Feeding from one breast only at each feed might encourage engorgement. But equally, many women find they get on very well by alternately feeding their baby from one breast at one feed, and the other at the next. See what works best for you and your baby.
- When your baby first begins to sleep through the night, you may have an erratic pattern for weeks, or even months, of having to feed them every three hours one night, then not for five or six hours the next, not for eight the next, then back to every three hours again. This can mean that sometimes your breasts will be producing more milk than is taken from them, and they may become engorged because of this. For ideas on sooth- ing sore breasts to help you through this rather uncomfortable erratic period, see page 28.

How to avoid engorgement in the first few days
- Feed as soon as you can after your baby has been born, preferably within the first half-hour.
- Feed as often as possible.
- Make sure your baby latches on well.
- Wear a firm and comfortable supporting bra.

Fullness versus engorgement: what's the difference?
Breast fullness is not the same thing as clinical engorgement, though the terms are often used as if they meant the same thing. Fullness happens to almost every woman who breastfeeds her baby. While it may be uncomfortable, it does not make it difficult for the baby to feed, nor does it cause the mother actual pain. Though your breasts are full, it is possible to press and compress them gently.

True engorgement really hurts and can give you a temperature. Your breasts will feel rock hard, and your nipples may be so distended that it is difficult to get your baby to latch on. This can happen anything from two to ten days after birth. Peak time is usually 3–6 days.

How to soothe engorged breasts
- A warm bath can help relax the stretched, sore breast skin.
- Put cool compresses – cold flannels will do fine – on your breasts between feeds, then warm compresses at the start of each feed.
- Very gently massage the breast, working from the chest wall towards the nipple, in a soft, circular motion with your fingertips. A good place to do this is in a warm bath or shower. Putting oil on your breasts to make them slippery can help. Try almond oil or baby oil.
- Put cold savoy cabbage leaves on your breasts. Store them in the fridge to chill, pull off some big leaves, crush them slightly with a rolling pin to release the enzymes they contain, and place them over your breasts tucked inside your bra – they fit quite well as they are naturally curved. This can be surprisingly soothing and many midwives and mothers recommend them.
- Take painkillers – such as paracetamol or ibuprofen – twenty minutes before feeding. Do not take codeine, as this can encourage constipation, and you may well be a bit constipated anyway in the first few days after your baby's birth.
- Try feeding your baby for longer periods. Do not hurry feeds or time them.
- Use a breast pump.
  You can use this to release some of your milk and so relieve the pressure inside your breasts, but make sure it has a really comfortable action. The electric breast pumps available in postnatal wards in hospital are useful here, and you can also hire these from the NCT or via the hospital itself. If you have a hand- or battery-operated one and are having trouble getting your milk flowing, try sitting in a warm bath to use it, or express gently by hand whilst in the bath. It can help to rub a little oil on your breasts first to relieve the tightness of the skin. (See Expressing Milk, page 20.)
- If your breasts are so full that your baby is choking and spluttering as the milk gushes out, express some by hand before you begin each feed.

INVERTED OR FLAT NIPPLES

Nipples come in all shapes, colours and sizes. It is not unusual for a woman to have one or both nipples which dimple inwards rather than stand out. These are called inverted nipples. It is also normal for a woman to have nipples which do not stand out when she is cold, sexually aroused or beginning to breastfeed and these are known as flat nipples. With both types of nipple it can be harder for a baby to latch on and draw the nipple in to suckle, but neither type need be a bar to breastfeeding. As one famous British midwife pointed out, babies don't nipplefeed, they breastfeed.

What helps

- *Nipple shells.* Some health professionals suggest women treat flat or inverted nipples during pregnancy by using glass or plastic breast shells or shields that fit over the nipple or part of the breast and are worn inside the bra to encourage the nipple to protrude, combined with exercises (known as Hoffman's exercises) to stretch the nipple using thumb and forefinger. No one has come to any conclusion yet as to whether the shells or the exercises really do work. But they're worth trying.
- *Expressing* for the first two or three weeks. Many women say that as their babies get bigger and their suckling action stronger, it becomes much easier to feed them from inverted or flat nipples. You may well find that if you keep your milk supply stimulated by expressing your milk, rather than trying to breastfeed, until your baby is two or three weeks old, they will then be able to feed from you just fine.

  If you do this, you may find you have to persist for a few days to teach them to feed from your breast, because having got used to a bottle they may not at first instinctively open their mouth wide enough to breastfeed. Ask your breastfeeding counsellor for support and advice during this time, and keep persisting.

  If you have an inverted or flat nipple on one side only which is causing you difficulties, there is no reason why you cannot express from this side for the first two or three weeks, and feed from the other. When your baby's suckling is stronger, introduce them to the inverted or flat nipple and they should be able to suck strongly enough to draw it out. They will know just what to do from their practice with your breast.
- To encourage your nipple to stand out more for feeding, you can also:
  — Wrap some ice cubes in a flannel and hold this against your nipple.
  — Try spraying cold water from an Evian or plant spray on the area.
  — Use a breast pump to express a little milk and draw out the nipple, then help your baby to latch on to it.
  — Make doubly sure your baby is latching on to your breasts correctly. Ask your community midwife or local breastfeeding counsellor to come over and see you to help assess this.

LEAKING

Milk may leak or spurt from your breasts when your partner caresses your breasts or when you become generally sexually aroused. This need not be a problem, but some couples find it feels inappropriate or messy and that it's a bit off-putting. Many women also find that their breasts begin leaking milk copiously when their baby cries, causing a large damp stain to spread across their clothing. This is more of a laundry problem if you are at home, but it can be embarrassing when you are out and about.

What helps

- To prevent a gush of milk, immediately cross your arms and press the heels of your hands firmly against your nipples and areolas.
- Make love *after* you have fed your baby, or express some milk from your breasts beforehand.
- Breast pads can absorb sudden spurts and leaks, so wear a pair all the time and always carry a supply with you. Change them as soon as they become damp or you may be setting yourself up for sore, cracked nipples. Many women always carry a couple in their handbag plus an emergency rolled up T-shirt in a colour that matches most clothes (e.g. black or white).

MASTITIS

Mastitis is an inflammation of the breast tissue which an estimated one in three breastfeeding mothers develops temporarily at some point. There are two types. *Non-infective* mastitis tends to be caused by something like a blocked milk duct. *Infective* mastitis is caused by a viral, bacterial or fungal infection. The latter is not that common in the UK, but if it does occur it tends to be as a result of bacteria, often from your baby's nose or from your own skin surface, finding its way into the breast via cracks in or around the nipple.

Symptoms

Early warning signs of mastitis include a temperature, a small reddish patch on the breast, a sore area but nothing visible, feeling as if you are coming down with flu, or feeling generally unwell.

You are more likely to develop mastitis if you are tired, according to a survey in 1990 of the reasons for mastitis given by 161 new mothers who had it (published in the *Journal of Human Lactation*). A quarter felt it was tiredness that had caused the problem, another quarter put it down to stress, 17 per cent to plugged milk ducts, and 15 per cent to a change in the number of breastfeeds they had been giving their baby. Other risk factors include cracked nipples, tight bras, underwired bras, sleeping so one of your breasts is heavily compressed, an infection such as a cold or flu in the family, and producing too much milk.

What helps

If the mastitis is not caused by an infection (and most of the time it is not) try:

- Stroking the affected area of your breast up towards your nipple. This may encourage the area to drain. It may be easier in a warm shower or bath.
- Continuing to breastfeed from the affected side as often as possible, OR
- Expressing milk from the affected side – both expressing and feeding can encourage the duct to clear. Some mothers report that when they do this a thick, yellowish-looking plug or lump of material emerges ('like a small strand of thin spaghetti,' as one put it). Don't worry, it's harmless if your baby swallows it.
- Asking your breastfeeding counsellor or community midwife or a good friend who has or is breastfeeding to come and see you and help you check your baby is latched on well when they feed. If they are not this may cause uneven emptying of your milk ducts, which can encourage the formation of small blockages.
- Checking for, and treating, any cracks in your nipples.
- Resting in bed as much as you possibly can, even if it is only for half an hour at a time. Get as much help as you can in the house until your breast is better. This can make a great deal of difference to recovery.

If self-help measures do not improve matters within 24 hours (they won't 'cure' mastitis in this time but you might start feeling better) and the problem is getting worse, go and see your GP right away as you may need a course of antibiotics. Suggest that the GP takes a sample of your milk and a swab culture from your baby's throat to see exactly which bacteria is causing the problem, so treatment can be tailored accordingly.

NOT ENOUGH MILK

Fear that their baby might not be drinking enough milk from them is given by mothers as a major reason for stopping breastfeeding. It is frequently unfounded, since most babies, if allowed to suckle for as long as they want to, take as much as they need. The actual time they spend suckling is not always a very reliable indicator of volume drunk. An efficient baby can empty one breast in ten minutes flat, while another will do so in fifteen or twenty minutes, but might carry on suckling for a further ten because they are enjoying the closeness and comfort so much.

If your baby shows all the signs of getting enough milk (see page 20), you need not worry. However, the following factors can reduce your milk supply. Might any of them apply?

Things that can cause a reduced milk supply
- Topping up your baby's breastmilk feeds with formula milk.
    Supplementing with formula is tempting if you do not feel you are

making enough milk, if your baby still seems hungry or it seems harder to satisfy their appetite than it used to be.

It may be that your baby is putting on one of the many growth spurts it will have (they grow fastest of all in their first three months of life) and needs more nourishment than usual, causing your baby to be irritable and cry for a feed after a couple of hours rather than the four you had previously both got used to.'

However, if you top up the breastmilk feeds with formula, you are not giving your own milk supply the chance to increase and catch up with your baby's hunger. The more your baby suckles on you, the more milk your breasts will be stimulated to produce. If your baby suckles less because they are being filled up on formula, your milk supply will fall accordingly.

So if your baby seems very hungry, let them suckle longer. Give them your breastmilk and nothing else, and within anything from a few days to a week or so you should be making more milk. Its composition might change too as it does throughout the breastfeeding months, becoming richer and more filling to cater for your baby's changing needs. It will most probably *not* be necessary to go out and buy a tin of 'formula for the hungrier baby' as a supplement to your own, which is what mothers in desperation often do.

However, if you are not too worried about maintaining breastfeeding and feel that introducing some formula feeds is the next logical step towards gently weaning your baby from your breast and on to bottles, you are on your way. Supplementing each feed or replacing *more than one* feed a day with formula milk is gradually going to reduce your own milk supply until it stops.

- Giving your baby a dummy when what they really want is a feed.
- Wearing nipple shields. Your baby can't suck as hard on the nipple through a shield (which is why they are sometimes used as a temporary measure for sore nipples).
- Rigidly scheduled feeding times.
- Shortening or hurrying feeding times.
- Tension and stress.
- Over-tiredness.
- Not eating well or drinking enough liquid yourself.
- Smoking.
- Some types of medication (check with your GP).
- The Combined Pill.

Ways to keep up or increase your milk supply
- Drink plenty regularly (milk, water or diluted juice rather than tea or coffee, both of which are diuretic).
- Express any milk you have left over from feeds (if you don't want to keep it, just pour it away).
- Eat properly.
- Try to get more rest, especially towards the end of the day.
  This is the time of day when you tend to be at your most tired and

Complementary therapy to encourage milk supply

There are many different natural and traditional medications for encouraging your milk supply to increase. Aromatherapy treatment would be with essential oil of lavender and aniseed oil; a herbalist might suggest goat's rue to increase both milk volume and the proportion of milk solids, or chaste tree to affect the relevant hormone levels; a homeopath might suggest Asafoetida if milk supply has begun well then suddenly stops, Aconite if shock caused the decrease or stoppage, and Chamomile if the problem is anger and irritation with life in general on your part. Acupuncture is also said to help increase milk supply.

It is vital that any therapist who treats you, especially if you are pregnant or breastfeeding, is fully qualified and has a special interest in pregnancy and postnatal mothers. Call the Institute for Complementary Medicine, or the therapy's own professional association (see Useful Addresses) for a suitable therapist near you.

harassed. This can, not surprisingly, reduce your late afternoon/early evening milk production. Have you noticed your baby seems hungrier or less satisfied with breastfeeding, or just plain ratty, in the late afternoon or early evening? If so, this may be the reason.

Do you have a partner who can, for a while, ensure he is home at night by 6 p.m. at the latest? If so, can you let him care for the baby and any older children you may have so you can go and rest, even for half an hour? If not, do you have a mother or sister or good friend living near, or a paid carer (nanny, childminder, mother's help) who could help you out by being around at this time of day?

- Offer both breasts at each feed. Some babies seem to like feeding from only one breast at each feed, but encourage them to have both. However, let them finish one before starting on the next. If they don't feed much from the second breast, start with that one at the next feed.

NO MILK FLOWING

This is a common problem when you first begin to breastfeed, but it rarely lasts for long. Usually the colostrum will begin to flow in response to their suckling as soon as your baby shows an interest. This nourishing fluid seems only to be present in relatively small amounts but it is actually all your baby needs in these first three or four days.

The fact that many babies seem to want to suckle for hours every day at first, partly in the hope of extracting more from your breasts, and partly for comfort, is just what you need for stimulating milk production. This prolonged suckling can initially make your nipples rather sore as they are not used to this much attention (see Sore Nipples, page 34). By day four, when the colostrum gives way to proper breastmilk, your baby should need to suckle for shorter periods of time, which will give your nipples a well-earned rest.

What helps

If your milk seems reluctant to start flowing at all (signs are that your baby cries, becomes impatient at the breast and clearly remains hungry – check to see if there's any milk at all in their mouth), try:

- Warm compresses, such as damp flannels.
- A covered, warm (not hot) hot-water bottle.
- Sitting in a warm bath so the water comes up over your breasts, or lying in the warm bath on your front and elbows, breasts hanging downwards.
- An electric breast pump.
  You can borrow one on the postnatal ward in hospital, or hire one from the NHS or NCT to use at home. Do not be discouraged if at first you seem to use it for hours and only the smallest amount of milk appears – this is normal, if immensely frustrating. Persist with it, and talk to your midwife or breastfeeding counsellor for as much help and support as you feel you need.
- Plenty of peace and quiet in your own familiar territory.
  Mothers often say it was easier for them once they came home from hospital. It is another good reason why it is probably worth persisting with breastfeeding at home if you can, even though you found it difficult in hospital.
- The relaxation exercises you learnt in antenatal classes.
- Asking your midwife or breastfeeding counsellor to help you check both your feeding position and the way your baby is latched on to you.

SORE NIPPLES

Your nipples may feel sore, especially in the first few days of feeding your baby, as they are unused to all the attention. This tenderness usually disappears within two or three weeks.

Dampness doesn't help either. Try to make sure your nipples don't stay soggy for long periods in between feeds. If you are using breastpads or tissues to absorb any leaking milk, change them often for the same reason that you wouldn't leave a baby's bottom in a wringing wet nappy for hours – it produces skin soreness.

Damp nipples can become sore nipples because moisture makes the skin swell up, and rapid air drying makes it shrink again irregularly. The resulting tension on the skin causes it to crack. Some suggestions for sore nipple treatment which concentrate on speeding up the drying process, for instance using a hair dryer on a cool setting, might make them dry out even further.

What helps

The two most important things you can do to avoid sore nipples are:

- Ensure your baby is latched on in the right position. Ask your midwife or breastfeeding counsellor to come and see you breastfeed, so you can make sure the positioning is exactly right.
- Keep your nipples dry. The following might help:
  — A drip-catcher device (available from larger branches of Mothercare, Boots and some department stores such as John Lewis). This will store any milk that leaks between feeds, rather than letting it collect in a soggy breastpad.
  — Absorbent breast pads tucked over your nipples and held in place by your bra when not breastfeeding. Change as soon as they become damp. Carry a small supply in your handbag or baby-changing bag.
  — It is not always possible or convenient to change your breast pads (perhaps while you are out and about), even if you feel they are becoming damp. Keep damp breast pads and soggy bras from sticking to the nipple itself by using the circular heads of two small plastic tea strainers inverted over your nipples, held in place by your bra. Don't worry – these do not give your breast an odd shape that is noticeable through a sweatshirt or even a T-shirt. You could also place a large breast pad on top of that. If your nipples leak milk, it will be soaked up by the pad as usual so your bra stays dry, but the pad's increasingly soggy surface will be held away.
  — When taking your baby off your breast, always do so by gently inserting your little finger into the corner of their mouth to break the suction. This will help prevent nipples becoming sore as well as protect those which already are.

Other ways to prevent sore nipples:

- Use a cotton bra rather than a nylon one.
- Try not to let your baby drag downwards on your breast and nipple when they feed. Support them well from below instead. Bring your baby up to your nipple, rather than letting them pull your nipple down towards them. Supporting them on a pillow can be helpful.
- Do not use plastic-backed breast pads. Although they do stop milk leaking through onto your bra and outer clothing, they also keep the moisture in against your breast and nipple skin. Save plastic-backed ones for occasions when you *especially* do not want any leaks, such as when you are going out.
- When breastfeeding, start with the least sore side first.
- Use a soothing cream such as calendula cream (one brand is Kamillosan, available from major chemists) as a protective barrier over your nipples between feeds. In fact it is not a bad idea to use a barrier cream between feeds whether your nipples are sore or not for the first few weeks until they toughen up a little. Plain lanolin cream can be useful too, but check first that it is guaranteed pesticide-free. (La Leche League sells one by

mail order – see Useful Addresses.) A hypoallergenic cream which is made primarily for clinical use may be the best option, and you can ask your GP to prescribe this for you. This too is available from the La Leche League.

If you use Kamillosan, which contains 10.5 per cent chamomile, it is best to wipe this off before your baby feeds from your breasts. It is generally accepted that it does not harm them, but there is at least one reported case of it causing severe contact dermatitis for one mother who used it, according to Peter Golightly, Director of the Trent Drug Information Service. To be on the safe side, it may be a good idea to do a patch test first and leave it for 24 hours to see if there is any reaction.

- Try gently rubbing in some of the richer hind breast milk, which comes in the later part of each breast's feed, into your nipples and areolas as this can be healing and moisturizing in its own right.
- Keeping feeding your baby as often as they want. Hospital staff often suggest to new mothers with sore nipples that they should limit their feed times to give their nipples a rest. In reality, this may just put off the time when their nipples become really sore until they have gone home and have no medical help instantly available.
- If they are so sore that breastfeeding makes you wince, try expressing for a while, giving your milk to your baby in a bottle. Do not worry if it seems you cannot express enough – baby's mouths are better at extracting milk from breasts than your hands are. Just express as much as you can, and make up any shortfall with formula for a few days. Try and do so by hand rather than with a breast pump, as the latter's sucking action may make your soreness worse, especially if you have one of the more enthusiastic types. When your nipples are comfortable again, feed as frequently as you can for several days to encourage your milk supply to build up again.
- If your nipples are very cracked as well as sore, a thin latex nipple shield, which you can buy from major chemists, may help protect them from direct suckling by your baby. You will find that feeds take longer, though, and if you need to use the shields for too long they might eventually reduce your milk supply. However, you can build it back up again after you have finished with the shields by feeding your baby very frequently for a week or so.
- Wet tea bags. This is a traditional remedy for both sunburn and sore nipples. Though there is no clinical research proving it works, it is thought to help because tea contains tannic acid, a mild astringent which can reduce inflammation. Pour boiling water on to the tea bag in a cup. Let it cool, squeeze some of the water out and apply the bag like a poultice.
- When practical, expose sore nipples to the fresh air by sitting with your bra flaps open, but with the supporting structure of your bra still in place.

BREASTFEEDING AND YOUR SLEEP

See page 317.

Nipples still sore?

The problem may be a thrush infection instead. Go and see your GP to check this. Thrush, a small fungal organism which occurs naturally in a healthy mouth, bowel, vagina and on the skin's surface, can occur in a newborn baby's mouth, which can then affect your nipples.

Symptoms of thrush

Check your baby for:

- Soreness around their anus or vulva which might be a thrush infection.
- White, irregular-shaped spots in their mouth which look like milk curds, but on closer inspection do not wipe away with your finger.

Check yourself for:

- Itching nipples.
- Reddened, sore nipples and areolae.
- Redness which spreads beyond the nipple and areola area.
- Vaginal thrush (redness and itching around the vulva, and a curdy white discharge from your vagina which does not smell offensive but crusts slightly on your pants).
- White spots in the mouth, and perhaps some soreness.
- Redness and itching around the anal area.

Remedies

Traditional. Your GP can give you a topical cream to rub on the affected areas, and possibly a treatment in pill form too. He will treat your baby orally. If you are having sex with your partner, he will need to be treated too, and he will need to use a condom until you are both clear. Thrush tends to be symptomless in men so they can keep passing it back to you without realizing.

Homeopathy. Tincture of Arnica can be useful for painful nipples, but if the skin is broken or cracked Calendula should be used.

Herbalism. A herbalist would recommend Calendula (available as Kamillosan).

Aromatherapy. Essential oil of lavender can help heal cracks and soreness, and is antiseptic too.

HOW TO STOP BREASTFEEDING

Stopping from the start

If you decide from the very start not to breastfeed, your doctor might offer you milk-suppressing hormonal drugs like bromocriptine, which are effective, but make some women feel sick. To help avoid nausea, take the first one before you go to bed at night (hopefully your baby will be asleep for two or three hours too) so you miss the worst of the effect of this dose. There is also a possibility of rebound engorgement after you have finished the medication, by which time you will be at home. (See Engorgement, page 26.)

The old-fashioned treatment of binding your breasts up firmly with a wide soft crepe bandage for a few days to support them firmly until the milk and engorgement ebb away of their own accord is still popular, as is its modern equivalent, a very well-fitted, supportive maternity bra, bought in advance so you can wear it straightaway. If either is too tight, or if the bra does not fit well or has supporting underwiring, it may encourage mastitis. If you would prefer a bra rather than a bandage, it is very important to buy it from a store which has trained bra fitters (such as a major branch of John Lewis) who can carefully estimate the size you will need if they see you late on in your pregnancy. It is astonishing how much the size of breasts can change temporarily during initial primary engorgement, and it can be difficult to assess this accurately without some expert advice.

Stopping later on

If you have been breastfeeding, but now feel that the time is right to stop, try to wind down slowly and gradually. Give yourself about a month if you can, as things do not always go according to plan. You may be putting both of you under unnecessary pressure if you try to do it more quickly, say within a week. If your aim is to stop before you go back to work, try not to rush it.

Drop one feed at a time, substituting a bottle if your baby is still very young but will accept this happily, or a beaker with drinking spout for an older baby (seven to nine months plus), or some food if they are already on solids. Try lunchtime first, then breakfast, then the teatime feed. It's important to go at your own pace over this, but as a very loose guideline, and if all is going well, you could try four or five days between each dropped breastfeed. Some babies may need longer intervals. Mothers often stop the night-time breastfeeds last of all, even if their milk supply has become very scanty, as their baby enjoys the closeness and comfort of a breastfeed before bedtime so much.

If you are stopping completely or cutting down substantially within a short time, perhaps over a week, you will probably find your breasts become temporarily very full and uncomfortable. Use cool flannel compresses and hot baths to soothe them until they adjust to making very little milk. (See page 28 for other soothing measures.) If you stop completely, it will probably take about five to seven days to reduce milk supply noticeably, and two to four weeks to tail off altogether. Some women are advised to bind up their breasts firmly, but comfortably, in bands of wide, soft crepe bandage while the milk is reducing, but a more modern equivalent is using a very comfortable supportive bra – your feeding bra, not an 'ordinary' one (see above).

Try not to express any milk, as this will encourage more to be made. You may have a heavy run on breastpads at this time. If your bra and clothes keep becoming wet, try using a couple of upturned plastic tea strainer heads with a double layer of breastpads over the top. Or tuck a drip catcher device (see page 35) into each bra over your nipple, and empty it regularly.

What to do when you want to stop but your baby doesn't

Many infants stop asking for the breast of their own accord, especially if you are already mixing breast and bottle. Some are easy to persuade as they seem to be ready for it. Unfortunately, others are not. If your baby or toddler is extremely attached to breastfeeding, resists all attempts to encourage them to turn to other methods of drinking, and is not satisfied with hugs and cuddling rather than suckling when they need comfort or are going to sleep, this can be a difficult one for both of you.

Your baby or toddler may be puzzled, upset or downright angry that you are no longer making your breasts available to them. They might refuse to drink anything else, constantly climb on your lap to try to unbutton your shirt or lift up your T-shirt, grab at your breasts – or anyone else's – at every possible opportunity, cry, have tantrums, gaze ardently and fixedly at other mothers who are breastfeeding babies, or refuse to go to sleep at night, especially if you used to give them a comfort breastfeed as part of their bedtime routine.

Even if you are confident in yourself that it is high time you stopped breastfeeding, this sort of reaction can be very upsetting for you as well as for them. You feel you are denying your child something that clearly gives them such comfort and pleasure, and which, worse still, *they still seem to want so much.* 'Never did I cry more broken-heartedly. Dreadful it is to ask in vain, but small is that hurt when compared with the pain of not giving,' wrote the French novelist Colette in 1912 of the time when she chose not to breastfeed her baby.

But breastfeeding is a two-way street, and you can only carry on for as long as *you* feel happy about doing so. If you really feel enough's enough, then it is, so feel confident in standing by your decision, keeping in mind the good reasons that have led to it. Be prepared if necessary for a prolonged transition – it may take weeks – from breastfeeder to cheerful bottle-feeder or willing cup-drinking. It is easier if your child is already happy to take a drink from a bottle. If they are not, they are unlikely to accept this easily as an alternative to your breast (despite what baby bottle manufacturers say the nipple does not really feel much like yours) and you may find it easier to persuade your child straight on to a baby beaker with a spout if they're old enough – six months or so.

There are no hard and fast rules about how to make the transition from breast to bottle or beaker, but there are several possible strategies to try. Frustratingly, none of the existing baby books or breastfeeding organizations is any help when you ask them about the best way to wind up breastfeeding, though they have plenty of advice on how to get going in the first place, or how to introduce solids.

'They all just told me she'd stop when she was ready in her own time,' said one mother from Edinburgh, whose 23-month-old refused to stop nursing. 'I'd been feeding both her and our three-month-old baby together, which was fine and loving for a while, and it prevented jealousy of the new baby too. But suddenly I just felt it was no longer appropriate. She was old enough to stop, but would she? I called up all the breastfeeding organizations who'd been so helpful when I had begun, my community midwife, saw the health visitor at the mother and baby clinic and our family doctor. I asked my friends who had breastfed their babies. No one had one *useful* bit of advice for me. Just what was I supposed to do? I felt abandoned and angry.'

The following suggestions come from mothers who themselves found that their babies simply refused to give up breastfeeding. All were six months plus; one was over two and a half.

Mothers' tips for a reluctant stopper
- Stop gradually.

  Cut out the daytime feeds first, beginning perhaps with the meal, if they are taking solids too, your child likes best (lunch?), and leave the comfort, going-to-sleep-at-night feed till last.
- Keep showing how much you love your child.

  Pay lots of attention to them, give them all the cuddles they could possibly want.
- Distract your child whenever the idea of breastfeeding comes up.

  'Let's go out for a walk to the park, let's read a story, play with water, sing a clapping song; hey look, it's *Sesame Street* on TV.'
- Replace former breastfeeding time – say first thing in the morning – with another happy routine activity which you do each day at the same time.

  Perhaps instead of a morning breastfeed, come downstairs, put some gentle music on, spread out a soft rug with toys on it and get down on the floor to cuddle and play with your baby. Offer them a bottle or beaker of warm milk as you drink your tea so they can see you could both enjoy an early-morning drink together. Try an extra long story and cuddle. The message you will be gently but persistently putting across is that they still have first call on your time, attention and love but that breasts are no longer on the menu.
- Make your baby or toddler feel as secure as possible in any way you can, even to the extent of being more protective than usual.

  For instance, when you stop breastfeeding, try to make sure you spend special time with them, perhaps by taking a few days off work or by letting them come on small errands with you when you might before have left them behind. Perhaps let them eat their meals sitting right by you, or even on your lap if they would like for a while. Stay with them for longer than usual when you put them to bed at night. Let your child see that comfort and security come from many different sources, not just from breastfeeding.
- Consider not letting them see your breasts naked for a little while until they are happier with cups and alternative comfort sources.

  This may apply at bathtime if you usually get in with them, or while you get dressed. When you sunbathe think twice about going topless. This may sound daft, but naked breasts, especially yours, can otherwise remind them powerfully of what they are missing.
- If your child keeps grabbing hopefully at your breasts, try saying 'No'

softly but firmly, coaxingly offering a beaker or bottle – keep some handy in the fridge – and a kiss, as promptly as possible instead.

If they refuse and keep grabbing, try putting them in a sling *on your back* and carry them about for a while, chatting and singing if you feel up to it, or just getting on with your tasks. Your child might enjoy the closeness and security riding on your back offers, but will be in the wrong position to try to undo your shirt, or put their mouth and hands very effectively on your breasts.

Older toddlers with a longer reach may still manage to continue grabbing and scrabbling, however, even if – or especially if – they sense this is winding you up. If they do, or if either of you is becoming angry, take them out for a while in the pushchair to distract them, or cuddle up together to watch a favourite video, read a much-loved story, or get them to help you with the washing-up by mixing and dabbling in the water – anything to take their minds off a breastfeed. In the early few days of breast-weaning a reluctant child, you may not get much done around the house and the day becomes a series of diplomatic scene avoidances and creative distraction therapy. But it will get easier, and surprisingly quickly too.

- Try getting your child a special feeder beaker.

  Let them know how special and grown up it is. Take them with you to buy it, let them choose it. Admire their choice.

- Use sleight of hand.

  One mother reported that she introduced her 18-month-old daughter to a bottle by waiting until she had suckled a bit from her breast, then breaking the suction gently with her finger and sliding the bottle teat in quickly instead, while still cuddling and rocking her.

  'She barely missed a beat and then took to the bottle like a duck to water, which cushioned the fact that I was weaning her off my breast. Unfortunately it then took another two years before she would give up her beloved bottle.'

- Have a weaning day celebration, if your child is old enough to understand.

  One mother gave her two-years-and-eight-months-old daughter plenty of warning every day for a month, and then celebrated with cakes, candles and presents when weaning day arrived. You could probably try this with a younger infant too; you yourself will know whether your child is old enough.

- Explain it straight, if you feel your child is old enough to understand.

  Some can take on board what you are saying about this from a surprisingly young age, even before they are two. You might say something along the lines of, 'I get really tired waking up at night to give you drinks. We could play and go out more in the day if I wasn't so tired. So can we just have one big drink before sleeptime instead?' and repeat this several times on consecutive days as a lead-in. It's worth a try.

USEFUL ADDRESSES

Aromatherapy Organizations Council, 3 Latymer Close, Braybrooke, Market Harborough, Leicestershire LE16 8LN. Tel: 01858 434242.

The umbrella body for the major professional aromatherapy organizations, with a register of professionally qualified members. Ask if they know if any of their members have a special interest in women's health and breastfeeding. An aromatherapy session will cost you anything from £17 to £50, but they can also suggest oils you can use to help yourself at home for specific problems.

Association of Breastfeeding Mothers, PO Box 441, St Albans, Herts AL4 0AF. Tel: 0181 778 4769.

Has national helplines offering telephone advice and support, as well as home visits, distance permitting, to help mothers with all aspects of breastfeeding. Also runs local support groups.

BLISS (Baby Life Support Systems), 17–21 Emerald Street, London WC1N 3QL. Tel: 0171 831 9393.

For parents of special care and premature babies. Help, support and information on all aspects of their care, including breastfeeding and giving them expressed breast milk.

Baby Milk Action, 23 St Andrews Street, Cambridge CB2 3AX. Tel: 01223 464420.

Campaigns against the inappropriate use and promotion of baby formula milks.

Caesarean Support Network c/o Yvonne Williams, 55 Cooil Drive, Douglas, Isle of Man, or (postal service only – send letter and s.a.e.) Sheila Tunstall, 2 Hurst Park Drive, Huyton, Liverpool

Offers non-medical and practical advice, support over the phone, and face-to-face help where practical on all issues surrounding Caesarean birth, including breastfeeding afterwards.

Institute of Complementary Medicine, PO Box 194, London SE16 1QZ. Tel: 0171 237 5165.

Can supply an extensive, though not exhaustive, list of properly qualified complementary practitioners of all types countrywide.

La Leche League of Great Britain, BM 3424, London WC1N 3XX. Tel: 0171 242 1278.

Offers encouragement, information, regular group meetings and support, both on the phone and, distance permitting, in person, to breastfeeding mothers with all types of breastfeeding problems. Has large list of helpful literature, and can supply mail-order products for comfort, such as hypoallergenic lanolin nipple moisturizing cream.

London Food Commission, 3rd Floor, 5 Worship Street, London EC2A 2BH. Tel: 0171 628 7774.

Monitors food policy and issues relating to the fitness of different foods for safe public consumption.

National Childbirth Trust, Alexandra House, Oldham Terrace, London W3 6NH. Tel: 0181 992 8637.

Help, support and information on all aspects of pregnancy, childbirth and breastfeeding. NCT counsellors will, distance permitting, visit breastfeeding mothers who are having difficulties, and can also offer telephone help. Large range of useful literature on everything from waterbirth to breastfeeding a toddler, and a postal catalogue of items catering for the needs of pregnant and breastfeeding women such as feeding bras and breast pumps.

You Can Do It Here!

National Childbirth Trust directory of 5,500 stores in the UK who are happy to have you breastfeed anywhere on their premises, many of which have dedicated mother and baby rooms. 50 per cent of Tesco stores, for example, have a special room for breastfeeding. Send £2 and a covering note to the NCT's press office.

TAMBA (Twins & Multiple Births Association), PO Box 30, Little Sutton, South Wirral L66 1TH. Tel: 0151 348 0020. Fax: 0151 200 5309. e-mail: www.surreycc.gov.uk/tamba/ TAMBA Twinline tel: 01732 868000.

Advice on all aspects of pregnancy, birth, and caring for twins (or more), including breastfeeding, which mothers of twins can do very successfully. Helpline operates 7 p.m. to 11 p.m. weekdays and 10 p.m.–11 p.m. at weekends.

Getting the Best Out of Bottles

Breastfeeding may be best for a baby's overall *health*, but the best way to feed your baby is the way that feels right for you. If you steel yourself to breastfeed even though you feel uncomfortable or unhappy with it, feeding times will be fraught rather than loving, nurturing and relaxing.

For most mothers, feeding isn't just a question of weighing up the pros and cons – you may feel very strongly about breastfeeding or bottle-feeding even before your baby is born. You might begin by breastfeeding and find you have problems – topping the list are sore nipples, difficulty latching on, lack of support from your partner and lack of help and advice from a sympathetic midwife when it's most needed. Or you might decide from the start that it simply isn't for you.

If you feel strongly that bottle-feeding would suit both you and your baby best, ignore anyone who tries to make you feel the least bit guilty about it. Millions of babies have grown up very happy and healthy on formula milk, and there is no reason why your baby should not make that many millions and one. The way you feed your baby is your own business – go ahead and enjoy feeding your child.

THE PLUSES OF BOTTLE-FEEDING

Although breastmilk is a unique substance, modern food technology is now so sophisticated, and the understanding of babies' nutritional needs so well-developed, that manufacturers can make formula milks which are almost identical to breastmilk in terms of nutritional composition.

Bottle-feeding has many advantages, one of the main ones being that your

---

How many women bottle-feed?
A 1990 government study for the Office of Population Censuses and Surveys found that although 63 per cent of mothers started to breastfeed their new babies, by six weeks around 40 per cent of them had stopped. Many mothers, even those who breastfeed, use supplementary bottles, and by four months three-quarters of babies are fully bottle-fed.

partner or another carer can feed the baby. For fathers, this is a great way to feel close. And it means that you can get a good six hours of uninterrupted sleep if he takes a turn at night. It also gives you a better chance of going out for a while since it is easier to leave a bottle-fed baby in someone else's care.

Added to this, it's easier to get a bottle-fed baby on to a regular feeding schedule since they go longer between feeds (formula takes longer to digest than breast milk), and they are likely to sleep through the night sooner than breastfed babies. You can also see exactly how much they are taking in, so you don't have the worry that they might not be feeding enough.

Bottle-feeding is more convenient, if you need to return to work, than expressing your own milk, and it can mean that your breasts stay in better shape. And whatever breastfeeding enthusiasts say to the contrary, some fatty tissue can be lost with prolonged breastfeeding and you may go down a cup size (though eventually the fat stores may be replaced).

WHAT IS FORMULA MADE OF?

Formula milk is cow's milk (unless it is a soya formula) which has been extensively adapted to make it more like breastmilk. In terms of the balance of fat and lactose, the total carbohydrate count and the presence of vitamins, minerals and trace elements such as sodium, potassium, calcium, magnesium, iron and others, breastmilk and formula are pretty much identical, although formula tends to be higher in protein.

The manufacture and marketing of formula is strictly controlled by government regulations. The main changes made to the cow's milk are:

- Carbohydrate is increased to the same level as breastmilk. It is added in the form of sugars such as lactose, or lactose plus maltodextrin (a starch).
- Protein is reduced, but the level is still higher than that of breastmilk. Extra amino acids may be added.
- All or some of the milk fat is replaced with blends of vegetable oils to help the baby absorb it more easily.
- The mineral content, especially sodium and phosphorus, is reduced so as not to overload the baby's immature kidneys – an important reason for making up the formula very accurately.
- A range of minerals and vitamins, such as iron, vitamin E, vitamin C and folic acid, is added.

However, there are still things in breastmilk that formula can't match, such as the antibodies and anti-infective factors that give a child protection against illness. But formula milks are continually being improved and refined in the light of new research. For example, some manufacturers now add certain essential fatty acids (EFAs) found in breastmilk which are known to be important for the development of the nervous system in young babies. Milupa's

> Don't ever give your baby cow's milk, goat's milk, powdered, dried, evaporated, sterilized or any other type of milk you can find in the supermarket or health food shop, as their digestive system simply won't cope with it and it could be harmful.

Aptamil was the first, and Farley's also have a formula containing EFAs. They are listed on the contents label.

THE DIFFERENT TYPES OF FORMULA

The huge number of brands available can be very confusing. Many mothers continue to use brands their babies were given in hospital. There are two types of standard formula, whey-dominant or casein-dominant. Many mothers try several brands before they find one that suits their baby.

Whey-dominant formulas
These are normally branded as first milks or stage one milks and most bottle-fed babies begin on them. They have a casein/whey protein ratio of 40:60, the same as in human milk, which is believed to be most easily digested and absorbed.

Brands are: *Cow & Gate Premium, SMA Gold, Milupa Aptamil, Farley's First, Boots Formula 1, Sainsbury's First Stage Milk.*

Casein-dominant formulas
These have a casein/whey ratio of 80:20, which is closer to cow's milk. This formula is said to be more satisfying for hungry babies since it takes longer to digest than the whey-dominant ones – the same amount of milk stays in the baby's stomach longer. Brands are marketed as second stage milk, or formulas for 'hungrier' babies. Many mothers change their babies to these formulas in the first six to ten weeks if they feel they are hungry or unsatisfied, although several studies have found no difference in a baby's level of contentment or weight gain between casein or whey-based formulas. Many mothers find that one brand suits their baby better than others.

Brands are: *Cow & Gate Plus, SMA White, Milupa Milumil, Farley's Second, Boots Formula 2, Sainsbury's Second Stage Milk.*

Soya-based formula milks
Soya-based formula is used for:

- babies who have an intolerance to cow's milk protein (which might cause eczema, asthma, crying, colic, diarrhoea)
- babies whose family has a history of allergic illness such as asthma or eczema

- babies who are lactose intolerant (see The Common Childhood Illnesses: Vomiting, page 229)
- vegan babies.

Soya-based formulas are based on modified protein taken from the soya bean and supplemented with vitamins and trace elements to make it as similar as possible to breastmilk. The formulas used in the UK are free of lactose (milk sugar, which some babies are intolerant of), so glucose, sucrose or maltose (other forms of sugar) are used instead. Some brands are also free of all animal products (it'll say on the contents label) and use only vegetable oils as the fat source (good for vegan babies).

The Department of Health (*The COMA Report on Weaning and the Weaning Diet*, 1994) advises against soya unless there's a specific reason for excluding cow's milk because:

- The sugars used are potentially more damaging to babies' teeth than lactose.
- Absorption of iron, zinc and calcium from these formulas seems to be low, although in practice babies fed them are not deficient in these nutrients because a little extra is added to compensate for this.
- Babies with allergies can also develop an allergy to soya protein. A formula using proteins modified by hydrolysis (see below) may be better.

Brands are: *Cow & Gate Infasoy, SMA Wysoy, Farley's Soya Formula, Mead Johnson Prosobel, Abbott Isomil.*

Protein hydrosylate
These formulas are based on cow's milk or soya proteins which have been broken down into simpler components that babies with food allergy or intolerance can digest without an allergic reaction, and are lactose-free. The soya-based ones are also used for babies who have fat malabsorption, which can happen in the case of prolonged diarrhoea, babies who have had gastro-intestinal surgery, or babies with inflammatory bowel disease. They are quite expensive and are given only on prescription to babies with proven food allergy or intolerance. They have a less pleasant taste and smell.

Brands are: *Cow & Gate Pepti Junior, Mead Johnson Pregestimil, Nutramigen, Milupa SHS Pepdite 0-2 Prejomin.*

Low birthweight/preterm formulas
The nutritional needs of premature babies and those of low birthweight are different from those of babies born at term. Premature babies grow very quickly and need a formula with more calories and higher levels of protein, fat, vitamins and minerals, while at the same time their digestive systems are immature, so the amount of lactose in the milk is limited. The milk used is whey-dominant cow's milk. Premature babies are especially in need of the essential fatty acids found in breastmilk, so these are often added.

Preterm formula milks are intended for babies who weigh less than 2 kg

(4 lbs 6 oz). Once the baby reaches 2 kg they can be swopped to a standard, preferably whey-based formula (which is easier to digest than a casein-based one).

Brands are: *Cow & Gate Nitriprem, Milupa Prematil, Farleys Osterprem, SMA LBW Formulas.*

Follow-on formulas

These are a fairly recent addition to the baby milk scene and are meant to bridge the gap between breast or bottle and ordinary cow's milk from six months to a year as part of a mixed diet. They are the casein-dominant 'hungry baby' formula with added protein, iron and vitamin D. Many paediatricians think they are unnecessary, and if your baby is taking enough ordinary formula supplemented by a well-balanced weaning diet, they probably are. However, given that high levels of iron deficiency have been identified in British children under two years across the UK, and that this formula contains substantially more iron than ordinary formula, it may be useful for babies who aren't eating a good range of weaning foods and so might not be getting enough iron (picky eaters, for instance).

Brands are: *SMA, Progress, Milupa, Forward, Boots Follow-on Milk, Cow & Gate Step-up, Sainsbury's Follow-on Milk.*

Ready-made formula

Most parents use dried formula milks which are made up with boiling water according to manufacturer's instructions. However, there's a small but growing market in ready-to-feed formula in cartons and – the ultimate in labour saving – ready-to-feed formula sealed into presterilized disposable bottles.

Ready-to-feed formula is made up and then heat-treated to sterilize it in the same way as longlife milk (UHT). It has the distinctive UHT smell and taste, but babies don't seem to mind this. At the moment, ready-to-feed formula costs about three times as much as powdered milk, so there's a high price to pay for the convenience, but it can be very useful if you're away on holiday, out and about or only need the occasional bottle.

A study at the Dunn Nutritional Centre in Cambridge found that ready-made formula has these additional advantages:

- It's always at the correct strength (it's not easy always to be accurate when you make up powdered milk).
- It's less likely to be contaminated with bacteria because you don't need to make it up.
- The babies in their study tended to produce softer stools.

THE GOOD BOTTLE GUIDE

Tips on feeding bottles

There is a huge variety available, but it's really a matter of personal choice which sort you buy. Normally you will need six to get you through a day's feeds (perhaps as many as eight in the early weeks) and have enough for making up a bottle for the night.

Look out for these points when you make your choice:

- Check that you can see the measuring guide clearly on the bottle and that patterns or designs don't obscure it. Making up the bottle accurately is the most important thing of all.
- Wide-necked bottles can be easier to fill (and easier to wash).
- Choose bottles that are easy to clean. Those with a central hole for the baby to hold are not a good choice (particularly for newborns, who can't hold them anyway). It's tricky to get the bottle brush round the hole and into the bottom.
- Disposable bottles can be extremely convenient when travelling. There are two sorts: one uses a roll of plastic bags which are torn off for each feed, and the other is a complete throwaway system with disposable teat.

Tips on teats

As with bottles there's a huge variety available, and there's a good deal of marketing hype about their alleged benefits. Again, it's a matter of personal preference which type you choose as your baby probably won't mind, though some mothers find they have to try a variety of different teats before their baby seems happy. Some babies do develop a preference, but that's probably only because they get used to a particular sort. There is not much evidence that they are particularly bothered that it should be as much like a natural nipple as possible, as the manufacturers would have us believe.

- Latex rubber teats (a yellow colour) are softer and thinner than silicone. The sides of the teat can squash together when the baby is sucking hard, which stops the milk flow.
- Silicone (clear) teats are harder and thicker, longer lasting and usually more expensive than latex teats. They keep their shape and don't collapse when the baby is sucking hard.
- Orthodontic teats are supposedly shaped to be more like a natural nipple. They go further back into the baby's mouth, as does a mother's nipple, which stretches as the baby sucks it.

Newborn babies can easily exhaust themselves if they have to suck too hard for their milk – breastmilk gushes out very fast, so a smaller baby may need a faster-flow teat.

> Boil new teats for five minutes before first use to get rid of any rubbery taste and to sterilize.
>   *As soon as a teat gets cracked or torn, throw it away.*

- Fast flow/slow flow teats have bigger or smaller holes which allow more or less milk to get through. Variflow teats respond to how hard the baby sucks, which is how the breast works.
- The hole in the teat should be big enough to let the milk flow at the rate of several drops a second when you tip the bottle upside down.
- Some teats have a slit in the side which is supposed to reduce air swallowing and keep the sides of the teat from sticking together. If your baby seems frustrated when sucking, it may be because they're not getting enough milk through. You can increase the size of the hole by nicking the edge of it with a razor blade (resterilize the teat before you use it).

WASHING AND STERILIZING BOTTLES

Bottles and teats must be very thoroughly sterilized as your baby is vulnerable to the slightest attack from bacteria. Traces of milk are an ideal breeding ground for bugs. Small babies have very little resistance to germs that are generally harmless to adults, and can become ill enough to be admitted to hospital if they get gastroenteritis. Thorough cleaning and sterilization of everything you use to feed your baby is absolutely essential until they are a year old to cut out this risk. Dummies and teething toys should be sterilized up to the age of nine months.

Washing – dos and don'ts
Whichever sterilization method you use, bottles and teats must first be very thoroughly washed and rinsed.

- Wash bottles as soon as you can after use.
- Rinse bottles in cold water first (hot water makes milk stick), then wash thoroughly in freshly run hot, soapy washing-up water. Formula milk is quite fatty and sticks fairly thoroughly to the sides of the bottle and teat. A good scrub is often needed to get rid of stubborn spots.
- Use a bottle brush to get right into the top of teats, the awkward angles

> *Germ Alert*
> Bacteria multiply cheerfully in a warm kitchen and can double their number every 20 to 30 minutes. Dirty bottles left for only four hours can have 256 times their original number of germs.

around the bottle neck and the bottom of the bottle. The brush itself should be kept very clean and be used *only* for bottles and teats.
- Wash the bottles in a good light. It's easy to miss spots and smears of milk if your sink is not well lit, or if you're washing bottles in the middle of the night and are very tired. You'll probably do a better job in the morning.
- Don't forget to do the lids and bottle covers.

GERM WARFARE: WHICH METHOD?

There are several ways to sterilize bottles. Even if you are breastfeeding, you will still need to sterilize spoons, dummies, teethers and juice feeders until your baby is about nine months old. All the methods are equally effective, so choose the one that suits you best.

1. Cold water
Bottles and teats are immersed in a solution made up with cold water and chemical sterilizing tablets or sterilizing solution for at least 30 minutes. You can buy sterilizing tanks which hold up to six bottles, or you can save yourself the expense and use a large plastic food box with a lid, or a bucket. Chemical sterilization isn't suitable for metal spoons or forks, so you'll need to steam or boil them instead.

Dos and don'ts
- Bottles and teats must be *very* clean. Traces of milk make the sterilization chemical less effective.
- Make sure the bottles are completely immersed in the sterilizing solution. Tanks come with a grid to hold the bottles and teats under water. Otherwise you could use a plate.
- Check that there are no air pockets in the bottles or teats by giving each one a gentle shake. Sterilization fluid can't reach the surfaces where bubbles remain.
- Rinse thoroughly with recently boiled water after sterilization. Don't run them under the tap or they won't remain sterile.
- Make up a fresh solution every 24 hours. You can use the old solution to sterilize tea towels or dishcloths before you throw it away.

Advantages
- You'll always have freshly sterilized equipment on hand ready for use.
- There needn't be any initial outlay for special apparatus.
- There's no need to carry bulky equipment if you're travelling – you can sterilize bottles in a strong plastic bag filled with solution hung up on a door knob or over the sink.

Costs

Can be just the sterilizing fluid or tablets used. Buying a special sterilizing tank which holds six bottles costs £10 to £15.

2. Steam

Steam sterilizers are becoming increasingly popular because they are quick and convenient. Bacteria or other organisms on the bottle surfaces are killed by the steam, chemicals are not needed, the bottles are free of taste or smell, and the timing takes care of itself, so you don't have to hang over it. The method is suitable for any equipment that can be boiled.

They come in two forms: an electric unit, designed to hold up to six bottles, which you plug in, add a small amount of water to and leave to turn itself off after ten minutes; or a microwave sterilizer, which is a purpose-made tub with tightly fitting lid designed to hold four bottles, which also takes ten minutes.

Dos and don'ts

- Make sure the bottles are very clean first.
- Place all items upside down in the unit, so the steam can get at all the surfaces.
- Leave to cool for a few minutes before opening. Units get very hot inside and you could scald yourself.
- Make up the milk within three hours as this is as long as the bottles and teats will remain sterile if left covered in the unit.

Advantages

- Very quick and simple to use.
- You don't need to rinse the bottles and teats before making up the milk, and there is no chemical aftertaste.
- Bottles stay sterile for up to three hours.

Costs

A six-bottle steam sterilizer costs around £30, but the running costs after this are minimal. A four-bottle microwave sterilizer costs around £10, with equally low running costs.

3. Boiling water

This was the traditional way of sterilizing before the advent of chemicals and steam sterilizers. It can still be useful if you don't have your normal equipment to hand. Washed bottles are immersed in a large saucepan of

---

Always wash your hands before handling sterilized bottles to make up feeds or you could transfer germs to them again.

If bottles need drying before use, make sure you do it with a freshly laundered tea towel or cloth. Tea towels are huge germ harbourers and can easily contaminate clean bottles.

water with a lid on, brought to the boil and boiled for ten minutes, making sure that everything remains under water. (If you let the bottles fill with water they won't bob up.) Teats need to be sterilized separately for five minutes only, because they are easily destroyed by prolonged boiling.

MAKING UP THE BOTTLES

The composition of formula milks is very carefully controlled to give your baby exactly the right quantities of energy, fat, protein, vitamins and minerals, *and depends entirely on you making up the feeds correctly*. Adding powdered milk to cooled, boiled water sounds easy, but when you're rushed or tired or your baby is screaming, it sometimes isn't.

One study published in the *Journal of the Royal College of General Practitioners* in 1989 asked mothers attending a child health clinic to measure out scoops of powder for bottles in the same way that they did at home. All the mothers had read the packet instructions and thought they were measuring correctly, but the weight of some scoops was nearly double that of others. Women who levelled the scoop by scraping it up the inner side of the packet especially were putting much more powder in than instructed by compressing it into the scoop and along the handle.

Over-concentrated feed increases the risk of overfeeding and is potentially harmful to your baby's kidneys because it gives them far too high levels of protein, fats, carbohydrates and salt. It will also make them constipated.

'Yellow labels yesterday, white labels today . . . or was it the other way round?'

This seems to bother bottle-fed babies more than those who are breastfed. The key is not to overconcentrate feeds and to give extra cooled, boiled water if your baby seems thirsty, especially in warm weather.

Step-by-step for accuracy
- First put the correct amount of cooled boiled water into the bottle or jug, then add the powder. *Never put the powder in first.* If you do this the feed will be overconcentrated because you won't be adding the full amount of water to the bottle.
- Measure the scoops of powder accurately by levelling off the powder lightly with a straight-backed (sterilized) knife. Never level the scoop off by scraping it up the inside of the tin, and never press the powder down into the scoop, or you'll be giving too much.
- Don't add an extra scoop or be even slightly over-generous to make the milk 'extra nourishing'. You'll be changing the composition of salts and minerals in the formula, which will make the baby thirsty and could be damaging to their kidneys.
- Never add anything like sugar or cereals to the baby's milk. It won't help them sleep or go longer between feeds, and it is potentially harmful. If your baby is hungry enough (and old enough) to need solids they are best given by spoon.

Dos and don'ts
- Always wash your hands before you start and make sure the work surfaces are clean.
- Let the boiled water cool a little before you pour.
- Don't use bottled mineral water or softened water for making up feeds, as it may contain salts and other minerals which are potentially harmful. Use mains tap water only (never softened water). If you're abroad and are worried about the tap water, boil it for *at least three minutes* to sterilize it before using it to make up a feed.
- Once you've added the powder, shake the bottle well with the top on to make sure the formula is completely dissolved before feeding.
- Cool bottles quickly by putting them straight into the fridge if you're not using them straightaway, or stand in a saucepan of cold water if you want to cool one down quickly for a feed.
- Don't keep made-up bottles for any longer than 24 hours.
- Never carry warm formula bottles with you when out and about, as they are dangerous breeding grounds for bacteria. Cool bottles thoroughly first

Many women find it's easier to make the whole day's feeds first thing in the morning and then store them in the fridge. This avoids the scramble to make a bottle with a screaming, hungry baby on one arm, but it does mean you may have to throw away any that aren't used at the end of the day.

and keep them with an icepack in an insulated coolbag. Warm them as you need them. You can always ask for an extra teapot of boiling water in a restaurant, or take a bottle warmer or flask of hot water with you.

How much do I need to make?

You'll soon be guided by your baby's appetite, but these quantities give a rough guide to how much milk your baby might take at each feed at different ages.

Age	Volume/bottles	
The first week	2 oz	55 ml
One month	3 to 4 oz	85 to 110 ml
Two to six months	4 to 6 oz	110 to 175 ml
Six months to a year	up to 8 oz	up to 225 ml

How do I know my baby is getting enough?

Most mothers worry that their baby may not be getting enough to eat, but there's a simple rule of thumb: if your baby is contented most of the time, active while awake, produces six or more wet nappies a day, and keeps growing on the right centile, then they are getting enough food.

Remember that breastfeeding mothers have no idea how much milk their babies are taking, and have no alternative but to leave it entirely up to them. Ideally, bottle-feeding mothers should do the same. The amount of milk each baby needs varies because each is unique. Some have an energy-efficient metabolism and grow well on less fuel than others, some are very active, others less so – their fuel requirements will differ accordingly.

Your baby's appetite may well go up and down depending on their rate of growth at a particular time, whether they are suffering from a minor illness such as a cold or cough, even how active they've been during a particular day.

However, a rough guide to quantity is to offer your baby 3 oz (85 ml) of milk for each pound of body weight a day. That means around 21 oz (595 ml) for a 7 lb (3.2 kg) baby (say approximately seven 3 oz (85 ml) feeds a day) and 27 oz (765 ml) for a 9 lb (4.1 kg) baby (say approximately seven 4 oz (110 ml) feeds a day). Don't worry if your baby doesn't take the same amount at each feed, but remember to make up a bit more than you expect them to take. On the other hand, don't worry if they take less than usual and don't try to force it on them if they don't want it. Provided they're growing, contented and healthy, they are getting enough.

Don't be tempted to push your baby to take more than they really need. It won't make them go longer between feeds, and you can over-extend their tummy and teach them not to be satisfied unless over-stuffed. They are also more likely to vomit some back up. Stop feeding when they're no longer sucking hungrily and are happy to let the bottle go.

Can I overfeed?

It is possible to overfeed a bottle-fed baby. Many want to suck for comfort when in fact they have already had enough, and they may continue feeding until they are so full that they vomit the extra milk back up. Babies can easily become used to feeling overfull and not feel satisfied until they are quite stuffed. If you are bottle-feeding, you may need more strategies to soothe and comfort your baby than a breastfeeding mother, who can offer an empty breast for comfort-sucking without the fear of the baby taking too much food. Offer them a dummy or some cooled boiled water if your baby wants to suck between feeds.

HOW OFTEN SHOULD I FEED MY BABY?

This is an individual matter, but there are two strategies:

- Demand feeding, where the baby is fed each time they cry for food.
- Scheduled feeding, where the baby is fed at regular, fixed intervals, usually every three or four hours. It's not usually possible to feed on schedule until six weeks.

Usually the baby prefers demand feeding and the parent scheduled feeding. Working out an arrangement to suit you both is a delicate compromise that can take a little while to arrive at. Many parents eventually settle on a type of semi-demand pattern where the baby has two or three of its bottles at fixed times each day, perhaps morning, noon and last thing at night, and then takes demand feeds at other times during the day.

Newborns

The food demands of babies in the first few weeks of life are very erratic. They may cry to be fed and comforted at frequent and unpredictable intervals while they adjust to the unfamiliar feeling of having a full stomach that gradually empties as food is digested.

Bottle-fed babies do best in the early days if they're treated just like breastfed ones – offered milk on demand and allowed to take as much as they like. Their tummies really are very tiny, about the size of a fig, which is one reason why they prefer to be fed little and often, and they may also want to feed for comfort and closeness. Don't worry that if you feed on demand you'll never get into a proper routine of regular feeding. Gradually,

---

Have plenty of bottles (at least eight in the first few weeks) and make them up with small amounts of formula – 2 oz (60 ml) is probably enough to start with – so that you don't waste so much milk if your baby only wants a small top-up.

as your baby grows and their digestive system matures, they will settle into a feeding pattern and get used to going longer between feeds.

After the first few weeks
Most babies settle down to a four-hourly routine of six feeds a day (per 24 hours) after the first eight weeks or so. Bottle-fed babies tend to settle more easily into scheduled feeding than those on the breast, because formula takes longer to digest than breastmilk and they can go longer between feeds.

The best feeding routine is the one that suits both of you, but a typical one, if you are aiming at regularity, might be feeds at around 6 a.m., 10 a.m., 2 p.m., 6 p.m., 10 p.m., 2 a.m.

As your baby gets bigger and their stomach capacity increases, they can take more milk at each feed and so last longer between them. Aim to drop one feed by about three months. Usually the night feed is the preferred one. You can then work on 'juggling' the feeds so that you give the last one just before you go to bed yourself. This way you stand more chance of getting an uninterrupted stretch of sleep before you're woken again by a hungry baby. If you give the last at 11 p.m., you might get to sleep until 5 or 6 a.m. if you're lucky.

A good tip in the early days is to dive into bed yourself by 8 p.m. (at least sometimes) and get your partner to give the 10 p.m. feed. You can then sleep until around 2 a.m. (six lovely hours) before you're woken again.

GIVING THE FEED

Feeding is a time for comfort and cuddling as well as giving nourishment. Cuddling is just as important to bottle-fed babies as breastfed ones, and some mothers unbutton their tops a little when they feed so that their baby can rest their cheek against their skin and enjoy feeling close and smelling their mothers.

Always cuddle your baby close when you feed them, make eye contact, and talk to them if they like this.

Dos and don'ts
- Warm the bottle beforehand to around blood heat.

  You can give milk cold, but most babies seem to prefer it warm. Stand the bottle in a saucepan of hot water or use a bottle warmer. You can use a microwave but you need to take extra care (see page 59). If you've just made the bottle up straight from the kettle, cool it down quickly by immersing it in a saucepan of cold water (keep the teat out of the water, though).
- Check the bottle temperature by dripping a little onto the back of your hand or the inside of your wrist. It should feel slightly warm, but not hot.
- Tilt the bottle up slightly as you feed so that the teat is full of milk all the time the baby is sucking and doesn't contain air. This is to prevent them swallowing air which may cause wind.

- Let your baby take as long as they like to feed.

    If they're very hungry they may finish quickly – some babies can demolish an 8 oz bottle inside ten minutes. If they're not so ravenous, they may simply want to suck longer for comfort and to be held. Breastfed babies sometimes suck for as long as forty or fifty minutes for pure comfort and pleasure; there's no reason why a bottle-fed baby should be denied the same luxury.
- *Always* throw away any unused milk at the end of the feed; never put it back in the fridge for later.
- Never prop up the bottle or leave the baby alone to feed – the baby could choke.

COMMON QUESTIONS ANSWERED

When can I stop sterilizing everything?

It's a good idea to carry on sterilizing bottles and teats until your baby is about a year old. This is because bacteria breed particularly quickly in traces of food. By one year your baby will have built up some resistance to germs, but a big dose from contaminated traces of milk can still cause gastroenteritis before then.

Normally you can stop sterilizing spoons, cups and other feeding equipment, dummies and teething rings at around nine months. By this age your baby will probably be mobile and shoving everything they meet on their travels into their mouth anyway. Even though you may not be sterilizing, it is important to keep high standards of hygiene with all feeding equipment. Wash it well in hot, soapy water and make sure no traces of food are left on it.

Does bottle-feeding make babies fat?

It can do, but it doesn't have to. Any baby can get fat if they're overfed, but this is possibly more likely with babies who are bottle-fed. Breastfed babies have a more controlled calorie intake. At the start of a feed the foremilk is low in fat, rather like skimmed milk. As feeding continues the baby gets the higher-fat hindmilk. If breastfed babies are simply thirsty they can suck for a few minutes and take only low-fat milk. Likewise if they need to suck for comfort after they've fed they take very little from the empty breast.

Bottle-fed babies don't have this luxury. All the milk they take is comparatively high in calories, so even if they are sucking for comfort only they will still be taking in calories. Bottle-feeding mothers need to find a variety of alternative strategies if they are to avoid comfort-feeding. Try offering a bottle of water or a dummy if your baby has been fed and still wants to comfort suck. Formula-fed babies also tend to begin on solids earlier than breastfed ones and this can increase the chances of chubbiness (as can sweet, sugary drinks). The chubbiness tends to fall away as soon as they get more mobile.

It's very easy to make up bottles with too much formula, so make sure you're using an accurate method (see page 54).

Can I heat bottles in the microwave?
Yes, but you need to take extra care. The concerns are that:

- The milk may heat unevenly so there may be 'hot spots' which could scald your baby's mouth.
- The outside of the bottle may feel cold even if the milk within is very hot.

If you use a microwave beware these risks. Time the bottle carefully, always shake it well, and always test the temperature by dripping some milk on the inside of your wrist before you give to the baby.

Do bottle-fed babies need water?
Yes, they may get more thirsty than those who are breastfed. Offer your baby a drink of cooled, boiled water at least twice a day. Try to avoid sweetened baby drinks as they add unnecessary extra calories. Formula milks have all the minerals and vitamins your baby needs.

Do bottle-fed babies sleep better?
Formula milks do take a little longer for a baby to digest than breastmilk, so a bottle-fed baby doesn't actually sleep *better* than a bottle-fed baby, but may sleep *longer* between feeds, up to four hours, sometimes quite early on, which means you will too.

Are bottle-fed babies more at risk of getting gastroenteritis?
Bottle-fed babies don't have the benefit of the antibodies found in breastmilk which protect against infection and help eliminate any harmful bacteria which may enter the baby's gut. For this reason it's doubly important that you're scrupulously clean when making and heating up bottles. Warm milk is an ideal breeding ground for bacteria and it's very easy to introduce germs from hands, cloths, utensils, or even from the air if you leave milk uncovered.

If you follow good hygiene rules there's no reason why your bottle-fed baby should suffer gastroenteritis.

Helping Your Baby to Sleep

You cannot *make* a baby go to sleep, or stop nightwaking, if they don't want to. But from about six months you can successfully *encourage* them to do so.

Most parents of young babies and toddlers will, at some time, find it increasingly hard to cope with the fact that they do not seem to have had a decent night's sleep since their child was born. They may find it hard to believe they'll ever get one again.

If this does not sound familiar, you are lucky. Skip this chapter. If it does – and according to Dr David Haslam, patron of the sleepless and crying baby charity CRY-SIS, between 20 and 40 per cent of parents with babies and small children do suffer repeated sleepless nights – read on. Though this is a complex area, in some cases infant sleep problems can be cured within a week.

A few obliging babies will sleep through most of the night, usually 11 p.m. to 5 a.m.-ish, from a very early age – six weeks in some cases. A few even do so within a week. Parents whose babies do so cannot understand what all the fuss is about and may assume either that you must be exaggerating, or that you are doing it all wrong. Nor do they understand the often devastating effect of sleep deprivation. My own (usually kindly) mother-in-law said, when my husband and I were hollow-eyed and desperate because our son was still waking us three times nightly at 11 months: 'But mine slept through at three weeks. Are you quite sure you're feeding him properly?'

How long do babies usually sleep?

It varies enormously, as all babies are as individual as is the mother who gave birth to them. The following figures are, according to Dr Richard Ferber – Boston-based paediatric sleep expert, and one of the first doctors to specialize in this area – purely a rough guide to the *typical* number of hours a baby might sleep in any given 24 hours.

Week 1	16½ hours
1 month	15½
3 months	15

6 months	14½
9 months	14
12 months	13¾
18 months	13½

But beware of averages. They can give new parents unrealistic expectations. Especially if you look at the list above and think that means your baby will, for the first few months, definitely be spending all that time asleep, because they may well not. Further, those sleep amounts are the average total number of hours slept per 24 hours, and may be broken up into two- or three-hour slots at night, plus half-hour naps during the day.

It's NOT your fault
A British GP, Dr Sundell, wrote, in 1922, that 'a sleepless baby is a reproach to its parents'. They're not. He has had a great deal to answer for over the years. Fortunately, medical experts – and parents – now know differently. If your baby's sleep patterns – or lack of them – are causing you problems, it's *very* unlikely to be your fault. Though there are many slight modifications you can try in your approach which might help (see below), it's perfectly possible that your baby is just Like That. Many are.

If this is the case, don't think you are somehow being an inadequate parent, or that you must be dealing with the sleep issue worse than anyone else. If another new parent you know says they're not tired, they are either being economical with the truth, or they are lucky enough to have a baby who sleeps most of the night – and some unaccountably just do – or the family is well off enough to afford a nanny who gets up at night *for* them.

Until you reach the six-month landmark, you can't do much about the broken nights, though there are lots of ways in which you can help yourself to cope with the tiredness that brings (see Beating Exhaustion, pages 311–35). But after this point, the good news is that there are a number of effective strategies you can follow.

Your sleep matters too
Sleep is essential to survival. Like all essential things, everyone tends to take it for granted until they find it is being regularly interrupted and they are losing too many precious hours. This is usually unavoidable for about six months with any new baby, but if it goes on for several months beyond this, the craving for a decent night's sleep can border on the obsessional. Any psychiatrist, parent or GP will tell you that too many months with few – or no – decent nights can turn any capable, loving parent into a glassy-eyed wreck.

Effects of sleep deprivation on you
If you have been sleepless for weeks – or months – it is perfectly normal to feel:

. . . and at the end of a long day, what we need is a good night's sleep . . .

- Constantly tired, becoming obsessed with the idea of sleep: how much you had last night and the night before; how to snatch a little bit during the day and whether your partner it getting more sleep than you.
- Inadequate as a parent.
- Depressed. Clinical depression is strongly linked to long-term exhaustion and sleep deprivation. According to the British Sleep Society, there is a 40-fold increase in your chances of suffering a mood disorder, such as anxiety or depression, if you have had interrupted sleep for the past year.

It is also perfectly normal to:

- Find it harder to be a 'good' parent, either to your baby or any older children you may have. You may be ill-tempered and have little energy left for parenting them or giving them special attention at a time when they especially need it because of the new baby's arrival.
- Start having difficulties in your relationship with your partner. You'll find you are arguing more (and not only about whose turn it is to get up this time or whether you are being 'soft' because you keep getting up to go to your baby rather than leaving them to cry at night), and have little energy left to talk, go out and have fun or make love.
- Feel resentment towards the baby as the cause of the problem – and then feel guilty about that too.

- Experience worse pre-menstrual syndrome symptoms (which may worsen after childbirth anyway, especially the birth of a second child).

You may also:

- Be more vulnerable to developing postnatal depression, which can appear at any time after birth between 0 and 12 months, though it most commonly makes its presence felt – if it's going to – around the 6 to 12 week mark (see page 415).
- Find you have lost the knack of sleeping through the night yourself – even when you get the chance (see Beating Exhaustion, page 312).

If you do feel any or all of the above *don't panic*. They are all completely normal reactions to long-term tiredness, which make the most stable personality disintegrate faster than an ice cube in a microwave. If anything, it is enormously to the credit of new parents whose nights are broken every two hours for several weeks, months, or, if you are really unlucky, years that despite getting so tired they do cope as well as they do. Dr Christopher Idzikowski, co-chairman of the British Sleep Society, says new mothers and fathers are actually very resilient and find extraordinary reserves of stamina.

A much-publicized case of what happens to people when sleep deprived was that of Peter Tripp, a top New York radio DJ, who stayed awake broadcasting continuously on air for two hundred hours to raise money for charity. He was assessed throughout by medical researchers. Though he showed few ill effects at first, Mr Tripp eventually began to hallucinate, and finally developed paranoid delusions that the research doctors were actually undertakers who had come to bury him. At one point he hared off down the corridor to try to escape them. Following his huge effort, he became quite seriously clinically depressed for a while, yet after just one single good night's sleep, he was able to function pretty well. Heartening news for exhausted parents who think they are never going to feel normal again. *You will.* And sooner than you think.

But in the meantime there is every reason to take your lack of sleep seriously. This means:

- Being confident that, no, you are certainly *not* making a fuss about nothing.
- Finding out how to work around temporary lack of sleep while your baby is small and you are concentrating on endurance rather than prevention (see pages 313).
- Tackling the problem as soon as they become old enough, and you have the necessary energy.

Why most small babies don't sleep through the night

Until a baby is about six to eight months old, it is par for the course in most cases that they *are* going to be waking up at night regularly needing milk. Babycare experts will tell you that you are just going to have to live with

---

The good news . . .
- If you get a few good nights in a row, you will feel enormously better immediately. You'll even start to feel better after *one*.
- There is a great deal you can do to encourage your baby to get a good night's sleep once they're a few months old, so that you can get some rest too (see page 74).
- There is no need to panic if lack of sleep is apparently turning you into a different person: your reaction is both perfectly normal – even healthy – *and* reversible.
- Sleep problems don't last. It really *does* get better eventually.

---

this one for a while. This may sound unhelpful, but unfortunately they are right. For the first few months, babies' stomachs are generally so tiny that they just cannot take in enough milk at the last evening feed to keep them going all night.

There are several other reasons why small babies tend to keep waking up at night:

- Their sleep cycles are shorter than adults'. The time when human beings of any age are most vulnerable to waking up is at the end of each sleep cycle. For adults this is every 90 minutes; for newborns it is 47 mins; for babies of three to eight months it is 50 minutes. So, biologically speaking, they have about twice the number of opportunities for night-waking as you.
- Babies and toddlers spend a greater proportion of the night in shallow sleep than adults do, and during these times they wake far more easily.
- Babies' sleeping habits are as much to do with their own individual temperament than anything their parents are doing (or not doing).

UNDER SIX MONTHS: HELPING YOUNGER BABIES TO SLEEP BETTER

If your baby isn't a sleeper (we've said it before and we'll say it again), it's very unlikely to be your fault. According to Dr Haslam, you can bring up two babies identically and still find that one will sleep beautifully and the other poorly. This can even apply to identical twins. But there are several soothing measures worth trying to help them sleep soundly between feeds.

Soothing sounds to go to sleep by
Some babies go to sleep better if they think they've got company:

- A clock with a loud tick.
- A radio tuned off-station so there is a gentle fuzz of white sound.
- A cassette playing soothing music so quietly it can only just be heard –

something like Mozart's violin concertos, Debussy, Chopin, Vivaldi or Brahms, or anything that has slowly rising and falling tempos, nothing too dramatic and sudden. Some young babies seem to love the rhythms of gentle reggae music (not the heavily dubbed variety).

- A ready-made tape of lullabies.
- Perhaps best of all, a tape of your own voice, and/or your partner's, just talking companionably, reading stories or singing lullabies. You may not think your voice is up to much, but to your baby it's their favourite sound and they will show a marked preference for *your* voice over the most musical of strangers' voices from three days (see *The Secret Life of Your Unborn Baby* by Nikki Bradford, Colour Picture Library, 1997).

  Get a cheap tape deck that has a repeating loop so you can have it on all night without having to rush in every forty-five minutes and turn it over. If the comforting sounds stop, babies have been known to wake up again promptly.

- Recordings of a mother's heartbeat or other womb noises (try health food shops, e.g. Holland & Barrett and the classified ads in the back of any baby magazine).
- A vacuum cleaner left on outside the room can help send some babies off to sleep, but you can't keep that on all night.
- A bubbling fish aquarium in your baby's room.

SETTING UP GOOD HABITS

At almost *any* age, you can take small steps to enhance your baby's sleep patterns. These include:

- Sleeping with your baby (see page 78).
- Not feeding them to sleep with a bottle or by breast, then putting them still sound asleep into their cot or cradle. It may seem a bit mean when they look so blissfully peaceful, but wake them just a little before you lay them down. This way they will hopefully get used to the feeling of dropping off by themselves, without depending on you as a comforter.

For breastfeeding mothers

A mug of warm milk (with honey, if you like the taste) drunk 30 to 45 minutes before the last breastfeed of the day – this is around 11 p.m. for most babies – can help your baby sleep really well. According to psychiatrist Dr Caroline Shreeve of Eversfield & Queen Charlotte's Hospital, St Leonards, milk is high in tryptophan, which has a sedative effect, and also in calcium, which has a soothing effect on the central nervous system. A snack high in tryptophan would have the same effect. T-rich foods include turkey and other lean poultry like chicken, cereals and seeds. You can also buy tryptophan supplements from health food shops.

- Making a distinction between day and night after as little as six weeks.

In the day:
Keep the lights on, curtains open, and a bit of background noise going. Feed your baby downstairs, surrounded by daytime activities like the TV or radio going quietly, other children playing nearby, adult voices. Interact with your baby, play and chat or sing to them, change their clothes and nappy.

At night:
Feed your baby peacefully upstairs in their bedroom (or yours if that is where they are sleeping) with the lights off or dim, everything quiet, no chatting from you, perhaps just singing them a lullaby or gentle song. Do not change their nappy or their clothes or otherwise disrupt them unless they are wet (rather than merely damp) or soiled.

Get a routine going
It is usually possible to get some sort of routine going from about six to eight weeks, and this helps reinforce the distinction between night and day.

Daytime
For instance: you might do something like start with a 6 a.m. feed, followed by a change of clothes, a play around 8.30 a.m., a walk in the pram at 9 a.m., another feed at 10.30 a.m., then carry them in a sling while you do a bit of housework or cooking. At 11.30 go out in the pram again to do some shopping, come back to cook lunch at 12.30 ish while your baby watches you from their pram or baby bouncer, or put them in the sling again. Let them kick on a rug with you until 1.30, give another feed at 2 p.m. – and so on. Develop whichever and as many routine activities as you wish to suit you both. It doesn't have to be that strict, as long as there is some sense of regularity for your baby to become aware of.

Many mothers say they find that once they have some sort of daytime routine, even a vague one (a regimented one can be hard to stick to when you have such a small baby to care for), their babies seem more settled and begin sleeping better at night too. This may be a reflection of their baby's increasing age, but it may also be that a familiar pattern each day has a calming influence. Perhaps it is also because as a mother regains a measure of control over what is, at least at first, a tiring, baby-driven, on-demand, routineless lifestyle, she feels more relaxed and her baby picks up on that.

Bedtime
Try to establish the sort of bedtime routine you feel your baby might like. Perhaps a warm bath in a dimly lit bathroom, then a cosy feed in their bedroom, again with dim lighting, a quiet cuddle or head-stroking session, and a particular lullaby tape or musical cot toy (always the same tune) as you settle them, awake, but happy and sleepy, in their cot.

COMMON CAUSES OF NIGHTWAKING

If your baby won't settle and sleep, there may be a physical cause. A single adjustment as simple as making your baby's bedroom slightly warmer, or curing a very low-grade ear infection that doesn't show up during the day, can make all the difference.

Here is a checklist of the most common causes of nightwaking:

- *Changing room temperature and humidity.*
  Keeping the room at a constant temperature is almost as important as how warm or chilly this is. For the first few weeks, new babies cannot adjust well to room temperature swings, so try and keep things at about 20–21 °C (69–70 °F). If you have no room thermometer, this is roughly the temperature you would feel warm enough in when dressed only in a nightdress or pyjamas without dressing gown and slippers.

  Having enough moisture in the air is very important too, as too-dry air can lead to a stuffy nose and dry throat (all common causes of repeated nightwaking). If you think this might be the problem – perhaps you've got the central heating on and don't want to open the window – consider getting a humidifier or a vaporizer (from larger branches of Boots or major department stores). At least make sure your baby's room gets a flush of fresh air through it once or twice a day.

  Unless it is very cold, turn any central heating in the baby's room right down low, or off altogether, at night, to avoid your baby getting overheated (see Cot Death page 301). If it's a very chilly night, consider putting on another light blanket an hour or so after the heating has gone off, when you get up for a late-night feed, or when you go to bed.
- *Irritating bedcothes and sleepwear.*
  As some babies just cannot seem to settle comfortably in polyester nightwear, a change of fabric is worth trying. If you don't want to buy new things until you're sure they will help, borrow a couple of cotton nighties or sleepsuits from a friend for a few days. Fold a single adult sheet into a size suitable for the cot and see if this makes a difference too.

  Another common culprit is the substance the baby's things are being washed in, particularly biological powders. They may be powerful cleaners, but children of all ages (especially babies) can be allergic to tiny deposits which may be left on their clothes. Try switching to a hypoallergenic, or at least a nonbiological, powder and conditioner. Give everything an extra rinse after each wash as well. (See Soothing Eczema, page 250 for a fuller explanation.)
- *Irritating airborne particles.*
  Keep your baby's environment as dust-free as you can. Regularly hoover the room, then damp-dust the furniture with a slightly wetted cloth to pick up as many particles as possible. Rinse well and wring out before also damp-dusting their cot or Moses basket. Remove any dust-collecting items, like feather pillows if your baby is sleeping in your bed, and any

fluffy toys. (See Dealing with Asthma, page 270 or Soothing Eczema page 249 for fuller explanations.)

- *Chilly bed.*
  Putting a warm, sleepy baby into a chilly bed is likely to wake them up again. A lambskin on top of the bottom sheet is a good option during cold weather. These wash easily, and are very comfortable for the baby to lie on outside the cot during the day too. Slightly textured, thicker cotton flannel sheets are warmer than plain cotton ones. Or wrap your baby in a light shawl when doing a nightfeed and replace them into their cot afterwards still loosely wrapped. Adjust the number of layers of bedclothes on top accordingly.

- *Baby too cold or too hot.*
  What does your baby wear at night? If they are sleeping on their own (i.e. not in your bed with you) they need as little or as much clothing as you would personally wear yourself, plus one extra light layer – cotton or polycotton sheets and cotton cellular blankets are best. So if you would usually be wearing a warm nightie, they need one too (or the equivalent type of sleepsuit with feet) plus a light cotton cardigan or cellular blanket. If they are sleeping with you and benefiting from the extra warmth this generates, leave off the cardigan layer and, avoid thick sleepsuits or they will get too hot. Leave off any woolly bonnets for night-sleeping as this will make them too hot, and use cotton blankets instead of a baby duvet (until they're at least one) or this could easily make them overheat too.

  If their nightwear has no feet, slip some socks or bootees on their feet,

---

Don't let your baby get too hot or too cold
- **Babies do not need hot rooms.**

All-night heating is only necessary in cold weather, when a thermostat may be needed to keep the temperature even.

- **Babies should never sleep with a hot water bottle or electric blanket.**

Equally do not put babies to sleep next to a radiator, heater or fire, or in direct warm sunshine.

- **Babies can be overheated because of too much clothing or bedding.**

The table below is a guide only. If a baby is sweating or feels hot take some bedding off. A nappy, vest and babygro are all the clothing that is needed.

°C	°F	
27	80	sheet only
24	75	sheet and 1 layer of blankets
21	70	sheet and 2 layers of blankets
18	65	sheet and 3 layers of blankets
15	60	sheet and 4 layers of blankets
13	55	
10	50	Remember a double blanket counts as TWO layers

(Taken from a leaflet produced by The Foundation for the Study of Infant Deaths)

> ### Sleeping safe
> Making sure your baby is neither too warm nor too cold is also one of the most important things you can do to help protect them against the possibility of cot death. The others are not smoking anywhere at all in the house, and lying your baby on their backs to sleep (see Cot Death, pages 298–307 for more detail).

as the circulation in a small baby's fingers and toes is not very good until they are about 18 months to two years old. If their bedroom air is cool, a light *cotton* night bonnet is a good idea in the early months for babies who have little covering hair. Make sure there are no dangling ties or strings on their nightwear, as this can create a risk of strangling.

The most comfortable material for babies to wear is pure cotton because nylon and polyester, no matter how cute-looking, soft and fluffy, can get uncomfortably sweaty.

When checking to see if your baby is too warm or too cold, feel the back of their neck, unless you're checking for fever, in which case feel their forehead as well. Their hands and feet are not good indicators of temperature at this age.

- *Colic?*
Colic is thought to affect up to 20 per cent of all babies during the first three months of their lives. If a baby has colic, they tend to be fine one minute and screaming inconsolably the next, clearly in considerable discomfort (some babies seem in real pain), drawing their legs up, their abdomen distended and taut. They may also pass a good deal of wind and have loud rumblings in their stomachs. The attacks are most usual in the evening ('six o'clock colic'), but can occur at any time of day, sometimes very late in the evening, waking up a previously peacefully sleeping baby. Colic bouts tend to last for two to three hours each time.

There is luckily a great deal you can do to make a colicky baby feel better (see Banishing Colic, pages 102–10).

SLEEP BREAKERS FOR BABIES OF ALL AGES

- *Soggy or soiled nappy.*
Some babies loathe soggy nappies at night, but most are not too bothered by them so there is no need to wake them for a nappy change unless you are treating them for nappy rash; the nappy is soiled or if it is really wet rather than a bit damp. Good quality disposables do appear to be far more efficient at keeping wetness away from the skin than washable ones.
- *Total silence.*
Your baby got used to a constant background of sound when they were in your womb – gurglings and rumblings from your intestine, the swishing of amniotic fluid, the sound of voices from the outside. In fact the womb

can be a noisy place, with levels reaching up to 90 decibels. So many young babies may need a little background sound to feel secure enough to go to sleep. This is especially true for premature babies who have recently come home from a special care unit in hospital where there were sounds (adult voices, machinery working, perhaps other babies crying) 24 hours a day.

• *Hyperactivity*.
There are no proven ways of identifying this as a cause of your baby's sleeplessness, but it *may* be *one* of the early signs, even in small babies. The Hyperactive Children's Support Group, see page 84, can advise you.

Is your baby ill?
If your baby is going through a particularly bad patch, or having a particularly bad night, they could be suffering from one of the following:

• *Stuffy nose?*
All babies get colds, sometimes when they are very tiny indeed. This makes it difficult for them to breathe, and even harder for them to drink their milk, so on top of everything else they are often hungry – both common nightwaking causes.

  A drop of aromatic decongestant containing Eucalyptus, Cajput or Menthol – or all three – (e.g., Olbas Oil, or Karvol, obtainable from the chemist) can be very helpful. Put it on the collar of your baby's sleepwear. In strict theory, babies under three months are not supposed to have Karvol or Olbas Oil, but in reality, check with your GP and they will probably say go ahead.

• *Nappy rash?*
If your baby has nappy rash, any urine or faeces may sting their skin, so they will need prompt changing. Keep the rash area very clean and dry and well-protected with a good barrier ointment such as plain zinc oxide cream, Kamillosan or, cheap and very effective, a petroleum gel such as Vaseline. (See Nappy Rash, page 120 for more details.)

• *Eczema?*
Might your baby have mild eczema? One baby in every ten does, says the National Eczema Society.

  Mild eczema is often missed as it can look like dry skin or nappy rash. It might not be bothersome in the day, but it can be very itchy indeed at night. Fortunately there is plenty you can do to make your baby more comfortable, and most children do grow out of it by the time they get to primary school. (See Soothing Eczema, pages 237–63.)

• *Ear infection?*
Have your baby's sleeping patterns suddenly changed from sleeping perfectly well to being restless and waking up a lot? Does your baby have a cold in the nose which is now producing thick, yellowish discharge? And, even more telling, is there also a yellowish discharge from their eyes?

  If so, the problem may be an ear infection. These vary from uncomfortable to very painful, and they are a fairly common cause of new nightwaking. A minor, subclinical ear infection which has been going on a long time, not very bothersome in the day but worse at night, is hard for patients to spot, but is also another quite common cause.

If you suspect an ear infection in the middle of the night – these can be *very* painful, as anyone who's had one themselves will tell you – give your baby an analgesic such as infant paracetamol syrup (e.g. Calpol) *now*. Continue four-hourly until you can get to see your GP the very next day. (See The Common Childhood Illnesses page 200 for more information on soothing earache.)

- *Teething?*

Babies may begin teething with their central front teeth as early as three months, though five to six months is more usual, and will continue on and off until they are two and have their back molars. This sounds like a very long time, but it tends to be the first couple of teeth which are the sorest.

Teething signs to watch for are:
— a wet patch on the sheet under your baby's head
— irritability and restlessness
— a red cheek, or cheeks
— a slightly raised temperature
— sore or swollen gums
— trying to chew at their fists, toys, feeding spoon etc.
— a reddened dribble rash around their mouth or down their chin.

If they are teething, homeopathic teething granules can be very sooth-ing. The granules available from the chemist (e.g. Nelson's Teething Gran-ules) are not as effective as a customized prescription from a homeopath (see page 131). Consider also giving your baby some infant paracetamol (e.g. Calpol or Medised) four-hourly to help soothe the discomfort. Topical soothing gels such as Teejel or Bonjela can be helpful too. (See Healthy Teeth – and Teething, pages 128–40, for more information.)

- *Constipated?*

Have your baby's bowel movements been hard and pebbly? Have they been less frequent than usual? Does your baby have to strain to pass them?

Constipation can make your baby very uncomfortable. It can be caused by fever, irregular eating habits, new foods, emotional upset, or not enough water. If they have not passed stools for four days or more, have a swollen abdomen or seem distressed, listless or generally unwell, it's time to take them to see your GP. (See Constipation, pages 183–6 for more details.)

- *Diarrhoea?*

If your baby's stools are watery, greenish, explosive and smell terrible, it's diarrhoea. It's usually more of a practical nuisance than a medical prob-lem, but it is important to avoid any risk of dehydration. See Diarrhoea, pages 195–7, for more details.

- *Urinary Tract Infection?*

Symptoms include poor sleep, unexplained temperatures, vomiting, and not growing very well. If your baby has two or more of these indicators, ask your GP to test for a urinary tract infection. If it does turn out that this is what is wrong, the problem can be treated very effectively with antibiotics.

• *Pinworms?*
These are reasonably common. They look like tiny pieces of pale thread about a third of an inch long and can be extremely itchy. They are unlikely in a very young baby but may well be the cause of nightwaking for an older infant of a year to 18 months or more. If you cannot spot any of the tiny worms themselves in the baby's bowel motions or around the anus, check for any itching around the back passage. Also look out for vaginal infection or itchiness in girls – and check whether any other members of the family, friends or friends' children have pinworms. They can easily be transferred under fingernails if hands aren't washed properly after going to the loo (one reason why washing hands is so important).

If you have your suspicions but have been unable to confirm them, try a night raid. In the dark, gently spread your child's buttocks apart and shine a flashlight on the area. If you still cannot find anything, ask your GP to take a clinical sample from the child's anal area and send it to the lab for testing – they may be able to find some of the little worms' eggs instead.

If your child does have pinworms, your GP can treat the condition with paediatric anthelmintic (de-worming) medication.

Nightwaking and illness – symptoms to look out for
There may be a medical cause for short-term nightwaking and poor sleeping patterns. Look out for the following signs:

• Your baby cries and cannot be comforted for long periods. (*Your baby is probably ill.* It could be *anything* from a high temperature to stomach pain, gastric spasm to meningitis. Or they might be coming down with something like chickenpox. Carry on comforting them with anything that seems to help – whether it's breastfeeding, rocking, walking about holding them or a warm hot-water bottle held against their abdomen. Keep a careful eye on symptoms and call the doctor if you're at all worried.)
• They seem very thirsty, and just as keen on plain water as on milk. (*Throat infection?*)
• They have slept badly since the day they were born. (*Possible compression of the bones of the skull during birth, which alters the pressure of the cerebro-spinal fluid circulating around between brain and skull, producing headaches and irritability?* If so, a cranial osteopath can often help by very gentle manipulation of the skull bones. See Useful Addresses, page 84.)
• A previously good sleeper becomes a poor sleeper. (*Infection?* Ask your GP to check your baby physically for signs of urinary tract or ear infections.)
• They wake up suddenly with stomach pains, or with a tight and gas-filled abdomen. (*Possibly a food allergy?* If breastfed, it may be something *you* are eating. The commonest culprit is cows' milk. Try dropping this from your diet for a couple of weeks and see what happens. If bottlefed, it

could be lactose intolerance. Ask your GP or health visitor about trying a lactose-free formula such as Wysoy, derived from soya.) Other possibilities include a stomach bug – any diarrhoea or vomiting? – or constipation.

- Your own intuition as a parent is telling you something is the matter. (*This is probably the most important alarm bell of all – you know your own baby.* Ring your GP and ask for an immediate appointment to check your baby over.)
- Your baby is pulling or swiping at their ear or the side of their head. (*Possible ear infection?*)
- There is an increasingly thick, yellow discharge from the nose (*ear infection, long-term cold?*) or ear (*long-established ear infection?*).
- Your baby does not want to lie down flat. (*Possible ear infection, or stomach pain?*)
- They have cold symptoms *and* are crying inconsolably. (*Ear infection?*)

If you suspect an infection, go and see your GP with your baby the same day. Doctors will always fit a young baby or toddler in immediately, without an appointment if necessary.

If your baby is clearly in considerable distress, or if you are really worried, call your doctor out even if it is in the middle of the night.

Developmental milestones

Previously good sleepers may start nightwaking for a while when they go through the first few days or weeks of any of the major developmental milestones, such as learning to sit up alone, starting to crawl or toddle. No one is sure why this affects infants' sleep. Perhaps they are receiving so much neurological stimulation down new movement pathways that their minds are becoming highly stimulated and they are dreaming about their new achievements at night, or even trying to enact them in bed, like the babies who are newly able to haul themselves up into a standing position using their cot bars, then cannot work out how to lie down again and have to shout for help.

Separation anxiety is also a possibility. Nine- to 19-month-old babies suddenly become far clingier, and if they wake up alone at night tend to want their parents, whereas before they might have felt secure enough to go back to sleep without being reassured. This is normal, psychologically healthy behaviour, and a part of all babies' development, to a greater or lesser extent. It usually fades away at around 18 months.

Some parents keep their babies in the next room during this time, calling out reassuringly to them when they wake. Others revert to the repeating loop tape trick of their parents' voices left on low all night. Others move the baby's cot into their room or take it in turns to sleep in the baby's room. Another option is to go in, lay a reassuring hand on your baby without picking up and cuddling them or turning on the light, or offering drinks or anything that would make the night-time visits especially interesting, then retreat quietly and promptly. The message is, 'We're here for you, it's OK. But if you call for us nothing exciting is going to happen.'

Emotional upheavals

Has there been any upheaval in your family recently? Has one parent had to go away for a while, have you moved house, have there been ongoing arguments between you and your partner about money or who is doing their fair share of parenting? Has your family's usual routine been disrupted in any way? Do you have an older child who is going through a difficult patch, or are you yourself exhausted, a bit depressed or feeling upset or anxious? Babies have finely tuned social radar and they pick up most changes in atmosphere.

You yourself will know the best way to help your own baby feel happy and secure, so whatever this is, do a bit more of it until things calm down, whether it's carrying them around far more in a sling, sleeping near them at night or paying them special attention. If it is you yourself who is upset or desperately tired, ask for help from your partner, relatives, GP, or a helpline (see also The First Six Months – How to Keep Going on Less Sleep page 313). It may well be that you are just depressed/anxious/angry/distressed because you are not getting enough sleep – and why not? That's a normal and reasonable reaction to sleep deprivation (see Lifesavers – How to Catch Up on Missed Sleep, page 316).

WHEN MIGHT MY BABY START TO SLEEP THROUGH THE NIGHT?

Some facts

Conventional baby wisdom states that babies should be sleeping through the night at six months. This 'fact' has depressed millions of parents with sleepless babies for the last forty years, since it was first quoted by Dr Richard Ferber, and Truby King, the New Zealand baby guru of the 1940s and 50s, amongst others. The only good thing about it is that it isn't true. At this stage babies' stomachs might be physically large enough to take sufficient milk to see them through the night, but that doesn't necessarily mean they will be sleeping through. According to the ongoing British 'Children of the 90s' Avon Longitudinal Study, out of the babies who had reached the watershed six- to eight-month mark, only 16 per cent were actually sleeping straight through. They found that half woke occasionally, 9 per cent did so on most nights, and 17 per cent woke more than once every night (between twice and nine times). So if your baby keeps surfacing, it's the norm rather than the exception.

- Top American paediatrician Professor William Sears, of the Southern California School of Medicine, says that babies usually wake up two or three times a night from birth to six months, once or twice a night from six months to a year, then once a night for one to two years.
- The strict medical definition of 'sleeping through the night' is a mere five-hour stretch.
- You cannot make a baby go to sleep if it doesn't want to any more than

you can make a baby who is determinedly falling asleep stay awake for longer.

SIX MONTHS PLUS: HOW TO HELP AN OLDER BABY SLEEP THROUGH THE NIGHT

If your baby is not sleeping through the night by the time they are six to eight months old, you can take steps to change their night-time behaviour by behavioural training, which means either leaving them to cry it out once and for all, or using a programme of gradual withdrawal. Other parents opt for co-sleeping, and others, as a last straw, use medication as a temporary measure.

First, don't even think about feeling guilty
Many parents are made to feel bad about taking action which some baby experts suggest interferes with a baby's own personal rate of adjustment. Disciples of the recent Attachment Parenting movement, which argues so persuasively for leaving the baby to take things at their own pace, accuse exhausted parents who try behavioural sleep programmes on their babies of using 'a method which trains babies with less sensitivity than we train pets', as one top pro-attachment parenting paediatrician puts it. Mothers and fathers who use this approach feel selfish, inadequate, and may be made to suffer enormous guilt about 'manipulating' their baby to suit their own convenience by other parents whose babies slept just fine, and so have no idea of the possible problems involved.

Almost all parents suffer from guilt. It is said to be nature's way of ensuring we fight to take the best possible care of our children, because no one else is likely to. The last two generations have also suffered from Babypanic because, in our era of 2.4 children per couple, we have not been brought up in big families where we could learn about babies simply by growing up with them.

Automatic parental guilt, combined with our haziness about the practical bits of babycare and our fear of doing it all wrong, leaves today's mothers and fathers vulnerable to strict *Do This, Don't Do That* rules offered by the 'experts', from midwives and GPs to paediatricians and child psychologists, who are making a bomb by writing baby how-to books. They seldom mention that there is more than one way – theirs – of tackling a problem.

'You see what power is! Holding someone else's fear in your hand, and showing it to them,' says Chinese writer Amy Tan, in her book *The Kitchen God's Wife*. Arguably, the baby expert authors are growing fat on our fears.

Everyone needs and welcomes some kindly advice. However, an experienced, friendly voice offering a balanced range of options from a wide variety of sympathetic sources so you can make informed decisions about what's best for *your* family is one thing. Baby-bossiness is another. Luckily, there really is only one rule at the end of the day: if it doesn't sound or feel right to you, forget it. It's your baby, not theirs.

Dr Benjamin Spock wrote in 1955 (boosting the confidence of generations of uncertain parents): 'Trust yourself. You know more than you think. The more people have studied different methods of bringing up children, the more they have come to the conclusion that what good mothers and fathers instinctively feel like doing for their children is usually best after all . . .'

As far as coping with a wakeful infant goes, the bottom line is that it is *you* who's getting up repeatedly night after night. Not the famous author of a baby manual which says you should respond to your baby's needs 24 hours a day, implying that if you don't you are a substandard mother. Not your next-door neighbour who happily carries her baby with her all day and sleeps with the baby as well, the better to breastfeed hourly in her sleep. This style of parenting may be right for her and her family, but that does not necessarily mean it's right for yours. If something sounds good and strikes a chord with you, try it. If it doesn't work or you don't feel comfortable about it, forget it. And if a particular strategy is clearly not working out, drop it and consider trying another one which makes more sense for you. This is how all parents find their way – a mixture of instinct, love, trial and error.

So if you reckon your baby's nightwaking has gone on too long, if you are becoming increasingly less able to function both as a parent and a person because of it, dealing with the problem makes you an extremely sensible mother or father, not a bad one.

METHOD 1: CRYING IT OUT

This means just what it says, and has worked fast for some parents. Others find they just cannot do it, or that it does not feel right to them. According to Dr Spock in his *Baby and Childcare* book, 'The cure is simple. Put the baby to bed at a reasonable hour, say goodnight affectionately but firmly, walk out of the room and don't go back.'

Most babies who have developed a pattern of nightwaking 'cry furiously for twenty to thirty minutes the first night, and when they see that nothing happens they fall asleep. The second night the crying is apt to last only ten minutes. The third night there isn't usually any at all.' Just like that.

Spock makes it sound very straightforward. Crying It Out may give quick results when it does work, but it can be more difficult than it sounds. Most parents cannot help but become very distressed indeed by the sound of their baby screaming, which a healthy baby can usually do for longer than its mother can stand. This means Crying It Out can be a tough method to be consistent about. Quite often, if the crying goes on and on, one of the parents' instincts (usually the mother's) will howl that they must go to their baby *now*, so they'll go to comfort them, giving completely the wrong message – 'My parents will have to come eventually if I can just keep crying.'

By this time the baby may well be so hysterical that they do not want to be left in their bed at all.

METHOD 2: GRADUALLY LEAVING THEM LONGER

Many parents feel better able to handle this more gradual approach. CRY-SIS reports that this method is successful in nine out of every ten nonsleeping infants, so long as they have no physical reason for nightwaking. You will begin to see an improvement, if you are going to at all, after two or three days, and most babies or toddlers should be sleeping pretty well after about a week. This method is not suitable or successful for babies under six months at the youngest (eight months plus is much better), and your baby needs to be completely well – no colds, snuffles or recent immunizations – when you try it.

The way GLTL works is that you *do* repeatedly go back in to see your child if they will not go to sleep in the first place in the evening, or will not go back to sleep at night. However, you time your visits at increasingly long intervals. Stay very calm if you possibly can, do not pick them up, cuddle them, feed them, sing to them or even make eye contact with them. Merely say something along the lines of, 'Hello, calm down, it's night-time – time for sleep now. Goodnight.' Perhaps give them a brief reassuring pat, then leave the room promptly. This is known as checking.

CRY-SIS suggests that your first visit could be after five minutes of crying, your second after ten minutes, your third after fifteen, your fourth after twenty, and so on. This way you can reassure your baby that you are there for them, but that nothing very rewarding will happen if they keep calling you back in. And you can reassure *yourself* that your baby is still physically all right, that they know you have not abandoned them, and that they are (you hope) learning that it is no longer worth calling for room service. If these intervals seem too long for you, decide on your own timings, *but it is very important to stick to whatever checking schedule you make*, or it will not work.

This method usually takes up to 7–10 days and may be hard work for all concerned. It helps to remember that:

- You should see *some* improvement after two to three days.
- You are not going to cause your child any psychological damage. Your baby sees that you do come back each time they call, and that you are not going to abandon them.
- It *does* usually work.
- You cannot continue as a parent with the sleep deprivation you have been fighting for so long.

Make a long list of all the things you will be able to do again once you get some decent sleep. Keep looking at it.

WAYS TO MAKE IT WORK

Before you start
- Talk things over with your health visitor or GP if they are sympathetic, before you begin GLTL, to see if they can offer any helpful advice.
- Clear a free week (or at least two or three days plus a weekend) to carry out the programme in, and start on a Friday night so that the worst days happen over the weekend when your partner will be around to help you get some daytime catch-up sleep. Many parents have even taken a week's compassionate leave if they are working, or taken one of their weeks' paid holiday, or, if all else has failed, simply phoned in sick for a few days. Three is the maximum allowed before you have to produce a sick note.
- Try to pre-arrange for someone (a good friend, relative, childminder, kind neighbour) to look after your baby for an hour or two each afternoon so you can catch up on sleep, if the nights have been bad.

While you're doing it
- Take it in turns with your partner. Perhaps you do the first four hours or the first entire night, while they sleep with earplugs and they do the second.
- Keep a watch or clock handy so you can keep track of the time.
- Read an easy book and wear earplugs (to *reduce* the noise – you'll still hear it) in between checks if your child's crying is really upsetting you. Or try to watch TV in another room with the baby alarm turned on very low.
- Keep a chart of what happens each night. Record how many times your baby woke up, at what times, and how long they cried before going back to sleep, plus any action other than checking which you needed to take. This way you will be able to chart the progress you are making very clearly, which will be extremely encouraging.

METHOD 3: SLEEPING WITH YOUR BABY

Now coming back into fashion with a vengeance, co-sleeping, sharing sleep, bed-sharing or three-in-a-bed, whatever you like to call it, can work beautifully.

Is there something else wrong?
If nothing works, there is a small possibility that your baby could have a specific disorder, which can still be solved but would need help from a specialist doctor. Ask your local mother and baby clinic to give your baby a thorough physical checkup to help eliminate from your mind physical causes such as specific sleep disorders, infections and allergies. If your GP proves to be less than helpful, and their practice doesn't have a mother and baby clinic, phone your health authority and ask them where your nearest major one would be.

The pluses

The friendly, protective warmth and soothing trust it generates can give new depth, delight and satisfaction to the relationship between parents and their babies.

It's not such an unusual thing to do, either. Medical anthropologist James McKenna of Pomona College in Claremont, USA, points out that in Sweden, the Netherlands, Israel, Switzerland and Japan, certain social groups' babies are sleeping in their parents' beds or rooms as a matter of course. What's more, these countries all have low levels of infant deaths (from Sudden Infant Death Syndrome and other causes).

One reason for this may be that the baby's breathing is stimulated by that of their parents during the night. McKenna suggests that the rhythm and touch factor probably plays a part in this, but it's also likely that the baby sleeping next to their parents will breathe in the carbon dioxide they exhale, which is an important stimulant for taking the next breath in.

Another reason for co-sleeping's apparently protective effect against ill health for a baby could be that they are kept warm, and receive TLC from their parents just being beside them all night – which any children's hospital unit would say is probably the most important thing that encourages sick children to get better. If constant love and parental closeness encourages very unwell children to heal faster, could it not soothe those who are healthy?

Finally, co-sleeping does solve nightwaking problems for many families who try it. Your baby may still wake up as often as ever, but when they do they are warm and cosy. You (and your partner) are right there next to them so they have the company they love best in the world. The result is generally that they go back to sleep without a murmur, and without waking you up, unless they are hungry, unwell or have a very wet nappy.

Co-sleeping may also mean your own sleep is disturbed less (if you are not troubled by any wriggling or snuffling). You may not notice if your baby wakes, then drifts off again peacefully, and night feeds are far less trouble. If you are breastfeeding your baby, it is really easy to roll over and do so if your baby is right next to you, and you wake up much less than if you go and get them, feed them, then put them back to bed, by which time you are possibly chilly and have to try and fall back to sleep again. If you or your partner are bottle-feeding, keep a fresh bottle in a bottle warmer (full of cold water until you need to heat it up) plugged in next to the bed for easy access. You might also want to keep some nappy wipes and a spare nappy there too so you can also change a wet bottom on site if necessary. Very soiled nappies are not so easy, and usually require a trip to the bathroom.

For mothers who work all day outside the home, there is another plus about having your baby or toddler sleeping with you in your bed. It may be the one time that you can both enjoy a long, satisfying stretch of the uninterrupted closeness you had to miss out on during the day.

The drawbacks

Bedsharing with a baby does not suit every family. Sleeping in their parents' bed actually *increases* nightwaking for some, who seem to prefer a certain distance to be kept between them and their parents. Other babies are active sleepers, meaning that they get a good night but you don't. Sleeping with a wriggling 11-month-old has been compared to 'sharing a bed with a cross between a puppy and a bicycle, which is taking up all the room.' As one father said, 'I didn't mind sleeping with our son in our bed if he only kept relatively *still*. But I'd cuddle him to sleep fine, then he'd lie curled against me using my testicles for all-night football practice.' Some babies are surprisingly noisy sleepers too, snoring and snuffling like small walruses – so if you or your partner sleep lightly this will keep waking you up. If you'd still like them in bed with you, try earplugs. You will hear them cry all right, but will not be aware of every nocturnal sniff and snort.

If you would like to have your baby right by you but are disturbed by their movements, try putting their cot flush next to your side of the bed with the side down. Or if they are still small enough to sleep in a basket, put it on its stand level with the side of your bed. This way you are comfortingly close, but not on top of each other.

If you have more than one child who likes to sleep by you, you could put a mattress at the end of your bed or on the other side and put the older child on that.

Is it safe to have our baby in our bed?

• Won't we somehow roll over and squash the baby during the night?

Unless you have had a lot to drink that night, or have taken drugs that might make you sleep very heavily (whether recreational drugs, tranquillizers or sleeping tablets) you won't. Sleeping parents tend to remain naturally aware of that small body next to them, like a mother labrador with a basket of new puppies: when one moves, the others automatically adjust their positions accordingly without even waking up. Think of how you react to the edge of the bed when you are asleep – you remain subconsciously aware of it so that you do not fall off it.

However, squashing (and overheating) may be a little more likely if your baby is very young and in bed *in between* you and your partner. The safest place is beside one of you and the edge of the bed, protected from rolling out by a low guard rail or the cot pushed next to the bed.

If your bed is very soft so your body creates a downhill slope when you lie down, put a board under your part of the mattress, so your baby does not roll down the dip and get stuck in a position where it's hard to breathe – i.e. face down – because they cannot push themselves back up. Young babies need to sleep flat, so do not give them a pillow.

Note: *Make sure there isn't a gap between the top of the bed and the wall or headboard too.*

- Will they get too hot?

  With your body heat adding to the warmth of the bed your baby will not need a warm furry sleepsuit or a shawl – a cotton vest and cotton sleepsuit should be enough.

- Once installed in our bed, will they ever want to leave it?

Co-sleeping enthusiasts say that children who sleep in or by their parents' bed become so emotionally secure that they grow up to be more confident than children who did not do this, and that they will cheerfully leave your bed in their own time. However, they also say that you should wait till *they themselves* show signs of readiness, which may be a bit too long for some parents' liking. Some are ready to move out at the toddler stage – perhaps to a cot next to your bed before moving into their own room. Others may not feel they want their own space until they are three or four.

This is fine for parents who are in no special hurry to get their territory back. But what do you do if you have had enough, and your child wants to stay put?

How to coax them back into their own bed

One option is to start a little night-time separation very gradually. Start playing in your baby's room with them a lot in the evening. Use it more (rather than your bedroom or the sitting room) in general, and especially for cuddles and stories or peaceful games so they become really familiar with it and associate it with happy things.

If you do not have one already, establish a bedtime routine, stick to it, and make sure that any pre-bed storytelling, hugging, lullaby singing or whatever you do happens only in your child's room, perhaps with them on your lap snuggled into a shawl. After a few weeks of this, the next step will be to try starting them off sleeping in their own bed, perhaps still comfortingly wrapped in the shawl (with fewer bedclothes to compensate) with a tape of their favourite songs, or the sound of your voice, running. Stay with them for a while without talking any more, then gently withdraw. Only take them into your bed if they wake and cry up later, and try to do so after increasingly long intervals. Some parents combine this with the GLTL method of sleep training.

If this doesn't work, your child will probably need to stay sleeping with you until they are old enough to be sold on the idea of being big enough for their own *special* bed, in their own cosy room, with all their favourite toys and books around them – probably around two years or more. As an interim stage, so your child is no longer actually in your bed but is very near to you, try a cot next to your bed, or, for an older child, a small mattress or futon, perhaps at the end of your bed. This can help your child learn to separate physically from you at night. They will still be comforted and reassured by the atmosphere of their parents during the night – but you will have got your bed to yourself again at last.

Co-sleeping, private space and sex

Co-sleeping is not everyone's cup of tea. One or both of you may feel that having given up all your waking hours to your baby, you need at least some personal space to call your own. Twenty-four-hour parenting is definitely not everyone's idea of reasonable. Other parents fear that three-in-a-bed will ruin what little sex life they have left.

If the idea of having your baby in your bed simply doesn't feel right to you for whatever reason, trust your instincts. Otherwise you may end up becoming resentful about what feels like an additional invasion of your nights. If you dutifully try it and your baby is delighted with the new arrangement, you'll end up feeling guilty as well when you call a halt to it.

As for making love, some small babies remain oblivious to what their parents are up to, but others seem to wake up promptly just as you are beginning to get going (even when they are in another room), possibly sensing a change in atmosphere. For many parents, making love while their baby is in the room feels completely inappropriate, almost indecent. Luckily there are many other places in a home that you can make love apart from your double bed. Many other times of day, too, even if you or your partner or both are out at work. It doesn't have to be at the end of the day just before you fall asleep.

If you don't like any of the alternatives, though, try temporarily moving your baby instead. I used to take my tiny son, asleep in his basket, quietly into another room, and bring him back again later. (It also has to be said that this didn't happen often during the years our babies were sleeping so little. We were usually too exhausted even to think about sex and would have swapped the opportunity to make love for even one good night's sleep anytime.)

METHOD 4: SLEEP DRUGS

Most GPs say they do not really approve of using drugs for infant sleep problems. So do most parents. However, possibly because their parents are the ones who are woken repeatedly, night after night, 25 per cent of first children have had night sedation by the time they are one and a half years old, according to research carried out in 1977. The 'Children of the 90s' study puts it higher at nearly 40 per cent.

Using medication for poorly sleeping children can give parents a vital breathing space and some rest so that they can face dealing with the problem – perhaps by trying the GLTL method, or rearranging the household so they can try sleeping with their baby at night. When you have been very tired for a very long time, you seldom have the energy to sort anything out. Occasionally, giving a child medication for a few days may break their habit of repeated nightwaking, but this is unfortunately not usual unless the period of sleep disruption was pretty short – perhaps brought on by a family holiday away from home, or a spell in hospital. For children with long-established

It is very important not to use drugs to control your child's sleep problems for more than a week – or at the very most, two weeks – unless this is under expert medical supervision from a hospital paediatric sleep clinic.

If you find that, with the best will in the world, you are unable to solve your child's sleep problems, consider asking for an NHS referral to one of these specialist sleep clinics. Your GP should be able to do this for you. If they seem unwilling or unable to help, either consult another GP, or call one of the help organizations (a specialist one like CRY-SIS, or a general one such as the Patients Association, or the Medical Advisory Service – see Useful Addresses) for advice on how to find one.

sleep problems, it might be worth trying medication for four or five nights, but in most cases this will not change matters.

After using sleep medication, parents often report their children are generally irritable and out of sorts the following day. Sedating your child *long term* may deprive them of some of their REM sleep, which is important for the development of their memory and learning, and for growth. Most parents only use mildly sedative drugs for their baby as a short-term solution or on the odd occasion. Under these circumstances there is no problem.

Over-the-counter medications you can buy in the chemist for short respite include antihistamines and cough medicines such as Medised (which anecdotal reports says is the most effective), Vallergen, Phenergen, Piriton and Benylin (Night Time formula).

Note: Phenergen and Vallergen are now only used for infants over the age of two years. They are no longer considered completely safe for younger babies.

Drugs your GP can prescribe include trimeprazine tartrate, dichloralphenazone (often seen under the brandname Welldorm and Restwel), promethazine and chloral hydrate (which tastes extremely bitter).

If you are exhausted and feel you have no alternative but to sedate your child for a few nights, try to have a word with your GP or health visitor before using medication, as there are some sedative cough medicines you can buy in the chemist which may cause hallucinations. Also, children become habituated to drugs very quickly, so, even if you're feeling a bit cautious, don't give them a lower dose than recommended, or the level that eventually has an effect may well be far higher than the real dose level they would have needed at the beginning.

Remember – it really does get better. And if you are now trying to tackle your child's sleep problems, you are already on the road to getting back the rest you so badly need.

USEFUL ADDRESSES

CRY-SIS, 27 Old Gloucester Street, London WC1N 3XX. Tel: 0171 404 5011.

A national helpline offering support and practical advice for parents or babies who cry excessively, have colic or sleep poorly. The counsellors are all parents who have formerly had, and solved, similar problems with their own babies. Also offers useful literature and a reading list.

General Council and Register of Osteopaths, 56 London Street, Reading, Berkshire RG1 4SQ. Tel: 01734 576585.

Can put you in touch with your nearest qualified osteopath, including those trained in cranial osteopathy.

Ainsworths Homeopathic Pharmacy, 36 New Cavendish Street,
London W1M 7LH. Tel: 0171 935 5330.

A homeopathic pharmacy which also offers a prompt mail-order service of homeopathic remedies. They will answer customer queries over the phone.

The Helios Pharmacy, 97 Camden Road, Tunbridge Wells, Kent TN1 2QR.
Tel: 01892 537254, or 536393 for mail order.

A homeopathic pharmacy which also offers a mail-order service for homeopathic remedies; will also answer queries over the phone.

The Hyperactive Children's Support Group, c/o Sally Bunday, 71 Whyke Lane, Chichester, West Sussex PO19 2LD. Tel: 01903 725182.

Institute of Complementary Medicine, PO Box 194, London SE16 1QZ.
Tel: 0171 237 5165.

Has an extensive (though not exhaustive) list of qualified complementary therapists of all types, countrywide.

The Medical Advisory Service, 38 Sutton Court Road, London W4.
Tel: 0181 994 9874.

A confidential telephone service operating 5 p.m.–10 p.m. weekdays, offer advice on a huge variety of health problems, including sleep deprivation.

Meet-A-Mum Association (MAMA), Cornerstone House, 14 Willis Road, Croydon CR0 2XX. Tel: 0181 665 0357.

A support group network of other mothers with babies/toddlers.
   Countrywide network of self-help, social and support groups for new mothers to make contact with others and share experiences and back-up.

National Institute of Medical Herbalists, 56 Longbrook Street, Exeter,
Devon EX4 6AH. Tel: 01392 426022.

Can put you in touch with your nearest qualified herbalist, who may be able to suggest sleep-enhancing herbs for an older toddler – or for you if your sleep patterns have been so shot that you too have lost your ability to sleep through the night – even though your baby may now be doing so.

The Patients Association, Union House, 8 Guilford Street, London WC1 1DT. Tel: 0171 242 3460.

'Listening to patients and speaking up for change.'

The Society of Homeopaths, 2 Artizan Road, Northampton NN1 4HU. Tel: 01604 21400.

Contact them for details of lay homeopaths who have had a four-year training – ask for those who have a special interest in treating babies.

TAMBA (Twins & Multiple Births Association), PO Box 30, Little Sutton, South Wirral L66 1TH. Tel: 0151 348 0020. Fax: 0151 200 5309. Tel: 01732 868000.

Help and advice on all aspects of bringing up twins, including suggestions and strategies for twins (either one, or both) who sleep poorly.

Calming the Crying

All babies cry, but some cry a lot more than others. They may just be Like That, says Dr David Haslam, GP and patron of crying baby helpline CRY-SIS, whatever their mothers do.

This chapter will explain why it's normal for small babies to cry, and normal that this crying should distress and exhaust their mothers. It will also outline how you can help calm your baby effectively, and also how you can help yourself to cope.

Mothers always feel uncomfortable when their babies cry, but the persistent crying of an inconsolable baby is an experience that goes way above and beyond this. Mothers of babies who cry and can't be comforted say they feel depressed, desperate, afraid they might hurt their baby, utterly exhausted and full of guilt. Most feel they're to blame for the crying and that they must be doing something wrong. Many come to believe they must be terrible mothers because they can't console their babies. *None of this is true* – but there is nothing like a crying baby to rob the most enthusiastic parent of their confidence.

'Women who have a crying baby do often feel very ashamed of it,' says Charlotte Preston, a former health visitor with twenty years' experience, 'and it can be a very isolating experience. I think there's a great deal of social stigma attached to being the mother of a crier because of our relatively recent heightened awareness of child abuse. For this reason crying is often a problem that's hidden or covered up. When my children were small a crying baby was regarded as quite a normal thing and it didn't seem to cause the amount of concern or anxiety it tends to now.'

How much do babies really cry?'
This seems a straightforward enough question, but finding an answer has taken an enormous amount of study and research. According to Dr Ian St James-Roberts of London University's Thomas Coram Research Centre, an internationally respected authority on crying:

- Babies cry more than you think. A couple of hours' worth a day is average in their first year. Three to four hours is not unusual.
- Babies cry most in the first 12 weeks of life.
- Crying reaches a peak at around six weeks.

'Doesn't she make you want one?'

'Several . . .'

- At six weeks about 25 per cent of babies fuss or cry for three or more hours a day.
- The evening, between 6 p.m. and midnight, is peak crying time.
- About 40 per cent of the daily total of crying takes place in the evening.
- Between the age of four months and 12 months, babies cry half as much as they did in the first three months.
- The evening crying peak disappears as babies get older, and at around nine months night-time crying becomes more common.
- Around 15 per cent of nine- to 12-month-old babies are reported to cry most at night.
- One in five families in the UK asks for professional help with a persistently crying baby – so if you are one of them, you are in good company.

All this may or may not be of any comfort to you if you're the mother of a crier. However, the good news is that both the evening crying pattern and general crying get less after three months.

The amount, volume and distress level of a baby's crying varies with age. If drawn on a graph the pattern looks like an upside-down U. The amount of crying peaks at about six weeks and tends to lessen considerably as the baby approaches his first year. There's often a big improvement as early as three to four months.

Why do babies cry?
These are some of the current theories:

- *It's normal.* From recent studies of babies in their own homes, it has emerged that they generally cry much more than has been believed up to now. Previous ideas about crying have been based on research by doctors in a hospital setting with sick babies. New research supports the view that it's probably *normal* for small babies to cry. Studies from non-Western countries which have found a crying peak at six weeks old and evidence of evening crying, even where there are big differences in the way parents care for their babies, supports this view.

'Crying can be related to a whole set of maturational changes that happen to babies at this time,' says Ian St James-Roberts. 'Virtually every system they have, digestion, excretion, liver function, temperature control, needs to adjust to life outside the womb. There's also a big neurological shift – the disappearance of the startle reflexes the baby is born with, among other things. Babies have to establish new patterns of waking, sleeping and functioning on every level.'

During this time a baby's body systems are disorganized and they may feel uncomfortable with what's happening to them. 'He may feel odd, cranky, unwell or have a headache, and of course there are differences in the way these adjustments affect different babies,' says St James-Roberts.

In other words, babies cry because they miss the warm, comfortable womb where their every need was automatically and easily met. Life outside is far less comfortable – upsetting, confusing, perhaps even painful sometimes. No wonder they cry.

- *The mother's behaviour affects crying.* Previous studies in hospital settings have suggested that anxious mothers cause crying babies, but these have largely been disproved. It's much more likely that crying babies cause anxious mothers.

- *Colic causes crying.* Probably the most popular theory is that a digestive or intestinal problem, usually termed colic, causes pain and discomfort which makes the baby cry. In fact, the terms crying and colic, or three months' colic, have become almost interchangeable. 'Colicky' is often used as a purely descriptive term for *any* baby who cries for more than three hours a day, even when there are no particular symptoms of abdominal pain, which is very misleading. 'The rule of three' which is sometimes used – a baby that cries for more than three hours, more than three days a week, for more than three weeks – describes a type of behaviour, not an illness.

- *Crying is part of babies' development.* Dutch researchers Hetty Van de Rijt and Professor Frans Plooij of the Universities of Amsterdam and Groningen have studied the development of babies for over twenty years. They claim that there are at least seven 'ages' during the first twelve months of a baby's life, major developmental stages which are quite upsetting to them, and three more between the ages of a year and eighteen months. They compare these to the physical growth spurts children have when,

---

Instead of seeing crying as an illness or disturbance, many experts feel it is a normal part of development which all small babies go through in their first three months.

Ages and stages – when might your baby cry most?

All babies go through at least *seven* developmental leaps in the first twelve months of life, and then more after that, according to Hetty van de Rijt and Professor Frans Plooij. They add that *every* baby experiences these stages, but calmer babies may be able to cope with them more easily than more anxious types. The early stages include:

5 weeks: Developmental changes affect senses and digestion. Baby is more awake and alert, breathes more regularly, cries real tears for the first time, startles and trembles less often. Expresses likes and dislikes more often, is more interested in their surroundings. After this leap babies are more cheerful and alert, more preoccupied with looking and listening.

8 weeks: Big changes in the way the baby experiences their senses. They see, hear, smell, taste and feel in a way that's completely new to them and this can make them feel puzzled, confused and upset. They may be fascinated by patterns and light, listen more keenly to sounds and discover their hands and feet. They may be more shy with strangers, want you to occupy them, sleep badly, lose their appetite or suck their thumb more.

12 weeks: Are able to co-ordinate their movements much more smoothly, are more perceptive about changes taking place in their environment, notice people's coming and going, experiment with vocal skills, in addition to crying. There may be another bout of shyness, sleeping badly, not wanting to feed, but wanting to suck a great deal.

19 weeks: Ability to understand the world around them becomes more developed. Begin to grasp that the world is made up of objects that continue to exist when out of their sight. May get clingy again.

26 weeks: Can perceive distance between objects. Climb up to reach things. Understand about distance between themselves and mother. May be more fearful.

37 weeks: Recognize categories of things. Experiment with foods and toys and want you to play constantly.

46 weeks: Begin to see things in sequences. String events together.

having not grown at all for many weeks, they suddenly shoot up by a few millimetres overnight.

The brain grows more rapidly in the first year of life than at any other time, doubling its volume and reaching 60 per cent of adult size by one year. As it grows, nerve cells called neurones, which are rather like tangled telephone wires, grow rapidly and connect up with each other to form more and more circuits that enable the baby to think better and do more things. Neurological studies have shown that dramatic changes take place in the brains of children at certain points, shortly after which there is a marked leap forward in learning and mental development. The researchers describe it as a type of rebirth, when the baby's familiar world is turned upside down with an unexpected jolt. This may cause them to feel so unsettled that they will do everything in their power to cling to the only safety and security they know – you. Which is why a normally cheerful baby will quite unexpectedly become tearful, troublesome, demanding and clingy. They also say that the anxiety, irritation and sheer exhaustion these stages induce in the baby's mother is perfectly normal.

According to this developmental view, babies who cry excessively are at the extreme end of a range of *normal* behaviour – they are *not* ill, and you are not looking after them badly. This confirms what doctors already know about 'colicky' babies – that the vast majority are healthy, thriving and not in need of medical treatment.

This doesn't rule out the fact that there is still a small group of babies who do suffer gastrointestinal problems which cause a particularly difficult type of crying problem. It may be more accurate to reserve the term colic for this sub-group (see page 102).

You're doing it right – how mothers are helping their crying babies
Our culture puts great value on 'good' babies. We tend to equate the good baby or good mother with a *quiet* baby. If you have a good baby, you must therefore be a good mother and by implication the reverse is true, isn't it?

It's not.

A major new study from Ian St James-Roberts has shown that you can be a highly sensitive, responsive mother and still have a crying baby. In fact the mothers of crying babies studied were exceptionally good mothers: responsive, sensitive to their babies' needs and very affectionate.

'We did some work to look at the effect of maternal responsiveness and sensitivity on the crying baby's behaviour. The idea that you must be a bad parent if you have a crying baby doesn't hold up. It must be the case that some babies cry because they've got rotten parents, but in the vast majority of cases that's simply not so.'

In an earlier study by St James-Roberts and colleagues, published in *Early Development and Parenting* in 1995, many mothers reported that whether their baby fussed or cried largely depended on their own (the mother's) response. Their babies cried if left alone, but if the mothers constantly intervened the babies fretted and were unsettled, but did not actually cry.

It seems likely, looking at this and other work, that the more sensitive and responsive a mother can be towards her crying baby the better. Attention and intervention seem to help babies cope more easily with the many developmental changes and adjustments they have to make in the first few months.

The moral of the story seems to be that however exhausted and thoroughly fed up you are with your crying baby, all the walking, dancing, bobbing up and down, clucking, cooing, rocking and soothing that you force yourself to do isn't a waste of effort because it's containing crying and preventing it escalating to the sobbing, hysterical unsoothable stage, which is the most distressing type of crying for both you and your child. Your baby would very likely cry much longer and louder without your attention.

Can you prevent crying?

It usually comes as a shock to new parents when a formerly easy baby begins crying behaviour. Newborns are often mercifully quiet in the first few days, sometimes weeks, of life. 'Real' crying normally doesn't begin until after two weeks.

Can quick intervention prevent your fussy baby becoming an outright screamer? Maybe. American paediatrician Professor Bill Sears suggests parents should try intervening early, before a baby learns that fussing and crying is the only way to get the attention they need. Sears suggests responding quickly to the baby's cries, feeding frequently, and what he calls 'babywearing' – carrying the baby with you in a sling as much as you can. In this way, he suggests, mothers learn to anticipate the triggers for crying and fussy behaviour and prevent it escalating.

The idea of carrying your baby in a sling against your back or chest (babywearing) as much as you can has gained great popularity in recent years. In many non-Western cultures it's normal to keep the baby close all day for the first months of life, and babies reared this way are thought to cry less. Babywearing gained support from a study carried out in Montreal in 1986 which found that babies carried for at least three hours a day cried and fussed far less than the noncarried group. The interesting point was that the carrying mothers did this as a matter of routine, not just because their babies cried a lot.

Most parents know that movement generally comforts a baby, probably by reminding them of the movement they experienced in the womb, but advocates of attachment parenting claim there are other important factors at work too. The baby benefits from close physical contact with their mother, they believe, because her regular heartbeat and breathing have a balancing effect on the baby's irregular rhythms of waking, sleeping and digestion. Her presence is thought to help the baby regulate their developing nervous and hormonal systems and promote day-waking and night-sleeping. Continual movement also has a regulating effect on the baby's sense of balance and their sense of themselves in space. Professor Sears claims that in his medical practice this type of attachment parenting actually reduced the numbers of fussy, colicky babies, but also helped parents cope better with colic and crying behaviour.

However, constant carrying doesn't suit everyone. Our society is very differently organized from those non-Western ones where you can wear a baby

Can I spoil my baby?
The short answer is no.

Mothers of crying babies are frequently warned that they will spoil their baby by responding to their demands to be carried, and that they shouldn't 'give in' to them.

This is not true.

Small babies do not deliberately cry to wind their mothers up or ensure they never get a moment's peace, though this is what it often feels like.

A baby's crying in the first three months is reflexive. They cry because they are utterly vulnerable and dependent on you, and crying is the only way they have of communicating their needs. A need for physical contact and comfort is as vital to a small body as their need for food.

Babies of this age are not yet capable of deliberately crying to manipulate you. It is therefore not possible to spoil them by giving them the attention they need. Nor will giving them attention make them more demanding. In fact it's likely the opposite is true. One well-known study, *Infant Crying and Maternal Responsiveness*, published in the journal *Child Development* in 1972, found that mothers who responded promptly and sensitively to their babies' crying during the first six months were rewarded with children who cried *less* than average and were more sociable and confident than others at the age of one.

If your instinct tells you that your baby will be soothed by being picked up and carried, this is the right thing to do. Don't let friends and relatives damage your confidence, and possibly your relationship with your baby, by accusations of over-indulgence.

to work in the fields all day. Most parents have other children to care for and tasks to do around the house that aren't compatible with carrying a baby in a sling. It's also true that, far from wanting to wear a screaming child, most people want to put as much space between themselves and their crying baby as possible. However, the idea of babywearing as a *preventative* measure might be worth considering in the first weeks if your new baby shows signs of being an unsettled or jittery type.

The anti-crying checklist
Having a mental checklist to work through when a baby starts crying can help you cope more easily. If one solution does not seem to help, try another.

- *Is your baby hungry or thirsty?* Offer breast or bottle, even if it's only been a short time since the last feed. Offer drink from a spoon or cup.
- *Are they in pain?* Offer dummy, breast or bottle, try a colic remedy, massage, changing the baby's position, walking, rocking.
- *Tired but fighting sleep?* Offer dummy, try swaddling, lie down and pat gently whilst rocking, leave to grizzle and settle.
- *Fighting at the breast?* Check they are latched on properly, check nose is

free of the breast and baby's head tilted back slightly, check to see nose isn't blocked, change feeding position, check whether there's too much milk or the breast is engorged, in which case express some off before feeding.

- *Trouble bottle-feeding?* Try a different teat, check the size of the hole (not too big or too small), try offering bottles more frequently for a few days, try warmed boiled water or a herbal remedy before feeds.
- *Too hot, too cold, uncomfortable?* Adjust heating or amount of clothing and/or bedding, change nappy.
- *Over-sensitive baby?* Try a quieter environment, handle and talk to baby gently, limit the number of visitors, don't pass the baby round to others, try swaddling.

What sort of baby do you have?

American paediatrician Professor William Sears and his nurse wife, Martha Sears, parents of eight children, prefer the term 'high-need' babies to the more usual description colicky, fussy or difficult. They say these are the most common characteristics mothers of such babies use to describe them:

Super-sensitive – acutely aware of their environment and easily bothered by changes. Startle easily during the day and settle poorly at night. Don't easily accept strangers or babysitters.

Doesn't like to be put down – unhappy left lying in a cot or chair, want to be held, fed and walked instead.

Not a self-soother – find it hard to relax by themselves. Won't accept cuddlies, dummies or toys as comforters.

Intense – in high gear all the time. These babies put a lot of energy into what they do. They cry loudly, laugh delightedly and are quick to protest if things are not to their liking.

Wants to nurse frequently – feeds more often and sucks longer than other babies, slow to wean, may breastfeed into second or even third year.

Wakes frequently – doesn't sleep for long periods either by night or by day.

Overactive – squirms a lot while being held and muscles feel tense and stiff. May arch back and wriggle while feeding.

Unsatisfied, unpredictable – changing needs, one set of comfort measures work well one day, but not the next.

Uncuddly – described as one of the most difficult types of high-need babies. Not comfortable with being held. May arch back, stiffen legs, withdraw from contact.

Demanding – strong personality who insists on having his needs met and won't give up until they are.

- *Generally cranky?* Talk and play with the baby, try babywearing, try bouncing chair or baby bouncer, go out for a walk, check for illness or infection, comfort by rocking or soothing noise, try baby massage or warm bath.
- *Still crying?* Go out with the baby, give to someone else if you can, phone a friend, relative or helpline. Put baby safely in cot, shut the door and go to another room for ten minutes.

Should you leave a baby to cry it out?

There really is no simple answer to this one, but it is worth knowing that in the first few months of life a baby's crying is instinctive: they have no real control over it and will cry until they are exhausted. Our grandmothers were taught that crying was good for babies and exercised their lungs. We now know this is not the case. Excessive crying is not good for babies: it raises their blood pressure, uses up their resources, and can arouse them to a pitch of hysteria.

However, by around four months you may notice that your baby sometimes stops crying when you approach and *before* you pick him up. Older babies gain more control over their crying and can *learn* that if they keep on crying a parent will respond. A vicious circle can develop, especially at sleep time – you leave your baby to cry a little longer each time but eventually pick them up for comfort, which means that they continue to cry when left, knowing that you'll come in the end. This way babies can learn to cry for long periods, and to keep up the crying for much longer than you can stand to hear it.

Avoiding the problem before it begins is the best tactic. 'Babies do have to learn to feel safe lying down in their cot without you,' says Charlotte Preston, 'and you need to teach them this in the kindest, most gentle way.' It can be worth leaving an older baby, who has been fed, watered and is quite calm, to grizzle and settle himself to sleep, especially at evening bedtime. (See page 77 for more on leaving babies at bedtime.)

HOW TO STOP YOUR BABY CRYING

Soothing strategies fall into three main categories: contact comforters, movement and motion, and sounds.

Many mothers of criers find something that works – but only for a short while. You may also find that what works one day is not so successful the next. Having a combination of different soothing techniques up your sleeve, and adapting them to suit your baby's mood, may help you get through the most difficult time of day more easily. Here are some ideas.

Contact comforters

When dealing with sleepless or crying baby, try and stay as physically relaxed as you can.

This is easier said than done, but well worth attempting because babies really pick up on their parents' emotions.

If you are trying to soothe a baby and you are tense or exasperated, deliberately relax your arm/shoulder muscles because they tend to go rigid when you are upset. Let them go looser, while still holding the baby; it is just as easy to hold your baby safe in a pair of relaxed arms as in a pair of arms wooden with tension.

Also, take long, deep, regular breaths – try breathing in for a count of six, holding for six, breathing out for six, 10 times. It will help calm you down, as slow steady breathing is the fastest way to gain control over your emotions, and over several important physiological processes such as heartbeat, blood pressure and metabolic rate too. Babies find slow deep breathing very calming too. If you learnt any breathing techniques for labour, they will come in very useful again now.

Both you and your baby will sense the difference quickly if you can manage either of the above.

- *Baby wrapping.* This is an age-old way to calm a fractious baby. Place their arms comfortably at their side or across their body, and wrap your baby up firmly in a soft shawl or blanket so they are held securely.
- *A warm bath* together can be soothing in the early evening when tension is at its worst. You can breastfeed your baby or hold them close. The extra warmth and skin contact can be very relaxing for you both.
- *Tummy to chest soothing.* Lie down, face up, and drape your baby across your middle, with their head mid-chest so they can hear your heartbeat. Press them firmly to you by gently rubbing their back up and down. The slight tummy pressure can help. If it's summer or you are in bed, skin to skin contact can be especially soothing.
- *The football hold.* Lay your baby face down along your forearm with their head in the crook of your elbow and their bottom resting in your hand, forearm tucked up against you. Hold them firmly between the legs. Gently pat or rub their back with your free hand.
- *The neck nestle.* Snuggle the baby into the gap between your chin and chest so that the underneath of your chin makes firm contact with the top of their head. Many babies seem to be comforted by feeling the top of their heads gently pressed (most will wiggle their way to press their head against the top of the cot during the night). You can then bob up and down, rock or gently croon.
- *Baby massage.* This won't work if the baby is in full flood or simply not in the mood, but gentle massage with warm baby oil can release tension before it builds. Many babies enjoy being massaged after a bath. You can begin at the toes and work upwards with the baby on their back, or turn them over and gently massage their back, thus putting some gentle pressure on the abdomen. Use firm, gentle strokes, and make sure the room is very warm. Some babies don't like being undressed or massaged all over, in which case just massaging their feet can be soothing.

Movement and motion

- *Swings and things.* Rocking chairs, baby bouncers, cribs on rockers, push-chairs, prams – you name it, parents have used it to relieve their aching arms of the burden of carrying their offspring up and down. Movement is one of the best baby soothers going. Walking plus rocking seems to score most highly.
- *The baby dance.* Walking with intermittent up and down rocking can be a very successful baby calmer. Research studies have shown the best rocking is quite fast, between 60 and 90 rocks a minute. Up-and-down rocking is best for calming, horizontal rocking is more likely to promote sleep. Try rocking to your favourite music (with your Walkman on if necessary); it helps relieve the monotony for you and may add an additional soothing element. Some babies apparently like gentle reggae or soft classical. South American pan pipes have also been used with some success.
- *Slings.* Carrying is very soothing for most babies. The advantage of a sling is that it leaves your hands free to do some simple jobs while you're soothing. The newer type of soft fabric sling which drapes over one shoulder and holds the baby close in front of you seems more comfortable for both mother and baby than the seat-like slings from which the baby's legs protrude on either side. These can be extremely difficult to get a very young, floppy baby in and out of on your own.
- *Riding out the storm.* Many's the parent who, literally driven to despair, has spent the evening driving round the block in order to get the baby to sleep. Car rides, pram and pushchair rides seem to have a soothing quality and can also be calming for you by getting you out of the house for a breather.

Sounds

- *Womb music.* There are many tapes available in shops and by mail order which mimic womb sounds, and these seem to be a great hit with babies. Alternatively, make a recording of your baby's favourite sounds. Many seem to like loud drones such as the sound of the Hoover, washing machine or hair dryer. Copy it several times to make a full-length tape and switch on when you want them to sleep.
- *Singing.* However awful you think your voice is, try it on your child: they'll probably like it because it's yours. Lullabies and soothing songs with repetitive melodies seem to have most appeal. You could try making a tape if you can't face giving a concert every night.
- *Musical boxes, mobiles or other toys* can condition some babies to sleep. Turn them on when you put your baby down into the cot. You may never, ever want to hear 'Rock-a-Bye Baby' or the Brahms lullaby for the rest of your natural life, but if it works you'll be grateful.
- *Other sounds to try* are: a loudly bubbling fish tank, a ticking clock, a metronome, tape recordings of waterfalls or sea sounds.
- Studies from Professor Peter Hepper at Queen's University, Belfast, have shown that babies respond positively to sounds they heard in the womb and have some memory for familiar ones which they seem to find sooth-

ing. Did you have a favourite soap you watched during pregnancy or a song you played a lot? Try it out.

The element of surprise

Sometimes the novelty factor can surprise a baby out of a bad mood. This is more likely with bored older babies who want your undivided attention the whole time and are miserable without it. You could try:

- Holding the baby up to a mirror to view their own antics. Some are so shocked they stop.
- Upside-down swings. Hold the baby firmly by the hips, never by the legs or feet, or you could dislocate their hips.
- Plenty of patting, clapping and singing games. This is the way the ladies ride, jogging the baby up and down on your lap, seems to amuse many.
- Peek-a-boo games are popular with some babies.
- Coloured paper, wrapping paper, pretty tissue paper, silver foil which the older baby can crumple, tear and shred with great satisfaction. Bear in mind the safety element: keep a watchful eye during paper play and don't ever give a baby a plastic bag as a plaything.

THE PARENTS' SURVIVAL GUIDE

- Concentrate on just getting through this difficult stage rather than desperately trying to discover why your baby's crying or what's wrong.
- Hang on to the fact that persistent crying generally doesn't last. Most babies are past the worst by three months and much, much better by the age of six months.
- Accept that however much you long for silence you may not actually be able to stop your baby crying – but you're doing a very valuable job if you are containing their distress and preventing it escalating.
- On the basis of what studies have shown, it seems worth trying to contain a baby's crying by soothing, picking up, carrying, rocking, whatever works for you. Your baby may then be just fretful and unsettled, rather than really crying. Although this is utterly exhausting, it may be worthwhile. Long crying episodes are more likely to become inconsolable crying bouts, which are the most distressing type for both you and the baby.

The way you think of your baby's crying may help you to cope with it. Remember that:

- Crying is simply normal in small babies.
- There's probably nothing wrong with your baby or with your mothering whatsoever.
- It's not your fault or theirs.

- If you can't, or don't want to, spend hours carrying your baby, don't feel guilty about putting them down gently and leaving them to cry for a while. If you feel very tense or angry, this is probably the best thing to do. You may both need a break from each other.

- Express your anger, resentment and frustration – but not at the baby. Shaking a small baby can damage fragile brain structures and may be very dangerous. If the crying is really getting to you, put the baby safely in their cot and then go to another room to shout, yell, beat up a cushion, kick the door. Then take five minutes' time out, somewhere where you can't hear the crying, or put in earplugs for a few moments' calm silence. These feelings are far better expressed than left festering away inside.

- When all else fails, put the baby safely in their cot or pram, close the door and retreat to another room. Use a personal stereo with headphones, if you've got one, to play some music to yourself and drown out the baby's noise.

- Try not to let the baby's crying come between you and your partner. The problem can cause a great deal of tension and often sparks disagreement over the best way to deal with it. Though there are exceptions, in general fathers tend to suggest you leave the baby to scream it out, while mothers find this harder to do and are pulled back to comfort repeatedly, or carry around long term. This is normal and it is nothing to do with mothers being 'soft'. There are powerful biological reasons why their own baby's cry triggers such distress in them – there is some evidence that it raises the mother's hormone levels and blood pressure – and why it is harder for them to ignore it than for fathers to do so.

   Try to decide on a plan for dealing with the baby that you can both agree on. Keep the lines of communication open, don't shut your partner out. Now more than ever you need his support and understanding. If you feel he's not doing enough to help you, tell him exactly what you'd like him to do and when. Don't expect him to read your mind.

- Make an effort to go along to your local parent group. If you feel embarrassed about your baby's crying, call beforehand and explain you've got a crier. Other mothers are generally very sympathetic and many offer to help by taking the baby off your hands while you have a cup of tea and a chat.

- Accept the fact that it's not possible for the house to be as clean and tidy as you would like, and make up your mind to ignore the temporary drop in standards rather than let it become something else to stress you out. If you can possibly afford it, a cleaner, even a temporary one, could be one of the most important investments you make at this time.

   Arranging a cleaner in advance of your delivery is even better. Otherwise, concentrate on essentials like sterilizing the baby's bottles, and keeping the kitchen food area and the bathroom clean. Accept that most other things will have to wait until this difficult stage is past, and talk this through with your partner before he begins to resent the fact that the service has gone off recently.

- Plan the evening meal ahead so you're not trying to cook when your baby's at their worst. Peel the spuds in the morning, or have a ready-made meal in the freezer that only needs reheating.

- Grab sleep whenever and wherever you can. Power napping – a quick ten or fifteen minutes – can be very restorative. (See Beating Exhaustion page 318.)
- Try to ensure that you eat nourishing meals, however hard it is to fit them in. They needn't be elaborate but should keep up your energy levels. (See page 314 for quick four-minute energy meals.)
- Feeling low, lethargic, irritable, worthless, still tired after sleep, unable to concentrate or get out of the house, experiencing panic attacks? All these are normal symptoms of long-term tiredness, but may also indicate post-natal depression. There are many effective treatments for it, so make an appointment to see your GP about *you*, not the baby, if you're feeling increasingly like this. (See Postnatal Depression, pages 413–29.)

MOST IMPORTANT OF ALL

Don't feel ashamed to ask for help. And don't pretend that everything's fine when it's not. A crying baby is not your fault. It's not evidence that you're an inadequate mother, either. No one will blame you or accuse you for your baby's crying unless they know very little about babies (and if that's the case you don't need to hear their opinion anyway). They will be sympathetic and want to help. It's not a sign of weakness, but of real strength to be able to ask for, and accept, help.

- See your GP, the paediatrician at your child health clinic, or your health visitor – they are there to help you. Be aware that there are limitations to what they can do if your baby is not ill or unwell; but be reassured that many health areas now have sleep clinics which offer help and expertise on crying and colic. Your GP or health visitor should know of these and be able to put you in touch. If not, call CRY-SIS or Parentline for advice (see Useful Addresses).
- Don't forget other organizations such as the NCT and Meet-a-Mum (see Useful Addresses). Take advantage of what they have to offer: a nonjudge-mental, friendly ear, and practical advice.
- Accept help from parents, in-laws, other relatives and friends to spread the load of coping with your baby. Ideally get them to commit themselves to offer help on a regular basis. Plan to have help when you most need it – in the early evening when you're tired, and crying is usually at its peak.

Coping with criticism

A new baby seems to act as a green light to people to offer advice – and criticism. Unfortunately, the mother of a *crying* baby is likely to get even more than her fair share of unwanted and unhelpful comments. The best plan is to consider any advice that sounds sensible, and try to ignore critical and upsetting comments. Here are some ways to cope with criticism:

- Most criticism is likely to come from parents and in-laws. Remember that they grew up in the era of feeding to a four-hourly schedule, no night feeds and the belief that it was spoiling to pick up a crying baby. These rigid handling ideas originated with the influential New Zealand doctor Sir Truby King in the 1930s, but persisted well into the 50s and beyond. Many mothers at that time put more trust in experts than in their own instincts. Remind them that because you do things differently it doesn't mean they were wrong, or that you're criticizing their mothering. Consider the possibility that they may wish they had had the courage to ignore the 'experts' and to follow their instincts to comfort or feed their baby when it cried, instead of leaving it to howl miserably.
- Be confident – even if you don't feel it. Take the wind out of critics' sails by declaring that the way you deal with your baby is beginning to work for you.
- Defend your child. They're not spoilt because they need holding or comforting a lot. It's very difficult for people who've not had a crying baby to understand the difficulties involved. You may need to do a bit of educating.
- Use the doctor as a scapegoat. It can take the heat off you if you answer criticisms with the reply that you're doing this or that on the health visitor's advice.
- If people ask why the baby's crying, say they've got tummy ache and it's very common in small babies, didn't they know?

USEFUL ADDRESSES

Ainsworths Homeopathic Pharmacy, 36 New Cavendish Street, London W1M 7LH. Tel: 0171 935 5330.

Supplies a full range of remedies as tablets, granules, pills and tinctures by mail order.

CRY-SIS, 27 Old Gloucester Street, London WC1N 3XX. Tel: 0171 404 5011.

For written help send an s.a.e.

Meet-A-Mum Association, Cornerstone House, 14 Willis Road, Croydon CR0 2XX. Tel: 0181 665 0357.

National Childbirth Trust, Alexandra House, Oldham Terrace,
London W3 6NH. Tel: 0181 992 8637.

Osteopathic Centre for Children, 4 Harcourt House, 19a Cavendish Square,
London W1M 9AD. Tel: 0171 495 1232.

The Osteopathic Information Service, PO Box 2074, Reading,
Berkshire RG1 4YR. Tel: 01734 512051.

Can give details of properly qualified osteopaths in your area.

Parentline, National Office, Endway House, The Endway, Hadleigh,
Essex SS7 2AN. Tel: 01702 559900 (Helpline); 554782 (Admin).

USEFUL READING

Crying Baby: How to Cope, Pat Gray, Wisebuy Publications. Available by mail
order from Cry-sis.

Homeopathy for Mother and Baby, Miranda Castro, Macmillan.

Why They Cry, Hetty Van de Rijt and Frans Plooij, Thorsons.

Banishing Colic

Babies suffering from colic show a very distinct and different type of crying pattern from the usual fussing and crying of small babies.

They tend to be tense and rigid during crying spells, they may pull their knees up to their stomach, scream piercingly, go red in the face and grimace, suffer wind and bloating and show all the signs of being in extreme pain. The crying of these babies tends to come in explosive bouts, sometimes described as paroxysmal, and during these types of crying sessions they are very difficult to soothe or console.

'Our studies have shown that it's the unsoothability of this type of crying that really upsets mothers most, combined with its completely puzzling nature,' says Dr Ian St James-Roberts of the Thomas Coram Foundation Institute of Child Health. 'Not being able to console their baby during colicky crying bouts seems to upset them more than the actual amount of crying a baby does or its loudness.'

A study of 160 infants by St James-Roberts and colleagues published in *Early Development and Parenting* in 1995 showed that babies with this type of colic behaviour cried for almost four and a half hours a day, compared with the average two hours a day.

The attacks can be exhausting and upsetting for both parents and baby. They are also very frustrating for the parents, as babies can be so hard to comfort during this time. The good news is that, according to Dr Haslam, one particular study shows that 54 per cent of all colicky babies had no more episodes of it after they were two months old, 85 per cent were fine after three months and 100 per cent by four months. This may sound a long time to wait while you are in the middle of it, but knowing there is a definite end in sight can be encouraging.

THE CAUSES OF COLIC

There is no conclusive research, but the possible explanations include:

Trapped wind
Although child care experts disagree on the importance of this, many parents of colicky babies say they seem to have trouble with trapped wind. Some babies have bloated tummies during a colic attack and appear to get relief

The colic checklist

How can you tell if your baby has colic? These are all typical symptoms:

* Are they crying inconsolably and nothing you do helps for more than a few minutes at a time?
* Are they tense and rigid during crying bouts, pulling knees up to tummy?
* Does the baby seem to have a painful tummy, are they drawing their legs up?
* Is the stomach bloated, does the baby pass a lot of wind?
* Does the stomach rumble loudly at intervals?
* Does the crying happen nearly every day at the same time, usually early evening?
* Is the baby between four and 12 weeks old?
* Are they otherwise well and gaining weight?

when wind is passed either up or down. Colicky babies often have trouble feeding and may fight at the breast or bottle. Often they seem hungry, but feeding seems to make their tummyache worse, possibly because they take in extra air. They may gulp air during crying bouts, and so excess wind could be an effect, not a cause, of crying. Food intolerance or allergies can also produce extra gas in the intestine (see below).

What you can do
* Hold the baby upright on your shoulder after feeding and gently wind them.
* Try gripe water or a herbal remedy (such as a chamomile and fennel drink, for example) before feeding.
* Massage their abdomen.

Digestive immaturity
Again, paediatricians disagree about the importance of this as a cause of colic, but this explanation chimes with the developmental explanation of crying. All babies' digestive systems are immature at birth and in some babies it may take some months before it begins to function smoothly and painlessly. The baby has few digestive enzymes for breaking down foods, and the muscle movement which moves food smoothly through the gut in adults is not yet present. Instead food is propelled forward in sudden spasms.

Sometimes food goes backwards, up from the baby's stomach into his windpipe, a condition called gastro-oesophageal reflux. This is due to lack of muscle tone in the sphincter which closes off the stomach from the oesophagus. Irritating stomach acids regurgitated up into the windpipe cause the baby pain, rather like heartburn in an adult. Often the baby will cry painfully after they've been fed, writhing or squirming in pain, and may spit up often, sometimes quite forcefully. This condition needs to be diagnosed by a paediatrician. Treatment consists of thickening the baby's feeds and prescribing a drug to speed the emptying of the stomach and increase the movement of the intestine. Regurgitation happens more if a baby is lying flat, so propping up can help. In most babies, GER improves by six months and is usually greatly improved by one year old. Breastfed babies seem to suffer less from this problem.

What you can do
- Use soothing strategies (see page 106).
- Check with your GP if you suspect a medical problem.

Milk intolerance – or allergy?
Intolerance of cow's milk or an outright allergy to milk seems to be a cause of colic in a small but significant minority of babies. This aspect of colic has been more researched than many of the others and has received support from two respected studies. 'It's difficult to put a figure on how many children could be affected,' says Dr Richard Turner, a GP and paediatric allergy specialist at one of the country's few NHS paediatric allergy clinics, at North Hampshire General Hospital. 'In my experience, approximately one in five babies who come to the clinic with suspected milk intolerance improve once taken off cow's milk formula.'

The terms allergy and intolerance are sometimes confused – the two conditions are quite different. An *allergy* is a chemical reaction mounted by the body's immune system in response to a normally harmless substance. Whenever the allergen is met the body releases histamines which cause symptoms such as a rash or itchy swellings. An *intolerance* is an inability to digest particular foodstuffs or a sensitivity to them. One of the commoner forms of food intolerance in babies is lactose intolerance.

Most baby milk formulas are based on cow's milk, and a baby with milk intolerance may have a sensitivity to either one of the milk proteins or the milk sugar (lactose) it contains. It's also possible for a breastfed baby to react to milk or dairy produce eaten by the mother and passed through to the breastmilk, although this is not common. The amount of antigens that pass into breastmilk from dairy produce is very small and an allergy is generally less likely if you are breastfeeding.

Normally, if a baby is milk *intolerant* there will be other symptoms besides crying and tummy pain. Diarrhoea with frequent mucousy stools and evidence that food is being passed very quickly through the gut is one of the most common. Some babies develop a sore-looking allergy ring around the anus.

Children who are *allergic* to milk will have much more troublesome symptoms, such as vomiting, skin rashes or eczema, sleeplessness and crying, excessive wind, wheezy chest, excessive dribbling or a constantly runny nose. 'Children who are clearly allergic have very obvious symptoms; eczema is one of the most common,' says Dr Turner. 'But the group who have milk intolerance are more difficult to diagnose.'

The usual test for allergy or intolerance is a skin prick test. A tiny drop of the suspect substance is put in a little skin scratch to test for a skin reaction. This is not always as helpful as it might seem: in babies with a straightforward allergy the allergic reaction is usually all too clear, but in those with food intolerance the skin prick test is often negative. Doctors may also carry out a challenge test, removing milk from the baby's diet for two weeks, and then putting them back on to it again to test if the symptoms start again. Swapping cow's milk formula for one based on soya milk can identify and help babies with this problem. Soya-based formula is a nutritionally sound alternative to cow's milk formula and can provide all the nutrients babies need. 'An improvement can take place within twenty-four hours in some cases,' says Dr Turner, 'but normally a week is enough to show a clear improvement if milk intolerance is the problem.'

In some cases a baby proves allergic to soya-based milk too (this tends to be among very allergic babies who also have eczema), and then specially formulated milks (Pregestimil or Nutramigen) in which the proteins and lactose have been broken down into smaller components, easier for the baby to digest and absorb, are used. These milks are very expensive but are available on prescription to diagnosed allergic babies.

'Babies who are milk intolerant don't necessarily remain allergic for good, and may not grow up to be allergic children,' says Dr Turner. 'Normally I will recommend they stay off cow's milk products for between three to six months. By this time they often develop a tolerance to food antigens. At the end of this time if milk is tried again the babies can often manage it without problems.'

If you have a colicky baby with tummy pain and any of the other symptoms listed above, it might particularly be worth considering the possibility of milk intolerance if either you or your partner suffers from allergies such as asthma, eczema or hay fever. An estimated 15–20 per cent of the population are atopic – suffering from allergic reactions – and this tendency can be inherited. The child of an allergy sufferer has a 50 per cent chance of being atopic and the chance is further increased if both parents have allergies. Ask the advice of your health visitor about changing the baby's formula to a soya-based one. You have nothing to lose by giving a new baby milk a try for a week or so.

What you can do
- If you are breastfeeding, cutting out dairy produce from your own diet may help. If the baby is weaning, it might help to exclude yoghurts, butter, milk, cheese and all prepared foods containing milk from their diet, but take a dietician's advice on this. These foods are an important source of nutrition and need to be made up elsewhere.
- Try changing the baby's formula for a week to see if there's an improvement.
- If you suspect an allergy, ask your GP or health visitor for advice.

Birth complications
It's not clear how much of an effect complications during pregnancy and birth – long labours, foetal distress, forceps or ventouse delivery, Caesarean section – may have on the baby. Clearly not all babies who have difficult

births are criers, but it's possible a difficult entry into the world may dispose a baby to a colicky, jittery temperament. Babies of low birthweight tend to cry more than normal birthweight infants. One major study indicated a negative childbirth experience on the mother's part to be associated with a higher risk of a colicky baby.

What you can do

- You might try carrying as a preventative strategy. Keep your baby close to you in a sling as much as you can.
- Handle gently, don't overstimulate.
- Keep noise levels down. Don't let too many people handle the baby in their first weeks.
- Try cranial osteopathy.

A baby's skull is slightly flexible and allows some movement during birth as it passes along the birth canal. According to advocates of osteopathy, in a long or difficult birth the skull may not return fully to its normal shape, and consequently the pressure of the cerebro-spinal fluid which bathes the brain and spinal cord may cause problems like colic, sleeplessness and crying. Although this idea has not yet been scientifically proved, many parents of crying babies, and children with other health problems such as glue ear or frequent infections, do report great improvement after treatment. It involves very gentle manipulation of the bones and tissues of the skull and is safe for even very small babies.

Many babies relax and sleep during or after treatment. Osteopathic training and practice will soon be regulated by law, but in the meantime check with the Osteopathic Information Service (see Useful Addresses) for a properly qualified practitioner who has additional training in cranial techniques.

Stephen Sandler, consultant osteopath at the Portland Hospital for Women & Children in London (also Director of the British School of Osteopathy's Antenatal Clinic), says that after treatments, 'mothers have come back to say "Thank you for giving me a normal baby." It is quite extraordinary how much, in appropriate circumstances, it can help.'

Illness or infection

A baby with an illness or infection will normally have other symptoms, such as raised temperature, diarrhoea or vomiting, or unwillingness to feed, in addition to persistent crying. The one exception to this is a urinary tract infection, where crying is sometimes the only symptom. It can be very difficult to tell if a baby who normally cries a great deal is in fact unwell. Your best guide is to try to gauge whether the amount of crying and type of crying is normal for your baby.

What you can do

If you suspect your 'crier' is putting in more than their normal quota, ask your GP to check them over.

How your doctor can help with colic

The health visitor may be your first port of call for help with a colicky baby. Many can be extremely helpful and offer practical and useful advice. Beyond this, your GP can help by ruling out the possibility of any underlying illness and set your mind at rest. They may suggest that they are admitted to hospital for observation.

The vast majority of crying, colicky babies are healthy and thriving. In these cases, 'colic' refers to their behaviour, not a medical disorder requiring treatment. If your baby is thriving and gaining weight, they are unlikely to be ill or unwell.

COLIC REMEDIES OLD AND NEW

- *Gripe water* has been the traditional standby for colicky, crying babies for decades. In the 1950s and 60s it was given as a preventative measure after each feed, and mothers often had a drop too. Until the late 1980s it contained alcohol, now it contains sugar, water, sodium bicarbonate and dill seed oil. Some mothers find it works, others that it's not much help.
- *Colic drops* are another variation on the same theme. Dentinox Colic Drops and Infacol are two products containing simethicone and anti-flatulent to soothe gut pain and wind. Some mothers swear by these medications, others find them of little value.
- *Dummies* can be a godsend if you have a crier. Sucking has a powerful pacifying effect on babies and many seem to need more sucking time than is necessary for just feeding. One study of fussy newborn babies showed that those who were given a dummy after feeding continued to suck for an average of one hour. Dummies avoid the need to put the baby constantly to the breast or bottle.

    Three cautions:

    — Don't sweeten them with anything, or give sweet drinks in dinky feeders. Constant exposure to sugars will rot small teeth.

    — It's also not a good idea to use a dummy as a form of gag and continually pop it back in when a baby spits it out. This can block the baby's only way of communication when they want their needs met in a different way.

    — If it becomes too much of a habit and continues when your baby gets older, it may be difficult to stop.
- *Herbal remedies*, such as fennel, dill, chamomile and catmint, are herbs especially recommended by herbalist and mother-of-three Anne McIntyre. (You can get the herbs from health food shops and herbal suppliers.) She suggests giving the baby 1 oz (30 ml) of tea before a feed to relax the digestive tract and ease digestion. After the feed if the baby is still uncomfortable give tea again.

Make the tea by pouring 3½ fl oz (100 ml) boiling water over ¼ to ½ a teaspoon of the (fresh) herb. Cover and infuse for ten minutes, then strain and use. Slippery elm powder mixed with warm water is also soothing.

If breastfeeding you can drink these teas yourself so that the volatile oils pass through your breastmilk to the baby. Keep to less than a litre a day, though, as too much can upset them.

You can use these herbs in a stronger infusion in a home-made herbal bath for your baby, or add a few drops of diluted essential oil of chamomile, fennel or lavender (get these from the chemist or health food shops) to the bathwater to relax the baby before feeding. Commercially prepared herbal baby drinks such as fennel and chamomile are also available. Be aware that these contain substantial amounts of sugar and should not be put in dummies or pacifiers for continual use because of the damage to developing teeth.

Homeopathic remedies
Homeopathic remedies can be safely given to even the smallest babies.

Giving a remedy
Remedies come in several forms and potencies. The most widely available to the general public is 30 potency, but there are several others which have a more powerful effect which a trained homeopath can prescribe for your baby. The liquid form given from a dropper is most convenient for babies (they can have up to five drops per dose), but you'll need to find a homeopathic pharmacist or mail-order service for these (see Useful Addresses, page 109). Hard tablets (babies can have one per dose), the most easily available (Nelsons is one brand), can be crushed between two spoons to a powder and given directly on the baby's tongue, which makes it harder to spit out. It's best if your baby doesn't eat or drink anything for ten to twenty minutes before or after taking a remedy.

The more severe the pain, the more often the dose – up to six maximum – should be given. The 'wrong' remedy will do *no* harm, but will fail to produce any improvement. In cases of severe colic pain, give a dose every five minutes and stop as soon as there's a marked improvement. For less distressing symptoms, a remedy might need repeating every half an hour, or be given three times a day.

The following remedies are suggested by homeopath Miranda Castro, the author of many books including *Homeopathy for Mother and Babies*:

Chamomilla (Cham.) German chamomile. Angry crying, may hit out, cannot be comforted, insists on being carried, unbearable pain, bloated abdomen, baby cries out when passing a stool, may have diarrhoea, green stools.

Colocynthis (Coloc.) bitter cucumber. Baby pulls legs up to abdomen and screams, bloated abdomen, severe griping pains in waves. Baby better for bending forward, pressure, passing a stool.

Dioscorea (Bios) wild yam. Rumbling, windy abdomen, cramping, twisting pain. Baby arches back and screams, doesn't want to lie down, is better for being held upright.

Milk of magnesium for colic

American doctor and nutritionist Leo Galland, MD suggests that colicky babies and those with behavioural problems may require more magnesium than others. Magnesium is an important mineral and a deficiency can contribute to the severity of allergies.

Human breastmilk normally contains about 2.8 mg magnesium per 100 ml. The government's RNI (reference nutrient intake) for magnesium for babies is 0–3 months 55 mg per day; 4–6 months 60 mg per day; 7–9 months 75 mg per day; 10–12 months 80 mg per day.

Dr Galland speculates that in colicky babies hormones secreted due to their high levels of stress trigger a greater than normal excretion of magnesium in the urine.

He suggests giving ½ teaspoon (2.5 ml) of milk of magnesia, equal to 100 mg of magnesium, either in milk or food each day. If you try this, bear in mind magnesium can cause diarrhoea if too large a dose is given.

'Magnesium generally has a calming effect and enhances sleep, a bonus in both colic and behavioural problems,' he says.

Magnesium muriaticum (Mag-m) chloride of magnesium. Cramping and sore with constipation or diarrhoea. For babies whose digestive upsets made worse or caused by milk.

If the homeopathic remedies you can buy over the counter do not help, consider taking your baby to a professional homeopath as they may well get far better results with remedies specially customized for your baby.

USEFUL ADDRESSES

Ainsworths Homeopathic Pharmacy, 36 New Cavendish Street, London W1M 7LH. Tel: 0171 935 5330.

A homeopathic pharmacist that also does mail order.

CRY-SIS, 27 Old Gloucester Street, London WC1N 3XX. Tel: 0171 404 5011.

Very supportive and helpful for crying, colicky babies.

G. Baldwin & Co., 173 Walworth Road, London SE17. Tel: 0171 703 5550.

Traditional supplier of herbs and essential oils at inexpensive prices.

Neal's Yard Remedies, 5 Golden Cross, Cornmarket Street, Oxford OX1 3EU. Tel: 01865 245436.

Suppliers of herbs, herbal remedies and essential oils. Also mail order.

The Osteopathic Information Service, PO Box 2074, Reading, Berkshire RG1 4YR. Tel: 01734 512051.

For a properly qualified practitioner in your area who has additional training in cranial osteopathy.

Nappy Matters – and Nappy Rash

Keeping your baby's bottom dry and clean is a never-ending job, although these days mothers are likely to get much more help with it than in the past. A magnificent 70 per cent of fathers claim to change their baby's nappy regularly according to a survey conducted by the Institute of Child Health at Bristol. It's been estimated that British parents spend an average of seven hours a week on nappy changing for the first two years of a child's life. Babies get through about 4,500 of them before the age of two and a half.

In our mothers' day, nappies were a relatively uncomplicated business – two dozen terry towels, two pairs of plastic pants and six or so nappy pins were all that was needed. With the birth of the disposable nappy in the 1970s and the huge boom in the market, there's now an overwhelming amount of consumer choice and information from the nappy industry regarding the relative merits of each brand.

More than 80 per cent of British mothers choose disposables. However, their ease and convenience comes at the price of a niggling conscience for many. The ecological consequences of the disposable became a high-profile issue in 1989 when the Women's Environmental Network (WEN), a London-based group of campaigners, took on the powerful paper manufacturers over the issue of chlorine bleaching to whiten disposables – and won. Now all the nappies sold in this country are bleached using an environmentally friendly oxygen process which doesn't have the deadly side effect of producing dioxins, which are both poisonous and carcinogenic.

WEN continue their campaign for a return to reusable nappies with some success. The terry towelling nappy is now seen as an eco-friendly, reusable product, and a small but growing number of mothers are turning to it. Several pilot schemes have been set up by midwives in maternity units to cut the cost of disposable waste and introduce new mothers to reusables. On one such scheme at Leicester Royal Infirmary, two-thirds of mothers in hospitals went for reusables in preference to disposables.

The disposable nappy manufacturers' counter-claim is that it's not simply a case of convenience versus conscience, since reusable nappies also consume resources – water and detergent for washing, fuel for heating and raw materials like cotton. So the choice for mothers is not cut and dried – each type has its merits. Here's what's on offer:

DISPOSABLES

The sheer convenience of disposable nappies has made them the first choice for the vast majority of mothers.

- According to Procter & Gamble, makers of Pampers, 98 per cent of British mothers use disposables, 80 per cent use them all the time, and 15 per cent some of the time.
- In Sweden the figure is practically 100 per cent and in France around 98 per cent.
- The disposable nappy first made its advent here in the early 1970s when a cellulose fluff pulp pad, originally designed for use inside a cloth nappy, was wrapped in plastic and fastened with sticky tapes.
- Sales of disposables continued to grow throughout the 1980s, and in 1994 the UK nappy market was worth £448 million, with a dozen or so different brands trying to outdo each other in terms of fit and absorbency.
- State of the art disposables now offer a snug fit in a wide range of sizes, elastic waist and leg bands, refastenable tapes, a boy or girl design plus 'ultra' technology, a gel-filled centre to the nappy giving extra absorbency.

What's in a disposable?
The core of the nappy is made of fluffed cellulose pulp, a fibre made from tree trunks. 'Ultra' nappies have AGM (absorbent gelling material) crystals added to the fluff pulp. These crystals are made from sodium polyacrylate, a high density polymer which can absorb about thirty times its own weight in liquid, compared with ordinary cellulose pulp, which only mops up about three times its own weight. When the baby's urine mixes with the crystals it forms a gel which 'locks' moisture away from the baby's skin and keeps it dry. The AGM forms a kind of chemical sponge that can't be wrung out.

Pros
- Very convenient to use.
- Easy to put on, no pins or folding, although if you have oily hands from using cream it's not quite so simple.
- Saves time – no washing or drying.
- Leaks are less likely, especially with 'ultra' brands.
- Manufacturers claim nappy rash is less likely, although there's little good published evidence to support this.

Cons
Disposable nappies are not environment friendly because:

- Each year around seven million trees are felled in Canada and Scandinavia to supply fluffed cellulose pulp for the three billion disposables sold annually in the UK.
- Although the paper companies point out that they plant three trees for every one felled, conservationists counter that ancient forests, wetlands,

moors and meadows have been destroyed to be replaced by single species plantations which are intensively managed with pesticides and fertilizers.
- Disposables pose a long-term environmental threat. Around three million are dumped in landfill sites that make a mess of the environment every year. Nappies contain plastic that may take generations to break down.
- 95 per cent of disposable nappies end up in household rubbish. Nappies contain untreated faeces and urine which is treated as domestic waste. At least a hundred viruses found in faeces can survive for over two weeks and can contaminate ground water supplies.
- Although manufacturers assure parents that AGM chemicals in nappies are safe, there has been no independent testing to verify this. In the US, consumer groups are lobbying the Food and Drug Administration to undertake government testing on the long-term health consequences for babies wearing AGM close to their skin twenty-four hours a day for an average of two and a half years.

The environment issue

Nappy companies have had to become more sensitive to the environmental disadvantages of their product and are taking some small steps towards damage limitation. Critics argue that these are too few and that far from having developed an environmental conscience they are merely worried about keeping their market share. However:

- Ultra nappies do contain between 30 and 50 per cent less pulp than ordinary nappies, although correspondingly more chemicals.
- Manufacturers are experimenting with compressing nappy packs to reduce volume and packing them in smaller, recyclable plastic bags.
- In America they have been experimenting with recycling and composting disposables, although without much success.

CLOTH NAPPIES

Fitted cloth nappies are fairly new to Britain although they're increasingly popular in America, Canada and Australia and they're catching on here fast. Mothercare, for example, have recently introduced them into some branches.

The new cloth nappies are a far cry from the terry squares our mothers depended on – a far snugger fit, much easier to put on, and they look much smarter too. Many brands come in sizes from extra small to extra large and have prettily patterned outsides. Some have additional nappy liners made from a variety of materials such as brushed cotton, wool or rayon. Most are available by mail order, see Useful Addresses.

Care is simpler than most people think – images of slaving over a boiling cauldron of nappies are outdated. 'A 60 °C wash is adequate to sterilize a nappy and many mothers wash them along with an ordinary family load after soaking,' says Gina Purrman of the Real Nappy Association.

A growing variety of shaped nappies are available which fit like disposables

and are fastened with ties, Velcro or poppers. Most are made from natural cotton. There are several systems:

- *All-in-ones* – shaped nappies with Velcro tabs and a waterproof shell which may be of coated polyester, cotton, felted wool or nylon so there's no need for overpants on top.
- *Quick-release nappies* – shaped nappies with Velcro closings, which need to be used with a separate overpant.
- *Two-piece nappies* – cloth nappies which fit a waterproof pant designed for it with Velcro closings.
- *Terry cloth nappies* – the traditional nappy folded and fastened with pins, although terries can now be pin-free thanks to a nifty new gripping device called a Nappi Nipper which is now widely available. Muslin squares are often used on newborns since they are less bulky, but they need a liner since they aren't very absorbent. Buy the best quality you can afford, as they will be more absorbent and last longer.

Pros
- Fast and simple to put on. Most don't need pins or folding.
- Cheaper than disposables, even taking into account initial outlay and the costs of washing and drying.
- Environmentally friendly.
- Need to change more frequently than disposables, but this may be beneficial in avoiding nappy rash since the baby's bottom won't be in contact with urine for as long.
- Can be used for subsequent babies.
- Don't pose the health risks associated with the disposal of disposables.

Cons
- Need soaking, washing and drying like terries.
- Initial outlay may seem expensive, ranging from £50 to £135 for around two dozen nappies, liners and covers, depending on brand.
- May not be as absorbent as ultras.
- When you're out you have to carry heavy wet or soiled nappies home with you to wash.
- Not as leak-proof as ultras and you may need an extra liner, or two nappies, and certainly plastic pants at night.
- Bulkier than disposables to carry about.

Extras needed with cloth nappies
- *Covers or overpants.* All cloth nappies, except the all-in-ones, need the addition of a pair of overpants to prevent leaks. These may be made of nylon, but traditional wool, which is a natural, breathable material and is also very absorbent, seems to be making a comeback.
- *Nappy liners.* Using a nappy liner makes real nappies much more convenient to use. Simply remove them from the nappy and flush them together with their contents down the loo. Many nappy liners are made

from polypropolene, which is not bio-degradable and defeats the object of the exercise if you're keen on being environmentally friendly, as well as keeping your baby's bottom away from chemicals. Taking the trouble to hunt down real paper liners, which are flushable, can make life much easier. The Real Nappy Association can help (see Useful Addresses page 127).

GETTING NAPPIES CLEAN

The nappy-washing service

If you don't want to use disposables but can't face the washing, or don't have a washing machine or the space to dry nappies, a nappy-washing service could be the answer. They deliver pre-folded 100 per cent cotton nappies, and pick up your soiled ones once a week. They usually also supply a bin and biodegradable bin liners. Many will 'rent' you the nappy wraps that go over nappies, or you can supply your own plastic pants or other nappy covers. Costs are around £6 to £7 a week for thirty nappies, comparable to disposables. Most services will ask you to sign up for a trial period of four to six weeks in advance. Because they wash loads of nappies at a time they are probably more environmentally energy-saving than home laundering, and may also sterilize more thoroughly because of washing at higher temperatures for longer.

There are around fifty nappy washing services nationwide. The National Association of Nappy Services (0121 693 4949) or the Real Nappy Association (see Useful Addresses page 127) can put you in touch with your nearest one. Members must sterilize nappies to the Department of Health's hospital laundry standard.

Washing at home

Reusables and terries need to be soaked, sterilized, washed and well rinsed, and the job needs to be done fairly thoroughly. Any remaining traces of ammonia or faeces may irritate or infect the skin, as can chemical residue from powders. This is the normal routine:

- You'll need a bucket with a lid to soak soiled nappies in.
- Both wet and soiled nappies need rinsing before they go into the soaking bucket. Scrape the worst off soiled nappies and flush it down the loo first.
- After soaking, soiled nappies are normally machine washed; wet ones can be just rinsed and dried if they've been soaked in a sanitizing solution.

Washing tips

Once you get into a routine with nappies the job need not be as onerous as it sounds. Finding a washing method which works for you will make life easier. Different methods of washing suit different people – it depends on what's important to you. Some mothers want their nappies very white, others

put a premium on speed and labour-saving. Babies also produce different types of stools. The Real Nappy Association gives this advice:

- The best idea is to experiment with your washing method to get the result you prefer.
- It's not necessary to boil nappies, although sterilizing at higher temperatures may help prevent nappy rash. Washing them at 60 °C is usually hot enough to sterilize adequately. Use the economy cycle to save energy.
- Always follow the manufacturers' washing instructions on care of nappies and the products to soak and wash in. Boiling can harm some types of reusables, and powders with bleach can damage Velcro fastenings.
- Otherwise, what you choose to soak nappies in is a matter of personal preference. You can use plain water or a mild solution of your normal detergent, or, to reduce odour and bleach mildly, you can use these alternatives:
  — Vinegar, about 2 tablespoons per bucket. Use white distilled vinegar and order in a 5-litre bottle from a friendly local grocer.
  — Bicarbonate of soda, about 1 teaspoon per bucket. Buy in large quantities from the chemist.
  — Bleach or nappy sterilizing solution. Follow the directions on the packet.
  Don't use:
  — Bio soaking powders with enzymes. They can irritate skin and are a major risk factor for infant eczema, which affects one in seven babies and toddlers. They are made to digest proteins and if any residue is left behind it is activated by contact with moisture on your baby's skin and may digest small areas.
  Also avoid:
  — Washing powders with biological enzymes, bleaches and optical whitening agents, for the same reason.
  — Fabric softeners – they will make your nappies water-repellent and far less absorbent.
- Washing nappies with an ordinary mixed load in your washing machine makes life easier. It's a more efficient use of the machine and makes nappies part of the normal family washing, rather than an additional chore.
- If you prefer to wash nappies only as a single load, you will need a bigger supply, since you'll need between 12 and 18 nappies to make up a full load.

Useful nappy tips
- If you're going for real nappies, take advantage of all the manufacturers' sample packs. Get one of each type in the newborn size. Send back the ones you don't like the look of and then try the rest to see which you prefer before buying more.
- Even if you use reusables, disposables may save a lot of trouble when out and about, at night or on holiday.

What's the cost?

The figures given below are from a survey prepared by the Women's Environmental Network in 1994. The price comparison is based on a two-and-a-half-year period making 5020 nappy changes. The cost of terries and reusables includes all accessories, washing agents, energy and £150 wear and tear on a washing machine. The washing service price includes delivery, nappies, wraps and accessories. The cost of disposables does not include delivery.

Type of nappy	Least expensive	Most expensive
Disposables	£703 (non-ultras)	£1104 (ultras)
Washing services	£816	£1076
Reusables	£346	£836
Terries	£250	£280

- Save supermarket carriers to wrap soiled nappies in and save yourself the expense of nappy sacks.
- If you want to try terries or reusables, don't invest in a whole two-dozen before your baby is born. Try a sample one or two on the baby to see how you get on first.
- If your baby seems to develop a rash when in contact with the chemicals in ultra nappies, get your pharmacist to order a bulk buy of the cheapest unbranded nappies they can find. These will be the least likely to contain chemicals and perfumes which irritate sensitive skin.

NAPPY CHANGING

Helpful hints

- A changing mat is a good investment. It protects surfaces from spills and stains, is easily washable and is comfortable for the baby. Cover with a muslin square or terry nappy to save a small baby's skin from contact with cold plastic.
- Put the mat on a changing surface at upper chest height so you don't need to bend, advises Stephen Sandler, senior lecturer at the British School of Osteopathy. Most changing tables are not made at back-friendly heights: raise yours up if necessary. If changing on the floor, ensure you are squatting or sitting so your back stays straight, not hunched over. Beds, especially hospital beds, unless you crank them up, are a terrible height for changing nappies on, and one of the main causes of early postnatal back strain.
- Everyone remembers to wash their hands after a nappy change to ensure they're not infected by the baby's waste products. But remember to wash your hands *before* as well so that you don't infect your baby – you'll notice that midwives and paediatricians always do. Our hands are great germ

The best nappy table ever . . . is a computer table. 'I turned mine over to a changing table when I moved over to a laptop,' says Gina Purrman of the Real Nappy Association. 'It's just ideal – the little pull-out shelf underneath is perfect for creams, wipes and other bits and pieces, I put two baskets on the bottom shelf for the nappies. It keeps everything beautifully neat, and it's just the right height too.'

carriers which can infect the baby's bottom if it's at all sore because the protective skin barrier is weakened or broken. If you don't have soap and water handy, clean them with a baby wipe.
- Make sure you have everything to hand before you start, including:
— a clean vest and stretch suit for a small baby – they may need a complete change after a bowel movement
— a bowl of warm water
— cotton wool, or wipes for older babies (use cotton wool only in the first month or so as it's gentler on a newborn bottom than wipes)
— barrier cream, if necessary (see below)
— a bag for a dirty nappy, if needed.
- Traces of cream on your fingers can ruin the adhesive fasteners on disposables (though some now have re-fastenable Velcro tabs), so wipe your hands well before putting on a new one. If a nappy has lost its stick, a fabric plaster does a very good job and saves wasting the nappy.
- Boys often wee unexpectedly when being changed. Be prepared and put a tissue over his penis while you're cleaning him up.
- Never be tempted to flush disposables down the loo, they will cause an instant blockage.
- When changing your baby, unless you are doing so on the floor, always keep one hand on them at all times. Even tiny ones can do astonishing split-second twists off the changing table the second your back is turned. Everyone has a story about the day their baby landed on its head having fallen off the changing table, and while small babies are surprisingly tough, they're not that tough.
- If your older baby tends to wriggle try:
— continuing to change them on a changing table – they'll wriggle less than if you do it on a bed or the floor
— keeping a special toy with your changing things for use only then
— hanging a mobile above the changing mat
— singing to them
— giving them something safe to play with while you change them.

How often should I change them?
All babies should be changed immediately after a bowel movement. Paediatricians suggest that newborn babies should be changed ten to twelve times a day. This may seem excessive, but newborn skin is incredibly fragile and

babies are especially vulnerable to nappy rash at around two weeks old. Older children should be changed at least six to eight times.

Estimates from disposable nappy manufacturers suggest that British parents change on average only five times a day. Manufacturers make much of the fact that their nappies keep babies drier and therefore lessen the chance of nappy rash. However, it's not wetness alone that causes rash, but bacteria too. It's easy to think that a dry nappy is also a clean one and not bother to change it. The result can be nappy rash. If a nappy feels at all spongy when you pinch the crotch, it's time for a change.

Nappy no-nos

- *Forget the talc.* Health professionals no longer advise it for nappy changing. They claim it cakes in the baby's skin folds, may cause irritation and provides a good medium for bacterial and fungal growth. Also, small babies have had to be taken to hospital after inhaling talc and choking.
- *Hold on the barrier cream.* A good thick layer of barrier cream to keep moisture away from the baby's delicate skin has always been advised after each nappy change. Many health professionals are now advising that this isn't necessary with the new type of 'ultra' nappy which draws moisture away from the skin, and that, in fact, over-use of unnecessary creams may promote nappy rash that's due to fungal (thrush) infection. You should still use a barrier cream if you're using real nappies, though.

NAPPY RASH

What is it?

Nappy rash is an umbrella term for several types of skin rash that appear in the nappy area. About one in three babies have nappy rash at any given time, and some with very sensitive skins seem much more prone to it than others.

Normally the skin is a naturally dry and slightly oily barrier against irritation and infection. However, a baby's bottom is almost continuously in contact with moisture which removes the skin's natural oils and makes it more vulnerable to damage. Bad nappy rash can make a baby very sore and cause them to cry because the urine stings whenever they wet, but normally it isn't painful and is quite easy to treat.

Newborn babies and those between the ages of eight and 10 months are the ones most likely to get nappy rash. Once babies are sleeping through the night without a nappy change, their bottom is warm, wet and airless for eight to 12 hours at a time, ideal conditions to spark a rash.

What causes it?

The cause of nappy rash is quite complex and is usually the result of several factors interacting on the baby's delicate skin to cause a type of dermatitis. In its mildest form it makes the skin slightly red. In severe cases the skin wrinkles, cracks or even develops ulcerous patches, making it more vulnerable to secondary infections like thrush.

- *Moisture* makes the baby's skin more vulnerable to all the causes of nappy rash outlined below. The key to preventing nappy rash lies in keeping the baby's skin dry. Waterproof pants, and possibly the use of disposables with their plastic backing, can promote nappy rash by providing hot, moist conditions.
- *Physical chafing and rubbing.* Wet skin is much more likely to be damaged by physical chafing, and chafed skin in turn is more vulnerable to infection and irritation from other causes.
- *Bacteria from urine.* Decomposing urine and bacteria together can cause a rash. When urine sits in the nappy for too long, bacteria begin to break it down and produce caustic ammonia. Ammonia irritates the baby's delicate skin and the longer the skin is left in contact with it the more likelihood there is of nappy rash.

  Breastfed babies tend to suffer less from this type of nappy rash as they produce a more acidic stool which discourages the chemical reaction responsible for it, whereas the stool of a bottle-fed baby is more alkaline, allowing the bacteria to flourish.

  This type of nappy rash tends to start around the genitals, not round the anus, but can spread.
- *Chemical irritants* from naturally forming micro-organisms in the bowel motions or urine, or any remains of artificial chemical irritant in the nappy itself, for example traces of detergent or fabric softener in which the nappy has been washed, can trigger a rash.
- *Enzymes from faeces*, when combined with the ammonia produced from urine, irritate the skin by making it more vulnerable to bile salts.
- *A change in diet.* New foods introduced when weaning can lead to rash due to food protein in the stool or additional acidity in urine.
- *Teething.* Urine often becomes more alkaline when a baby is teething and leads to more irritation.
- *Some medicines* such as antibiotics.
- *Diarrhoea.*
- *Allergies.* This is most common in babies with a family history of allergy. The rash can be caused by food intolerance, perfumes from baby wipes, or chemicals in nappies or creams.

Treating simple nappy rash

Most mild nappy rash should clear within a few days if you follow these simple steps. If it doesn't settle or keeps coming back, seek your doctor's advice.

How to prevent nappy rash

You probably can't entirely prevent it, but certain precautions make an outbreak less likely.

- Change your baby's nappy often. Babies who are changed at least eight times a day get less nappy rash.
- Experiment with different types of nappies to see which causes less rash in your baby. Try reusable nappies as well as different types of disposables if rash is a problem.
- Clean your baby's bottom very thoroughly before every nappy change with cotton balls moistened in plain water. Take special care to clean thoroughly after a bowel movement – you may need to use some mild soap to make sure. Where possible change the nappy immediately after a baby has dirtied it. Make sure that the skin is thoroughly and gently dried with cotton wool.
- If your baby's skin looks even slightly sore, go easy on the baby wipes. Many contain alcohol and perfumes which may irritate. Stick to plain water for cleaning up whenever you can.
- If you are using real nappies, always use a good thick layer of protective barrier cream with water-repelling qualities, such as petroleum jelly or a branded product containing dimethicone (a silicone-based water repellent), after each nappy change. Apply it thoroughly over the whole nappy area. Barrier creams aren't necessary with disposable nappies and may in fact encourage the growth of thrush.
- Rinse reusable nappies really well to remove all traces of detergent and chemical irritants. Add half a cup of vinegar to the rinse cycle of your machine. The acetic acid it contains will remain in the nappies and help prevent bacteria from making ammonia.

- Change your baby's nappy very frequently.
- Cleanse the nappy area very gently and thoroughly at each change.
- Apply a treatment cream (see below) and rub it in carefully. Then apply your normal barrier cream over the top if you use one.
- Let your baby kick around in a warm environment without a nappy on as much as you can. If they're lying in a crib or a cot, put them on several thicknesses of terry towels. A crawling baby could wear a pair of cotton pants to protect their bottom area, but you will need to watch out for puddles and change them as soon as they get wet or the object of the exercise is defeated.
- Changing the brand of disposable can sometimes help if the baby is sensitive to the chemicals or deodorizing agents it contains. The cheaper brands of non-ultra nappies can be better for some babies because they are made using fewer perfumes and chemicals.

What sort of cream?

- **Barrier creams** are used to keep moisture away from the nappy area and so prevent nappy rash. Vaseline does this job. There are also many other branded products which contain water-repellent substances like dimethicone or other silicones.
- **Emollient cream** are used to treat existing nappy rash by adding moisture to sore skin. Zinc and castor oil cream do this job. Some branded products contain antiseptics. They do not prevent nappy rash.
- **Anti-fungal creams**, e.g. Canesten, are used to clear up thrush infection in the nappy area. Use only as directed. Overuse can sometimes *cause* thrush.
- **Hydrocortisone** is a mild corticosteroid that reduces inflammation and is present in certain nappy rash treatment creams that your GP might prescribe. Generally it's not advisable to use these on babies under one year. Babies are especially susceptible to side effects and the active ingredient is particularly well absorbed across a sore area of skin. If your GP does feel this is necessary, use with great care. Apply the cream thinly and use for no longer than seven days.

NAPPY RASH AND BABIES WITH ECZEMA

Babies and children with eczema have very sensitive skin so you need to pay special attention to the nappy area to keep it dry and well moisturized. The skin will be more vulnerable to infection from bacteria and candida (thrush) if it is already sore. Eczema is not infectious, but children with eczema easily get skin infections. It's sensible to take precautions to protect them from the bacterial infection impetigo, which can be serious because it spreads so rapidly, and from infection with the herpes virus which is transmitted via cold sores.

Simple steps you can take are:

- Avoid commercial nappy rash creams and products. Use instead simple aqueous cream from your chemist for moisturizing the nappy area. It is cheap, easily available and almost never causes an allergic reaction in babies with sensitive skin.
- Always keep a separate face flannel and towel for each member of the family. Put them all in a hot wash every week.
- Don't let anyone with a cold sore kiss the baby, and don't let your baby touch children or adults with impetigo.
- Always wash your hands before you change your baby so you don't pass on bacteria.
  See Soothing Eczema, pages 237–63, for more advice.

Infantile seborrhoeic eczema

This is a common type of eczema that makes the skin look red, inflamed and flaky. It's not sore or itchy, unlike other types of eczema, so babies with it will play, feed and sleep as normal. It usually starts in the nappy area, or on the baby's scalp, but may spread to the face, neck, armpits and body. This skin problem can begin at any time between two weeks and six months, but it's unusual in babies over the age of one year.

Treatment

It should clear up on its own if you keep the skin dry and well moisturized. If it becomes infected, it will need extra treatment from your GP with an antibiotic cream.

Atopic eczema

This makes skin dry, red, sore and scaly, and is very itchy. Small blisters may form on the skin and these can burst and weep, leaving a raw surface. Eczema can be very upsetting for small babies and their mothers. A recent study funded by the National Eczema Society at Wrexham Maelor Hospital in Clwyd found that 86 per cent of pre-school-age children with eczema suffered sleep disturbance due to it.

Treatment

Good skin care is very important to make the skin more comfortable and prevent flare-ups and infection. Treatment, supervised by your GP, may be with:

- *Topical steroids* – a cream, lotion or gel containing 1% hydrocortisone to damp down inflammation and reduce the risk of infection from scratching, although this is normally avoided with children under two if possible.
- *Oral antihistamines* – these medicines, taken by mouth, make the skin less itchy.
- *Antibiotics* – as a cream or by mouth to treat infection.
- *Medicated bandages* – can be applied to bad patches to moisturize the skin and protect it from more damage.
- *Gamma-linolenic acid (GLA)* – found in evening primrose oil. Taken by mouth it may help make the skin less itchy.

Special nappy care for eczema babies

The National Eczema Society advises the following for babies with eczema:

- Check nappies often if the skin is sore and change them as soon as they become wet or soiled.
- Disposable nappies are good for babies prone to nappy rash because they keep their bottoms drier, but they still need changing often.
- At each nappy change clean the baby's bottom using water with a little medicinal bath oil added (such as Oilatum or Balneum, available at good

chemists). Apply a good moisturizing cream, preferably simple aqueous cream, available from the pharmacist. Avoid talc and other barrier or nappy rash creams as they can irritate the skin.

- Avoid putting plastic pants over a nappy.
- If the skin is sore, try to leave the baby out of nappies as much as possible.
- Babies and children with eczema usually benefit from a lukewarm bath or wash each day to keep skin clean, remove scales and crusts and moisturize, especially if a medicinal bath oil is added (Oilatum, Balneum). Don't use soap or bubble bath, even those advertised for sensitive skin, as they can still dry it out and irritate.
- Biological washing powders contain enzymes which can make skin problems worse. Ordinary non-biological powders are better for washing nappies and baby clothes.

WHEN NAPPY RASH WON'T CLEAR UP

If nappy rash doesn't clear within a few days following the steps outlined above, it's likely there's a secondary infection from thrush or bacteria which needs additional treatment.

Thrush
Thrush is the common name for the candida fungi which are present in the mouth and gastrointestinal tract and are normally quite harmless, but if something causes them to multiply very rapidly – moisture is a common cause, or a course of antibiotic treatment which kills off the bacteria in the body that normally keep candida under control – it can become a problem.

The result is reddened, sore skin in the nappy area. Unlike ordinary nappy rash, the soreness goes right into the skin creases of the groin, sometimes inside the vulva or onto the penis, and may cover the thighs. The rash may also have raised edges, although this isn't always easy to spot. You'll notice small, pimple-like red spots which extend out from the main sore area. It can be very itchy and uncomfortable.

Treating thrush
Follow the steps given above for ordinary nappy rash – change the nappy often, clean the nappy area thoroughly and let the baby go nappy-free whenever practical. Additionally:

- Thrush needs treating with an anti-fungal cream containing the active ingredients clotrimazole, nystatin or miconazole. You can buy an effective cream at the chemist without a prescription. If the baby is very sore, your GP can prescribe an antifungal cream that contains hydrocortisone which calms skin inflammation.
- Apply treatment cream sparingly two to three times a day and then smooth protective barrier cream over it.

> Take these precautions while you are carrying out thrush treatment:
>
> • Boil any teats, toys or dummies that have been in the baby's mouth for twenty minutes to avoid reinfection. Ordinary sterilizing solutions don't kill candida.
> • Try to keep your nipples clean and dry. Change breast pads frequently.

• It's important to continue to use the cream for at least a week after the soreness has gone since thrush can be very persistent and flare up again if it hasn't been completely routed.
• Fungal spores can linger in terry nappies and cause reinfection. If you use terry nappies you'll need to boil them, or else switch to disposables for a few weeks.

Oral thrush
Nappy rash caused by thrush sometimes goes together with the oral version and it can be very persistent unless both are treated at the same time. In this case you'll notice white patches inside your baby's mouth which look like little scraps of milk but won't budge if you try gently to wipe them away. The areas round the patches may look red and sore.

Breastfeeding mothers can get thrush on their nipples which makes them very sore and also means mother and baby reinfect each other, so make sure both of you are treated.

Treating oral thrush
Your GP will normally treat your baby with an oral antifungal, usually nystatin, and your nipples with an antifungal cream. Wash and dry them gently after each feed and apply the cream.

An old-fashioned remedy for the problem is to swab your nipples in a vinegar solution (a teaspoon of vinegar to a cup of water) after each feed.

Bacterial infection
If a baby's skin is very sore or chafed, it's easier for bacteria to gain a foothold and set up an infection. This is even more likely if your baby has been suffering from diarrhoea and their bottom has been in contact with bacteria from stools more frequently than normal. Using a nappy cream with antiseptic ingredients may help, but if the rash persists you'll need your GP's advice and probably a prescription for an antibiotic cream.

Impetigo
This is a very common and highly infectious skin rash, easily spread on fingers, which you should not attempt to treat yourself. It needs prompt treatment by your GP with an antibiotic ointment, or, in severe cases, medication by mouth.

Impetigo is caused by the bacteria *Staphylococcus aureus* which very easily infects broken skin. It can appear anywhere on the body, not just in the nappy area. Children who have eczema are especially easily infected, and a sore area of dribbler's rash round the mouth is another prime site.

The first sign is a small itchy spot which quickly enlarges to a weepy rash with a golden yellow crust.

Treatment
Carefully wash the skin with mild soap and water. Treat with antibiotic cream as directed by your GP. Keep all the baby's towels and flannels separate from those of other family members to avoid the risk of cross infection.

Special care for girls
Some little girls, especially if they have a tendency to eczema, have trouble with a sore vulva in their early months and this can continue into childhood. Girls with very sensitive skin may have stinging when they pass urine, and the vulva can look red and sore. A sore bottom is also common at the toilet-training stage when the child dribbles or may not wipe herself very well. Careful cleansing with baby oil, careful drying, and using a simple moisturizing or barrier cream after each nappy change or trip to the loo can help.

Some girls seem more prone to vaginal thrush than others and may get repeated troublesome bouts. A very sweet or sugary diet can make the problem worse – holidays with an above average intake of ice creams and sweet drinks can often spark off an attack. A thrush infection causes soreness and stinging urine, itching and sometimes a curdy-white discharge which dries to a yellowish-looking stain on pants. Discharge should also be checked by a doctor. Treatment is with an antifungal cream such as Canesten.

Special care for boys
A boy's foreskin cannot usually be pulled back until the age of two or three. Don't try to force it back before then – just clean the penis and genital area gently but thoroughly with warm water, not soap.

When should I see a doctor about nappy rash?
If your baby's skin seems hot or inflamed, weeps, smells odd or develops any unusual-looking rash it should be checked out by your GP. In fact, any persistent or recurring type of rash needs to be checked by your doctor. A baby with eczema should see the doctor at the first sign of a skin infection because it needs to be treated promptly.

USEFUL ADDRESSES

The National Association of Nappy Services, tel: 0121 693 4949.
Can give details of local nappy laundering services.

The Real Nappy Association, PO Box 3704, London SE26 4RX.
Send a large s.a.e. for parents' information pack.

Healthy Teeth – and Teething

All children can grow up with strong, healthy, decay-free teeth. You need to begin the process of dental care which makes this possible as soon as the first tooth pokes through your baby's gum.

Tooth formation begins extremely early on in life – the buds of your baby's twenty primary teeth begin to develop three months after conception. At birth, these teeth are sitting under the gums ready to come through in around six months' time, and some parts of a baby's permanent teeth are already developing higher up in the gums.

During pregnancy your diet provides the calcium, phosphorous and other minerals needed to help form your baby's teeth. Provided you are not actually undernourished, this process is entirely automatic and the baby will get everything they need. However, there are three things that can directly affect the development of your child's teeth:

- A high temperature from a viral or other infection while you're pregnant can upset the delicate balance of calcium and phosphorus salts in your bloodstream, affecting the tooth structure that's forming at the time in the foetus. Obviously there is little you can do about this except take the usual precautions to avoid infections in early pregnancy.
- The antibiotic tetracycline can stain and discolour developing foetal teeth. This doesn't happen often now, since doctors are advised not to give it to women who are, or might become, pregnant.
- If your baby is born prematurely, they may be more at risk of dental decay because they may have defects in their tooth enamel. Only the baby teeth are affected.

Your baby's mouth at birth

A few days after birth part of the baby's health check includes their mouth to see that the lips and palate are properly formed. Defects such as cleft palate or harelip are rare, affecting only about one in 870 babies, and can be very successfully treated by surgery when the baby is three months or more.

You might notice in your baby's mouth:

- *Epstein's pearls.* These are little white spots like grains of rice on the roof of the mouth and are made of keratin, the fibrous protein found in hair

and nails. They are not important and will disappear in around 14 days.

- *Eruption cysts.* These small cysts can develop on the gum pads shortly after birth. They are sacs surrounding a developing tooth and tend to disappear after a few days. Don't pierce or cut them, as they can easily become infected.
- *Tongue tie.* At birth, and for a few days after, the baby's mouth has a little membrane that 'ties' the tongue to the gum midway back in the mouth to keep the tongue in the proper position for the baby to begin to nurse. It usually disappears in a few days and the baby can then stretch his or her tongue forward.

A teething timetable

The timing of teething depends a great deal on the individual baby. By the time your baby is two and a half years, they will probably have all of their 20 primary (baby) teeth, 10 in the upper, and 10 in the lower jaw. Some children get their teeth early, some later, and some babies are occasionally born with one or more teeth already through. Girls often teethe earlier than boys. The timing of the appearance of teeth is really not important and is influenced slightly by hereditary factors, so if you were a late teether, your baby may be also. A baby who teethes earlier is not any more advanced or intelligent than one who gets their teeth later on, contrary to old wives' tales.

The pattern of teeth appearing is generally as follows. It is perfectly normal for teeth to appear six months earlier or later than the timings shown here:

Age in months	Upper jaw	Lower jaw
6–7	–	4 incisors
7½–9	4 incisors	–
12	–	2 first molars
14	2 first molars	–
16	–	2 canines
18	2 canines	–
20	–	2 second molars
24	2 second molars	–

The first tooth will usually be a bottom incisor, and will appear at around six months. The teeth push through in lower and then upper pairs, and the general rule is to expect four new teeth every four months until around two and a half years, when all the baby's 20 primary teeth should be through.

Teething pain

There's disagreement on how much teething hurts babies. Some experts maintain that sharp teeth pushing through the baby's gums do hurt, others that teething produces nothing but teeth, is a gradual and natural process and doesn't cause much discomfort at all. Teething is sometimes blamed – falsely – for every outburst of crying and irritability in young babies, when it is actually due to other causes. However, a short report published in the

Archives of Disease in Childhood in 1992 found that among 46 healthy babies, 20 had a temperature higher than the normal 37.5 °C (99.5 °F) on the day their first tooth came through.

The truth is that some babies have more and others less discomfort. Some babies produce one tooth at a time steadily every month or so with no trouble at all, while for others it can be a very painful time. If several teeth come through together, for example, it's likely to be more painful. The teeth most likely to cause discomfort are the first molars, which usually appear between 12 and 14 months, and the second molars, which appear between 20 and 24 months.

It's not always easy to tell when your baby is teething, but it is worth trying to spot the signs, which include:

- Gums which look irritated, red and puffy.
- Swollen ridges under the gums when you run a (clean) finger along them.
- The tip of a tooth poking through the gum.
- Much more saliva and dribbling than normal.
- Wanting to bite and chew on everything much more than usual.

Common teething troubles

There are some common problems you might notice when your baby is teething

- *Dribbling.* A teething baby produces much more saliva than normal and young babies don't have the muscular control to keep the saliva in their mouths. The result can be a teething rash round the lips and chin caused by constant moisture. Wipe away the saliva gently as often as you can, wash the area gently with lukewarm water, and apply a gentle moisturizing cream, such as E45 cream, to stop the skin drying out.
- *Fever and irritability.* Teeth pushing through gums can sometimes cause inflammation and a slightly raised temperature (in the region of 38.3 °C or 101 °F). Give a dose of infant paracetamol if your baby seems especially flushed and irritable.
- *Night waking.* Painful gums may cause your baby to wake more often in the night.
- *Loss of appetite.* Your baby may not want to feed as much as normal. Try offering cool foods like chilled apple purée to see if these are more acceptable, but don't force them if they don't want to eat as much as usual.
- *Biting more than normal.* Chewing hard on anything that comes near is one way that babies help relieve sore, painful gums.

> Although teething can be painful, it should not make a baby ill. A high temperature, rashes, vomiting or diarrhoea, or refusal to feed, are not usually symptoms of teething and should be checked by your doctor.

- Use just a smear of children's paste – it's all that's needed. Some babies dislike the 'stinginess' of mint toothpaste, so use the very mildest you can.
- Most babies don't like having their teeth cleaned, however much you try to be jolly and make it fun. Toddlers get very vociferous, want to clean their own teeth, and may cry and snatch the brush away. They can clean their own teeth, but you must clean them too, brave the yells and even pin them down if needed so that you get the brush around the back teeth. Be as gentle and considerate as you can as it can make them gag, but make it clear that teeth have to be cleaned twice every day, however much they protest.

  It may sound harsh, but it's far worse to find – and many mothers do – that when the dentist has a good look at the molars at around the age of two or three there are already signs of dental decay.
- You'll need to continue to brush your child's teeth for them until they're at least five and have the patience and dexterity to brush thoroughly for long enough every day on their own.

Fluoride

Children's dental health has improved dramatically during the last 20 years, which is largely due to the use of fluoride. According to the latest 10-year national survey from the Office of Population Censuses and Surveys, since 1973 tooth decay in the primary teeth of five-year-olds has declined by 55 per cent, and in the second teeth of 12-year-olds by 75 per cent. The Department of Health's 1994 publication *An Oral Health Strategy for England*, proposes that by the year 2003 the average five-year-old should be 70 per cent caries-free and have on average less than one decayed, missing or filled tooth. The sour note on these encouraging figures is that there's an increasingly large gap between the dental health of the most and the least privileged children: around 20 per cent of the nation's children have 80 per cent of the dental caries.

Many studies have shown that dental decay is reduced by half in areas where the water has fluoride added. In Chicago, which was one of the first major American cities to fluoridate its water supply in 1956, tooth decay dropped by 50 per cent among school-age children in the first 15 years afterwards. Unfortunately, only 12 per cent of the population in England have fluoride added to drinking water, so the fluoride in toothpaste – most brands of children's toothpaste now contain it – is most likely the reason for the drop in dental decay here.

What fluoride does

Fluoride is naturally present in some water, some plants and animal life, and most foods. It helps prevent tooth decay in two main ways:

- During the formation of teeth, fluoride is incorporated into tooth enamel, making it stronger and more resistant to attack from acids in the mouth.
- In the mouth, fluoride from toothpaste protects teeth by interfering with

---

When should I take my baby to the dentist?

Take your baby to the dentist with you every time you have your own six-monthly check-up just to establish the idea that dentists' visits are a normal part of family life. Once your baby's teeth start to come through, your dentist can sit them up in the chair and begin to accustom them to the idea of their teeth being looked at and counted.

---

the growth of bacteria and by modifying the action of acids which cause tooth decay. When enamel has been weakened by acid attack and lost some of its minerals, fluoride can also prevent decay by encouraging remineralization and the rebuilding and reinforcing of tooth enamel. In effect, it can actually 'heal' the early stages of tooth decay.

However, too much fluoride can be harmful.

Should I give my baby fluoride drops?

The British Association for the Study of Community Dentistry recommends that babies should not receive fluoride supplements until six months, if they are necessary.

Fluoride is a very potent mineral and should be treated with caution. A tiny amount too much can be as bad as too little. The agreed beneficial dose of fluoride is 1 part per million (ppm) of water – that's 1 mg per litre, which is the equivalent of adding a grain of salt to a cup of water. Two parts per million – two grains of salt – is enough to do damage. Overenthusiastic use of fluoride can result in permanent brown mottled stains or white flecks on tooth enamel, called fluorosis, where fluoride has displaced calcium in the tooth enamel, and teeth will be weaker, not stronger as a result. The OPCS survey quoted earlier found that 20 per cent of 12-year-olds had markings on their tooth enamel possibly associated with taking fluoride.

In America fluoride drops for babies are only available on prescription. Here you can buy them at the chemist, but do use them with care and only if you need to. Talk to your dentist if you're in doubt.

Take the following precautions:

- Telephone your local water authority to find out if your water supply contains any natural fluoride or has fluoride added. If your water supply has 0.7 ppm or above, you don't need to give your baby drops.
- If you do use drops, measure the dose with extreme care and dilute it in as much fluid as your child is likely to drink in a day.
- Treat fluoride as a medicine. Keep it safely locked away.

It is generally believed now that topical application – toothpastes, mouth rinses and dentists' treatments such as gels painted onto the teeth – is more important than drops.

Keeping your child cavity-free

Despite improvements in dental health, 45 per cent of all five-year-olds still have some dental decay. But it is possible for your baby to grow into a child who is filling-free. Follow this three-point plan:

1. Make sure they brush twice a day as soon as they have teeth to brush with fluoride toothpaste to remove debris and keep enough cavity-fighting fluoride in contact with their teeth.
2. Cut down on contact with sweet foods.

   It's not the amount of sugar in foods but the length of time the plaque-forming acids are in contact with the teeth that does the damage. You don't need to be a dragon about sweets, but don't let them have the type that linger in the mouth all day such as boiled sweets or lollipops. The same goes for sweet drinks. Don't let sipping go on and on.

   Bear in mind, also, that it's not just confectionery that contains sugar. Dairy products contain a sugar called lactose, fruits contain fructose, and starches like pasta and bread are broken down in the mouth into other sugars, glucose and maltose. Any foods that stick to the teeth and stay there for a longish period, including fruit, biscuits, crisps, raisins and cake, provide fodder for bacteria to get to work on. Cutting down on snacking, and brushing teeth after meals, are two ways to prevent this.
3. Take them to visit the dentist regularly, at least every six months. If you stick to points one and two, there should be very little for your dentist to do.

Serious teeth rotters

- *Nursing bottle caries.* This is an alarming phenomenon caused by frequent use of very sugary drinks like fruit juices, commercial baby drinks, sugary milk, and even breast milk. The worst effects are caused when a baby is allowed to sip these drinks over a long time, especially at night. Don't give any drink but water in a bottle at night or let your baby's teeth be exposed to sweet liquids for long periods.
- *Dental erosion.* This is a very serious threat to the health of children's teeth. It doesn't involve bacteria like dental decay does, but happens when

---

Baby drinks – beware of misleading labelling

All sugars, including the 'natural' or 'fruit' sugars glucose and fructose, have pretty much the same effect on acid production and plaque as ordinary sugar. *They are not any better for teeth.*

Beware 'unsweetened', 'pure' fruit juices. Fruit juices are high in sugars and very damaging to teeth. 'No added sugar' means no sucrose has been added, the implication being that the food/drink is better for teeth, but this is not so if there are high levels of other sugars. Drinks containing artificial sweeteners (which shouldn't be given to small babies) can be just as damaging as the high acidity levels cause dental erosion.

acids in certain drinks or foods directly attack the outer tooth enamel and dissolve it, making the teeth sensitive and brittle. Even drinks with 'no added sugars' or containing artificial sweeteners have high acidity and can cause dental erosion.

The 1993 OPCS Child Dental Health survey of 17,000 children aged from 5 to 15 found a shockingly high level of dental erosion in children of all ages. Their findings were that:

— About half of five- and six-year-olds had some dental erosion. In a quarter of cases the tooth enamel was worn away right through to the inner pulp of the tooth.

— Nearly a quarter of children over 11 had erosion of the tooth surfaces.

Dentists blame dental erosion on the consumption of fizzy drinks, colas and fruit drinks, and also pickles and other foods which contain high levels of acids that eat away at the tooth enamel. Most fizzy drinks and fruit-based drinks have a pH balance of between 2.7 and 3.7, and many have citric acid added. 'Anything with a pH scale level of less than 7 is acidic,' says Linda Shaw, senior lecturer in paediatric dentistry at Birmingham University. 'Below 5.5 is the critical level at which teeth start to be dissolved.' It's easy to see why fizzy drinks damage children's teeth so badly.

The British soft drinks market is worth £6 billion a year and has grown by a third in the last five years – children consume around two-thirds of its products. The government's *National Diet and Nutrition Survey* of 1995, which looked at over 1500 children under four and a half, found that 24 per cent had fizzy drinks and 43 per cent had sweets on most days of the week. A Swedish study has identified the main risk factors for dental caries and high on the list are sugar-containing beverages consumed more than twice a day, and sweets eaten more than once a week.

Watch out for chemical sweeteners

The use of artificial sweeteners such as saccharin, aspartame and acesulfame K is forbidden by law in foods for babies. However, these sweeteners are used in many commercially prepared foods and drinks that you may offer your baby when they are past the weaning stage – crisps, jellies, lollies, tomato soup, rice pudding, baked beans, ketchup, custard and toothpaste are just a few of the foods that use them, and many low-sugar and regular brands of drinks have them added too.

There's evidence that children as young as two and three are exceeding acceptable levels of saccharin. The 1995 National Diet and Nutrition Survey of children aged one and a half to four and a half found that one in 40 was having more than the recommended intake. Be aware of this possibility, and check labels on the drinks and foods you offer for how much chemical sweetener you're giving, if any. If you use concentrated soft drinks (a major source of saccharin), dilute them more than you would normally for yourself.

Preventative measures
Taking the following steps will help prevent decay from the start:

- Only ever offer your baby plain water to quench thirst.
- If you do use baby juices, follow the manufacturer's instructions about dilution, and try diluting them more than that.
- Dilute fruit juices half and half with water. Remember that fruit juices, even 'natural' juices which claim to have no added sugar, also contain sugars and damaging acids.
- Don't let your baby continually sip sweet drinks from a bottle. The longer teeth are in contact with sugar, the more damage can be done. Keep drinks from bottles short.
- Move your baby on from bottles to drinks from a cup as soon as you can.
- Be aware that all baby drinks are sugary and acidic. A 1996 article in the *British Dental Journal* in 1996 from Leeds Dental Institute pointed out that drinks marketed as 'healthy' herbal baby drinks have the same potential as other baby drinks to cause dental decay, and the same rules about not letting them suck too long apply.
- Never give a baby a sweetened bottle to go to bed with at night or during the night as their teeth will be in prolonged contact with sugar. Be very strict and give plain water only as a bedtime drink.

What to do if your child injures a tooth
Accidents and injuries to teeth are usually due to falls, and are quite common among unsteady toddlers – about one in 12 children under the age of five suffers accidental damage to their teeth. An injury that causes damage, or knocks out a tooth altogether, needs immediate action.

- Take the child to a dentist, or a hospital with a dental department, without delay.
- If a tooth has been completely knocked out, put it in some milk and take it, with the child, to a dentist immediately.
- Any injury to a primary tooth has the potential to damage the developing tooth underneath, especially if any infection develops. Don't be surprised if the dentist recommends having a damaged tooth taken out to avoid this possibility.
- If a tooth that's been previously injured turns black or discoloured, take the child back to the dentist. It's likely that the nerve of the tooth has died, in which case infection is a possibility, so it may be better to have the tooth extracted.

DUMMIES – THE CASE FOR AND AGAINST

Should I give my baby a dummy?
There's nothing quite like a dummy for provoking guilt and unease in mothers. Years of powerful propaganda against their use have given them

an image as a germ-laden, jaw-damaging, lower-class evil. The Truby King school of child care, which was so influential in the 1920s and beyond, fostered the belief that dummies were bad for a baby's character because they were 'giving in' to the dangerous desire for pleasure and comfort, when learning self-control was the order of the day.

Anti-dummy prejudice is still around, and controversy continues among doctors, dentists and paediatricians over whether they really are damaging to children's teeth, speech or health, or whether they are any worse than thumb-sucking, since most babies will use a thumb if they're not given a dummy. There have been very few good studies on dummies, and a great deal of nonsense talked about them. A study published in the *Lancet* in 1996 concerning a chance finding on the IQ of babies who'd been given dummies as children over 30 years ago provoked a storm of tabloid headlines proclaiming dummies made babies stupid. In fact the study showed nothing of the sort.

It's entirely a matter of personal preference and convenience whether you choose to give your baby a dummy or encourage thumb-sucking instead – nearly all babies do one or the other. Most of the arguments against dummies apply equally to thumbs.

The advantages
- *Comfort.* All small babies have a need to suck even when they don't need any food. This 'non-nutritive sucking' is easier to provide for the breastfed baby who can suck on an empty breast for comfort, but it's not so easy if you're bottle-feeding. A dummy can satisfy the intense need to suck, especially in small babies.
- *You can take a dummy away.* Most babies will give up the dummy at around six months if you remove it. Thumbs can't be removed or 'lost'.
- *Thumb-sucking can persist for longer than a dummy.* It's very unusual for dummy-sucking to go on until nursery school age because of the social embarrassment, if nothing else. However, thumb-sucking may easily persist in real devotees until well past five and can be quite difficult for some children to give up. It distorts the permanent teeth if it continues past the age of seven.

The disadvantages
- *They may cause 'nipple confusion'* in the early weeks of breastfeeding (see page 21). Some experts advise against them when you're trying to establish breastfeeding. Your baby needs to suck a lot – on you – to establish your milk supply. Use a finger if the baby still needs to suck and your nipples are sore.
- *Dummies can become a comfort habit.* The need to suck normally gets much less in babies at around three or four months. If you pop the dummy in as soon as your baby whimpers, it can become a comfort habit that they – and you – get attached to for years.
- *Dummies need to be sterilized* and kept scrupulously clean for the first year to avoid the risk of infection. Thumbs don't fall on the floor.
- *Dummies can interfere with speech development.* According to some speech

therapists, it may prevent a child vocalizing or making certain speech sounds at the front of the mouth. But this argument, if true, applies equally to excessive use of bottles or thumbs. There are probably other underlying problems in children who have real speech problems.

- *They can be abused.* Dummies shouldn't be a habitual substitute for nurturing. A baby who cries often needs to be held and comforted. Always using a dummy as a 'plug' isn't a good idea.

When should I encourage my child to give up their dummy/thumb?

The sooner the better is the real answer to this question, but it's not worth making a child's life a misery about it until the second teeth arrive. It's better to let the process happen naturally.

There's no doubt that prolonged sucking, past the first year or two, can push the front teeth out of place quite considerably – and it doesn't make a bit of difference whether it's a thumb or a dummy. Protruding first front teeth really aren't that serious, but when the second teeth begin to come through you'll either have to work on getting the child to give up the habit, or resign yourself to orthodontic treatment later on to correct misaligned front teeth.

Obviously it's better if your child can give up the dummy or the thumb as soon as possible, and the less they suck the better. Two years is better than three, two hours a day better than five. Removing the thumb or dummy from the child's mouth every night after they've gone to sleep is one way of cutting down the amount of sucking, although many will pop a thumb back in again when they stir.

To help your child break the thumb-sucking habit you could try:

- Painting the thumbnail with bitter antinail-biting solution.
- Offering 'rewards' for not sucking before breakfast/after tea time.
- Keeping the child as busy as possible as a distraction.
- Holding the 'sucking' hand when out walking.
- Negotiating with an older child.

Dummy safety

- Never tie a dummy round a baby's neck because of the risk of strangulation.
- Choose a dummy that's sturdy and made all in one piece so there's no chance of the nipple becoming detached from the base.
- The base must have ventilation holes and be too large to swallow.
- Check the dummy regularly for signs of wear. Make sure that there's no chance of perished parts breaking off.
- Never be tempted to dip the dummy in anything sweet. It encourages a sweet tooth in a baby without teeth, and tooth decay in one with them.

YOUR OWN DENTAL HYGIENE

Your own dental hygiene has an important part to play in keeping your baby's mouth cavity-free when their teeth do appear, and not just by the example you set.

At birth your baby's mouth is completely free of bacteria, including those kinds which have the potential to cause dental decay later on. Several studies, including a 1995 study from the Department of Oral Biology at the University of Alabama in America, have found that children under three acquire the major caries-forming bacteria, *Streptococcus mutans* chiefly from their mothers. A 1995 Swedish study published in a dental journal called *Caries Research* found that in children of three and a half dental decay was four times more likely if the children had *mutans streptococci* colonies in their mouth.

Transferring saliva through kissing and cuddling is the main way mothers can infect their babies. Of course no one is suggesting that you shouldn't kiss your baby, but keeping your own dental hygiene good will benefit both of you.

Prevent the transfer of harmful bacteria to your baby's mouth by:

- Sterilizing anything you put into your baby's mouth before they are one year old, including dummies, teething rings and any spoons or cutlery you use later on when they're weaning.
- Don't be tempted to use saliva to dampen a tissue to clean a spot from the baby's face, or to hastily wipe a speck from a dummy or teething ring.
- Don't share food with them, nibbling, biting or tasting their food first.
- Never let them use your toothbrush, or that of another family member. If a toothbrush has been lost or forgotten, rub a little paste around their teeth on a clean finger instead.

Taking good care of your baby's teeth right from the beginning really is worth the trouble. It hugely improves their chances of staying cavity-free later on, and lays the foundations for good dental health for life.

USEFUL ADDRESSES

Ainsworth Homeopathic Pharmacy, 36 New Cavendish Street, London W1M 7LH. Tel: 0171 935 5330.

The British Homeopathic Association, 27a Devonshire Street, London W1N 1RJ. Tel: 0171 935 2163.

Helios Homeopathic Pharmacy, 97 Camden Road, Tunbridge Wells, Kent TN1 2QR. Tel: 01892 537254, or 536393 for mail order.

Neal's Yard Remedies, 15 Neal's Yard, London WC2H 9DP. Tel: 0171 379 0705.

The Society of Homeopaths, 2 Artizan Road, Northampton NN1 4HU. Tel: 01604 21400.

Introducing First Foods

Most mothers look forward to introducing their baby to their first foods, because it can be one of the most rewarding stages of development. Equally it can be irritating, messy and frustrating. The easy baby who's content to have you slip a small spoon of purée between their lips quickly becomes the independent nine-month-old who wants to feed themselves and enthusiastically flips their food everywhere.

Many books pass lightly over the weaning and first food stage as if it's simply a matter of progressing smoothly from slush to solids. In fact it can be a disheartening dance of one step forward and two back, and many parents worry about their baby's apparent lack of progress. It's worth remembering that at the same time as learning to accept and enjoy new foods and developing a sense of what they like and what they don't – a reflection of their strengthening personality – babies are also mastering a whole range of developmental and social skills. They need time to experiment and plenty of encouragement to enjoy their new experiences.

The whole area of food and eating is heavily loaded, both emotionally and socially. Mothers are programmed to nurture their babies, so when your baby literally throws the food you've taken the trouble to prepare back in your face, it's hard not to take it personally, feel you've failed, worry that they'll become ill, won't grow and will never learn to eat well – never mind being fed up about having to mop up the mess again.

The process of moving through the weaning stage and on to family foods will absorb considerable amounts of your energy and patience, but it is time well spent. There's strong evidence that good eating habits start young, and that the diet babies are weaned on influences their food preferences in later life. Given that eating good, healthy food can play an important part in the prevention of major illnesses like heart disease, high blood pressure, diabetes and some cancers, remind yourself that, as with so many aspects of bringing up your baby, your hard work now will help to pave the way for a healthy future for your child.

The information and advice in this chapter is based on the latest government report on the subject of weaning and first foods. In 1991 an eminent group of dieticians, paediatricians and medics came together to review all the latest scientific evidence. In 1994 they published their findings as the COMA (Committee on Medical Aspects of Food Policy) report 45, *Weaning and the Weaning Diet.* This report is the nutrition bible for baby and children's food and diet at this stage.

WHEN SHOULD WEANING START?

Milk, either breastmilk or formula, can provide everything your baby needs for growth and development until they are between four and six months old. By this stage most babies have doubled their birthweight and will continue to grow rapidly. Eventually their stomach is simply too small to hold the amount of milk they need to meet their energy requirements, so more energy-dense foods are necessary. This is when they will start to seem extra hungry. You may notice that they begin to want to feed more often, or are not as satisfied by a full feed for as long as before.

Babies reach this point at different times, but whether your baby is breast- or bottle-fed, by six months they will need to be taking some solids to provide enough energy and protein and the vitamins A and D. From six months onwards, the extra iron and zinc in foods is also important to avoid the risk of iron deficiency.

Not earlier than four months . . .

In the past, many babies were given their first taste of solids as early as six weeks. You may find your mother or mother-in-law raising her eyebrows if you're not weaning your baby this early on, but the thinking on when to wean has changed drastically over the last 20 years, and the COMA report recommends that most babies should not be weaned before the age of four months. Premature babies should wait until four months after their expected date of birth.

The reasons are:

- Babies of less than this age don't have the neuromuscular co-ordination skills that allow them to keep their head upright or still enough to be fed solids, nor can they move solid foods from the front to the back of their mouth. They will spit out foods put in the front of their mouth to save themselves from choking because they are not able to do anything else with them. This is called the extrusion reflex, and it begins to fade at around four months.
- The kidneys of babies less than four months old can't cope with highly concentrated foods.
- The digestive systems of babies under four months are immature. They don't yet produce the gastric juices and enzymes from the pancreas which aid the digestion of proteins and fats. Several of the enzymes which digest starches don't begin to be active until nine months or later.
- Giving early solids can make a baby more susceptible to allergic reactions. The gut wall in babies under four months is quite immature and highly permeable and hasn't yet developed the ability to screen out large protein molecules. If large molecules pass into the blood stream they can provoke

an allergic response. This is especially likely in babies where tendencies to allergic illness such as asthma and eczema run in the family.

- Early weaning may increase the risk of coughs and other respiratory illness, according to one 1993 study led by consultant paediatrician Dr Stewart Forsyth, from Ninewells Hospital and Medical School in Dundee.

... But not later than six

There is some evidence that if babies don't begin to learn to bite and chew at around this age they find it difficult later on, and resist moving on from bottles and purées to real food. Late weaners often 'nibble' at food and keep it in the front of the mouth because they don't seem to have the skills to pulverize it at the back. They often want to stick to sweet, sloppy foods for this reason.

How do I know if my baby is ready for solids?

Every baby is different and each is ready to begin tackling solid foods at a different time, but yours may be ready to begin weaning if:

- their birthweight has doubled
- they seem hungrier than usual
- they suddenly stop gaining weight
- they start waking again during the night wanting to be fed.

If you offer food and your baby pushes most of it back out again, they are probably not ready. Don't force the issue – just give it a break, and try again in another two or three weeks.

GETTING STARTED ON SOLIDS

Your baby doesn't need to consume vast amounts when you first start to introduce solid foods. Until they are between six and nine months old their main source of nourishment will still be milk. Weaning is partly about helping them to learn to chew and bite and experience new tastes and textures. Of course the nutrition is valuable, but a teaspoon or two may be all they want and need. Never force food on your baby if they refuse it – food should be fun, not a punishment.

There are several ways of helping your baby enjoy their first experience of eating:

- Try to choose a quiet, relaxed time to offer the first solids. Mornings are often very rushed, and by the evening you may both be tired. Midday is often the best time to start.
- If your baby is ravenous, offer a little breast or bottle first. A very hungry baby won't have the patience to mess around with spoon-feeding, and will just get frustrated.

- Make sure the food is at the right temperature – check carefully that it's not too hot.
- Offer the first taste of food on a small plastic spoon or the tip of a clean finger. Encourage your baby to open their mouth first – some get the idea if you also open yours wide – and help them suck the food off by gently tipping the spoon upwards so the purée slips off the spoon and down into their mouth, or brush your food-filled finger against their tongue. Don't push the spoon or finger right into their mouth or they will gag.
- If your baby enjoys the taste, offer more. If they clearly dislike the whole experience, don't force them. Try again tomorrow or, if you feel they're not yet ready, leave weaning for another couple of weeks. It won't hurt.
- Most mothers offer solids just once a day to begin with. After a couple of weeks (depending on your baby's progress), offer something at breakfast too, then finally move on to three meals of solids a day, aiming to fit in with family mealtimes.

Tips for happy feeding

An important part of weaning your baby is to encourage a good attitude towards food and eating. This means being patient, letting your child go at their own pace, and allowing them some control over what and how they eat. Most babies get very frustrated if you pin down their arms and simply shovel in mush. They need to be allowed to learn to feed themselves, however much mess they make to start with – they will eventually find their mouth.

- *Encourage self-feeding.* Self-feeding is an important part of the weaning process. Babies who are allowed to hold the spoon themselves, allowed to enjoy finger foods and are not over-controlled about the way and amount they eat seem to manage the weaning process better.
- *Go at your baby's own pace.* Allow your baby to take their own time getting used to different foods. Some adapt quickly, others take longer to learn to bite and chew rather than sip and suck. Don't rush them.
- *Be prepared for the mess.* There's no way to wean a baby without it. Babies put their hands in food, they smear, spatter and spit it – think of it as part of the learning process. Some sheets of newspaper underneath the high chair, a large bib for them and an apron for you are essential equipment.
- *Forget fast feeding.* There's no way a baby or toddler can eat in a rush – they need to be able to dawdle and dabble, so try to aim meals for when you're not in a hurry.
- *Don't force feed.* If your baby turns their head away, purses up their lips and closes their mouth, *they don't want to eat.* Don't force it. They may not be hungry, they may not be interested in food at that moment, or perhaps they simply don't like what's on offer.
- *Look at your baby's face.* Don't just look at the bowl while you're feeding them. Their expression will tell you if they're enjoying what they're eating or have had enough. Your baby is a better guide than the amount of food left in the dish.

Safety first
- **Never leave a baby alone with food and drink.**

Nearly all babies will gag or choke from time to time, especially if they bite off more than they can chew or don't manage to grind down a stubborn lump small enough to swallow. Usually a choking baby will manage to cough up what's stuck – leave them alone to do it if they're coughing or crying and don't panic and start thumping their back. If an offending lump *does* become stuck, dislodge it by putting them face down across your knees and gently patting or rubbing their back upwards.

- **Always strap a baby into the high chair.**

However much they protest, it's a long way down.

- **Always check how hot the food is.**

You should always check the temperature before offering it to your baby. Check it especially carefully if it has been heated in a microwave – stir it first to make sure there are no hot spots, and make sure the food is heated through thoroughly.

THE THREE STAGES OF WEANING

One of the aims of weaning is to introduce your baby to new textures of food. To them, the texture and consistency of the food is as important as the taste. They also need to master the skills involved in moving food around their mouth and making it ready to swallow. This seems simple enough, but in fact it involves considerable muscular and nervous co-ordination.

During weaning your baby will progress from sucking and swallowing to biting and chewing, and will develop the skill of moving food from the front to the back of their mouth and using the gums at the back (and later their molars) to grind food and mix it with saliva to make it soft and liquid enough to swallow.

Weaning has traditionally been described in stages according to the age of the child, though this is only a guide. Babies vary considerably in their

'That's not sweeties'

'I only eat sweeties'

There is no benefit in rushing a baby before they are ready, but you should aim to have them eating a good, varied diet by the age of one year. By this time milk should no longer be their main source of nourishment.

abilities to cope with new foods, and in their interest in them. Some are quick to wean, gallop through new foods and are soon chomping away. Others are less adventurous and more naturally suspicious about unfamiliar tastes and textures.

What should my baby not *eat*?

Provided foods are well cooked and mashed or minced in a way your baby can manage, they can try most things. The aim of weaning is to encourage enjoyment of a wide variety of foods, so don't feel the suggestions given below are the *only* foods you should give your baby.

However, there are just a few foods you should avoid giving. They are:

- *Soft boiled eggs*, because of the risk of infection with salmonella. Eggs cooked until both white and yolk are hard can be safely given to babies over six months.
- *Chopped or whole nuts.* They may cause choking and should be avoided until age five.
- *Chilli and spices.* These can cause stomach upset.
- *Pâté and soft ripened cheese*, such as Brie, Camembert or blue-veined cheeses, because of the possibility – though a very rare one – of contamination with the food poisoning bacteria listeria monocytogenes. Hard cheese and other soft cheeses such as cottage cheese, processed cheese triangles and cheeses spread are fine.
- *Salt.* Babies' immature kidneys are not able to excrete salt until after four months, and they can easily become overloaded if extra salt is added to food. The amounts that occur naturally in foods are enough for their needs. Discouraging a taste for salty food may protect your child's long-term health by helping to avoid the risk of high blood pressure in later life. Generally, it is not necessary or desirable to add salt to children's food, though a tiny amount here and there won't harm them.
- *Sugar.* Although it provides energy, it is in the form of 'empty calories' –

Listeria
There is always a risk of poisoning with contaminated foods. Small babies and children (as well as the elderly and those with compromised immunity) are advised to avoid pâté and soft ripened cheese because such poisoning can be fatal.

in other words, it provides no other nutrients, vitamins or minerals. You might need to use sugar sparingly to sweeten very sour fruit, but try to give your baby unsweetened foods also, so they don't expect everything they eat or drink to be sweet.

Stage one: four–six months

The first stage of weaning aims to introduce your baby to the idea of food that isn't milk and to get them to accept it from a spoon. This may take a short while or several weeks, depending on their taste and enthusiasm. At this stage, breast milk or formula still provides the main part of the baby's nutritional requirements.

- Offer them smooth food that has the consistency of a sloppy purée and is quite wet so that they can almost sip it. If it's too dry and sticks to the roof of their mouth it will frighten them.
- A cereal such as baby rice is often the first food given. The COMA report recommends that cereals for babies under six months should be gluten free – i.e., not made from wheat, rye, barley or oats. This is because some studies have shown that in babies who have inherited a tendency to coeliac disease (an allergy to gluten), giving gluten-free cereals can prevent early onset of the illness.
- Food should be bland in taste. You can mix purées of fruit or vegetables with milk to give them a milder taste.
- Try first with purées of just one fruit or vegetable at a time, then move on to mixing, say, carrot and potato, or apple and pear.
- Mothers used to be advised to introduce one food at a time, leaving several days before going on to a new food. This advice doesn't hold any more, since there's no good evidence of any benefit, unless your child is at risk of food allergy (see page 161 below). It is quite safe to mix and match your baby's foods – in fact, it's a good idea to broaden your baby's repertoire of foods quite quickly, provided they enjoy it.

What to give

Your baby will still need at least 600 ml (21 fl oz) of breast milk or formula a day.

Try the following foods.

- **Baby cereals** – thin porridge made from rice, cornmeal, tapioca or millet.
- **Starchy vegetables** – like potato or carrot.
- **Dairy foods** – plain fromage frais, custard, cheese sauce, yoghurt.
- **Fruit** – apple or pear purée, apricot, banana, peach, nectarine.
- **Protein** – try a little well-cooked meat purée, or pulses like lentils.

Don't give yet

- Cow's milk as a main drink – your baby needs the extra iron in breast and formula milk until they are a year old – but you can use (pasteurized) cow's milk for sauces, custard or to mix other foods with.

- Bread or cereals with gluten (wheat, rye, barley, oats).

Stage 2: six–nine months
Once your baby is happy taking foods from a spoon, they can begin to try different textures and stronger tastes.

- Most foods can now be mashed or roughly liquidized leaving some lumps, provided they are soft ones.
- Meat will still need to be coarsely puréed.
- Your baby will be ready to start trying finger foods at some time during these months. Try cubes of Cheddar cheese, toast, pieces of banana or pear (see more finger food ideas below). Introducing finger foods is an important part of development towards self-feeding.
- Encourage a taste for savoury, not sweet, foods. You are in charge of directing your baby's food preferences. If you don't offer sweet food too often, they won't expect everything to taste sweet.
- Now the taste of foods can be less plain. Try well-mashed or blended family foods, for example a few teaspoons of meat and vegetables from a family casserole, or some peaches and custard from your own pudding.
- Begin to introduce your baby to drinking water or juice from a training beaker with a spout and two handles.

What to give
Continue to give 500–600 ml (18–21 fl oz) of breast milk or formula a day.

- **Cereals (2–3 servings a day).** You can begin to introduce a wider range of cereals, including the ones that contain gluten (wheat, rye, oats, barley). Try breakfast cereals such as porridge, Rice Krispies or Weetabix, avoiding the sweetened ones which have a very high sugar content. Also try breads and pasta shapes, which are quick and easy to prepare and most babies love them. Avoid tinned pasta in tomato sauce, as it's usually very sweet and contains additives and quite a lot of salt.
- **Vegetables and fruit (2 servings a day).** Try pieces of raw soft fruit or vegetables like banana, pear, melon, tomatoes, boiled potato, soft green beans. Your baby will probably suck them rather than bite or chew.
- **Meat and meat alternatives (1 serving daily).** Soft minced or puréed meat, liver, lentils, poached white fish (take great care to remove small bones and avoid very oily, rich fish like sardines for the moment) and hard-boiled egg.
- **Dairy foods.** Yogurt, custards, fromage frais, cheese cubes or grated cheese.

Don't give yet
- Cow's milk as a main drink.
- Whole nuts – but you can try nut butters like peanut butter, unless you have a tendency to allergy in your family, when it would be wise to avoid them. (See food allergies and intolerance, page 161 below.)

Finger foods
Finger foods are ideal for developing the skills of biting and chewing. They are also fun.

Make sure the foods you offer are:
- free of pips, stones, small bones, strings and tough membranes
- big enough for small fingers to handle
- not too hard
- large enough for your baby to realize the food is to be nibbled at, not swallowed whole.

Let your baby try:
- cubes of hard cheese, tofu, cooked cold chicken
- pieces or slices of almost any kind of fruit. Most babies seem to love pears, melon slices, apples, oranges (with the skin, membranes and pips removed), peaches, nectarines, slices of kiwi, strawberries, and slices of avocado.
- pasta shells or shapes (for the older baby who has a good grip)
- quarters of hard-boiled egg
- ready-to-eat dried apricots or prunes (not too many)
- flakes of fish, chunks of tuna (be careful of bones).

Softened vegetables
Vegetables can be a little hard if given raw. Blanch small pieces in boiling water for three minutes or so to soften them first. Try:
- small florets of cauliflower or broccoli
- carrot sticks
- courgettes, Brussels sprouts, baby sweet corn
- strips of sweet peppers
- cucumber.

Breads
Babies enjoy bread from six months on. Exclude granary bread and any others with hard grains, but try:
- ordinary wholemeal bread or toast 'soldiers'
- pitta bread, ciabatta, chapatti, soft rolls or plain bread sticks
- fruit breads, malt loaf, herb or garlic breads, light rye breads or pumpernickel.

Sandwiches
These make excellent finger foods and good high teas for the older baby. Try fillings like hummus, tuna fish, grated cheese, cream cheese, ham, mashed hard-boiled egg or mashed avocado.

Stage 3: nine–twelve months
Your baby is now developing the skills of self-feeding and learning to join in with family meals.

• Your baby should be moving towards a pattern of three main meals a day with small snacks and/or drinks in between if they need them.
• Start to give some foods chopped or minced – like cooked carrots, eggs or chicken – to help your baby develop the ability to bite and chew.
• Don't encourage them to eat biscuits and cake. Although they're convenient to offer as a snack or quick filler, there are better alternatives. Try rice cakes, malt loaf, ordinary bread or crispbreads instead. These are not as sweet, are lower in fat, and generally provide more nutrients.
• Continue to expand the range of finger foods – they are very popular with this age group. You could try putting a selection of different foods in an ice-cube tray and let them pick and choose as they wish. Small sandwiches are ideal (see above) and are a good way to introduce different tastes.
• Introduce your baby to a plastic cup with two handles instead of the trainer beaker. Don't let them carry on with a trainer beaker for too long as they need to learn the skills of sipping fluids from a cup, instead of sucking.

What to give
Continue to give 500–600 ml (18–21 fl oz) of breast milk or formula a day.

• **Cereals and starchy foods (3–4 servings a day).** These can now be normal adult breads and cereals.
• **Fruit and vegetables (3–4 servings a day).** Continue to expand the variety of foods you offer. Finely mince or chop vegetables and fruit and gradually move towards a coarser texture if your baby can cope with it.
• **Meat and meat alternatives (1 serving of protein from an animal source, or 2 from a vegetable source every day).** Meat or fish can be a little less finely ground and can even have soft lumps. If you are raising a vegetarian child, ensure you give a variety of vegetable proteins to ensure that your baby gets the full complement of amino acids (see Weaning a Vegetarian Baby, page 154 below).
• **Dairy foods.** Use a little butter or margarine on your baby's toast or bread and continue with the dairy foods they are already having.

Don't give yet
• Cow's milk as a main drink.

After one year
Your baby should now be able to cope with many of the foods you serve for family meals, provided they are chopped or cut up well enough. By the age of two you should aim to have them eating a normal family diet. If your normal family diet relies heavily on convenience foods or ready-made meals, try still to offer them plenty of fresh fruit and vegetables – and eat them

yourself too. Feeding a baby can be a good way of improving your own diet.

- Your baby can now have cow's milk as a main drink. Try to give around 350 ml (12 fl oz) a day. If they don't want to drink this much, you can make it up in custards, sauces, yoghurts, cheese or soups.
- Keep up the variety of foods your baby eats. Don't be put off if they appear not to like certain foods – continue to offer them from time to time. Babies are very changeable in their tastes, and may seem to hate a food one day, then devour it the next.
- Don't add sugar to your baby's drinks or breakfast cereals, even if you use it yourself.
- Don't continue to give your baby a bottle after the age of one. Prolonged sucking can encourage dental decay and they need to learn how to drink from a cup instead of suck.
- If you have stopped giving your baby infant foods and cereals which are iron-fortified, be aware of the need to give them iron from other foods (see The Importance of Iron, page 156 below).

Still don't give
- Whole nuts, because of the risk of choking. Wait until your child is five.
- Soft-boiled eggs, to avoid the risk of salmonella.
- Extra salt and sugar in their food.
- Strong spices and chillies.

WHAT IS A GOOD DIET?

This simple question causes a great deal of confusion. The basics of healthy eating are, in fact, pretty straightforward. It's knowing how good or bad individual foods are that's more confusing. In general, simple, fresh, unprocessed foods are far less likely to contain the hidden fats and sugars which are the villains of the dietary world.

A good diet is one which includes foods from each of the four main food groups and offers a variety of foods within them. Nutritionists advise that, ideally, a balanced diet should include several servings from each of the four food groups every day. In the real world, children's food tastes are notoriously fickle, and it works better not to worry about what they've eaten each day but to look at the balance of their diet over, say, a whole week.

The four main food groups are (see page 152–3):

Fatty and sugary foods
Foods that are high in fats and/or sugars (the two often go together) should only be eaten sparingly, or not introduced at all. Your child will start demanding biscuits and sweets soon enough when they start mixing with other children. Until then you can get away with not giving them any.

This group includes butter and margarines, sugar, biscuits, cakes, crisps, savoury snacks, mayonnaise and bottled sauces, cream and ice cream,

Bread, cereals and potatoes

The foods in this group provide energy (calories) mainly in the form of starch (carbohydrate). Bread is rich in B vitamins and provides some protein, calcium and iron. Many breakfast cereals are fortified with vitamins and iron.

This includes white, wholemeal and granary bread, pitta bread, chapatti, crispbread, rice cakes, crumpets, breadsticks, breakfast cereals, potatoes, rice, pasta, noodles, yam, oats and grains such as maize, cornmeal, millet.

Offer your child at least one food from this group at each meal.

Milk and dairy produce

These are the most important source of calcium, which is needed for strong bones and teeth. Because of their rapid bone growth children have high calcium requirements relative to their size. COMA recommendations are: for babies four to 12 months – 525 mg per day; for babies over one year – 350 mg per day. One pint (570 ml) of milk contains 700 mg, 2 oz (50 g) of hard cheese or a small carton of yoghurt each provide around 233 mg.

Dairy foods are also an important source of energy from the calories in the fat they contain, and of protein and B vitamins. Although adults are urged to cut fat in their diets, the under-twos need full-fat milk because of the energy it provides.

This group includes all types of milk, pasteurized, longlife or powdered, yoghurts, fromage frais, crème fraîche, all hard and soft cheeses, cottage cheese, cream cheese, processed cheese and cheese spreads.

Aim for two to three servings daily

Fruit and vegetables

An important source of the vitamins and minerals your child needs for good growth and development, especially iron and vitamin C. The antioxidant nutrients provided by fruit and vegetables – the vitamins A, C and E, the mineral selenium and the many phytochemicals found in the coloured

chocolate, sweets, jams, marmalade, sweet spreads and sugary drinks, including fizzy drinks.

Don't give these foods too often, and if you do, use only small amounts. For example, spread butter or other spreads very thinly, and add only a little sugar to sweeten sour fruits. Your child will be healthier if you avoid sweets, crisps and fizzy drinks altogether.

Why 'health' foods are not good for babies

Babies grow at an incredibly fast rate compared with adults. Most have doubled their bodyweight by the age of four or five months and they continue to grow very fast in their first two years. For this reason their calorie pigments of red, yellow and orange fruits and vegetables – are being seen as increasingly important in protecting against degenerative diseases such as heart disease and certain cancers in later life. Encouraging your child to eat a variety of fruits and vegetables is one of the best things you can do to help them enjoy good health as an adult. Fruit and vegetables are also an important source of dietary fibre which helps bulk food out and pass it along the digestive tract.

Dark green leafy vegetables like broccoli, cabbage, sprouts and spinach are good sources of B vitamins, vitamin C, iron and other essential minerals. Citrus fruits, fruit juices, kiwi fruit and berries such as blackcurrant are good sources of vitamin C.

This group includes all fresh fruit and vegetables, frozen, canned and dried vegetables, all salad vegetables, and unsweetened fruit and vegetable juices, whether fresh, tinned or longlife.

Offer your child at least one food from this group at each meal. If they don't like vegetables, and many small children don't, give extra fruit instead.

Meat, fish and vegetable proteins

These foods provide protein – a good supply is vital for the growth and repair of the body's tissues. They are also a source of certain minerals which are essential for your child's mental and physical development. Meat, especially red meat, is one of the most easily absorbed sources of iron. Children during the weaning stage are especially at risk of a low iron intake (see page 156 below).

This group includes meat of all kinds and meat products such as bacon, ham and sausages, poultry and game, eggs, also fresh fish, canned fish and fish products such as fish fingers and fish pies, pulses such as beans, baked beans, lentils, smooth peanut butters and nut spreads, tahini (sesame spread), and also meat alternatives – vegetable proteins such as TVP (textured vegetable protein), soya protein and Quorn.

Offer your child at least one to two servings daily from this group.

requirement is very high. A three-month-old baby needs around 100 calories a day per kilo of bodyweight. A nine-stone woman eating at this rate would be packing away a massive 6,300 calories a day – at least three times more than her needs. Children continue to need more calories than adults until their teens. Combine this huge energy requirement with the fact that babies' stomachs are very small, and you'll see why they need to eat foods which give them energy in a very compact form.

The high-fibre, low-fat foods which are considered a healthy diet for adults – skimmed milk, polyunsaturated margarines, beans, low-fat yoghurt, high-fibre cereals or muesli – are not suitable for babies because they fill up their small stomachs without giving enough calories. Bran can interfere with the

---

The babyfood blacklist

These foods are all high in sugar, salt or fat, and shouldn't form the main part of your child's diet. Give them only sparingly, if at all. However, if your child eats poorly, they can provide an extra source of calories.

- biscuits
- fizzy drinks
- crisps
- packet pudding mixes and toppings
- commercially prepared burgers and pies
- synthetic and sugared fruit drinks and squashes
- high-sugar breakfast cereals

---

absorption of nutrients such as iron. Paediatricians have coined the term 'muesli-belt malnutrition' for babies who are fed these adult foods by well-meaning, health-conscious parents. Full-fat milk and yoghurt, butter, cheese, and ordinary cereals are all much better for babies under two. Don't begin restricting their fat intake until after then.

This is not to deny the very real dangers of high-fat diets. Recent research has shown that children as young as seven can have evidence of the furred up arteries that ultimately lead to heart disease if unchecked. The increase in obesity, a major health concern, is also linked with a high intake of fatty foods. However, general advice on cutting down fat in the diet shouldn't be strictly applied to pre-school children.

Weaning a vegetarian baby

Most parents who raise a vegetarian baby are already eating this way themselves and are pretty well informed about vegetarian eating. Becoming a vegetarian doesn't just mean removing meat from your diet, it involves learning some new nutritional rules about what constitutes a balanced meal, and this is especially important with babies.

The nutritional requirements of a vegetarian baby are just the same as those of a meat eater and the main concerns are just the same – to ensure you meet your baby's requirements for protein, calories, iron, calcium, vitamin C and the B vitamins.

Protein is formed from amino acids. There are 22 known ones – 14 are produced by the body, the remaining eight we need to get from foods. Animal protein contains the eight essential amino acids in about the right proportion. Vegetable proteins need to be carefully combined to make up the full complement of eight.

You can make a complete protein by combining the following vegetarian food groups:

- grains (rice, wheat, oats) + legumes (chick peas, beans, lentils, split peas, kidney beans, soy beans)
- grains + milk products

Food myths
- Cereal bars are better for children than chocolate and sweets because they have less sugar.

Not always. Many muesli-type bars have sugar as the main ingredient and are just as bad for teeth as any other sugar-loaded sweet. Always check the label.

- Products with 'no added sugar' won't damage children's teeth.

This isn't necessarily true. Sucrose isn't the only form of sugar. Concentrated fruit juice, glucose, dextrose or maltose are all sugars that are added to foods for sweetness and can cause tooth decay in just the same way as cane sugar.

- Diet or reduced-sugar drinks are better for children.

No they aren't. The artificial sweeteners used in these drinks – such as aspartame, saccharin, acesulfame – are banned by law from foods for babies and small children because of possible health risks. Many of these drinks also have high acidity levels, which can cause dental erosion.

- Dried fruits like raisins don't hurt children's teeth.

These sweet snacks do have high levels of fruit sugars and have the added disadvantage that they stick to teeth. Eaten in large amounts they can cause tooth decay.

- seeds + legumes or nuts

In practical terms this means that you could offer your baby meals such as:

- brown rice with dal (lentil soup)
- hummus (chick pea spread) with bread or toast
- cheese or yogurt with wholemeal pancakes

There are several excellent books on vegetarian eating for babies and children (see Useful Reading page 171). It's a good idea to brush up on your nutritional knowledge and get some ideas for weaning foods and the weaning diet from them. Alternatively, contact the Vegetarian Society for information (see Useful Addresses page 170, for details).

Does my baby need extra vitamins?
It's always been known that during the weaning stage children are at risk of going short of essential vitamins. This is because they start to take less breast or formula milk, which up to now has provided all the essentials, but may not yet be eating a great enough variety of foods.

Vitamins A and D can be especially difficult to get from food sources for children. The COMA Report recommends supplements of the vitamins A and D for:

- All children between the ages of one and five, unless you are certain they are getting enough of these foods from their diet and from time spent outside in sunlight.
- Babies from six months who have breastmilk as their main drink. Breastfed babies under six months don't need vitamins provided your own diet is good and varied.
- Babies who are taking less than 500 ml (18 fl oz) of formula or follow-on milk a day, or whose main drink is cow's milk.

It also suggests that you try to give your baby plenty of vitamin C from fresh fruits and vegetables, or, if this is difficult, by including vitamin-enriched drinks at mealtimes. Vitamin C is an important vitamin in its own right, and also helps with the absorption of iron, another essential nutrient (see below).

The risk of young children going short of vitamins A, C and D has always been recognized by the Department of Health, who make children's formula vitamin drops available at child health clinics. If you claim Income Support the drops are free, but if not you can buy them quite inexpensively. There are also many commercial children's vitamin drops available at most chemists. The Department of Health's recommended intake for children of one to two years is vitamin A 400 μg a day, vitamin D 7 μg a day, and vitamin C 30 mg a day.

THE IMPORTANCE OF IRON

Iron deficiency is the most commonly reported nutrition problem among small children in the UK. According to the 1995 National Diet and Nutrition Survey, one in four children aged between 18 months and two and a half years were iron-deficient, and many other reliable studies have supported this finding. The lack of iron is especially common in this age group – the risk becomes less as children get older and eat a more varied diet.

Iron is an essential nutrient for young children. They need it for the formation of haemoglobin which carries oxygen in the red blood cells, and also for the production of white blood cells, an important part of the immune system.

Babies are born with their own iron stores in the liver, but by around six months these stores have been exhausted. Breastmilk and baby formula both provide a good source of easily absorbed iron, but once a baby begins to take less milk this safety net is gone and iron must come from other foods. Iron-rich foods such as meat and green leafy vegetables are not ideal first weaning foods, and so it is easy for a baby to fall short of iron in the time between weaning and the ability to eat a good varied diet at around the age of 24 months.

Premature babies *don't* have good iron stores and are particularly at risk. And if you are raising a vegetarian or vegan baby who is not getting iron from meat sources, you need to pay special attention.

Signs of iron deficiency include:

- tiredness and irritability
- listlessness, lack of energy
- poor appetite
- low resistance to common infections like coughs and colds
- poor physical co-ordination, clumsiness.

The effects of iron deficiency can be quite serious if it continues for some months and is not reversed. Studies of iron-deficient children in Chile and Costa Rica have shown that lack of iron can affect children's intellectual development at age five, and they may score lower on developmental and IQ tests.

It is therefore vitally important to spot iron deficiency early and treat it. Low iron can be quickly reversed with drops taken by mouth or, in severe cases, by injection.

Some experts such as paediatrician Dr Anne Aukett of the Children's Hospital, Birmingham, have called for routine screening of children at 14 months (the time of the MMR vaccination) for iron deficiency. Dr Aukett conducted a study of 1,000 families. Half of them were given advice on avoiding anaemia in their children, but at 18 months, over 28 per cent of toddlers in *both* groups were iron deficient. Her work showed that it's not always easy to tell which children are at risk. If you have concerns that your child could be low on iron, you can request a simple blood test from your GP.

The recommended iron intake is:

Babies of 6–12 months – 7.8 mg a day

12 months to 3 years – 6.9 mg a day

4 to 6 years – 6.1 mg a day

You can improve levels of iron in your baby's diet by:

- Not giving your baby tea. The tannins in it hinder iron absorption.
- Giving your baby a piece of citrus fruit, or a citrus fruit drink, with meals. Vitamin C helps the uptake of iron from foods.
- Continuing to give breastmilk or baby formula until 12 months – these both have a good iron content. Don't give cow's milk as the main drink under one, as it's low in iron.

Iron alert

Never give a child iron supplements except under the supervision of a doctor. Iron is poisonous in overdose and there have been cases of children dying from swallowing iron pills. If you have iron supplements for your own use, keep them safely locked away.

- Giving fortified baby cereals, and later ordinary breakfast cereals, which also offer useful amounts of iron. Stick to the less sugary ones such as Weetabix, cornflakes and Rice Krispies.
- Making sure your baby is offered plenty of iron-rich foods (see below).

Iron-rich foods include:

Food	Quantity*	Iron (mg)
Minced beef	50 g (3 tbsp)	1.6
Liver	50 g (3 tbsp)	5.0
Lamb	50 g (3 tbsp)	0.9
Pork	50 g (3 tbsp)	0.7
Chicken	50 g (3 tbsp)	0.4
Sausage	20 g (1 small)	0.3
Fish fingers	60 g (2)	0.5
Cooked lentils	40 g (1 tbsp)	1.2
Baked beans (or other cooked beans)	40 g (1 tbsp)	0.7
Egg	50 g (1)	1.0
Vegetables (e.g., green beans, cabbage, peas courgettes, broccoli)	60 (2 tbsp)	0.2–1.0
Dried fruit (apricots, raisins, prunes)	30 g (1 tbsp)	0.4–1.1
Avocado pear	50 g (half small pear)	0.2
Bread	1 slice (35 g)	0.5–0.9
Digestive biscuits	1 large (15 g)	0.5
Rusk	18 g (1 large)	2.5–3.0
Weetabix	20 g (1)	1.5
Cornflakes	20 g (1 small bowl)	1.3
Rice Krispies	20 g (1 small bowl)	1.3

* Cooked weights unless food normally eaten without cooking

Offering plenty of iron-rich foods should prevent an iron deficiency, but if you think your child is showing signs of deficiency, ask your GP for a blood test.

Avoiding fights over food

Mealtimes should be as enjoyable and relaxed as you can make them. The whole topic of food and eating *can* become quite highly charged. If you are anxious about what your baby does or doesn't eat, it's very easy for them to pick up on this later and use mealtimes as a way of pulling your strings.

You can help avoid this possibility by trying to keep the whole area of food and eating emotionally neutral. Try not to use food as a threat, bribe or reward. This doesn't mean you shouldn't express pleasure and enjoyment in food and eating, but rather that you should aim not to confuse food with other emotional or behavioural issues.

- Let your baby eat what they want without fussing or forcing.
- Don't make eating up their food a way of expressing love for you with comments like, 'Eat just this one for Mummy.'
- Avoid passing any judgemental comments at all about what they eat or don't eat. This is easier said than done, because of course you will be pleased when food vanishes, but you can say, 'I'm glad you enjoyed that,' instead of, 'There's a good boy for eating it all up,' or, 'You're naughty not to eat your supper.'
- If your baby won't eat what's on offer, just take it away without recriminations, threats or bribes and don't offer an alternative. This seems tough, but it is a good policy in the long term, otherwise food fads can make meals a misery. Your baby won't starve between breakfast and tea.
- Don't threaten 'No pudding if you don't eat your first course.' Give them their pudding anyway. If you're worried that all your child will ever eat is sweet foods, make pudding some fruit and a cube of cheese.
- Never replace uneaten meals with a biscuit, drink or chocolate, as it can set up very bad patterns. If your child hasn't eaten a meal and is grumpy because of hunger, offer a piece of fruit or other healthy snack like a cube of cheese.
- Don't put them in the high chair until the food's there too, or they'll get fed up and restless.
- Let small children get down from their high chair or table once they've finished. Sitting until everyone else has finished out of politeness comes later.

WHAT SHOULD MY BABY DRINK?

Milk, either breast or bottle, is still your baby's most important drink during the weaning stage.

The amount of milk your baby needs will get less as they increase the amount of solids they eat, but even at 12 months they're still likely to be getting at least half their energy intake from milk. Children under one need 500–600 ml (18–21 fl oz) of milk (breast or formula) a day. After 12 months a minimum of 350 ml (12 fl oz) is needed to make sure they get enough calcium. Discourage your baby from drinking much more than this, otherwise they will be too full to take solids.

Water
Ordinary mains tap water is suitable for babies of over six months; before then it should be boiled and cooled. Take tap water from the mains tap – it's usually the one that feeds the kitchen sink. Other cold taps around the house, for example the bathroom tap, are often fed from storage tanks so there's a slight risk of contamination from bacteria which won't hurt an adult, but could possibly make a baby ill.

Milk

The Department of Health recommends that babies up to the age of one should continue to be given either breast or formula milk as their main drink, because ordinary cow's milk is low in iron and vitamin D. Cow's milk isn't bad, and it won't make your baby ill, but it won't give your baby what they need before this age.

Fruit juice

Unsweetened natural fruit juice can make a contribution to your baby's diet by providing vitamin C. It can also aid the absorption of iron from foods if given with meals.

You can use ordinary juices, either freshly pressed or squeezed, or UHT longlife juices in cartons – you don't need to buy expensive 'baby juices'. Orange and apple juice are favourites. Both contain fruit sugars, so make sure they are very well diluted, at least half and half with water.

Drinks to avoid

- *Fizzy drinks of all kinds.* They contain large amounts of sugar, colourings and flavourings and some, like Coca-Cola, contain caffeine, which is unsuitable for babies. They are also very filling and blunt a child's appetite for food.
- *Diet drinks and sugar-free adult drinks.* Many mothers think these are OK because they are sugar-free and so avoid the risk of dental decay, but the artificial sweeteners used in place of sugar are not suitable for babies.
- *Fizzy natural mineral waters* are not a good idea for small children. Natural mineral waters don't have to conform to the same safety standards as those for the public water supply. Many contain levels of sodium and other minerals which are potentially dangerous for small babies.
- *Tea and coffee.* Tea contains tannins which hinder the uptake of iron from foods. Coffee contains caffeine, a powerful central nervous system stimulant, which shouldn't be given to babies or children.

Beware of special 'baby' drinks

The best drinks for babies are water and milk. However the huge market in baby drinks has convinced many mothers that water alone isn't enough, and that 'enriched' drinks are better. A 1994 study from the University of Southampton showed that an amazing 70 per cent of pre-school children never drank plain water.

Sweetened drinks are one of the main causes of 'nursing bottle caries' – dental decay caused by constant exposure to sweet foods and drinks (see Healthy Teeth – and Teething, page 135). Many 'natural' or 'herbal' baby drinks also contain sugars, and manufacturers go to some lengths to conceal the fact.

- Don't be fooled by drinks that boast 'no artificial sweeteners' and 'no added colours', as both of these are banned by law in baby foods anyway.
- Beware the 'no added sugar' sell, as it probably means other sorts of

Squash-drinking syndrome

A small 1995 study from the University of Southampton showed that failure to thrive can be linked with excessive squash drinking. Eight toddlers with poor weight gain, loose stools and difficult behaviour at mealtimes improved and gained weight when their parents weaned them off too much squash. Food diaries showed that the children were getting at least 30 per cent of their calorie intake from drinks. The parents said it was hard work reducing the juice, but the results proved worthwhile.

sweeteners are being used instead. Fructose, glucose, dextrose and maltose are all sugars and are just as bad for babies' teeth.
- If you do use baby drinks, make sure they are well diluted.

Sensible drinking habits
- Give drinks just to quench your child's thirst. Don't let them fill up with milk or juice, as it will blunt their appetite for more nutritious food.
- Don't give sweet drinks too often. The length of time a child's teeth are in contact with sugar is just as important as how sweet a food or drink is when it comes to tooth decaying potential.
- Never give a child a sweet drink at bedtime or during the night. Sugar can really get to work when the natural anti-bacterial saliva flow is reduced at night-time.
- Don't use 'dinky feeders' which children keep in their mouths for long periods. Keep contact with sugar to a minimum.

Drinking cups
Trainer beakers made in plastic and with a spout help make the transition from breast or bottle to cup easier for babies.

- Choose one that's made of plastic because it will certainly end up on the floor from time to time.
- Some have weighted bottoms which help them stay upright.
- Many babies find a mug with two handles easier to hold.
- Most trainer beakers have a removable lid so the baby can use it as an ordinary cup, without the spout, when they've mastered the art of sipping.

FOOD ALLERGY

The range of illnesses associated with allergy and food intolerance is very wide. It can cause, or contribute to, eczema, bronchial asthma, hives, hay fever, failure to thrive, diarrhoea, vomiting and possibly hyperactivity and glue ear.

The whole topic of food allergies and intolerance is highly controversial. Research on the subject is often conflicting and contradictory, and different doctors and health professionals may offer different advice. Some conservative paediatricians dismiss the role of food in allergic illness altogether.

The terms allergy and intolerance are frequently confused and used interchangeably, but the two conditions are quite different. An allergy is a chemical reaction mounted by the body's immune system in response to a normally harmless substance. On contact with the allergen, the body releases histamines which cause symptoms such as a rash, wheezing or itchy swellings. An allergen which provokes this response may be eaten (as with foods), inhaled (in the case of pollens, or the droppings of the house dust mite which provoke hay fever and asthma) or come into contact with the skin (as in a rash caused by stinging nettles and some plants).

Food intolerance, on the other hand, is an inability to digest particular foodstuffs, or a sensitivity to them. The most common examples of this are lactose intolerance, where children are not able to digest the natural sugar found in milk, and coeliac disease, a condition in which gluten, a protein found in wheat, rye, barley and oats, damages the lining of the bowel and prevents other nutrients being absorbed.

Food allergies are more common amongst babies and children than adults, and babies are particularly vulnerable to becoming sensitized to allergens in their early months. This is because the baby's immature gut is highly permeable – in the first three to four months very large protein molecules are able to pass through the intestine wall directly into the blood stream. These molecules are sometimes identified as 'invaders' by the body's immune system, which then releases antibodies in a defensive reaction against them. When the child next eats these foods, they have a full-blown allergic reaction. Gut permeability does become less as the baby grows bigger – by the age of six months the gut has 'closed' and developed enough to prevent large molecules passing through its walls. If a sensitivity has developed it is likely to persist, but delaying the introduction of certain things can prevent a sensitivity developing.

The foods most commonly implicated in allergy are:

- cow's milk protein
- eggs
- nuts
- wheat
- shellfish.

A family tendency to allergic illness is a much higher risk factor than the food itself. The normal chance of a child developing an allergic illness is 10 per cent if neither parent suffers from allergies. This figure rises to 50 per cent if one parent has an allergic disorder, and to 60 per cent if both parents do. An allergic child doesn't necessarily develop the same type of allergic illness as its parents.

Some common signs of food allergy

Many of these symptoms can also be signs of allergy to inhaled allergens.

Respiratory	*Skin*	*Intestinal*
Runny nose	Red, dry facial rash	Mucousy diarrhoea
Sneezing	Swelling in hands and	Constipation
Wheezing	feet	Bloating, gassiness
Watery eyes	Dry, scaly, itchy rash	Excessive possetting
Persistent cough	Dark circles under eyes	Poor weight gain
Recurring ear infections	Puffy eyelids	Rash around anus
	Lip swelling	

A weaning plan for babies at risk of allergic reaction

If you think your baby might have inherited a family tendency towards allergy, you might like to try the weaning plan outlined below to try to avoid problems with foods in the first year. You should always seek medical advice if you are contemplating making restrictive changes to your child's diet; unless you are an expert it's easy to get things wrong and it is very important that small children get the right balance of nutrients for their growth and development. Ask to be referred to an NHS paediatric dietician at your local hospital.

Allergic illnesses don't normally show any symptoms until the child has been exposed to an allergen at least twice.

The general principles to follow are:

- Breastfeed for at least six months to avoid cow's milk proteins.
- Delay weaning until after six months.
- Reduce exposure to inhaled allergens such as the house dust mite in the first year of life. (This is for children who are susceptible to asthma, and

---

Avoid peanut butter and nut products

Nut allergy is becoming increasingly common and more and more children under one year are becoming sensitized to it. It can cause a rare but serious allergic reaction, anaphylaxis, which causes serious swelling and breathing problems. Baby milk formulas used to contain peanut oils, but most now don't – apart from some specialized formulas, and these are currently under review by the companies who make them.

According to one study from Addenbrooke's Hospital's allergy clinic, published in the *British Medical Journal* in 1996, peanuts were the most common cause of allergy in children under a year, and this was followed by Brazil nuts, almonds and hazelnuts.

Don't let your child eat nuts or peanut butter until they are at least five. If they are allergic, they may never be able to eat them.

in practical terms is pretty difficult to do, see Dealing with Asthma, pages 264–78.)
- Introduce solids slowly one by one and leave three or four days before going on to a new food, to check for allergic reaction.
- Avoid smoking in the house and don't keep pets.
- Avoid peanut butter and nut products.

The weaning plan

Age	Foods to be introduced
0–6 months	Exclusive demand breastfeeding
6–8 months	Root vegetables, non-citrus fruits (grapes, melon, banana), other vegetables and cereals (except wheat), supplementary breastfeeding
8–10 months	Wheat, citrus fruits, meat (leave beef and chicken until last), supplementary breastfeeding
10–12 months	Cow's milk and dairy products, fish, eggs

Source: *Cant Food Allergy and Intolerance, Textbook of Paediatric Nutrition,* Churchill Livingstone, 1991.

Food additives and hyperactivity

Some children are sensitive to additives and may develop skin rashes or hyperactive behaviour in response to them. The relationship of hyperactivity to diet is controversial and not generally well accepted by conventional doctors. An American paediatrician and allergist Dr Ben Feingold found that many of the hyperactive children he treated were sensitive to substances called salicylates, which are chemically related to aspirin. Salicylates are found in many food additives such as colourings, and also in most fruit, including apples, apricots, oranges, strawberries. Although Feingold's work is still considered 'fringe', a strictly controlled scientific trial at Great Ormond Street Hospital in 1983 found that the behaviour of all the hyperactive children put on Feingold's low-allergy diet improved. The Hyperactive Children's Support Group recommends this diet and can give more information (see Useful Addresses page 170). More recently, oil of evening primrose has been used to treat hyperactive children with some success, especially among those who have a tendency to allergic illness generally.

Many food additives are banned from baby foods by law – these include most colourings, some preservatives and artificial sweeteners. However, they are not banned from other foods and drinks which small children consume, such as fish fingers, fruit squashes and biscuits. Bear in mind that not all additives are bad. Some are necessary preservatives. Vitamins and minerals are also important 'additives' to children's food. Check the label if you want to know what's in a product.

These are the most common additives children react badly to:

Artificial colours

E102 Tartrazine
E104 Quinoline Yellow
E110 Sunset Yellow
E122 Carmoisine
E123 Amaranth
E124 Pontceau
128 Red 2G

Preservatives

E210–219 Benzoates
E220–227 Sulphites
133 Brilliant Blue
E151 Black PN
154 Brown FK
155 Chocolate Brown HT
Natural colour
E1619b Annatto

Antioxidants

E320–321 BHA and BHT

PREPARING FOOD – AND PREPARED FOOD

Whether you make your own foods or give your baby commercially prepared ones is largely a matter of your own preference and lifestyle. If you're at home and cooking for other children, making something for the baby at the same time may not be much extra effort. If it's your first child and you're out and about a good deal, or you're a working mother and arrive home in the evening with a starving child in your arms, opening a tin or packet is simpler and quicker.

Home-made foods have the advantage of containing none of the starches, thickeners, preservatives and extra sugars in commercially made baby products (see below), and they taste better too. But not all mothers are willing or able to find time to shop for foods and then make it up and freeze it in advance, or make something fresh for each meal.

Mix and match

The amounts of food a baby takes during weaning, especially the early stages, are very tiny, so if you haven't got the time or inclination to cook home-made foods, don't feel too guilty about it. Babies should be eating the majority of their foods from family meals by the age of one year, so they won't need to consume bottles or jars for ever.

Many mothers use a mix of ready-made and home-made foods for their babies and choose whichever is most convenient at the time. If you're having just a sandwich for lunch, for instance, and your baby's not yet ready for this type of food, a ready-made meal will be easier to give than making something separate. And you can mix and match – packet cereal at breakfast time can be followed by some mashed up banana or a little bit of boiled egg or a finger of toast, depending on your baby's age.

It's not a good idea to rely *entirely* on commercial foods. Fresh foods are important, both for nutritional reasons and to get your baby used to eating what the rest of the family have.

Home-made food

Pros

- It contains only the food you want your child to eat – no starches, thickeners, preservatives, extra sugars or other additives.
- It will accustom your baby more easily to the family foods they'll eventually eat.
- You can vary the texture more easily, leaving more or fewer lumps.
- It's cheaper.

Cons

- It can be fiddly to make in small amounts.
- You may need to buy extra equipment like a mini-mouli or small liquidizer to get the right consistency.
- It's much more time-consuming to make.
- If your own diet isn't that good, commercially made foods, which contain all the vitamins and minerals the baby needs in the right amounts, can be better.

Commercial baby foods

Pros

- They're convenient and labour saving.
- They're easy to carry with you if you need to travel.
- They're easy to make up special foods or meals for your baby.
- You'll probably only need to use them for a few months.
- They provide the baby with all the important vitamins and minerals they need.

Cons

- They're expensive and can be wasteful if a baby takes only a few mouthfuls from a jar.
- They might encourage a taste for over-sweetened foods.
- Some contain bulking agents and additives not found in home-made foods.
- Your baby may have trouble making the change from baby foods to family meals, since the tastes and textures are so different.

Making baby meals in advance

Making a batch of food in advance then freezing it can speed up the process of feeding your baby home-made foods. Once you've got going, it's quite easy to stockpile a good variety of home-made foods in the freezer. It means you've always got something ready if what you're eating won't adapt itself to your baby's needs or you haven't got time to cook that day.

You will need:

- A liquidizer, food processor or baby food mill like a Baby Mouli for grinding food finely. You can use a sieve, but it takes ages and is quite difficult for fibrous foods such as meat.
- Several ice-cube trays.
- Storage pots that can go in the fridge or freezer.
- Airtight freezerbags.

Storing it

Cool the food you've made quickly and either purée it or chop it up finely, depending on what stage your baby's at.

Put it into containers and freeze it or put it in the fridge straightaway. Don't leave warm food standing around because of the risk of food poisoning.

Ice-cube trays are great for the first stages of weaning as you can press out a cube or two at a time – just the right amount for the early stages of weaning. Fill the trays, freeze straightaway, then transfer the cubes to freezer bags when they're hard. For babies with larger appetites, small plastic pots or jars (many manufacturers make freezer-proof food jars), well-washed yoghurt pots with foil lids, plastic food boxes or foil pastry dishes for individual pies or tarts (no good though if you're going to heat food in the microwave) are ideal.

Heating and serving

Pull what you need for the baby out of the freezer in the morning to defrost – small quantities don't take long. Heat the food in the microwave or put it in a basin and heat it in a saucepan of water on the stove. Make sure you heat it through thoroughly (especially if you're in a rush and want to warm food up straight from frozen), and test the temperature before serving.

Choosing the best commercially made babyfoods

'Many commercial baby foods are tinned pastes and polyfilla. The purpose of weaning is to introduce a baby to real food, not start a habit of eating sweet, over-processed pap. Some manufacturers now offer better products and we welcome this. Meanwhile, parents should look at products carefully and buy the best, or make their own,' says Dr Tim Lobestein of the Food Commission.

If you're using commercially prepared babyfoods, it pays to check the labels and make sure you know what you're really buying. A 1995 survey of over 400 babyfoods by the Food Commission, an organization that campaigns for safer, healthier foods, found that the majority of them were failing to live up to the recommendations of government health advisors on at least one point. Over 70 per cent of the products were using low-nutrient starch fillers like modified starch and maltodextrin to cut costs. The Food Commission also warned that under forthcoming EU legislation, a baby lamb dinner may be permitted to be up to 90 per cent low nutrient starch and water. The Commission also criticized the practice of adding extra unnecessary sugars to food, including savoury foods.

Make sure you know the facts when choosing preprepared foods for your baby.

- Added starches, water and sugar are all ingredients of commercially made babyfoods. They're used to improve the texture of foods and extend shelf life. These cheaper ingredients are added at the expense of more nutritious ones.
- Look for babyfoods that don't use extra starches or thickeners (Baby

Food safety

Because babies' immune systems are less well developed than those of adults, they are at greater risk of illness from harmful bacteria in foods. Notified cases of food poisoning have multiplied fourfold in the last 10 years, partly because of salmonella in chicken and eggs, and partly because of poor food handling. Avoid the risk of food poisoning when preparing babies' foods by following good hygiene rules in the kitchen:

- Store food carefully in the fridge. Avoid cross-contamination by keeping cooked foods away from fresh ones. Don't let raw meat drip on to other foods – keep it in the bottom of the fridge.
- Always make sure that any meat you give your baby is very thoroughly cooked.
- Cook eggs until the white and yolk are solid. Don't give babies foods containing raw eggs, such as homemade mayonnaise or ice cream.
- Thoroughly wash and peel fruits and vegetables before giving them to a baby.
- Cook food thoroughly – always heat it until it's piping hot and then allow it to cool before feeding.
- Don't give babies their leftovers at the next meal. Throw away all unfinished food and drink.
- Store freshly prepared foods in a clean, covered container in the coldest part of the fridge, between 0–5°C (32–41°F), and always use it within 48 hours.
- Never put food in cans in the fridge. Decant it into a dish or plastic pot, and put a lid on it.

Keep things clean

- Always keep food preparation surfaces clean, and don't let animals walk on kitchen counters.
- Wipe high chairs, bibs and eating areas with an anti-bacterial cleaner after every meal.
- Teach young children to wash their hands before touching food and after using the potty, and make sure you do too.
- Keep dirty nappies well away from food preparation areas. Always wash your hands after handling them.
- For babies under one year, you should sterilize spoons and dishes. Once they're over a year, wash them very well in hot soapy water and make sure utensils are perfectly clean before your baby uses them.

Organix is one, Heinz frozen baby meals another – they tend to be the more expensive products, but at least you'll know that your baby is getting some real food). Maltodextrin, modified cornflour, modified starch, starch and wheatstarch are all starch 'fillers' which have no nutritional value at all – no protein, vitamins or minerals, only empty calories. Check labels carefully.

- Labels can mislead. Ingredients are listed in descending order. The main ingredient is listed first, so choose a product with a first ingredient such as carrots or bananas, not sugar, water or starch.
- Don't be fooled by foods that boast 'no artificial sweeteners' or 'no added colours', as both of these are banned by law in baby foods anyway.
- If the claim is that there is no added sugar, other sorts of sweeteners are probably being used instead. Fructose, glucose, dextrose and maltose are all sugars, and are just as bad for babies' teeth, as well as encouraging a taste for over-sweet foods.

Are you passing on your food preferences?

There's increasing evidence that our food tastes are developed very early on in life. Although there does seem to be some inbuilt genetic preference for sweet and salty foods our natural preference for them can be enhanced, especially when exposure starts very young. Babies who are given sugary liquids will consume increasing amounts when the concentration of sugar is increased. One study from Professor Leanne Birch for the University of Illinois found that children with a greater than average preference for high-fat foods were more likely to have overweight or obese parents. As well as passing on their weakness for fatty foods, the parents were also more likely to encourage the consumption of these foods and make them more easily available.

The message for parents is simple – you can play a large part in influencing the foods your child likes or doesn't like. Given that there's increasing evidence that many of the killer diseases of our society are linked to dietary choice – high blood pressure, certain cancers, diabetes, obesity – you can set your child up for good health by what you give them now.

- Give your child the foods you want them to like more often, and keep giving them even if your child seems not to like them – they will eventually learn to. Toddlers are notoriously fickle over foods, but don't force them to eat foods they don't like, simply keep offering them.
- Don't give the foods and drinks that aren't healthy – or at least severely restrict them. Fizzy drinks, sweets, crisps, chocolate and biscuits can all quite happily be banned in the first few years of life. Your child won't even notice (until they start getting them at other people's houses).
- Dilute baby drinks and juices very well, until they have only a little sweetness to them.

BSE FEARS

Should I feed my baby beef?

At the time of writing, the Department of Health still maintains that British beef is safe to eat, although a large proportion of the British population remain unconvinced. These are the facts according to the British Government's Departments of Agriculture and Health:

- 'There is no good evidence that BSE is transmitted from cattle to humans.' There is no evidence that it is not, either.
- 'Children are at no greater risk of CJD, the human form of BSE, than adults.' This is a difficult argument to accept, since babies and children are normally at greater risk of every kind of infectious illness than adults.
- 'The infectious agent in BSE is found only in the spinal cord and brain of infected animals and effective steps are being taken to remove this from the food chain.' The current method of removing these parts of the body is crude, and some concerned scientists feel it is not good enough.

At present the truth about the BSE problem is that many questions remain unanswered, and it is not clear what the real risk of infection may be. In the meantime, many parents have voted with their purses and chosen not to give their children beef. The Health Visitors Association is advising parents who are worried about the situation not to give children beef products until there is proof that they are completely safe.

Unfortunately, beef is a very useful source of iron in the diet. Some parents are choosing to feed their children organically reared beef as an alternative, or using organic baby foods (Baby Organix and Hipp are two organic brands available). For meat to be called organic, the animal's mother needs to have been fed organically for the last three months of its pregnancy, and the resulting young animal reared entirely organically. Even then, 'There is no absolute guarantee, but so far there have been no cases of an organically born animal contracting BSE,' says the Soil Association, who certify organic products. You can check for suppliers of organic beef who are registered with a certifiable body by calling the Soil Association (address below).

USEFUL ADDRESSES

Action Against Allergy, PO Box 278, Twickenham TW1 4QQ.

Has useful information about doctors and clinics who specialize in the diagnosis and treatment of allergies, a comprehensive booklist and library with reference materials for members. Please write enclosing an s.a.e.

London Food Commission, 3rd Floor, 5 Worship Street, London EC2A 2BH. Tel: 0171 628 7774.

A campaigning organization for safer, healthier food. Publishes the *Food Magazine*.

The Hyperactive Children's Support Group, c/o Sally Bunday, 71 Whyke Lane, Chichester, West Sussex PO19 2LD. Tel: 01903 725182.

Advice on the Feingold diet to help with hyperactivity. Also offers a support network and information.

The Soil Association, The Organic Food and Farming Centre, 86 Colston Street, Bristol BS1 5BB. Tel: 0117 929 0661.

Information·on organic foods and farming methods. Certifies growers and farmers who reach organic standards.

The Vegetarian Society, Parkdale, Dunham Road, Altrincham,
Cheshire WA14 4QG. Tel: 0161 928 0793.

Information on vegetarian diets and feeding vegetarian children.

Viva, PO Box 212, Crewe, Cheshire CW1 4SD. Tel: 01270 522500.

Campaigning vegetarian organization. Offer information and leaflets on raising a vegetarian baby.

USEFUL READING

Baby and Toddler Foods, Liz Earle, Boxtree.
The Baby and Toddler Meal Planner, Annabel Karmel, Ebury Press.
Children's Food – the Good, the Bad and the Useless, Tim Lobstein, Unwin
    Paperbacks.
Food Fights, Dr David Haslam, Cedar Mandarin.
Healthy Eating for Babies and Children, Mary Whiting and Tim Lobstein, Hodder
    and Stoughton.
Superimmunity for Kids, Leo Galland, MD, Bloomsbury.
Vegetarian Baby, Sharon Yntema, Thorsons.

The Common Infant Illnesses

The up side of childhood illness

Your baby or toddler has just come down with chickenpox – or measles – or croup – or German measles – or mumps – or flu. Don't panic. Not only is there an enormous amount you can do to soothe them and help them get better as fast as possible, but instead of these few days or couple of weeks being at best a nuisance or at worst a miserable time, there is actually a positive side to it all.

For one thing, if it is measles/mumps/rubella/whooping cough/chickenpox, your child will (almost) certainly now be immune for the rest of their life – something which vaccines cannot ensure as their effects may either wear off or the vaccine may not 'take' in the first place. Catching these illnesses as an adult is far more severe. Natural health practitioners feel that many minor infections, such as colds and coughs, can also be beneficial in the long run as they help to prime an infant's immune system and strengthen it for a healthier adulthood in which they can fight off infection more easily.

As homeopath Miranda Castro writes, it's possible to 'look on the whole experience as *improving* their health. Often a child who has had a common childhood illness and come through it successfully will be stronger afterwards. Many children put on a growth spurt, either physically or emotionally.'

Then there is the closeness factor. Can you remember back to when you were small and ill? How did your mother and father look after you? Do you remember a special time of being allowed in your parents' bed, of long stories, songs, privileges, cuddles, being permitted, for once, endless ice cream for your sore throat, and long dreamy afternoons lying bundled up on the sofa while your mother pottered about or your father worked at a desk nearby (or vice versa?) If you do you'll have a rich store of memories to draw upon for your own child. If you were not so lucky, and remember illnesses more as times when you were dealt with rather dismissively or regarded as a bit of an inconvenience, you probably won't be making the same mistake with your own children.

Many parents find that, contrary to what they had been expecting, they actually *like* many aspects of this nurturing time because it can allow a special emotional closeness that there isn't always so much time for in the ordinary, busy run of things. Children deserve special treatment when they are unwell as they will certainly be feeling uncomfortable and fretful. They may even

A note on complementary therapies

Complementary therapies such as aromatherapy, homeopathy, herbalism and the Bach Flower Remedies are often especially helpful for childhood disorders. The things that respond best include croup, coughs, colds, the 'itchy' diseases like chickenpox and measles, thrush, diarrhoea, ear infections, cradle cap, teething, sleep problems and constipation. The various therapies, which can be used by parents for their children, can offer really effective additional options to the range of other home treatments parents can use to help heal and soothe a small child.

It is important to be aware, however, that in some circumstances complementary medicine is not appropriate. For instance, if your baby has a roaring ear infection causing them acute pain they will need a course of antibiotics – and quick – rather than some gentle herbal infusions or a rub with essential oils.

The suggestions given in this chapter are *examples* of the type of approach a qualified therapist is likely to suggest. As they treat all their patients on a very individual basis according to their health history, circumstances and personality, your child might be given something different instead.

This is why it is important *always to seek advice from a professionally trained therapist* before treating your child at home with these remedies. See A Note on Complementary Medicine, pages 1–7, for addresses and telephone numbers to get in touch with qualified practitioners.

We have mentioned the therapies which lend themselves best to helping each different childhood illness. If none is mentioned at the end of a section, it is because our complementary therapy advisors did not feel they were especially useful for that particular disorder.

feel afraid some of the time, especially if they have, say, a breathing disorder such as croup or bronchiolitis.

With the combined skills of you, the parents, your GP and home-nursing suggestions from complementary practitioners, there have never been so many ways of giving your child that special treatment, making them comfortable and helping them to get better again quickly.

Comfort sleeping

If you are happy to do this, let your child sleep next to you when they are unwell. Sometimes it is easier – and less hot – to put a mattress down in their room and have them on it with you rather than have three (one of whom has a roaring temperature) in the parental bed. Or try having a mattress flush next to their cot in their room so you can reach out and gentle them at night without them being in the same bed. That way, mothers and fathers can, if they wish, take turns at night-time parenting. And if the carer needs to get up repeatedly to comfort the baby, offer drinks, change bedding and cuddle, or if the baby is sleeping very restlessly or noisily, at least only one of you will be disturbed.

Working days permitting, the other can take over the next night or for part of the next day to allow the night-time parent some catch-up sleep. This may sound like musical beds, but it works.

Many mothers and some fathers say that they prefer to sleep in their baby or child's room when they are ill as they feel strongly that they just need to be near. And from a purely practical point of view, comfort sleeping means the night-nurse parent can look after their sick baby more easily as they are not inhibited about having to be very quiet, and not move much in case they disturb their partner.

BRONCHIOLITIS

What is it?

A viral infection of the bronchioles, the tiny tubes which branch off the main airways to the lungs, and it is most often caused by a bug called the respiratory syncytial virus (RSV). The tubes become inflamed and blocked with mucus, which makes it difficult for the baby to breathe properly. Around one in every ten babies develops this in their first year, but those especially at risk are babies born prematurely or those with heart/lung disease or any type of disorder of the immune system.

Symptoms

The virus can be hard to recognize at first because:

- Its first signs are similar to those of a cold.
- It may follow on from a cold as a complication.
- Later symptoms are similar to asthma.

However, apart from the coughing and snuffling, babies with bronchiolitis then go on to develop:

- A dry, high-pitched cough.
- Wheezing.
- Rapid or difficult breathing.
- Some babies experience long pauses in their breathing, which can be alarming.
- About 10 per cent may also suffer from shortage of oxygen (because they cannot get enough down into their lungs through their narrowed airways). This may show as a slight bluish tinge to their skin, and difficulty feeding.

A common scenario is that an older brother or sister passes their ordinary cold on to the baby, who gets a chesty cough accompanied by a slight temperature. Their breathing then suddenly becomes more difficult, or more rapid, than usual. If this happens, call your GP, as in one case out of every ten a baby with bronchiolitis needs a brief period of care in a hospital.

Treatment

Because this is a viral rather than a bacterial infection, antibiotics are of no help. If your baby does develop bronchiolitis, all you can really do is keep them as comfortable and calm as possible, giving them small, frequent feeds or meals as they will not be able to manage large ones.

What you can do

- *Propping up.* It may help their breathing to keep them sitting upright, or to carry them upright against your body in a sling for as long as you have the strength to do so. If carrying them in a babysling with shoulder straps for long periods, tuck a couple of clean tea towels folded into thick pads under the points where the straps dig into your shoulders to avoid muscle tension and shoulder pain developing.
- *Ensure they sleep semi-reclining rather than flat.* Many mothers find that if their baby has a cold, or blocked airways, they all get the best night's sleep by propping themselves at the angle of a reclining Tourist Class aircraft seat, up in bed on many pillows, or against a beanbag or huge (clean, dust-free) floor cushion, with the baby lying against their mother's upper chest. Many parents whose babies suffer from asthma also report this position helps at nights. You may not sleep all night for eight solid hours, but at least you will get some unbroken rest in groups of two or three hours together – and even this makes a great deal of difference for mothers who have to be up and about looking after their baby and family the next morning.

    If you want to prop them up in their own cot, put a cushion or pillow *under* the mattress. Giving your baby a pillow to sleep on increases the risk of suffocation.
- *Increase your baby's fluid intake and feed them milk or water as often as you can.* If you are breastfeeding, you will not need to supplement the milk with water. Plenty of liquid helps thin out any mucus secretions and makes it easier for the baby to cough them up.
- *Do not smoke in the house while your baby has a cough or cold.* If possible, try not to smoke in a house where there is a young baby or child even when they are well, as there is such a powerful link between smoking and serious breathing or coughing problems of all types. Have a doorstep light-up routine for inhabitants of the house and all visitors. Or smoke when your child is safely in bed, and ventilate the room thoroughly afterwards.

What your GP can do

If your baby experiences severe breathing problems they would need to go to hospital for a few days. If you are worried, either go to your GP, who may refer you, or go directly to casualty with your baby yourself. Babies are a top priority at all Accident & Emergency departments and you will be seen very promptly.

Acute bronchiolitis is the commonest cause for babies being admitted to hospital, where they are given oxygen either through a box placed over their head, or through a small prong placed directly inside their mouth. If the illness has stopped them from feeding, they might also be fed by a tube passed down through their throat or nose. If they have become very dehydrated, they may need to be given extra fluids via a drip in their arm for a while.

Babies or toddlers with bronchiolitis usually get a bit worse before they start to get better, but they do also begin to show an improvement after about five days. It might take up to three weeks for them to be completely better. After the infection has cleared up, they might still suffer from attacks of wheezing occasionally, which are seldom severe but may require treatment. (Prolonged, repeated wheezing may mean asthma – see Dealing with Asthma, pages 264–78.) As they grow older, the wheezing should become far less frequent, and most medical research suggests that very few babies or toddlers who have had bronchiolitis even go on to develop asthma.

Currently there is some research under way at the University of Newcastle Medical School to try to develop a vaccine against RSV.

CHICKENPOX

What is it?
A viral infection which is still very common in childhood. According to the ongoing 'Children of the 90s' study in Britain, 36 per cent of toddlers between the ages of 18 months and two and a half years have had it. Chickenpox takes 12 to 20 days to develop after contact with an infected child or adult, and is highly contagious. The disease is infectious a day before the child comes out in the rash in the first place until all the spots have crusted over – usually between seven and ten days. Because it tends to be mild for young children and worse as they get older, many mothers actively encourage their toddlers to contract it when they are very young, taking them to play with a small friend who is recovering, but still infectious.

If a pregnant woman contracts chickenpox, there is a possibility of her developing a serious lung infection.

Symptoms
Symptoms include generally feeling unwell, a headache and a temperature for the first 24 hours. Then the spots begin to appear, usually on the body first, gradually spreading over the arms and legs during the next few days. They can and do pop up anywhere, including in the mouth, on the scalp, on the penis, in the vagina, around the anus and in the ears. Small and red to begin with, they enlarge and fill with fluid to become small blisters

'Have you tried dabbing on whisky and marmite?'

When all else fails, try a traditional remedy . . .

which rapidly burst and crust over, eventually drying up completely to form a scab.

The spots can be miserably itchy and it is very important to stop the child from scratching at them because this may cause scarring, and bacterial infection where the skin is broken.

Chickenpox is one of the herpes virus family, like shingles. The difference is that chickenpox affects the skin, while shingles lies dormant in the nerve roots, and when it breaks out will do so across skin supplied by that particular nerve. It is possible, though unusual, for a child to catch chickenpox from an adult with shingles.

Though invariably mild in childhood, chickenpox also carries the risk of rare but serious complications such as pneumonia and encephalitis (inflammation of the brain and sometimes the spinal cord too).

Spotting encephalitis
The signs are drowsiness, fits and possibly a bad headache and irritability if the membranes surrounding the brain and spinal cord – the meninges – are involved. If you're worried, call your GP. For more details of encephalitis see page 204.

What you can do

- *Cut your child's fingernails so they cannot scratch sharply.* Consider buying them some cotton mitts to tie on for the same reason. Baby equipment shops have them in baby sizes, and sometimes to fit older children too.
- *Dab calamine on their spots to help reduce itching.*
- *Add sodium bicarbonate or salt to their bath water*, enough that you can taste it in the water – it relieves itching.
- *Help reduce fever by keeping the room fairly cool with some fresh air supply.* Sponge them down at regular intervals with warm (not cold) water, then pat dry with a soft towel. If this does not work, try giving an appropriate dose of infant paracetamol.
- *Give plenty of cool water or diluted fruit juice to drink.* If spots in your child's mouth make even swallowing drinks uncomfortable, give small amounts of fluid regularly using a plastic syringe (available at the chemist), and deliver any medicine in the same way.

What your GP can do

Not much, apart from prescribing anti-itch cream, or treating secondary infections with antibiotics if appropriate. Very rarely, a child may be ill enough with chickenpox to need your GP to refer them to hospital – if they have developed rare complications such as pneumonia, meningitis or encephalitis. Staff would keep them under careful clinical supervision, possibly in intensive care, and the drug aciclovir might also be used.

Complementary therapy

Homeopathy

A homeopath might suggest Belladonna or Aconite for mild fever and general discomfort of the chickenpox's first stage. For later on, if your child seems very whiny and simply doesn't want to be left on their own at all, try Ant tart. If they are very feverish and restless try Rhus tox, or Sulpher if they are thirsty/hungry but won't eat.

Aromatherapy

An aromatherapy mix can be very soothing to itchy spots. Try a blend of equal amounts of tea tree, lavender, and Roman chamomile essential oil, mixed 2.5 per cent with a bland carrier oil like almond oil, and rubbed gently

---

Never, ever put a feverish child in a cold bath.

If your baby or toddler still has a high fever after two days, if you think they have developed an infection in their chest, or if they are excessively coughing or vomiting, call your GP.

over all areas of skin affected by the spots. Avoid the eyes, mouth, vagina, and urethral exit from the penis.

Bach Flower Remedies
Chicory, hornbeam or cherry plum – not rubbed on the spots, but two drops taken in a small drink of water – every half an hour or so may help relieve the intense irritation caused by the rash.

COLDS

What are they?
A very common infection of the breathing passages (nose, throat, sinuses, ears and breathing tubes of the lungs) that parents become rapidly familiar with, because most babies have had at least six to eight common cold infections by the time they reach their second birthday. Possibly more, if they are in regular daycare nurseries with several other children, or attend regular playgroups two or three times a week.

There is a good deal of confusion over just when, once and for all, a baby or toddler with a stinking cold is actually contagious to others. According to Linda Rufer, Assistant Professor of Paediatrics at the Rush-Presbyterian St Luke's Medical Centre in Chicago, it is for three to four days *after* symptoms have appeared. If you need to let other parents, whose children your child's been playing with, know, one day before the symptoms appeared counts too.

Colds are caused by both airborne viruses and bacteria propelled into the atmosphere by being sneezed out in fine droplet form. If your baby catches a cold, it will take at least two to four days to incubate before breaking out. So if they developed a cold after playing with a friend's child yesterday who was sneezing – that wasn't where they caught it.

The fact that colds are more common in the chill winter months has less to do with the weather than with the fact that children tend to stay inside more when playing with other children. In modern buildings which are double-glazed, roof-lagged and centrally heated, the air inside only changes about one and a half times in every 24 hours, which means that any cold germs sneezed into the air get a chance to build up. In summer, when the doors and windows are open, it's nearer eight times in every 24 hours.

Symptoms
Symptoms include coughs, sneezes, a runny nose, then later a stuffed up nose, watery eyes, slight fever, irritability, general aches and pains, lethargy, clinginess, and sometimes diarrhoea as well.

When to call the doctor

If your baby or toddler has a nose running with clear mucus, seems fairly cheerful, and is playing, eating and sleeping well with no temperature, there is no problem.

However, go to see your GP if:

- they are increasingly miserable and unwell
- their nose is discharging thick yellow or green mucus
- they have a temperature, and are waking at night (more than is usual for them)
- their eyes are exuding yellow discharge from the corners
- they are ratty and seem generally pale and peaky
- they are uninterested in food or playing
- the cold is worsening and shows no signs of wearing off
- the cold is still persisting after two weeks (most are over within three to seven days).

What you can do

- *Give your child plenty of plain fluids to drink – as much as they will take.* This helps keep dry sore throats lubricated, and may help to thin their mucus secretions too. Feed little and often.
- *Keep some moisture in the air where your baby is.* Dry air leaches moisture from the mucus being produced in the airways during a cold, making it thicker, stickier and harder for your baby to get rid of. Use a humidifier or vaporizer in their room at night, washing it out daily and, if still in use after a week, sterilizing weekly with bleach solution. Boiling and reboiling a kettle in their room to create some steam clouds, or creating a mother and baby steam bath with the shower curtain drawn around the bath and you both sitting and playing in warm water are both good alternatives.
- *Keep them semi-upright.* Ensure they sleep semi-reclining (perhaps on your chest with you propped up in bed if necessary) and are sitting upright or

---

Is it something else?

Certain cold symptoms – or very persistent cold symptoms still hanging on in there after two weeks – may suggest other health problems, and need to be checked carefully by your GP.

For instance, yellow discharge from the corners of your baby's eyes might indicate a sinus infection. Increasingly thick, snotty nose discharge or sudden worsening of a cold may indicate an ear infection, which can be miserably painful and needs prompt treatment (see page 198). Persistent coughing may be due to babyhood asthma (see page 267). Puffy eyes, or a continuously runny nose might mean your child has an allergy rather than a cold.

How to unblock a stuffy nose

Breast- or bottle-feeding young babies find it very difficult to suck when their noses are blocked, so this can be a long, frustrating process for both of you, repeated every couple of hours, because they can take so little milk at a time. However most babies find suckling immensely comforting if they are unwell, even if they can only take a little.

Before each feed, it helps to clear their noses using a small glass or plastic pipette with a rubber bulb on the end. This is called a nasal aspirator and you can get them from your pharmacist. To use it, squeeze the rubber bulb, then insert the tip of the other end into your baby's left nostril gently, but firmly enough to form a seal. Slowly release the rubber bulb, drawing out the mucus stuck in that side of the nose. Repeat. Then tackle the right side in the same way. This will at least free the nose of mucus for long enough for your baby to feed more comfortably. Always wash the pipette well after use by drawing hot soapy water into it, and then rinse well with plain water.

- Try also laying your baby face down, head a little lower than feet, across your lap. Gently rub, stroke or massage their back to soothe them as you do so as they might not like this much either. Some mothers report they find this encourages mucus to slowly slide down the nasal passages, then you can wipe or gently aspirate it away.

- If they are really blocked up, there is often nothing for it at night but for you to sleep propped up with your baby on your chest. Use huge pillows/a soft beanbag to support your own back and neck, only reclining about as far back as the average Tourist Class aircraft seat does. Place your baby face on your chest to sleep, with their head just below your chin, bedclothes tucked comfortably over both of you. This semi upright sleeping position really helps stop mucus running down into your baby's nose and blocking it, so they will be far more comfortable and able to night feed more easily.

    Another advantage of the Aircraft Position is that your baby will be very soothed by sleeping against you if they are feeling unwell. Your gentle regular breathing will not only help calm them to sleep and relax, it will also help keep their own breathing stimulated – very important if the baby is still under five months old.

being carried in a sling upright during the day to stop their noses from becoming bunged up.

What your GP can do

Give your baby a full physical examination, checking to assess whether:

- any infection has descended into the chest, or affected the ears
- it's a cold that is likely to go away on its own, or whether it might benefit from an antibiotic in case it is caused by a bacteria

- the infection has taken up residence in the throat, lungs or sinuses
- there are signs of asthma, if the cold is a continuous one
- there may be an allergy connection, and if so whether it is worth referring your child for hospital tests to see what it is they may be allergic to. (See Soothing Eczema page 237 and Dealing with Asthma page 264, for more information, as testing for allergies in the under twos is pretty inaccurate.)

Complementary therapy
Homeopathy
There are many different homeopathic remedies for colds in children, but they depend very much on the child's own constitution and personality and upon the symptoms they are showing. Possible remedies might include Aconite for the first runny stage of the cold, Bryonia if your child is very irritable, thirsty and just wants to be left alone, Pulsatilla if they are tearful and their nose is producing thick, greenish catarrh, or Mercurius if their cold started off as a sore throat, they have an earache, and the glands in their neck are swollen and sore.

Aromatherapy
Essential oils such as the eucalyptuses (there are five different types, but Eucalyptus Smithii is the gentlest) can help act as decongestants, while lavender and tea tree are both anti-infective and can help fight infections caused by both bacterias and viruses. For a baby, put one drop of lavender, one drop of Eucalyptus Smithii and one of tea tree in the bath for a soothing warm soak; or place two drops in either a kettle or boiling water or a humidifier/vaporizer in their room. Alternatively, use one drop each of lavender and tea tree mixed with a palmful of plain carrier oil such as almond oil, and massage into the glands at the neck and groin, and into the palms of the hands and soles of the feet, morning and evening.

Bach Flower Remedies
These will not treat your child's cold in the traditional sense of making it go away faster, but will help your child cope with it emotionally while they have it. Some of the remedies may help keep your child calmer (Rescue Remedy mixture, Cherry Plum), or soothe extreme rattiness and irritability (Impatiens). Willow might help if they are feeling thoroughly miserable and sorry for themselves, Vine if they are being very demanding and bossy, wanting all your attention, Aspen if they feel anxious and apprehensive and

---

For *parents* who are feeling drained from looking after a small child who is unwell, Olive can be a very good supportive remedy. It's not dramatic, but you suddenly realize you are not feeling quite as exhausted as you thought you were. You may need to take it regularly over two or three days.

don't want to be left alone, and Chicory if they are feeling exceptionally clingy.

CONSTIPATION

What is it?

Constipation is broadly defined as passing hard, pebble-like, infrequent stools. However, bowel movements vary hugely from baby to baby. It may be normal for one to open their bowels once every three days, and for another to do so two or three times a day. Bowel habits also vary according to the baby's age. Newborn babies pass several stools a day, which are soft – especially if they are breastfed – and often slightly grainy like French mustard. Bottle-fed babies usually have firmer and smellier stools. As babies begin to eat more solid foods such as cereals and puréed fruit and vegetables, the stools become more formed and less frequent.

Symptoms

Your child is constipated if:

- Their bowel movements are hard and pebbly, and it seems to hurt to pass them out.
- There are any streaks of blood on the outside of the stool – or on the cotton wool or loo paper you use to clean their bottom.
- Your child really has to push and strain to pass their stools. If they are a baby, they go pink in the face with effort, grunt, and draw their legs up to their abdomen or take a long time to pass the stool out.
- If they are a newborn baby, they have firm stools once a day only or less, again straining hard to pass them.
- They appear to have tummy ache, plus hard infrequent bowel movements.

When to go to the doctor

- If they have not passed any stools for four days or more.
- If their abdomen is swollen.
- If they are clearly uncomfortable – being plugged with an increasing amount of bowel waste is pretty unpleasant.
- If they become clearly distressed, or listless, or generally unwell. It is possible, if waste stays in the bowel for some days, that some of the toxins in the bowel waste due for expulsion are leaching back into the body through the bowel wall. These waste poisons may make your child feel ill.

Possible causes

Treating the problem depends on finding the cause. It may be physical or emotional, and can include:

- *New foods or a different type of formula milk.* Have you introduced your child to anything new in the last few days? If you suspect a particular food or formula, remove it from their diet and see what happens. If your baby is bottle-fed, try different formulas and see which one suits them best.
- *Irregular eating habits.* Regular bowel movements are helped by regular eating patterns. Try to give the same size meals at the same times each day and avoid between-meals snacks. Even very small babies could do with about two hours between feeds, even when they are feeding completely on demand.
- *Particular foods that have a constipating effect on sensitive children.* Bananas, white rice, rice cereal, rice pudding, milk – unfortunately, all favourite first foods – and cheese are common culprits.
- *Too much hard-to-digest fibre.* It seems logical if you want your baby or toddler to have more fibre in their diet to give them plenty of brown bread, bran-based cereal, muesli cooked with milk, and raw vegetable sticks to chew on. However, babies and toddlers find these difficult to digest, and if they eat a lot of them the foods may build up in their intestines, which are not yet mature enough to cope with so much roughage. Wait until they are at least three years old to introduce them to brans and mueslis, and go easy on the raw vegetable sticks (cook them lightly, perhaps?) and wholemeal toast fingers.
- *Not enough water.* Breastfed babies should not need extra water unless they are dehydrated, but bottle-fed babies might need some to supplement their milk. It's easy to make formula milk a little too strong, so this may be a contributing factor in itself (see Getting the Best Out of Bottles page 59). Water is the cheapest and most easily available stool-softening agent there is.
- *Emotional upsets.* Toddlers have a lot of life changes to adapt to, and babies have several distinct episodes of intense neurological development and disturbance which are a healthy and normal part of their growing up (see Calming the Crying page 88, for more detail). They may react to some of these by holding on to the contents of their bowels.
- *External upsets* might include the arrival of a young brother or a sister, starting daycare if their mother is returning to work, any severe upset or fright, an illness which causes temporary constipation which seems to have dragged on after they have recovered, or potty training.

Potty training marks an important new stage in the relationship of a toddler with their parents. You are hoping – and after a certain age, feeling it is high time – that your child will behave in a particular way, but they may react by rebelling and doing the opposite – retaining their stools rather than depositing them tidily in the required place, as a way of asserting their own independence.

What you can do
- *Add more easily digested fibre to your baby's diet.* Try peas, broccoli, green beans, pears, apples, plums, peaches – mashed if necessary.
  How do you get a reluctant baby or toddler to eat more fruit without

making a big deal out of it? As soon as they are old enough to eat a piece of soft pear safely, every time you take them out in their buggy or in the car, or they're sitting watching their favourite video or listening to you read a story, give them a chunk in each hand and keep a further supply to offer in a plastic bag. When relaxed and with their attention elsewhere their mind slips comfortably into neutral and they will often nibble fruit happily without really thinking twice about it.

- *Offer more water drinks*, perhaps very slightly flavoured with fruit juice if they are old enough.
- *Cut down on constipating foods*, for instance eggs and bananas.
- *Check you're not making up formula too strong.* Stick religiously to the making-up instructions. Do not be tempted to guess, even if you are in a hurry. Put water in *first*, powder in last.
- *Try different types of formula* to see if there are any which are easier on the bowel. Try one for 7 to 10 days to see if it helps. If it doesn't, move on to the next one.
- *Try natural laxatives.* Start off gently with prune juice diluted half-and-half with water. The doses are 1 to 2 tablespoons for a four-month-old baby, and up to 6 or 8 ounces, if they will drink that much, for a constipated toddler.
- *Try Lactulose.* This is a very gentle over-the-counter laxative made of indigestible sugars which draw moisture into the stools. Do not use any other laxatives unless it is on the specific advice of your GP. Laxatives are not really a good idea for small children and babies, and should not be used unless absolutely necessary.
- *If there is blood streaking the stools* or a little appears on the toilet paper or cotton wool used to clean your child's bottom and you suspect a small anal tear, wash the anal area well, pat dry with cotton wool and use a tiny bit of Savlon cream to disinfect the area.
- *If your child has been trying to go all day* and still can't, you may be able to relax the gut muscles with a warm bath. Afterwards, keep them warm, lay them down comfortably on their back, put a favourite gentle tape on if you feel this would help them lie still, and try massaging their abdomen with very gentle stroking movements (not kneading ones), following the track of their colon. The colon forms a squarish C-shape on its side, going *up* to the stomach along the right-hand part of the child's lower abdomen, *along and across*, then *down* on their left side. Always follow this pattern or you will be stroking bowel waste backwards in the wrong direction.

What your GP might do
Your GP can offer laxatives, an enema or glycerin suppositories, and will examine your child physically to exclude the possibility of any physiological abnormality.

Complementary therapy
Homeopathy
There are many different remedies, depending on the child's personality and constitution and the precise type of constipation, and any other symptoms they have. Some of the remedies a homeopath might suggest include Nat mur, if the stools, when they do come, are hard and dry, and if your child is sensitive and touchy and tends to withdraw or hide away if their pride is hurt. If the urge to pass stools only comes every few days, they are hard and dry when they come and the child often seems to want to pass more but cannot, try Alumina. If the child does not seem bothered by their constipation, and the stools are pale and bad smelling, Calc carb may be suggested.

Herbal medicine
Soak a teaspoon of linseeds (budgie seed, basically, from a health food shop) in 70 ml ($^1/_8$ of a pint) of water overnight, drain and mix in with your toddler's cereal or fruit/vegetable purée the next day. Do this each morning until the constipation eases, then as necessary. They act as a gentle laxative because they are a bulking agent in the gut.

Bach Flower Remedies
Because chronic (long-term) constipation may have a strong emotional component, the Bach Flower Remedies can be extremely useful for children of all ages from babies upwards, though the older the child, the easier it is to work out the reason behind the problem and find the most appropriate remedy. However, even if you do not get the right one, the remedies at least do no harm.

If you feel your child may be having some trouble adjusting to a new stage in their life or to a change, try Walnut, for helping people of all ages cope with change. If you think they may be jealous and resentful of a new baby, try Holly, to help with envy. If they have started some day care, try Larch to give confidence, with Walnut. If they seem to put off or worried about trying to open their bowels (perhaps as it is painful when they are constipated), try Aspen, for apprehension and nervous anticipation.

COUGHS

What are they?
This sounds like a daft question, but a cough is the body's attempt to get rid of any blockage or irritation in the airways, so, annoying as it may be, it is actually trying to do a very useful job. Most colds produce coughs as part of your baby's natural defence system to get rid of the mucus blocking up the airways. According to the ongoing British 'Children of the 90s' survey, 73 per cent of babies between the ages of eighteen months and two and a half years will get a cough which lasts for more than two days.

Coughs you don't need to worry about
- If your baby coughs during the day, but sleeps well with only minimal coughing at night.
- They seem well apart from the cough – it is not interfering with their eating, playing or sleeping.
- They have no fever.
- After two or three days it is improving steadily.
- No green or yellow or brown sputum is produced.

Coughs you need to see your GP about
- The cough is waking your baby up repeatedly at night.
- The cough comes on suddenly, persists, and you are worried your baby might have something lodged in their throat or airways.
- Your baby has a fever and is generally unwell.
- They are coughing up thick yellow green mucus. Phlegm this colour usually means it has become infected.
- The cough is getting steadily worse.
- The cough is accompanied by an obvious allergy.
- If a cough has lasted more than two weeks, go and see your GP.

What you can do
If your baby has a hacking cough, you can:

- *Keep the mucus thin so it is easily moved (sneezed out, coughed up).* You can do this by ensuring there is plenty of moisture in the air. Use:
  — a vaporizer or humidifier if you've got one. If you haven't, try
  — a mother and baby DIY steam bath in the shower cubicle, or
  — sit with your child in a warm bath with the hot tap or shower running and the curtain pulled around and/or the door shut to keep the steam in, or
  — keep boiling and re-boiling a kettle in your baby's room so clouds of steam are sent into the air.

  Steam helps because dry air otherwise soaks up moisture from all parts of the body, including the mucus lining the nose and airways. The result is that the mucus starts accumulating in sticky deposits, which are both harder to cough loose from their moorings and also act as a very good breeding ground for germs. The result is swollen clogged airways and even more difficulty breathing.
- *Choose the right cough medicine.* There are three sorts:
  — Expectorants. These help liquefy the mucus secretions so they are easier to cough up.
  — Cough suppressants. They help stop a cough because they inhibit the cough-reflex in the brain.
  — A mixture of both.

  If the cough is interfering with your baby's eating, sleeping and playing, try giving an expectorant *only* medicine. If this doesn't make any difference, try an expectorant/suppressant combination medicine.

All these medicines are available over the counter without a prescription – check with your pharmacist about the brands they have in stock, but one particularly time-honoured range is Benylin, and another popular one is Tixylix.

- *Do some gentle chest physiotherapy.* Cup your hands slightly and 'clap' gently about a dozen times on each side of your baby's back, four times a day. This may help dislodge mucus from the airways.
- *Do not let anyone smoke in the house.* This is a good rule anyway if you have a healthy young baby and want to keep them that way, as smoking by parents at home is a number one cause of breathing problems of all types for young babies and children. *It is an unbreakable rule if you have a baby with a breathing problem*, whether it's a long-term one like asthma or a short-term one like a cough or cold. If it's simply not possible, make a doorstep-light-up-only rule, or have the smokers shut themselves in one room in the house when they want to enjoy a cigarette, then ask them to open the windows and fully ventilate the room afterwards. They may think you are fussing, but let them. It's you who is the mother of a baby who can't breathe properly, not them. If they were, they might feel differently.

What your GP can do
- *Give your baby a physical examination* to check that there is no lung problem brewing, such as asthma or bronchiolitis.
- *Advise on appropriate types of cough medicine*, if necessary prescribing a stronger formulation, perhaps for night-time use, than you could get over the counter for yourself.

Complementary therapy
Homeopathy
There are dozens of different types of cough, and an equally large number of remedies for them, though persistent or recurrent coughs need constitutional treatment from the homeopath (see Homeopathy page 2). The remedies for acute coughs, depending upon their characteristics and how the child is reacting to them, include Belladonna, Bryonia, Aconite, Pulsatilla, Chamomilla and Kali carb.

Aromatherapy
A therapist might suggest a really gentle type of eucalyptus essential oil called Eucalyptus Smithii. Ordinary eucalyptus is too strong for a baby or toddler with a hacking cough, and far from soothing it would probably irritate their airways even further. Do not put the oils on their pillow or clothing as again this would be too much for them. Instead place two drops in a kettle of boiling water in their room, or in a vaporizer or humidifier.

CRADLE CAP

What is it?
A form of seborrhoeic eczema (sometimes still called sebhorrheic dermatitis). It is very common, especially in boy babies under a year old – it is thought that male hormones are partially responsible as it also occurs in boy teenagers and middle-aged men.

Symptoms
Cradle cap's symptoms are a crusty, greasy, scaly rash which starts on the baby's scalp, often around their soft spot. In more severe cases, it may spread to the eyebrows, neck, groin (where it may aggravate any existing nappy rash) and underarms.

What you can do
In mild cases the cradle cap just looks a bit like dandruff – slightly flaky and scurfy. If it takes this form it does not need any special treatment, just gentle washing once a week in mild shampoo (more often will encourage the area to dry out further), and it will disappear of its own accord.

If your baby has more marked and extensive cradle cap:

- *Massage cold-pressed olive oil into the crusty scales* to soften them up. Let the oil soak in for fifteen minutes and then shampoo the baby's head. You can do this every day. Another useful oil treatment is almond oil (available from local health shops, or the Neals Yard chain, also via mail order from there, or from your local chemist, which is likely to be cheaper). Leave the oil on overnight and then wash the baby's head well the next morning.
- *Try to resist the primitive grooming temptation*, which kicks in with most parents at the sight of any imperfection on their child, to pick at it the cradle cap scales as you might a scab on your own knee. Satisfying though this feels, it won't help in the long run and it may make things worse by introducing infection. When the cradle cap scales have either been softened and loosened from their anchor on the scalp, or have dried so much as to be only very weakly attached, try a soft wide-toothed baby comb to remove some of the scales instead.
- *Try a shampoo such as Dentinox Cradle Cap Shampoo* which you can get from your local chemist. It helps dissolve the crust a little more with each application over a few days.

What your GP can do
Cradle cap can be persistent and may also be itchy. If it won't go away, is getting worse, or is irritating your baby, go and see your GP, who may prescribe a very mild tar shampoo. In severe cases they may also prescribe a gentle steroid for short-term use to help control the itching, or a mild anti-fungal cream, as some dermatologists feel that the condition is caused by a fungus called *Pityrosporum orbiculare*.

Complementary therapy

- Try calendula (marigold extract) cream rubbed into the scalp to both reduce itching and moisturize the area.
- Many skin experts feel that cradle cap has similar underlying causes to eczema, so complementary therapists often suggest parents check to see if intolerance to cow's milk may be the problem. The source may be:
  — formula milk if they are bottle-fed. Try changing to a soy-based formula such as Wysoy.
  — cow's milk if they are old enough to be drinking or eating cow's milk or its products (yoghurts, fromage frais, cheese). Avoid these products if you think they might be the problem.
  — the culprit may be proteins, if you are breastfeeding, in the cow's milk *you* drink or cheeses and yoghurts you eat. Breastfeeding mothers may be consuming a fair amount of these as they are told to keep up their calcium levels. (See Soothing Eczema, page 248 for suggestions on alternatives to cow's milk and dairy products.) Try substituting non-dairy products and see if it helps. If it does, and you plan to do so for longer, check with a nutritionist to ensure that both you as a breastfeeding mother, and your breastfeeding baby/toddler, will still be getting all the nutrients you need. According to Dr Chakravanti, consultant immunologist at the Portland Hospital for Women & Children in London, if changing to non-dairy products is going to help you will notice an improvement within a week or so.

CROUP

What is it?

A coughing disorder caused by a virus which affects the vocal cords (larynx). It is common – there are about 100,000 cases a year in Britain. There are two types of croup which affect children of five and under. In both, the same things happen – the baby's windpipe (trachea) narrows, so it is difficult for them to take air into their lungs; and the small muscles which encircle that windpipe go into spasm. The lining of the trachea swells up and thick mucus forms inside.

Symptoms

The baby or toddler has to fight for each breath, and as they labour to draw air down into their lungs the air makes a rasping noise which doctors call stridor. When they cough the sound of it is unmistakable – a harsh, honking noise which one parent described as 'like a seal barking for its bucketful of fish'.

Croup is commonest in children aged six months to three years, and as with any breathing difficulty (such as babyhood asthma) it can be very alarming for both parents and baby. Parents often worry that if their child has had croup they may also be vulnerable to asthma because what is happening in a croupy child's airways is very similar to what happens during an asthma attack. However, there is not thought to be any connection between the two. Croup is not a chronic condition, whereas asthma is, and a child may only ever have a single attack of croup in their life, whereas a child with asthma will probably have several, plus general breathing difficulties.

Croup may follow on from an ordinary cold, but sometimes there is no warning – just a sudden night-time attack. One of the most difficult aspects of croup for parents is working out when it is serious, and when it can be treated at home.

Treat-at-home-croup
- Does your baby seem, apart from the coughing, fairly cheerful?
- Is the cough not bothering them – are they taking it in their stride?
- Are they able to play, be interested in their surroundings?
- Are they sleeping OK? Does their cough seem not to be waking them (though it is probably waking you)?

Call-the-GP croup
- Is your baby's sleep disturbed at night? Do they seem unwilling to lie down at all, instead sit up and bark-cough all night?
- Are they having difficulty catching their breath?
- Are they less active than usual, not very interested in play? Do they seem to be concentrating instead on getting enough air into their lungs?
- When you look at the small indent at the base of their neck just above their breastbone, does it seem to sink in with each laboured breath in? This is called indrawing, and usually goes with a rasping sound as they let their breath out again.

What you can do
There is a great deal you can do to help soothe a croup attack, and to try, if you get any warning signs, to head off an attack.

- *Calm your baby.* Stay as calm as you can, keep your voice quiet and evenly pitched, and try to relax your baby or toddler. If they sense you are calm, or are at least fooled into thinking that you are (even if you are getting worried) this will help them greatly, as anxiety makes the airways tighten up even further. If you can relax them, their airways may also relax a bit too.

  Sit up with them cuddled on your lap or across your shoulder, walk slowly with them on your shoulder, patting at one pat/step per second – this is the rhythm parents often seem to adopt instinctively as a calming technique and it can be very soothing. Play gentle music, sing, sit them upright watching a favourite nursery video, and if you are feeding them yourself offer breastfeeding as this often works when nothing else will do. Otherwise offer small amounts of diluted milk, juice or pure water in a bottle.

- *Use humidity.* Run a warm bath, and if you have one, pull the shower curtain around it so you and your baby can get in and have a soothing, steamy soak. Or run the shower on full heat so the bathroom fills with warm steam. Sit on a chair and read your baby stories, sing, or listen to their favourite music tapes for as long as they seem happy to be in there with you. If you have no shower, shut the bathroom door and run a scalding hot bath. Leave it in so clouds of steam rise from it, and sit on a chair next to it with your baby, topping the bath up at intervals. You may notice an improvement quite rapidly, within half an hour or so.

  If it's night-time, the steam is helping, and you feel you do not want to put your child back in their room in case their breathing worsens again, there is nothing to stop you both bedding down for the night on the bathroom floor with duvets wrapped round you, well propped up on a bank of pillows, a beanbag or a big squashy (dust-free) floor cushion. You might get a bit damp but at least you should both get some sleep. If you would like to venture back into their bedroom or take your child into your bed, fill up a vaporizer or humidifier if you have one. If not, repeatedly boil a kettle as near to the bed as the socket arrangements of the room allow (be careful of being too near so as not to scald either of you).

  Alternatively, if your baby has a cot with tall sides, drape a cotton sheet over it and direct any steam underneath to form a humidity tent. Some hospitals will treat croup this way too, only with a rather more sophisticated arrangement. Children may not want to go to sleep under it – it may look like fun, or rather claustrophobic, depending on their frame of mind. If they do not like the idea, let them fall asleep in your arms then gently put them in the tent, propped upright.
- *Watch their temperature.* Give them the appropriate dose of infant paracetamol if necessary. Let them take frequent drinks.
- *Do not smoke in the house when a baby has, or is prone to, croup.* Do not let anyone else, including visitors, do it either. If you are smokers, instigate a doorstep or garden light-up rule. If you possibly can, stop altogether, as there is such a powerful connection between serious coughing and breathing problems in children of all types and parents smoking. If this is not possible, try to smoke only when your child is safely in bed, and ventilate the room thoroughly afterwards.
- *Take your baby for a slow car ride in the evening with the window open.* Often the slightly misty, cool night air will help. This is, in fact, why babies with croup often improve en route to the hospital.

Do not give cough medicines to a child with croup unless it is on the advice of your GP. They may make things worse, as some, especially those containing decongestants, can dry the airway passages further, causing them to narrow even more.

When to take your baby to hospital

Most cases of croup can be treated very effectively at home, but about 7 per cent of children need hospital treatment. If, after the self-help measures suggested above, there is no improvement at all, or if your baby's croup is getting worse, go promptly to the casualty unit of your local hospital. Specific signs of worsening croup are:

- The muscles below the breastbone, between the ribs, and above the collarbone are sucking in and out with the effort to draw breath down into the lungs.
- The honking, harsh stridor sound has also diminished. Far from meaning the croup is better, this can be a danger signal meaning that hardly any air is going in and out of the airways at all – they have become so swollen that your child is at risk of severe oxygen starvation.
- Your child is very pale, their skin has a grey or blueish tinge.
- They are frightened, and if old enough to talk, can no longer do so.

If possible, either get someone to drive you to the hospital while you hold and reassure your child, or call a cab. If you need to do the driving yourself, keep reaching over to pat and reassure your child, talking calmly, singing their favourite songs, doing whatever you know will help to reassure them. Keep a window open for humidity and fresh air. Do not turn the car heater on (wrap your baby instead if it's chilly) as this dries the air. When you arrive at your local hospital, be assured that your child will be seen immediately, as young babies are a top priority – in its most severe form croup can occasionally be fatal.

Hospital treatment might include placing your baby in a humidifer tent, with ventilation assistance if necessary. More usually, they are merely kept in under observation. If it is the latter, *ask* for a humidifier tent.

Up until 1995 there was no specific medicine for treating croup in hospital, but recently one of the drugs which help to open up the airways of children with asthma is being used successfully for croup too. Called budesonite, it is administered via a small face mask, or with a machine called a nebulizer which delivers the drug as a fine mist. Because croup is usually caused by a virus, no antibiotics are given unless a test done from a throat swab shows that the culprit is a bacterium after all. The exception to this is if a secondary complication such as pneumonia develops.

The good thing about croup is that, though it can develop rapidly, it can also disappear fast too.

Complementary therapy

Homeopathy

A homeopath may suggest Aconite, Hepar sulph, or Spongia.

Herbal medicine

A traditional croup-soothing remedy is a teaspoon of Coltsfoot and Vervain in a cup of boiling water, left to steep for ten minutes then the liquid strained. When it has cooled to a merely warm temperature, a teaspoon of it may soothe children under three. For babies under one, check with a qualified herbalist first.

Aromatherapy
Croup may respond to a couple of drops of a very gentle type of eucalyptus essential oil called Eucalyptus Smithii placed in a vaporizer or boiling kettle in the child's room, or five drops in a bath if you are sitting in the bathroom inhaling steam from it. Do not put directly on the child's pillow or clothes.

Bach Flower Remedies
Rescue Remedy could be useful to help calm a child's anxiety during a croup attack where breathing is difficult, or given at regular intervals (perhaps once an hour) to help keep them generally calm and so help avoid airway-tightening anxiety while they are unwell.

Mix it with a plain water drink, or if the child cannot take this, try to place one or two drops underneath their tongue. If this is not possible either, rub a drop on each of their temples. Rescue Remedy is also helpful for parents who feel alarmed, tense and anxious for their children: take four drops in a glass of water as needed. The effects are not dramatic, but it seems to calm without your realizing – you suddenly realize that you aren't feeling nearly as wound up as you were.

DIARRHOEA

What is it?
Loose or positively liquefied stools. The term comes from the Greek word meaning 'to flow through'. In toddlers, the most common causes of diarrhoea are:

- colds
- food intolerances
- antibiotic treatment.

In babies, the culprit is usually gastroenteritis, an infection and inflammation of the intestine. The stools resulting are very frequent, watery, greenish, explosive and usually smell terrible. They may also occasionally be blood

Rescue Remedy is a composite of five of the Bach remedies: Star of Bethlehem for shock, Rock Rose for fear and panic, Impatiens for mental and physical tension when the sufferer cannot relax, Cherry Plum for loss of emotional control, and Clematis. It's very subtle but can be so effective that many independent midwives offer it to women in childbirth (and to their partners).

tinged. Diarrhoea usually creates a sore red rash around the anus, and your baby may also show signs of general infection – a temperature, irritability and generally looking and feeling unwell.

Most diarrhoea illnesses are more of a practical nuisance than a real medical problem. They tend to be dealt with quite easily, using fairly straightforward measures like giving extra liquids and making small alterations in diet, and those caused by colds and antibiotic treatment tend to disappear on their own after the chills and pills have finished. The major problem with diarrhoea is the risk of dehydration and loss of vital body salts, especially in babies.

What you can do
- *First, is your baby getting dehydrated?* Basically, if your child is not losing weight, there is nothing to worry about. Signs of *mild to moderate* dehydration are:
  — weight loss of about 5 per cent of their total bodyweight (that's 1 lb in a 20 lb baby). This is cause for careful monitoring rather than real worrying, but remember, your baby will put that weight back on again rapidly once they have got over the diarrhoea.
  — nappies are not as wet as usual
  — dry mouth – keeps wanting drinks
  — quieter than usual
  — when they cry, there are not as many tears as usual.

  Keep an eye on them, encourage them to drink water and milk, and report to your GP straight away if the weight loss increases or signs of dryness get worse.

  Continue to manage your baby's diarrhoea by:
- *Preventing dehydration.* If you are breastfeeding, let them have as much as they can possibly take – breastfeeding is enormously comforting too when a baby feels ill. If they vomit after feeding, try feeding far more slowly (perhaps express a little from your breast first so it is not so full). If it only stays down for a quarter of an hour they will in fact have absorbed quite a bit of nourishment from it already. If they refuse even your breast for a while, try and give them electrolyte solution instead. You can get this under the brand name Dioralyte from the chemist without prescription. It comes in different flavours, but babies under a year old tend to reject any except the non-flavoured solution, whereas toddlers tend to prefer the blackcurrant flavour.

  If your baby is on formula milk, substitute the electrolyte solution and check up with your health visitor or GP how much you should give your baby. The minimum is about 2 fl oz (60 ml) of solution per 1 lb (450 g) of baby, given at each feed. The solution contains the right balance of water and body salts to replace what your baby is losing.
- *Working out what started it.* If it was antibiotics, try a little acidophilus powder (available from health food shops) for 2–6 weeks to replace any of the naturally occurring, beneficial stomach flora and fauna which antibiotics can so easily wipe out.

Signs of danger dehydration
It's *severe dehydration* if:

- Their eyes look sunken.
- Their soft spot, if it has not yet closed up, seems sunken too.
- They are irritable or listless.
- They have a dry mouth.
- Their skin is pale and dry.
- They are urinating less often as well as less volume than usual, and when they do it is dark yellow (i.e. concentrated) in colour.
- They have a fever.
- They are vomiting.
- They have abdominal pains.

Take your baby to see your GP right away.

Has your baby started eating anything new recently? Try removing it. If that's the culprit you should see an improvement within the week.

Are they having a lot of one particular food or drink? For instance, some fruit juices contain a sugar called sorbitol which is not absorbed by the intestines but draws water to itself, soaking up moisture from the intestinal lining and into the stools, making them runnier than ever if there is existing diarrhoea – or it may even be the cause in the first place. Prune juice contains sorbitol, which is why it is such a good natural laxative, but so does apple juice (a toddler favourite) pear and cherry.

- *Altering what they're eating.* Is your baby vomiting as well? If so, carry on breastfeeding but *stop all foods and formula milk for 12 to 24 hours only*, depending on how bad the diarrhoea and vomiting are. Offer dioralyte instead.

Then resume your baby's former diet but slowly, offering half as much, twice as often for a few days until their stomach regains its balance. Begin with bland foods like baby rice, rice cereal, puréed vegetable (soft boiled eggy fingers if the child is older) and bits of toast without butter.

What your GP can do
They will recommend you continue with the electrolyte solution, and may suggest an anti-diarrhoea medication which is safe for infants (few are) like Imodium. Many parents understandably would like their GP to send a sample of their child's stool for examination in a lab, to see if the bug causing the infection can be identified. Retrovirus is responsible in 30 to 50 per cent of all

Most paediatricians now reckon that the old tradition of starving out diarrhoea for more than 48 hours is unhelpful, and that your child needs at least some nutrition to give their body the energy it needs to heal itself.

cases, but as many as 40 per cent of cases have no identifiable cause. It is not generally worth getting a stool check because by the time the results find their way back from the lab – 7 to 10 days later – the chances are your baby will be better anyway. If the diarrhoea persists, then ask for a stool analysis.

Complementary therapy
Homeopathy
There are many different remedies for diarrhoea depending on what caused it, the child's exact symptoms, their own personality, the way they are reacting to illness and the nature of their stools. Call or see your homeopath for advice, but Dr Julian Scott, who established the Foundation for Traditional Medicine Children's Clinic in 1984, suggests the following remedies:

If your baby/toddler has both vomiting and diarrhoea (both of which are grass green in colour) try Ipecacuana; when the child also has a colicky pain, is thirsty and their lips are dry, try Bryonia. If the diarrhoea seems to have exhausted them, try Carbo veg, but if their stools are green and watery, the child is fearful and nervous and has recently been out in the cold wind, try Aconite. For emotionally related diarrhoea, Borax is good for a child who is very highly strung; try Arg nitricum if they have had an emotional upset.

Bach Flower Remedies
As there is such a strong link between bowel patterns and the emotions, Bach Flower Remedies, which help deal subtly and gently with emotional problems and imbalances, may be very helpful here. They may be especially useful for stopping a short-term acute attack of diarrhoea from developing into a chronic problem. Try Chicory if your child is exceptionally clingy; Walnut if you think that recent change may have upset them and might have a bearing on the problem; Clematis if they are listless, aspen or mimulus if they are nervous or fearful, Centaury if they are a gentle child who finds it hard to stand up for themselves.

EARACHE AND GLUE EAR (0–2 years)

What is it?
Earache is usually caused by inflammation of the middle ear. Glue ear is a long-term ear infection producing thick, sticky secretions.

Ear infections are far more common in babies (30 per cent have had antibiotics in their first six months of life, and a high proportion are for ear infections) and toddlers than they are in adults because their Eustachian tube is not yet fully developed. This tube connects the throat to the middle ear and so helps equalize the pressure on both sides of the eardrum. In a baby or toddler, the tube is shorter, does not open and shut so efficiently and is set at a lesser angle than an adult's to the throat – all of which allows germs easier access from the throat, where they may have been breathed in, to the delicate inside of the ear.

The most common type of ear infection in children is called *otitis media*. There is very little space inside the ear for swelling, and so while this type of ear infection can be very mild, it can sometimes become extremely painful very fast.

The most common type of chronic or long-term ear disease in small children, *secretionary otitis media*, is better known as glue ear because of the sticky yellowish-brown discharge it produces. According to the Medical Research Council, it affects four out of every five children at some time. Figures gathered by the Royal College of Physicians show that there is a peak number of cases in children aged six to twelve months, and another soon after they begin school.

Glue ear tends not to be painful as such, but toddlers old enough to talk will probably say their ears feel 'full', and children of any age will find they cannot hear very well (try putting your fingers lightly in your ears to find out what it sounds like). It impairs an infant's ability to learn to talk, as they hear words indistinctly and so cannot copy them properly. Toddlers with glue ear are often labelled disobedient because they don't respond well (because they don't hear clearly) to what their parents and carers ask them to do. With long-term glue ear, it is not unusual for children to become so frustrated, because they cannot hear what is going on properly, that they develop behavioural problems. These may range from giving up on social interaction as a bad job because they have trouble working out what is going on, to withdrawing into themselves, to becoming disruptive.

Causes of short-term earache
The most common causes for short-term acute ear pain are:

- A brief infection which, besides causing swelling and soreness, can also produce pus.
- An ordinary cold. The same thin mucus streaming from your baby's nose may also find its way behind their eardrum. This may merely give them an uncomfortable sensation of pressure in their ears which could wake them at night and make them feel irritable, or it may actually be painful. If the fluid becomes trapped in there it is likely to become infected.
- Exposure to cold winds may also play a part, as they can inflame the membranes lining the ear.

The good news about acute ear infections is that there is a great deal parents can do at home to soothe their child's earache, and the problem tends to clear up fast on its own (without the use of antibiotics). According to one leading ear specialist, George Browning of the Institute of Hearing Research at the Royal Infirmary in Glasgow: 'More than 85 per cent of children will be pain free within 24 hours – irrespective of whether they have been treated with antibiotics or not.'

Causes of long-term ear pain
Long-term ear pain may be caused by:

- Chronic infection.
- Inflammation produced by food allergy. Unlikely as this may sound, in 1993 the Royal National Throat, Nose & Ear Hospital in London found that with a group of 200 children with glue ear who also suffered from allergic disorders such as asthma, eczema and hay fever, their hearing improved once their allergies were treated.

Symptoms
It can be hard to tell why, where or even *if* your child is in pain, especially if they cannot yet talk. However, you know your own baby better than anyone, so if your baby is behaving in a way that is unusual for them or they seem very discontented and you feel instinctively that they have an earache, they very probably have.

Some common signs to watch for include:

- Frequent night-waking or a sudden change in sleep patterns.
- Crying or screaming which you cannot seem to soothe for long.
- Your baby doesn't like lying down flat.
- An existing cold suddenly gets worse.
- Increasingly thick discharge from the nose.
- Discharge from the eyes too.
- Anecdotally, many parents report that ear pulling, rubbing and fiddling seems to mean ear infection. However, many child health experts argue that most babies pull and play with their ears experimentally anyway, especially when they are teething (perhaps because teething pain can sometimes spread to the ears as referred pain).
- Increased irritability.
- Problem worse at night. This is because when the baby lies down, fluid or pus builds up in their middle ear and puts extra pressure on the eardrum, so it hurts more.

What you can do
- *Help soothe the pain with heat.*
  Either: Partially fill a hot-water bottle with water of a temperature only high enough to make the outside comfortingly warm, rather than hot. Slip a soft cover over it or double up a clean, soft adult cotton T-shirt and wrap that around it. Cuddle your baby semi-upright on your lap, leaning them with their sore ear nearest your body, and put the hot-water bottle between their ear and yourself. Do this for about 10 minutes at a time.
  Or: Dip a clean flannel in very hot water, wring it out, and fold over into a slim pad. Place it over the baby's ear (checking it is not too hot for them) and hold in place with a cotton bonnet. Do this as often as seems helpful.
- *Sleep semi-upright.* When it is time for your baby to go to bed, partially

prop them up on pillows and ensure the sore ear is not pressed against the pillow. If it is difficult for them to remain semi-upright (they tend to keep sliding down), take them into your bed, prop yourself semi-upright, and lay your baby on your chest. This way they should remain in a more comfortable position, and your presence will comfort them throughout the night.

- *Carry them around with you.* As you go about the house, keep them semi-upright or sitting fully upright against your body in a babysling. Keep putting warm flannels on their ear under their bonnet.
- *Place two or three small drops of warm oil inside their ear.* Hold them with their sore ear tipped to one side for a few moments to encourage the oil to trickle as far inside as possible. Use almond or olive oil.
- *Give them the appropriate dose of infant paracetamol four-hourly.*
- *Give them a soothing steam bath.*
  It helps mucus drain from the nasal passages – and perhaps the Eustachian tubes too. Run an ordinary warm bath, but if you have a shower curtain fixed above it, pull it all the way round the bath to create a steam tent, and get in with your baby. Keep topping up the water to create more steam. Take in plenty of bath toys, bubble-blowing rings – anything to encourage your baby to remain here happily for 20 minutes or so.

Ways to prevent earache

- *Breastfeed your baby, if you can, for as long as possible.* Breastfed babies do get fewer ear infections. Research carried out at Southampton University in 1994 found that children who had been bottle-fed as babies were twice as likely to suffer from glue ear as breastfed ones. And another survey of 315 babies in America found that while two-thirds of the breastfed group had had a middle ear infection at some point, nearly every single one of the bottle-fed group had. One possible explanation for this is that breastmilk is high in gamma-linolenic acid, which converts to a powerful anti-inflammatory agent called prostaglandin.
- *If your baby is bottle-fed, always feed them upright.* Avoid prop-feeding at all costs. It can encourage air, fluid or even small amounts of milk to travel into the Eustachian tube. Trapped air can cause earache, trapped fluid or milk could become a breeding ground for germs and infection.
- *Do not smoke.* This may help prevent ear infection in the first place, but it most definitely increases the chances of a child who already has glue ear getting better without needing surgery. According to a study of 222 three- to nine-year-olds carried out by the Bristol Royal Children's Hospital in 1994, if the parents of glue ear children didn't smoke or gave it up their children were three and a half times more likely to get better without needing ear surgery.
- *If your baby has needed a course of antibiotics,* American nutritionist and doctor Leo Galland suggests mixing some acidophilus powder with their food or milk (see Useful Addresses page 236, for suppliers). It contains *lactobacillus*, the 'good' bacterium which lives naturally in the gut, which is, like other bacteria, destroyed by antibiotics. Replacing it in freeze-dried

supplement form helps avoid the possibility of an overgrowth of candida fungus – which also lives naturally in the gut, and does no harm unless it multiplies too fast. If the bacteria which usually keep candida in balance are wiped out, this gives the tiny fungus the chance to breed rapidly, and an overgrowth can produce digestive problems and general ill health. This problem is far more common in children or adults who have taken multiple courses of antibiotics than in babies who have only had one or two.

Give them acidophilus powder for two to six weeks, depending on the length and strength of the antibiotics course.

• *Treat colds early.* If you have noticed that if your child develops an especially snotty cold it often turns into raging earache:

— Help keep your child's nasal passages as clear as possible with steam treatment, regular wiping with a very soft cotton handkerchief (as paper handkerchiefs can create redness and soreness), and nasal aspiration or saline drops (see Colds page 181).

— Check with your GP when the cold starts developing in the direction you would usually associate with later ear infections, and ask about possible options such as a brief course of preventative antibiotics.

• *If your child suffers from recurrent ear infections* or chronic long-term glue ear, it is worth checking for allergies. The most common culprits are dairy products and wheat products – see if it helps to remove them from your child's diet for a few weeks, replacing them with soya products and rice-based products instead. For swap suggestions to maintain good nutrition on this type of trial exclusion diet, see Soothing Eczema page 247.

It is not easy with babies and toddlers as the tests for allergy often give inaccurate results at this age and you may be told it is not worth it. However, it is well worth the effort if you can put a stop to your child's ear problems. See Soothing Eczema pages 237–63 for details of the different allergy tests, their problems and the options available.

What your GP can do

Most GPs, when faced with a screaming baby or toddler with an inflamed ear, will offer antibiotics. This is partly because they feel it is their role to do something positive to help the child in pain, and partly to avoid the very slight chance of mastoiditis developing. Many parents, anxious to help their baby and distressed by the pain they are in, would not be too happy about leaving the surgery without a prescription, so the GP might feel under pressure from mothers and fathers too.

However, the latest medical advice on what to do about ear infections for babies and toddlers is starting to swing away from instant antibiotics towards a more balanced approach: hold off the antibiotics for the next 24 hours, treat your child at home with warm oil ear drops and gentle applied heat (for instance a hot water bottle wrapped in a towel), upright sleeping, carrying and infant paracetamol, and see if it improves. If it doesn't, then go for the antibiotics.

According to Oxford GP and researcher Dr Peter Burke, who is helping set up a major research project into the best way to treat very young children's ear disorders (see TARGET, below), antibiotics should not be given automatically to every child with acute earache. However, he adds that there is still a good case for them if your child is under two years old, if the GP can see, looking into their ear, that the·membranes in their middle ear are bulging outwards with the pressure of the fluid or pus building up on the other side, or if the child has been in pain for more than 48 hours.

Some doctors agree with George Browning that children hardly ever need antibiotics for ear problems. One Dutch study in 1991 suggested the drugs were no more help than dummy pills and the course of nature. And, according to the doctors' magazine *GP*, only one in 10 of all mild ear infections are caused by bacteria, and treatable with antibiotics, anyway. Another problem is that some popular types of penicillin such as amoxycillin are becoming increasingly ineffective because earache-inducing bacteria are developing a stubborn resistance to them.

The TARGET trial for glue ear treatment

As for the best treatment for glue ear, controversy has been raging for several years, but there is a British medical trial of three-year-olds now under way called TARGET (Trial of Alternative Regimes for Glue Ear Treatment) which should soon settle the argument once and for all. At the moment the options are:

- Wait-and-see. It might go away of its own accord.
- Antibiotic treatment during acute infection times, but no surgery.
- Surgery – inserting a slim tube about the size of a ballpoint pen tip, called a grommet, through the eardrum to even out the air pressure between the middle ear and the air outside.

  'The glue of the ear builds up because its Eustachian tube is in some way blocked. This may be because of swelling of the adenoids, an infection producing discharge, an allergy, an inflammation or anatomical variability. This can create a partial vacuum inside the ear,' explains Manchester GP Ivan Benett, who is currently working to develop a medical blueprint for standardizing good practice in the treatment of glue ear for all the children within the Manchester Health Authority area.

  'The discharge prevents the ear bones from passing sound vibrations into the ear so the child cannot hear well – and it also encourages infection, which not only hurts but makes the whole situation even worse. The solution is in theory to equalize out the pressure in the middle and outer ear by perforating the ear drum temporarily and artificially using a grommet tube.'

  The grommet usually stays in place for six to twelve months. It also means that the child is able to hear properly again. The problem with grommets is that they can fall out, and also carry a risk of hardening of the ear drum.

- Surgical removal of the adenoids. The child may have a grommet inserted as well.

Complementary therapy
Homeopathy
For earache, homeopathic treatment is highly individual and varies according to the child's personality, their constitution, the way they are reacting to the illness, and their exact physical and emotional symptoms. However, natural practitioner Dr Julian Scott suggests that often, for acute attacks with severe pain when the child is screaming, Chamomilla helps; for acute attacks when the child is red in the face with a temperature and considerable pain, Belladonna. Hepar sulp may be calming if the ear pain is sharp and there is yellow pus discharge with it, and he recommends Aconite as a useful general remedy for earaches if they are worse at night (most are) and says that there are some reports of Pulsatilla being useful for glue ear too.

According to top homeopath Dr Andrew Lockie, the following remedies may also be appropriate for 14 days after the glue ear sets in: Graphites for thick, honey-coloured discharge; Calcarea if there is ear discharge with swollen neck glands and the baby/toddler is also prone to night sweats; and Kali bich if there is some thick stringy mucus down the back of the throat.

Herbal medicine
The anti-inflammatory herbal agents include chamomile, echinacea, marigold (calendula) and garlic oil. St John's wort (hypericum) is helpful for acute attacks, according to Dr Julian Scott.

Chinese herbal medicine
According to the Chi centre for traditional Chinese Herbal Medicine in London, Chinese herbalism has been successful for many cases of glue ear. Doctors at the Chi Centre are qualified both in traditional Chinese herbal medicine and orthodox clinical medicine (see Useful Addresses, page 236).

Aromatherapy
For earache, try a drop of German Chamomile essential oil, which is both cooling and anti-infective, on a cotton bud, wiped gently in the ear. Do not try to push it deep into the ear under any circumstances, nor even to probe just a little with it (this would hurt a baby with an ear infection and may increase the chances of further infection). Lavender oil is a good cheaper alternative which is also anti-infective and healing.

Bach Flower Remedies
These do not dull the pain of earache as such, but they do work in subtle but surprisingly effective ways to help the baby or toddler cope emotionally with the illness and become calmer. If they are very upset by the ear pain, Rescue Remedy or one of its ingredients, Rock Rose, may be helpful; Willow if they are extremely sorry for themselves, Chicory if they are reacting by being very clingy and whiny. Crab Apple might be appropriate if the ear discharge is very purulent and unpleasant (described by its inventor Dr Bach as 'the cleansing remedy – which helps us get rid of anything we do not like either in our minds or in our bodies').

If you have been up for one or several nights and are parenting a baby who is screaming intermittently with earache during the day, one of the remedies such as elm 'for usually capable people who at times find the pressures or responsibilities of their work or family commitments overwhelming', olive for exhaustion, or Rescue Remedy may help maintain your equilibrium – not always easy if you are very tired and have a sick child.

ENCEPHALITIS

Encephalitis is an inflammation of the brain. It is rare, but can very occasionally be the result of a prolonged high temperature associated with many different things, including measles, chickenpox (see page 178) and flu. Vaccinations against childhood diseases, such as the MMR (Measles, Mumps, Rubella) vaccine, have also very occasionally been associated with it.

Symptoms
Headache, neck pain, fever, nausea and vomiting, seizures, lethargy, weakness, irritability and paralysis.

Treatment
The condition can be very dangerous and its outcome – and treatment – depend greatly on what has caused it and upon the age and general health of the child. If you notice some of the symptoms above, take your child directly to the nearest casualty unit where they will be seen straight away. Don't waste potentially vital time going to your GP surgery first. Your baby may not have encephalitis, but it is best to be on the safe side.

EYE DISCHARGE (STICKY EYE)

What is it?
A yellow or green sticky discharge from the eyes which forms crusty deposits in the corners and on the lids overnight. Eye discharge tends to have slightly different causes depending on the age of your baby or toddler. There are several common causes of sticky eyes in infants.

The most usual cause
A blocked tear duct is the most common cause in the first few weeks of life. What can happen is that at birth, the end of the tear duct nearest the nose may be covered by a thin membrane. Generally this breaks open soon after birth so tears can drain out. If the membrane does not break open properly, the tear fluid builds up in either one or both eyes, providing a splendid breeding ground for viruses and bacteria. When tear fluid becomes infected it develops into a yellow, sticky substance, some of which is able to drain into the baby's eyes.

What you can do

The tear duct is under that tiny lump at the nose corner of each eye. Unclog it by gently massaging it with a clean finger upwards towards the nose. Do this half a dozen times every two to three hours – a good time is just after each feed, or before each nappy change. If the yellow discharge persists, or both your baby's eyes are now watering, let your GP know.

It also helps to clean any discharge away with cooled, boiled water and cotton wool.

What your GP can do

Prescribe antibiotic ointment or drops to help treat the infection. Blocked tear ducts may recur but should usually be resolved between six and nine months of age. If they do not, it may be necessary for a doctor to open them using a tiny metal probe.

Other causes

- *The common cold.* This is a very frequent cause of sticky eyes. For how to help your baby get over it fast, and make them as comfortable as possible while they have it, see Colds pages 179–83.
- *Ear infection.*
- *Irritation.* This can be caused by contact with maternal blood or amniotic fluid during birth. An eye swab will determine whether the problem is caused by infection or short-term irritation.
- *Contact with mother's genital infection during childbirth.* If a mother has a genital infection such as chlamydia, genital herpes or gonorrhoea – which may be symptomless for her so she may be completely unaware of it – this can be passed on to the baby as it travels down the birth canal and out into the world, causing eye inflammation and infection.

  If a baby's eyes are sticky with pus and the whites inflamed, it is vital that a doctor should take a medical swab of the discharge and have it checked in the lab, so it can be treated promptly and appropriately to prevent serious eye damage.
- *Conjunctivitis.* This is a common cause of eye discharge in older babies and toddlers. Conjunctivitis is an infection of the membrane that covers the eyeball (conjunctiva) and it can be caused by a wide variety of germs and irritants – from viruses and bacteria to irritants like dust and pollen, or allergies. Strictly speaking, the condition is known as pinkeye if it is caused by a bacteria.

To clean sticky eyes, use cotton wool dipped in warm water, perhaps with a little salt added. You can bathe the eyes with breastmilk rather than plain or slightly salted water if you like. Some mothers say it works wonderfully.

How to give eye drops

It's not always easy to give eye drops to a squirming, reluctant baby. For best results, try and get someone to help you hold your child's head steady while you hold the dropper in one hand, resting it against your child's forehead. Then, using the index finger of your other hand, gently pull down their lower eyelid and drop the liquid medication between the eye and lower lid curve – avoid touching the eye with the dropper at all.

For eye ointment, use a similar method, rolling down your baby's lower lids and squeezing a small amount of ointment along the inside of the eyelid. Your baby will then blink rapidly which will distribute the ointment all over the eye's surface.

Symptoms

Symptoms are watering, bloodshot eyes which your baby tries to rub all the time, sensitivity to light, and a yellow sticky discharge from the eyes which dries to a golden crusting in the corners and on the lash ends. It is highly contagious and will spread rapidly to the other eye – and to other people's.

What you can do

- *Try not to let the child rub their eyes* if possible. Wash their hands well if they do to avoid cross-infection.
- *Regularly wash eyes with cool water.* Use your left hand to wipe the left eyelid, then get a new piece of cotton wool and use your right hand to wipe the right eyelid. Wash your hands well afterwards.
- *Help your child avoid suspected allergens.* For instance, if you think house dust is the culprit, try damp-dusting their room, washing all bedclothes, beating the mattress outside and covering it with a microporous cover (see Dealing with Asthma page 270).

What your GP can do

- *Prescribe antibiotic drops or ointments.* The infection drops from being highly contagious to only mildly contagious from 24 hours after treatment begins. This is especially relevant if there are other children in the family or if your baby/toddler goes to daycare for all or part of the day.
- *Take a swab from the eye* and get it checked in a laboratory to try to identity the germ causing the infection. They will probably prescribe an antibiotic.

Complementary therapy

Homeopathy

General remedies for older children, which can also be used for babies under a homeopath's supervision, include Euphrasia (eyebright) if their eyes are watering heavily but occasionally also get gummed up with sticky mucus. If the child is a toddler and can indicate to you that their eyes feel burning as well as looking red and watery, that they feel better in warmer air, but they are also sneezing, Allium cepa may be the right remedy. For really thick yellow discharge with itching burning eyes that your child seems to want to rub all the time, Pulsatilla may help.

Herbal medicine
A traditional remedy for eye infections is to wash them in soothing, cooled herbal teas made from any of the following, as directed by a herbalist – Purple Loosestrife, Marigold (Calendula), Golden Sea, Eyebright or Marshmallow plant.

FEVER AND CONVULSIONS

What is a fever?
Any temperature above normal – that's 37 °C or 98.6 °F – is classed as a fever. It is the body's way of helping to kill invading germs which are causing infection. They are usually viruses, such as chickenpox, measles or upper respiratory tract infections.

The way fevers usually behave, if you let them run their course, is that they build in intensity until they reach their crisis – the point at which the germs causing the illness start to be destroyed by the toxins they themselves are producing – and after that the fever gradually dies away again.

Fever is not dangerous in itself. The two main reasons for treating it with cooling measures or infant paracetamol (see below) are to make your baby or toddler feel more comfortable and to avoid the possibility of febrile convulsions, also known as fever fits or seizures.

What is a convulsion?
Infants' immature neurological systems can react to even moderate rises in temperature or rapid temperature fluctuations with a convulsion. The key factor seems to be not how far the temperature rises, but how fast it does so. Febrile convulsions, as they are called, tend to run in families, and are very common in babies and small children between the ages of six months and two years. According to the ongoing 'Children of the 90s' study in the UK, one in twenty children have had a convulsion by the time they are just a year old, half of which are due to a fever, and a fifth to deliberate breath-holding. Though these fits can be extremely alarming for parents, doctors do not feel fever fits are a problem if they last for less than 10 minutes, and if no persistent neurological problems follow.

In only about 2 per cent of cases is there a later link with epilepsy.

According to a Danish study in 1995, babies' intelligence is not impaired

---

If a baby's or toddler's temperature rises past 38.8 °C (102 °F), this is cause for monitoring and concern, so always let your GP know. If it rises past 40.5 °C (105 °F), delirium may occur.

by convulsions. The study followed up 300 children who experienced febrile convulsions, and when they did IQ tests at the age of 14 researchers found virtually no difference between them and children who had never had a fit in their lives. Doctors say that the outlook for babies and children who experience these fits is very good, and that usually they simply grow out of them.

Symptoms
Just before a febrile convulsion, there will sometimes be a warning – twitching lips or a shaking arm or perhaps simply a blank stare. If your baby has had a convulsion before and you recognize the signs, now is the time to cool your baby down – perhaps under a light, barely warm shower if there is no time for gentle sponging down with warm water – as this can avert the fit. Signs of a full-blown convulsion include your baby shaking all over, eyes rolling back in their head, becoming limp and skin going pale. Most fits only last 10 to 20 seconds, but as they can appear very alarming it may seem far longer. This is not nearly long enough to do any harm to your baby, but it may upset you considerably. Your baby is likely to fall asleep promptly afterwards.

What you can do

For fevers
- *Give infant paracetamol* in the appropriate dose.
- *Give extra fluids.* Let your baby suck on home-made ice lollies of frozen diluted fruit juice and sip cool liquids on and off all day. This is a good time to breastfeed on demand for a day or two, if you are feeding your baby yourself.
- *Avoid heavy fatty foods* as digestions tends to slow down during a fever, but offer your baby light alternatives such as puréed fruit or thick home-made soups – many children love messily dunking bread in them and eating the resulting mush.
- *Sponge down to cool.* Expose and sponge with lukewarm water just one limb at a time until it feels cool, replace it under the covers then start the next one. (Do not strip your baby naked and sponge all over at once unless in an emergency, such as a dangerously high temperature, or if you see the warning signs of a fit approaching.) Just sponging the face and forehead can bring relief.
- *Splash in a lukewarm bath.* Get in too, if necessary. Take toys, bubble-blowing kits, anything so your baby can play happily for a while or be amused by you while they cool down.
- *Stand under a lukewarm shower with them*, if they enjoy showers. This works even better than a bath because of the cooling water on their heads and faces.
- *Do not over-dress them.* Try to dress them in light layers so one or two can easily be removed or added again to help control a fluctuating temperature.

- *Keep the environment cool.*
- *Do some comfort sleeping.* At night, it is immensely comforting for a sick child if you lie down next to them and stay with them while they sleep – in fact some sick babies will only sleep at all if their mother's body is close to theirs. Keep the bedclothes light and layered.

For convulsions

Try to head off the convulsion with rapid cooling if you can. Some parents report that after a known warning sign, such as a twitching mouth, they do not wait to sponge the child down gently. Instead, they take them direct to the shower, turn it on gently (as a slightly warm not cold temperature) and get in there immediately with their baby or child fully clothed if necessary.

If you cannot carry out any cooling measures, or do not get the chance (sometimes there is no warning at all).

- *Place your baby or toddler on the floor* face downwards or on their side so that their tongue can fall forwards and any phlegm drain easily down their throat.
- *Do not try to restrain them.* Allow them to shake, and quickly clear a space around them to guard them from banging themselves accidentally on anything while this brief period lasts.
- *Do not give them anything to drink or eat* during or immediately after the fit.
- *As long as their lips are not turning blue and they are breathing normally, you do not need to worry.* In the unlikely event that their lips are turning blue, indicating that they are becoming short of oxygen, give them mouth-to-mouth breathing.

It is not unusual for an infant to have another fit just after the first. Help prevent this by cooling them down immediately after the first fit is over by removing their clothes and sponging their skin down with slightly warm water.

When to call the doctor

Generally it's a good idea to call your GP immediately after the convulsion. If it is the middle of the night and you are able to keep the fever down successfully, you can probably safely sit tight until the morning. However, if your baby *either* had a convulsion without a fever *or* seems very unwell still, take them directly to the casualty department of your local hospital without waiting until the day begins. If going to hospital after a fit, take cool flannels in a plastic bag with you or a cooling water spray if you've got one to hand, to help ensure their fever does not climb again on the way there, causing yet more seizures.

What your GP can do

- *Prescribe paracetamol or ibuprofen* to reduce the fever, especially if the measures you have been using have not been enough.

Mouth-to-mouth breathing
Clear their mouth.
Put them on their back.
Put one of your hands on their head, your fingers under their chin.
*Clear their tongue from the back of their throat by lifting their chin with one
    hand and pressing their forehead with the other.*
Tilt their head slightly upwards towards the ceiling.

Now begin mouth-to-mouth breathing:
1. Cover the baby's nose and mouth with your mouth.
2. Blow into their mouth just using the air in your cheeks rather than
   taking a deep puff. (Forcing too much air into their lungs can distend
   their stomach, encourage vomiting or compromise their breathing still
   further.)
3. Watch their chest rise gently as you blow. If you can see this happen,
   you know their airway is clear and that you are doing it right.
4. Continue to give one steady 'cheek breath' every three seconds until
   your baby is breathing again on their own. Let the air come out under
   its own pressure between breaths – don't press the child's chest.

If the convulsion occurred soon after any vaccinations your baby has had,
let your GP know and insist that this is reported to the Committee on the
Safety of Medicines (your GP has to fill in and send off what is known as
a Yellow Card). Ask to see a photocopy of this notification, as the majority
of reactions to vaccinations such as the MMR do, in fact, go unreported,
giving the Department of Health the impression that they happen far more
rarely than they do. (See Infant Vaccination, pages 279–97, for further
information.)

• *Prescribe antibiotics* if there is a bacterial infection.
• *Give the tranquillizer diazepam* rectally if your child is prone to febrile
  convulsions, as this medication can prevent a fit occurring. Anti-
  convulsants are seldom prescribed for infants.

Complementary therapy
Homeopathy
Some of the specific homeopathic remedies which might be useful include
Aconite if your baby's fever has come on suddenly and is worse around
midnight; Apis if they feel chilly, will not drink and seem worse in hot
rooms; Arsenicum if the fever is worse between midnight and 2 a.m. and
your child is restless, exhausted and anxious and chilly; Belladonna if the
fever came on suddenly and violently and your baby is hot and flushed,
with staring eyes and a pounding pulse; Gelsemium if they feel fluy, with
heavy eyes and aching muscles.

Herbal medicine
Treatments include infusions of herbs such as Borage, Marigold, German Chamomile and Willow bark.

Aromatherapy
Add a few drops of essential oil of Pettigrain and Roman chamomile to lukewarm water and either sponge your baby down with it, or use it as a cooling bath to help bring the fever down.

GENITAL AND BREAST ODDITIES IN NEWBORN BABIES

The genital area and breasts of newborn babies may, for a couple of weeks, look rather different from the way you had expected. The concerns new parents mention most often are:

Enlarged testes
They may be enlarged at, and soon after, birth. This could be because some watery fluid has accumulated around the testicle(s), or because of the increased amounts of hormones present in the baby's system at birth. This slight enlargement is usually normal and subsides within about ten days of its own accord.

There is, however, one clinical condition called a hydrocele which causes the testes to enlarge and this, though not harmful, can be uncomfortable and does not go away on its own. So if the enlargement is still there after three weeks, ask your doctor or health visitor to check it.

Undescended testes
The testes are initially produced inside the baby boy's abdominal cavity and generally drop down (descend) into the scrotal sacs just before or soon after birth. Sometimes one will come down but not the other, which arrives later. If either of your son's testes still has not descended by the time they are a year old, your GP may suggest surgery to correct this, as undescended testes are linked with fertility problems and testicular cancer in young adulthood.

Breast enlargement
Sometimes newborn babies have slight swellings in their nipple and breast area, and small beads of fluid (which used to be called 'witches' milk') may appear on the nipple too. This is called neonatal mastitis and can affect both newborn baby girls and boys. None of the symptoms are anything to worry about. They are caused by some of your hormones having crossed the placenta into your baby's own system just before or during their birth, and are a natural response to a natural process.

The condition does not need any treatment, as the swelling usually reaches its peak within about four days – about the same time as your own milk comes in to your breasts – then fades away again. It will generally have disappeared completely within a few weeks.

Slight bleeding from the vagina

Some baby girls shed a few tiny drops of blood from their vaginas, which you may find dried on to their nappy or as fresh blood when you clean their genitals and bottom during a nappy change or in the bath. Again, like the swollen infant breasts mentioned above, this slight bleeding is the result of the sex hormones they received from your own mature system via the placenta. It is nothing to worry about and will stop within a few days.

GERMAN MEASLES (RUBELLA)

What is it?

This is a very infectious but usually mild viral disease with an incubation period of two to three weeks.

Symptoms

It starts with what appears to be a cold, then comes loss of appetite, sometimes accompanied by a sore throat and swelling up of the lymph nodes in the neck, and a temperature. There is a very tiny possibility of encephalitis (brain inflammation) as a potential complication (see page 204 for signs of encephalitis).

The rash appears about one day after the cold-like symptoms. It tends to start on the face and spreads rapidly to the body. Your child is contagious from a few days before to seven days after the rash disappears. It is mildly itchy and consists of tiny pink spots that can be so concentrated that the entire area seems red and inflamed. It is not that easy for a GP to diagnose German measles accurately, and it may be confused with other similar-looking conditions such as roseola. However, with the latter the rash appears *after* the fever has gone down.

If a woman contracts German measles during the first four months of pregnancy, there is a serious risk of miscarriage and birth deformities. This is one reason why women in their mid to late teens need a bloodtest to check that they have definitely had rubella or still nave the antibodies produced by their babyhood (MMR) vaccine to it. If they are no longer immune, revaccination can be offered. A homeopathic GP could do this homeopathically using the rubella nosode.

What you can do

Children need to be kept at home and have a quiet time when they have rubella, even if they appear perfectly well.

Dab itchy spots with cider vinegar or bicarbonate of soda (one teaspoon of either to a pint of water). If your child is not too sick, let them soak in a lukewarm bath to which you have added one cupful of the vinegar or a handful of bicarbonate.

What your GP can do

No treatment is usually needed, unless to confirm the diagnosis with blood tests.

GPs administer the standard MMR (Measles, Mumps, Rubella) vaccination at around 15 months as a preventative measure. If your baby has any reaction to the MMR other than a slight temperature – such as a rash, a fit or a temperature with high-pitched crying, or appears unlike themselves to you, *this is not normal*, though parents are often told that it is. Insist that your GP reports this via the Yellow Card system to the Committee on the Safety of Medicines, and ask to see a photocopy of the relevant documentation (a 'Yellow Card' report). See Infant Vaccination, page 288, for more information about this.

Complementary therapy

Homeopathy

According to Dr Andrew Lockie, likely remedies include Phytolacca, if your baby or toddler has swollen glands, their ears hurt when they swallow and if these symptoms are soothed by cold drinks; or Pulsatilla when the rash appears, if the child is tearful, red-eyed and has yellow catarrh.

Bach Flower Remedies

Chicory, Hornbeam or Cherry plum may help relieve an itchy rash. Impatiens can soothe extreme rattiness and irritability, Willow might help if they are feeling thoroughly miserable and sorry for themselves, aspen if they feel anxious and don't want to be left alone, Rescue Remedy and Cherry plum if they need calming, vine if they are being demanding and bossy, and chicory if they are feeling exceptionally clingy.

Aromatherapy

Massage oil containing a 2.5 per cent blend (2.5% essential oils in 97.5% carrier oil) of a mix of Tea tree, Lavender and Roman chamomile essential oils, to help reduce any itching.

HERNIA

Hernias are often associated in people's minds with men in late middle age, but they are also surprisingly common in babies, especially a type called an umbilical hernia which appears underneath the baby's navel. A small loop of intestine has pushed its way through a weakness in the muscle of the abdominal wall and is seen as a firm lump on the smooth surface. If it's in the groin it's called an inguinal hernia. The lump may come and go, but tends to be especially noticeable if the baby is crying. Hernias require a small surgical procedure to close the gap in the abdominal wall and push the protruding loop of intestine back inside. The operation is usually delayed until the baby is a suitable age, around two.

Emergency hernia treatment

There is a slight chance that a baby's hernia may strangulate, which means it twists and cuts off its own blood supply. Should the lump become larger, darker coloured or tender, or if your baby is vomiting and suffering unusual colicky pains, contact your GP straight away. This is a medical emergency so it needs immediate attention, but it can be repaired extremely successfully with surgery.

IMPETIGO

What is it?

Impetigo is an itchy, highly infectious skin infection caused by the bacterium *Staphylococcus aureus* (also implicated in eczema, see page 239) or by *Streptococcus* – the germ which also causes sore throats.

Symptoms

It usually begins as one small itchy spot resembling a pimple that has been picked at, and rapidly becomes a cluster of small red spots of differing sizes which enlarge into blisters the size of 1p, 5p or even 2p coins, oozing pale honey-coloured liquid. They tend to break out on the face (especially around the nostrils and corners of the mouth), cheeks, and nappy area, but can appear anywhere at all on the skin surface.

What you can do

*   *Take your baby for a prompt appointment with your GP.* This is not going to clear up on its own. You may want to consider giving your baby small amounts of lactobacillus powder if your doctor prescribes them a long course of antibiotics (see page 215).

The 'scalded baby' syndrome

Some small babies develop another form of skin eruption from *staphylococcus* bacteria – if they already have impetigo and the skin barrier is broken, the germ has easy access. The syndrome's symptoms are blistering red marks that look like boiling water scalds, though they have been nowhere near hot water, and if it is not treated promptly with antibiotics, the rash spreads and the surface of the skin peels off, as if the child has experienced serious burns. This condition was highlighted by a doctor writing in the *British Medical Journal* in 1990 whose own small daughter had suffered from it, and she warned both parents and GPs to be on the lookout for it. Scarring rarely occurs with this, though it looks dramatic. Your baby needs antibiotics, loose clothing and warm soaking baths to help slough off affected skin, and perhaps additional fluid intake too. Go to your doctor straight away if you think your baby might have it.

- *Ensure your baby has their own towel and flannel*, because impetigo is highly infectious. Better still, use throwaway paper towels instead of a flannel. Wash their towel on a hot cycle daily. This is vital, otherwise the entire family will probably get impetigo.
- *Wash any loose crusts off the skin* with warm water and a paper towel (not loo paper as it disintegrates when wet), and pat dry carefully. Do not pick at the crusts to remove them, though this may be tempting.
- *Try not to let your baby infect others* by touching and kissing if they have impetigo on their face or a skin surface not hidden by a nappy or clothes. Recommend a cuddle without cheek to cheek contact – perhaps from behind with the person kissing or resting their cheek on the top of the baby's head – instead.
- *Wash their hands in soap and water* if your baby has been picking or touching the impetigo areas.
- *Wash your own hands well* in soap and water after cleaning the impetigo areas, and dry them on a throwaway paper towel.

What your GP can do
Prescribe antibiotic cream or, if necessary, oral antibiotics.

Complementary therapy
Aromatherapy
Tea tree oil will help treat the acute infection, and Roman chamomile will help soothe the itching. For a baby or toddler, put two to three drops of each in a warm bath, and squeeze water from a clean flannel over the areas of impetigo. Or add one drop of each oil to a palmful of carrier oil such as apricot (which has slightly different properties from almond oil), and apply gently using a small piece of cotton wool soaked in the mixture.

JAUNDICE

What is it?
Neonatal (baby) or physiological jaundice is very common in newborn babies, and about half will develop it to some extent by the third day after their birth. The appearance of jaundice tends to coincide with the third day blues when you may be feeling particularly vulnerable and emotional anyway. But though the term 'jaundice' sounds alarming, unlike adult jaundice it seldom proves to be a problem – it is part of the new baby's normal adjustment to life outside the womb. A new baby's liver is not immediately efficient enough to carry out one of its jobs – removing from the blood the yellow-coloured waste pigment called bilirubin which is produced when red blood cells are broken down – which is why the skin looks yellow. It can take a couple of weeks for the liver to get into its stride. Not surprisingly, the condition tends to be more common and last longer in premature babies, who may need some additional help, and whose jaundice may take longer to subside.

Jaundice is eminently treatable. Even on the rare occasions when it is caused by a serious liver disorder or a structural problem, treatment can be very successful if the condition is detected early.

Symptoms
The symptoms of normal, no-worry neonatal jaundice include:

- An increasingly yellow tinge to the skin, or what looks like a slight suntan, after about three days.
- Yellowish whites of the eyes. In darker-skinned babies, this is the only visible sign.
- Your baby may be rather drowsy and slow feeding.
- It clears up within 10 to 14 days.

What you can do
Normal physiological jaundice usually disappears without any medical treatment, and generally the following measures are all you need to help clear it:

- *Give your baby as much to drink as possible* to help wash the yellow pigment through their system. Feed breastmilk or formula (water with glucose supplements, which used to be suggested, is no longer recommended) on demand until the condition clears. As babies with jaundice can be rather sleepy and not that interested in milk, or will only take a little at a time, you may initially find that you need to rouse them to encourage feeding every two hours. As their jaundice subsides, they become less dozy and will take more milk at a time.
- *Keep a sharp eye on your baby's symptoms*, noting any improvement or lack of it.

What your GP can do
- *Refer your baby for hospital phototherapy.* This is artificial light treatment, which usually lasts from two to four days and needs to be carried out in hospital. Problem jaundice may be noticed before you are due to leave hospital (if that is where you gave birth to your baby), in which case you both simply stay where you are for a couple of days or so longer. Your

---

Danger signs
Prompt medical help is needed if:

- Your baby develops jaundice *in the first 24 hours after birth.*
- They become very jaundiced-looking very quickly.
- They seem listless, unwell, do not want to feed.
- The condition is still present after two weeks. Your baby will need blood tests to check the cause (see below).

baby can often have the light therapy in their own cot next to your bed, with the light unit placed over the top. But if you had your baby at home or went home before any jaundice was noticed, you will have to take them to hospital now for a short period.

A jaundiced infant has phototherapy treatment lying naked, except for their nappy and eye shields, beneath the light for a few days. You can take them out and cuddle them at feeding times with their eye shields removed. Your baby will need plenty of drinks (either breast or formula milk) or they can become dehydrated beneath the lights, so you may need to wake them up for a feed every two hours. Their stools will probably be very liquid under phototherapy, but this is nothing to worry about and ceases when the treatment is over.

Babies often dislike the phototherapy setup at first – perhaps because lying so exposed without even a blanket between them and the air makes them feel vulnerable after being curled up and confined in the soft comfort of the womb. But there is nothing to stop you holding your baby's hand, or stroking their body and talking to them through the circular open windows in the side of the special cot if you feel they are missing contact with you, and this often helps greatly.

- *Arrange for liver and blood tests* to be carried out by a specialist hospital department if there seem to be other more serious, or continuing, problems.

If it hasn't cleared after 14 days
Your baby will need to be tested promptly to find out the cause – see below. Possibilities are:

- Being born early.
- A condition in which their blood cells break down more rapidly than is usual. This is often discovered very soon after the baby has been born, and further treatment may be necessary.
- They may have an infection.
- The jaundice may continue because of breastfeeding (see breastmilk jaundice, below). This is not a harmful form of jaundice and it resolves of its own accord.
- Your baby's thyroid gland may not be functioning properly.
- In rare cases, there may be a problem with their liver such as an obstruction of the bile duct.

Breastmilk jaundice
This condition is very seldom cause for concern and it does not mean you should stop feeding your baby yourself. It can last for several weeks, or, in some isolated cases, for months.

No one really knows why it happens, but frequent suckling helps disperse it. If it seems to be getting worse, tell your community midwife or health visitor and they will arrange for regular blood tests to monitor its progress. If the amounts of bilirubin reach problem levels, you can stop breastfeeding for 24 to 72 hours, and encourage your baby to accept formula milk from a bottle instead, without interfering too much with your milk supply, says Catherine Parker of the National Childbirth Trust's research and information group, and levels should drop rapidly. Apparently they do not rise as high again once you start breastfeeding again.

If you opt for the 72-hour take-a-break approach, help keep your own breastmilk supply going – and your breasts comfortable – by expressing milk regularly at the times when you would normally be breastfeeding (see page 21). Perhaps do some expressing before you feed your baby by bottle, otherwise the sight and sound of a hungry baby and the act of seeing them suckling can cause substantial leakage from your breasts which saturates the stoutest of breastpads, and then wets your shirt.

Your milk supply may diminish if you do not breastfeed for a week, despite expressing, as it is very much based on supply and demand. But when you begin breastfeeding again, your output, if you feed your baby as often as possible on demand, should be back to normal within a week or so.

The Split Bilirubin Test
Any baby who has been jaundiced for more than 14 days needs to be given this inexpensive test. Insist upon it, and do not settle for reassurances from either your health visitor or your GP that it is 'only breastmilk jaundice'. They cannot tell for sure simply by looking at your baby, no matter how experienced they are.

When it is more serious
It is vital that a baby who has had jaundice for two weeks or more is checked out because, while liver disease is rare, it still happens. And though it is eminently treatable if diagnosed in time, it will be fatal if it is left too long. There are, for example, 5,000 babies born with a congenital infection of the liver every year, and 1 in 7,000 are deficient in a vital enzyme usually made by the liver called alpha-1-antitrypsin. If your baby does have any of these problems, early diagnosis is vital so treatment can be given to avoid any irreversible liver damage. If this has happened already, the only option then is a liver transplant, which may or may not be successful.

Early diagnosis of possible liver disease is very important.
Liver disease in babies is rare, but if you notice any of these additional symptoms, tell your GP or health visitor right away:

- very poor feeding
- fretfulness
- dark yellow urine (it is usually very pale or colourless)
- pale, clay-coloured stools (they are usually yellow, or sometimes greenish, in a healthy new baby)
- unusual feeding patterns (feeding very poorly or excessively)
- failure to thrive and put on weight
- a tendency to bleed – perhaps from the umbilicus, or your health visitor/

midwife might notice an abnormally long clotting time after a standard heel prick blood test.

Your doctor must arrange for prompt testing to work out what the problem is. If you are still concerned for any reason after having seen your doctor, and would like to talk further about infant jaundice, or if you have a baby who has liver disease, contact the Children's Liver Disease Foundation (0121 643 7282) or send an s.a.e. to the foundation at 138 Digbeth, Birmingham B5 6DR.

Possible reasons for serious jaundice include:

- Your blood group is not compatible with your baby's.
  For instance, if you are rhesus negative and your baby rhesus positive then haemolytic jaundice may develop within the first 24 hours after birth. This happens because you have developed antibodies against your baby's red blood cells, which were then destroyed by your own blood cells as the baby was developing in the womb. Fortunately this type of jaundice rarely occurs these days as all rhesus negative mothers are carefully monitored during pregnancy and treated to prevent them developing the problem antibodies.
- A metabolic disorder, such as an underactive thyroid gland or low blood sugar.
- Too many red blood cells are being broken down by your baby's system.
- A structural problem with their liver and bile equipment. If no bile is able to get into the bile ducts because of an obstruction or malformation, this would need urgent surgical correction.

MEASLES

What is it?
A highly infectious viral disease which is usually spread through the air in droplet form, after an infected person coughs or sneezes. It takes about 14 days to incubate and once the disease has started, it runs its course within seven to 10 days. Young babies are protected by their mothers' antibodies which are still present in their bloodstreams for three to six months. The most common time to catch it is between one and three years of age. Despite routine immunization, it is still reasonably common – according to the ongoing British 'Children of the 90s' study, one in 20 infants between the ages of 18 months and two and a half years still gets measles (which is surprising, since the uptake for the MMR vaccine for 15-month-old infants is around the 95 per cent mark in the UK. See Infant Vaccination, pages 279–95).

In developed countries like Britain, America and Australia, measles has lost some of its traditional bite, but children are still likely to feel very unwell with it, and 1 in 10 develops additional complications such as bronchitis, ear infection, gut problems, conjunctivitis, croup, diarrhoea or fever fits. There is also a very small risk of far more serious complications such as encephalitis (inflammation of the brain) and pneumonia. See page 204 for how to spot encephalitis.

Symptoms

Measles begins like a cold, with a running nose, sneezing, watering eyes, a cough, followed by a fever and characteristic little white spots called Koplik's spots which appear inside the cheeks. This is followed rapidly by a higher temperature still (40 °C (104 °F) is not unusual) and a rash of deep red flat spots on the skin, often starting behind the ears and face and later spreading to the trunk, arms and legs. In mild cases, these may just take the form of a few red dots here and there. In severe cases the spots proliferate fast and join up, so there seem to be entire areas of red skin with pale islands breaking them up. Your child will probably feel thoroughly unwell when this rash first appears, and they are thought to be infectious until the rash has gone.

Other symptoms: the lymph glands may swell up, your child may have little or no appetite, may find bright light hurts their eyes, and may have some vomiting and diarrhoea. Phlegm can accumulate in the lungs during measles, too, forming an ideal breeding ground for bacteria, which is why respiratory infections such as bronchitis and even pneumonia sometimes develop.

Measles spots are not especially itchy, but your child might feel miserable and listless while the virus is at its height.

When to call the doctor

If your child has a chest pain or has trouble breathing, call your GP right away as they may need antibiotics if this indicates a chest infection.

Also call them if the temperature remains high despite your efforts to cool it (see Fever, page 208, for ways to help cool a temperature), or if they have a fever fit (see page 209 for ways to cope with a fever fit).

What parents can do

- *Stay near your child to comfort them* if you sense this is what they would like, keeping them quiet and calm.

  This may mean tucking them up on the sofa downstairs if they are old enough, or in their pram if it is large and comfortable (buggies are not so comfortable unless the baby is very small) so they can be near you while you work in the house or kitchen. One mother mentioned that she brought the travel cot into the kitchen, and propped her toddler up snugly in it so she could see her cook and move around the area, but was lying completely comfortably with toys and books around and could just snuggle down when she had had enough.

- *Try to ensure they have as much undisturbed sleep as they need.* If your child seems to prefer to stay quiet in their room for a while, leaving the door wide open so they can hear you and making regular visits every 20 minutes or so helps strike a balance between being left alone and knowing you are there for them. If you feel comfortable with the idea, try sleeping with them in your room or theirs at night (perhaps you already do) as this is very reassuring. Some sick babies will not go to sleep at all unless they can feel their mother's body close by.

- *Keep the room they are in fairly dim* if light seems to be hurting their eyes. Rest their eyes by reading stories to them and playing story and song tapes rather than letting them watch TV or a video.
- *Give them as much as they will accept to drink* – keep offering a lot of little drinks if necessary. If you are breastfeeding or bottle-feeding, do so on demand for comfort, and to keep up their energy for fighting the illness.
- *Cool them down by sponging or bathing* if their temperature is high (see page 208 for other cooling methods).
- *Dress them in cotton* as this is more comfortable if they are feeling sweaty, and cover them with a cotton or polyester-cotton sheet and a cotton blanket or two. If they have no cotton nightclothes, a cotton T-shirt and nappy is fine – or a skimpy cotton T-shirt of yours might do as a makeshift long nightgown.
- *If their rash is itchy, try:*
  — A tablespoon of cider vinegar or bicarbonate of soda in a pint of water. Mix well and dab on the rash.
  — Mix Lavender and Roman chamomile essential oil together and dilute in a 2.5 mixture with a plain carrier oil such as apricot (even vegetable cooking oil will do if nothing else is available). Massage lightly over the rash to help reduce itching.
  — Some of the Bach Flower Remedies – Chicory, Hornbeam and Cherry plum – may help reduce itching too.

What your GP can do
There isn't a treatment as such for measles, but your GP will be able to treat any complications that sometimes come with it, such as bronchitis and ear infection, with antibiotics if appropriate.

Complementary therapy
Homeopathy
A homeopath might recommend Aconite or Belladonna for cold-like symptoms and when the fever is beginning; Euphrasia if the baby or toddler has a fever, watering eyes or swollen eyelids; Pulsatilla if they seem feverish but chilly, and very miserable, have thick green catarrh and light hurts their eyes. When the rash emerges, Sulphur or Bryonia may be helpful.

Herbal medicine
Fever-relieving herbs include infusions of Elderflower, Yarrow and Boneset. For aching limbs and restlessness, Chamomile is good.

The Chinese view of measles

The philosophy and practice of Chinese medicine sees measles as being very special amongst all the childhood illnesses – an important milestone in the development of every small child's physical, emotional and spiritual health. Traditional Chinese practitioners write that often a child can be restless or irritable for many weeks before the disease breaks out, 'as though a storm were brewing' and that the family will greet measles' arrival with relief because to them it explains the child's recent behaviour. They explain the rash of measles (and the other eruptive diseases like chickenpox) as the process by which poisons accumulated in the womb are pushed outwards into the skin, so the child can at last expel them from their body.

When he or she recovers, the Chinese also believe that the child's outlook on life will be rather different – that much negative behaviour will be gone, that they will be more emotionally sensitive to others, open to new influences and perhaps even able to express their own individuality and independence better.

Overall, according to their philosophy, measles is a positive developmental milestone, and when a child of any age has passed it, they take another major step towards growing up into a happy and contented adult. At a higher level, they also believe that measles is a rite of passage which helps the child throw out many of the forces of greed and self-centredness (which Westerners weaned on Freud would call the Id) that are a natural part of a very small children's makeup until they learn, by trial and error, that there are other people besides themselves who matter too.

MENINGITIS

What is it?
Any inflammation of the meninges, the triple layer of soft membranes enclosing the brain and spinal cord, caused by either bacteria, virus or yeast organisms.

Symptoms
There are many different types but one of the commonest is bacterial (spinal) meningitis which may start like either a cold or flu-like illness, or even an ear infection but the child becomes progressively more ill, with a temperature of 38.8–40 °C (102–104 °F), feels drowsy, may vomit, complain of neck pain or a stiff neck. If their fontanelle space in the top of the skull has not yet closed over this may bulge outwards, you may also notice the infant's legs seem unnaturally stiff, perhaps when you are changing their nappy. The baby will also be very pale, and simply look extremely unwell. Viral meningitis shows itself rather differently in that your baby does not appear to be as ill as with the bacterial form of the disease described above and does not deteriorate as fast.

What you can do
Suspect possible meningitis if your child is fast becoming worse, i.e., getting more drowsy and responding to you less, becoming increasingly hard to rouse, does not seem to want to move, and if the usual cooling and mild medication measures cannot bring the fever down. If any or all of these are happening, go directly to your nearest casualty unit where your baby will be seen and treated straight away.

What the doctors will do
Take a sample of spinal fluid (a lumbar puncture or spinal tap test) to check for sure whether it is bacterial meningitis, and if it is the treatment will be intravenous antibiotics in hospital for at least a week while your baby is closely monitored. If it is viral meningitis, your baby will also remain in hospital for close monitoring but the treatment will be more like that given for severe flu.

Note: Meningitis is rare. It is also something that all parents dread – but you are by no means helpless against it because the quicker it is diagnosed, the better and faster children recover and that is where you come in – you know better than anyone whether your child is 'really' sick. You are also the best judge of whether they are getting better or worse on an hour-by-hour basis, and can act very fast on this.

MUMPS

What is it?
Mumps is caused by a viral infection which produces fever and swelling of the main salivary glands (the parotids) on one or both sides of the neck, creating the unmistakable chipmunk face. These glands are just beneath the earlobes and above the jawbone and can be confused with other glandular infections which cause swelling *underneath* the jawbone.

Mumps is rarely seen in children under two to three years old, takes about two weeks to incubate and is infectious from the day before the glands start swelling up to a few days after they have subsided – which should happen within 7 to 10 days.

Symptoms
Symptoms are flu-like at first, often accompanied by an upset stomach, then earache, tenderness around the neck, discomfort on swallowing, a sore throat and dry mouth. Though this sounds like a lot, the child does not usually

---

Suspect possible meningitis if your baby has a cold or ear infection – but begins to be progressively more lethargic, developing a fever which you simply cannot shift.

feel that unwell, and any temperature they have is usually a low one. Mumps is usually a mild illness, but if a teenage boy gets it, there is the possibility that they may develop inflammation of the testes too, which can lead to fertility problems in a minority of cases. Other – rare – complications may include inflammation of the ovaries in girls, inflammation of the pancreas nerve, deafness and a mild form of viral meningitis.

What you can do

- *Offer cooling, easy-to-swallow foods* like softened ice cream, cool yoghurts, fromage frais, puréed banana.

  Avoid acidic foods as they stimulate the salivary glands and this hurts when someone has mumps. Drinking milkshake through a straw is an idea if your child is old enough. If you have a blender or mixer, whizz some banana into the shake for added food value. Soups (bland and not salty or spicy), perhaps with small pieces of soft bread dunked into them, are another favourite, as is baby rice cereal or Ready Brek. Breastfeed or bottle-feed on demand if this is still an important source of nourishment for your baby.

- *Get a plastic syringe from the chemist* if swallowing hurts so much it is temporarily stopping your child taking liquids, and use it to gently squirt water or milk down the side of their throat, as many times as necessary. Use Dioralyte mixture too, which provides the right balance of salts and electrolytes and water, if you think they are becoming dehydrated rather than just thirsty (see Preventing Dehydration page 195). The plastic syringe trick has kept many a baby out of hospital and off a drip.

- *Apply cooling compresses* to the glands of the neck (add herbs to the water – see below).

- *If they have a temperature, use cooling measures* – see cooling fevers on page 208.

- *Give as much TLC as you have the energy and time for* – this is where parents really come into their own. Keep your child company, tell them stories, give plenty of cuddles. Let them stay near you as you move around the house as they may not be able to talk much, but just being around you will be immensely comforting for them. Tuck them up on the sofa, set up a travel cot in the kitchen, let them sleep in your room, or sleep in theirs, if they want to be with you – most sick babies and toddlers do.

If your child develops a severe headache, their neck becomes stiff, light seems to upset them or they become very drowsy, call your doctor right away. Although these signs can be caused by other factors, they could mean meningitis. Tell your GP too if your child vomits or has a stomach ache, as this can be a sign of an inflamed pancreas.

What your GP can do
Treat complications, such as inflammation of the saliva glands, with anti-biotics if appropriate, or with hospitalization in the very unlikely event of encephalitis developing, or dehydration which cannot be managed at home.

Complementary therapy
Homeopathy
If the course of mumps is normal, there are several remedies which could be given every four hours, such as Aconite at the onset of the fever, Bella-donna for high fever where the right side of the child's neck hurts more than the left, or Phytolacca if their glands feel rock hard and their ears hurt when they swallow.

Herbal medicine
Infusions of Yarrow herb and Elderflower help if your child's temperature is rising, and a Marigold infusion may help relieve swollen glands. Cool it and use it on a compress.

ROSEOLA INFANTUM

What is it?
Its name means literally 'a pink rash seen in infants'. It is often confused with German measles, though the baby's temperature tends to soar higher.

Symptoms
Your baby or toddler suddenly develops a high fever, 39.4–40.5 °C (103–105 °F) out of the blue, when they were fine an hour or two previously and have not been obviously sickening for anything. The fever may cause fits too. They may have a sore throat and swollen neck glands. After between three to five days the fever tends to drop abruptly, and your baby will seem almost well again until you notice a faint pink, flat-to-the-touch rash appears around the neck, body and thighs which may last for a few hours or up to two days.

What you can do
- *First concentrate on helping to control the temperature by at-home cooling measures* (see Fevers page 208 for full details of sponging down) and dose with Calpol. Though high sudden fevers like this can look alarming, these measures will help make your baby feel far more comfortable (high tem-peratures make anyone feel rotten) and will help avoid the possibility of a convulsion.
- *Encourage your baby to drink as much fluid as possible.*
- *If the fever persists after five days and/or a rash appears, contact your GP right* away and ask them to come to examine your baby. It is not possible to

be certain that this is roseola infantum – and therefore fairly harmless – until the rash has broken out.

What your GP may do
May offer antibiotics initially when the high temperature is still present and before the rash has come out – but these are not of much help against a virus. Will offer advice on cooling measures, and will always come and see you, day or night, if you become especially worried about your baby.

See sections on homeopathy, aromatherapy and herbal medicine page 211 for advice on what complementary therapists may recommend to supplement cooling-down measures, and help prevent convulsions.

SCARLET FEVER

What is it?
A rash and fever caused by the same virus as a sore throat. Full blown cases are now very rare in Britain but a milder form known as scarlatina has made its appearance. This is uncommon in infants, more likely in school-age children.

Symptoms
A sunburn-like rash over the trunk, face and hands and/or feet which feels slightly rough to the touch. This is caused by the toxins released by the invading streptococcus bacteria. Other signs are swollen tonsils, swollen neck glands and what can be a very sore throat. You may also be able to see a moustache-like area of contrasting pallor around the mouth. Vomiting is also common.

What you can do
Give your child plenty of fluids, encouraging them to drink as often and as much as possible. If breastfeeding, do so on demand and try to encourage as frequent feeds/drinks as possible – suckling will also be very comforting for your baby. Older infants who can hold an ice lolly enjoy sucking these, as both the cold and the liquid bring relief. Try making some in some plastic ice-lolly moulds (available at many supermarkets) from diluted fruit juices and water, or a mix of yogurt or fromage frais and milk. If they are hungry for solid food, offer them a very bland diet.

What your GP may do
Offer antibiotics, usually penicillin for about 10 days. May also suggest preventative antibiotic treatment of immediate family and close contacts if they have not had the infection before.

Note: scarlet fever or scarlatina is contagious for 24 to 48 hours after antibiotic treatment has begun.

Complementary treatment
See suggestions in Mumps section (page 225), and Bach Flower Remedies suggestions for emotional distress the illness may be causing in German Measles (page 213) and Colds sections (page 183).

THRUSH

Thrush is not an infection but an overgrowth of the fungus called *Candida albicans* which lives naturally on the skin and in the gut of every healthy body. It thrives in moist damp places such as the vagina, in enclosed folds of the skin, such as the typical nappy creases of a baby, and in the mouth.

In infants, nappy rash often lays the ground for thrush because the sore inflamed areas break up the usually excellent barrier of the skin, allowing candida access (see Nappy Matters, page 124). A hefty course of antibiotics can do the same by wiping out much of the naturally occurring candida-regulating bacteria in the gut along with the bug your baby was receiving the medication for, thus allowing the candida to multiply out of control.

Symptoms
If thrush develops in the nappy area it tends to take the form of an itchy redness, possibly with small, irregular-shaped red spots round the edges. You would probably also notice flaky white patches. The area may be itchy or sore (especially when urine stings it) or may cause your baby no discomfort at all. If your baby develops thrush in their vagina, you may notice the skin is red and itchy with some white, thick, curdy discharge when you change their nappy. This area too will probably be sore or itchy.

If your baby develops thrush in their mouth, it looks as if they have small amounts of milk curds clinging to the insides of their cheeks, which on closer inspection cannot be wiped off as usual. From here the condition transfers easily to your nipples if you are breastfeeding them. Symptoms of nipple thrush are red, sore, swollen nipples which may also crack, and which are not helped by the usual soothing emollient creams (see Happy, Successful Breastfeeding, page 37).

What you can do
- *If it's nappy thrush,* keep the area as clean and dry as possible (change their nappy more often) and allow your baby to kick free in a warm environment without a nappy on whenever practical (see Nappy Matters, page 124).
- *Try giving acidophilus powder* from the health shop. This is a freeze-dried mixture of the live beneficial bacteria which live naturally in the body,

balancing out the candida fungus and preventing it from multiplying too fast.

Top American paediatrician Professor William Sears suggests parents use it as follows: pierce one of the capsules so the powder runs out, and, with a very clean finger, spread a little of it onto the thrush areas in the nappy area twice daily for a week. Don't apply it in this way to infant vaginal or mouth thrush – you need anti-fungal oral drops or a cream for these. Remember to keep the capsules in the fridge as heat kills the bacteria.

- *Spread cool, plain, natural, live yogurt on the rash* – you can get it from most supermarkets and all health food stores. It has a cooling, soothing effect and again contains the live acidophilis bacteria needed to balance out the candida overgrowth. Women can use this vaginally when they have a thrush infection there.
- If your baby is clearly in great discomfort from itching, sit them in a bath or basin full of warm water, and encourage them to stay there for at least 10 minutes. This can act as a valuable soother.
- *Buy some Canesten cream from the chemist*, as you can do so without a prescription, if you are sure it is thrush. Apply this to the nappy or vaginal area three times a day and when you change a night-time nappy, having first cleaned the area with plain warm water and patted it dry. Use the cream on your nipples too if they are affected.

What your GP can do
They may prescribe antifungal drugs such as nystatin or clotrimazole (Canasten) in cream or ointment form for the nappy area, or in the form of oral drops for the mouth. If your nipples are affected, antifungal ointment would be prescribed for these too.

Complementary therapy
Herbal medicine
A therapist might use localized treatments which have anti-candida action such as Aloe Vera mouthwash (also available from selected chemists without prescription).

Aromatherapy
For thrush in the nappy area, use one drop of antifungal Tea tree oil in a palmful of plain carrier oil such as apricot oil (or plain vegetable oil will do if there is nothing else to hand) and spread gently on the affected areas.

VOMITING

There is a wide spectrum of vomiting behaviour in babies and toddlers. Some, such as spitting up or possetting milk, are perfectly normal – this is just what babies do sometimes – and can be resolved at home by you with a few feeding modifications. Others, such as the impressive-looking projectile vomiting, or vomiting which looks as if it is caused by a gut infection because it is accompanied by a temperature and colicky pain, need help from your GP.

Possetting or spitting up milk

What is it?
Most babies tend to bring back small amounts of milk several times a day during their first few months of life. As American paediatrician Professor William Sears writes: 'This is more of a laundry problem than a medical problem. Dress for the occasion ... wear prints, avoid dark-coloured clothing ...' and keep a cotton nappy or nappy liner handy as a burp-up cloth at all times.

Babies bring back milk because they tend to gulp down air along with it as they feed, and that air then settles underneath the milk in their stomach. When their stomach contracts, the air is pushed back up their food pipe and into their mouth, landing in a sour-smelling, partially digested splodge on your shoulder. Some enthusiastic babies drink too much milk too quickly and the excess tends to get returned rapidly by their over-full stomach.

Mothers of champion possetters often worry that their baby is not keeping enough milk down to nourish them properly. But if your baby looks well and is steadily gaining weight there is no problem – and spilled liquid always looks rather more than it is. Try pouring a dessert spoonful over the kitchen work surface. It makes a surprising amount of mess, probably considerably more than lands regularly on your shoulder after each feed – it is thought that most spitting up is in fact only about a teaspoon or two's worth. Possetting generally subsides after six to eight months, when babies start sitting upright on their own and are taking more solids.

Gastro-oesophageal reflux and pyloric stenosis

What are they?
Vomiting in younger babies is usually caused by straightforward possetting. However, sometimes the culprit is gastro-oesophageal reflux (GER) and occasionally a progressive structural problem affecting the lower stomach valve called pyloric stenosis (PS).

GER is very similar to adult heartburn – irritating stomach acids are regurgitated from the stomach where they belong and up into the oesophagus (foodpipe) causing considerable discomfort. GER has usually lessened by six months, and gone altogether by the time the baby is a year old.

PS is the narrowing of the stomach's lower end, which is called the pylorus, and needs an urgent operation to correct it. The problem does not usually start to make itself known until the first week or two after birth, when the muscles encircling the pylorus start growing thicker, until they clinch the lower exit from the stomach like a fat rubber band. If the pylorus is only partially obstructed, some milk can still trickle through and it seems as if the baby is just spitting up, as many babies do. However, towards the end of the first month the pylorus has usually become very narrow, and when the stomach tries to push milk down through what is left of the pyloric exit, most of it comes gushing back powerfully as projectile vomit.

Sometimes, babies who do not have pylroic stenosis may vomit up a projectile of milk if they have drunk too much or been bounced about too soon after feeding. You do not need to worry about the occasional once or twice.

Symptoms
Suspect gastro-oesophageal reflux if, alongside the vomiting, which may take the form of possetting or more forceful regurgitation, your baby:

* is also suffering colic pain
* seems happier when they are carried or sitting upright
* seems unhappy and uncomfortable if laid down after a feed.

Suspect pyloric stenosis if your baby:

* is losing weight or failing to gain weight
* is vomiting up more and more often
* is developing projectile vomiting – the regurgitated milk shoots across you in a powerful stream, to land perhaps as much as a couple of feet away on the floor.
* Your baby's abdomen is swollen and hard after feeding, and deflated after vomiting.
* is showing signs of dehydration (see page 195 for checklist).

Suspect a gut infection if, alongside the vomiting, your baby has:

* painful colic
* a temperature
* diarrhoea.

What parents can do

About possetting
* *If bottle-feeding, check the hole or holes in the teat* are not too big or allowing milk through faster than your baby can comfortably handle. If in doubt, try using a teat with a smaller hole to see if this helps.
* *Feed your baby upright*, and keep them upright for half an hour afterwards. If you do not have the time to sit with them quietly on your knee for 30

Vomiting is also a possible sign of other conditions including ear infections, urinary tract infections, encephalitis and appendicitis. If your baby appears to have symptoms of any of the above, go and see your GP, or better still your local mother and baby healthcare clinic, right away.

minutes after each feed, and few new mothers do, carry them upright in a babysling instead.

- *Slow down feeding time.* Consider giving smaller amounts of milk more often to see if this helps. Young babies have very small stomachs.
- *Burp your baby gently after every 2 to 3 ounces of milk,* if bottle-feeding, or when you switch from one breast to the other if you are breastfeeding. If feeding from one breast only at each feed, wait till there is a natural pause in your baby's suckling and burp your baby then instead.
- *Regular weekly weighing* helps confirm that your baby is getting enough milk to thrive.

About GER
- *Give a little rice cereal* before, during or after they have had their milk from a bottle or from your breast – or thicken up a bottle-feed with tiny amounts of rice directly. Tiny amounts of rice will help neutralize the milk's richness and damp down acid production by providing a gentle 'stomach lining'. Do this for as long as they have GER *at each feed*. Stop every couple of weeks if it seems to be working to see if the condition has ceased entirely.
- *Offer smaller feeds, more often.*
- *Keep your baby upright and their stomach down against your shoulder,* either held in your arms or nestled in a sling, for half an hour after feeds. If it is in the middle of the night, prop them up at a 30° angle in the prone position in their cot or your bed, depending on where they are sleeping. Just placing your baby upright in a baby bouncer, buggy or baby seat is no help – it is the combination of propping up and being on their stomach which helps avoid GER.
- *Carry your baby close to you* in a sling as much as you can. This does get harder as they become heavier – there is a great deal of difference between carrying an eight-week-old baby around for a long period and doing the same for a hefty six-monther. If your shoulders are being hurt by the sling straps digging in, wad up two clean tea towels and place them between the straps and your shoulders as padding.

  Carrying your baby helps GER partly because of the position they are in, but partly because it is thought that the gentle rocking motion, your heartbeat and perhaps the occasional gurgle from your own stomach might enhance a young baby's intestinal development and function.

About a gut infection such as gastroenteritis
This can be treated at home in the same way as diarrhoea (see pages 195–7) by home rehydration methods, and by giving electrolyte solution to replace lost liquid and vital body salts.

Traditionally, infants with gastroenteritis have always been taken off food and given rehydration therapy (Dioralyte with water) instead for 24 to 48 hours. But in 1996, researchers in Bristol found that giving them some very plain, bland food – such as baby rice mixed with water, boiled potato or rice, clear soup or, believe it or not, Rice Krispies *plus* the Dioralyte – but keeping them off all milk and wheat products for a few days, is better for them. They do not lose weight, have some energy from food with which to fight the infection, and get better from their gastroenteritis just as fast as the babies who are being deprived of food altogether.

- *Watch carefully for signs of dehydration* (see page 195) and begin to treat it at home if you think it's occurring. If it is not improving within 24 hours, take your baby to see your GP right away.
- *Offer small, very frequent doses of fluids* – a teaspoon or half a plastic syringe full every 10 minutes if they cannot keep anything larger down. If you are breastfeeding your baby, offer them the chance to suckle very frequently for short periods, say a minute or two at a time every 20 to 30 minutes.

What your GP can do

For GER your GP can prescribe anti-acid medicines. If regular projectile vomiting is the problem, they will give your baby a careful physical examination to check for pyloric stenosis and, if there is any doubt, order an X-ray of the area or ultrasound check. If it is PS, your baby will need a couple of days' rehydration, probably intravenously in hospital, then an operation to deal with the pyloric obstruction, which will produce an immediate improvement.

A GP can also offer an anti-vomiting prescription.

If matters are becoming progressively worse despite your efforts, if your baby vomits consistently for more than 24 hours and seems not to be able to keep anything down, speak to your GP straight away.

Blood in vomit

Do not panic if you see a small amount of blood staining your baby's or toddler's vomit. This is usually due to a tiny tear in the lining of their foodpipe (oesophagus) which has burst a small blood capillary because of the force at which the vomited liquid thundered past.

Give your baby some cold liquid – a home-made fruit juice ice lolly if you have such a thing is ideal, or a manufactured popsicle stick or tube ice lolly – and the bleeding should stop rapidly.

However, let your GP know straight away if there is an increasing amount of blood in your child's vomit.

WHOOPING COUGH

What is it?

A highly infectious disease caused by the bacterium *Bordetella pertussis* and passed on by an infected person coughing or sneezing moisture droplets into the air. Three-quarters of all the children who catch whooping cough are under five.

Whooping cough's incubation period is between one and two weeks, and it tends to last three to four weeks, though the coughing and whooping may continue for as long as 10 weeks.

The younger the child, the more serious the illness is. Whooping cough can be especially worrying in young babies – if they get it at around three months or less there is a 1 in 200 death rate. It is therefore very sensible to go and see your GP right away if you know your baby or toddler has not been immunized against whooping cough, but has been exposed to it in the last few days. There is some evidence that the drugs erythromycin or co-trimoxazole given preventatively may avert the illness altogether, says Dr Douglas Jenkinson, a Nottinghamshire GP who has studied the disease for the past 20 years. There is also some clinical evidence that giving these drugs may shorten a bout of whooping cough that has already begun.

Symptoms

In textbook cases, whooping cough begins as a normal cold, and develops into a cough. The airways produce thick mucus and gradually the coughing becomes severe, developing into long bouts which begin with a spasm and end with the characteristic whoop as the child fights for breath. It is not unusual for the child to cough so hard that they vomit. Young babies may have brief periods of not breathing, either instead of coughing bouts, or after them. This is called apnoea and it can be thoroughly alarming for both parents and child. There is a possibility that babies may also develop a hernia from the strain of coughing, or fits due to shortage of oxygen during the coughing bouts (see Convulsions, page 208).

The disease actually goes unrecognized much of the time as lab tests are unreliable, and the coughing may only come occasionally with the child seeming otherwise well with a clear chest. The other problem with diagnosis is that most younger GPs may never have seen a case of whooping cough, or heard what it sounds like, as the disease is now so uncommon, thanks to blanket childhood immunization, whereas older GPs may find it easier to recognize – before immunization was introduced about 75 per cent of people had it. Finally, it is easy to confuse whooping cough with other breathing problems which involve coughing, such as croup, asthma and bronchiolitis, all of which are increasingly common in small children.

Additional complications may include middle ear infections and, in about 1 per cent of cases, pneumonia. The cough may recur briefly if the child develops any ordinary coughs or colds for the next couple of years.

What you can do

- *Keep your child calm and comforted during coughing bouts.* Even if you are worried, you will give them confidence by not showing it. Fear and anxiety tighten up the already partially blocked airways and make it even harder for your child to breathe. Relaxing your child will possibly have the opposite effect.
- *Babies should be laid to sleep in a semi-prone position,* chest down, head to one side, to avoid the danger of choking on vomit or mucus during the night.
- *Sleep in your baby's room* so they will be comforted by your presence and you can be there to help them instantly if necessary. Consider taking it in turns with your partner, if they are at home, as your sleep is likely to be badly affected if your baby coughs a lot at night.
- *Consider reducing their intake of mucus-producing foods.* Complementary practitioners say these include dairy products, rich fatty foods, foods high in sugar and bananas.
- *Give warming vegetable soups daily* if your child is old enough to enjoy them, perhaps with small pieces of soft bread dunked in them which they can suck or swallow easily without hurting their throat.
- *Try to keep their main meals earlier in the day,* so they eat less in the late afternoon and evening. This is not easy if you're breast- or bottle-feeding every four hours – but the principle is that this allows their stomach a chance to empty by bedtime and therefore reduces the chances of them vomiting after coughing at night.
- *Keep your child calm and quiet during the day.*
- *Do not smoke in the house,* or let anyone else do so either. Have a doorstep light-up routine if anyone does need a cigarette, or smoke at night when the baby is in bed and fully ventilate the room afterwards. This is a must while they are ill as the connection between parents smoking and children's coughs and breathing problems is so powerful.

What your GP can do

Give antibiotics as mentioned above to help prevent, or try to shorten, the course of the whooping cough. Treat any secondary infections such as ear infections, as necessary.

The DTP (Diphtheria/Tetanus/Pertussis) vaccine is offered to babies from three months of age. Unfortunately, as Dr Jenkinson points out, the protective effect of the vaccine can wear off, which is why the average age at which people now get whooping cough has shifted upwards.

Complementary therapy

Homeopathy

Possible remedies include Drosera if your baby or toddler's throat is very ticklish; Kali carb if they have a hard, dry, hacking cough that starts in earnest at around 3 a.m., and if they are chilly and exhausted with puffy eyes; Caprum if the paroxysms of coughing are leaving them worn out and short of breath, if their fingers and toes are cramping and drinks of cold water seem to help.

Herbal medicine
Remedies the herbalist may recommend for your child include relaxants like lavender and hyssop, and expectorants to help bring up the phlegm such as infusions of Mullein flowers, Thyme and White horehound.

Aromatherapy
Run a warm bath and add two drops of Roman chamomile and lavender essential oil, and let the child soak and play in there – adding plenty of toys to keep them interested or getting in too, if necessary, for about 20 minutes.

Colour therapy
Colour therapists suggest that the colours pink and pale blue are calming, so recommend pale blue or pale pink bed covers and pillow covers and perhaps a warm pink light bulb in the room to soothe and calm.

USEFUL ADDRESSES

Action Against Allergy, PO Box 278, Twickenham TW1 4QQ.

Write enclosing an s.a.e. for information on all types and aspects of allergy for both adults and children.

The British Allergy Foundation, 23 Middle Street, London EC1A 7JA.
Tel: 0171 600 6166.

Helpline staffed by nurse counsellors trained in all aspects and types of allergy.

The British Liver Trust, Central House, Central Avenue, Ransomes Europark, Ipswich IP3 9QG. Tel: Non-medical enquiries 01473 276326;
Helpline 01473 276328.

Advice, information and support for all those with any type of liver disorder, including parents of babies with jaundice.

The British Lung Foundation, 78 Hatton Garden, London EC1N 8JR.
Tel: 0171 831 5831.

Information and literature for children and adults with all types of breathing problems, including the parents of babies with bronchiolitis.

The Chi Centre, 10 Greycoat Place, Victoria, London SW1P 1SB.
Tel: 0171 222 1888.

The doctors here are qualified in both traditional Chinese herbal medicine and orthodox clinical medicine.

The Children's Liver Disease Foundation, 138 Digbeth, Birmingham B5 6DR. Tel: 0121 643 7282.

Information and support for parents whose children have liver disease.

The National Deaf Children's Society, 15 Dufferin Street, London EC1Y 8PD. Tel: Freephone 0800 252380 2 p.m. to 5 p.m. weekdays.

Information and support for all aspects and types of hearing problem which can affect young children, including glue ear.

Nature's Best, 1 Lamberts Road, Tunbridge Wells, Kent TN2 3EQ. Tel: 01892 552117 for orders or 552118 for enquiries.

Stockists of acidophilus powder and many other nutritional supplements. Mail-order service available.

Soothing Eczema

Eczema, or to use its proper name, atopic eczema, is an inflammation of the skin, characterized by dryness, redness, flakiness, and often blistering which weeps and crusts over. It can be miserably itchy but it is not infectious.

The most common time for it to appear is between two and four months. Like childhood and baby asthma – which is often linked with eczema – it is becoming increasingly common and there are five times more cases today than there were 40 years ago.

Generally, babies with eczema have perfectly calm skins until they are eight to 12 weeks old, when the first small patch appears, usually on their cheeks. Initially it tends not to bother them at all, but as the weeks go by it will begin to make its presence felt. The baby begins to rub, perhaps against objects like their cot bars, and the rash grows and reddens further until their cheeks may be weeping and raw. If it does spread, it tends to do so slowly, moving next to the body, and then, between nine and 18 months, to the knees and feet, aggravated by crawling. In toddlers, the lesions tend to settle in the body crease areas of the buttocks, backs of the knees, insides of the elbows and wrists.

Doctors sometimes refer to it as dermatitis (*derma* – skin, and *itis* – inflammation). It should not be confused – though it often is – with other non-infective red rashes which may appear during the first few weeks of a young baby's life, such as napkin eczema (straightforward nappy rash), which is easily treated, or with seborrhoeic eczema (cradle cap), which can also be itchy, though not as much as eczema itself, and disappears within three to 12 months.

Symptoms

- *Itching.*
  This is the worst aspect of eczema, and ranges from mildly uncomfortable to unbearable. It can be so mild that your baby may not notice it until

---

People of all ages can develop eczema but it usually affects very young children and babies. One in four (24 per cent) of toddlers under the age of two and a half either have, or have had, eczema in the UK, according to the ongoing 'Children of the 90s' survey.

they do something like paddle in the sea for the first time and the salt water makes their legs sting. Or they may only have small, thickened, itchy patches on the elbows or knees that come and go occasionally and can always be dealt with by additional moisturizing for a couple of weeks, or perhaps by avoiding too much cow's milk. But for some parents and their infants, it goes much further.

Unless you have watched or cared for a child with serious eczema, it can be difficult to imagine just how severe it can be for both babies and parents. David Atherton, Britain's top paediatric eczema specialist, of Great Ormond Street Hospital for Sick Children, writes: 'In an attempt to relieve this itching children will tear at living flesh ... the child may appear to be in a trance-like state, and may seem not to hear or respond to onlookers. One feels that were one to throw the child into the sea he would sink to the bottom still totally engrossed in scratching. This is all devastating for parents.'

According to clinical research psychologist Val Lawson, one mother told her in 1994: 'Nothing works ... by 3 a.m. my baby has heated up to boiling point ... I try to hold his hands when he is asleep but he pulls them away. It is like a magnet when you hear him ripping his skin.' A father of a 14-month-old little boy said: 'It looked as if someone had lacerated his poor skin with a cheese grater in the night, yet still he tore at the bleeding areas as if by doing so he could strip them off his body and his itching would at last be still. I would do anything, anything in the world to help him, but I can only watch, catch his hands and try to stop him.'

Comments like these are not reported here for effect, but because they may help other people who are trying to understand just how desperate parents and their babies really do become; and also how important it is to take into account the effect a baby's eczema is having on *the entire family*. It can cause exhaustion, frustration and ultimately resentment too, no matter how much the parents pity and love their baby, or how readily they would give everything they owned if only the eczema could be cured.
- *Sleep deprivation.*

Paediatric dermatologist Sue Lewis-Jones of the Wrexham Maelor Hospital in Wales carried out extensive research in 1995 on the sometimes devastating effect a baby with severe eczema has on the entire family. She found that sleep is probably the biggest casualty. Due to the warmth of bed coverings, which aggravates the eczema, the child's sleep is often profoundly disturbed, as is that of any brothers and sisters who share a room with them, and parents, who are woken repeatedly by sounds of the baby's scratching and distress.

It is also very common for even mild cases of eczema to interrupt sleep at night. 'I often see the children who come to see me (and their parents) asleep on their waiting-room chairs in the middle of the day, they are both so exhausted,' reports Sheffield dermatologist Dr Michael Cork. 'Not only does lack of sleep make everyone very irritable but it impairs children's intellectual development of all ages, because they are not very responsive or receptive to new information, whether this is how to balance building blocks on top of each other for a 10-month-old, or how to do simple sums at school for a five-year old.'

Sleep interruption may be temporarily reprieved by remissions in the eczema, as the condition tends to ebb and flow.

Apart from constant tiredness or exhaustion, symptoms of sleep deprivation for you range from intense irritability, inability to concentrate and reduced ability to be a good parent, to a deterioration in the way you feel about your eczema baby, worsening of your relationship with your other children and partner, clinical anxiety, depressive states, and lack of libido (see Beating Exhaustion page 311). Work by Oxfordshire health visitors in 1980 has also clearly linked long-term parental sleep deprivation with complete marital breakdown, violence and child abuse.

These are all reasons to take infantile eczema very seriously indeed. Even though it is not life threatening and children do usually grow out of it, the distress it can cause should mean its treatment is one of the top priorities for GPs, practice nurses and health visitors across the country.

- *Redness.*

This is the most constant visible sign of eczema. For some children, there is no crusting or weeping of the affected areas – just redness (erythema) and scratch marks (excoriations). When eczema gets worse the first warning sign is a deepening redness as blood flow increases through skin in that area. This can be a useful early warning sign for parents to begin preventative treatment or start looking for recent triggers.

- *Crusting.*

The chemicals that make blood vessels expand (causing redness) also make their walls leaky so fluid (serum) can seep out of the vessels. The fluid first oozes into the surrounding tissues, producing swelling (oedema) and then up into the skin itself producing a crop of fluid-filled blisters as if the skin itself were boiling. The very word eczema in fact comes from a Greek word meaning 'to boil over'. The blisters burst, the fluid spills out on to the surrounding skin and it is this that makes eczema rash weep. It rapidly forms a protective scab or crust.

These oozing areas are very vulnerable to infection. The fluid acts as a form of culture broth for bacteria. One of the most common bugs to infect them is a bacteria called *Staphylococcus aureus*, *aureus* meaning 'gold' in Greek and describing the rich colour the crusts now become. Skin broken open by weeping eczema lesions is also vulnerable to a wide range of other infective agents, including fungi and viruses.

- *Scaliness.*

Children with eczema often have dry scaly skin. Some of this is as a result of the eczema, but sometimes this is their natural skin type, which is perhaps what made them more vulnerable to the disorder in the first place.

- *Thickening (lichenification).*

If skin is repeatedly rubbed at and scratched over long periods of time, its outer layers thicken in response. This tends to happen when people have been affected by eczema for many years rather than in babies or very young children.

- *Changes in skin colour.*
Eczema interferes with the skin cells responsible for making the skin's natural pigmentation, temporarily switching off their production. This can cause a marked effect even in fairly mild cases, though it does tend to resolve within a few months after the eczema has been successfully treated. With lighter-skinned children, former eczema areas may not tan well. For darker-skinned children, such as those of Indian or Afro-Caribbean origin, the skin thickening associated with eczema can produce deeper dark patches which may look unsightly, but these too will resolve.

- *Poor appetite.*
Babies and toddlers with eczema sometimes have poor appetites, which can make mealtimes difficult, particularly if the child is tired and drowsy from antihistamine medication too, says clinical nurse specialist Sue Donald of London's Chelsea & Westminster Hospital. If the condition is moderate to severe, the child may fail to thrive not only because of their poor appetite, but perhaps as a result of a restrictive diet which avoids foods which exacerbate their condition, or because they are burning up calories at night tossing, turning and scratching.

There is some good news

First, there is an enormous amount that can be done, often by parents themselves, to make babies and children with eczema feel comfortable and help them live perfectly normal lives. Second, children usually find their eczema improves as they get older, and many grow out of it completely.

David Atherton says:

- If your baby is one of the 80 per cent who develop their eczema in their first 12 months of life, they have a 50:50 chance of being free of it by the time they are five and begin primary school.
- After this the rule of thumb is that every four years, another 50 per cent of the remaining children will be saying goodbye to their eczema too – so about 25 per cent of sufferers will still be affected by it by the time they are nine years old, 12 per cent around the age of 13, 6 per cent at

---

Will the eczema scar my baby?

Eczema does not cause permanent scarring. Though it looks alarming and can reach quite deeply into the dermis, it does not reach down as far as the basal membrane which lies between the dermis – the living layer of skin – and the epidermis – the dead, protective upper layers. Any actual skin damage is caused by scratching on the skin's surface, and this is easily repaired.

17 and 3 per cent at 21. The risk of the condition coming back again after this is, happily, small.

However, when children get older, the fact that they have had a history of eczema still puts them more at risk of irritant skin reaction, especially on their hands, if they choose certain careers such as hairdressing, working with animals, some branches of the armed forces, catering and mechanics – all of which involve oils or damp heats which can irritate.

CAUSES AND RISK FACTORS

To quote a famous (retired) dermatologist from Harvard Medical School in Boston, America: 'If I could tell you what caused eczema I'd be sitting on the right hand of God writing *How To* books.' No one is quite sure what causes eczema in the first place, but there are plenty of theories. There are also several factors known to be major culprits in triggering an attack of pre-existing eczema. The general 'why?' theories include:

- *Genetics.*
  Genetic research shows that people with eczema do have an abnormally functioning immune system which means their response towards invaders, whether they be germs or pollutants, is way over the top. This is also why those with eczema react more strongly than usual to a whole range of environmental triggers.
- *Allergy.*
  Many specialists believe eczema is an allergic response to substances in the person's surroundings which do not seem to bother other people. There may be several of these substances. Interestingly, this is also the most popular theory about asthma, where the airways respond to the allergen rather than the skin.
  Common eczema provokers in the early years, include:
  — *Foods.* Cow's milk and dairy products, eggs, nuts, fish and wheat tend to top the list. The reaction may come an hour or two or even a day or two after consuming the food – and may appear as a form of contact urticaria rash (red weals at the site of contact, for instance around the mouth and cheeks). According to paediatric immunologist Dr Chakravanti of the Portland Hospital for Women & Children, 'Up to 20 per cent of children with eczema may have a food allergy of some sort, though the top two are wheat and milk.' Some of them may cease to be a problem as the child gets older – you can 'try rechallenging the child with the food at appropriate times,' says the National Eczema Society.
  — *House dust mites*, or rather their droppings. The mites themselves cannot be seen by the naked eye, but they are around throughout the year, especially between August and October. They accumulate anywhere house dust does, feeding off skin scales. Mattresses, pillows, duvets, carpets, soft furnishings, and cuddly toys are all good harbourers. If any of these places

are slightly damp (a child's mattress may be damp from sweat or regular body warmth), they like it even better.

— *Pets* – the hair, feathers and dead skin (dander) they shed, and their saliva, which can remain on their coats in substantial amounts when they've licked and groomed themselves for hours.

— *Moulds*. These flourish in house dust, bathrooms and other damp places such as cellars, toilets and sauna rooms, and in rotting garden vegetation or house timbers. They release spores into the air, especially during autumn.

— *Bacteria*, and yeasts such as *Pityrosporum* found naturally on the skin surface, find it easy to infect the eczema-damaged skin of a baby or infant. It is thought possible that a child may develop an allergic response to the antigens in these micro-organisms' waste products.

- *Irritants.*

Babies and children with eczema react to a wide variety of potential skin irritants. An irritant is different from an allergen in that it does not provoke an allergic response (involving the body's immune system) but has a more directly harmful effect – one example of an irritant reaction would be the effect a mild bleach solution has when poured over the skin. An irritant response involves pain, itching and burning. The irritants that upset your child's skin are very important because if you can identify them you can protect your child from them, and so stop them aggravating your child's eczema.

The high-irritant list includes:

— *Infant soaps*, detergents, shampoos, bubble baths, washing powders, especially biological action varieties which don't stop at digesting hard-to-shift stains such as blood, egg and gravy but attack any form of protein they come into contact with, including skin. If any tiny dry flakes of these powders are still clinging to sheets or clothing after washing (and there usually are some) they will be reactivated by the moisture on your baby's skin, and so begin attacking that too.

— *Climate* – any sudden changes in either temperature or humidity. Very warm (summer) or very cold (winter) air contains little moisture. Coupled with central heating and/or air conditioning, it means what little moisture there is in eczema-dry skin is soon drawn out.

— *Plain Water*. Even if you do not add in any soap to bath water, it can leach some of the natural minerals and salts out of the skin, and remove the natural skin oils. The effect can be seen after an overlong bathtime soak – the skin of areas with little subcutaneous fat underneath, such as the hands and feet, become as wrinkled as a raisin. Baths are helpful for babies and toddlers with eczema only if they have oil added to them (see Moisturizers, page 251).

— *Cigarette smoke*. No one should be allowed to light up in the same house as a baby or child with eczema. It's worth knowing that three-quarters of any cigarette you light up at home disappears into the surrounding air for your child to smoke passively. That passive smoke – the smoke drifting around in the air of the room – is far more toxic than what the smoker is inhaling, because the filter stops some of the poisonous compounds from the mainstream reaching the smoker's own lungs, but the airborne smoke contains them all.

— *Certain fruits and vegetables:* the acidic ones such as oranges and grapefruit; raw onions are another example.

— *Household chemicals:* aerosols, solvents, dry-cleaning fluid. Petrol can be a problem if you have an integral garage in your home, as petrol fumes seep through to the main house easily.

— *Antiseptics.* These kill germs but they can also harm human cells and be irritating to sensitive skin. Many households still add gentle antiseptics to baths (perhaps a little Savlon liquid) but this would be very irritating to anyone with eczema. Any traces lingering in the bath after cleaning with such fluids could also cause problems for a baby with eczema.

— *Pure wool.* This should never be worn right next to eczema skin – though it's fine if a pure cotton layer separates them. The same goes for nylon – nylon bed sheets should also be avoided. Pure cotton can be hard to care for (it tends to need ironing) and it is expensive. Cotton mixtures offer a good, less costly solution. Carpets of all kinds tend to be very irritating, so if a baby or child with eczema is playing on one, cover the area with a large cotton sheet first.

• *Routine childhood vaccination.*

There is a small but growing number of respected complementary and orthodox health professionals who are beginning to suspect that blanket routine babyhood vaccination may actually weaken infants' immature immune systems for life.

They include eminent names such as Dr John Mansfield (allergy specialist), French obstetrician and childbirth educator Michel Odent (who introduced water birth to Britain and is now specializing in infant health), Dr Alan Franklyn (consultant paediatrician on the National Task Force for Children with ME), and Dr Andrew Wakefield, consultant gastroenterologist at the Royal Free Hospital, London, author and homeopath Miranda Castro, and many other respected medical homeopaths. The vaccinations in question include the MMR (Measles, Mumps, Rubella) shots given to toddlers from 12 to 15 months of age, and the whooping cough or pertussis vaccine given from two months, which in itself has had a checkered history.

The think-again vaccination contingent argues that blanket immunization of young babies represents a major assault on their as yet immature immune systems which they are ill equipped to cope with. They further suggest that any initial adverse reactions (usually a fever, but very occasionally more serious) are not the end of the story, as the procedure leaves the babies more vulnerable to a wide range of immunity-related disorders which have – unarguably – become far more common in recent years. Specialists such as Dr David Baxter, Senior Lecturer in Public Health at Manchester University and Consultant in Communicable Disease Control for Stockport Health Authority, actually separate the multiple vaccines out into single-spaced doses for vulnerable children to minimize the shock and therefore likelihood of adverse reaction. These include children with a personal or family history of allergy-related disorders such as asthma, eczema and rheumatoid arthritis. In theory, single doses could be administered by any doctor – including your GP, but it does not occur to most of them and would be time consuming for both GP and parent, with many more clinic visits.

The disorders which these specialists feel may have a connection with blanket childhood immunization include a wide variety of allergies such as hay fever (which has increased fourfold in the last 20 years), asthma (which has doubled over the last 30 years), and eczema (which has increased three- to fivefold in the last 40 years). The list also includes diseases which appear to have emerged for the first time during the past 15 years – 'new' diseases such as HIV infections and AIDS, ME, and systemic candida (thrush) infection.

That the autoimmune diseases are rapidly becoming more common is something no one can argue with. It is the reasons *why* this is happening that are fuelling such a heated debate on both sides. Many conventional experts in the fields of both asthma and eczema suggest that increased pollution of the air, water and food are making people's immune systems in general 'twitchier' and this is at least part of the story. But vaccination doubters are taking this one step further by arguing that the immune system is being made more reactive in the first place by routine immunization damage and that the increasing number – and level – of pollutants around is merely providing them with more things to react *to*.

Though the full range of arguments is beyond the scope of this book, see Infant Vaccination (page 279–97) for the basic details of the cases being put by both sides and suggestions for further, more detailed reading.

DIAGNOSIS – AND FINDING THE CAUSE

Eczema is generally fairly straightforward to diagnose in the first place. If there is any doubt, ask your GP to refer your baby to a good dermatologist as soon as possible.

If the waiting list seems unacceptably long and you are unwilling to delay because your child is in distress, consider asking your GP for a private referral to a consultant dermatologist if you can possibly afford it, so that you can at least get an accurate diagnosis quickly and begin the right treatment as soon as possible. A private appointment costs between £50 and £120 depending upon the consultant and where they are practising. Armed with an expert diagnosis, you can then return to the NHS system where your child can be treated.

The tests associated with eczema are designed to find out what is causing it or why it isn't clearing up. Swab tests check any oozing fluid for infection by bacteria, viruses or fungi, and there are several tests to find out whether the condition is caused by an allergy which might be treated or avoided.

Is your child's eczema caused by allergy?

'About 40 per cent of the many hundreds of children I have treated with eczema have had a food allergy problem,' says Dr John Mansfield. If you feel that your child's eczema could be due to an allergy, there are several ways to try to find out, within both orthodox and complementary medicine, though none of them are foolproof.

The skin prick test and the RAST blood test

There is no specific test available on the NHS for identifying foods that may produce an allergic eczema reaction, and the results of those which do exist such as the skin prick test, or the more highly respected (and expensive) RAST blood test, can be inaccurate or confusing.

The problems are that:

- The RAST test is only available at a very few specialist centres, mostly private.
- The skin prick test's reaction can be more pronounced in some places on the body than on others.
- Skin prick tests tend to be done in batches of several at a time, so if there is more than one thing your child is allergic to, the results can be muddling.
- Results may also be affected if the baby or child has taken any antihistamine drugs over the last 24 to 48 hours.
- The composition of a food after it has been cooked and found its way into the stomach to start being broken down is usually very different from its composition when it is raw, especially in the likeliest allergy-producing foods such as wheat products, milk or eggs. Skin prick tests involve solutions of the *raw* product, so a child who is allergic to that may not be allergic to its cooked form, which is the state they are more likely to eat it in. The same is true of the RAST test. Again, this can therefore produce misleading results.

As if that were not enough, even a positive result at best only implies that your child *might*, under certain circumstances, be allergic to that substance, so you could end up putting them on an unnecessarily restrictive diet. A negative test shows that skin contact with a substance is not likely to upset your child, but doesn't prove that your child won't have an allergic response if the food is eaten.

Dr John Mansfield, a private allergy specialist in Banstead, Surrey, who works with many cases of infantile eczema (and asthma), estimates that skin prick tests are about 15 per cent accurate. Many other specialists in the field of paediatric dermatology and respiratory medicine also reckon the tests are not really worth doing. So if you want your child tested but your GP is stonewalling, this is probably why.

This is not much help to parents frantically trying to discover the cause of their child's skin problems. However, there are some other allergy tests you can try.

The Vega test

This involves using a mild electrical current to measure the body's electrical resistance. Differing levels of resistance are said to indicate a body's allergy response, but there is as yet no convincing clinical evidence that it is accurate at diagnosing allergy.

Hair analysis

There are several commercial allergy-testing companies who advertise in the back of health magazines, offering to work out what you are allergic to by testing a clipping of your hair. Sounds very promising. So promising, in fact, that in 1987 Guy's Hospital in London decided to try them out. They sent the hair of nine people whose skin prick tests indicated an allergy to fish to five hair-test companies to see what they came up with. Hair clippings from nine more non-allergic patients were also sent for good measure. Unfortunately, not only were all five labs unable to detect any of the cases of fish allergy, but they reported several other allergies in the apparently non-allergy group too. When sent the same samples of hair again under different names, they managed to provide quite different results.

Applied Kinesiology

There are some encouraging anecdotal reports of AK, but no published clinical evidence to back them up as yet. The only bit of published clinical research we could find was a small study of 11 people evaluated for shortages in four different vitamins, carried out in 1988. It appeared in the *Journal of the American Dietetic Association*, and the three experienced kinesiologists involved had consistently got things wrong.

The ALCAT

This checks the immune system's white blood cells. A sample of these cells is put with different foods and their responses noted. If they get larger when exposed to a particular one, it is thought to be an indication that the person has an allergy to that particular substance. This test is only available at private specialist clinics.

IDP Test

Intra Dermal Puncture testing is routinely done in approximately 5,000 American clinics. In the UK, it is currently only available through the NHS Middlesex Hospital in London in limited circumstances, and through a dozen private allergy clinics. According to Dr John Mansfield, the IDP is extremely useful for pinpointing allergies in general, including those related to both infant asthma and eczema.

The test involves checking one possible allergen at a time. A diluted dose of a suspected substance, whether it be a food or an environmental pollutant, is injected under the skin. If it provokes a positive reaction, it is repeated using ever smaller doses until the clinic finds the smallest possible amount that can still provoke a reaction. This is called the Neutralizing Dose, and it is said to be the one which 'turns off' the child's allergic reaction. It is then used to desensitize the child. Some have no further problems, says Dr Mansfield. Others may need to return occasionally for similar treatment.

The treatment remains controversial in Britain. Most doctors feel the test is not sufficiently reliable, and deny that the technique can be successfully used as a treatment for allergy.

But according to Dr Mansfield, and to the parents whose children's eczema (and asthma) he has helped to cure, this type of allergy testing is far more accurate and well worth doing. Unfortunately, the private fees may well prove a stumbling block to many parents, as they range from £60 to £100 for a full consultation, with the cost of any tests on top of that.

Note: This treatment is not to be confused with a practice called desensitization, a method of treating allergy which is now largely out of favour as it occasionally sent patients into serious shock. The therapy involved injecting progressively larger amounts of the suspected allergen, and the starting dose was far higher than that which is used for IDP, which has so far not been associated with any cases of shock reaction.

WHAT YOU CAN DO

Combating food allergy

An elimination diet

It is not so much a question of 'Does cow's milk cause eczema?' as 'Is cow's milk causing or exacerbating *my* child's eczema?'

Perhaps the least expensive way to try and find out if your baby or child has a food allergy or, according to the *Lancet* medical research journal in 1994, a food intolerance as 800,000 Britons of all ages have, is one by one to remove suspect foods from the diet. Leave each one out for a couple of weeks at a time, see if there is an improvement, then reintroduce it and see if the eczema worsens. 'If the culprit is milk in your child's diet, or in your own if you are a breastfeeding mother, you should see an improvement a week or so after cutting it out,' says Dr Chakravanti. If you are trying this, let your GP or health visitor know what you are doing and why. If an important food such as milk, eggs or wheat does seem to be the problem, speak to a nutritionist (see Useful Addresses, page 261) about what foods to substitute in your child's diet so they continue to receive good all round nutrition.

According to Ms Lewis-Jones, 'Dietary treatments for eczema have been tried for many decades with very disappointing results and the vast majority of children do not benefit from special diets. They should be reserved for severe cases of eczema which are unresponsive to conventional therapy and they should always be undertaken with the help of a dietician.'

Diet adjustment does, however, appear to work for many children (from babies to teenagers) with eczema, and research suggests it works best of all for children under the age of five. 'In the very young, food allergies do sometimes seem to be the major cause of atopic eczema, and avoidance diets may occasionally be dramatically beneficial,' writes Dr Atherton. His department's own work suggests that an ordinary elimination diet can help up to 40 per cent of babies under a year old, and 30 per cent of children between the ages of one and four.

One study carried out in 1984 by a paediatric dermatologist named Dr Pamela Graham at Brighton's Royal Alexandra Hospital for Sick Children found that most of the three- to 12-year-olds this was tried on improved when the suspected allergic foods were taken away but relapsed when the foods were reintroduced to their diets after three weeks.

Cow's milk

Experts disagree on whether it helps to cut out milk, and if so whether you need to leave it out completely or not – the answer depends on who you talk to (see also Banishing Colic, page 104).

According to most allergy specialists, you need to cut *all* dairy products out – of your own diet if you are breastfeeding, as the antigens do cross into the baby's system in breast milk, and out of your baby's own food. It may be one of the first self-help measures progressive GPs and health visitors suggest.

Talk to your GP or health visitor about it first, or better still a community dietician or a professionally trained nutritionist. Start by cutting milk back by half for two weeks to see whether reduction rather than total elimination of so important a food is sufficient. If there's no improvement, try cutting out all dairy products (and that means *all* – check for dairy produce in all packaged and prepreared foods) for another two or three. If *that* doesn't work, forget it.

No milk means leaving out many of the sources of calcium breastfeeding mothers need, and some of the important nutritional building blocks babies need. Replacing the calcium and proteins cow's milk provides means eating more meat, fish, lentils or beans and complete milk substitutes, which include soya milk, goat's milk and hydrolysate formulas.

Soya milk is not really milk at all, because it is made from soya beans. Soya milk brands suitable for babies and infants include Wysoy and Nutrilon (which you can get on prescription from your GP, which will save money). It smells and tastes different from cow's milk or breast milk, so your baby may refuse to drink it altogether. For older children (but not infants as they are unable to digest it) you can try using flavoured soya shakes, which can be found in health food shops and big supermarkets.

The other alternative to cow's milk is goat's milk, but this cannot be used for babies under six months old. It is not subject to the strict controls that dairy cow herds have and is seldom pasteurized, so it needs to be boiled to kill any bacteria it may harbour, then cooled. Not the easiest of things to find in the local supermarket, it also tastes very strong and distinctive, which your baby may not appreciate. Many of the proteins it contains are similar to those in cow's milk, so using it as a substitute may make little difference to your baby's eczema.

Hydrolysate formulas are produced by breaking down one of cow's milk's main proteins (either curd protein or whey protein) so it can no longer cause an allergic reaction. Formulations you can buy in the chemist include Nutramigeñ and Pregestimil. Again, they can be prescribed by your GP which is useful because they are also quite costly.

Wheat

Cutting wheat out means no pasta, bread, biscuits, rusks, cakes or wheat-based cereals like Weetabix for breakfast. This is not nearly as troublesome as it sounds as there are many ways around it. Try using rice instead of pasta, rice cakes, rye bread or crispbreads instead of bread slices; and rice flour or potato flour in cooking. Make sure you read lists of ingredients on prepre-pared foods carefully to check, for instance, that there is no wheat on the bread crumbs of fish fingers or in sausages. See Useful Addresses page 261, for a list of companies who do special foods for allergy-free diets by mail order. Health food shop chains such as Holland & Barrett are good sources, as is any independent health food shop.

Combating allergens in the environment
House dust mite

Allergy to dust mites – or, to be strictly accurate, to their droppings – is probably the number one cause of allergy in this country. Ninety per cent of children with asthma are also allergic to it. It is a sobering thought that 10 per cent of the average bed is entirely composed of living dust mites, their dead bodies, their eggs and their faeces – along with sundry moulds and other allergens. This includes your baby's bed too, especially if it was given to you secondhand by a kind friend whose own children had grown out of it. Should you be offered a secondhand bed, get a new mattress or a microporous mattress cover, which will not let mite droppings through but does allow for moisture and air exchange (see Useful Addresses page 262).

There is a much fuller explanation of how to make your child's room – and your entire home – as allergen-free as possible in Dealing with Asthma (page 270), but the main things to look at when making the environment of an eczema child as hazard-free as possible include:

- *Toys*. Soft toys harbour dust mites. Try not to have a dozen or more sitting companionably in your child's cot. Perhaps keep it down to two or three special favourites, but de-dust mite them by either regularly putting them in a plastic bag in the freezer for 12 hours, or washing them at 60 °C or more. If you rotate the toys, your child will always have one with them. Hanging a soft toy on the washing line in hot summer sun or tumble drying it also kills the mites.
- *Pets*. Technically a child with eczema or asthma should not have pets, especially furry ones. This includes not only cats and dogs but rabbits, hamsters, mice and gerbils too. Sometimes a tank or bowl of goldfish or tropical fish can be the answer instead. Be careful, though, that the tank doesn't grow any mould, not just for the sake of the fish but because this may also irritate your child's eczema and asthma.

If you already have much-loved pets whom your child is very attached to, do not allow them anywhere near the child's bedroom, and ensure that they stay out of the linen cupboard (a favourite place for cats). Though they won't like it much, wash your dog – or, even more hazardous, your cat – weekly. One Swedish study found that this reduced the amount of house dust mite in the home by 40 per cent. If they fight too hard for you to wash them, try damp-dusting them as a halfway measure instead.

Use a cotton sheet to cover the carpet when your child sits on the floor to play to avoid contact with animal dander, which sticks to carpet fibres. If you go to the house of a friend where there are animals, try to keep your child from touching them, take a cotton sheet with you to put down on the floor, and do not allow pets near or under their bed if they are staying overnight. Unfortunately, contact with pets can increase your baby's chances of developing asthma.

- *Beds*. Use microporous covers for both mattress and pillows. Try to use a foam mattress, avoid feather duvets and pillows, and do not place toys or books on shelves above the bed as they collect dust which harbours dust mites. Damp-wipe any mobiles hanging above the cot weekly, and vacuum your child's room, especially around and under their bed, *daily*. If you can afford it, a special vacuum cleaner that does not blow out any dust into the air is an excellent idea for cleaning the entire house, as dust mite droppings can pass straight through the bags of ordinary vacuum cleaners. If cost is a problem, you can get special filters for ordinary vacuums (try a company such as Medivac – see Useful Addresses page 262). Vacuum the surfaces of sofas and armchairs in the sitting room too.

  Allow a good supply of fresh air to the room at least twice a day, and do not allow the child to get too hot at night as heat is the great eczema provoker. Use cotton bedcovers, and do not leave central heating on overnight unless it is very cold weather, in which case keep it turned down very low. An ionizer by the bed might help by attracting house dust particles. Some people find air filters helpful – if you are going to try one, use a high efficiency (rather than electrostatic) model. Consult The National Eczema Society (see Useful Addresses page 262) who advise that machines which produce positive ions may damage the lungs. Also ask at major branches of Boots for one to be ordered for you.

  Consider bright, attractive linoleum as a floor covering in your child's room rather than carpet, and avoid scatter rugs and cushions. Use vinyl or material blinds rather than curtains or Venetian-style blinds, and painted or plastic chairs rather than upholstered ones.

- *Linen*. Always use non-biological washing powders, and do not add conditioner to the water. Tiny dried traces left on the fibres rehydrate and start to irritate skin on contact. Use 100 per cent cotton or cotton/polyester mix sheets (not pure polyester or nylon ones) as these let your baby's skin breathe, and help ensure they do not get hot or sweaty in bed. Wash all your child's bed linen on a hot cycle (60 °C or more) to kill the dust mites.

- *Baths*. Consider installing a water softener if the water in your area is hard, as there is some evidence suggesting that there are more cases of eczema in hard water areas of Britain (see Useful Addresses page 261). The water should be comfortably warm, not hot, as heat of all types makes eczema worse.

- *Humidity*. Dust mites do not like dry air, so parents are sometimes advised to use a dehumidifier inside the room of a child with eczema. Unfortunately, the dry air this produces also leaches water from skin. Consider a humidifier instead, especially in winter when your baby's skin will be dried both by cold air outside and central heating inside, at least for the child's own room at night.

Other helpful measures

- *Moisturizers*. Moisturizing the skin of a baby or child with eczema is, after finding the trigger in the first place, the single most important thing a parent can do to help their child feel more comfortable and control the disorder without the use of drugs.

Whether the moisturizers are in cream, gel, oil, lotion or ointment form they are known as topical (because they are put on top of the skin) treatments. Creams and lotions are a mixture of oils and water, ointments are made from just oil, usually a type of mineral oil such as white soft paraffin (e.g. Vaseline), and gels are a mixture of oil, water and collagen (jelly protein).

They can be given in bath form, coating the water's surface so they cover the body as the baby emerges from the water, or applied to the skin afterwards. It is always easier to get the cream to sink into the skin if the skin itself is damp, so just after a bath and before dab-towelling (do not rub dry) is an ideal time. Moisturizers not only treat dryness, which is both a symptom and a predisposing risk factor of eczema, but also prepare the skin to receive other treatments such as mild topical steroid cream. This cream is not as effective if put onto dry skin because the scales and crusts act like a sponge, soaking up the cream and preventing it from going deeper where it could begin to help reduce the itching and inflammation.

There are many excellent skin moisturizers helpful for eczema available from chemists, ranging from Keri lotion, which is the least greasy, to Coconut oil BP, 50:50 cream, and Neutrogena Dermatological cream, which are the most oily of all. Some contain certain special ingredients, such as lactic acid which improve their moisturizing qualities – but this is not suitable for eczema – and a natural body waste product called urea which both penetrates the skin fast and can attract water, which is suitable for dry but not inflamed eczema as it can sting.

The best time to apply moisturizers is immediately after a bath when the skin is still damp. For best results it needs to be applied every two hours. Dampen the skin with warm water wrung from a clean flannel first – the prospect of immersing a baby in a bath every two hours, unless the eczema is really bad, is not very practical. It may not be such a problem when your child is a baby, but becomes much more difficult when they begin nursery school.

If the skin is weeping, a very watery cream such as aqueous cream is best. As the skin gets less raw, one of the other, oilier, creams mentioned above may be more suitable.

• *Evening Primrose Oil.* There is a form of evening primrose oil called Epogam Paediatric which has been clinically tested and pronounced safe for use on any child over 12 months old. The oil is taken internally by mixing it with the child's milk or into their food. One two-year-long study at the Charing Cross and Chelsea & Westminster Hospitals in London in 1993 found 'significant, all-round improvements in all the symptoms including itching'. There are thought to be no major side effects of EPO, though *occasionally* some nausea, indigestion, loose bowel movements and head-ache have been reported. Epogam Paediatric is available on prescription from your GP. Other rich sources of EPO include borage oil, starflower oil and blackcurrant seed oil. They are available over the counter from health food shops, as is EPO, but buying them yourself can work out quite costly as children need between two and four 40 mg capsules twice daily.

The oils help eczema because they contain essential fatty acids (EFAs) which are vital for the normal functioning of many tissues in the body, including the skin. Essential fatty acids such as linoleic acid (LA) cannot be made in the body, they have to be eaten in the form of food and *then* converted into gamma-linolenic acid, which is the form in which the skin can use them. Research carried out as long ago as 1937 found that people with atopic eczema do not metabolize LA normally.

• *Baths.* Some bath oils, such as Oilatum Emollient bath liquid, contain lanolin, a fatty substance derived from sheep's wool which is a possible cause of allergy in itself. The research work on this is being hotly disputed, so the NES recommends that lanolin is a good moisturizer and should not be rejected out of hand: try it and see. Recent research on peanut (arachis) oil suggests children with a history of atopic allergy are more likely to have a peanut allergy too. Again, do not reject out of hand, try a little and see, or try an alternative such as Aveeno (oat based) or Balmium bath oil or Diprobath instead.

There are several lanolin-free moisturizers, if lanolin proves to be a problem, such as E45 cream or bath oil. Balneum Plus, which is made from soya oil, also contains an anaesthetic ingredient.

If your baby or toddler objects to baths or hates being covered in cream, try making it into a bit of a game. If they are old enough to appreciate the gesture, let them take a doll into the bath and dollop her with cream too, or better still, let your child do it themselves, no matter how haphaz-ardly. Try dotting the moisturizer all over their body to make patterns, to tell stories with, link the dotting and rubbing in with songs or rhymes with their name in them – anything to make it fun rather than a chore.

Babies and bath surfaces are both very slippery during and after emolli-

---

Do not use EPO if your child has been diagnosed as having temporal lobe epilepsy.

ent baths, so line the bath with a towel and place your child on it, and take special care when lifting them out.

For cleaning skin directly, gently massage aqueous cream BP, which is a plain, moisturizing clinical cleansing cream, into their skin and rinse it off by squeezing a sponge over them or using a plastic pourer to remove dead skin, crusting and dirt. This will make them feel a lot more comfortable and also less vulnerable to infections which can easily find their way in through cracked, dry skin.

- *Wet wrap bandaging.* This involves moistening light, stretchy, tubular bandages with water and fitting them over the areas of eczema after you've put ointment or cream on. You then put a dry layer of bandage over the top. The wet dressing helps cool and soothe the inflamed hot skin and so reduces itching, and also encourages the skin's absorption of the creams. The bandages also stop the child scratching and tearing at the skin.

Talk to your GP first about avoiding infection with this method if the area is weeping.

You might want some help from a specialist nurse initially to show how the bandaging is done, but you can easily do this at home. With small babies, the creaming and bandaging-up process may be a two-person job until you become practised at it. Some parents feel it is not kind to bandage up a child with eczema fearing they may get even hotter and more uncomfortable. This may be so with dry bandages, which should not be used except over a wet layer, but because wet bandages are so cooling, children usually feel very much more comfortable in them and may be able to sleep well for the first time in months (which means you can too).

If the eczema is really severe, it is advisable to keep the wraps on 24 hours a day, changing them morning and evening. When they begin to dry out and become less blessedly soothing, remove the outer layer and spray or squeeze water from a sponge to rewet the inner layer again. When the eczema begins to calm down again, probably after about a week, they can be used just at night. Most infants and children with eczema will invariably have a particular start time in late afternoon when they begin to become itchy again – this can be a cue to put the dressings on for the night, redampening them at bedtime.

- *Fingernails.* Keep your child's nails short, with no jagged edges, and very clean. Pure cotton tie-on 'scratch mitts' safety-pinned onto the end of your child's sleeve can give good protection, especially at night, if you're not using bandages.

Wash any flannels you use on your child's skin on the hot machine cycle (60 °C plus) every couple of days, or boil them every couple of days, otherwise they will become a good breeding ground for the bacteria to which your baby's cracked, dry skin is so vulnerable.

WHAT YOUR DOCTOR CAN DO

Paste bandages

These are impregnated with soothing substances such as zinc paste, ichthammol or coal tar, and are very helpful for relieving itching as well as preventing a baby or child from scratching and further damaging their skin. Some contain calamine, which is often used instead of tar products for very angry, inflamed areas. A second securing bandage keeps the paste-impregnated layer in place. Your doctor or a specialist nurse can show you how to apply these, and will give you a supply to use at home. Paste bandages, especially tar ones, are often used to break down areas of thickened skin.

Antibiotics

The weeping lesions of eczema can easily become infected with a variety of different bugs. *Staphylococcus aureus* is the commonest, and once installed produces its own toxins which make the infected areas itchier than ever. Strong topical steroids alone halve the bacteria count, so stubborn eczema needs to be treated with a combination of both topical steroids and antibiotics for maximum effect.

Infected eczema tends to be soggy and weeping, in which case oily baths are not appropriate. Your doctor may suggest adding potassium permanganate to the bath instead (in a ratio of 1:10). When the weeping areas dry out, the oily baths can be started once again. Alternatively, you can use a bath oil which contains an added antiseptic ingredient, such as Oilatum Plus.

Steroids

Topical steroids

Steroids are a group of hormones which the body naturally produces from several different glands. Corticosteroids are the type produced by the middle part of the adrenal glands called the adrenal cortex. One particular type of corticosteroid are called cortisols, and their function is to soothe inflammation. They can be used to treat several different skin diseases, including eczema, by rubbing them directly onto the affected areas.

Unfortunately, if present in stronger concentrations than usual, cortisols can also suppress certain parts of the immune system and inhibit bone growth. (But see The Myths, below.)

The myths

There has been, and still is, a good deal of confusion about steroid treatment (amongst doctors and nurses as well as parents) which ultimately does the children they are trying to help a severe disservice. There are three main misunderstandings:

- *They are wonder drugs and do little harm.*

WRONG. During the 1960s, cortisone drugs were revolutionizing the treatment of several skin disorders. The medical profession was not then aware of the problems they could cause, so they were often *overused* without proper caution and some unpleasant side effects resulted. Corticosteroid treatment does great good, but may also be harmful – what is 'safe' for one child may not be for another – and the drugs are still occasionally overused, or used inappropriately, by non-specialist doctors.

- *Corticosteroid drugs used for skin disorders are the same thing weight trainers take to make their muscles grow.*

THEY AREN'T. Corticosteroids used for eczema and asthma are wrongly linked in people's minds with a different type of drug called *anabolic* steroids, which some weight trainers use (illegally) to increase their muscle bulk. These can have very unpleasant side effects, such as testicular shrinkage. But the steroids used to treat eczema are *completely different* from the steroids weight trainers use.

- *Mild hydrocortisone creams which are applied to the skin cause the same side effects as the very strongest creams, and as the powerful steroid treatments which have to be taken by mouth.*

THEY DON'T. In normal circumstances, the only cream that should ever be used on babies and infants is Hydrocortisone, as this is the mildest there is. According to top paediatric eczema specialist Dr Atherton, it never causes skin thinning or damage, unlike the medium to strong creams which may do so. It is very rare that it causes any internal effects such as immunosuppression or growth retardation, unless it is applied very liberally all over the body of a very small baby at least twice a day for a very extended period of time. Stronger creams may occasionally be used for infants for a very few days, under the supervision of a dermatologist, to bring a severe flare-up under control.

With the *prolonged* use of *strong* topical steroid treatments, which may be suggested for older children with severe eczema, there is a potential risk of some serious side effects. These may include:

— Growth retardation.

— Blanching of the skin on the areas treated, followed by a rebound time when the skin's blood vessels widen again, which, though usually temporary, can also become permanent – the end result may be pale areas of treated skin marked with noticeable red veining.

— Skin atrophy, when the skin becomes transparent and fragile.

— Stretch marks on the skin.

— Glaucoma – increased pressure inside the eye which can result in visual disturbance or impairment.

The use of such creams in babyhood eczema is not usual. If they are used on an older child, their effect depends upon where they are being applied – they are less likely to have serious side effects on thicker areas, more likely on thinner areas such as the face or hands.

Striking the balance with steroid creams

Balancing control of eczema with as limited a use of steroid creams as possible is a delicate, ongoing process. It is more harmful to your child's skin not to control flare-ups of eczema when necessary with mild steroid cream, as long as it is used sensibly.

It is *overuse* that causes side effects such as skin thinning. It is now easier to overuse the cream on older children because it is now available from your local pharmacist without any prescription as 1% hydrocortisone cream – but pharmacists will not sell it to you for use on a child who is under 10 years old.

However, the opposite problem of *underusing* the creams for fear of their side effects will mean that any eczema continues to develop. This is not only likely to cause great distress to both baby and parents, but it also means that the condition could become severe and that the baby will probably eventually need longer courses of far more potent steroid preparations.

Oral steroids

These may be used for short periods of time to treat severe eczema flare-ups in children, but they are never used on babies under two. Even for older children their use is seldom justified because the drugs can adversely affect growth and may also interfere with the immune system's ability to fight off infections. (For further information on their appropriate use, safeguards and potential side effects see Useful Addresses page 261, at the end of this chapter.)

Antihistamines

Antihistamine medicines (available for babies and toddlers in syrup form) and on prescription from your GP can help reduce itching, and many types also make the child sleepy, so they can be valuable at night (though in some children antihistamines have the opposite effect and seem positively to stimulate them).

If you use them or if your doctor prescribes them it is a good idea to administer the medicine about an hour before your child goes to bed so they do not lie there feeling itchy (and probably scratching) while waiting for the drugs to take effect. It also reduces the likelihood of their feeling grumpy, sleepy and 'hung over' in the morning.

There are many available over the counter at the chemist such as Piriton, Vallergan and Phenergan, but often quite high doses are needed to have any effect on a child with eczema. These drugs are not addictive, but over time they can become less and less effective. They are therefore best used intermittently for short periods of a couple of weeks or so at a time, or just on particular nights when you feel your baby is going to find it especially difficult to sleep. If you are using them every single day, they are going to be less effective when you badly need them. Other sedative drugs do not seem to be much help for eczema as they do not reduce the itching. (See also Sleep Drugs section in Helping Your Baby to Sleep, page 82.)

OTHER REMEDIES

Chinese herbal medicines

In China, medicinal herbs made from dried bark, roots, flowers, seeds, and twigs as well as herbs have always been used to treat illnesses. At the time of writing, an estimated 80,000 children and adults have been treated with this form of medicine in the UK. Practitioners do treat young babies and toddlers, and have been doing so for at least 2,000 years. Some will treat babies who are only a few months old, others prefer to wait until they have reached their first birthday.

The herbs can be:

- Added to water, boiled and 'cooked', and then left to stand (steep). You then drain them and give the resulting strong liquid to the child to drink. For the straining part of the process, use a nappy liner or an old pair of tights (throw away afterwards). Large coffee filters, which is what people often try to use, are not very suitable.
- Made into washes, ointments or creams which might be used directly on the skin or as impregnated dressings, compresses or wet wraps secured with tubular bandaging at bedtime.

A traditional Chinese herbal practitioner will usually use between eight and 12 different herbs, and the combination and strength they are used in will depend on the child's particular constitution, their age, and their symptoms. A practitioner may give the baby one type of mix for two or three weeks, then reassess them by checking their pulses: (they can identify over 12 different ones relating to the different major organs of the body, whereas Western doctors are only taught to check one) and looking at the condition of their tongue (tongue diagnosis is also an important everyday tool for assessing health in Chinese medicine). What is given to one infant may differ from that which is used for another.

Trying to ensure a reluctant toddler or baby drinks a herbal medicine can be difficult, as the mixture taste bitter. Young infants may only need as little as 20 mls (less than a fluid ounce) three times a day, and this – or larger amounts – can be put in small plastic medicine syringes and delivered in a slow, gentle stream towards the back of their mouth, bypassing their taste buds altogether, advises the Chi Centre in London, one of the top centres for Chinese medicine in the UK. Using a bottle or a feeding beaker with a spout also directs the liquid to the back of the baby's mouth, again avoiding most of the taste buds.

Who says it works?

Chinese herbal medicine does work for many cases. It is the first effective new treatment for eczema since topical steroids were introduced 40 years ago. There have been many encouraging success stories of children whose eczema is controlled or even cleared up using traditional individualized Chinese herbal medicines.

There have also been two positive clinical research studies (in 1989 and 1993) using a standardized version of the herbal mixture. Both compared the use of dummy herbal treatment with the right herbal treatment for children and adults with hard-to-treat eczema. One study of the medical trials was based at the Great Ormond Street Hospital for Sick Children in London, under Dr David Atherton. Of the 47 children who began in the trial, 37 were to finish it. Of the children who dropped out, half did so because the medicine was so bitter-tasting. New research is currently under way to give the treatment in the form of tiny pills. The other hospital trial was carried out on adults with eczema at London's Royal Free Hospital.

The results? More than 60 per cent of those who had been taking the real herbs instead of the dummy mixture found their skin was less inflamed and itchy. After the trials the standardized real herbal mix was patented under the trade name Zemaphyte. It is licensed to be used for children who are aged *two years or more*, but doctors are not allowed to give it to babies. However, some traditional Chinese herbal practitioners do treat the under-twos with mixtures similar to this. Others will only do so once the child is over 12 months old.

Is it safe?

Just because a substance or medicine is natural doesn't necessarily mean it's completely harmless – you get prussic acid from cherry stones, for instance. There is no list of possible side effects for other Chinese herbal eczema treatments, but for Zemaphyte, researchers noted that there were some possible ones (though they did not affect everyone), including nausea, looser bowel motions and some stomach bloating. Two of the children out of the 40 who took part in the Great Ormond Street Zemaphyte trial developed a change in their blood, suggesting that the herbal mix was affecting their liver. For this reason, everyone taking Chinese herbal medicine for eczema (whether it is Zemaphyte or another non-licensed mixture) needs to have regular blood and urine checks at the hospital where they are being treated. No one yet knows if there are any long-term side effects if the treatment is continued over several years.

Five things you need to know about Chinese herbal medicine for eczema

- Zemaphyte is one particular herbal mixture, available in granular form, but there are many other different ones which have not been subject to any clinical tests or trials, so the fact that this mix is seen as safe does not necessarily mean the others are too.
- The same applies to the creams and ointments which traditional Chinese medicine clinics offer. Some of the latter have been found to contain

potent but impure steroids, as well as herbs. These can be damaging to vulnerable eczema skin, especially on that of babies and toddlers. In the UK, only medically qualified doctors are allowed to prescribe strong steroids.

- All the creams' ingredients should be listed on the tube or pot they are contained in. If they are not, ask the clinic to tell you exactly what they are made from. If the clinic staff are evasive, think again before using their medicines.

- It is not always easy to establish whether doctors at a traditional Chinese medicine clinic are medically qualified in the way in which orthodox Western medicine understands the term. How do you know? They should have a certificate of professional qualification. The Register of Chinese Herbal Medicine will tell you of a professionally trained practitioner in your area (see Useful Addresses page 262). Two clinics with good reputations are the Chi Centre and the Chrysanthemum Clinic (see below).

  Generally, a *practitioner* of Chinese herbal medicine is someone who has been trained to diagnose patients and treat them using herbal remedies, and a herbal *pharmacist* is someone trained to dispense these herbs but not prescribe them (i.e. decide which ones a patient should have). A practitioner may be qualified in Western medicine as well as Chinese herbal medicine, or they may just be trained in the latter. In Britain, it is the law that only doctors registered with the General Medical Council are allowed to use the title 'Dr', but many Chinese practitioners, though neither medically trained nor registered with the GMC, are still addressed as 'doctor' by their staff and patients as a mark of respect.

  There are a handful of clinics where the doctors are medically qualified in Western medicine as well as being trained in traditional Chinese herbalism, such as the Chrysanthemum Clinic in Ealing, London and the Chi Centre in Victoria, London. For information on where to find other such practitioners and clinics, contact the Institute of Complementary Medicine (see Useful Addresses page 262).

- Your child can only be prescribed Zemaphyte on the NHS under the direct supervision of a consultant dermatologist, either in private practice, or in an NHS hospital. Unfortunately, some hospitals will not do this, because the treatment is expensive. You could ask your GP to write out a private prescription for it, but the treatment would still need to be supervised by a dermatologist, who could ensure the necessary blood tests and urine checks were carried out during its use.

Anti Candida Treatment

Dr John Mansfield of Banstead, Surrey, says that between 10 and 20 per cent of the children and babies he sees with eczema have an overgrowth of the naturally occurring gut fungi candida, and are allergic to the toxins the candida is producing, which causes the eczema. The treatment for candida infestation of the gut is the anti-fungal drug Nystatin taken by mouth, and avoiding sugars and yeasts in the diet for a while. This diagnosis can be made by an allergy specialist or a clinical nutritionist.

Homeopathy

A homeopath would probably address the immune system, the workings of the kidneys as well as the skin itself. Common remedies include Graphites for 'moist' eczema with a yellowish discharge and dry, cracked skin; and Sulphur for 'dry' eczema that is rough, red and itchy. It is important to take your baby to see a fully qualified homeopath – see Complementary Therapies page 2 – rather than to try to treat this at home with remedies from a health food shop, as a homeopath's medication would be very specific and customized especially for your baby for maximum effectiveness.

Preventing eczema before birth

If you have a child with eczema and are worried that a second baby might develop similar problems, there is plenty you can do to try to ensure this does not happen.

Babies can become sensitized to external allergens while they are still in their mother's womb, as certain substances (such as the proteins from cow's milk) cross the placenta into the baby's system intact. Work by Professor John Warner at the University of Southampton, and (other research at) St Marys Hospital on the Isle of Wight, found that if mothers were exposed to allergens like dust mites and pollen during their pregnancy, it could influence whether or not their baby developed asthma. As asthma is so closely related to eczema (children with the latter are three times more likely to develop the former, and a high proportion of the trigger factors are identical in both disorders), it is not unreasonable to assume that if the unborn baby's airways can be sensitized to allergens in this way, so might their skin.

If you, your partner or your family has a strong family history of atopic problems (asthma, eczema, hay fever), it is a good idea to try to avoid the most common allergenic foods – cow's milk, wheat and eggs – in the last three months of pregnancy. Try very hard never to binge on anything (especially peanut butter, as there are many anecdotal reports of this also pre-sensitizing an unborn baby, so that when it is born it is allergic to peanuts).

Another sensible precaution is to de-dust mite the entire nursery before the baby arrives, using commercial anti-mite spray – contact the NES for mail-order suppliers (see Useful Addresses page 262) – or even strong milky tea on non-staining areas like wooden floors, as the tannin in it kills mites. Keep all pets out of the room after you have done this, for good.

Breastfeeding

Breastfeeding will help protect your baby against many types of allergy-related disease, including eczema, food allergy and asthma, although it will not guarantee they definitely won't develop them – some breastfed babies do have eczema. Breastfeeding experts are always advising new mothers on the benefits of feeding your baby yourself and often mention its protective effect, but though it sounds too good to be true, it is backed up by some long-term, thorough medical research. One 17-year-long study which bears out the 'breastfeeding protects' story was carried out by the Children's Hospital at the University of Helsinki, following 150 children from birth to their seventeenth birthday, and another similar 20-year-long British study found exactly the same.

No one is entirely sure why, but it is thought that perhaps human milk encourages both the immune system and the formation of the barrier of soft protective mucus which lines the gut to mature. The second most popular theory is that breastmilk reduces the exposure of the baby's gut to several potentially harmful substances, including food allergens and bacteria.

USEFUL ADDRESSES

The Allergy Shop, PO Box 196, Haywards Heath, West Sussex RH16 3YF. Tel: 01444 414290.

A wide range of products, retail and mail order, for those with allergies to food or other substances such as pollen and dust mites, including less expensive anti-dust mite bedding covers. Also has useful booklet: 'How to Ease Your Child's Eczema Without Drugs'.

The British Allergy Foundation, 23 Middle Street, London EC1A 7JA. Tel: 0171 600 6166.

A helpline staffed by qualified nurse counsellors specializing in allergy of all types.

The British Dietetic Association, 7th Floor, Elizabeth House, 22 Suffolk Street, Queensway, Birmingham B1 1LS. Tel: 0121 643 5483.

It should be possible to refer your child to a nutritionist on the NHS. However, many nutritionists have been made redundant during the last few years under NHS cuts, so there may be a long waiting list. To contact a private nutritionist who has had the NHS-accepted three-year training, call this Association (consultations cost from £15 to £50 depending on where in the UK they are).

Chinese medicine
There are more than 600 clinics in the UK offering Chinese medicine for eczema. They are not all equally professional. Traditional Chinese herbal medicine clinics with properly trained practitioners, also qualified to prescribe Chinese herbal medicines, include:

The Chi Centre, 10 Greycoat Place, Victoria, London SW1P 1SB. Tel: 0171 222 1888.

Doctors here are qualified in both traditional Chinese herbal medicine, and orthodox clinical medicine, and are on secondment from teaching hospitals in the People's Republic of China.

The Chrysanthemum Clinic, 3 Station Parade, Burlington Lane, Chiswick, London W4 3HD. Tel: 0181 995 1355.

Dr Ding-Hui Luo, 15 Little Newport Street, Soho, London WC2.

It was she who helped so much with the trials carried out at the Great Ormond Street Hospital for Sick Children. She does not arrange appointments by telephone. In the traditional Chinese style you have to turn up at 8 a.m., take a ticket and queue.

The Register of Chinese Herbal Medicine, PO Box 400, Wembley, Middlesex HA9 9SZ. Tel: 0181 904 1357.

Cotton-On Ltd, Monmouth Place, Bath BA1 2NP. Tel: 01225 461155.

Specialist pure cotton clothing company. Has a wide range, including cotton mitts, special cotton sleep suits with closed-in hands and feet, buttoned up the back, for babies.

The Institute of Complementary Medicine, PO Box 194, London SE16 1QZ. Tel: 0171 237 5165.

Holds a large, but not exhaustive, register of professionally trained complementary therapists of all types in the UK.

Medivac Healthcare Ltd, Market House, Church Street, Wilmslow, Cheshire SK9 1AU. Tel: 01625 539401.

Manufactures vacuum cleaners whose collection bags do not let dust mite droppings through (supply by mail direct, from £199). Also supplies microporous bed and pillow covers, which do not let dust mite droppings through.

The National Eczema Society, 163 Eversholt Street, London NW1 1BU. Tel: 0171 388 4097.

Advice and support for people with eczema at all ages, including parents of babies and children with eczema. Large range of useful literature on treatments and coping strategies. It also funds research.

Seton Healthcare Group plc, Tubiton House, Oldham, Greater Manchester OL1 3HS. Tel: 0161 652 2222.

Produces two booklets and a video especially for children on wet-wrap bandaging techniques, to reassure them and help them understand what is going on ('Thomas Wears Tubifast').

USEFUL READING

Eczema in Childhood – the Facts, David Atherton, Oxford University Press, 1994. This is invaluable.
The Eczema Handbook, Jenny Lewis with the National Eczema Society, Vermilion, 1994.

Dealing with Asthma

Asthma is a long-term (chronic) breathing disorder in which the airways have become hypersensitive, and narrow temporarily when they come across substances which upset them. These substances – and doctors reckon there are about 200 of them at the last count – are referred to as irritants. The airways are the hundreds of tiny tubes in the lungs ending in minute air sacs called alveoli that pass oxygen into the blood. They react to irritants, whether pollen or exhaust fumes, by going into spasm (tightening up), swelling up inside and making sticky mucus. The narrower the airways become as a result, the harder it is to breathe. The wheezing of a person with asthma is the sound of air trying to get through these partially blocked tubes. Watching a small child fight for breath can be one of the most alarming things in the world, for the parents and the child, and a severe asthma attack can be very frightening.

The good news is that the majority of babies and toddlers grow out of their asthma by the time they are around five, and there is a great deal that both parents and doctors can do to help them cope with an asthma attack, prevent or reduce the attacks in the first place, and perhaps track down the triggers of the problem so they can be avoided.

Asthma is divided into two types.

- *Viral asthma* is caused by a virus infecting the airways so they become inflamed and swell up. This variety is by far the commonest in babies and toddlers. It is also the type which they are most likely to grow out of by the time they reach primary school age.
- *Allergic asthma* is where the airways narrow in response to an allergy to a substance which the person has taken into their body, either by breathing it in (more usual), or by eating it (less common). Infants are less likely to grow out of this sort.

Some children with asthma may also have related conditions caused by an overreactive immune system. For instance, two-thirds of babies and toddlers with eczema will also develop asthma at some time in their lives, and the triggers which set off asthma attacks or eczema flare-ups are remarkably similar. Many children will also have hay fever, and there may be a link with glue ear (see Glue Ear pages 198–204).

How common is it?

Infant asthma *is* common. Far more common than people usually imagine. Eighteen per cent (that's nearly one in five) babies have had wheezing attacks by the time they are two and a half, according to the ongoing child health survey 'Children of the 90s'. Two-thirds of these toddlers will carry on wheezing but outgrow their symptoms by the time they are five years old, but the other third will go on to develop significant asthma which they may have for life. And just for the record, one in five children (from 0 to 12) will, by the time they quit primary school, have had asthma formally diagnosed by their doctor at some point.

It is also on the increase. The number of young children who need emergency admission to hospital because of it has risen alarmingly – between three- and fivefold in the last 20 years, according to Professor Stephen Holgate of the University of Southampton/Southampton General Hospital.

Asthma triggers

Some of the commonest *allergic* triggers are:

- House dust mites, or to be strictly accurate, their droppings.
- Furry or feathered pets' dander, which is the dead skin flakes shed by animals and birds.
- House dust itself, in which dust mites live. It consists of a splendid cocktail of dead human skin (each adult sheds about a gram of this a day), mould spores, insect fragments, animal dander, animal fur, bacteria, food particles, soil, fibre fragments, insecticide residue and pollen of many different types during spring, summer and early autumn.
- Moulds, especially in late summer and through the autumn.
- Some foods and drinks. Any one can be implicated in asthma, but the commonest are the ones which also tend to trigger eczema flare-ups – cow's milk, eggs and wheat products.

Common *non-allergic* triggers include:

- viral respiratory infections, including ordinary coughs and colds, and bronchiolitis
- air pollution
- cigarette smoke
- exercise
- emotional stress
- sudden weather changes
- cold air
- cigarette smoke
- perfumes
- chemical fumes
- thunderstorms – especially when combined with high pollen counts. One particular storm in 1994 in London saw ten times the usual number of emergency asthma admissions to hospital.

Why are so many more small children developing asthma?
There is no single cause, but there are several factors all making a difference.

- *About 50 per cent of all families in Britain own a furry pet.* According to top paediatric asthma specialist Mike Silverman, Professor of Child Health at Leicester Royal Infirmary, 'There is *no doubt* that cats, and to a lesser extent, dogs, are major asthma sensitizers. If the family owns a furry pet in the child's early babyhood (and possibly in late pregnancy too) it increases the risk of the child developing allergic asthma later very significantly. For babies and children with really troublesome asthma – not just a mild wheeze – in 40 per cent of cases this is caused by their furry pet. Pet owning is the second most important factor in children's asthma, after dust mites.'
- *The rise in indoor pollution.* This is increasing because homes are often effectively sealed, by double glazing, because windows are kept closed, and because homes are insulated to retain heat.

  This means that stale air containing allergens such as dust mites and mould spores can remain trapped and start to build up. The furnishing trends over the last 30 years towards fitted carpets, which also trap dust mites and their droppings, has also made a difference, providing an extra hiding place and breeding ground for dust mites. Central heating is now far commoner than it was 25 years ago, and this too can encourage dust mite breeding. If the air is damp as well as warm, it encourages the growth of moulds which act as allergic triggers. Polluting gases such as nitrogen dioxide are emitted from indoor gas cookers, solid fuel and gas fires and these too may remain trapped within the sealed houses.
- *The rise in outdoor pollution.* Especially from traffic fumes discharging nitrogen dioxide and sulphur dioxide into the air. As a result there are also increasing amounts of ozone gas at ground level.

  According to one report by St George's Hospital Medical School in London in 1996, when the air pollution is high, actual *deaths* from breathing disorders such as asthma go up by nearly 6 per cent.
- *Changing diet.* Both adults and young children are eating fewer fresh vegetables and fruit, which contain anti-oxidant vitamins such as Vitamin A, C, and E, which may be helpful in reducing the likelihood of allergy.
- *More women are smoking while pregnant.* This is thought to damage the formation of an unborn baby's lungs, as the chemicals from cigarettes are absorbed into the mother's bloodstream and enter the baby's bloodstream via the placenta. Smoking may also stunt growth overall so the baby is born smaller than it should be. Smaller babies have smaller lungs, which are less robust than those of a baby of average weight.

  Smoking during pregnancy also increases the likelihood that the baby will be born prematurely. The biggest problem premature babies have is that their lungs are seldom mature enough to cope with breathing without help. Even when they are born at full term (40 weeks), only 50 per cent of the air sacs in their lungs have developed. If they arrive at 28 to 34 weeks, they are dependent on oxygen therapy and a ventilation machine until enough of these air sacs have formed to allow them to breathe unaided. Premature babies are often short of a substance called surfactant which lines the lungs and stops them from collapsing. Even after they no longer need additional support from the intensive care unit, premature babies' lungs remain more vulnerable to recurrent breathing problems (including asthma) than a full-term baby's. About one baby in every 10 is now born too early.

- *A decrease in childhood infections.* According to the Idling Immune System Theory, this leads the immune system to target other 'ordinary' substances – the ones people are most often allergic to, such as pollen, dust mite droppings, pet dander and so on.
- *Blanket vaccination of babies and toddlers against childhood diseases.* Critics of the vaccination system, of which there are a small but growing number, suggest that the vaccination programmes are a major assault on children's very immature immune systems, and are leaving them vulnerable to auto-immune and allergy-related diseases. This theory is controversial – for further information see Infant Vaccination – The Pros, the Cons and the Facts, pages 279–97.

Does my child have asthma? The parents' checklist
The classic signs are:

- *Wheezing alone, or wheezing with coughing.* According to Mike Silverman, there are several different illnesses which can obstruct the airways, causing wheezing and persistent coughs in babies and the under twos. They include acute bronchiolitis (inflammation of the tiny airways), wheezy bronchitis (occasionally called 'episodic viral wheeze' – about 80 per cent of all wheezing in small children is caused by a virus), and classic allergic asthma.
- *Coughing on its own*, especially at night, with colds. A cough *with* wheezing is far more likely to indicate asthma.
- *Shortness of breath.* This is the most distressing aspect of asthma. As the child's airways shrink and fill up with mucus, they find it an increasingly uphill struggle to get enough air into their bodies – or to get it out again – and the lungs gradually become distended with air. No matter what age they are, the child becomes alarmed as they feel they are suffocating, and the physical effort to get air in or out can be terrific. Any baby or child having a severe asthma attack will undoubtedly be frightened – their face may be pale, their eyes wild, their skin may be clammy and there may also be some sweat on their foreheads. If they are old enough to talk, their breathlessness may become so severe that they can no longer say more than one word at a time. Even moderate breathlessness can be disruptive and disconcerting.
- *Wheezing and a chronic (long-term) cough which tends to be started off by coughs and colds.*

All the symptoms above may be made worse, or brought on, by:

- Emotional upsets and stress, or even gales of laughter and rough-and-tumble games.
- Exercise, especially out of doors in cold air – perhaps playing in a playground on a frosty day in winter. It is normal for airways to tighten when exposed to cold air, but in asthmatics this response is greatly exaggerated.
- Contact with things that your child is allergic to (you'll learn which they are) such as house dust, pollen, furry pets, particular plants, chemical fumes or occasionally certain foods.
- High air pollution levels, especially on hot, smoggy, summer days in cities. Again, it is quite normal for healthy airways to tighten up when they come into contact with dust, smoke and fumes, but people with asthma respond far more strongly than those who don't suffer from asthma. Sometimes the irritation of inhaling these substances is made worse by chemical reactions in the body. For example, nitrogen dioxide gas belched out by car exhausts combines with the water content of mucus in the airways to become diluted nitric acid, and sulphur dioxide from industrial emissions turns into sulphuric acid in the airways in the same way. Both are highly irritant.
- If the child also has hay fever, eczema or glue ear. Two-thirds of babies with eczema will go on to develop asthma at some point, though the greater proportion of them will grow out of both by the time they reach adolescence. Asthma is also one of the three allergic conditions which run in families – the other two are eczema and hay fever. Generally speaking, if one parent has asthma the chances of one of their children having it are doubled. If both parents have asthma or one of the other two family allergies, the chances of their baby developing asthma are increased fourfold.
- A change in behaviour. Many parents report that they can often see an attack coming and make preparations for it, because their child seems to become drowsy and rather listless before an attack of asthma, or may fidget and become irritable, even feeling apprehensive or sad for no apparent reason. A few children, though this is less usual, may become remarkably talkative (if they are old enough) or lively.

Why can asthma be so hard to diagnose?

Asthma can be difficult to diagnose, especially in babies and toddlers. In fact, one study by a Harrow GP found it took no less than an average of 16 visits to the GP to get it diagnosed in children. Professor Silverman, top medical advisor on infant asthma to the National Asthma Campaign, adds: 'Diagnosis by GPs can still take a long time and things are not really improving much. Despite the energetic health education campaigns over the last few years, children are still being given antibiotics for asthma because the GP thinks it's just a chest infection, when what they really need is bronchodilator medicines to help open up those airways. For instance, 15 per cent of schoolchildren wheeze regularly, but only 10 per cent of them have actually been diagnosed as asthmatic.'

Reasons for reluctant or slow diagnoses may include the fact that GPs may not wish to alarm parents. They may also be unclear themselves about what actually constitutes asthma. As a result, your doctor might be reluctant to use the label 'asthmatic' and may, confusingly, talk about wheezing, wheezy bronchitis, persistent chesty coughs, and colds that move to the chest instead. Some paediatricians have yet another (affectionate) term for babies who wheeze constantly yet never seem to be upset by it, in other words have little trouble actually catching their breath in the way asthmatic children can – they call them 'fat, happy wheezers' because the infants are usually plump as well.

Then there is the problem of how to test for asthma in babies and very young children. From about six or seven years of age, children can be tested for breathing capacity, a good indicator for asthma, using a device called a Peak Flow Meter. It cannot be used by babies and infants, as it involves blowing as hard as possible into it, as if inflating a balloon, and most babies or toddlers cannot do this. The only reliable way of measuring how well an infant's lungs are working is by using a non-invasive, simple device, which is only available in hospitals, called an oximeter. It clips painlessly onto the child's finger or toe and shines a strong light through it. The amount of light actually getting through indicates how much oxygen the blood contains. The more severe the blockage of the lung's airways, the lower the oxygen content of the blood.

If there seems to be some confusion, the following checklist of points and questions can help you and your GP work out whether your baby actually does have asthma or not:

- Does the baby have the symptoms listed above on a regular basis?
- Do they tend to be brought on by the situations listed above?
- Does it seem to be brought on or made worse by other allergens such as pet dander or certain foods?
- Is one or both parents asthmatic? If not, is there any history of it in your immediate family?
- Do one or both parents have eczema or hay fever?
- Does the baby/toddler have eczema or hay fever?

If asthma is diagnosed, GPs tend to use the terms mild, moderate or severe to describe it.

Mild asthma tends to mean that your child may cough and wheeze, but they also play happily, feed well, and their symptoms do not wake them up at night.

Moderate asthma usually means that the symptoms do wake your child – and you – at night, and they cannot run about and play without wheezing and coughing.

Severe asthma means that the child is too restless and uncomfortable to sleep at night, they do not seem to want to play or interact with others very much, are listless, often too breathless to feed or (if they are old enough) talk, and their asthma attacks, if extremely severe, are serious enough to produce cyanosis, where their lips, and sometimes extremities, take on a blue tinge because of shortage of oxygen in the blood.

TREATMENT

The type of treatment the child needs for their wheezing depends upon what is causing it, how they are in themselves at the time and how severe their symptoms are.

What you can do

* *Ban smoking from your house and steer your child away from smoky atmosphere when you are out and about.* Cigarette smoke is extremely irritating to asthmatics, especially to very young ones. A survey carried out by the TV programme *Blue Peter* and the National Asthma Campaign in 1996 found that, of the 10,000 children who replied, 74 per cent said that cigarette smoke made their asthma worse (of these a third lived with someone who did smoke), compared with 43 per cent who said air pollution – which gets far more media publicity – made breathing more difficult for them.

    Parents, frustratingly, have no control over the quality of air outside where they live – but they do have control over the quality of air inside their home, so this is probably one of the single most important things the mothers and fathers of asthmatic children can do to help protect them (see Soothing Eczema page 242).

* *Ask for allergy testing, to try to find out if there are any particular triggers for your child's asthma.* Even if you have already identified one or two major ones, such as air pollution and pollen, there may be others which you could help them avoid if you only knew what they were. All the allergy tests for eczema apply – see pages 245–7 for details.

    The most common food allergies implicated in asthma are eggs, cow's milk products and wheat, the same ones that are linked with eczema. The official line is that food allergies are seldom the reason (or even a factor in) asthma. However some allergy specialists, and anecdotal reports from parents, suggest otherwise, so it is still an avenue worth investigating.

* *Wage war on dust mites.* Eighty to 90 per cent of asthmatic children are sensitive to dust mite droppings. A vigorous programme of dust reduction will probably produce a major improvement in your child's asthma. Try turning at least your child's bedroom – because they spend more time in here than in any other room – into a dust mite-free haven.

    — *Put microporous covers on the mattress and pillows* – wipe-clean or, less

---

There are over 200 substances recognized by doctors to provoke asthma. Unfortunately we cannot cover them all here, so we have concentrated on the two worst – dust mites and pollen. These are arguably the two which parents can do most to protect their baby or toddler against.

expensively, washable polyester are the best anti-dust mite pillows as feather or down ones are highly allergenic. The microporous covers let moisture and air in and out, but not dust mites or their microscopic, allergy-provoking droppings. It is a sobering thought that 10 per cent of any mattress or pillow is composed entirely of dead or live dust mites, their droppings and the dead human skin they live off. Microporous covers and special anti-allergy bed covers and duvets are not cheap, but they last a long time. Single bed covers cost from about £35 to £50, wipe-clean pillows about £60 for two, pillow covers about £12 each. A single bed anti-allergy duvet costs about £190, the covers from about £25 for a single (see Useful Addresses page 278 for stockists).

If the covers are too expensive, vacuum your child's mattress twice a week, paying special attention to button-down areas and seams (see below). Or cover it in heavy duty plastic sheeting held in place at the ends of the mattress by staples or sticky tape. To avoid the sweatiness sleeping on plastic can produce, cover it in two or three cotton sheets, changed at least once each week. According to Professor Silverman, new baby cot mattresses with washable covers are a perfectly good option.

If the wipe-clean pillows are too expensive, don't try encasing the pillows you do have in thick plastic too, as this makes them less yielding to lie on and therefore uncomfortable and sweaty against the face, no matter how many cotton pillowcases you put on top. Instead, buy ordinary polyester-filled pillows and put them in the washing machine on a hot cycle (60 °C or more) every two weeks to kill off any mites.

A cheaper and very comfortable alternative to a special non-allergenic duvet is cotton sheets and cotton cellular blankets washed in a hot cycle every two weeks to kill dust mites.

— *Wash any soft toys in the hot wash every week,* or put them in the freezer for 12 hours – both methods kill dust mites. Do not have several sitting companionably on your child's bed, as they are great dust and mite gatherers – perhaps have two or three, de-mited regularly, instead.

— *Keep their room very, very clean.* Damp-dust your child's room twice a week like one possessed; do the walls once a fortnight. Go over any mobiles hanging above the child's bed and any shelves in their room twice weekly. Avoid lots of books standing on the shelves – try having just a few and put the rest downstairs. Do not have lots of shelf ornaments – dust gatherers, again.

— *Make their room quite Spartan.* It doesn't mean it can't be bright and cheerful: happy, bright posters add colour and friendliness to the walls in place of toys and books, and you can use flat clip frames instead of dust-prone moulded ones. If your child's bed has a padded headboard, throw it out, and use lino (it can be a cheerful colour) rather than carpets and rugs which harbour dust mites. Have a small, bright, washable rug by their bed or cot to put their feet on first thing in the morning and last thing at night if you feel it's not very comforting standing on a chilly lino floor. The same goes for material curtains – go for vinyl blinds instead (not Venetian ones – again, a great source of dust). Remove upholstered furniture, and have plain wooden or plastic brightly coloured little play chairs or tables instead. Put all toys away in a covered box at night. Wall coverings should ideally be plain and wipable – avoid wood chip and textured wallpaper.

— *Vacuum with a specialist medical vacuum cleaner if you can possibly afford it.* The ordinary type tends to increase the amount of dust in the air, letting through dust mites and their droppings and redistributing them into the atmosphere. Ordinary vacuum cleaners may not be powerful enough to dislodge the mites as they cling onto the crevices in carpets and upholstery anyway, but the clinical models can shift them, and the machines' collection bags contain them properly. Some models have official approval from clinicians specializing in asthma. Prices range from about £250 to £500 (see Useful Addresses, page 278, for suppliers). Check with the National Asthma Campaign for other specialist products which may be helpful.

- *Keep the pollen down.* The light pollen from wind-pollinated plants like grasses and trees gets just about everywhere. It has even been found 400 miles out into the ocean and two miles up in the atmosphere. If you know that pollen can trigger asthma for your child, keep your child's bedroom window closed at night during the pollen season (which runs from April through May right up until late season in September).

If your child has a *proven* pollen allergy, further measures include:

— *Driving with car windows closed.* Some roads and motorways are long and straight and act like pollen traps – as many as 5,000 pollen grains per cubic metre of air have been recorded (a mere 25 grains per cubic metre can be enough to set off symptoms). Avoid walks down canalsides or riverbanks for the same reason.

— *Putting a little Vaseline inside your child's nostrils* three times a day, as this will help trap any pollen on the way up their nose before it can upset them.

— *Do not let your child sit or play outside on long warm summer evenings* – pollen levels are highest first thing in the morning and in the evening. Wait till mid-morning before any trips to the park or playground. Better still, save park trips for still days (when pollen is not being blown about) or after it has just rained, as the water washes the air clean.

— *If you have a lawn, keep it well trimmed.*

— *Keep your child indoors with windows closed in bright sunny weather in June or July,* or at least well away from large grass expanses like football and cricket pitches. To avoid stuffiness, use a fan, or tape two layers of butter muslin or gauze over all the window openings in the house. Keep spraying them with water to keep them damp, and this will trap a good many of the pollen grains.

If grassy parks are off limits, trips to an outdoor lido (as long as it is not in the middle of the local grassy park) or indoor swimming pool with a transparent roof or large concrete patio outside may be good alternatives.

— *Avoid camping holidays or canal barge holidays,* and instead try to stay near the seaside where pollen levels are lower. If possible (this will be easier with a baby or toddler as you have no school terms to coincide with), take your summer holiday in May, in Britain.

— *If you've been on a trip outside with your child,* brush down their clothes, and yours, with a damp cloth on the doorstep. Do the same to the buggy and both your pairs of shoes before coming in. Some parents extend this to undressing their children for bed in the bathroom and ensuring all outdoor clothes are left in there and not taken into the child's room bearing pollen grains.

What else helps?

- *If you have a furry pet, consider giving it away* to another kindly family to look after. Technically, as there is such a strong connection between allergic asthma and furry pets, a household with an asthmatic child should not have any pets at all, except perhaps a bowlful of drifting goldfish or a tank of tropical fish.

  However, pets are often there before the baby arrives, and are therefore much loved and valued members of the household, so it's not necessarily a viable option to let them go. If you do keep a cat or dog, wash them without fail once a week. They might not like this much, especially if they are a cat, but according to allergy expert Dr Platts Mills, 'Cats certainly will tolerate washing and there is no question that it's a great help.'

- *Invest in an ionizer,* if possible for both the child's bedroom and your own sitting room. Ionizers give out negatively charged air molecules, which attack airborne particles like pollen and dust, settling them down out of the air so they are less likely to be breathed in. Asthma experts are divided on whether these help – could you borrow one on trial for a couple of weeks and see if it helps your child? Health shops, chemists and specialist outlets supply them, from about £20 to £70 each.

  Give your child plenty of fluids to drink to help thin out any mucus they are producing. According to one of America's top paediatricians, Professor William Sears of the University of South California Medical School, this makes it easier for your baby to cough phlegm loose from their airways.

- *Give vitamin C.* One study carried out in Nigeria in 1980 found that if asthmatic adults took 1 g or 1,000 mg daily, they had 75 per cent fewer asthma attacks. This was actually done as a double blind crossover trial, which means that both dummy pills and the real vitamin C pills were used on volunteers in such a way that neither the patients nor the doctors conducting the study knew until afterwards who had what. It is thought that about 50 mg a day would be safe for children of six to 12 months, and 50 gm a day for one- to three-year-olds. Vitamin C may also help your child avoid the repeated colds and coughs during winter which can cause asthma.

- *Evening primrose oil.* Anecdotally (it is not medically proven), this appears to help some asthmatic children. Perhaps given them one 250 mg capsule three times daily – prick the capsules with a pin and squeeze into food or milk. You may need to wait about eight to 12 weeks before noticing any improvement, even if it is going to help. EPO is very safe to use, and suitable for children from four months old, but should not be given to children who have been diagnosed as having temporary lobe epilepsy. The only recorded side effects are, occasionally, some diarrhoea and headaches.

- *Give lots of magnesium-high foods.* New research from Dr John Britton of the Nottingham City Hospital suggests that a diet rich in fruit, vegetables and whole grains may help protect against asthma. These foods are high in magnesium, and when magnesium levels of the blood rise, any allergic response falls. If you are interested in the idea of also giving your toddler magnesium supplements, it is important to check potential dosage, and what age it should be safe to start, with a professional nutritionist first (see Useful Addresses, page 278).

- *Try to keep your home as calm as possible.* Some parents report that a calm home environment really seems to benefit their child's asthma – yet more asthma specialists would argue strongly that any asthmatic child should be treated as normally as possible.

    You know your baby's own temperament best, and from experience what seems to make their asthma worse or better, so it is up to you whether you choose the 'no special treatment' approach, or opt for trying to keep your home life as calm, low key and routine as possible. Parents who find the latter helps suggest it does so because emotional stress is one of the major triggers for asthma and eczema flare-ups in all age groups, and that a baby benefits from calm because they have finely tuned emotional antennae which can pick up on *any* nuances of atmosphere, good or bad.

    Measures for keeping things calm can include ensuring the house isn't packed with a constant stream of exciting, noisy visitors and friends, trying to avoid quarrelling with your partner when the child is there too, keeping overhead lighting softish, keeping any noise from music, TV or radio fairly muted (no blaring house music or deafening, hysterical football commentaries), and having a regular routine.

    Children, including very young babies, like routine. They know where they are with it. This applies as much to babies who don't have asthma. The fact that you have instigated a daily timetable with particular (approximate) times for meals, going out to the park, naps, playing, bathing and bed is not going to bore them rigid – they will actually find it very reassuring and soothing. They feel comfortable when life is predictable.

- *Colour therapy and aromatherapy.* Colour therapist and medical aromatherapist Dr Vivienne Lunny, formerly a pathologist at the Harefield and Mount Vernon hospitals, suggests decorating the child's room and bed in blues and greens, as she says this may these help reduce anxiety and muscular spasm. Dr Lunny has been head of the Aromatherapy Organizations Council and is still on their Medical Research Board – she suggests using the essential aromatherapy oils Roman chamomile and Helichism in a vaporizer in the child's room (not on their clothing or pillow as they could irritate the airways) to help relieve bronchial spasm, soothe and help get rid of catarrh. For where to find the oils, see Useful Addresses page 277.

- *Take care of yourself too.* It is very important to try to get time off for yourself if humanly possible, even if it's only half an hour that's yours alone every day. Looking after a baby or toddler can be tiring for most women, but having a baby or toddler with asthma can be even more so (as sleep may be interrupted regularly) and stressful too. Unfortunately it tends to be mothers who get up more often at night when their children are sick, beating even the most willing and (technically) liberated of fathers by about 30 per cent.

  Time for yourself is not self-indulgence. You can parent your child better and help keep them calmer by staying calm yourself, and you can only do that if you have some breaks and rest.

What your GP can do
Orthodox medicine cannot yet cure asthma. Treatment is based on easing and managing its symptoms, and on preventing full-blown attacks, so that children can lead full, active, happy lives. Nearly all medicines for asthma are taken by inhaler (breathed in). There are two main types:

Preventers
These help prevent asthma attacks and breathing difficulties from occurring in the first place, but they are no use for treating an attack once it is under way – for that you would need a reliever (see below).

Preventers work by protecting the linings of a child's airways so that they are less likely to constrict when they meet an asthma trigger, be it cold air or car smog. The medication needs to be used on a regular basis, even if your child is well. Once your child's asthma symptoms are back under control, your GP might suggest reducing the preventer treatment to smaller doses. Preventers are far more effective in chronic allergic asthma than for a wheeze caused by a virus. Finding the right one is often a case of trial and error.

There are two different types of preventer drug. One is a non-steroidal one called sodium cromoglycate, which is breathed in. Side effects might occasionally include temporary spasm of the breathing tubes (just what you are trying to avoid). The other drugs are corticosteroids, also inhaled, such as Beclomethasone and Fluticasone, whose side effects can include some oral thrush and voice hoarseness. The thrush can be treated with antifungal creams, so let your GP or specialist know (also see oral thrush, in The Common Childhood Illnesses page 227). Inhaled steroids can also cause mouth thrush, but this is very unusual if they are given using a spacer or face mask. The steroid doses are very low, so they do not affect your baby's growth as heavy doses of steroid pills can.

For babies and toddlers these asthma-preventing drugs need to be administered using a small funnel-like device which fits comfortably over the nose and mouth, called a spacer. Some infants and very young children may be given face masks instead. Very occasionally, a hospital doctor may prescribe a child a device called a nebulizer instead. These are much bigger and bulkier than spacers, and deliver the anti-asthma medicine in the form of a fine mist.

Relievers

These are the treatments used to deal with an actual attack of asthma, or to help a child when they are experiencing general breathing difficulties. They work by relaxing the airways so they open up again. They may also offer protection against triggers if you know your child is going to be coming up against one.

The drugs used as relievers include Salbutamol (side effects may occasionally include a headache, overactivity or hand tremors – report any signs of these to your GP or specialist) and ipratropium bromide, which is often given to younger children (side effects include a dry mouth). Unfortunately, not all relievers work very well for infants under a year old, so your GP needs to be patient and use some trial and error to find the one which suits your baby best.

If your baby or toddler has asthma, always keep a reliever with you so you have the reassurance should you ever need it. Some mothers have four – one kept permanently in the medicine cabinet at home, one kept in the car (if they have one), one in their handbag and one in the baby's changing bag. If the child is looked after by another carer too, or spends regular time in a nursery, there should be one left there too.

Call your GP and ask to speak to them right away if:

- Your child has a rapid pulse rate (it varies from child to child, but consistently above 120 beats a minute is a danger signal).
- They have a rapid breathing rate.
- They have a dry, unproductive, hacking cough.
- They are clearly frightened.

If you are not reassured by your talk with your GP, take your child to the local hospital's casualty unit instead. You will probably be seen very

---

Staying calm when your child has an asthma attack

This is easier said than done, but it is extremely important that, no matter how worried you are, you at least *pretend* to be calm. If your child senses that you are frightened, this will make them worse. If they see that you are not panicking but are trying quietly to help and comfort them, it will help give them some much-needed confidence.

It helps considerably to know beforehand:

- Exactly where all the medicine is kept, and what amounts should be used in which circumstances.
- Your GP's phone number (keep it stuck to the telephone).
- The quickest route to your local casualty unit. Keep the telephone number of a friendly local minicab company handy as a fallback option.
- What danger signs to look out for so you can judge the situation with more confidence.

Dial 999 for an ambulance if:
- At the height of a wheezing attack, your baby's chest goes silent. Far from the attack having suddenly eased off, this may mean there is very little air moving in and out of your child's lungs at all, and they are in danger of suffocation.
- The medication your child has been given does not help their symptoms, which are rapidly worsening.
- They develop bluish lips or fingertips – these are signs of oxygen starvation.

If there is more than a 10-minute delay, take your child to the nearest casualty unit yourself.

promptly as infants are a top priority. Do not be afraid of being seen as a worrying mother. That's your job – and you know your own child best. If you don't ensure that no chances are taken with your child's health, who else is going to?

USEFUL ADDRESSES

G. Baldwin & Co., Herbalist Health Foods, 173 Walworth Road, London SE17 1RW. Tel: 0171 703 5550.

Herbal supplies, about half the price of Neal's Yard.

The British Allergy Foundation, 23 Middle Street, London EC1A 7JA. Tel: 0171 600 6166.

A helpline staffed by trained nurse counsellors specializing in allergy-related conditions.

The Institute of Complementary Medicine, PO Box 194, London SE16 1QZ. Tel: 0171 237 5165.

For further information about, and local contact numbers of, properly trained complementary medicine practitioners, such as homeopaths and acupuncturists, who may be helpful in alleviating your child's asthma.

National Asthma Campaign, Providence House, Providence Place, London N1 0NT. Tel: 0171 226 2260.

Advice, information and support on all aspects of asthma for people of all ages.

Neal's Yard Remedies, 15 Neal's Yard, London WC2H 9DP. Tel: 0171 379 0705.

Retailers and mail-order suppliers of high quality essential oils and herbs.

Quitline
0171 487 3000

Sensible, practical and sympathetic advice to help people cut down their smoking. Can also direct you to stop-smoking groups countrywide.

Suppliers of asthma prevention products

The Allergy Shop, PO Box 196, Haywards Heath, West Sussex RH16 3YF.
Tel: 01444 414290.

Has a wide range of products for people of all ages with asthma and eczema; also a good booklet called 'How to Ease Your Child's Asthma Without Drugs'.

Medivac Healthcare Ltd, Market House, Church Street, Wilmslow,
Cheshire SK9 1AU. Tel: 01625 539401.

Suppliers of medical vacuum cleaners whose collection bags do not allow dustmite droppings through; also of microporous bed coverings, and anti-allergy pillows and duvets.

Nutritionists

If you suspect your child's asthma may have a link with food allergy and would like to see if a gentle exclusion diet might help, either speak to your GP and ask if they can refer you to a community dietician on the NHS (these are an increasingly rare breed these days) or, if you can afford the fee for a private dietician (from £20 to £50), contact the British Dietetic Association, 7th Floor, Elizabeth House, 22 Suffolk Street, Queensway, Birmingham B1 1LS; tel: 0121 643 5483 and they will put you in touch with one of their members locally.

Vaccinating Your Baby: The Pros, the Cons – and the Facts

Considered up until now by most patients and health professionals to be the single most important thing you can do to protect an infant's health, a small but growing number are now having their doubts about vaccination.

What is vaccination?
The principle behind immunization – artificially induced protection against infectious disease – is that if a tiny amount of an infectious disease, or a small amount of some of the chemical toxins it produces, are introduced into the body, the body will fight back by producing its own antibody defences against it. If it ever encounters this particular bug again, these antibodies will recognize the invader and be able to fight off the infection.

Why is it done?
Your baby may be born with their own effective natural immunity against the major infectious diseases, because your own antibodies to these bugs usually pass into their systems during pregnancy and if you breastfeed. The word usually is used advisedly here because, according to Dr David Baxter, vaccination expert and Consultant in Communicable Disease Control at Stockport Health Authority, 'This passive transfer of maternal antibodies does not always occur. Nor does it depend on whether the mother has high or low levels of particular antibodies. I have seen babies who have no antibodies to anything – yet both their parents had.'

In most cases, however, young babies have substantial protection against infections – not so much colds and coughs, as the viruses and bacteria causing these tend to mutate quite fast, but rather against any infectious diseases which you yourself have had at one time or another (with the exception of whooping cough). But this immunity wears off. After a few months, the protection they get from you against diphtheria, tetanus and polio fades. By the time they are a year old (unless you are still breastfeeding), their defences against measles, mumps, polio, and rubella or German measles will have faded too – measles protection, for instance, is thought to peter out between five and seven months. These antibodies are not replaced, so from now on your baby is vulnerable to these infections. This is why there is a comprehensive immunization programme for babies and infants.

The fact that diseases which formerly killed and crippled children have largely been eradicated in countries which have had comprehensive child-hood immunization programmes is given as an excellent reason to continue to immunize. Vaccination is one of the cornerstones of modern medicine, as basic to our current approach to the prevention of infectious disease as antibiotics are to treating certain infections. There is no doubt whatsoever that it has saved many hundreds of thousands of lives over the last 50 years, and, worldwide, prevented many more cases of illness in children which might otherwise have resulted in serious, life-long side effects.

As the basic building block of the preservation of a child's good health, the vaccination programme is an immensely emotive issue, both for doctors and for parents. This is why, now questions are being asked about the effectiveness and safety of multiple routine immunization, such very strong feelings are being roused. One particular female doctor went on record in the National Childbirth Trust's magazine *New Generation* saying that *not* giving a baby every injection recommended is 'tantamount to child abuse'. Many GPs react strongly when the vaccination programme is questioned. Several have threatened to strike families off their registers if they do not have their children fully immunized. Some have actually done so.

What vaccinations should my baby have?

Doctors recommend five different sets of vaccines for your child, some as triple doses, others as a single dose. Each offers protection against a specific disease. Most of them are given by injection, either in the upper arm or outer thigh. The polio vaccine is given as drops placed on the baby's tongue. They are currently given from six weeks of age.

So what is the problem?

The possibility that vaccination may not always be a good thing for every child may come to parents as a shock. With so many other uncertainties about the best way to raise our children – do we let them cry it out if they will not sleep? When can we give them eggs? Is beef safe? Is bottle-feeding second best? Is it dangerous to have them in our beds at night? – this has always been the one thing parents have always assumed they could be quite clear about.

The medical establishment is not always right

It is worth remembering that even during the last generation many standard medical practices in the field of infant health have had to be discontinued. At the time they were carried out in good faith, but some have now been proved useless, others to be downright dangerous.

For instance, in the 1970s it was standard paediatric advice that small babies should be put down to sleep on their fronts. Yet in 1993 our own government's Back to Sleep Campaign advised that babies should sleep on their backs because of overwhelming evidence that the prone sleep position was a major factor in cot death. The cot death rate in the UK has halved as a result. Scores of thousands of antibiotics prescriptions are still given out in 1996 for infants' earache, despite the fact that it is now well accepted

Immunization schedule currently recommended
(Source: Health Education Authority 1996)

When due	Which immunizations		Type
At 2 months	Hib		One injection
	Diphtheria		
	Whooping cough	–DTP	One injection
	Tetanus		
	Polio		By mouth
At 3 months	Hib		One injection
	Diphtheria		
	Whooping cough	–DTP	One injection
	Tetanus		
	Polio		By mouth
At 4 months	Hib		One injection
	Diphtheria		
	Whooping cough	–DTP	one injection
	Tetanus		
	Polio		By mouth
At 12–15 months	Measles		
	Mumps	–MMR	One injection
	Rubella		
3–5 years (around school entry)	Diphtheria		Booster injection
	Tetanus		Booster injection
	Polio		Booster by mouth
	Measles*		Booster injection
	Mumps		
	Rubella		
Girls 10–14 years	Rubella		One injection
Girls/boys 13 years	Tuberculosis		One injection (BCG)
School leavers 15–19 years	Tetanus		One injection
	Polio		Booster by mouth

* Addition to immunisation schedule 1977

that nine out of 10 such cases is caused by a virus which would be unaffected by this type of drug, and that repeated courses of antibiotics may adversely affect a baby's gut. The practice of operating on premature and newborn babies without painkilling anasthesia because they do not feel pain as we do' was only discontinued 10 years ago, though it is now accepted as barbaric.

There are dozens of such examples. This does not necessarily mean that the medical profession makes a lot of mistakes – considering the complexity of the human body it is surprising that they do not make more than they

'It's just a teeny weeny jab . . . baby won't feel a thing . . .'

do. But it does suggest that medicine is very much an ongoing learning process for both clinicians and the consumers of healthcare services. Good medical practice means continuing to ask questions, assess practices and treatments and keep an open mind. The status quo is the starting point, not the last word.

This is why immunization deserves serious reconsideration, even from its most enthusiastic supporters. It also deserves far more space than we have room for in this book (there are several others devoted to the issue entirely – see Useful Reading page 296). However, we have tried to summarize the pro and anti blanket immunization arguments put forward by both sides, drawing up a comprehensive list of further reading and sources of information so that when you are asked to have your own child vaccinated, you will know what all the fuss is about, will have had a chance to read up on the subject, will have the ammunition to discuss the issue fully with your child's doctor, and so be able to make an informed decision, rather than an automatic one.

The compromise solution

It doesn't have to be a straight either/or choice between having your child fully vaccinated with every jab available or not allowing them to have any vaccinations at all. A small but growing number of parents is choosing a middle way. Your compromise options include:

- *Considering each immunization separately*, perhaps choosing some and not others. It makes sense to some parents, for instance, to let their child be vaccinated against diseases such as diphtheria, polio and TB, which are regarded as more severe – but not against mumps, measles and German measles, some of whose side effects can occasionally be severe but which have always generally been seen as 'ordinary' and usually fairly mild childhood illnesses.
- *Requesting each immunization be given separately*, one at a time. At two months, for instance, babies are normally given five vaccines at once (Hib, diphtheria, whooping cough, tetanus and polio), which is felt by some to be a great deal for the child's immature immune system to cope with. A paediatric immunologist or a vaccination expert like David Baxter would advise you how these vaccinations could be spaced out, and you could ask to be referred to such a doctor by your GP.
- *Beginning your children's immunization programme later* when their immune system is a little more developed. Dr David Baxter rightly points out that babies are being bombarded with bugs and potential allergens from their environment from the minute they are born and seem to manage perfectly well most of the time. But this being so, some parents wonder whether, in that case, this is the best time for their babies to cope with yet more, which are injected directly into their bodies rather than simply breathed in?
- *Assessing your child's own individual health and family history* carefully before deciding exactly which vaccines you feel would benefit them most, and which might be more likely to be problematic for them.

For instance, some mothers whose babies or families have a history of allergy, whether to a food substance or pollen, or who have other potentially allergy related problems such as asthma, rheumatoid arthritis and eczema, are opting not to have any vaccines which have been cultured in eggs, such as the measles vaccine. The reasoning behind this is that egg is in itself a common allergen for susceptible individuals, and that the introduction of even tiny amounts into a 12-month-old baby's system might encourage an exaggerated immune response to develop to a range of other substances too.

Note: Pro and con discussion has been largely limited to using the MMR vaccine as an example of the type of arguments surrounding the others. This is partly for reasons of space, but also because the childhood diseases the MMR is intended to prevent are not generally serious, and usually pose far less of a threat to a child's health than polio, diphtheria and whooping cough, which are the other major diseases vaccinated against. It is therefore the vaccine whose necessity is most often questioned, and the one there is currently the most debate about. It is also especially topical at the moment because the Department of Health is doing another blanket reimmunization of all children aged five to 16 in the autumn of 1997 – a practice which may become routine. The Department of Health is also considering introducing a measles shot for all 11-year-olds, whether they have previously had their two MMRs or not.

Note: Operation Safeguard, which is mentioned several times in the coming pages, was the campaign which reimmunized all five- to 16-year-olds with the measles and rubella (MR) vaccine, whether or not they had already had it done, or had the diseases it was intended to prevent. It was implemented at very short notice for autumn 1994, officially to avert a forthcoming measles epidemic. There were many questions raised about the need for it by pioneering publications such as *The Bulletin of Medical Ethics,* and about whether there really was an epidemic pending, and about the financial interests of the drug manufacturer that supplied the eight million doses of the vaccine – which had remained unused for a while and was approaching its sell-by date. The episode has since provided considerable material for the vaccination debate.

THE ARGUMENTS FOR VACCINATION

1. Vaccines are responsible for the eradication of dangerous infectious diseases such as polio and diphtheria.
Today's parents of young children have never known a society in which dangerous diseases like polio and diphtheria are an ever-present threat. Older health workers remember only too well when 'every street had a child with an iron lung, and every mother knew of a baby who had died of whooping cough or measles'. Because these diseases are now so rare we have forgotten what their worst results can be, and faced with the news of the possible serious side effects of vaccines, we may find it easier that we ought to shy away from the idea of vaccines altogether.

However, according to a World Health Organization report in 1974 by the Director of the Institute of Nutrition for Central America et al. ('Malnutrition & Infection – Deadly Combination') the eradication of the major infectious diseases has as much, if not more, to do with the wider availability of clean drinking water, proper sewage management and an improved diet than with vaccination programmes. The report states that 'Diet is a more effective vaccine against most of the diarrhoea, respiratory and other infectious diseases.'

2. Stop vaccinating children and the diseases will return, says the Health Education Authority.
This is true. When Sweden banned its whooping cough virus because of the unacceptably high rate of neurological difficulties it was causing, case numbers did indeed go up, which is why their Government would like to reintroduce a vaccine and are trying to produce a safer form of it. The same happened in Britain in 1975 when the rate of side effects of the whooping cough vaccine caused a drop in uptake so that only 30 per cent of children were receiving it. Two epidemics followed, with a total of 100,000 notified cases in 1977/9 and 1981/83. By 1988 vaccine uptake was back up at 73 per cent and case notifications had dropped to 5,027.

However it is also true that:

1. Epidemics of particular diseases are still tending to occur, though on a far smaller scale, even when the population has been vaccinated against them. For instance, America has recently had epidemics of measles (the most serious for decades). Despite the fact that vaccination against the disease has been implemented since 1957, cases steadily doubled from 1988 to 1989, then again from 1989 to 1990.
2. All infectious diseases appear to work on a cyclical basis anyway. They have their natural highs and lows over a number of years. Based on former outbreaks, it is possible for epidemiologists and local health workers to predict with some accuracy when the next one may be coming.
3. If children catch what used to be the common childhood diseases naturally – measles, mumps, German measles (which nearly all children would catch at some point before immunization was introduced) or whooping cough (which three-quarters of all children used to catch) – their immunity is almost always for life. These diseases are usually mild.
4. Some of these childhood diseases are also becoming less severe. This may be due to mutation over time, as with scarlet fever, which was once a potential killer and now usually appears in a mild form, rechristened scarlatina.
5. In young children, many 'childhood diseases' – such as German Measles and Mumps – usually appear only in a mild form.

3. We need to continue to vaccinate all children to preserve the 'herd immunity', otherwise the unvaccinated ones put the rest of the population at risk, says the HEA.
If the majority of the population's parents has chosen to have them vaccinated, and if vaccines work, vaccinated individuals should not be at risk from unvaccinated children catching the disease and passing it on. The only people at risk of contracting the infectious diseases are those who have not been vaccinated.

An interesting point
GPs are paid bonuses to ensure as many babies as possible are vaccinated. The system is quite complex, but essentially those who achieve the upper target of 90 per cent immunization of babies within their practice receive a payment of £2,235 a year. For those who immunize 70 per cent, it is £545.

Critics of this system fear that the payments may encourage GPs to pressurize the (currently) few parents who are reluctant to have their babies immunized, preferring them to gain their immunity to the ordinary infectious diseases of childhood such as German measles naturally. They also fear it might discourage a GP from retaining a family which did not want its children immunized on their register of patients, lest that family suffer more illness – or influenced other parents too, preventing the GP from reaching his or her immunization targets.

THE HOLES IN THE PRO-VACCINATION ARGUMENT

The following quotations are taken from the main points in the Health Education Authority's parents handbook 'A Guide to Childhood Immunizations' (June 1996) unless otherwise stated.

1. 'Vaccines provide almost all children with long-lasting and effective protection.'
- If this is the case, why does America's Centre for Disease Control (CDC) in Atlanta estimate that between 5 and 15 per cent of children they had vaccinated between 1957 and 1967 had no immunity?
- If the MMR's protection lasts, or if it 'takes' and is effective, why did Britain's Operation Safeguard in autumn 1994 want to immunize all of our seven million five- to 16-year-olds with the MMR vaccine, including the 60 per cent who had already had the shot or had had the disease naturally?
- Why is the British Government implementing a further MMR immuniz-ation campaign, again for all five- to 16-year-olds, when virtually all the children will now already have been vaccinated twice, once between the ages of 12 to 18 months, and again in 1994? The MMR is meant to be a one-off immunization jab.
- Why, if immunization lasts and is effective, are outbreaks of these diseases still occurring regularly?

There are many examples (see also Further Reading) but they include:

1. There was an outbreak of measles in 1986 at Corpus Christi in Texas where 99 per cent of the children had already been vaccinated against it and 95 per cent were meant to be fully immune (*New England Journal of Medicine*, 1987).
2. In 1987, the CDC reported 2,440 cases of measles in previously vaccinated children (*Paediatric Infant Diseases Journal* Newsletter, September 1987).
3. According to Professor Gordon Stewart, formerly of the University of Glas-gow's Department of Community Medicine, amongst British whooping cough cases in 1974/5 and 1978/9 (and in 1974 in Canada and America), between a third and a half of all those who succumbed to it had been fully vaccinated.

Theories as to why this happened include:

- The immunity conferred by the vaccine just wears off in time. 'I wouldn't be at all surprised, and this means that people will need regularly revaccin-ating as they get older,' comments Dr Pan Chakravanti, Consultant at the Department of Paediatric Immunology at the Portland Hospital for Women & Children in London.
- Some versions of the vaccine are less stable than others.
- The shots were given too early, or were given when the child was unwell.

'The protective immunization effect [of whooping cough] wears off rapidly. The average age of incidence has shifted upwards,' according to Douglas Jenkins, a GP from Keyworth in Nottinghamshire, who has spent the last 20 years studying whooping cough in general practice.

2. *'If the child does develop any of the diseases some time after being immunized, it is likely to be in a milder form.'*
All of the formerly common childhood diseases – measles, mumps, rubella or chickenpox are far more severe if caught as a teenager or young adult.
What the MMR vaccination at 12 to 15 months is currently doing is:

• Shifting the age at which children are likely to catch the 'childhood' diseases (if they are going to) upwards, so if they do catch it, they get it more severely and have a correspondingly greater risk of suffering from the more serious complications.
• Creating a new population of young mothers who may not pass measles antibodies on to their bodies. Today, the greater proportion of younger mothers (up to the age of 29) have had the measles vaccine, and so have lower levels of antibodies to pass on to their babies than they would if they'd caught measles naturally, according to the Unité d'Immunologie at the Pasteur Institute in Paris, leaving them unprotected at the most vulnerable time in their lives. They cannot be given any artificial protection until they reach of the age of 12 to 15 months.

3. *'The risk of harmful, lasting complications from the vaccines themselves is extremely small indeed. The risks of harmful effects from the diseases themselves are much higher and more serious.'*
(*Note:* Britain's Chief Medical Officer has put the chances of measles vaccine causing encephalitis or brain inflammation as 'one in a million'.)

• *The risk of serious side effects may not be as small as we are led to believe.* The Swedish Government dropped the whooping cough vaccine because of fears of its side effects several years ago. However, they are trying hard to develop alternatives to the live whooping cough vaccine. The Japanese

---

Chickenpox vaccine
The Department of Health is, at the time of writing, considering introducing the vaccine for chickenpox into the UK. Already in use in America, it does not yet have a licence for use in this country except on a named patient basis. Chickenpox is a characteristically mild childhood disease, but can be severe if caught in adulthood. The vaccine's staying power and effectiveness level is uncertain. If it either fails to 'take' (produce an immune response) or wears off after a few years, as can happen with the MMR, this could lead to a shift from mild infant and childhood chickenpox to more severe teenage and adult forms of the disease.

Ministry of Health gives parents the choice of whether to give their babies the formerly compulsory childhood immunizations such as measles and polio.

• *The long-term side effects of vaccines against common childhood diseases have not been researched.*

After Operation Safeguard in 1994, the Public Health Laboratory of Britain announced that in order to assess the long-term effects of the vaccines they would be following up all the children who had had this second MMR jab for the rest of their lives. This is exactly the type of study needed to determine whether these vaccines are, indeed, safe and effective.

The safety/side effects part of it was stopped after three weeks. According to the Public Health Laboratory, this was all that was necessary, any side effects of the MMR vaccine would have shown up by then. Concerned GPs and specialists feel this is inadequate, because if no one monitors to see if there are any side effects beyond this point, it is not possible to say with any confidence that there aren't any because some may take months or even years to show up.

• *Clinical studies have repeatedly confirmed that the side effects of drugs (and vaccines are drugs) are often not reported to the administering doctor.*

Different sets of clinical research have variously reported the number of adverse reactions getting reported back to the Committee on the Safety of Medicines as between 13 and 25 per cent.

Doctors readily accept that immunizations may cause a bit of fever – and indeed parents are routinely advised to have Calpol on hand should their child develop a temperature. But that is all. Most reactions to drugs in general (average of 83 per cent) go unreported. If vaccines are regarded as drugs, it is not unreasonable to assume a similar low level of reporting any side effects. Even if they are reported to a GP by a parent, the doctor must then fill in a 'Yellow Card' and send it off to the Committee on the Safety of Medicines. This is happening much less now that GPs are under increasingly heavy administrative pressures in their practices following the last six years' health service reforms.

Many doctors are coming under legal fire from families for failing to warn them about the potential side effects, and for the vaccine damage which they feel has been done to their children. The reactions parents attribute to vaccine damage range from children 'not being themselves since vaccination', becoming noticeably withdrawn or less sociable, catching one cold and ear infection after another, profound brain damage, MS, ME, paediatric Crohn's disease, full-blown epilepsy and acquired autism.

• *The British Government appears to be misleading parents by overstating the dangers of formerly common childhood diseases like measles and mumps.*

This is (presumably) to encourage vaccination uptake. The reason behind it is probably that to achieve the desired 'herd' immunity, 95 per cent of babies need to be immunized (whereas for some other diseases the critical mass figure is only 70 to 80 per cent). Currently the MMR uptake rate in Britain is 90.9 per cent.

Consumer watchdog observers of 1994's Operation Safeguard noted

with interest the way in which measles appeared to become more dangerous with each successive press report. In 1989 Dr Norman Begg, then
Director of the Public Health Laboratory, stated that the chances of a
child developing encephalitis – one of the most dangerous complications
of measles and the one responsible for a variety of different degrees of
brain damage and neurological impairment – was one in 5,000. As the
revaccination scheme got under way in the autumn, most newspapers and
magazines covered it, using source material from the Health Education
Authority, amongst others. A figure of one in 500 was later quoted in *The
Times*. Finally, at the height of the campaign, the *Daily Mail* said it was
one in 17.

These figures might have had something to do with the literature given
to journalists (including us) in January '94 by the HEA immunization
promotion entitled 'Immunization – facts for life'. The first item in their
Press Notes reads: 'Measles is a highly infectious disease. In one in 15
cases complications occur. These include pneumonia, convulsions and
encephalitis, a swelling of the brain.' It doesn't mention the other, far
more common and much milder complications – a sore throat or an ear
ache – which you might well see in one in 15 cases, therefore giving the
impression that the serious complications happen far more often than is
in fact the case.

This type of information is passed on by journalists – in good faith –
to their many millions of readers, without being seen to come from the
HEA's promotional campaign itself. It appears to be designed to mislead
parents deliberately by giving them the impression that these childhood
diseases are considerably more dangerous than they really are.

Not surprisingly, the campaign to persuade parents that measles is a
very dangerous disease is making its mark. In April 1994 15 per cent of
mothers polled considered it to be 'very serious'. By the end of Operation
Safeguard's advertising campaign, it was 55 per cent.

• The Department of Health appears to be playing down the extent of
serious vaccine damage in babies.

Though their own vaccine information unit told us that it had 'no idea
how many British children had received the MMR – we don't collect the
figures like that', other sources put it at around the ten million mark, plus
the seven million from the 1994 campaign, making approximately 17
million in all. The risk of vaccine-induced encephalitis is given as 'one in
a million'. If these figures are correct, there should be about 17 children
suffering the consequences of vaccine induced brain inflammation.

But there are more than this. The pressure group Justice Awareness
and Basic Support (JABS) has the names and addresses of more than 325
children whose parents believe they have suffered MMR-induced brain
damage due to encephalitis just from the MMR (never mind the standard
DPT jabs as well), plus another 170 from 1994's Operation Safeguard.
There are many different types of disorder – from epilepsy to restricted
limb movement. As not all parents are aware of JABS and therefore have
not contacted them, the real figure is likely to be higher still.

That vaccines can on occasion do long-term damage to children's health is now well established. What is currently under ferocious debate is how often this happens, to what extent, and which symptoms are produced. Some particular long-term side effects have been proven by the type of traditional, careful, published clinical research accepted by the medical profession. However, some parents are saying that their children have experienced other side effects too, some subtle, some very obvious, which have not yet been proven to have definite links with vaccines but which, anecdotally, appear significant. This type of side effect is far harder to prove, but it does provide food for thought.

THE PROVEN HEALTH PROBLEMS

The serious long-term, vaccine-linked health problems include:

Crohn's disease
This painful inflammatory gut disorder has increased in developed countries over the last 30 years. There has been a 500 per cent increase in the number of cases seen in children since the introduction of MMR.

Research from around the world has identified an association between early exposure to the measles vaccine and Crohn's. In 1995, research at the Royal Free Hospital in London showed a three times greater likelihood of Crohn's disease and a 2.5 times greater likelihood of ulcerative colitis in people who had been vaccinated against measles or had had the disease naturally. So if vaccinated, you'll definitely be exposed to this increased risk, but if not vaccinated, you may well not catch measles naturally and so you avoid an increased risk of Crohn's.

Arthritis
Pharmaceutical giant Wellcome, the MMR vaccine manufacturers, note in the 'Datasheet Compendium', which is one of the reference books for British doctors on drugs and their side effects, that the German measles component of its vaccine causes arthritis in 3 per cent of children. The company admits to a similar side effect for 12 to 20 per cent of the adult women who are reimmunized pre-pregnancy as part of a preconceptual care programme, or who come into contact with German measles when pregnant. It also adds that this vaccine-induced form of arthritis 'may persist for a matter of months, or on rare occasions, years'.

Childhood diabetes
Following New Zealand's drive since 1988 to get its children vaccinated against Hepatitis B, there has been a 60 per cent increase in cases of childhood diabetes. The key factor, according to research published in the *New Zealand Medical Journal* (24 May 1996) seems to be the timing of immunization. The Baltimore-based Classen Immunotherapies Inc. research institute, which

investigated this, suggests that the vaccine appears to increase the risk of diabetes if it is begun after six weeks.

Seizures
In 1994 Britain's Public Health Laboratory had completed research studies on three health districts, examining hospital admission rates with severe vaccine reactions. They found that children who had had their MMR were three times more at risk of seizures, and two-thirds of those seizures were directly related to the measles component of the vaccine. This mirrored research carried out by America's Centre for Communicable Diseases in Atlanta.

Multiple Sclerosis
The link between measles vaccine and MS has in fact been properly researched, but is seldom mentioned.

The first work to connect the two was carried out by Professor Charles Poser at Harvard Medical School in Boston, beginning in the late 1960s, and is ongoing today. There are tiny molecules of a substance called myelin, the protective sheath covering the nerves, present in live measles vaccine. When babies are born they have very little myelin, but begin making it in earnest around the age of 15 months, completing the task by the time they are 10 years old. In some cases a baby's body responds to the vaccination by attacking the myelin they themselves are making as if it were a foreign substance – because myelin antibodies have been injected into their system with the vaccine. This can lead to the progressive nervous system degeneration characteristic of MS.

WHAT YOU CAN DO

Parents' action plan
Vaccination is an immensely complex issue and there are no straightforward solutions. Questioning the usual medical thinking on vaccinations is still seen by the establishment and mainstream press as a radical area.

Whether or not to have your own child fully vaccinated as recommended is something that no responsible parent can afford not to question – whatever your final decision. It's not something that health workers, whether they are local practice nurses, health visitors, GPs or top consultant paediatricians and immunologists, should ignore either, as it's a major, though discomfiting, issue that is not going to go away.

1. Learn as much about the subject as you can
Read up on it, talk to information groups such as The Informed Parent, and try to get a general picture of the issue.

Though there is a fair degree of pressure to get babies started on the immunization programme from two months of age, you are not necessarily putting your child at risk if you take another month or two to become as informed as you feel you need to be to make your decision.

2. Talk to a homeopath about the alternatives
Ask what additional support they could offer your child if they were being immunized in the usual way.

There are two main types of homeopath:

- Medical practitioners who are doctors (usually GPs) who have also had standard training in homeopathy. They tend to belong either to the Faculty of Homeopathy or to the British Homeopathic Association, and generally have a six-month-long training in homeopathy.

  Both officially agree that the vaccination programme as it currently stands should be kept to, but the medical homeopaths own professional association says its members would be prepared to treat children homeopathically as and when they encountered any infectious childhood diseases. A few might also be prepared to treat infants preventatively for the infectious childhood diseases using a homeopathic form of immunization. There has been no research on how effective this is.
- Non-medically trained homeopaths who have a four-year training in homeopathy but are not qualified as doctors as well.

These homeopaths would belong to the Society of Homeopaths or the United Kingdom Homeopathic Medical Association, or to the Institute of Complementary Medicine. They have a more flexible approach than medically trained homeopaths, and are more willing to:
— Support parents with as much information surrounding vaccination as possible so they can come to their own decision in an informed way.
— Treat homeopathically any of the infectious childhood diseases encountered as they come up, just as they would treat any other disease.
— Practise homeopathic immunization or prevention of the common infectious diseases. Again it must be emphasized that there is no published research showing that homeopathic immunization works. However, many homeopaths say they have carried out this type of treatment and feel confident that it does.

3. Consider each vaccine separately
Ask your GP for the data sheets on each vaccine. Precisely how effective is it? How safe is it?

They should be able to give you a copy, but if they seem unwilling or unable to do so, you can get them from your local pharmacist at the chemist.

4. Would you know how to identify a bad reaction to a vaccine?
The most common bad reactions – they are certainly not 'normal', as parents are often told – include prolonged high temperature, not wanting to be touched and high-pitched screaming (suggesting a degree of brain inflammation or encephalitis). A rash is another common reaction. If your baby

does have one or more of these reactions, make absolutely sure the GP reports it to the Committee on the Safety of Medicines via the Yellow Card system. Ask to see a copy of this to make sure it has been done.

5. If your child has had a bad reaction to the last vaccination, make sure it is properly investigated

Various approaches could be offered, including giving the next vaccines singly, or even leaving one or more out altogether.

'It is important to seek expert medical advice with a view to having them separated out,' explains Dr Baxter. 'Ask your GP to refer your child to a consultant immunologist with a special interest in vaccination.' Separating them is perfectly possible to do as the vaccines originally come as individual doses, but it tends not to be offered because it is more time-consuming to do and therefore not considered cost effective.

It is important not to continue with any further shots of any vaccine which has caused your child problems until this investigation has been carried out and you are happy with the advice you have been given. If you are not, contact one of the vaccination help and support groups (see Useful Addresses, page 295).

6. Does your child have any allergy-related disorders such as asthma or eczema?

If they do, they may react more strongly to vaccination.

If there is any history of these types of problems – including rheumatoid arthritis – in your child's immediate family (parents, grandparents, uncles or aunts), you may want to think carefully about certain shots.

The suggested connection between an allergy history and a bad vaccine reaction appears to be supported by an ongoing survey of 700 families who have contacted the organization Justice Awareness and Basic Support (JABS) on behalf of their children, whom they feel have been harmed by the routine childhood vaccines. The survey is, amongst other things, looking to see if there are any common factors for the children who react so badly to immunization.

There are. Two-thirds reported a history of allergy and disorders which are often allergy-related, such as asthma and eczema or hay fever in their family or in the child itself. 'It may be that children who are more susceptible to allergy are more likely to have problems with some of the vaccines,' suggests coordinator Jackie Fletcher.

Herself the mother of a four-and-a-half-year-old son who was brain-damaged in 1992 by a vaccine, Mrs Fletcher states that the organization is not antivaccination as such: 'They have been developed for good reasons – but we must get back to treating children as individuals. You choose a washing powder, which only affects the surface of the child's skin, carefully to eliminate any problematic elements. Why not take the same care with your child's vaccines, which are injected right underneath their skin?'

7. Make sure your child is well enough to have their vaccination

If, for instance, they have a cold or even a runny nose, this suggests they are already fighting off one type of bacteria or virus. You may prefer to wait until they are clear before introducing anything further for their immune system to deal with.

8. Ask yourself whether your child really needs this particular vaccine at the moment

This could apply, for instance, to tetanus, usually given with the diphtheria and whooping cough vaccines at two, three and four months. Children can contract tetanus from soil, rusty nails and animal bites. Is your baby, constantly being carried or lying in a cot, pram or bouncing seat, really at risk from these things just at the moment? Would it be more suitable to have it when they are able to crawl and more likely to come into contact with tetanus-carrying agents, and have a stronger immune system to deal with the effects of the vaccination?

9. Boost your child's general health as much as possible

A good diet, sufficient exercise and possibly childhood vitamin supplements will help.

10. Consider allowing your child to catch mild childhood diseases naturally while they are young

If mild diseases such as chickenpox or German measles are around and your child has not been vaccinated against them, they will probably experience these diseases mildly, and develop strong, lifelong immunity. Depending on how robust your child is, they should not be subjected to these diseases if possible below the age of about 18 months.

The same could be done for measles, but because this can occasionally become serious, consider asking a good homeopath for help after exposure to the virus and during the time when your child has the disease (see Measles in The Common Childhood Illnesses, page 222).

If they catch measles naturally, give Vitamin A – but take care as it can be toxic in overdose. Research carried out with pre-school Indian children by Boston's New England Medical Centre suggested that Vitamin A ought to be given a children wherever there was evidence of deficiency or the likelihood of complications from measles. Clinical nutritionists (medical doctors trained in nutrition) also recommend it. Contact the Society for the Promotion of Nutritional Therapy (see Useful Addresses page 295).

11. If you do decide you don't want your baby to have one or more of the standard infant vaccines, ask your local Family Health Authority to tag your child's records.

Every baby is registered on their Birth Computer. If there's a note in your file, you will not be sent continuous reminders or receive visits and calls from your health visitor about having the shots.

What if your GP will not accept your child as a patient without full vaccination?

This has happened on occasion, though the threat of it alone is more common. It will probably continue to happen more often as the vaccination debate gathers momentum. Your GP has the right, just as you do, to change you to another doctor without needing to give you reasons, or to remove a patient from his or her list. However, unwillingness or outright refusal to vaccinate is not officially considered a valid reason for a GP to remove anyone from their patient list. According to the British Medical Association, the reason for a GP dropping parents must be 'if relations between the two have irrevocably broken down'. The Chief Medical Officer Dr Kenneth Calman went on public record on national television in 1995 (*Newsnight*) that 'for a parent to be struck off for the vaccination issue is not acceptable'.

Your local Family Health Authority is obliged to find you another GP if your current one no longer wishes to be responsible for you.

USEFUL ADDRESSES

Association of Parents of Vaccine-Damaged Children, 2 Church Street, Shipston-on-Stour, Warwickshire. Tel: 01608 661595.

The British Homeopathic Association, 27a Devonshire Street, London W1N 1JR. Tel: 0171 935 2163.

Medically qualified homeopaths.

The Health Education Authority, Hamilton House, Mabledon Place, London WC1H 9TX. Tel: 0171 383 3833.

A Government-funded organization giving information on all aspects of health, including the recommended childhood vaccinations.

The Informed Parent, PO Box 870, Harrow, Middlesex HA3 7UW. Tel: 0181 861 1022.

Promotes awareness and understanding of childhood immunization, to help parents make a fully informed choice.

JABS (Justice Awareness and Basic Support), 1 Gawsworth Road, Goldborne, Warrington, Cheshire WA3 3RF. Tel: 01942 713565.

An organization which supports and informs parents whose children's health has been harmed by vaccination.

The Society of Homeopaths, 2 Artizan Road, Northampton NN1 4HU. Tel: 01604 214000.

The British non-medical (professional) homeopaths' organization.

The Society for the Promotion of Nutritional Therapy, PO Box 47, Heathfield, East Sussex TN21 8ZX. Tel: 01435 867007.

Contact for nearest professionally qualified nutritional therapist.

INTERNATIONAL ORGANIZATIONS

Vaccination, Information & Alternatives Resource Group, 49 Benlamond Avenue, Toronto, Ontario M4E 1YB, Canada.

National Vaccine Information Center, 512 West Maple Avenue, Suite 206, Vienna, Vancouver, VA22180. Tel: +1 703 938 0342.

Immunization Awareness Society Inc., PO Box 56 048 Dominion Road, Auckland, New Zealand.

Australian Council for Immunization Inc., PO Box 177, Artarmon, NSW 2064. Fax: +2 419 2573.

USEFUL READING

Adverse Events Associated with Childhood Vaccines, Institute of Medicine, National Academy Press, Washington, 1994
'Health – the only immunity', Ian Sinclair, 1995, available from The Informed Parent organization.
   This Australian book gives a clear explanation of how to prevent childhood illness and keep children in optimum physical health without vaccines and drugs.
Immunisation Against Infectious Disease, Dept of Health, HMSO, 1992. Available from libraries.
   This is the textbook for GPs, health visitors and other primary healthcare workers on the immunization programme as it currently stands in the UK. A new edition should have been published some time ago, but the Department of Health has not yet decided what to say about the MMR.
'Mass Immunisation – The Point in Question', Trevor Gunn, available from The Informed Parent for £3.50.
   A booklet by a homeopath, which suggests vaccines are not as safe as originally thought.
'Measles: the disease, the vaccine, the homeopathic treatment', R. D. Micklem, available from the Helios Pharmacy (01892 537254)
Modern Vaccines: A Lancet *Review*, ed. Edward Arnold, 1990
   This is an overview of clinical research into vaccination published up until 1990 in the premier British clinicians journal the *Lancet*. It will be rather out of date by now as around 100 papers are being published on different aspects of vaccination – from the trial development of vaccines against cervi-

cal cancer and herpes or HIV to chickenpox and measles – worldwide. But it is very valuable historically.

The Role of Medicine, Thomas McKeown, Blackwell, 1979

This looks at the changing aspects of disease and the causes of death over the last few centuries – and at the impact of vaccination, improved diet and better sanitation.

'Vaccination – a sacrament of modern medicine', Richard Moskowitz, 1991, available from the Society of Homeopaths.

Vaccination and Immunisation: dangers, delusions and alternatives, Leon Chaitow, Minerva Books, 1991

'Vaccines – are they really safe and effective?', Neil S. Miller, New Atlantean Press, 1993

Cot Death – Helping to Keep Your Baby Safe

Cot death is the sudden and unexpected death of a baby, for no apparent reason. It is the major cause of death in infants between the ages of one week and 12 months. The commonest time for it to happen is in the winter when a baby is between two and four months old, but the 'winter high' is no longer as pronounced as it used to be – approximately 60 per cent of cot deaths now fall in this group. Eighty per cent of all cases occur between one and six months of age. Cot death affects a slightly greater number of boys than girls (60:40), and premature babies are more at risk. It does not run in families, and research shows that less than one per cent of cases are due to inherited disorders, such as enzyme deficiency.

If a family has suffered the loss of one baby by cot death, there is only a slightly increased risk of it ever happening to them again. Out of every 500 subsequent babies born for former cot-death parents, 495 will survive and grow up happily and healthily.

Going in to pick up your baby from their cot and finding they are no longer alive is every parent's worst nightmare. Luckily cot death *is* very rare – it affected only 531 babies in 1994. Twenty-two of those babies were over 12 months old. But for any mother or father, and also for the doctors researching the syndrome's causes, this is still 531 too many. And unusual or not, the possibility of cot death remains at the back of most parents' minds, and is probably the reason why they find they repeatedly check up on their new baby to the point of obsession, especially if the infant is unwell, hovering anxiously over the cot or basket several times during the day and night just to check that they are still breathing.

Though most babies who are victims of cot death are indeed found in their cots, it is a slightly misleading term because some parents have also experienced an apparently well baby dying in their arms during a cuddle, in the pushchair, or even on a journey in the car, so doctors have another phrase for it – Sudden Infant Death Syndrome (SIDS). The common denominator apart from the babies' age is the suddenness and unexpectedness of the death, and the fact that no obvious reason could be found for it, which makes parents' trauma and distress even greater.

Risk factors

There is no single cause of SIDS, but experts have found several different risk factors which are worth avoiding. And knowing there is plenty that you can do to help protect your baby can help you feel more confident as a parent. Risk factors within your control include:

- *Smoking during pregnancy.*
- *Smoking around the baby after they are born.*
- *The baby's sleeping position.*

The Department of Health's 'Back to Sleep' campaign and The Foundation for the Study of Infant Deaths' (FSID) 'Reduce the Risk' campaign, which advised against putting a baby to sleep on its front, have brought cot death rates in the UK tumbling down to a third of their former level (0.7 per cent per 1,000 live births compared with 2.3 per cent before). Unfortunately, by the end of 1994 the fall had stopped. This suggests that sleep position was an important part of the puzzle, but that there are other elements which remain a problem too.

- *Overheating.*
- *Infections and illness.*
- *The baby's mattress.* An oversoft mattress, a secondhand mattress, or the chemicals in a mattress can all be risk factors.
- *Feeding.* Some studies have found breastfeeding has a protective effect, but the evidence is very muddled because several research studies contradict each other. See What you can do, below.
- *Where your baby sleeps.* Some studies suggest that if your baby sleeps in bed with you this has a protective effect against SIDS by making your baby's breathing patterns more stable. However, others suggest bed sharing is a risk factor in itself. See What you can do, below.

What you can do

There may be no surefire guaranteed ways to eliminate cot death entirely yet, but there are several things you can do to considerably reduce the risk of it happening to you.

1. Lay your baby down to sleep on their back or side. Use a firm mattress and no pillow.

This is the safest position for your baby to sleep in, and the 1992 campaign to promote it in Britain cut cot death rates by more than two thirds. No one is quite sure why it helps but theories include:

- If very young babies sleep on their tummies (prone) with their head to one side, they may have the neck strength to turn their heads face down into the mattress, but they may not, especially if the mattress is very soft, be able to turn their heads back again if they are finding breathing difficult.

This could lead to suffocation. For the same reason, babies should not be given pillows.

- Lying prone with their face close to the mattress may increase the risk of them being in close contact with any germs which might be breeding in the slightly damp warmth created by the baby's body temperature. These could encourage both respiratory and general infections. Both breathing problems and having a temperature have been implicated in a raised risk of cot death. The latter is also more likely if the baby is also becoming too hot, and therefore sweaty.

Propping your baby up when they have a cold
If your baby does need propping up at night because a really bad cold is stuffing up their breathing tubes, do not pile pillows into the cot and lay the baby against them.
    Either:

- Raise up the mattress by putting some phone directories or a wad of rolled up towel *underneath* it, and/or raise the head of their bed on some piles of big books. Then put your baby in the bed so they are sleeping in the Feet to Foot position currently being recommended by the Foundation for the Study of Infant Deaths (see below).
    Or:
- Take your baby into your bed, prop *yourself* up on a few pillows so you are lying with your head and shoulders raised, and lay them, still on their back or side, with their head on your chest, feet pointing down towards your lap.
    If your doctor tells you that for medical reasons your baby needs to sleep on their side, place one of their arms in front of them to stop them rolling onto their tummy, and perhaps a small rolled-up towel at their back.

When prone sleeping is helpful
There are sometimes certain reasons why your midwife or GP may advise you to put your baby to sleep on their front:

- Babies who suffer from gastro-oesophageal reflux should sleep on their tummies with their head elevated at an angle of 30° as they face the side.
- Premature babies in special care units in hospitals are placed tummy downwards, as this increases breathing efficiency in premature babies.
- Babies with small or imperfectly-formed jawbones or other structural airway abnormalities should also sleep prone, but your doctor will advise you about this. If they seem unsure, or if you are, call the FSID helpline for advice (see Useful Addresses page 307).

2. Use the 'Feet to Foot' sleep position.
Make the bed up as if it is only half its real length and tuck your baby in halfway down, so that their feet are almost touching the bottom. This way they are far less likely to slide down the bed and will avoid the risk of their

Babies who sleep on their backs seem to gain other health benefits too. According to the ongoing British study 'Children of the 90s' (which is following 14,000 children as they grow up), back sleeping babies need fewer antibiotics, have fewer earaches, fewer temperatures and need to be visited less often by their GP at home than front or side-sleepers.

bedclothes ending up over their head, which could cause overheating or straightforward suffocation. As a double safety check, it is very important to tuck in the bedclothes so they do not come up any further than the baby's shoulders.

3. Keep your baby's mattress clean and well aired.
Wash it every couple of months. Wipe down with liquid Fairy or Dettox, wash with very hot water and dry well. This will help stop a build-up of sweat, urine, skin flakes and all the other substances which potentially problem-causing bacteria and fungi enjoy. The same applies if you have a pram with a wipe-down mattress in it. There is a type of mattress by Mothercare called Sleep*right* which is especially easy to clean as its top section zips off, and you can wash it in your washing machine at 40 °C.

If you have a Moses basket for your baby to sleep in for the first few months, always buy the mattress new if you possibly can (they are not PVC-covered and can't be given a good wipe down). If you do get a second-hand one, wash it as well as you can in very hot water and Dettox. Then wash off all traces of detergent and dry well. Cover in one or even two stretch cotton towelling sheets or a couple of cotton blankets. The same goes for secondhand wash-and-wipe pram mattresses. The concern is that, after being slept on, wetted, and sweated on for months or even years, it may harbour germs and fungi, which may be harmful to your baby. Don't be tempted to put it in the washing machine, though, as it will probably begin to disintegrate.

4. Ensure your baby never gets too hot.
Several reports suggest that too warm a room, too much wrapping and too many bedclothes are risk factors, but especially for babies over 10 weeks old. The fact that slightly more cot deaths still happen in winter may be partly to do with the fact that parents put more blankets on babies' beds in winter, whether or not the house temperature remains largely unchanged thanks to central heating. It may also be linked to the fact that babies tend to catch more infections in winter, and many parents wrap them up more snugly when they are not well – sometimes a bit too snugly.

Keep your baby comfortable and cosy but not too hot:

• Put a thermometer on the wall of their bedroom and ensure the room temperature remains at about 65 °F or 18.3 °C. It's only really necessary to leave the heating on all night in very cold weather.

- Do not give them a hot-water bottle or electric blanket to sleep with. A warm bottle wrapped in a towel for a little while for them to lie against to comfort earache is all right, providing you check them every half-hour or so to ensure they are not overheating.
- Babies should not sleep in thick padded or fluffy sleepsuits, as they will get too hot. A nappy, vest and babygrow are enough.
- Don't put woolly bonnets on your baby when they go to bed at night, because they lose a great deal of the excess heat they do not need via their scalps. Avoid using thick padded cot bumpers too for the same reason.
- If your baby has a temperature, they need fewer clothes. Cool them gently by taking off some of the bedding, don't wrap them up in too many clothes, and sponge their bare skin with warm water (not cold as it is too much of a shock to their systems). For more help with cooling down a feverish baby, see Fevers in The Common Childhood Illnesses, page 208.
- Although you certainly do need to wrap babies up warmly to go out, especially in cold weather, *always* remove their hats and extra outdoor clothing as soon as you are inside a building (whether it is a shop, café or your own house), a warm car, train or bus, even if it is only for a short period – and *even if your baby is asleep.*

  If you really do not want to wake them and feel that removing any of their clothes would do so, place them, if possible, still sleeping and wrapped up in their pram outside the back door to your patio or garden, if you have one, with the door wedged open so you can hear them if they wake.
- In your baby's cot, go for layers of cotton baby blankets, with cotton or polycotton sheets. Baby duvets, sheepskins and babynests are such good insulators that they all carry a risk of overheating.

5. Don't smoke, and avoid smoky atmospheres.

Smoking is physically addictive and so can be very hard to give up, especially if you are stressed and tired or worried. Unfortunately, if mothers smoke during their pregnancy, their babies do run a higher risk of cot death. Any smoking anywhere near the baby increases the risk of cot death.

- Try to give up smoking if you possibly can. If you feel that you might like some help with this, call Quitline (see Useful Addresses, page 307), who can offer a great deal of practical advice, and find out where your nearest stop smoking group is. Many are free, and run by local hospitals.
- If you are not able to give up, never smoke anywhere near your baby and do not let your partner or visitors do so either. If you or anyone else in your house needs a cigarette, either go into the next room to have one, then open the windows to disperse the smoke, or nip outside. If you smoke while pushing the buggy along or sitting peacefully on a bench in a park, this will not affect your baby as the smoke disperses rapidly in the open air.

6. Keep a close eye on your baby if they are unwell
There is not much you can do to prevent a tiny baby catching coughs and colds apart from keeping them out of the way of others who have them, especially when they are between the ages of two and five months. However, you certainly can keep a sharp eye on your baby's progress if they have an illness which either gives them a temperature or causes them problems with breathing – which includes anything from an ordinary cold to bronchiolitis.

If your baby is not only unwell, but does not 'seem right' to you, contact your GP right away. This goes for night-time as well as daytime. A visit may not be necessary, but you can explain your baby's symptoms over the phone, and exactly why you are concerned, and the doctor will decide whether they need to come and see you or whether you need to go into their surgery.

Never be afraid that you are bothering your GP, despite the posters in GPs' surgeries about 'thinking twice before you call your doctor' and 'Can't it wait till morning?' The health service gives top priority to all children, especially new babies, and any good GP would rather be called up a hundred times over about a baby who was not in danger than miss a single one who really was.

It is important to give your baby plenty of fluids if they are not well. Even if they are sleeping a great deal, wake them regularly for a drink.

When to call your doctor
The following are all signs that your baby may be seriously unwell:

- An unusually pitched cry, either high or weak.
- Being less responsive or less active than is usual for them.
- Being floppier than usual.
- Has a high temperature, or is sweating.
- Appears very pale all over.
- Is finding breathing difficult – seems to be sucking in the upper tummy area and/or between the ribs as they draw in each breath, are grunting as they draw breath, or their chest is barely moving at all as they breathe (which suggests very little air is finding its way into their lungs).
- Takes less than half their usual volume of fluids, and passes far less urine than is usual for them.
- Vomits greenish fluid.
- Their stools contain blood.
- Has had a fit, but failed to recover from it fully.

If your GP cannot come right away, and you are not reassured by speaking to them on the phone, go straight to the nearest hospital casualty unit where you will be seen very promptly.

7. Breastfeeding.
Breastfeeding may well help reduce the risk of cot death – certainly the existing evidence has convinced other countries such as New Zealand (where breastfed babies had only a third as many cot deaths as bottle-fed babies)

> **When to call 999**
> - Their breathing stops.
> - They turn bluish.
> - They are unresponsive, and show no apparent awareness of what is happening around them.
> - They cannot be woken up.

to advise mothers to feed their babies themselves to help reduce the risk. Large-scale studies from America's National Institute of Child Health & Human Development also found there were fewer cases of SIDS in breastfed babies.

The protective effect may be because breast milk, as well as being the perfect form of nutrition for babies, also contains antibodies to infection which are passed on to your baby. If they are less prone to infections, and therefore less prone to temperatures and respiratory problems, this cuts down two of the important risk factors for cot death. Babies are less likely to have an allergy to anything in your breast milk than they are to formula milk, and this low 'allergenicity' may help keep their breathing passages clearer and blockage free. Breastmilk also contains the hormone progesterone – studies show breastfed babies have a higher level of it in their bloodstreams than bottle-fed babies – and this is, amongst other things, a breathing stimulant.

The very closeness of mother and baby during breastfeeding has such a nurturing and positive effect that it helps sick babies get better faster (this is often observed in premature or sick babies on hospital wards) and may also help prevent well babies becoming ill.

Breastfed babies are also more likely to sleep in bed with or right next to their mothers as it's much easier to feed a baby at night this way. Breastfeeding mothers are also a bit more likely than bottle-feeding mothers to be comfortable with natural parenting – what American paediatrician Professor Bill Sears of the University of Southern California School of Medicine calls attachment parenting. This essentially involves keeping your baby close to you at all times, perhaps carrying them in a sling around the house and when out and about, and feeding on demand. Both these things might have a protective effect against illness in general, and against SIDS.

Britain's official guidelines on avoiding SIDS do not include advising breastfeeding as a protective measure, as UK experts feel much of the available evidence is too confusing. In Hong Kong, for instance, where almost all babies are happily bottle-fed, the number of SIDS deaths is still very low. Researchers feel it is the entire package of precautions rather than just breastfeeding alone which has the protective effect.

8. Sleep right alongside your baby – or consider having them in your bed – for the first six months.
This can have several advantages. Medical anthropologist James McKenna of Pomona College in Claremont, USA, points out that in Sweden, the Netherlands, Israel, Switzerland and Japan, babies from certain social groups

sleep in their parents' beds or rooms as a matter of course. What is more, these countries all have low levels of infant death from all causes, including SIDS.

One reason may be that the babies' breathing is stimulated by that of their parents during the night. McKenna suggests that the rhythm and touch factors probably play an important part in this, but that it is also likely that the baby will be breathing in the carbon dioxide their mother and father exhale, an important stimulant for taking the next breath in.

One of co-sleeping's positive effects on a baby's ill health may be that they are kept warm. This is not promoted as a protective measure against SIDS in this country as experts fear that a baby might well become too hot (a major SIDS risk factor) because of the extra body heat. However, child sleep specialists such as Dr David Haslam suggest that all you need to do is ensure the baby does not wear too many clothes – just a nappy plus cotton Babygro, no extra vest or cardigan, and certainly not a padded sleepsuit, and that you do not put your baby in your bed in a padded baby nest. He also adds that there is no danger of parents inadvertently squashing the baby during the night either, unless they have been drinking heavily, or have taken drugs which dull their awareness, such as sleeping tablets or rec-reational drugs with a sedative effect. Sleeping parents tend to remain natur-ally aware of a small body next to them.

Then there is the constant love, parental closeness and protection which the baby would be conscious of all through the night. If this can encourage children who are unwell to get better faster and comfort those who are miserable, what could it not do for the healthy baby to help prevent them from becoming ill? (See Help Your Baby Sleep Through the Night, pages 78–82.)

Baby breathing alarms – are they worth having?
The FSID does not recommend that monitors are used for babies unless it is under a paediatrician's supervision.

There are three main types:

- Small sensor pads are attached to a baby's stomach, or on an elastic belt which can be slipped on over clothing. They detect pressure changes due to movement (i.e. the baby's breathing).
- The baby lies on a battery or mains-operated pressure pad or mattress which detects changes in the distribution of their weight due to breathing movements.
- Two electrodes are attached to the baby's chest and a mains-operated electronic monitor which records the small electrical current changes caused by the baby's breathing movements.

All will ring an alarm or flash a light when these breathing movements stop for more than around 20 seconds.

Other varieties use a heat probe attached to the baby's skin, or measure the oxygen content of their blood with a clip, or detect airflow through the baby's nose, or monitor heart rate instead. There is so far no good impartial evidence that any one type is more effective than any other.

For parents who have experienced one cot death and now have a new baby, or for parents very aware of the possibility of cot death and wishing to do everything possible to avoid it, these monitors can offer some reassurance. The drawbacks are that:

- Even if little or no oxygen is reaching the baby's lungs because of an obstruction in their windpipe, the slight breathing movements may be enough to ensure the alarm does not ring.
- They are likely to give a great many heart-stopping false alarms, because other body movements such as twitching or increased heartbeat, which are nothing to do with breathing, can continue to stimulate the monitor so it does not ring.
- Some parents find they are so anxious for their baby's safety that they become dependent on the monitor and may refuse to stop using it even when the baby is well past the age when cot death may occur. Others find they come to rely so much on the monitor's reassurance that they do not spot other signs of illness.
- Sadly, a baby whose breathing ceases and then is revived might still have sustained brain damage due to oxygen starvation.

Alarms cannot necessarily do anything to change the cot death rate. There are over 50,000 of them in use in American homes, but there has been no decline in US cot deaths since their introduction. And a study of these monitors by the FSID in conjunction with paediatricians around the country found that, of 130 monitor users, 16 per cent experienced a baby dying even despite using the monitor.

Whether to monitor or not is very much a matter of your own personal choice and what you would feel most comfortable with, and surveys suggest that 96 per cent of paediatricians will make one available to parents if they ask. They can also be bought commercially (and expensively) or hired via the FSID. The latter also has a scheme called CONI (Care of the Next Infant) which operates in conjunction with the district health authorities, and offers parents a total package of general support including the choice of a breathing monitor for their next baby.

Helpline support

If you are a parent, relative, carer or friend who has been affected by the cot death of a baby, ordinary words will never describe just how you felt at the time or even some time later – and few other people can imagine it. Many people in this situation have found it immensely comforting to speak to another parent who has had the same experience, and who is now spending their time as a counsellor to help others who have lost a child in this way. They may not only be able to offer a befriending ear, but may also be able to help with practical details and the medical issues which can surround SIDS. The number, should you or anyone you know ever need it, of the

Child Death Helpline is Freephone 0800 282986. It is open 7 p.m. to 10 p.m. every evening and 10 a.m. to 1 p.m. on Wednesdays. The FSID also has a 24-hour helpline.

USEFUL ADDRESSES

The Foundation for the Study of Infant Deaths, 14 Halkin Street, London SW1X 7DP. Tel: 0171 235 0965.

Advice, help and information on all aspects of SIDS. They also have a 24-hour Cot Death Helpline 0171 235 1721.

Parents Anonymous: 0171 263 8918.

Helpline in total confidence for parents with any type of problem, with children of all ages from newborn babies upwards.

Quitline: 0171 487 3000.

National stop-smoking help and advice organization.

Guildmaster Works (FSID Sales), Desborough Road, High Wycombe, Bucks HP11 2QA.

Supply very clear, easy to read wall thermometers for babies' rooms for £2.50.

You

Beating Exhaustion
How to Get Your Energy Back

Being tired when you have a new baby is an occupational hazard. It's unfortunate but true that unless you are very lucky a baby will deprive you of your normal quota of sleep, probably for at least the first six months of its life. If you're unlucky and have one that won't settle into a regular sleep routine, it could be for much longer.

In the first few months of motherhood most women keep going on a mixture of energy reserves, raw willpower and the novelty of looking after a newborn. But by the time the baby is six months old, continual sleep deprivation can begin to make you feel mad and bad, waking irritable and exhausted in the mornings and wiped out before lunchtime.

Feeling tired all the time isn't life-threatening, but it can be very depressing. Dr Peter White of the Department of Psychological Medicine at St Bartholomew's Hospital runs a clinic for chronic fatigue sufferers. 'Women with new babies or young children are in the highest risk group for getting TATT [tired all the time],' he says. 'All child-related activities, from pregnancy to breastfeeding, deplete your energy levels, and disturbed nights can leave you feeling totally exhausted.'

It's a tribute to mothers' extraordinary stamina and devotion that most still manage to care for their baby and themselves, keep the house in reasonable order, get some food on the table, provide clean clothes and, often, contribute to (or provide) the family income at the same time. Small wonder, though, that many find themselves often functioning on autopilot, wondering what on earth happened to their powers of clear thought and concentration and, occasionally, crying tears of pure fatigue.

The suggestions given below won't *prevent* you being tired – this is normal for the majority of new mothers at least in their baby's first year. But complete exhaustion and draining fatigue is not. It's important to know what you can do to avoid getting to this stage, both for your own and your baby's sake, and to know how to get help if you've already reached it.

It's terribly easy to fall into the trap of putting the baby's needs first, second and third, but paying attention to your own requirements – for good food, relaxation and adequate rest – isn't selfish, but vital, for you, for your baby and for the whole family.

The causes of tiredness in mothers

The main causes of fatigue among mothers with small children, says Dr Peter White, are:

- *Sleep deprivation.* This is at the top of the list, and can be caused by:
  — Lack of sleep and/or disturbed sleep because of the need to wake and feed the baby. Breastfeeding mothers report more fatigue than those who bottlefeed, irrespective of the number of times they are woken. Repeated nightwaking can also get you out of the habit of falling asleep easily when you *do* have the chance.
  — Subconsciously listening out for your baby, even when you're asleep, makes your sleep lighter and less refreshing.
  — A child with a sleep problem who continues to disturb your nights into the second year. The answer to your tiredness is to sort out the child's sleep patterns. There are voluntary sleep help organizations (such as CRY-SIS) and paediatric sleep clinics around the country which offer practical help. See Helping Your Baby to Sleep, pages 83–7.
  — A partner who snores or disturbs your sleep in addition to the baby waking you.
- *Postnatal depression.* Exhaustion and poor sleep are strongly associated with this illness. You should go and see your GP, either to rule this out as a cause of fatigue, or to get the correct help for it. (See Postnatal Depression, pages 413–29.)
- *Lack of physical fitness.* Most women become less fit during the last stages of pregnancy and don't keep up normal activity levels. Studies have shown that just one week of bedrest results in a 10 per cent loss of muscle power. Regaining your fitness with exercise will help you both to feel less tired and to re-establish normal sleeping patterns.
- *Emotional adjustments.* The many complex changes and adjustments to your lifestyle and self-image due to pregnancy, childbirth and becoming a mother put a great strain on most relationships. Problems with your partner, older children and other family members are common. Emotional difficulties are tiring and stressful and make a big contribution to fatigue. Mothers of overactive and hyperactive children or those with behavioural difficulties report more tiredness than others.
- *Over-dependence on caffeine.* This can be due to drinking too many cups of tea, coffee or cola drinks, which you may be drinking in an attempt to keep yourself going.
  A 70 kilo person (11 st) taking more than 500 mg of caffeine a day (that's around 8–10 cups of coffee) has a 50 per cent chance of caffeine poisoning.
- *Your weight.* Being either underweight or overweight can make you more tired. A study of 200 nurses at St Bartholomew's Hospital found that the more underweight they were the more fatigued they became. Being overweight will also make you more tired.
- *Poor nutrition.* Missed or skipped meals, and dieting to lose weight, can contribute to fatigue.

> **Five basic ways to fight fatigue**
> - Cut down on caffeine and alcohol or cut them out altogether. You'll probably find you feel much less tired.
> - Eat regular, nutritious meals.
> - Try to get enough sleep. Catch up with catnaps during the day if nights are disturbed.
> - Take some regular exercise – even a 20-minute walk a couple of times a week will make a lot of difference.
> - Learn a relaxation method and use it.

- *Postnatal back pain or back problems.* See Getting Rid of Back Pain, pages 396–412, for ways of dealing with this.
- *Certain medical conditions.* Thyroid function can be temporarily disturbed after the birth of a baby. Normally no treatment is needed for an underactive thyroid, but it can cause temporary fatigue. Anaemia (see If You're Anaemic, page 337) and diabetes can also add to your tiredness at this time. If you're concerned that your feelings of exhaustion could be due to more than just normal tiredness, see your GP and ask for a check up.

THE FIRST SIX MONTHS – HOW TO KEEP GOING ON LESS SLEEP

According to parents whose babies did not sleep much, the following can all be invaluable:

- *Take no notice of mothers whose babies are Good Sleepers.* Whether they are sympathetic, smug or silent they will probably have not the slightest idea of how you are feeling. Do not feel you need to ask their advice unless you really want to because it is very doubtful their baby sleeps well because of something they are doing right, and you are doing wrong. (But see Common Causes of Nightwaking page 67 to check.)
- *Catnap, catnap, catnap.* When and if your baby sleeps during the day, you do so too. Even if you only curl up on the sofa under a blanket for half an hour, it can be just about enough to top you up for the rest of the day. (See Power Napping, page 318.)
- *Let the housekeeping go for a while.* Try to resist the temptation to use your precious catnap time for catching up on any household chores that have been stockpiling. Your household can do without a tidy house/ironed clothes/interesting home/cooked food for months if necessary, but *you* cannot function without enough sleep for that long. So what if clothes are clean but slightly crumpled, and the food fishfingers with frozen peas (again)?
  This does, however, go very much against the grain for many mothers. Novelist Fay Weldon hits the nail on the head when she writes: 'Down among the women, we don't like chaos. We will crawl from our sickbeds

to tidy and define'. Lower your standards for a while. Let everyone know they cannot expect a tidy household or great food for a bit.
- *Small, regular meals of complex carbohydrates.* These will slowly and evenly release energy into your system, unlike a Penguin bar or sticky bun, which gives you a rapid lift of glucose that dies away fast.

Lack of food to turn into energy will make you feel even tireder, and it's easy to forget to eat – or just not be able to find the time – when caring for a small baby. I didn't manage to drink a cup of tea which hadn't been reheated in the microwave at least once, or eat food that was more than lukewarm, for eight months after my son Ben was born. It's especially important you eat regularly if you are breastfeeding. If you do not eat enough, the milk you produce for your baby will probably contain all the nutrients they need, but there won't be enough left for you.

Four-minute energy meals
Here are some suggestions for nutritious meals, tried and tested by mothers who report they are the easiest, fastest way to eat food to keep your energy levels up. You can even eat them on the run, or while feeding your baby.
— Porridge – topped with raisins, banana, nuts, dried apricots or all four. You can also make excellent porridge using muesli instead of plain oats.
— Muesli with a chopped banana and a handful of raisins added. Optional: spoon some thick Greek yoghurt over and top with honey and a handful of nuts.

These will keep you going for a good four hours, and don't need to be confined to breakfast.
— Dried fruit. You can keep a supply in a plastic bag in your baby's changing bag, or your handbag to eat when out and about, e.g., figs, dates, dried bananas, apricots, raisins, nuts. Or prepackaged bags of peanuts and raisins.
— Baked potatoes cooked in the microwave filled with a wedge of cheese and butter. Another filling option: tinned tuna mixed with nuts and real

---

How to keep house when you don't have the time
Here are five easy tips for keeping a household going on the barest minimum of work from you.
- Hoover floors whenever they need it.
- Make beds roughly immediately after you get up.
- Use low wattage light bulbs, or have an overheard lighting dimmer switch turned down lowish. (You don't see the dust and smears.)
These 3 make the biggest difference, to a house's appearance fastest and with least effort.
- If all your food's all burgers and TV dinners, adding just one fresh, lightly cooked or raw vegetable makes a lot of difference nutritionally. Forget puddings completely. Offer fresh fruit and pots of yoghurt instead.
- Leave all the washing up for your partner.

'My maternal instinct said "Hand the baby over – have a day off"'

mayonnaise or thick yoghurt. This will keep in the fridge for three days.
— Baked beans on toast.
— Banana and peanut butter sandwiches. Or honey and peanut butter. Use thick wholemeal bread and plenty of filling. Put with an apple and a bit of cheese they make a good stopgap lunch in just two minutes.
— Pasta. Use a quick-cook variety and top with some ready-made tomato pasta sauce from a jar. The remainder will keep in the fridge for a week after opening.

• *Identify any friends and relatives who really mean their offers of help.* Let friends who offer do babyminding for a couple of hours so you can sleep, shop, cook or whatever you want to do. Accept help to conserve what energy you have.
• *Get the odd night off.* If you feel comfortable about doing this, accept offers from someone you really trust (your childminder, your mother, sister, neighbour, good friend, nanny) to come and look after the baby occasionally for a whole night while you and your partner go and sleep at their place. Do not try and stay in the house unless impregnably earplugged up, as you will probably only wake when your baby cries anyway and feel furious because it is hard going back to sleep.
• *Try to avoid taking on anything stressful until you are getting a reasonable*

amount of sleep once more. That includes new work projects, job changes, house moves, redecorating, friends to stay, having the entire extended family over to your place for Christmas Day. It also includes holidays abroad. With a non-sleeping baby, these often turn out to be more of the same somewhere far less convenient, with too much sun. Going away can also start sleep problems off again once you thought you had them settled. Use the money for home-based treats instead.

GETTING MORE SLEEP

Good sleep is obviously central to preventing exhaustion. Yet broken nights and changed sleeping habits can mean that, when you finally do get to bed, sleep eludes you. Either you have a problem getting to sleep, or you wake in the early hours. Many mothers have trouble getting back to sleep once they've been woken for a feed or nappy change.

Sleep hygiene
In recent years the tide has turned against the use of sedatives and tranquillizers for sleep problems because of their potential for establishing dependence and the unwanted daytime side effects some cause. Good GPs will advise a programme of sleep hygiene for sleeping troubles, before they reach for a prescription pad.

The basic rules of sleep hygiene are outlined below. It's easy to see why small babies cause poor sleep, since they make many of these guidelines practically impossible to follow. However, the guidelines are a useful point of reference – even if you can't follow them right now, you'll know what you're eventually aiming for.

Lifesavers – how to catch up on missed sleep
* *Go to bed as soon as your baby has had the mid-evening night feed – it doesn't matter if it's 8.30 p.m.* Be very strict with yourself and leap into bed right

---

The basic rules of sleep hygiene
* Go to bed at a regular time each night and get up at a regular time each morning. The aim is to establish a regular sleep pattern.
* Wind down an hour or so before going to bed. Try not to start a heated 'discussion' with your partner or watch anything too upsetting or exciting on TV.
* Don't eat too late. A large meal can take three to four hours to digest.
* A hot, milky drink can help soothe you to sleep.
* Establish a bedtime routine, such as teeth, bath, tidying the bedroom, organizing clothes/nappies/bottles for the next day.
* Avoid stimulants like tea, coffee, chocolate drinks, too much alcohol.
* Try not to take your worries to bed.

away. Don't tidy up, finish the washing up, fall asleep in front of the television or linger in the bath for hours. If you can get at least three hours' uninterrupted sleep before you're woken again, you'll feel far better. It's being woken in the first hour or so, just as you've fallen into the deep sleep stage, that's the killer.

Better still, your partner can do the next feed at 11 p.m. or so by bottle, as this will give you perhaps six hours' uninterrupted sleep. You can take it in turns to do this, thus protecting each other's sleep quotas. If you feel bed so early is antisocial because this is usually very precious time you would spend with your partner, try it every other night.

To doubly protect your sleep, you may find it necessary to bed down in another part of the home (if it is big enough – this isn't so easy in a one bedroom flat) with earplugs. Most mothers are automatically woken if their baby cries even slightly. As Dr Idzikowsi, co-chairman of the British Sleep Society, explains, women sleep more lightly than men and most mothers are spiritually fine-tuned to the sound of their small babies – many so much so that they report they always seem to wake up a minute *before* their baby starts crying.

After your partner has done the feed, he then quietly opens your door and the door to your baby's room, and puts in his own earplugs and shuts his door so that you take turns. It may sound absurdly complicated, but it works.

- *Bottles.* Even if you are breastfeeding, they are invaluable from the point of view of catching up on your sleep, to also introduce your baby to feeding from a bottle.

  They can then either drink your own expressed breast milk or formula, given by your partner (or other helper). Having someone else do the odd feed for you, especially some night feeds, can be a godsend. It will also free you if you sometimes want or need to go out on your own for a little while during the day.

  Purists object to offering a small breastfeeding baby a bottle on the grounds it may cause what is known as nipple confusion, when the baby may become muddled by the different shapes, textures and smells of breast and rubber teat and as a result is put off suckling altogether. Though this may happen, there is no good evidence to suggest it does very often.

- *Take cat naps.* Go back to bed for an hour when your baby has a morning nap. Put your feet up on the sofa after lunch when they sleep again. It's very tempting to catch up on chores while they're settled, but if you're exhausted it's counter-productive.

- *Make sure you get more than a full night's sleep every week or so, if nothing else.* It's enormously restorative and can make up for three or four lost nights in one go. Take yourself off to the spare room, or make up a bed on the sofa – just make sure you're out of earshot. Let your partner/ mother/friend look after the baby. Obviously if you're breastfeeding this is more difficult, but it's worth expressing milk and trying a bottle.

- *Get a babysitter for a Saturday or Sunday lie-in, an early night or an afternoon's extra sleep.*

Power napping

According to James Maas, Professor of Psychology at Cornell University in the US, who runs corporate sleep seminars for industrial giants such as IBM and Pepsi, a nap need only last 20 minutes (no more) to be effective, and has its highest recharging potential between 2 p.m. and 5 p.m., when your energy naturally dips.

Snatching a quick nap for 15 minutes or so when the baby is sleeping can be very restorative and make up for lost sleep at night. Try napping after lunch or in the late afternoon before you gear up for the baby's feed, bath and bed.

- Take yourself to a quiet place where you won't be disturbed.
- Take the phone off the hook, and shut the door.
- Lie down if you can, or sit in a comfortable chair. Let yourself completely relax and drift off. If you're lacking in sleep this will be surprisingly easy.
- Set the alarm to wake you up if you're worried you'll sleep on.

Don't underestimate the importance of rest and relaxation. If you can't replace missing sleep, or you find it hard to catnap, it's doubly important that you put your feet up at least once a day and take time out from chores. Avoid physically exhausting yourself in addition to coping with lack of sleep.

EXERCISE FOR ENERGY

Exercise is probably the last thing you want to do if you feel tired, but if you can manage some the benefits are enormous. If you've become less fit during pregnancy and childbirth, as many women do, regaining your physical fitness will help you:

- Reduce the amount of muscle fatigue you suffer. Stronger muscles don't tire as quickly or ache as much after exertion as flabby out-of-condition ones.
- Cope with stress more easily. Fit people do not seem to experience the same rush of adrenal hormones (adrenaline, cortisol, noradrenaline) in response to everyday stresses as those who are out of shape. The explanation for this is that exercise itself actually acts as a stress. When you begin an exercise programme the adrenal glands secrete increased amounts of hormones, but after a couple of months they produce far less in response to exercise stress as the body's tissues become more sensitive to them. The result is that fit people can face ordinary stress without a big hormone production. They also seem able to rid the body of unwanted stress hormones more quickly.
- Cope with depression and anxiety better, and improve your self-image.

Regular exercise appears to benefit people in emotional as well as physical ways. One explanation is that exercise raises the level of endorphins in the body – natural substances which control the body's response to stress and lift mood.
- Increase your resistance to disease. Exercise appears to play some part in increasing general immunity – fit people are less prone to minor illnesses and infections like colds.

DEALING WITH EMOTIONAL DIFFICULTIES

Because body and mind have such a profound effect on each other, it's never easy to separate out where the physical ends and the mental begins. Fatigue is a major symptom of psychological illnesses such as depression and anxiety states, and can also be part of the cause.

Postnatal depression
Lack of sleep and sheer exhaustion can be an important factor in sparking off postnatal depression in some women. Some doctors argue that the condition would be far less common if mothers got more rest in the early months after childbirth.

You may not realize you are suffering from postnatal depression. Some of the warning signs are:

- Finding it increasingly difficult to cope.
- Crying more easily than you normally would.
- Waking very early.

What sort of exercise?
To get the benefits outlined above you will need to do aerobic (oxygen-burning) exercise which benefits the whole body, not just individual muscles. Any exercise is aerobic if:

- It lasts at least 12 minutes without stopping.
- It gets you breathing deeply, but not out of breath.
- It raises your heartbeat to more than 100 beats a minute.
- It uses muscles in the thighs and buttocks.

Swimming, fast walking, jogging, running, cycling, skipping, stair climbing and stepping are all forms of aerobic exercise. To improve your overall level of fitness, three 20-minute sessions a week are recommended, but any amount of exercise you can manage to fit in will be better than none.

If you have recently had a baby, you must take particular care to protect your joints and ligaments from injury for the first five months. See How to Get Your Body Back, page 456, for suggestions on safe exercise in the postnatal period.

- Yelling at your partner/other children more than you used to.
- Overwhelming fatigue – a feeling of being too tired to bother that spills over into all areas of your life.
- Lack of pleasure in things you would normally enjoy.
- Feelings of tension, panic and not being able to cope.
- Feeling very sad, down and morbid, closed off and alone.
- Fearing you don't love your baby.
- Feeling guilty, worthless and useless.

There are many different ways to cure postnatal depression. It is possible to get over it quite quickly – but it's important to get help for it. See Postnatal Depression: Breaking Through, pages 413–29.

Relationship difficulties

Having a baby, especially your first, makes a major change to your lifestyle and normally involves considerable adjustments to your relationship at a time when you have little spare energy to cope. All of the following are likely to be affected by a new baby:

- Your sexual relationship with your partner – your enthusiasm, or lack of it, for sex (see Your Sex Life after Childbirth, pages 477–98).
- The amount of time and attention you are able to give to your partner's emotional needs.
- The amount of time you spend at home – it will probably be much more than before, especially if you were working pre-baby.
- Your relationships with friends, especially those who don't have children.
- Your finances – there will probably be some drop in income, or greater expenditure.
- Your self-confidence and self-image. You may feel worried about your ability to cope with a baby, and upset by the physical changes of childbirth.

All these changes require adjustment, reorganization and rethinking in many areas of your life. It's easy to lose your sense of perspective when you're exhausted, and more stress can lead to even greater fatigue.

It's likely you'll be wanting more support and understanding from your partner than you have in the past, but your partner will also be making adjustments to the new responsibilities of fatherhood and the practical and emotional changes a baby brings into his life. The potential for misunderstanding and emotional difficulties between you is huge at a time when you probably have less opportunity to spend time together discussing ways to tackle problems and less energy to stand back and review things calmly.

Good communication with your partner is essential to prevent resentments building up which can damage your relationship. Making time to talk through difficulties in a clear, non-accusing way, expressing your wishes and needs simply and directly, and listening to your partner's feelings and wants is vital. Counselling can help if problems between you become too difficult or too touchy to discuss without argument and bad feeling. But a little talking things through sooner is much better than loads later.

HOW TO COMBAT STRESS

Not all stress is bad. A certain amount peps you up and improves performance. However, too much makes you feel exhausted and irritable, means you cope less well with the tasks you need to do, and makes you more prone to anxiety and possibly depression, especially if you have other worries – financial, personal, or social – as well.

Caring for a small baby involves many stresses and pressures which you can't do much about in the short term. Scientists like Dr Martin Seligman from Cornell University in the US claim that the important underlying factor in how stressed you feel is the amount of control you believe you have over events. This idea may go some way to explain why new mothers so often feel extremely fraught. The behaviour of newborns can be puzzling and unpredictable to the extreme. Most new mothers can remember feeling utterly helpless at times in the face of the baby's erratic crying, sleeping and feeding patterns. They rush each time the baby opens their mouth to soothe, feed, comfort or change, and are entirely at their beck and call. You may feel you have absolutely no control over your babies' behaviour and the way it affects your life. There's no question who is pulling whose strings in the early days. Perhaps it's a desire to establish a measure of control that makes many mothers so anxious to establish a routine for their new babies as quickly as they can so that they, not the baby, are in the driving seat.

The good news is that after a few weeks, when your baby has grown and developed, and you have learnt more and begun to understand each other, the feelings of helplessness and lack of control diminish. The baby's cries begin to have meaning and life assumes a more predictable, controllable shape, with feeding and sleeping falling into a routine.

Until this begins to happen, remind yourself that current stresses are not permanent or personal – the baby *will* grow up and become less demanding, they are *not* crying to wind you up or annoy you. Try to hold on to the fact that things really do become far easier.

Reduce other sources of avoidable stress in your life, or cut them out entirely if you can. It's not being selfish to refuse to be involved in things which add to your stress levels – it's a lifesaver. Try these:

Say no to:
- Unwanted visitors who tire and exhaust you, mentally or physically.
- Imposing the same routine of domestic chores that you had pre-baby.
- Chores, errands or duties which give you extra work. It's OK to drop your commitments to other people for now.
- Worrying about your social life, or keeping up with friends or relatives who don't keep in touch with you.

- Being burdened with the emotional troubles of others. You've got enough to get on with for the moment.
- Always replying 'I'm fine' when people ask how you are. Be truthful instead and say, 'I'm extremely tired,' or 'I'm finding it hard to cope.' You will hopefully be offered some practical help.
- Criticizing yourself about the state of the house, your clothes, your appearance, your weight, the meals you serve, your career progress. Give yourself a break from worrying. You have a new baby to care for and this is the most important thing right now. Everything else will fall into place later.
- Feelings of resentment towards your partner which sap your mental energy. Try to address any problems with him and work out a compromise on difficult areas that you can both live with.
- Low self-esteem. Feeling vulnerable, that you're not coping well, are not up to the job of motherhood and can't manage all the changes in your life is quite common in the early days. Try listing all your good points and all those things you *do* accomplish in a day to boost your confidence. Getting through the day with a newborn baby and a household, perhaps also with other children and a partner to look after, is a major achievement in itself.

Say yes to:
- Extra sleep and rest as often as you can. You aren't being lazy, you're being sensible.
- Social contact you enjoy. Outings with friends, NCT group teas, one o'clock clubs in the local park, any events where you can get some emotional support, have fun, and share problems and ideas. Social isolation can be stressful.
- Any kind of enjoyable activity that gets you out with the baby – walking, swimming, shopping if you enjoy it. Forget the chores and go out.
- Any practical help anyone offers you, any time – with shopping, cleaning, looking after other children, cleaning out the fridge, doing some ironing.
- A cleaner or domestic help once a week if you can possibly afford it, or maybe a friend or relative could lend you a hand with the chores for a few weeks.
- Offers to take the baby off your hands for a short time. Let go – they will be fine without you for a few hours. Don't feel you are imposing, if people offer help. They want to do something for you. Give them a chance to feel good, don't reject their offers. Don't be shy to ask for a favour when you need help. People are often very flattered to feel needed, and you can return the favour later on.
- Any chance you have to grab some time to yourself.
- Whatever help your partner can give. Don't feel guilty that he's been working all day, does so much already, has been very supportive so far and don't worry that he must be losing patience with you. If he offers, he wants to help – so don't refuse. Also, try not to criticize or complain if chores don't get done the way you would do them, or he may stop offering.

WAYS TO RELAX

A progressive relaxation exercise

In this exercise you contract each body area in turn and then relax it. This gives a feeling of deep relaxation. It need only take 10 minutes, but spend longer if you can.

- Lie comfortably, legs outstretched, in a warm room.
- Focus on your right foot and lower leg, and tense the muscles by pointing your toes towards your face. Hold the muscles strongly for five seconds and then tense even harder for a few more before releasing totally. Repeat with your left leg. Tense each leg the other way by curling your toes under and tightening the muscles at the back of the leg.
- Tense the muscles round your kneecap, then relax. Next tense the muscles behind your knee by pushing it down against the floor, and relax. Do each leg in turn.
- Strongly contract your thigh and buttock muscles, and relax.
- Draw your lower abdomen in tightly, tense, then relax. Then push it up towards the ceiling, tense, and relax. Push your lower back against the floor, tense, and relax, then arch it up towards the ceiling, and relax.
- Work on your upper body in the same way, tensing then relaxing your fists, arms and shoulders. To relax your neck, tighten the muscles as much as you can, and relax.
- Finish with the facial muscles – purse your lips tightly, and relax. Open your mouth wide, and relax. Do the same with your eyes, jaw muscles and forehead.

Meditation

There are many forms of meditation which lay down different rules about how and when you should meditate, but the underlying principle is the same. The aim is to reach a state of relaxed awareness that stills and calms both mind and body, allowing the release of stress and tension and generating better energy and concentration afterwards.

Many clinical studies such as one conducted by Dr Herbert Benson at Harvard Medical school showed that meditation decreases blood pressure and breathing rate, slows heartbeat and lowers metabolic rate.

You can easily practise meditation at home yourself. Ideally, do it regularly, twice a day, for fifteen minutes. Following these steps.

- Find a quiet place where you won't be disturbed. Make sure the room is warm and your clothes are comfortable.
- Sit upright in a chair with your feet on the ground and your hands loosely in your lap. Close your eyes and relax.
- Breathe steadily and slowly in and out through your nose and down into your abdomen.
- Decide what you will allow your attention to rest on. It could be your

Headaches

Feeling constantly tired and stressed makes you more prone to headaches. Many migraine sufferers find that lack of sleep makes them much more vulnerable to attacks. Painkillers are the remedy most of us reach for, but sometimes they can be counter-productive and have a rebound effect that only makes a headache worse. If you find you're taking painkillers most days for a thumping head, try these alternatives instead.

- Massage the base of your neck or ask your partner to.
- Lavender oil can offer relief. Try rubbing it neat into your temples on either side, or sprinkle a few drops on a tissue and inhale.
- Eat regularly – missing food can sometimes spark headaches.

---

breathing, the repetition of a simple word (a mantra) like 'peace', or 'one', or a phrase.

- When your thoughts wander, bring them gently back to the object of your meditation. You are aiming for a state of passive awareness or mindfulness, noting what passes through your attention but not thinking about it or mentally pursuing it.
- At the end of your time, gently open your eyes and allow yourself a few minutes to come back to your surroundings. You may feel dizzy if you get up too quickly because your blood pressure has dropped.

De-stress tapes

There are many tapes available which teach relaxation exercises for general wellbeing, or as an aid to overcoming insomnia. Others play relaxing music or soothing sounds such as birdsong or the waves on the seashore. You may be able to borrow some from your local library to find one you enjoy. Alternatively they can be bought from charitable organizations such as Relaxation for Living, Mind, and the Pain Relief Foundation (see Useful Addresses page 335).

Breathing exercises

Breathing well can give you more energy by oxygenating the blood. It can also help release emotional and stress-related tensions. Try to practise this breathing exercise twice a day for five minutes at a time, if possible near to an open window.

- Always breathe in through your nose and out through your mouth.
- Lie in a comfortable position on the floor, knees bent. Rest your hands lightly on your lower rib cage.
- Breathe in gently for a count of three to four so your abdomen rises, pushing your hands slightly towards the ceiling.
- Exhale on a count of four or five. Apply slight pressure at the end of the breath to complete the exhalation.

- Repeat the exercise 15 times. Give yourself a few minutes to rest before you get up since you may feel a little dizzy if you do so quickly.

THINGS THAT CAN MAKE YOU MORE TIRED

Drugs
Many types of drugs can cause fatigue. This includes both prescribed medicines and illegal recreational drugs, including cannabis, amphetamines and other stimulants, and hallucinogens such as LSD.

Long-term use of sedative drugs such as diazepam and lorazepam, used to treat anxiety, can cause depression, headache and insomnia, all of which can be linked with feelings of chronic fatigue.

If you have recently been prescribed medication by your GP and there's a noticeable increase in your feelings of tiredness, check with them to see if what you're taking could be making your fatigue worse. In many cases there's another drug you could try instead.

Caffeine, alcohol and cigarettes
Understandably many sleep-deprived new mothers drink tea, coffee or alcohol or smoke cigarettes to keep them going through exhausting days or to unwind in the evening. Yet these stimulants can quite easily end up contributing towards the problem they're designed to help, making you feel even more tired.

Alcohol, nicotine and caffeine can all alter sleep patterns, affecting your ability either to fall asleep or to stay asleep. If you find you are getting poor sleep, in addition to the baby waking you, and you smoke, drink or have a lot of coffee or tea to perk you up during the day, it might be worth thinking about cutting them out.

Caffeine
Large amounts of caffeine cause overstimulation, anxiety, irritability, restlessness and poor sleep. Caffeine could be what's making your tiredness worse if:

- You drink large amounts of tea or more than five cups of coffee every day.
- You rely on it to keep you going. As with alcohol, your tolerance to caffeine increases and you'll find you need more and more to experience the same lifting effect.
- You feel drowsy and irritable on waking, even if you've had a decent night's sleep. For some people too much caffeine has a hangover effect.
- You have trouble getting to sleep at night and/or you wake frequently during the night, even when the baby's not crying.

However in emergencies ('I have got to keep going until this evening or else') Dr Idzikowski recommends taking your coffee with a glass of grapefruit

---

Cutting out caffeine

If you do decide to cut out caffeine, and you've been drinking quite a bit, do it slowly, otherwise you may experience withdrawal symptoms for a couple of days. Cut down slowly over a period of three weeks, gradually replacing tea and coffee with decaffeinated substitutes or other drinks such as herbal teas or fruit juices.

Caffeine withdrawal symptoms include headaches, tiredness and irritability, and can be quite unpleasant, depending on how much you've been used to.

---

juice afterwards. Apparently this slows down the rate at which your body metabolizes the caffeine.

Alcohol

In small amounts alcohol gives a feeling of relaxation and confidence, but in larger doses it can lead to irritability, depression, sleep disturbance and fatigue.

A few glasses of wine are a great social pleasure but if you're suffering from fatigue and exhaustion, and you drink every day and/or use alcohol regularly as a way of giving you a quick lift, it's possible it could be making your tiredness worse. Even three or four units a day may be enough to lower energy levels in some people. Dr Alan Stewart, author of *Tired all the Time* and founding member of the British Society for Nutritional Medicine, suggests that people who are suffering from fatigue might do best to avoid alcohol altogether. Although it is a sedative and promotes sleep, the sedative effect wears off during the night and there's a rebound effect when alcohol blood levels fall to zero, usually in the early hours of the morning. More than two glasses of wine in the evening generally cause waking, and sometimes sweating and headache.

There's absolutely no harm in enjoying a glass of wine with your meal in the evening – in fact a small amount of alcohol has positive health benefits for the heart and circulation, and red wine contains iron which many women are short of after childbirth. But it might be time to try a few weeks without alcohol if:

- You find you've been drinking more without feeling the effects.
- The thought of a day without drink seems difficult.
- You're becoming unusually irritable or argumentative.
- You feel muzzy-headed in the morning or vaguely depressed.

The double whammy – coffee and alcohol

Because of their opposing actions, coffee and alcohol taken together can particularly effectively produce early morning insomnia. The sedative effects of a few drinks reverses the arousing effects of caffeine to begin with, but by the early hours of the morning most of the alcohol will have been cleared

> **Giving up cigarettes**
> If you've been a fairly heavy smoker and you stop suddenly, you'll probably find you have disturbed sleep – but this should only last from two to four nights.

from the system. The rebound effect of this normally causes wakefulness and, added to the stimulating effect of caffeine, will almost certainly wake you from sleep.

Cigarettes

Smokers usually use cigarettes as an aid to relaxation – nicotine in small doses is a mild sedative and can promote sleep. However, in heavy smokers the reverse is true and the sedative effect is quickly overtaken by feelings of arousal and agitation. If you smoke more than a few cigarettes a day, nicotine could be contributing to poor sleep.

NUTRITIONAL SUPPLEMENTS TO KEEP YOU GOING

Guarana capsules

Guarana is a substance taken from a Brazilian rainforest plant, which is pharmacologically similar to caffeine. However it appears not to have the latter's addictive effect, nor does it give you caffeine's very rapid energy hike for an hour followed by a rapid letdown. Instead, a couple of capsules will fuel you slowly and steadily for four to five hours.

If you have to keep going – say it's 3 p.m., you are becoming very tired and wondering how to make it through to 8 p.m. that night, this is a good standby. Do not take it too often though, as you may end up using energy you don't biologically have, becoming even tireder after several days constant use. Available from health food shops.

Floravital tonic

A palatable tonic in the well-known Floradix range of vegetable sources of iron and the B group of vitamins, which can enhance energy levels. Double the dose suggested for a general wellbeing maintenance, and after a few days you will notice you are not feeling as tired as usual. Available from most health food shops, at approximately £6.75 for 250 ml.

Rescue Remedy

The most famous Bach Flower remedy, made from a distillation of several British wild flowers. Rescue Remedy can help combat the extreme irritability and distress you may feel when constantly very tired. Four drops are taken as needed in a glass of water. Independent midwives often suggest it for women in labour, and their partners. Again, the effects are not dramatic but suddenly you notice you are not feeling quite as bad as you thought you were. Available from health food shops, and some chemists, at approximately £3.99 for 15 ml. Olive is useful for long-term tiredness, or Oak for usually strong and competent people who are 'temporarily exhausted by their responsibilities'.

GETTING ENERGY FROM FOOD

Your diet can help or hinder you when it comes to general tiredness and fatigue. Good nutritious food helps your body meet the extra demands made on it by pregnancy, childbirth and breastfeeding and keeps up your energy levels. Eating regularly is important if you are to avoid the temporary fatigue and irritability which overtake you when blood-sugar levels dip dramatically.

However eating nourishing, regular meals is much easier said than done, especially in the first few months after childbirth when you may find you hardly get a chance to wolf down a packet of chocolate digestives, never mind shop for and prepare all the fresh fruit and vegetables you know are so good for you. But once you and the baby have settled into a routine, you will find it easier to shop and cook more thoughtfully.

If you find your eating habits go completely awry after you've had your baby, don't make food another thing to feel guilty about. Work towards eating a better diet gradually, try to make good food choices when you can. Aim to eat a balance from the four main food groups so your body gets four-star fuel and is firing on all cylinders.

A good balance
The four main food groups are listed below. Try to have two-thirds of your diet from groups 1 and 2 and one third from groups 3 and 4. Eat foods from group 5 sparingly or as an occasional treat.

1. Bread, other cereals and potatoes

2. Fruit and vegetables
Dark green leafy vegetables like broccoli, cabbage, sprouts, and spinach are good sources of B vitamins, vitamin C, iron and other essential minerals. Citrus fruits, fruit juices, kiwi fruit and berries such as blackcurrants are good sources of vitamin C. Aim for five servings a day of fruit and vegetables.

3. Milk and dairy produce
This group includes all types of milk – pasteurized, longlife, powdered, yoghurts, fromage frais, crème fraîche, all hard and soft cheeses, cottage cheese, cream cheese, processed cheese and cheese spreads.

Don't skip breakfast
A good breakfast prevents blood sugar levels plunging mid-morning and keeps energy up. Try museli porridge, it lasts and is quick to make.

---

4. Meat, fish and vegetable proteins

5. Fatty and sugary foods

Foods that are high in fats and/or sugars (the two often go together) should only be eaten sparingly. This group includes butter and margarines, sugar, biscuits, cakes, crisps, savoury snacks, mayonnaise and bottled sauces, cream and ice cream, chocolate, sweets, jams, marmalade, sweet spreads and sugary drinks, including fizzy drinks.

How's your nutrient intake?

Pregnancy, childbirth and breastfeeding make huge demands on your body for extra nutrients, in particular for the minerals iron, zinc and magnesium. If you were well nourished before pregnancy and you ate a good, nutritious diet throughout, your body will have risen to the nutritional challenge. However, if that wasn't always the case, the growing baby may have depleted your stores. The effects of this can become apparent after childbirth in problems such as excessive hair loss, frequent colds or infections and poor skin. Less obvious is feeling tired the whole time, lacking in energy and stamina.

There is well-documented research about the contribution that a lack of certain minerals can make to ill health and tiredness. A good, well-balanced diet which includes a variety of foods from the main foods groups is the best way to meet your dietary requirements, but missed meals, lack of time and the general stress of caring for a small child can mean that you're missing out on what you need, just when you need it most. Vitamins and minerals don't actually work in splendid isolation but depend on complex interactions between them for proper absorption and use by the body. If you feel you're not managing to eat as well as you'd like to, a good multivitamin and mineral supplement can provide a useful backup.

Energy boosters	*Energy bombers*
Cereals – fortified breakfast cereals, muesli, porridge	Very sugary cereals
Fresh fruit and vegetables	Biscuits, cakes, sweets, chocolate, ice cream
Nuts, seeds, dried fruit	Crisps, salted peanuts, savoury snacks and biscuits
Wholemeal bread, pasta, rice, starchy vegetables	Pot noodles, chips, shop-bought pies
Fruit juices, water	Alcohol, too much tea, coffee, fizzy drinks
Lean meat, animal proteins, eggs, fish, cheese	Fatty meats, sausages, prepared meat products

You can boost the most important nutrients naturally by concentrating on the following:

The B vitamins

Plenty of B vitamins are essential for lots of energy and general wellbeing – and they are often lacking in the average diet. The B-complex vitamins are especially important if you're breastfeeding. Poor supplies have been associated with tiredness, weakness, fatigue, insomnia and irritability. Fatigue with depressive symptoms and anxiety is especially connected with lack of B12. The B vitamins (except for B12) are all water-soluble and aren't stored by the body, so a good daily intake from food is important.

B vitamins are found in:

- Bread and fortified breakfast cereals.
- Meat (especially liver and kidneys), eggs, milk, dairy produce.
- Dark green leafy vegetables.
- Vitamin B12 is only found in meat, eggs and dairy produce. You'll need to take a supplement if your diet doesn't include these.

Iron

Tiredness due to lack of iron is a particular risk after pregnancy and child-birth. During pregnancy the growing baby needs plenty for its own growth and development, and if we don't get enough iron from our diets – and most of us don't, according to government figures – the baby draws on its mother's reserves, leaving her at risk of anaemia.

Iron can be provided from meat and vegetable sources – but the iron from meat is more readily absorbed than that from vegetables. Iron is found in:

- Red meats, especially beef, liver and kidneys.
- Egg yolk.
- Haricot beans, kidney beans.
- Green vegetables.
- Shellfish, parsley, dried figs.

Increase your uptake of iron by:

- Including plenty of fresh fruit in your diet and drinking a glass of orange juice with meals. Vitamin C increases the body's absorption of iron.
- Avoiding drinking tea for at least an hour after food – the tannins it contains reduce iron absorption from vegetable sources. Coffee also reduces iron absorption.

Magnesium

The body's demand for magnesium increase during pregnancy and breastfeeding, so it's a good idea to check that your diet gives you adequate supplies. A mild deficiency could make a contribution to fatigue and tiredness.

Make sure you drink enough fluids

Low-level dehydration is thought to contribute towards fatigue. You need plenty of fluids, especially if you're breastfeeding. Aim for at least 2 litres (4 pints) a day. Try to keep your drinks simple – plain water, diluted fruit juice, herb teas rather than too much tea, coffee and fizzy drinks because of their caffeine content.

The main sources of magnesium are:

- Cereals, nuts and seeds.
- Green vegetables.
- There are small amounts in meat and animal products.
- Some mineral waters have good amounts of magnesium – check the label to see.

The overall quality of your diet affects the way the body is able to use and store magnesium. Improve your uptake by:

- Eating enough protein, especially animal protein, meat, fish and eggs.
- Sprinkling a handful of nuts (almonds and brazils are especially good) on your breakfast cereal, or choose a muesli mixture that includes them. Add dried apricots for an extra magnesium boost.
- Restricting the amount of alcohol and sugars in your diet, as these increase the amount of magnesium lost in urine.

Zinc

Pregnancy and breastfeeding increase the body's need for zinc, another important mineral for a healthy immune system and resistance to infection.

Good sources of zinc include:

- Red meat and offal.
- Vegetarian proteins like split peas, beans and nuts.
- Wholemeal bread.

COMPLEMENTARY THERAPY ENERGY BOOSTERS

Complementary therapies can help with tiredness. Many of the treatments are in themselves very relaxing – an hour of peace and quiet while someone works on your body or listens attentively to your feelings and needs can be therapeutic in itself.

If you're feeling stressed and under pressure it may be difficult to find the time and energy (and money) to investigate alternatives and find a qualified local practitioner. However, several therapies offer ideas for relaxation, meditation and massage which you can adapt for yourself at home.

Aromatherapy

Aromatherapy has particular benefits for fatigue and stress-related conditions. Some aromatherapy oils are invigorating (for instance rosemary, juniper, peppermint, lemon, eucalyptus), and some relaxing (try sweet fennel, linden, valerian, marjoram). Jasmine, clary sage, ylang-ylang, bergamot, neroli and rose all lift the spirits, and are especially recommended for postnatal depression.

Self-help
- Try an invigorating body rub. Mix three drops each of lemon, grapefruit and rosemary essential oils with 20 ml (4 teaspoons) of carrier oil. Vigorously rub the mixture for a moment or two into the parts of yourself you can reach – thighs, arms, buttocks, legs, abdomen.
- Ask your partner to give you a simple, relaxing back, neck, shoulder or foot massage. Choose one or more oils from the list above, depending on whether you want to be relaxed or invigorated, and mix them with around 20 ml (4 teaspoons) of carrier oil. A gentle foot massage doesn't take too much effort on his part (he can do your feet while he watches TV) and is very relaxing and enjoyable. Five drops each of lavender, rosewood and clary sage added to 20 ml of carrier oil can make you deliciously sleepy.
- Relaxing in an aromatic bath before bedtime is one of the best ways to promote a good night's sleep. Add six to eight drops of lavender to the bathwater as it runs, lie back and relax for at least 20 minutes. Lavender is the best essential oil for promoting sleep, but if you don't like it, you could try rosewood, clary sage or sandalwood. Add five or six drops of oil to your bath.
- When a relaxing bath is not possible or practical, inhale the vapour of a few drops of essential oils on a tissue, or sprinkle them on your pillow.

Acupuncture

Acupuncture is not a self-help treatment. You need to consult a properly qualified practitioner (through the British Acupuncture Council, see Useful Addresses page 334).

Self-help
For sleep improvement an acupressure kit called Isocones is available at high-street chemists. The disposable cones are applied to the Heart 7 acupressure point inside the wrist and held in place by a plaster while you sleep. A French study which monitored subjects with EEG found a decrease in wakefulness and an increase in non-REM (dreaming) sleep in users. These cones have also been used with some success in children with sleep disorders.

Chinese herbal medicine

Fatigue, headaches and insomnia are all said to respond well to this type of herbal medicine. You will need to see a qualified practitioner (see Useful Addresses on page 335).

Herbal medicine

Herbal medicine cannot cure chronic conditions such as long-standing fatigue overnight – it may take some months before you feel the benefits.

Self-help

Although medical herbalists prepare the most potent herbal remedies, there are many simple over-the-counter herbal preparations such as teas and tinctures you can try to help overcome the effects of exhaustion, nervous anxiety and stress. Alternatively you can buy loose herbs to make your own teas – there are several suppliers (see Useful Addresses page 7).

One word of warning: it's not a good idea to drink large amounts of some types of herbal teas if you are breastfeeding. One study showed that two babies whose mothers were drinking large amounts of herbal teas (over two litres a day) to stimulate breastfeeding had symptoms such as poor feeding and reduced growth.

Anne McIntyre, Director of the National Institute of Medical Herbalism and author of many books, including *The Complete Woman's Herbal*, recommends the following remedies for the post-natal period:

- *As a tonic after childbirth*
  — Dang gui as a tea or tincture taken three times daily during the first few weeks.
  — False unicorn root to restore vitality after childbirth. Take as tea three times a day.
- *For exhaustion and stress*
  — Make a remedy from equal parts of False unicorn, Dang gui, Ginger and Nettles. Take three to six times a day.
- *For fatigue and stress*
  — Choose from among the following herbs and make your own tea to sip several times a day: Lavender, Rosemary, Camomile, Linden blossom, Lemon balm, Wild oats, Passion flower, Vervain, Valerian, Skullcap, Catmint.

Medical herbalist Andrew Chevalier recommends Dandelion root coffee drunk at lunchtime to avoid the mid-afternoon energy dip. 'The best way is to get the roasted root form which you can buy in a pack and then grind up. It works on the liver to improve the absorption of your lunch and helps improve blood sugar levels.'

- Rosemary tea is a gentle stimulant and increases alertness, and is thought to have a stimulating effect on the adrenal glands, so improving your ability to cope with stress. Don't drink more than two cups a day and avoid it if you have high blood pressure.
- Fennel aids digestion and is a gentle-acting herb that is generally calming.
- A cup of peppermint tea can help to get you going in the morning. It's an invigorating alternative to tea or coffee and can help you cut down on your caffeine intake.

Herbal remedies for sleep problems

There are a number of herbs which are known for their calming and sedative properties. Some are stronger than others. Ideally begin with the mildest remedy, then if you find that doesn't help much, move up a notch, but allow two or three days for the herbs to work before moving on to a stronger one.

- Camomile is a mild relaxant. A cup of Camomile tea before bed can be soothing.
- Linden and Lime flower are both mildly sedative and tranquillizing. They can be taken as tea in the same way as Camomile.
- Valerian, a herbal remedy from the root of the plant *Valeriana officinalis*, has been traditionally used by herbalists as a relaxant to help soothe the nervous system and ease tension. It's a non-addictive tranquillizer that can be used both for daytime stresses like anxiety and panic, and for night-time insomnia.

  Valerian is often combined with other sleep-inducing herbs such as Passion flower (*passiflora*), Hops (*humulus lupulus*) and Lemon balm (*melissa officinalis*) in many of the herbal remedies and supplements found in health food shops.

Homeopathy

Homeopathic remedies can be helpful if you're having trouble sleeping or are feeling stressed. Generally a homeopath would regard sleep problems as part of an overall constitutional problem, and would not treat them in isolation. However, there are some remedies worth trying. The general advice is to take the remedy every night for up to a week. If you see no effect, stop – it's the wrong remedy.

- Sulphur may help if you have trouble falling asleep despite daytime tiredness. It's also appropriate if you wake in the early hours and then can't get back to sleep.
- Nux vomica is sometimes prescribed for people whose sleep is disturbed by lively thoughts, or if it takes a long time to get to sleep.
- Calcarea is for those whose sleep is disturbed by frightful vivid visions when they close their eyes or horrid thoughts that create restless sleep.
- Coffea can help if you find you wake at the slightest noise, or racing thoughts prevent you from sleeping.
- Lycopodium is used for those who fear being able to cope with the stress of change in their lives.

USEFUL ADDRESSES

The British Acupuncture Council, Park House, 206 Latimer Road, London W10 6RE. Tel: 0181 964 0222.

The British Holistic Medical Association, Rowland Thomas House,

Royal Shrewsbury Hospital, South Shrewsbury, Shropshire SY3 8XF.
Tel: 01743 261155.

Have a selection of relaxation tapes on stress, meditation, sleep and relaxation.

The British Homeopathic Association, 27a Devonshire Street.,
London W1N 1RJ. Tel: 0171 935 2163.

MIND (National Association for Mental Health), Granta House,
15/19 Broadway, Stratford, London E15 4BQ. Tel: 0181 519 2122.

The National Institute of Medical Herbalists, 56 Longbrook Street, Exeter,
Devon EX4 6AH. Tel: 01392 426022.

The Pain Research Institute, Pain Relief Foundation, Rice Lane,
Liverpool L9 1AE. Tel: 0151 523 1486.

Has a selection of stress-reduction tapes which give advice and instruction on learning to unwind.

The Register of Chinese Herbal Medicine, PO Box 400, Wembley,
Middlesex HA9 9SZ. Tel: 0181 904 1357.

Contact for a professionally trained practitioner.

Relaxation for Living, 12 New Street, Chipping, Norton, Oxon OX7 5LJ.
Tel: 01608 646100.

The Women's Nutritional Advisory Service, PO Box 268, Lewes,
East Sussex BN7 2QN. Tel: 01273 487366.

Dietary information and advice for women.

USEFUL READING

Coping with Chronic Fatigue, Trudie Chalder, Sheldon £4.99
Get Up and GO! Self-Help for Fatigue Sufferers, Anne Woodham, Headline £5.99
Nutritional Medicine, Dr Stephen Davies and Dr Alan Stewart, Pan
Tired All the Time, Dr Alan Stewart, Optima

If You're Anaemic

Anaemia after childbirth is far more common than most people think. It responds very well to treatment but if it is not dealt with, it can make you feel tired (more than tired – physically ill) and generally pulled down for many months. Anaemia often develops during pregnancy. Pregnant women are routinely given a blood test at their first antenatal (booking in) appointment. This is repeated at 28 and 34 weeks of pregnancy as the demands on your iron stores are highest towards the end of the second trimester of pregnancy and all through the third, when the baby is growing most rapidly. Any anaemia would be diagnosed then.

However, anaemia may not be diagnosed after delivery because:

- You are not generally offered a blood test then.
- Feeling tired is so common. Since this is rather how many health professionals expect busy new mothers to be feeling for a few months, due to probable lack of sleep, considerable new demands on their energy and the recent effort of pregnancy and childbirth, they do not always think to check you for anaemia.

According to one recent (1995) study of women in the Grampian region an astounding quarter of all new mothers were anaemic after they had given birth to their babies.

What is anaemia?

Mention anaemia to most people and they would associate it with being short of iron. Strictly speaking, anaemia is the blanket term for a whole range of disorders of the blood, which all involve a lack of haemoglobin. Haemoglobin is the substance which carries oxygen in the bloodstream. For women who have just had babies, anaemia may be due to:

- *Blood loss*, perhaps following heavy bleeding such as after placental abruption when the placenta begins to peel away from the womb wall.
- *Megaloblastic anaemia.* This is caused by folic acid (one of the B group of vitamins) deficiency during your pregnancy. According to a survey by Leeds General Infirmary in 1994, the average folic acid intake of a British woman was 200 μg a day – half the amount recommended by the Govern-

ment – and eight out of every 10 women coming to their first antenatal appointment there were not taking any extra. Folic acid shortage may also be made worse by prolonged breastfeeding afterwards on what is perhaps a not-very-nutritious diet.

Folic acid is vital for the formation of the DNA of all new tissues, both yours (your growing womb, enlarging placenta and, after your baby is born, breastmilk if you are breastfeeding) and your baby's. If you do not have enough folic acid in your system, you cannot make enough of any of the new cells you personally might need, including red blood cells.

- *A general iron shortage.* This can begin as a result of the nutritional demands pregnancy places on your body, but may be continued because of breastfeeding and poor diet afterwards. If you vomited a good deal throughout your pregnancy, this may also have contributed. So can having eaten a diet low in iron while you were pregnant (see Eating to Beat Anaemia: High Iron Foods, page 338), being pregnant with twins or triplets, having had several pregnancies; or pregnancies which were close together.
- *An inherited blood disorder.* One example of these is sickle-cell anaemia, in which the red blood cells are moon-shaped instead of fat and round, and cannot carry sufficient haemoglobin. This is only a problem for Afro-Caribbean mothers. The other possibility is thalassaemia, a condition in which red blood cells are easily destroyed, and which tends to affect only people from Mediterranean countries.
- *Pernicious anaemia.* This can develop when there is a lack of a particular stomach enzyme. The condition prevents your body from absorbing enough vitamin B12 to make an adequate supply of blood. It can affect people who have a strict vegan diet, and those with blood group A in particular.

How much iron do I need anyway?

The total amount of iron in your body is usually about 3500 mg. However when you are pregnant this rises, as you need a further 500 mg for your enlarging uterus, and 500 mg more for your growing baby's needs. That would leave you an average of 1,000 mg down on your usual iron stores after the birth. However on the plus side, you would not have had any periods while you were pregnant, and if you were breastfeeding none for a few months after that either. If you remained periodless for say, 15 months, that would be about 255 mg iron saved. If you breastfed for six months, according to clinical biochemist Dr Len Mervyn, that's about another 180 to 200 mg of iron which needs to be replaced. If you are a bit short of iron to begin with, or not absorbing the amount you are getting while pregnant very well, this could easily lead to post natal anaemia.

Symptoms

These vary slightly depending on which type of anaemia you have, although there may be none at all which are obvious. They can include:

- Tiredness – ranging from feeling slightly below par, to constant dragging fatigue.
- Headaches.
- Insomnia.
- Breathlessness.
- Swollen ankles.
- Loss of appetite.
- Vision disturbance.
- Pale 'reds' of the eyes if you pull the lower eyelid downwards. Some clinicians also report that checking the colour showing through your fingernails (whether a very pale tone or a healthy pink) is another indicator.

EATING TO BEAT ANAEMIA

High-iron foods
Even if you are being given iron supplements, it is important to get as much iron in your diet as you can. Iron-rich food groups are:

Meats
Beefsteak, lamb chops, liver from all the main sources, goose, duck, grouse, partridge, pigeon, hare, kidneys from the usual sources, tongue and liver sausage.

Cereals
A high-iron cereal means sprinkling wheatgerm on ordinary cereal, or making up a tasty muesli with oatmeal flakes, wheatgerm and All-Bran in it, plus chopped dried fruits (see below) such as apricot, figs or peaches.

Wheatgerm, raw oatmeal, All-Bran, puffed wheat, Ready Brek, Special K, Weetabix, wholemeal bread.

Vegetables
Red kidney beans, parsley, boiled spinach, haricot beans, mung beans, split lentils, laver bread, horseradish, leeks, potato crisps.

Fruit
Best iron sources are dried fruits rather than fresh.

Raw dried apricots, raw dried green figs, raw dried peaches, raw dried prunes, stewed dried peaches.

Also:

- All types of nuts especially almonds, barcelona nuts, walnuts and dried coconut and peanuts.
- Liquorice allsorts sweets.
- Bovril, dried yeast, Oxo cubes, brown sauce and tomato purée.

OTHER TREATMENTS

For iron deficiency anaemia
You can take iron supplements, either in tablet or liquid form. You need to remember to:

- Take them persistently and regularly. When you are taking supplements it is usually six to eight weeks before you notice an improvement.
- Take them with a glass of real orange juice each time as vitamin C improves the absorption of iron greatly. One study in 1973 reported in the *British Journal of Haematology* by a Dr M. H. Sayers found 50 g of vitamin C – what you'd probably get from the juice of one and a half squeezed oranges, upped iron absorption by a factor of four. Other ways of taking iron with vitamin C include a tonic like Floradix, which is sold in health food shops and has good amounts of iron and vitamin C in it, or a vitamin C tablet, giving you about 50 to 100 mg worth. One of the problems with iron supplements is that not everyone's system absorbs them very well and if this is the case with you, taking iron pills is pretty useless. So the vitamin C may be the key to successful treatment.

For Folic Acid Deficiency
- Take folic acid supplements.
- Eat more foods which are rich in folic acid, such as dried brewer's yeast, foods made from soya flour, wheatgerm, wheat bran, nuts, pig's liver, green leaf vegetables, wholegrains and pulses.
- If the anaemia is marked, you may be given oral iron tablets or liquid to take as well.
- In very severe cases, you may need a blood transfusion. A transfusion is seldom necessary for postnatal anaemia, but you may be more likely to need one if you had a Caesarean section, and/or an infection after your baby's birth too.

USEFUL READING

Beat the Iron Crisis, Leonard Mervyn, Thorsons, 1988

Loo Problems and How to Sort Them Out
(Constipation, piles and incontinence)

CONSTIPATION

What is it?
Small, hard, pebble-like stools which are infrequent, uncomfortable and difficult to pass. There is such a wide variation in how often different people usually move their bowels that infrequent is usually defined as being only once every three or four days.

It is extremely common to be constipated in the first few days after you have had a baby. Christine Norton, former Director of the Continence Foundation and how a specialist research nurse in this area, based at St Mark's Hospital in London, suggests this is because all the nerve receptors in the muscles, and the usual neurological pathways, can be disturbed by the tremendous stretching which labour involves, and it may take anything from a few days to a few weeks to re-establish the system again. Caesareans can often produce temporary constipation too. This is because all abdominal surgery of any sort disrupts your bowel habits for a while.

Causes
- *Pregnancy hormones.* Around delivery time your body produces high levels of two hormones in particular, progesterone and relaxin. Both relax muscle and ligaments. The stretchier and softer these become, the more flexible the cervix and birth canal down which your baby passes to be born. Unfortunately the hormones affect the whole body, including the smooth muscle fibre in your bowel.

  Your bowel usually works by squeezing hard to help slide bowel waste along its length, and, when required, pass it out of your body altogether in a voluntary (rather than accidental) bowel motion. When it temporarily loses its ability to do so because its muscle fibres are so relaxed, you get waste building up and packing together in the bowel so it becomes harder and more difficult and uncomfortable to move along. The long it stays there, the more likely the bowel is to start absorbing water back out of the waste, so in addition to being packed hard it becomes drier too, which makes you even more constipated.

This effect may last far longer than the expected few days. According to Stephen Sandler, Senior Lecturer at the British School of Osteopathy, new research which he has been involved with at the Chelsea & Westminster Hospital in London shows there are measurable traces of relaxin to be found in the body months after childbirth (which is why women may be more prone to back injury in the first year after giving birth.)

Further, any type of change in the ratio of the sex hormones can affect bowel habit – as women who regularly experience either mild constipation or diarrhoea every month premenstrually could tell you. According to Dr Michael Brush, Honorary Consultant at St Thomas's Hospital London and medical advisor to PMS help organization PREMSOC, it can take many months – even, for some very hormonally sensitive women, years – for their normal sex hormone ratios and cycles to re-establish themselves after childbirth. And 'in some cases, they never quite re-synch.'

- *Disturbance of the pelvic organs.* If you have had *any* type of operation in the pelvic area, including a Caesarean, the physical trauma this produces affects the way your bowel operates for a while. The tremendous rhythmical, muscular activity of the womb during normal childbirth can also create a measure of disturbance in the general pelvic area as all the organs – bowel, womb, etc., fit closely together in this limited space.
- *Worry that your stitches might burst open.* Though constipation will generally disappear rapidly after your baby's birth, the fact that you may, as half all new mothers do, have perineal stitches can mean the constipation lingers for several days. Often women fear that if they do strain to open their bowels they might burst an episiotomy or tear repair stitches open, and so are very reluctant or nervous to try it. If she has developed any haemorrhoids during pregnancy or labour this can make things even harder, leading in turn to a build-up of yet more faeces in her lower intestine – and more constipation.
- *Women tend not to eat much in labour* (and not feel like doing so for a little while afterwards either), and may only have drunk a little liquid over several hours. This means they have very little bulk in their bowels to pass, so it may stay there for longer than usual, and become quite hard as some of its water content is gradually reabsorbed by the bowel lining.

What helps
The first few days:

- A gentle laxative like Lactulose (which does not affect your baby if you are breastfeeding). You might find it helpful to carry on taking a very mild laxative like this for a few days, until your bowels are working completely normally again.
- A gentle glycerin suppository to help loosen any waste matter it comes into contact with, and also to lubricate the inside of the rectal passage. You can get these from your pharmacist.
- Drinking as much water as you possibly can. This helps bulk out and soften faeces.

- Eat foods with both water and fibre in them. Fruit is ideal. Ask for a basket of grapes (do not eat too many of these if breastfeeding as there may be a connection with colic), apples, pears and satsumas, keep it by your bed and dip into it as often as possible throughout the day.
- Do not strain for long on the toilet, but keep going back and trying again at regular intervals.
- If your perineum hurts as you push, or you are frightened your stitches will give way, try holding a soft sanitary towel gently but firmly against the areas as you push, for extra support.

If you still have not opened your bowels after the fifth day or so and are now feeling very uncomfortable, ask the hospital staff, or your GP if you are now at home, for a stronger laxative or for an enema.

Long-term measures

- Eating ordinary All-Bran (or a cheaper supermarket own-brand variety – it tastes the same) every morning can be surprisingly effective. If it tastes boring, mix it in with another favourite cereal. Or have a smaller bowl as a night-time snack. If you hate bran-based cereals, the new fruit and fibre drinks are a reasonably palatable option. Ask your local health food shop or major Boots.
- Eat at least four pieces of fruit a day, one with each meal. If you are breastfeeding your baby, take each daytime feed as a cue to munch on an apple, banana, a pear or some grapes. This helps keep up your energy levels too, which is vital for new mothers constantly on the go.
- Drink plenty of plain liquid like fruit juice, milk, spring and spa water. Try and avoid tea, coffee, cola drinks and alcohol as they are all diuretic and encourage water loss rather than replace it. Have water or juice to drink each time you feed your baby, and drink when you are woken at night too. This is especially important if you are breastfeeding, as it depletes your body's water resources.
- Take regular exercise. It's not an old wives' tale that lack of exercise makes you constipated, though the first piece of medical evidence to support the idea only came to light in 1991 when some hearty South African volunteers found that jogging or cycling an hour a day meant food sped through their intestinal tracts in a snappy 37 hours, compared with a dragging 57 when they spent their exercise times with their feet up on

---

If you have an enema

If you have an enema, you will suddenly, and without much warning, have a desperate need to go to the toilet. The longer you can hang on, the better the treatment will work to relieve your constipation. If you are worried you might not reach the loo in time, go and sit there with a magazine or book 15 to 20 minutes after you have been given the enema, so at least you will be close to base when you need to be.

the sofa. Walking is fine – you will probably be doing a good deal of pram pushing around the neighbourhood anyway. Swimming is ideal if you can find the time.

- Mix linseeds (yes, that stuff budgies eat) in with your cereal, salads, even stews. They help the passage of stools out of the body, as they act like small ball bearings mixed in with the bowel waste. Take a tablespoon two or three times a day for any effect. Linseed is available from health food shops and is said to be beneficial for hair growth – a useful side effect if your hair appears to be doing a dramatic postpregnancy moult (see Hair Loss, page 449).

- Avoid sitting for ages on the loo straining, because those old stories about sitting on the pot and piles are unfortunately true. A study carried out by the John Radcliffe Hospital in Oxford in 1989, which looked at the early morning habits of 100 women and men with piles, found half of them did indeed sit on the lavatory for at least six minutes each morning, reading the newspaper or magazines and straining intermittently.

Lumps and bumps

The vagina and the rectum lie next to each other, with a thin, muscular wall separating them. If your vaginal wall was weakened by childbirth, this dividing wall loses its tone, so that you can occasionally feel the lumpy mass of bowel waste contained in your rectum bulging out against the vaginal canal.

Sometimes, if you are pushing on the loo to pass a hard bowel motion, some of this waste can pop into that small weakened area, which balloons into the vagina as a small pocket. The piece of faeces then becomes trapped and simply won't come out if you are trying to open your bowels. Many women find the easiest option is to simply slide a clean finger into the vagina and push the small ball of waste matter forward so it can pass out.

If the problem keeps happening, it can often be dealt with by a vigorous regime of pelvic exercises to strengthen the area (see page 350 for the most effective way to do them). If this is not sufficiently helpful and the sensation is worrying or uncomfortable, a surgical tuck can be done in the vagina (see pages 369–70).

PILES (HAEMORRHOIDS)

What are they?

Piles may be a standing joke, but not if you've got them. They are caused by enlarged blood vessels in the wall of the anus and can be very uncomfortable, especially if you are sitting for long periods. Unfortunately, new mothers do a lot of sitting, as a tiny baby needs frequent feeds.

Symptoms

Apart from feeling the presence of small lumps around your rectum, they can also be itchy. Piles may feel uncomfortable or downright painful when you pass a bowel motion, and they may even bleed. They can also protrude outside the anus and if they don't return on their own you may need to push them gently back inside using a clean finger.

Causes
They can be caused by strenuous pushing during the second stage of labour, to help the baby out into the world. Generally they subside within a couple of weeks of the birth, but some never quite disappear and may worsen with additional pregnancies.

What helps
Your GP should be able to prescribe haemorrhoid-shrinking ointment for you. These also contain an anti-irritant to help calm any itching. If this is not really very helpful and the haemorrhoids are not disappearing of their own accord, they may need minor surgical treatment such as ligature, which involves tying off the individual piles tightly so that they wither away and slough off gradually. This would not be done until about six months after the birth of your baby.

While you are waiting for them to subside, it can help to use a child's blow-up swimming ring for sitting on, just as many women do if they have a sore perineal stitches site, perhaps after an episiotomy. Try not to get constipated (see What Helps Constipation, page 341) as this means you have to strain more to empty your bowels, which can make the piles worse. Hard faeces are especially uncomfortable to pass if you have haemorrhoids.

HAEMATOMAS

What are they?
Haematomas are small sacs filled with clotted blood. They feel like small lumps underneath the perineal skin, and can be very tender to touch.

Like piles (see page 343) haematomas may develop as a result of strenuous pushing to help the baby out but they should subside within a week or two of the birth. Some however remain. When haematomas refuse to diminish, they may go on to develop fibrosis and form scar tissue around themselves. They may also become infected, and so a stubborn haematoma lump may need removing by minor surgery.

What helps
- An injection. One way to try and get rid of these is to inject fluid into any fibrous tissue which has formed, to spread it out. This can be done under local anaesthetic but it is better to have a general anaesthetic as the injection can make you very sore.
- Manual stretching. It is also possible for a surgeon to try stretching the haematomas manually to break down the fibrous tissues surrounding them. Again, this can be most uncomfortable and is best done under

general anaesthetic. If neither of these works, they can be removed surgically.
• Cold treatment (freezing the area) under local anaesthetic.

INCONTINENCE

This is the second most common loo-orientated problem after childbirth after constipation, but tends to be longer term.

What is it?
Passing water, or bowel waste, when you don't want to. Neither is a disease – they are just a sign that there is a problem, which needs sorting out. One in three women has some measure of urinary incontinence at their six-week postnatal checkup. This may range from feeling a little leaky or experiencing two or three drops of urine loss when you laugh or lift something very heavy on a full bladder, to frequent urine loss even when your bladder is not full which means you are having to use special pads as protection.

The other variety, faecal incontinence, is not as unusual as everyone seems to think, so if this is a difficulty for you, you are certainly not alone. According to Clare Fowler, consultant neuro-urologist at the National Hospital for Neurology in London, as many as 1 to 3 per cent of mothers experience some degree of faecal incontinence postnatally.

New mothers report that this can be anything from needing to reach the loo within a couple of minutes once you have the urge to empty your bowels – which may not sound like much but if you are out and about with no known toilet in sight it can be very disconcerting – to needing to void immediately and not being able to hold back at all. The latter is very unusual, though if it does happen it is exceptionally restricting and upsetting.

However, most women who experience a degree of this are so embarrassed that they tend not to tell their GP about it at all unless asked directly. Some manage to get round this by saying they have frequent diarrhoea. 'But there really is no need to feel embarrassed,' assures Christine Norton. 'Your GP should already be aware that women may have faecal problems after childbirth and be very sympathetic and ready to help.' If you find you cannot discuss this comfortably with your GP, speak to a trained continence nurse instead (see Useful Addresses page 359) over the phone or in person.

Bladderworks and waste plumbing
To understand the causes and cures for incontinence, it helps to know a bit about the way in which the bladder and the anal sphincter muscle operate when they are working properly.

Urine is stored in the bladder, which is essentially a balloon-shaped structure with a ring of muscle around its neck to keep it closed. You usually get the signal to open your bladder and empty it every two to three hours when it has collected about half a pint's worth. If necessary, the average bladder can hold about three-quarters of a pint.

'In fact your bladder has a pretty limited range of behaviour,' says Dr Fowler. 'It spends 99 per cent of its time collecting and storing urine until you can find a socially appropriate moment to get rid of it. And if anything goes wrong with this process, you are likely to be incontinent.'

Your rectum is the final port of call for any undigested matter, and is situated at the far end of your gastrointestinal tract, the long tube which begins at your throat, passing into your stomach, small then large bowel, then rectum, whose exit is at the muscular ring of the anus.

When there is enough waste bulking out the rectum to distend it, the neurological sensors there relay messages to the brain that it is time to defecate. In newborn babies, the sensory nerve signals trigger an automatic reflex so the anal sphincter opens of its own accord. This reflex is brought under voluntary control during most toddlers' potty-training period, so defecation only happens when you make a deliberate effort to open your anal sphincter and expel some waste matter, perhaps with a few good muscular pushes.

If anything damages the nerves that run from the anal sphincter to the brain, or if the structure of the rectum itself is damaged, this produces a continence problem.

Causes of incontinence

Incontinence always has a cause. It isn't something that just happens, and it is certainly not (as some unhelpful GPs have suggested to new mothers) an inevitable result of being a woman or having a baby.

Basically, the background cause is a fundamental design fault in women's anatomy. As Professor Linda Cardozo of King's College Hospital in London puts it: 'You rarely see four-legged animals with incontinence, do you? The trouble is that female humans have to support all their internal pelvic organs with their pelvic floor muscles. In pregnancy this means holding up the increasing weight of a growing baby, placenta and womb; and then it needs to withstand the physical stress of childbirth as well.'

Urinary incontinence after childbirth is usually either what is called *stress incontinence*, when the muscles of the pelvic floor have been weakened by physical stress of pregnancy/labour so that you tend to leak some urine when you cough/sneeze, or *reflex incontinence*, the result of slight damage to the nerves supplying the bladder during labour and birth.

Faecal incontinence after childbirth tends to be caused by the same things. It may also occasionally be the result of a severe or third-degree tear, created as your baby was emerging into the world. This tear can extend from your vagina into your rectal passage, which is next to it. These can heal very well indeed, as long as they are repaired promptly (within half an hour or so) by a *skilled* person, probably a senior obstetrician – it is not a job for an inexperienced doctor or junior midwife. If the repair was not a very good one, you may experience problems until the area has corrective surgery to put everything right.

60 per cent of first-time mothers find they have some degree of incontinence while they are still pregnant. *After* the birth, one study of 1,000 new
mothers carried out in 1984 found that one in five of them was losing
some urine by accident three months after having her baby, and three
years later one in eight was still doing so.

Factors that contribute to incontinence

- *The high levels of hormones*, especially relaxin and progesterone, which
  your body produces while you are pregnant act on all the muscle tissue
  in your body to soften and loosen it, so that your pelvic joints will be
  flexible for childbirth, and your vagina and cervix will expand gradually
  and easily to allow the baby to squeeze past. This temporary, general loss
  of muscle tone includes both the muscles relating to your bladder and
  those controlling your anal sphincter.
- *You have higher than usual levels of relaxin* in your body for some weeks
  after the baby has been born, which discourage your muscle system's
  return to normal.
- *The act of pushing your baby out into the world*, especially if this takes a long
  time or happens over-rapidly, can also cause physical trauma to your
  pelvic floor. It may even cause a small amount of pelvic nerve damage,
  which can affect your control over your bladder after the birth.
- *A poorly repaired third-degree tear* can make bowel problems far more likely.
  Fortunately, tears like this do not happen very often. If they do occur,
  they can be the result of a very rapid, uncontrolled delivery or because
  your baby was particularly large. A badly done episiotomy going beyond
  the designated perineal area might also produce a third-degree tear.
- *Not doing enough (or any) postnatal pelvic lifts.* The exercises can help prevent
  urinary stress incontinence. They can also improve any mild difficulty
  you are having in holding on to bowel motions, so long as this is not due
  to nerve damage.
- *Constipation.* It sounds ridiculous that constipation could make a urinary
  continence problem any worse, but straining repeatedly to pass a hard
  bowel motion can further stress a pelvic floor that has already been temporarily weakened by pregnancy and birth. If there is a good deal of
  hardened faeces packed into your bowels, this puts extra pressure on your
  bladder or urethra neck.

Are you incontinent?

If you are experiencing any of the following regularly, you probably have a
degree of incontinence.

Urinary symptoms include:

- Leaking a little urine when you cough, laugh, lift, sneeze or exercise. The
  acid test is whether, according to Professor Cardozo, you can do star jumps
  on a relatively full bladder without any spillage whatsoever.

- Leaking urine when you make love, or when you have an orgasm. This never gets talked about openly but it is extremely common. New research published in 1996 shows that one in four women who have urinary continence problems is suffering from a sexual problem as a result.
- If you have very little warning of needing to pass water, sometimes perhaps not quite reaching the lavatory in time.
- If you find you are needing to pass water increasingly often, and this is starting to make you think twice about going out and about, or you find yourself checking where the public toilet is each time you are out and feeling uneasy if you cannot locate one.
- If you find you have wet the bed slightly when you wake up in the morning.
- If you notice that you seem to be dribbling urine without realizing it.

The following back passage symptoms do not mean you have faecal incontinence – only that your control may have been impaired and needs your attention to regain it. They may also be warning signs of incontinence developing later if you don't do something now.

- Finding that you cannot hang on for long – or even long enough to reach the toilet in time – when you feel the urge to empty your bowels.
- Finding that when you urinate, you often seem to empty your bowels too without intending to.
- That you sometimes have faecal strains on your pants without realizing that you had passed anything.
- That you need to void your bowels very often.
- That you are uneasy when out and about if you do not know where the nearest toilet is.
- That your behaviour is becoming increasingly adaptive – that you are emptying your bowels frequently 'in case' rather than because you feel you actually need to.

Speak to your GP or continence nurse (see the Continence Information Helpline, page 359) if you are experiencing any of the above. They will be able to suggest measures such as pelvic exercises concentrating on the back passage area, which may well improve matters dramatically.

Full faecal incontinence is rather a different problem and involves actual soiling.

Needing to pass water frequently can also be a symptom of a bladder or urethral tube infection like cystitis. When you go and see your GP about the problem, ask them if they could do a urine test to check for this.

Tests

It is important that your doctor finds out precisely what is causing your continence problem so that they can offer you the correct treatment. It's no good being given a stiff regime of pelvic exercises when the problem is actually a degree of nerve damage due to trauma during childbirth. Any or several of the following tests can be used, and except for the chart, which is a DIY monitoring technique, would be carried out at your local hospital's urology or gynaecology department, usually with a specialist nurse helping you.

Urinary

They can include:

- A How Often?/How Much? chart, filled in by your at home, with the help of a measuring jug kept by the loo.
- Perineometer test, a device which is inserted gently inside the vagina to check how strongly your internal pelvic muscles can squeeze, and therefore, how strong your pelvic floor is and the extent of any damage or slackness there.
- Pad testing to see how wet it becomes with urine over a day. This is not very exact or reliable, though.
- Ultrasound picture to see what your bladder capacity is after you have emptied it.
- Urine flow rate test, to see how fast you can pass water.
- A cystometogram and video-urodynamics. The former shows the amount of pressure the bladder creates when it has urine inside it. The latter is a cystometogram with X-rays. It is often carried out when your continence problem has not responded to simple measures, but before any surgery, to check whether this is what you need.
- Neurophysiological investigation – often done if doctors suspect that incontinence is being caused by a nerve damage because of physical trauma during childbirth.

Faecal

For faecal problems, the tests would probably be done in a different department of the hospital, perhaps gastroenterology, whose clinicians specialize in the workings of all parts of the bowel, including the rectum. They would try to assess whether the difficulty is due to a weakened anal sphincter muscle (perhaps as the result of a third-degree tear) or to neurological damage. They include checking your perineum, checking how well the muscles of the anal sphincter are working, neurological investigations to check the perineal and pudendal nerves, and forming a visual ultrasound image of the muscles of the area.

URINARY INCONTINENCE

What helps
Incontinence is not always a matter of leaking a single discrete drop when you do scissor jumps at an exercise class. It can rule your life if you let it. Research in 1988 published in the *British Medical Journal* found half all women with urinary incontinence avoided sex because of it, 60 per cent avoided trips away from the home if they possibly could, and 45 per cent said they would not use public transport for fear of being too far from a toilet.

The good news is that there is *always* something which can be done either to cure this type of incontinence altogether or improve it considerably. Encouragingly, you can do most of the treatments yourself, with a bit of professional help and guidance.

Pelvic floor exercises
These are the cornerstone of treating stress incontinence. Many women find that no further treatments are needed, and some who have been scheduled for corrective surgery find that a vigorous regime of them can prevent the need for an operation altogether.

Experts say that you are supposed to do 300 to 400 a day postnatally for three months or so. This may seem an awful lot, especially if you start trying a few days after the birth and find that not only are you rather sore there and can only do them very gingerly, but the muscles don't seem to be responding very well to your instructions and it is a major effort to get any done at all. If this is still a problem even after any stitches in the area have healed, go and see your GP and ask if they can refer you to a specialist physiotherapist.

It helps to start with doing just a few four times a day. If that is uncomfortable, try again in a few days' time. It's encouraging that generally the more you do the easier it gets until you can do 30 or 40 at a time without thinking twice about it. Two other pluses are that these exercises encourage perineal healing because they stimulate blood flow to the entire area, and also tone up your vagina after the stretching of childbirth.

As with most new exercise regimes, it may feel for the first few weeks that you seem to be expending a lot of effort and getting nowhere. If you do feel this way, try keeping a daily diary of how many you can do and how often, and how much urine you lose involuntarily during each day even if it is only a drop or two. You will probably be able to look back at your progress over the weeks and be encouraged by just how much improvement you have made.

How to do pelvic lifts
To get the most out of them, do them *at least* three or four times a day. To help you remember to do them in the first place (it's not usually the first thing in your mind when you have a new baby to look after and are short on

sleep), do them when you do other routines, every-morning, every-evening things like brushing your teeth, and also at any time you encounter water (e.g., boiling a kettle, filling the bath) – the sound of running water often triggers a desire to go to the loo anyway. Or even better, do a few of them each time you sit down to feed your baby (that means at least six times a day).

The National Childbirth Trust suggests sticking coloured adhesive dots in strategic places – the fridge door, the mirror, the telephone – and doing some exercises each time you spot a dot. One woman in Wakefield recently reported she had become so conditioned to seeing a green dot and instantly responding with pelvic lifts that she's still doing it three years later, and probably has the most powerful pelvic floor in Yorkshire. Another tip, advises Judy Hakin, the Continence Nurse Advisor at King's College Hospital in London, is to get yourself a cheap bleeping watch and set it to bleep hourly during the day. Every time it does, you do some pelvic lifts.

Finding the right muscles
You need to locate three different sets:

1. The sphincter muscles which open and close the neck of your bladder. Next time you pass water, try stopping the flow of urine – the muscles you are using are those of your bladder sphincter.
2. The muscles that control your anus. Pretend that you badly want to empty your bowels (or wait until you actually are). Now try and make yourself hang on for a little longer. The muscles you are using to do this are the ones controlling your anus.
3. The muscles you use to squeeze and relax your vagina. Flex the muscles you usually use in your vagina to grip or squeeze your partner's penis when you are having intercourse. If you are not quite sure that you are flexing the right ones (there are so many different bands of muscle in the area that it can be hard to separate the action of one from another) slide a tampon applicator or a clean finger into your vagina and try squeezing that.

It takes a bit of practice at first, but once you've got the technique you've got it for life. If you are not quite sure whether you have identified the right muscle groups, it is well worth making a one-off appointment to see your local continence advisory nurse (your health visitor, midwife, practice nurse or GP will be able to tell you where to find them) to make sure. Thousands of women have spent weeks, sometimes months flexing the wrong muscles, usually in their buttocks or upper thighs, and become very discouraged when this did their pelvic floors no good at all.

An added plus of doing regular pelvic exercises and toning up the entire vaginal and pelvic area is that this can feel very good to a male partner during intercourse, and also contribute to more powerful orgasms for you, too.

> ### The long-term benefits of pelvic exercise
> Pelvic exercises are a very good life-long habit to get into. If physiotherapists had their way, the exercises would be taught at 'every girls' gym class at every school in the country' so women got into the habit of doing a few every single day of their lives. Pelvic lifts don't just help you restore your bladder control after childbirth. Done regularly, they can go a long way to helping you avoid continence problems and prolapse of the womb, which so many women experience to some degree after their menopause.

Catch the rhythm – smile inside

To do one full pelvic floor exercise, you need to squeeze each set of muscles in turn. Hold for a count of four and release each set in turn, then tighten them all together and pull up the entire sling of muscle running sideways across your pelvic floor. This is called The Pelvic Smile, because that is the shape it is making inside you.

Try to get into a steady, easy rhythm for doing this, saying something like: '**Front** [urine-stopping muscles] **Back** [bowel-stopping ones] **Middle** [vaginal muscles] **Pull Up** [all of them together].'

Repeat three or four times a session at first – or as many as feel comfortable, and stop if it hurts. Work gradually up to 10, 20, 30 then 40 or 50 at a time. Do the sessions at least four times a day, or if possible, each time you sit down to feed your baby.

Extra measures to strengthen the pelvic floor

Machine power

Pelvic exercises can be augmented by passive exercise, using low-level electrical stimulation to help the relevant muscles contract. This can be arranged with a hospital physiotherapist, and carried out under their supervision. You can either work with the machine, consciously flexing in time with it, or let it do it for you. Even with the latter, your muscles can end up working hard and you may find you actually feel quite tired afterwards. As to how it feels, comments vary from 'quite relaxing really' to 'like a dead frog kicking in one of those 5th form lab experiments at school.' Women also report that when the machine stimulated the right muscle groups, it helped them identify which ones were which: 'I was never quite sure I'd found the right ones before.'

The machines work along the same lines as the Slendertone passive exercise machines at health farms and beauty/exercise salons. You use them while lying down comfortably, attached via slim, insulated wires ending in soft, flat, rubber pads kept on your skin either by suction, or, with the old-fashioned type, with tape. The pads are placed *over* the muscle groups they are going to work on – for instance, your pee-stopping and sex-squeezing muscles would be stimulated by pairs of pads against either side of your lower abdomen. They are not used internally.

Though they can enhance the work you are doing yourself, passive exercise

Size inside – and sex

Many women fear that after childbirth their vagina is wider and looser than it was before and that this will affect the quality of their partner's sexual enjoyment, as well as their own. Though it is completely normal for there to be some change in tightness and dimension, it is often not enough for a male partner even to notice, though a woman may worry he can. And even if he does, the most usual male comment is that sexual entry is easier but he can feel *no* difference once the penis has actually slid into the vagina.

If there *is* a change which is significant enough for both partners to find it a problem, pelvic exercises can improve matters considerably. If there has been extensive stretching and loss of tone, a regime of regular internal exercises plus minor surgery involving a small tuck in the vaginal tissue, like a dart in a dress, can improve matters dramatically.

However, this can be an uncomfortable operation to recuperate from (similar to having another episiotomy), and it does involve a general anaesthetic so it is very much a last resort. (See Sex page 483.) It is therefore not really worth having it done unless you have completed your family, as any subsequent births may do the same damage all over again. If a woman does feel very strongly that she would like the tuck operation before she has finished childbearing, it would probably mean subsequent births would have to be by Caesarean section.

is not a substitute for it and you need to carry on faithfully with your own active exercise regime.

Biofeedback

This can improve the results of ordinary pelvic floor exercises too, and has a success rate of about 80 per cent. It involves using electrical equipment to see and feel exactly when you are clenching specific pelvic floor muscles, and so retraining yourself to control the process. Some urology departments of the major teaching hospitals offer this therapy. Ask your GP if they can refer you to a unit in your area. If they cannot find one, ring the Continence Foundation to find out where it is and let your GP know.

Internal Weight Training

This involves doing pelvic exercises – with weights. These are usually slightly cone-shaped or tampon-shaped, covered in plastic or perspex and weighted inside with aluminum. A single set would have several different weights ranging from light to medium to heavy.

You begin by holding one of the lighter ones inside your vagina for half an hour or so, gradually progressing to the heavier ones for longer. Check with your doctor before you begin using these. You will begin to see improvements after only a few weeks. According to a small study of 39 women who were on a waiting list to have surgery to correct their stress incontinence at

St James and St George's Hospitals in London in 1988, after four weeks of cone training 70 per cent reported either a considerable improvement, or a complete cure. Other research suggests that pelvic tone improves faster if you are using vaginal cones than with plain pelvic floor exercises alone.

You can buy your own sets for home use: one type called Femina Cones are about £40. But it is cheaper to borrow some from the hospital physiotherapy department, so ask your therapist or your continence nurse about this.

Lifting devices

These are short-term interim measures, designed to help control incontinence while it is being treated. These days they are not usually given to young sexually active women. They include:
— Vaginal rings, small ring devices or ring pessaries which help lift up the bladder neck if it is dropping down slightly. These are available from your GP, specialist hospital department (either obstetrics and gynaecology, or urodynamics department) or continence nurse. Continence nurses have had specialist training in this area. They may be attached to a large GP practice, or working at a hospital department. They can be a fund of invaluable, completely confidential practical advice and support. The Continence Foundation has a list of where to find your nearest one.
— Tampons. Inserting an ordinary tampon into your vagina has the same effect as a pessary device or, temporarily, as surgery – it lifts up your bladder neck. This can be useful when you are out and about or exercising, but do not wear them all the time as apart from anything else they absorb the natural moisture from the vaginal lining, leaving it dry and vulnerable to infections like thrush. When you are wearing them, make sure you change them every three to four hours, again to avoid the risk of infection or the unlikely but potentially serious toxic shock syndrome.

It is important to wait until it feels entirely comfortable to use tampons, as sometimes the perineal area and vagina may still be a bit sore following any stitches or mechanical trauma from the recent birth. Many women also find that their baby passing down their vagina has stretched it so that it has not yet returned to its former size, and the tampon will not stay in place very well. Don't worry, as while you will never be quite the same size as before down there, the area will soon return virtually to normal, especially if you continue to do enough pelvic exercises.

Pads and Pants

If you feel you would like the added security of a protective pad to wear in your pants while waiting for continence treatment to take effect (and you won't need to wear these for long as nine out of 10 continence problems can be completely cured) check with the trained nurses on The Continence Foundation's helpline, who are all sympathetic, helpful and advise in total confidence, as to the best types to get.

One recent survey suggested that about 60 per cent of women were using ordinary sanitary towels to catch any involuntary urine flow. But unless it is only a matter of a couple of drops or so these are not really the best thing to use as they do not mask urine odour. There are currently about 100 different companies making special slim, discreet pads which have been specially treated with gel to neutralize any possible urine smell, and they are available from large chemist outlets such as Boots.

Self-help for incontinence

- Start pelvic exercises as soon after childbirth as you can.
- Ring any of the relevant helplines (see Useful Addresses page 359) for some confidential practical advice – and encouragement.
- Go back to your GP if matters are not improving, or if you find you cannot do pelvic lifts. Don't give up on it – you may just need a little bit of expert help, perhaps from the hospital physiotherapist, to sort things out.
- Try and keep your weight down (see How to Get Your Body Back page 470). You will probably lose weight quite fast after the birth to the end of the first three months, but may well find you get stuck with about half to one extra stone for months after that. If you are a stone or more overweight it can put additional unwelcome pressure on your bladder.
- Avoid diuretic drinks like tea and coffee, colas or alcohol as these can make you produce more urine. But do not restrict the overall fluid intake because that may make continence problems even worse, and produce other difficulties for your kidneys as well. Try to drink seven to eight mugs of liquid a day – diluted fruit juices or squashes, milk, plain water or herb teas.
- Avoid becoming constipated by eating plenty of fibre (see Constipation, page 342).
- Clothes: while you are dealing with any continence difficulties, it helps to wear the sort of clothes which can be easily and quickly adjusted so you can pass water or empty your bowels without delay when you reach the loo. Loose skirts, trousers without complicated fastenings, French knickers are all good options. Wearing leotards, teddies or tight Lycra leggings could cause a delay that makes all the difference.
- If matters are not improving, go to see your local continence nurse (again), The Continence Foundation has a list of where they can be reached countrywide). If you and the nurse still feel you need more professional help, see your GP and insist on a referral to a good gynaecologist specializing in this area, or to a urologist.

Getting a bit discouraged?

Even if things are not going very well, don't ever feel that there is nothing you can do to improve the problem – because there is plenty – nor that you are just going to have to put up with this because you aren't, and there is no reason why you should. There is always something which can be done either to improve the situation or cure it altogether, and it is your right to have access to whatever assistance or treatment you need. Keep talking to the continence advisors, who can offer both vital moral support as well as advice, and if necessary, keep on pushing for specialist referral.

DIY Check Up

Been pelvic smiling for weeks and want to see if it's working? Try stopping your flow of urine halfway through next time you are on the loo. Note how promptly it halts. If you have difficulty cutting it off, see how long it takes you to do this – or if you can do so at all.

Try this self test the second time in the day you pass water. The first time your urine will contain high levels of bacteria which have built up overnight, and leaving a little behind in the bladder might encourage a urinary infection such as cystitis. And if you leave it till late in the day it's not a fair test of bladder strengthen as all the muscles of your body, including those of your bladder sphincter, will have become tireder by then and you will have more pee-stopping difficulty than you should. Do this exercise once a week – say each Monday – and keep a chart of the results, so you can see your progress clearly week by week. This can be very encouraging as many women discover they are improving far faster than they had ever thought.

Don't leave the problem to sort itself out, no matter how tired or busy you are at the moment. It won't.

Never give up!

Surgery

The final option for severe stress incontinence is an operation, carried out under general anaesthetic, which usually lifts up the neck of the bladder, including the bladder sphincter muscle itself, to a higher position in your body. This may also involve correcting any sagging of the pelvic floor.

There is also a new form of minimally invasive surgery which involves injecting collagen (the natural material which forms the scaffolding of skin and muscle) into the neck of the bladder, to strengthen it. This is usually done under local anaesthetic. About 100 hospitals in the UK are now using this method, which is suitable for urinary stress incontinence caused by childbirth. So far, it looks as if the results offer some long-term (up to five years, perhaps more) improvement for about six out of every 10 women. As it is so easy to do, doctors say it can always be done again if the effects are wearing off.

FAECAL INCONTINENCE

Back passage problems

These include any damage to:

- The rectal passage, which solid waste (faeces) passes down just before it is expelled from the body. It may have been torn as the baby was pushed out of the birth canal (vagina) which lies alongside the rectum, separated by a muscular wall. This type of damage is called a third-degree tear, and it need not cause any problems if it is properly repaired, by a skilled person, in the same way as an episiotomy cut would be sewn up, straight away after the birth. If it is not properly repaired, then it can cause you problems afterwards, including the possibility of some faeces passing out via your vagina instead of the usual route.

- The anal sphincter itself. This is the powerful little ring of muscle which acts like a thick elastic band at the end of the rectum, keeping any waste material held back until you decide to empty your bowels. According to Christine Norton, former Director of The Continence Foundation, now the first research nurse for the area in the UK: 'The type of problems this may cause show no symptoms at all for years – often the first time you notice anything is the menopause, when muscular tissue (in the pelvic floor especially) starts to lose its tone. When you do finally experience difficulties, it can be anything from being unable to stop yourself breaking wind all the time, or needing to reach a toilet within just two or three minutes once you feel the urge to go, to slight soiling, and full-scale faecal incontinence.

There is also a possibility that all the stretching during childbirth can damage the pudendal nerve in the pelvis. Recent research at St Mark's Hospital in London using ultrasound to look at the anal sphincter muscles of 200 women both before and after they had had their babies, has now shown that the problem of incontinence was usually as a result of a rip or weakened area in this ring of muscle.

What helps
If the problem is only a weak area in the anal sphincter muscle, internal exercises you can do yourself, plus some gentle electric stimulation in the area at a hospital physiotherapy unit, can do the trick. If the muscle has actually been torn, it's not going to get better, either on its own or with exercises. You will need some corrective surgery. You will also need surgery if the rectal passage was torn and was either not properly repaired at the time or has not healed well.

Pelvic muscle exercises
If you are just getting minor symptoms, ask your GP to refer you to a hospital physiotherapist, who can teach you how to do some active pelvic exercises. They may supplement those with passive exercises, the muscles stimulated to contract involuntarily with a very gentle electrical current (like a Slendertone machine), a couple of times a week. These can help you re-establish the right neurological pathways for controlling, and voluntarily emptying, your bowels once more.

In case of emergencies – small amounts of bowel motion making an unwelcome and involuntary appearance – in the meantime, during the weeks when you are working on the area and waiting for the exercises to take effect, there are protective pants you can wear which both contain the waste and help absorb the odour. These are available from major chemists, or by mail order. The Continence Foundation's nurses can advise you over the phone as to which might be the most helpful, and where you can get them from, and how to get them via your local district nurse, because the costs can mount up.

Biofeedback

This is a gentle, conservative treatment which retrains your body to recognize voiding signals, and thus regain voluntary control over the process.

As with biofeedback for urinary problems, it involves being connected to a small unit which electronically measures even the tiniest muscle activity around the anus. By watching the unit's dial, you can see, even if you cannot feel, signs that you are about to move your bowels. It also enables you to observe how much difference your own muscle flexing (even if it is very weak) is having on the process. Thus week by week you can, with practice, rebuild your body's ability to respond appropriately to a bowel-opening reflex and also see with your own eyes how much stronger you are becoming at controlling it.

Biofeedback sessions are carried out in the privacy of a special room in the hospital outpatients department, with a fully trained and highly sympathetic continence nurse to help and encourage you. This gentle therapy may take several weeks worth of practice but it can work very well indeed. One study reported in the *Nursing Times* in 1995 following up 109 people who had received biofeedback therapy for faecal incontinence found that it is highly effective in the *long* term – the acid test of any treatment. Five years on, former biofeedback patients were getting five times fewer problems as those who had not used BF.

Surgery

If gentle measures are not helpful, or if it's clear from your symptoms that you need something stronger, DO NOT JUST PUT UP WITH IT.

For more severe problems, or for those which have not been improved by about three months of the exercises, the solution is almost always a small surgical repair. Ask your GP for a referral to a type of surgeon who specializes in this area – he or she will be called a coloproctologist, and there are 30 or 40 of them in the UK. Referral to such an expert is important as a general surgeon who does not do this type of operation very often is unlikely to do such a good job.

Using ultrasound, the surgeon will pinpoint the exact areas in the anal muscle ring which need repairing, then sew those muscle ends back together under general anaesthetic. These repair operations (called an anterior anal sphincter repair) can be very successful. Encouragingly, the 1995 report from the Royal College of Physicians on the subject found that the results are good in about eight out of every 10 women who were having the operation as a result of damage during childbirth. In most cases it completely solves the problem.

New treatments on trial for urinary and faecal incontinence

- Electro-stimulation of the nerves at the base of the spine (the ones which control the rectal passage and anal sphincter ring of muscle). Very small initial studies (reported in the *Lancet*, October 1995) in elderly people only, have suggested this can help two out of three, though the technique is still very experimental.
- A new weapon in the battle against women's urinary stress incontinence is the urethral balloon. It is about one-fifth the size of a sanitary tampon. You insert it with a reusable applicator, use it once, then throw it away afterwards. The device's tip is inflated to press the vaginal wall on to the urinary canal lying next to it, so blocking any unwanted urine flow. With 20 minutes' training from a specialist nurse, the patient can easily put these in and remove them herself, and the device can be useful if a woman is about to go out and about and fears a leakage. The balloons were expected to be on sale in the UK in summer 1996.
- There is some experimental work being carried out at a few British hospitals to see if injecting collagen can help strengthen areas in the back passage which have been weakened or damaged during labour or soon after delivery. Doctors are not yet sure whether it could help here in the same way as it can with childbirth-induced urinary stress incontinence.
- High-tech experimental solutions, such as repairing the anal muscle ring by grafting some muscle from your leg, implanting some tiny electrodes and having a tiny magnet which can cause them to stimulate the new muscle either to open (if you want to go to the loo) or remain shut (if you don't). A sort of pacemaker for the bottom.

USEFUL ADDRESSES

Aquaflex, Depuy Healthcare, Millshaw House, Manor Mill Lane,
Leeds LS11 8LQ. Tel: Freephone 0800 614086. Confidential helpline: 0800 526177.

System of pelvic exercise cones worn internally costs from about £32 a set.

Chartered Society of Physiotherapy, 14 Bedford Row, London WC1R 4ED.
Tel: 0171 242 1941.

Offers advice and information on exercises to help correct continence problems. They also advise on antenatal and postnatal exercises of all types.

The Continence Foundation, 2 Doughty Street, London WC1N 2PH.
Tel: 0171 404 6875.

The Continence Information Helpline, tel: 0191 213 0050.

Both staffed by trained specialist nurse counsellors who can offer support and practical advice on any aspect of postnatal urinary or faecal incontinence.

Intravent Orthofix Ltd, Burney Court, Cordwallis Park, Maidenhead, Berks SL6 7BZ. Tel: 01753 860378.

Manufacturers and suppliers by mail order of the small sets of vaginal weights for internal pelvic toning exercises. £35 a set including P&P.

National Childbirth Trust, Alexandra House, Oldham Terrace, London W3 6NH. Tel: 0181 992 8637.

Advice/literature on all aspects of childbirth and postnatal issues, including continence.

Why Can't I Sit Down?

The good news is that around 50 per cent of all new mothers do not experience any particular discomfort or pain at all after the birth of their babies, according to the ongoing Britain Avon Longitudinal Study. The less good news is that the other 50 per cent or so do. If you are one of them, this chapter is about the types of problem you may come across, and what to do about them. Because whatever the problem is, minor or more severe, there is always something that you, the medical staff, or both, can do to make it very much better – or, as usually happens, get rid of it completely.

Note: Some researchers feel the above figures are too low. Aberdeen Maternity Hospital, for instance, questioned about 200 newly delivered mothers in 1992, and found that 72 per cent needed some form of painkilling treatment the day after they gave birth; 77 per cent of first-time mothers said their biggest problem was pain around their perineal areas from tears or stitches. The same number of mothers who had had babies previously reported that it was uterine cramps that caused them most difficulty. Even so, that still leaves an encouraging quarter of mothers who reported no painful problems after the birth.

The most common source of discomfort in the first few days after you have had your baby is:

Most common types of postnatal pain/discomfort Taken from the ongoing British Avon Longitudinal Study.		
What is sore?	*Almost always* %	*Sometimes* %
1st most common: Painful stitches	9	40
2nd Backache	8	58
3rd Headaches/migraine	2	56
4th Haemorrhoids	7	32
5th Breast/nipple problems	1 to 2	34

A SORE EPISIOTOMY OR TEAR SITE

An *episiotomy* is a sterile scissors cut made in your perineum, the muscular area between your vagina and anus. It would usually be done during a contraction – when the baby's head is stretching the perineum as far as it can go. Although the area is generally already numbed by this extreme stretching, the hospital will probably have given you a local anaesthetic too. A *tear* occurs naturally, where the tissue of the birth canal may give way along the line of least resistance, to make way for the baby's descending head. Minor to moderate tears are thought to heal more easily than an artificial episiotomy cut.

Episiotomy is often carried out in the final stage of labour by the doctor or midwife to:

- Create more room for your baby's head to get past, especially if the baby was in a difficult position for delivery.
- Ease delivery of a premature baby, whose skull is softer than that of a full-term infant – the procedure would reduce pressure on their head as they passed down into the birth canal.
- Speed up the delivery itself if the pushing stage has been going on for a long time and the mother and baby are becoming exhausted.
- Allow more room for an assisted delivery with forceps or vacuum extraction.

Episiotomies are routinely done in about half of all births in the UK. Two-thirds of first-time mothers, and a third of mothers who have had babies

'Harriet, I've been meaning to ask you . . . those words you were shouting during the birth . . . where did you learn them?'

before, will have one of these incisions. Perineal tears are also more common in first-time mothers.

Whether episiotomies are done too readily and too often or not is a subject of an ongoing and very heated debate between natural birth groups/progressive obstetricians and midwives, and the more mainstream medical establishment. However, it is interesting that in the 1940s, if a woman attended by a midwife needed an episiotomy the midwife was, as Beverley Beech, chairwoman of AIMS, The Association for Improvement in the Maternity Services puts it: 'On the carpet – and called upon to explain herself.' There is also a substantial difference between a routine episiotomy (done perhaps because of rigid hospital policy limiting how long a woman may remain in the second stage of labour) and a necessary one, carried out because of a labour complication, such as a baby being too large to pass comfortably down and out of the vaginal canal or being in an awkward delivery position.

How well and easily yours heals depends upon the depth and extent of it, as well as how promptly and skilfully it was sewn up. There are varying degrees of tear/cuts which can appear in, or be carried out on, the perineum as the woman reaches the late pushing stage of her labour. They include:

- First-degree tears. These just affect the skin. If they are promptly well stitched they rarely cause any problems at all, and tend to heal within just two or three days. Often they don't need any stitching at all. They may affect the skin of the perineum itself, or the skin of the labia.
- Second-degree tears. These go through the muscle as well as the skin. Again, if stitched properly within half an hour, they rarely cause problems. Usually the area is no longer sore after 10 to 14 days.

   An episiotomy is usually equivalent to a second-degree tear.
- Third-degree tears. These reach from the vaginal and perineal tissues into the rectum. They may be an extension of an episiotomy if the mother has had an especially difficult birth with a big baby. Third-degree tears heal well if they have an experienced member of staff repairing the area promptly after the baby is born.

   These too can, very occasionally, extend to the rectal passage as well, but will also heal well if skilfully repaired. However, it is very important that an expert does this, otherwise the woman may experience bowel incontinence.

   From a doctor or midwife's point of view, a neat episiotomy is easier to sew up than an uneven tear. However, if a tear involves only skin and muscle – i.e. it is a second-degree type, which are the most common – it tends to heal more easily and rapidly than a cut.

   Sixty per cent of new mothers have no problem with pain from the stitches in such a cut or tear site, but the other 40 per cent do. Fortunately the area usually heals well and quickly because its blood supply is so good, and there is an enormous amount which you can do to reduce any discomfort while it does so, and to encourage rapid recovery.

How long does it take to heal?
About three-quarters of all women will no longer be sore in this area after 10 days, but for 8 per cent of them the discomfort may persist for three months. Some women are uncomfortable for much longer than this, and may experience sexual difficulties as a result. If the area has not been properly stitched then it is likely to cause you problems and need additional repair treatment at a later stage (see page 483).

What helps?
Back in the 1920s, well-meaning maternity unit staff used to tie new mothers' knees together and keep them in bed thinking this helped the perineum to heal better. Fortunately they now know better, and the readily available comforting and healing treatments available range from crushed ice packs and herbals baths to local anaesthetics and ultrasound.

In the short term
The following can be helpful for sore stitches sites for problems during the first couple of weeks after you have had your baby, whether they are result of an episiotomy cut or a natural tear.

Though there is no conclusive evidence that any one of them helps every single mother, there are many reports saying they have each helped some, so they are all options worth trying:

- *Crushed ice packs*, wrapped in a clean cloth and held against the area. Do not hold the bare ice packs directly against the skin or you may develop ice burns. It is important to crush the ice as finely as you can, so that it can mould itself comfortably to the contours of your perineum. If you have no crushed ice, packs of frozen peas or sweetcorn will do just as well, but smash out any frozen lumps in the pack first. These DIY fanny-freezer packs need constant renewal because they are obviously less effective as they begin to warm up. Do not try to cook the contents afterwards either. The constant melting and refreezing will encourage bacterial growth so on top of not being able to sit comfortably you could possibly develop food poisoning.
- *Cooling sprays* can help, though they may also cause initial stinging.
- *Epifoam*, a mildly anaesthetizing foam sprayed on the area. It contains a mild steroid and anaesthetic, and the hospital can prescribe this for you.
- *Lignocaine gel*, an anaesthetic gel which the hospital can also give you. Also available in spray form.
- *Cold sitz baths*. There is some evidence that these are more effective at reducing the pain for half an hour afterwards than warm ones – but few people like taking cold baths.
- *Warm baths of plain water*, though some women said that hotter baths are also very comforting, especially if your muscles and ligaments are also aching from the recent major physical effort of labour. Soak for 20 minutes if possible. Women have found the following additives useful:
  — Savlon lotion, which can be soothing though it can make the bath quite slippery.

— 10 drops of good-quality Lavender essential oil. Try brands like Neal's Yard or Tisserand.
- Tincture of the homeopathic remedy Hyper cal. Place a few drops on a soft sanitary pad, as this is also thought to help reduce soreness, encourage cooling and aid the healing process.

Note: you will need to wear sanitary pads for several days to protect your pants from lochia discharge, the blood which comes from your womb as the area where your placenta was attached heals. It diminishes steadily, and disappears altogether within two to six weeks.

Tips for comfort and healing
- Keep the area scrupulously clean, and as dry as possible.
- Change your sanitary pads very often and regularly.
- Wash area in warm water and pat area dry gently with a soft tissue – *not* cotton wool, as though it is wonderfully soft, the area is too sensitive to wipe firmly, and dabbing gently with it can leave strands behind which may encourage infection.
  Do this both after passing water or opening your bowels, or if you are feeling sticky with lochia discharge.
- Comfort pads. Though the newer firm, slim-line pads can be ideal for ordinary menstrual periods, if you are sore around the genital area and have healing tears or stitches, the old-fashioned, large soft cotton wool and loose lint covered ones are particularly comfortable. The packet labelling will say 'Night Size' or 'Maternity Pad'.
- Try KY gel. Though stitches heal better when kept dry, and this also reduces the risk of infection, according to Caroline Flint, President of the Royal College of Midwives, if your stitches are very sore indeed, some KY gel on a clean sanitary pad can be very soothing.
- Put some large handfuls of salt in your warm bath, enough so the water tastes quite salty, and soak your lower regions in there.
- Enhance the healing power of your warm water baths by adding herbal infusions.
  Visit a herbalist, or ask your partner to go for you if trips to hunt for your local shop are impractical, which they well may be at the moment. Many reputable ones also have a rapid 24-hour mail order service (see Useful Addresses page 378). You'll need three types of loose dried herbs – Comfrey, Uva ursi and Shepherd's purse.
  For a single healing bath, you can then make up an infusion from a big handful of this herbal mix. Put the herbs in a bowl, pour over four pints of boiling water, stir and leave to steep for 30 minutes, stirring occasionally. Drain off the liquid and use this in your bath. Caroline Flint suggests adding an entire head of crushed garlic to the above mixture too as it is both antiseptic and healing. The only drawback is that it takes for ever to peel and will probably make the concoction smell strong – and it is a smell that tends to travel around the house.
- Witch hazel soaked into pads, and applied directly onto the perineum

may help, as it can soothe and cool swollen or inflamed tissue. This is the reason why it is also sometimes used for sunburn. Some midwives say that witch hazel and glycerine together are more helpful.

• Paracetamol can be useful for mild perineal pain. If this does not help, try a non-steroidal anti-inflammatory drug like aspirin. However, strong painkillers which contain a good deal of codeine are not so suitable because they can encourage constipation. Straining to empty your bowels is the last thing you need if you have perineal stitches, and many women find they are constipated after giving birth anyway.

• Ultrasound, and pulsed electromagnetic energy. These are often used for many types of soft tissue injury, especially sports injury, but there is conflicting evidence as to whether they really do help. Despite conflicting reports, most maternity units do offer the treatment. It needs to be given by a physiotherapist, and it can be given through a sanitary towel.

Theoretically, ultrasound treatments may help reduce swelling by increasing the permeability of cell walls, so fluid can flow back into them, as well as out to the spaces betw.'en the cells. Pulsed electromagnetic energy, though, is to help heal damaged tissues by restoring the electrical balance of damaged cells.

More comfort-increasing techniques

• It may help to sit on a child's plastic swimming ring, or a foam ring of the sort which used to be used in elderly people's wards, to reduce pressure on your stitches while they are healing. The foam rings are no longer available in NHS maternity wards, as from clinical observations on elderly people's wards where the rings were also used, it is thought that they can prevent blood returning to the heart by compressing the major veins in the legs if used for long periods. However, this need not stop women buying their own (see John Bell & Croyden, Useful Addresses page 372) and using them just for a week or two.

Cushioned seating rings may be especially useful if you are trying to breastfeed for the first time, as it is easier in the beginning to get your baby latched onto your breast in the right position while you are sitting down. Lying down to feed is very comfortable once you have both got the hang of it, but it can be difficult and frustrating in the first day or so, trying to get the baby at exactly the right level to suckle effectively.

If you cannot sit to feed, and find it initially difficult to do so lying down, the only other option is to do so standing up. This can be very tiring, as you may have to do it for hours. Newborn babies often like to suckle for comfort as well as a drink for an hour or more at a time. Some may want to do so at hourly or two-hourly intervals throughout the whole day and night – as even though your milk does not come through until the fourth day or so they will still be getting small amounts of highly nourishing colostrum. If your baby likes to suckle for long periods, try to get some help with the lying down feeding position. If you are in hospital keep asking the nurses or midwives; if you are at home, ask your local community midwife to drop in to see you more than once a day to begin with if she can, or contact your local breastfeeding counsellor from the NCT, or La Leche (see Useful Addresses in Happy, Successful Breastfeeding page 42).

- Keep the area very clean to help avoid infection. Wipe or pat dry from front to back after passing water or emptying your bowels.
- Soothing cold compresses help. Try making a frozen compress sandwich and keeping it in the freezer. The recipe is to take half a dozen wetted men's handkerchiefs, lay plastic layers between them (cut up supermarket bags will do) then freezing the cotton and plastic layers. They are then readily available for use one at a time, twisted into a slim, flexible, and very cold pad, on the episiotomy site.
- Keep the stitches as dry as possible between cooling, soothing treatments as soggy stitches become more easily infected. After baths, showers, urinating while pouring over water to prevent stinging, etc., some women use a hairdryer on a cool setting rather than a potentially abrasive and less than sterile towel or loo paper. If you are drying your stitches manually, pat dry with soft tissue, or keep a separate clean towel for your genital area.

  The only problem with this is that hairdryers may harbour germs best not blown over a healing wound. A potential alternative is to have an electric light bulb shone over your perineum to dry the area with radiating heat, instead of a stream of hot air. Try removing the shade from a lamp which you can pick up and move about – an angle-poise lamp would be ideal.

- Lying on your front is an effective way of relieving pain from episiotomy and tear repair stitches, piles and backache. Put one or two pillows under your waist so your pelvis is raised up slightly and your back flattened comfortably. An extra pillow or two under your front or shoulders is helpful to protect your breasts.

  If the cut or tear is a small one it may well heal on its own without stitching. Because the area would be sore, women tend to keep their legs fairly close together and move carefully so as not to stretch and put any tension on the perineum at all, which would also encourage healing. In many parts of Australia, small cuts and tears are not routinely sutured unless the mother especially wishes it, but kept very clean and dry, and left to heal on their own instead.

Your stitches should be feeling considerably better within 7 to 10 days. If they are not, tell your GP or midwife and ensure they investigate the reason for this as there may be several potential causes. These include infection – which can be swiftly treated with antibiotics – and that the stitches that have been done too tightly, in which case they can be removed.

In the long term

If the sore episiotomy/tear site appears to have healed but is still uncomfortable around three months after childbirth, ask your GP to refer you to a good consultant gynaecologist or obstetrician because it may be that you will need a small operation to put the problem right.

Many problems causing pain and discomfort after childbirth will resolve within a couple of weeks, and most within three months. However, for about one in every 100 women, childbirth may cause some structural damage to the pelvic area which does not resolve on its own within six to 12 months, and needs to be corrected with surgery. Unfortunately only about half the women who need this type of help ever get it. An episiotomy site which has not healed properly is thought to be the problem most often requiring later treatment. The area may be uncomfortable even when touched firmly, and can cause pain which may be acute if you try to have sexual intercourse.

Help for a badly healed episiotomy or tear

There are different types of discomfort associated with a poorly healed or problematic episiotomy site, including:

- Pain, ranging from the area being slightly sensitive to touch, to it being extremely painful to touch.
- Itching, especially if the scar has become lumpy and keloid (overgrown).
- Feeling as if your vagina is too small, or that there is a constant slight pulling and overtightness of the skin. This is likely to be because the episiotomy site was stitched up too tightly. It tends to happen when there was no room left for the tissue swelling which always follows injury, and perineal tissues can swell up considerably.

A poorly healed episiotomy site remains very sore to touch and can make intercourse impossible, or at the very least, uncomfortable rather than pleasurable for any woman.

What might have gone wrong?

- Poor stitching technique. Occasionally, if the stitching has not been done by someone who was competently trained, plain bad suturing may cause the underlying muscles to distort so the labia, perineum and vaginal lining are unevenly aligned.

   Both doctors and midwives who are learning how to do suturing should ALWAYS be carefully supervised. Some of the former may never have done this type of stitching before and the technique is very different from the standard stitching up of a cut, say on a patient's arm or leg, that a new doctor would have been using during their standard stint at the hospital's Accident & Emergency department.
- Granulation and fibrosis over the stitched area so it has not healed flat, and the scar remains raised.

   These tissue overgrowths may also become supplied by tiny new blood vessels, and so develop into living lumps. This is more likely if the area is not kept dry, although it is difficult (and uncomfortable) to keep a vagina completely moisture-free.

- Another reason for poor healing of cuts or tears around the vagina, perineum and labia is that the edges have not been brought together so they lie flush with each other, and they have overlapped or shelved, which is especially likely if the tear is a jagged one rather than a clean cut done by the obstetrician or midwife as an episiotomy.

Treatment

If your episiotomy or tear scar has healed badly and is still painful, it may need to be recut along its original site and sewn up once more, carefully and evenly. This needs to be done under general anaesthetic. It will be as sore as it was originally for a few weeks, but then should gradually begin to improve until it no longer causes discomfort.

It will help to do all the things you did to soothe the pain it causes that you tried originally, such as having regular herbal or saline baths, using cool crushed ice packs on the area, and keeping the stitches dry.

If the problem is that a small nerve had been trapped when the episiotomy repair was done, the treatment would also be surgical. Though this problem is not usual, it can be difficult to detect as there is nothing actually to see even if a woman is examined carefully, and sometimes women have had to seek several second opinions from different consultant gynaecologists before the trouble was pinpointed and dealt with.

But if it is hurting, it is hurting, and you are the best judge of that. So if you are dismissed because the doctor cannot find anything the matter, always ask for referral to one of their colleagues, and keep persisting. Even if the original stitches area has healed months ago, you are not imagining your pain (though having been told a few times there is nothing the matter with you, you may begin to think that perhaps you are). If you are having any trouble being taken seriously, call up a help organization such as AIMS or the Episiotomy Support Group (see Useful Addresses page 371–2) for support and advice.

Help when the vagina feels 'too tight' or scar tissue is painful

This can involve an entire scar area, or an isolated small lump of tissue anywhere along the vagina's length. Either can cause pain, and make penetration during intercourse difficult. This may be due to tissue tenderness, or there may even be a nerve in the area that has been trapped by suturing.

Symptoms

Pain when the area is touched at all for some women; for others they are more aware of pain when trying to have intercourse.

Treatment

Steroid creams may be useful to help soothe tenderness or itching along the scar site.

However, poorly healed or badly done episiotomy or stitch sites usually need to be corrected surgically. A lumpy scar along the vagina's length can be recut and sewn up again carefully. The general term for an operation to repair a vagina is colporrhaphy. Any of these procedures might involve the slight loss of some vaginal tissue, as they are done in much the same way as a dressmaking dart is sewn into a piece of material to conceal a tear.

The operation can be very successful. However, it is not always an easy one to do, as it is possible for a surgeon who does not have good experience in this sort of repair to sew a vaginal repair up 'a little too well' – with the result that the passage is made too tight. This may also be a problem if they were trying to do a small tuck because the vaginal tissues had been very stretched by the baby's descent, leaving the passage far slacker than it was before. The latter is not usual, but is more likely to happen with an extremely rapid delivery. It is therefore worth checking that the consultant who is operating on you has a great deal of experience in this specific area. If they have not, politely ask for referral to one of their colleagues who has. A tactful way of putting it is to ask to see a consultant who 'has a special interest in this area'.

However, even if the vaginal passage is now too small, it is usually possible slowly to restretch it over a period of time by massage or gentle, careful lovemaking. This process may take months and means you need a gentle, understanding partner to help make it work.

Again, aftercare from this type of operation includes all the things that help heal a post-delivery tear or cut (see What helps? page 364 and Labial Tears below.)

WHAT ELSE CAN MAKE SITTING DOWN UNCOMFORTABLE?

Labial tears
Your baby's birth may have caused some small, shallow tears and grazes in the labia, the soft, fleshy lips around your vulva which close around and protect the entrance to your vagina. They do not usually need to be stitched up as they are generally quite small and heal within a few days. However they can be very sensitive while they are healing, especially when you pass water, as urine can make them sting furiously.

What helps?
If the tears are large enough to need it, they will be stitched. If they are not, they will be left to heal by themselves. While they are doing so, all the anaesthetic and cooling sprays, ice packs, and warm soothing salt, aromatherapy and herbal baths which can be helpful for a sore episiotomy site, can help.

Self-help
- Soothing baths and ice packs (see suggestions on pages 364–7).
- Pouring water over your vulva while you are passing water, or doing so in the bath, bidet or shower to avoid the scalding sensation of urine on the soft tissues of the labia, which may be either sore, swollen, slightly grazed or have some minor tears. You can also pour over some cold

comfrey tea. Keeping a supply in the fridge for up to three days when not being used. Or use some of your cooled, diluted herbal bath mix, made as on page 365.

- Another option is to urinate on a bidet with the water spraying gently upwards, or in the bath (clean both bath and bidet well afterwards though). Some women find it helpful to pass water in the bath, running cool water from a showerhead very gently over their perineal area as they do so, but it has to be gently or the force of the water can hurt the perineum too.

A swollen vulva
This is often the result of a long labour with strenuous pushing at the end but it tends to resolve quickly, within a few days at the most.

What helps
- Try taking homeopathic tablets of Arnica as soon as possible after labour, as these can help prevent swelling, bleeding and bruising of all types. For best results (though it is probably a bit late by the time you are reading this) take the Arnica before and during labour too if you can.
- Hold ice packs against this area. This helps reduce, and anaesthetizes the area slightly. It is important to change them every 30 minutes, as they warm up fairly rapidly. Do this lying down if you can.
- Bathe the area in a solution of three teaspoons salt to one tumbler of water.
- Lie down rather than sit when possible. Try to feed your baby while you both lie down together. This will cut out several hours of sitting time. Ask your midwife to help you find a comfortable position so your baby can latch on well, as though this is very comfortable and restful for both of you, it may take a little practice.
- Sit on a child's swimming ring or a foam ring (see page 366) for a few days to help keep pressure off the area.
- Wear loose cotton pants (or your partner's cotton pants if they are good and baggy on you and do not fit too snugly into your crotch) to keep your sanitary towel in place rather than tight bikini pants.
- Choose a soft sanitary towel of cotton wool covered in wide mesh gauze (which says 'Night Size' or 'Maternity Pad' on the packet) rather than a slim-line one.

USEFUL ADDRESSES

AIMS (Association for Improvement in the Maternity Services), 40 Kingswood Avenue, London NW6 6LF. Tel: 0181 960 5585.

Campaigns for better maternity and post-natal care; offers advice and information on women's rights and health issues in both areas; has a free publication list available (please send s.a.e.). Also information on the risks and benefits of ultrasound.

G. Baldwin & Co., Herbalist and Health Foods, 173 Walworth Road,
London SE17 1RW. Tel: 0171 703 5550.

Mail order service and advice.

John Bell & Croyden, Chemists, 50–54 Wigmore Street, London W1H 0AU.
Tel: 0171 935 5555.

Foam rings and other medical supplies.

Culpeper Ltd., Hadstock Road, Linton, Cambridge CB1 6NJ.
Tel: 01223 894054.

Mail-order service of herbal remedies.

Episiotomy Support Group, 100 Holmesdale, Waltham Cross, Herts EN8 8RA.

The London organizer is Sally Barrett, and she can pass you on to a contact in
your area. Send sae with your letter.

Health Rights, Unit 405, Small Businesses Centre, 444 Brixton Road,
London SW9 8ES. Tel: 0171 501 9856.

Works for the rights of all those who use the NHS and provides independent
advice and information on all aspects of health care. May have helpful suggestions if you are having postnatal problems which need correction (e.g. a *still*
painful scar area after many months) but are coming up against a brick wall so
far as being taken seriously or getting a specialist referral are concerned.

National Childbirth Trust, Alexandra House, Oldham Terrace,
London W3 6NH. Tel: 0181 992 8637.

Advice, support and information on all aspects of pregnancy, childbirth and
post-natal care.

Neal's Yard Remedies, 15 Neal's Yard, London WC2H 9DP.
Tel: 0171 379 0705.

Chain of natural remedy shops selling good quality aromatherapy oils and dried
herbs. Also supplies Bach Flower Remedies. Prompt mail-order service.

Relate Marriage Guidance, Herbert Gray College, Little Church Street, Rugby,
Warwickshire CV21 3AP. Tel: 01788 573241; fax: 01788 535007.

If the soreness of a repaired episiotomy or stitches area is causing you sexual
problems even after it should have been better.

Royal College of Midwives, 15 Mansfield Street, London W1M 0BE. Tel: 0171
872 5100.

Advice and information on all aspects of maternity, childbirth and post-natal care.

Preventing Prolapse

What is it?

Prolapse is damage to an organ or internal part of the body so it drops down-wards from its usual position, usually because its supporting tissues have been damaged or weakened. This drop can be so slight as to be unnoticeable by the woman herself, or it can be quite dramatic. Childbirth is a very common cause of a prolapse *later in life* for women and there are several different types which can be caused by labour. It is unusual for a womb actually to prolapse in the classic sense soon after childbirth, but what is more common is that the groundwork for a full prolapse later in life can be laid down now.

Whilst a postnatal prolapse is seldom enough sufficiently marked to cause any problems until 20 or 30 years later, in a few cases the symptoms might be sufficiently marked for you to notice there is something wrong: including the following:

Prolapse of the womb

Its symptoms can include:

- A very slight dragging feeling, if the problem is minor. If it is more severe, you actually feel something bulging out at the top of your vagina, by the cervix.
- A dragging ache around your lower abdomen.
- Backache.
- Fatigue.

Prolapse of the rectum or bladder

This is caused by damage to the tough, fibrous wall between the rectum and vagina. If you feel something bulging through into the back wall of the vagina when you have a full bowel and need to empty it, it is called a rectocele. If you can feel something bulging through the front wall of the vagina, that is the bladder when it is full, and the condition is called a cystocele.

Symptoms, if you are aware of them, may include:

- You may feel a slight bulge in the vagina on either the back or front wall if you slide your finger gently in.
- Some vaginal discharge.

- An aching or dragging feeling around your perineum, the muscular area dividing the entrance of your vagina from the entrance to your rectum.

Vaginal prolapse

This is caused by structural damage to the vagina so that this moves downwards, protruding slightly into the labial area.

Symptoms, if you notice any, may include:

- A slight but continual awareness of what is described by women who have experienced it as 'drooping' or 'a feeling of bagginess' in their vagina. You can pull the dropping area back up into position by doing a pelvic lift movement. Wearing tampons may be uncomfortable because they drag at the already stretched vaginal tissue when they are removed.
- You may find you are more prone to vaginal infections.
- The prolapsed area itself may be uncomfortable – perhaps it may be rubbed by tight pants and become sore. The fact that something is in the labial area which shouldn't be there can in itself be unpleasant. Even if it does not actually hurt, it simply does not feel right and a woman may be constantly aware of it.
- Feeling as if you need to pass water frequently.
- You may be more prone to developing urinary infections, like cystitis.

Prolapse of the cervix

This may drop down slightly from its usual position during pregnancy, and not fully return after delivery.

Symptoms, if you notice any, can include:

- A bulge about the size of a cherry at the top of your vagina.
- An aching, dragging feeling in your lower abdomen.

What helps

Pelvic exercises

See pages 350–2 for the easiest and most effective way to do these.

Pelvic exercises can help mild prolapses of certain types, but as they do not benefit all types, it is important to check with your gynaecologist or obstetrician first that the type of prolapse you have can be helped this way. However, pelvic lifts are often the first line of treatment to try, and they can mean you avoid surgery altogether.

As a bonus they can also be useful if, on top of everything else, you are also suffering from stress incontinence (see page 346), which is caused by the same types of damage to the pelvic soft tissues and suspensory ligaments as a mild prolapse.

This is because the brunt of the force with which your baby descends is taken by the pelvic floor, the sling of muscles which holds up all the internal abdominal organs, including the womb, bladder, intestines and rectum.

Pelvic exercises can be practised at home but they need to be done properly to be effective. It's not just a matter of clenching your bottom or squeezing your urine-stopping muscles as often as you can – so it helps if you have someone to describe in detail the right way to do them. See also Extra Measures to Strengthen the Pelvic Floor, page 352.

To get the most out of pelvic floor exercises you will need to do them as many times a day as you can, at least three or four.

If despite all your efforts, the exercises do not seem to have made much difference after another three months, return again to see your obstetrician and ask them to re-examine you, and insist that they consider a surgical repair for you.

Temporary measures
Wearing a pessary
If you have a prolapsed womb and it has not been improved by at least three months' worth of rigorous pelvic floor exercises, or is too severe to be suitable for these, you will need surgery to correct it but may have to wait a few months for it.

In the meantime your GP or gynaecologist can fit a pessary which is placed at the top of the vagina. It is a circular ring of soft rubbery plastic about 1 cm thick, which fits around the cervix, holding the womb upwards and back while allowing the round cervix to protrude through a hole in the middle, so any menstrual blood can flow out normally. It needs to be fitted by a doctor who has experience of this type of device, and many GPs will refer you to a hospital outpatients department for this (family planning clinics are not equipped to do it either).

The ring stays in until it needs replacing, for between three and six months, so it's very important that it fits well. To make sure of this, it comes in a variety of different sizes – so tell your doctor if it is at all uncomfortable. It does protrude down into the vagina slightly and though you will probably not be able to feel it, your sexual partner will. Watch out for signs of infection when you wear one, though – the main signs are any bad-smelling discharge or itching – and if you have any report them straight away. Pessaries can also cause a certain amount of vaginal inflammation which may turn into

---

Some women find it very difficult if not downright impossible to do pelvic lifts after giving birth because their perineum has been damaged by a bad tear or episiotomy. The area may also feel numb and refuse to respond to your efforts to mobilize it for a few days.

The rule is to do these exercises as soon as possible. Even if you only do a few in the first few days very gingerly indeed it will improve the circulation to this area, which in itself can help promote healing. However if it really hurts, wait another couple of days until the area has healed a little further and you can use the muscles more easily. If you are still unable to flex your pelvic muscles even after the area has healed, tell your GP and ask to be referred to a specialist for help. These muscles need using to avoid problems such as prolapse and incontinence.

an ulcer, due to constant pressure on the delicate tissues, so again report any feelings of discomfort.

Surgery

Surgery for any sort of prolapse involves a general anaesthetic and a stay in hospital of about a week. Just exactly what the surgeon does depends on what is wrong. In the first six to 12 months after you have had your baby, doctors may be unwilling to do any surgery at all, even though it is clear that there is a problem. One reason is that despite the distress and discomfort this type of problems can cause, the operations to correct them are not usually considered a priority within the NHS, especially as now budgets are so tight.

However the basis of most treatments is to take a surgical tuck in whatever muscle or ligament has been overstretched, basically by cutting it, removing any excess tissue and sewing it back up again. Prolapse operations are successful in about 80 per cent of all cases.

In about 20 per cent of cases, the problem returns later, but usually any pelvic tissue repair of this sort is quite strong because where a tuck has been taken in muscle or somewhere like the thick, tough wall between rectum and vagina, a certain amount of fibrosis (overgrowth of tough fibrous tissue) would cover the area which has been stitched, reinforcing it further.

Occasionally if the prolapse of a womb is severe a surgeon may suggest a hysterectomy if you have completed your family.

There are also some clinical reasons for not doing such a repair too promptly, including:

- The fact that many structural postnatal problems, including prolapses, can improve considerably on their own within six to 12 months with pelvic exercises.
- Prolapses do not usually happen until several years later, following further pregnancies, the effect of the menopause and general ageing, so it is unusual for younger women to need an operation to repair one. The seeds of a prolapse can be sown now – but it will not develop fully into a condition needing repair for some years. The best way to prevent one is to do pelvic exercises several times a day, every day.
- After body tissues are repaired, whether they are the knee ligament or the pelvic floor muscles, they may be left permanently weakened by the surgery and stitching. There is therefore a chance that the problem may recur. A proportion of postnatal prolapse repairs do need redoing around the time of the menopause, because the pelvic tissues are then losing elasticity and strength as their supply of oestrogen diminishes naturally. So if there is an existing weakened area, it may well break down again, and the second repair form an even weaker link than the first.
- If a woman wants to have more children, and there it is clear that her pelvic floor has been weakened so as to produce the beginnings of a prolapse there, she is advised to use temporary measures, such as a vaginal

support ring pessary for a womb prolapse or vaginal prolapse, until she has completed her family – and then have the repair operation.

- If she has already had a repair, either of a stitches site or pelvic floor damage, and it is feared that pregnancy and labour would damage it all over again, she would be advised to give birth to her subsequent babies by Caesarean section. Further, the weight of the developing baby and growing uterus could, together with the relaxant effect of pregnancy hormones upon all muscles and supporting ligaments, put you at risk of another prolapse.

USEFUL ADDRESSES

Aquaflex, Dupuy Healthcare, Millshaw House, Manor Mill Lane, Leeds LS11 8LQ. Tel: Freephone 0800 614086/Confidential Helpline 0800 526177.

System of pelvic exercise cones worn internally, cost from about £32 a set.

Chartered Society of Physiotherapy, 14 Bedford Row, London WC1R 4ED. Tel: 0171 242 1941.

Will offer advice and information on exercises to correct pelvic problems such as prolapse, associated with pregnancy and birth. Have information on all the latest treatments and research work into the area too, and a range of helpful literature. Can put you in touch with a specialist physiotherapist in your area.

Intravent Orthofix Ltd, Burney Court, Cordwallis Park, Maidenhead, Berkshire SL6 7BZ. Tel: 01753 860378.

Manufacturers and suppliers by mail order of the small sets of vaginal weights for internal pelvic toning exercises. £35 a set including P&P.

The National Childbirth Truth (NCT), Alexandra House, Oldham Terrace, London W3 6NH. Tel: 0181 992 8637.

Help, support and information on all aspects of pregnancy, childbirth and post-natal health and wellbeing, including upon pelvic exercises.

Pelvic Pain – the Treatments

There are many different causes and types of persistent pelvic pain (PPP), and it is a common problem which women often do not tell their doctors about. The pain may feel different for different women, depending on whether it is the result of a short-term, acute condition – perhaps a temporary pelvic spasm produced during or after sexual arousal which happens each time you make love – or a long-term problem associated with something like a grumbling pelvic infection, or even chronic stress.

Women usually report that theirs feels like a dull, persistent ache if they have the grumbling, long-term types of PPP. Others also report that if the pain is associated with sexual arousal it feels sharp, can be exceptionally unpleasant, both in the deep pelvic region in general but also around the perineal areas, and may last for anything from minutes to a couple of hours.

Causes

These are many and varied – but the list includes being more highly strung and stressed than the average woman, and childbirth – and some women do indeed report their PPP began soon afterwards. Childbirth could be associated with pelvic pain for several different reasons.

- *Stress.* Caring for a new baby day and night will make you feel more tired than usual, at least for several months. It may also be quite stressful, especially if you have a demanding baby and/or other small children/ a job/all three to manage as well.

    Stress can cause muscular tension all through your body, especially around the shoulders, and the abdomen – and pelvis. Permanently tensed abdominal/pelvic muscles will squeeze the blood vessels running through them and supplying them, so they receive less oxygenated blood, and can eliminate fewer muscular waste products than usual. This will make them sore, just as muscles hurt when overused for a short period (e.g. running a couple of miles if you are not used to it) or when they do not get enough oxygen (as with the pain of angina because not enough oxygenated blood is reaching the heart to feed its muscle mass).
- *Dilated pelvic veins.* It has been suggested that this is due either to the body making too much oestrogen in general, or to recent pregnancy and childbirth when levels of oestrogen soar.

The theory is that for some women, their pelvic veins dilate substantially during pregnancy under the influence of relaxing hormones such as oestrogen and relaxin, to accommodate the extra 30 to 40 per cent of blood in your body in general, and the need for a far greater supply to the pelvic area for your enlarged uterus and your growing baby. This is perfectly normal, but it's thought that for some women, these pelvic veins do not return to their former size afterwards. This means that after you had had your baby, there would be a relatively small (i.e. normal) volume of blood flowing through these permanently enlarged pelvic vessels, which moves more slowly, giving rise to oxygen deficiency and therefore pain.

Professor Richard Beard of St Mary's Hospital in London has pioneered this theory of pelvic pain for many years and has a well-known pelvic pain clinic (possibly the only specialist one in Britain).

He points out that he and his staff looked at PPP women's pelvic areas by ultrasound scan, it was plain that in 80 per cent of cases, they had enlarged veins in the area – sometimes up to five times the usual diameter. About half also had small cysts on their ovaries. Professor Beard feels that this confirms the theory, and adds that the best way to encourage those veins back to their normal size is to reduce the body's supply of oestrogen, which may be keeping them enlarged. However, other specialists disagree with his ideas.

Treatments

Treatments for PPP include many different approaches such as:

- The Pill, which would flatten out your natural oestrogen production levels.
- Danazol, which suppresses oestrogen production but may have some unpleasant masculinizing side effects such as increasing body hair, weight gain and acne. Usually at the lower dosages at which it is given for PP these are not so marked, though.
- Provera, which also suppresses oestrogen production. Side-effects may include a drier vagina, which can be counteracted by using a lubricant like KY gel, or oestrogen cream if your doctor can assure you that even tiny amounts of local oestrogen would not affect the action of the Provera treatment.
- Pain killers, ranging from a couple of aspirin to stronger measures such as Solpadeine.
- Counselling, to help reduce stress, establish whether there is anything especially distressing you which might be indirectly causing your pelvic pain, or to help you understand the cause of the stress and manage it effectively.
- Antibiotics, if the pain is due to a pelvic infection following childbirth.
- Relaxation techniques to help reduce stress.

Women with persistent pelvic pain which is not responding to these usual treatments should be offered a laparoscopic investigation. This involves a slim fibre optic tube being inserted into the pelvic area via a small incision, while you are under general anaesthetic. The tube enables the doctor to see inside the pelvic cavity, and look for anything that might be causing the pain such as adhesions (a sign of endometriosis), inflammation, which would indicate there was an infection which needed treating, or even a benign tumour. Even if there was nothing to be seen, at least you could then be assured that there was no sinister physical cause of the pain.

Finding the right help

Though it is a relief to know you have nothing unpleasant lurking which is causing your pelvic pain, it may also be discouraging when doctors cannot find any cause for it at all and many women report they have been made to feel as if they are merely imagining it all, and bringing it on themselves. Nor is it uncommon to have to search persistently for a doctor who is both sympathetic to your difficulty, and has the experience to help you do something effective to deal with it.

But don't give up – the pain is real enough if you are feeling it, and you are fully entitled both to competent treatment and someone to take you seriously. If necessary, ask your GP or gynaecologist to write to the St Mary's Hospital clinic (their new head of obstetrics is Professor Lesley Reagan) asking if they know of any gynaecologist in your area who has a special interest in PP, or even if the clinic can take you as a referral. If you feel you are being stonewalled, contact a consumer advisory group like the College of Health or the Patients Association (see Useful Addresses) for advice.

Self-help

Relaxation techniques can be extremely helpful for PPP. Try anything you can fit in to what is currently probably very limited free time. An hour's yoga class each day might not be much help if you would seldom be able to get there, but briefer techniques, which could be fitted in to the odd 10 or 15 minutes of quiet, might be viable. Options include:

- A hot bath with one of the relaxing aromatherapy oils added to it (such as lavender). You need to soak for about 15 to 20 minutes to get the benefit.
- A 20-minute brisk walk or jog around the block on your own – much quicker than having to go to an exercise class, but still raises your endorphin levels, the natural opiates your body produces in response to physical effort, and which have a soothing effect for some time afterwards.
- Ten minutes of deep, calm breathing – the type you might have learnt at antenatal classes. Gaining control over your breathing pattern is easy to do, and a very quick way to relax as it also slows your heart rate and general metabolic rate too. Try lying flat on the bed, eyes shut, breathing in for a count of eight, holding it for eight, then breathing out for eight, and concentrate just on that rather than allowing any thoughts to intrude into your mind. Do this at least once a day if you can.
- Self-hypnosis, so you can send yourself into a calm, relaxed state quickly and easily. You can learn this in one or two sessions with a professional hypnotherapist (see Useful Addresses page 382 for how to find a properly

qualified one). Ten to 15 minutes of self-hypnosis can, from a soothing and re-energizing point of view, make you feel as if you have had a couple of hours' nap. While in a hypnotized state – which is nothing more than deep relaxation – you can also give your mind instructions which it is likely to follow when you wake – such as 'My pelvic pain will be soothed when I get up', which can often work.

- Getting to see a sympathetic doctor can make all the difference, as many are at a loss as to how to help a woman with PPP. If you come up against a brick wall, write to one of the general women's health advisory services for advice such as The Women's Health Concern, or call the College of Health or the Patients Association for suggestions (see Useful Addresses page 382).
- Don't take no for an answer. According to gynaecologist Kevin Ganger of Ashford Hospital (who formerly worked at St Mary's) 'There is always something which can be done to improve pelvic pain, or to get rid of it altogether. There is no reason why you should have to suffer in silence. This is a common condition, and it's treatable.'

Sexual self-help

If you find that after having had a baby – or two – you experience sharp pelvic pain, which may radiate around the vulva and perineal areas too – as soon as possible after sexual arousal, try rhythmically clenching your vaginal, perineal and/or entire pelvic area several times. Some women say they find doing this virtually straight away after orgasm helps the most, and also that the more rapidly they orgasm (perhaps by masturbating rather than making love with a partner) the more likely they are to experience pelvic pain. Try taking it more slowly if this is true for you.

Try squeezing different areas of the pelvic muscle complex to see which work best for you. Another good way to do this is to perform pelvic floor exercises a few times, as powerfully as you can and holding them for as long as possible. The reason this helps is that if the area has become short of blood (ischaemic, as in angina pain around the heart) this can help pump more into the area, so relieving the discomfort.

For how to do them, see page 350.

USEFUL ADDRESSES

The British Association for Counselling, 1 Regent Place, Rugby, Warwickshire CV21 2PJ. Tel: 01788 578328 (information) or 01788 550899 (administration).

If your pelvic pain is causing you sexual problems too, a relationships counsellor may be able to help you. To find one who is professionally qualified and fully trained send an s.a.e. and covering note to either the BAC, or to Relate (see below, or phone them). The BAC has a list of professionally trained counsellors specializing in all types of sexual and marital problems. Private fee system.

British Hypnotherapy Association, 1 Wythburn Place, London W1H 5WL. Tel: 0171 723 4443.

Chartered Society of Physiotherapy, 14 Bedford Row, London WC1R 4ED. Tel: 0171 242 1941.

Advice and information on pelvic exercises following childbirth.

College of Health, St Margaret's House, 21 Old Ford Road, London E2 9PL. Tel: 0181 983 1225.

The Patients Association, Union House, 8 Guilford Street, London WC1 1DT. Tel: 0171 242 3460.

'Listening to patients and speaking up for change.'

Relate Marriage Guidance, Herbert Gray College, Little Church Street, Rugby, Warwickshire CV21 3AP. Tel: 01788 573241; fax: 01788 535007.

This organization has a large network of professionally trained counsellors countrywide who can help you with a very wide range of sexual problems, and would also have helpful advice for pelvic pain around lovemaking or orgasm. They also have a sliding scale of fees based on ability to pay.

St Mary's Hospital, Paddington, London W2 1NY. Tel: 0171 725 6666.

A pioneering pelvic pain clinic. Ask your GP for referral to this clinic, or ask that they speak to the department to see if there are any other specialist clinics they know of in your area. (If there are, as this is as yet a fairly small field in medicine, they would probably know about them.)

Women's Health Concern, helpline: 0181 780 3007.

Recovering Fast from a Caesarean

You are in good company if you had a Caesarean because in Britain, about 15 per cent of mothers (the World Health Organization recommends 10 per cent at most) have their babies this way, and the number is continuing to rise. There are probably several reasons for this and they include:

- Obstetricians becoming increasingly nervous about the possibility of being sued by parents if a baby is harmed during vaginal childbirth. In fact such harm is most unusual, and if it does happen, it is generally the result of medical negligence (though in each case this has to be proven, often with difficulty). However, Caesareans are seen as a 'safer' option *for the baby*. Obstetric staff are becoming increasingly wary of blame and litigation as consumers of medical care, in their turn, follow the trend already well established in writ-happy America where the Caesarean rate is 22.5 per cent, and patients are increasingly ready to sue if any problems do arise.
- As the C-rate rises, an increasing number of younger doctors and midwives are no longer so confident about helping women whose babies are in the breech (bottom first) position give birth naturally. They just haven't seen enough of them done, and have not therefore had the practice they need.
- There are still a few myths around which suggest to first-time mothers who have had little contact with other new mothers and childbirth organizations that Caesareans, especially those done under a general anaesthetic, are somehow an easy way out. (As Kathy Lette puts it in *Fetal Attraction*: 'The wake-me-up-when-the-hairdresser's-here approach.') They aren't. They are one way to have a baby, but they are certainly not an easy option.

Most antenatal classes tend to concentrate on the mechanics of ordinary labour and vaginal delivery. They do not usually mention Caesareans except in passing, which is unhelpful because some advance information would be very useful for the 100,000 mothers a year who have one.

Though the operation is very common and very safe, it is also major surgery because both your abdominal wall and then your womb need to be cut open so the baby can be lifted out, then the incisions carefully sewn up. The significance of this is something which obstetricians tend to play down.

Once a Caesarean mother, always a Caesarean mother?

There are many reasons why you might have had a Caesarean delivery, but they do not all have to mean that you must have a C section next time as well, unless this is what you would like. Up to 85 per cent of all mothers who had their previous baby by Caesarean can go on to deliver their subsequent babies vaginally, according to obstetrician and holistic physician Dr Christine Northrup, of the Woman to Woman clinic in Maine, USA. This is worth knowing if you have just had your first baby this way and would like to have more children one day.

However, it is not a matter of routine for the mother herself because the medical care you will need straight afterwards, the possible emotional effect of the procedure and the longer postnatal recovery time may raise special issues or bring their own specific problems. The good news is that there are many strategies which you yourself can use to help enormously with any post-Caesarean difficulties you may have.

Women's reactions

Having a baby by Caesarean is not a problem for many women. Some sail through the procedure and its aftermath, and say they would not want to give birth any other way. Many take a very calm, pragmatic approach to childbirth, feeling it's the baby that matters, not how they arrive.

Other mothers, however, feel very differently about it. 'I cannot cope with the sense of loss at not being awake when my son came into the world,' explains one. And another: 'I feel not quite "a whole woman" for not being able to give birth normally – deep down, that still hurts.' 'I don't know why I feel so angry, but I do,' says another. 'I'm furious about what that hospital did, and it's eating away at me still, months later.'

As for recovery rates, according to Gina Lowden, one of the three national co-ordinators for the Caesarean Birth/Vaginal Birth After Caesarean group for the National Childbirth Trust, who has been working with Caesarean mothers for several years: 'I have known some women who were virtually back to normal within a week. However, you cannot assume a link between physical and emotional recovery. Mothers who recover fast physically may well have emotional scars which last for years. On the other hand, those who have problems such as postoperative infections may not feel at all negative about their Caesarean.

'But for most, they may not feel back to normal for a year. The truth is that the first year with a new baby is always hard work, but that it is often especially hard work for Caesarean mothers.'

There is a third group of Caesarean mothers too, though – the very few who had such births but remain deeply distressed for years and suffer from a form of post-traumatic stress disorder. PTSD is rare, but can in fact occur after any form of childbirth.

There is no such thing as an average reaction to a Caesarean any more than there is an average ordinary childbirth. Just individual mothers and their babies, coping and reacting in different ways.

GETTING COMFORTABLE FAST

What helps
The level of discomfort you may have depends upon:

- Your own pain tolerance levels.
- How rapidly your body recovers after the type of anaesthesia you've had.
- Whether or not you had your Caesarean after a long period of labour.
- Whether or not you develop an infection afterwards, which according to the NCT 40 per cent of Caesarean mothers do.

But however you are feeling, there is a huge amount of practical and sympathetic advice available from the Caesarean Support Network on everything from the easiest way to get up out of bed on day one to which positions you can breastfeed twins in that will not put pressure on your stitches site. The following are some of the most important and helpful suggestions – but perhaps the number one piece of advice is: *accept all help you are offered, as long as you are not finding it interfering. Then ask for more whenever you need it, every time you need it.*

If you can possibly pay for help for a few weeks, even someone to come in a couple of hours a day, tidy up and cook a family meal, it's worth every penny. If you cannot afford this, do you have a mother or sister (as long as you get on well with them, as they can be either the best or the worst people to have around you after having a baby, depending on your relationship) who could pop in daily or even come to stay for a couple of weeks?

Home helps
In theory, newly delivered mothers have the right to a home help to assist with the cooking and cleaning or shopping for up to 10 days after delivery. The Social Services Department has a legal obligation to provide you with one: maternity cases take priority. (You can quote the NHS Act 1977, Schedule 8, paragraph 3 (I) when you phone up your local Social Services Department to ask about this.) So if you are reading this before you go in to have a Caesarean which has been preplanned, call up the social services. In some cases it may be possible to get some help for an extended period but this would depend very much on your local authority. If you are reading this from hospital and planning to come home say around day five, get your partner to chase up social services for you.

In practice, you will need to fight for these rights. As one VBAC campaigner put it on reading the above, 'If it's that easy, how come I don't know more than one mother who managed to get it?'

STRAIGHT AFTER YOUR OPERATION

You will probably stay in hospital for five to 10 days afterwards, depending on how you are feeling and on the policy of the hospital. Currently a five-day stay is more common as long as there are no problems. There are also a few units who will allow you home within a couple of days if you had a spinal or an epidural anaesthetic, and home is where you would rather be, as long as you take adequate pain relief with you and have daily visits from your community midwife. If you are not happy in hospital you can also, in theory, discharge yourself.

Day one

Your incision site will either be a bikini cut just within your pubic hair or, less usually, a vertical cut running down the centre of your abdomen, and covered in a light dressing. There may also be a draining tube in place for a few hours to draw off any excess fluid or blood loss from the area.

What helps

- *Strong pain relief.* If you had an epidural this may be left in place and stopped up a little. You might be offered a push-button system of drug delivery that you work yourself as and when you need it, which sends painkilling drugs directly into your arm. Painkilling injections or tablets are offered by all units. If you want to breastfeed your baby, check with the hospital staff that the drugs will not affect the baby too. The NCT – see Useful Addresses page 395 – has a leaflet listing breastfeeding-compatible drugs.
- *Sleeping tablets at night.* These can be very helpful for the first few nights, especially in a place which has 24-hour noise levels like a maternity ward. If you would like some help sleeping but are not offered any, ask the hospital staff. They may however make breastfeeding your baby awkward, especially if they are suckling frequently on demand – less of a problem if bottle-feeding, in which case the hospital staff can feed your baby for you if you are sleeping heavily or are exhausted and feel you need a night or two's uninterrupted sleep.
- *Antibiotics.* These may either be given preventatively to avoid the possibility of a postoperative infection developing, or they may not be offered until one does. If you do take them they might also encourage thrush, so ask about a preventative antifungal pessary to use. Alternatively, your partner can buy both pessaries and anti-thrush cream for you direct from the pharmacist (the tradename is Canesten). But tell him to make sure they let the pharmacist know the treatment is for vaginal thrush because a report in the *Drug & Therapeutics Bulletin 1994* found most pharmacists were selling women the wrong one, giving them the type for athlete's foot instead.

Self-help

- *Gentle movement.* On day one restrict this to sitting up slowly with help, cuddling your baby, and wriggling your toes or doing gentle foot circling every hour or so for about 30 seconds at a time, to encourage the circulation. Carry on doing these for the first week. Encouragingly, some women are up and walking (albeit rather gingerly) within hours of their Caesarean.

- *Tummy protection.* If you are going to laugh or sneeze this will make your newly stitched abdominal muscles tense, which will hurt. Protect the area by lacing your fingers together and placing your joined hands gently but firmly over the area to support it.
- *Homeopathic remedies.* Arnica tablets or granules taken about four times a day will reduce swelling, bruising, bleeding and trauma (see Useful Addresses page 494 for suppliers who can offer further information too). According to homeopath and midwife Bridget Cummins of the Homeopathic Midwifery Service in West Cork, Ireland, Bellis perennis is very helpful for deep abdominal surgery such as a Caesarean.

Day two
Self-help
- *Walking.* This is the day when you will probably be encouraged to get up out of bed and try to walk around a little if you have not already done so – most mothers are encouraged to try within the first 24 hours. Unkind as this seems at the time, as you will probably still be very sore, movement is vital to improve your circulation. It helps avoid any blood clots forming, and encourages your mobility to return faster.

  Ask a nurse or your partner to help you walk slowly, a few steps at a time, if this is the first time you have got up since your baby's birth as you may feel a bit dizzy and unsteady at first. It helps to keep stopping for rests, and taking slow, deep breaths. Try not to overdo the first few excursions out of bed, and if you possibly can, try not to do the Caesarean Shuffle (head down, shoulders dropped, hands supporting the abdomen as you walk for fear that your stitches are going to burst open). Feeling protective and tentative about the incision site is very natural, but it really will not break apart. And walking gets a little easier each time you try it, so walk as tall as you can.
- *Bathing.* No matter how much you are longing for a hot bath, you may find it too difficult to clamber in and out of one for the first couple of days. However, a long hot shower can be very soothing and uplifting too. This is because the hot water encourages the release of the body's natural opiate-like chemicals, endorphins, in the same way as a hot bath does, which is why both are so helpful as a natural method of pain relief in the first stage of labour. Check the shower's temperature first before you stand under it because if it is scalding hot, you will not be able to jump out of range quickly. Ask someone to be there to help you dry and put on your slippers and nightdress so you do not have to stretch up your arms above your head or bend over to your feet.
- *Getting in and out of bed.*
  This may be uncomfortable too for the first few days, but it helps to:
  — Arrange for your bed to be lowered.

— Take it in stages. The Caesarean Support Network says that this routine may be helpful:

1. As you try to get up, tuck your chin into your chest, push your palms into the bed close to your sides, lifting your bottom slightly to shuffle your body sideways.
2. Keep going until you have reached the left-hand side of your bed.
3. Using both hands, lift your left leg at the knee to place your foot on the floor. Do the same with your right leg.

Keep stopping for rests, and taking gentle deep breaths as often as you need to. Go at your own pace.

- *Exercises.* Keep doing the hourly foot circling from day one. In addition, try these two if they feel comfortable to you. If they hurt, stop immediately and try again in a couple of days. Also ask to see the hospital physiotherapist for alternatives and advice.

— Bend and stretch your feet from the ankles briskly. Keep doing this for 30 seconds. This one helps avoid swollen feet and ankles.

— Lie on your back with your knees bent, feet resting on the bed, breathing slowly in and out. Do this three or four times. This is helpful for your general circulation.

- *Sitting.* Initial sitting is likely to be in bed, propped up on pillows. When it's time to try sitting up out of bed, choose a chair which is high and upright, preferably one with arms. Avoid comfortable, squashy sofas and deep armchairs even if there are any in the hospital day room. To sit down comfortably, try putting one leg behind the other, bending at the knees. To get out of the chair again, lean forward gently, put one leg behind the other and bend your knees. Use arm rests, if there are some, for gentle leverage and balance.

- *Going to the toilet.* You can usually pass water as soon as your catheter has been removed.

To sit yourself on the loo, bend your knees to lower yourself, and if there are any side support rails, which there often are in hospital, use them too. You will probably be asked to try to pass water and open your bowels within two days of your Caesarean. Bowel movements may not be easy as:

— You might not have eaten or drunk anything for a while.

— Any abdominal surgery can disturb the bowel and the neurological signals to empty it.

— Your abdomen will be sore, and you will not want to strain much for fear of breaking open your stitches (you wouldn't, but it may certainly feel as if you could).

It can help greatly to:

— Drink as much water as you can throughout the day, starting as soon as possible after your operation. Stools absorb water, making them easier to pass. Do not overdo it though, as some breastfeeding experts suggest that excessive water intake can actually reduce milk production though you do need a decent intake to produce a good milk supply in the first place.

— Ask for a gentle laxative such as Lactulose. It consists of a nondigestible sugar which absorbs water from the gut wall and so bulks out faeces, and it does nòt affect your baby if you are breastfeeding.

— If your stitches site is feeling vulnerable as you strain on the toilet, support the area gently and firmly with the flat of your hand as you push.

— Ask for gentle action suppositories (e.g. glycerine ones) if there are problems, if you have not already had them offered to you.

If your bowels have not opened by the fifth morning, some hospitals will suggest an enema of plain water to soften any waste matter in the rectum.

- *Gas and wind.* You might find that you have wind pains for two or three days after your Caesarean, which can be mild, or severe enough to be positively painful. The Caesarean Support Network suggests the following breathing exercise, recommending that you begin it as soon as possible after your baby is born and repeat it four times every waking hour.
  1. Lace your fingers together, folding your joined hands over the incision to support it.
  2. Breathe in deeply, and breathe out slowly.
  3. Take another deep breath and hold it there for a count of 5–10 if you can manage it comfortably. Then breathe out slowly.
  4. Take a final deep breath and let it flow back out.

  It might also help to drink peppermint water, fennel tea, eat some arrowroot biscuits or some extra strong mints. But avoid all fizzy drinks, including the varieties visitors often bring friends in hospital – sparkling pure spring water and Lucozade.

Feeding your baby

Your baby can begin to suckle colostrum – the rich, nourishing fluid which is the forerunner to breastmilk – from your nipples as soon as you like from day one. However there are some special issues associated with breastfeeding for Caesarean mothers, who may have some difficulties to overcome resulting from their operation before beginning to breastfeed successfully and easily. The National Childbirth Trust has counsellors who can come to visit you at home (or while you are still in hospital if you ask them to) to help you become confident about feeding your baby yourself after your operation, and the La Leche League can offer support and advice over the phone (though they too will come and see you, distance permitting). The Caesarean Support Network will be able to put you in touch with other Caesarean mothers who have breastfed their babies, and they may have invaluable practical advice and support to offer. (See Useful Addresses pages 393–5 for contact telephone numbers.) Hospital staff will also be on hand to help.

You can begin feeding your baby immediately after an epidural Caesarean, as long as you are both feeling well. If you have had a general anaesthetic you may both take some time to come around fully from it and may feel groggy for a day or two. For your baby, this can mean they are very sleepy and do not suckle well at first, needing only very short, frequent feeds until the anaesthetic's effects have worn off – and this can be very tiring for you, especially if you are feeling the anaesthetic's after-effects yourself. However, your baby will soon settle down and feed for longer, and at longer intervals too, if you can just get through the first two or three days with support from the nursing staff.

If you are bottle-feeding, try to give your baby their feeds yourself and ask the nurses to help you get into a comfortable position for doing so. If you are sitting, make sure your back is supported by a pillow or cushion, that your legs are not crossed and that your baby is resting on a pillow on your lap to keep their weight off your incision site.

If you have a vertical scar, you might find it comfortable to:

- Sit up with pillows across your stomach to absorb the pressure of your baby's small body.
- Lie down on your side with your baby snuggled in next to you. It can take a bit of practice to get a bottle, or especially a breast, at the right height but once you have developed the knack of it this is a very comfortable feeding position especially if you are feeling tired or you are giving a night feed.
- Put a pillow on the meal tray which fits over your bed, and place your baby on this, drawing them up near to you.

If you have a bikini scar, it might be comfortable to:

- Tuck your baby underneath your arm lying on a pillow, with their head facing your breast/bottle and their body beneath your arm. This is called the American Football hold, and it helps prevent your baby from accidentally kicking you. It is also a good way to feed twins.
- Sit up with a pillow supporting you on either side, their head on one of these and their feet on your thighs.
- Place your baby on a pillow on your meal trolley and draw them close to you for feeding, as above.
- Sit upright on the edge of your bed with a chair on the floor for your feet to rest on so your knees are *higher* than your incision. Place a pillow across your lap to support your baby's weight and ensure you lean forward a little while feeding.

Day three
General comfort
The top part of your pubic hair will be shaved (time permitting) before you have a Caesarean. While the hair is growing back it can be very itchy. If this is the case for you, it helps to sprinkle the area with plain baby powder, or with zinc or Calendula talcum powder.

The pain or discomfort of your stitches site soon fades into itchiness and sensitivity instead, then stops causing you any problems at all. Initially, it helps to wear waist-high soft cotton pants to avoid chafing a bikini scar, and larger, floppier clothes with loose or no waistbands while healing.

What helps
More exercises
Some additional exercises to add to the first three. Though you may feel that you already have more than enough to worry about without having do these as well, the first really does help tremendously to strengthen your pelvic floor, so helping to avoid loose vaginal tone, prolapse and stress incontinence. The second and third will strengthen the three major groups of muscles in your abdomen to help you get your figure back. Or as one new mother put it: 'If they will stop my stomach from looking like a bin liner full of yoghurt, I will certainly manage to fit them in somehow.'

Speak to the hospital physiotherapist, who will be visiting you on the ward anyway, about the type of exercises she would recommend and how many. If she does not come to see you within the first two or three days, ask your staff nurse to contact the physio department for you.

The secret of the success of any exercises, postoperative or otherwise, is to start gently with whatever you can manage, build up very gradually and persist with them regularly or they will not make any difference. The other golden rule is if anything hurts, leave exercising it for several days before trying again.

Pelvic power
If you are not quite sure you are flexing the right muscles – and for many women it is the first time they have ever tried to locate their pelvic floor – turn to page 351 for a very full explanation and some simple DIY location tests.

Basically all you need to do is lie down with your knees bent, feet resting flat on the bed.

Tighten your back passage as if trying to stop a bowel movement, then your vagina as if squeezing your partner's penis when having intercourse, then tighten your front passage as if trying to stop yourself passing water. Now pull up all three, as if the entire sling of pelvic muscles is making a smile shape inside you, hold for five seconds and release slowly. Try to do five repetitions, 10 if possible. Do this six times a day – perhaps to coincide with starting to feed your baby so you won't forget. Increase the number you can do week by week until you can manage 50 without any trouble.

Abdominal strengtheners:
- Lie down with your knees bent, feet resting on the bed, pull in your tummy as well as you can and press the middle of your back into the bed. Only press as hard as is comfortable for you. Hold for a count of five, then let go slowly. Repeat six times. This exercise also helps ease away backache.
- Lie down with your knees bent and together, feet flat on the bed and arms stretched sideways level with your shoulders. Draw in your tummy muscles as strongly as is comfortable for you and push both knees gradually over towards the right, twisting from the hips and waist. Begin this exercise very gradually, only moving your knees a little at first. Over the

next few weeks gradually increase your range of movement until your knees touch the bed. Repeat this exercise six times. If it is at all uncomfortable leave it for several days and then try again.

Further information on post-Caesarean exercises after you have come from hospital, from the NCT or the Chartered Society of Physiotherapists.

EMOTIONAL HEALING

Many women have a very good experience of Caesarean birth. They were fully involved in the decision to have their baby in this way, and able to be awake during the procedure itself, which they found exciting and fascinating. They were supported joyfully by their partner, pleased by the way the birth was handled by the medical staff, and recovered fast physically. These are the new mothers who are unlikely to have any emotional issues arising from their baby's birth that they feel they need to resolve. Other mothers however find they are struggling with a wide range of negative emotions ranging from feeling rather taken aback and confused, to disempowerment, shock, anger, deep lasting distress, or sheer personal frustration that they were unable to give birth naturally, especially if their Caesarean was an unplanned emergency.

If you feel that you might welcome talking to someone in total confidence who could provide an informed and sympathetic ear, think about contacting the Caesarean Support Network. All their contact mothers have also given birth by Caesarean, and while no two Caesareans are exactly alike, they will understand from personal experience at least some of what you are feeling, and may have many invaluable practical suggestions as well as being able to offer friendly support.

If you feel as if you have been traumatized either physically or emotionally by the way in which you had your baby, contact Birth Crisis. This organization has a countrywide network of counsellors (other mothers) trained by birth educator and pioneer Sheila Kitzinger, who can both support you and listen. If your feelings are affecting your relationship with your partner, a Relate counsellor may be able to help you, and so could the resident psychosexual women's counsellor at one of the major family planning centres (call the Family Planning Association for where to find your nearest one). See Useful Addresses pages 393–5 for all these telephone numbers.

Bach Flower Remedies

As a small self-help measure, which may be surprisingly effective in the meantime, consider using these natural and gentle remedies. They can help soothe a wide variety of sometimes very deep-seated emotional and mental states – and at worst they are so very gentle that even if they do not do you good, they certainly will not do any harm either. Call The Bach Centre (see Useful Address page 394) for where to find a properly qualified practitioner, but as a self-help measure you could also try:

- Gentian, for those who are convalescent but feeling discouraged and despondent.
- Heather, if you find you are becoming obsessed by your own physical ailments and problems post-Caesarean.
- Holly, if you find you are feeling full of simmering anger perhaps towards the medical staff of the hospital, if they handled your Caesarean badly, insensitively, or went directly against your wishes.
- Pine, if you are feeling full of guilt or self-reproach.
- Olive, if your Caesarean and its aftermatch of physical and emotional recovery coupled with caring for a new baby has left you long-term exhausted, especially if you also had a tiring pregnancy leading up to it.
- Star of Bethlehem helps treat the effects of shock, which many women may feel afterwards, especially if their Caesarean was an emergency procedure.
- Sweet Chestnut, if you are feeling very upset and weepy, as this is the remedy for 'extreme mental anguish and distress'.

Note: remedies are chosen on a very individual basis so the above are guideline suggestions only, which may well help, but for best results it is still advisable to contact a trained practitioner. Remedies are taken a few drops at a time in water, and are available in health shops and independent chemists, £2.99 each.

Homeopathy

This can also be very helpful for healing the emotional side of a Caesarean. Commonly used and useful remedies include Pulsatilla and Hypericum. However, as this therapy is a very complex one, and homeopathy prescribes on a very individual basis according to both your personality and the precise type of symptoms, for best results contact a qualified homeopath who should be able to prescribe exactly what you will need (see Useful Addresses page 394).

USEFUL ADDRESSES

AIMS (Association for the Improvement in the Maternity Services), 40 Kingswood Avenue, London NW6 6LF. Tel: 0181 960 5585.

A free publication list is available (please send s.a.e.). Also information on the risks and benefits of ultrasound.

Association of Post-Natal Illness, 25 Jerdan Place, London SW6 1BE. Tel: 0171 386 0868.

Support, information and advice for women experiencing all degrees of postnatal illness or sadness. Women who have had their baby by Caesarean can be especially vulnerable to postnatal depression because of the special physical recovery and emotional issues it can involve.

The Bach Centre, Mount Vernon, Bakers Lane, Sotwell, Wallingford, Oxfordshire OX10 0PZ. Tel: 01491 834678.

For details of a therapist near to you. The remedies themselves can be bought at most health food shops like Holland & Barrett or from independent chemists.

Birth Crisis Network, Sheila Kitzinger, The Manor, Standlake, Nr Witney, Oxford OX8 7RH. Tel: 01865 300266.

Write or phone to contact a counsellor in your area.

BLISS (Baby Life Support Systems), 17–21 Emerald Street, London WC1N 3QL. Tel: 0171 831 9393.

Help, support, information and advice for parents whose babies are born prematurely and need special care for a while.

British Association of Sexual and Marital Therapy, PO Box 62, Sheffield S10 3TS.

BASMT has a register of approved therapists countrywide.

British Homeopathic Association, 27a Devonshire Street, London W1N 1RJ. Tel: 0171 935 2163.

Has register of medical doctors who are also homeopaths.

The Caesarean Support Network, c/o Yvonne Williams, 55 Cooil Drive, Douglas, Isle of Man. Tel: 01624 661269 and Sheila Tunstall, 2 Hurst Park Drive, Huton, Liverpool.

Send letter and s.a.e.

Chartered Society of Physiotherapy in Obstetrics & Gynaecology, 14 Bedford Row, London WC1R 4ED.

For information and advice about postnatal exercises after a caesarean.

The Family Planning Association, 2–12 Pentonville Road, London N1 9FP. Tel: 0171 837 5432.

Helios Homeopathic Pharmacy, 97 Camden Road, Tunbridge Wells, Kent TN1 2QR. Tel: 01892 536393. Or Ainsworths Homeopathic Pharmacy, 38 New Cavendish Street, London W1M 7LH. Tel: 0171 935 5330.

For rapid mail-order supplies of homeopathic remedies and basic over-the-phone advice.

La Leche League of Great Britain, BM 3424, London WC1N 3XX. Tel: 0171 242 1278.

Encouragement, information, regular group meetings and support for breastfeeding mothers. Counselling is usually by phone contact, though, distance permitting, a LLL member will also come to see you.

National Childbirth Trust, Alexandra House, Oldham Terrace,
London W3 6NH. Tel: 0181 992 8637.

Support and information covering all aspects of pregnancy, childbirth, breastfeeding and postnatal issues, including Caesarean birth and breastfeeding after a Caesarean. A counsellor will usually be able to come and see you to offer help and support. Countrywide network of other contact mothers who have similar experiences to you, and a wide network of postnatal groups too.

Relate (formerly the Marriage Guidance Council).
Your local phone book will have the address and phone number of the nearest branch to you, or contact their head office on 01788 573241. Helpline open 10 a.m. to 3 p.m. weekdays.

VBAC (Vaginal Birth After Caesarean), 8 Wren Way, Farnborough,
Hampshire GU14 8SZ. Tel: 01252 543250.

Help and information on *all* aspects of Caesarean birth.

USEFUL BOOKS

Bach Flower Remedies for Women, Judy Howard, C. W. Daniel, 1992.
Homeopathy for Women, Dr Andrew Lockie, Hamlyn.

Getting Rid of Back Pain

One in two new mothers has no back problems at all. The rest however find they do have some low back pain, which may be either short-lived or more persistent, down around the sacro-iliac joint, where the spine joins the pelvis. If that sounds familiar, this chapter is for you . . .

According to the ongoing British midwifery Avon Longitudinal Study in the first few days after giving birth six out of 10 women say they have intermittent postnatal back pain and one in 10 reports constant problems. Eight weeks after delivery this has risen rather than dropped – to two-thirds of new mothers getting backache, around one in 20 reporting it is constant. You normally feel it over the joint itself, which lies just underneath the two dimples on either side of your lower back, above your buttocks.

You may first notice it as a gnawing ache or the occasional sharp twinge just after your baby is born. This may be all you have, and it could well go away on its own. However it might also continue, either as intermittent or constant pain, which may range from merely uncomfortable (so you try to avoid making certain movements or sitting in certain ways which trigger it) to the downright immobilizing.

RISK FACTORS

During pregnancy
Possible triggers include factors which date back to your pregnancy, such as:

- The way every pregnant woman's posture changes to accommodate her growing baby. This tends to involve hollowing out your lower back, pushing your knees back and rounding your shoulders.
- The softening of your ligaments which hold all your joints, including those in your back, together. The growing levels of hormones during pregnancy do this to help your entire pelvic area to become supple and stretchy enough for the baby to pass through when it is being born.
- Your abdominal muscles being weakened by having stretched so much during pregnancy. A waist measurement that starts at 26 inches usually reaches 46 inches, but the good news is that it tends to go back again all the way, except possibly for the last inch. This matters because your

abdominal muscles help support your back. Weak abdominals mean a more vulnerable back.

This is why it is very important to do the ante- and post-natal exercises which your midwife or hospital physiotherapist suggests, though they are probably one of the very last things you feel like at the time. Most maternity units will either make sure one of the hospital physiotherapists comes round to see you to explain them before you leave, or at least gives you a leaflet showing how to do them. If they do neither, either ask to see the physiotherapist, or contact one of the childbirth or physiotherapy organizations (see Useful Addresses page 411) for information on abdominal strengthening, back protecting postnatal exercise. Quite apart from reducing your risk of having backache for the next year or so they will help you get your figure back far faster. See diagrams on pages 406–8 for some of the most popular ones.

There is not enough room in this book to show them all in detail as there are many possible ones you may be given, and you need to do different ones at different stages – some you can begin the day after you have had your baby, such as foot flexing and gentle pelvic rocking. Others like situps should not be tried until at least three months later, and only after you have been practising the gentler moves up until then or you might hurt yourself. See Useful Addresses page 411 for where to get the most helpful leaflets and books which show the postnatal exercises in detail.

- Because of the position or positions you actually laboured, and gave birth in. Being able to move around freely greatly reduces the chance of later back problems, as may squatting-style birth positions.

Epidurals to blame?

Many women blame having had an epidural for their later back problems but the medical juries are still out on this one and the few clinical studies which have tried to find out for sure have come up with conflicting evidence.

To summarize their findings, it is very possible that having a *traditional* epidural is associated with later back trouble. And if this is true it is a major issue for the 650,000 pregnant women a year, when they are thinking about which type of pain relief, if any, to use during their labour.

One particular study by the University of Birmingham Medical School in 1989 showed that 18 per cent of new mothers who had had epidurals during their labour had long-term backache, compared with 10.5 per cent who had not. Another survey of 1,000 mothers carried out by St Thomas's Hospital got similar results. However the most recent study that has surfaced at the time of writing is by the Royal Victoria Hospital in Montreal, suggesting that the back pain reported by women who have had epidurals is just local soreness due to the injection itself. Now no one is sure what to think. Suggestions include the possibility that:

- It is something about the epidural's method of delivering anaesthetic drugs – into the fluid inside the sac of membrane surrounding the spinal cord – that might cause the problem, because people given epidurals for pain relief in situations other than childbirth also suffer backache later. One particular survey of 9,000 patients given epidurals for surgery other than Caesareans found one in 50 later complained of backache.

- You have to stay semi-reclining or sitting in one place for several hours, often with inadequate back support. Mothers who have had the newer style walkabout epidurals which allow you to change positions fairly freely, sit in a rocking chair or even go for a visit to the loo are associated with fewer postnatal back problems.

The softening hormones of pregnancy and labour

Even after the baby is born, new mothers are still more vulnerable to back strain than usual because their ligaments remain softened by the hormones of pregnancy for up to five months later. Levels of both relaxin and progesterone are also high premenstrually, which may explain why women tend to strain their backs and necks more at this time of the month than at any other.

It is also common to develop back trouble, even when you never had any before, three or four months *after* delivery. According to Stephen Sandler, consultant osteopath at the Portland Hospital for Women & Children in London, this is because of the additional new strains your back is having to cope with (see How to Avoid and Beat Backache page 399).

During labour and delivery itself

- *Being in any positions which placed excessive strain on your back.* These can include sitting for hours, then giving birth, with your knees up and back inadequately supported, as may be the case with an epidural, for instance.
- *Having had a very long, tiring labour.* Tired muscles are far more susceptible to being strained and ripped, as any sports medicine specialist or athlete knows to their cost.
- *Straining your back during the pushing stage.*

After the birth – the first hours and days

- Breast or bottle-feeding your baby without enough back support. You can be sitting in the feeding position for several hours every day, so it is vital to be comfortable.
- Changing nappies, bathing or dressing the baby at an uncomfortable height for your back.
- Exhaustion – due to a tiring labour, or the lack of sleep that nearly all new babies bring. Again tiredness = tired muscles = muscles more likely to be strained.
- Lying down to rest so that your vulnerable back is strained or twisted in some way, or simply not supported well enough. This is why it is important to have proper back support (perhaps a pillow tucked behind it) if feeding your baby lying down, which is very comfortable and soothing especially if you are very tired, it is night-time or you cannot yet sit down comfortably.

HOW TO AVOID – AND BEAT – BACKACHE

The best thing about new mothers' backache is that you *can* generally deal with it successfully or, at the very least, reduce it to become much more comfortable, yourself.

What helps
- Being very careful about the way you sit, whether you are eating a meal, watching TV or working – use a cushion or two to support your back.
- Breastfeeding or bottle-feeding your baby as you sit comfortably in a rocking chair, or with your feet up on a footstool.
- Pram pushing with the handles at the right height. Try out several in the shop before you buy one – you are going to be using it a very great deal.
- Changing, bathing and dressing your baby at a comfortable height for your back.
- Lifting and standing so as not to strain your back.
- Not carrying your baby, either on your hip or in a sling, for long periods.
- Doing gentle but regular exercises to strengthen the muscles supporting the back – persist with them for at least six months if you possibly can.
- Some gentle, yoga-based stretching, such as the Cat Arch and the Frog Stretch (see page 406). Continuing with any back soothing stretches, yoga-based or otherwise, which you found helped during your pregnancy.
- Get some specialist back help and advice. It may also be very helpful to see an osteopath or chiropractor who has a special interest in postnatal back care (many do – see Useful Addresses) to have any joints or vertebrae which have become twisted out of alignment gently put right again. In fact, it may be a very good idea, in the interests of catching any problems before they get the chance to develop, to have a back check-up from a chiropractor or osteopath anyway six weeks or so after you have had your baby, in the same way as you would go for a postnatal check-up with your doctor.

In detail
Your posture
Posture is the way you hold your body whether you are sitting, standing, walking, pushing. Try to correct any changes in the way you do these things which may have developed gradually while you were pregnant without your even noticing them. For instance, the way you stand.

'I can do the back exercises – I just can't get up again.'

Mothers do a lot of standing with young babies. Rocking them, holding them on a hip or over your shoulder, cooking, telephoning and washing-up holding them. Some are far more reluctant to be put down than others and may cry loudly and persistently until you pick them up again. A baby who won't be quiet unless they are constantly carried is very hard on your back. If yours does it is not your fault and it is very unlikely to be related to anything that you as a parent are doing, or failing to do. It is simply that your baby may just be Like That, in the same way as some simply do not sleep.

Action
Knowing it won't last
Keep reminding yourself that this phase will probably NOT last long. But it is best anyway to get your child checked by a cranial osteopath as, if this treatment is needed, it can mean that instead of three or four months' worth of constant crying there may be only a couple of weeks.

According to Stephen Sandler, Director of the Expectant Mothers Clinic at the British School of Osteopathy, 'If babies have had forceps or ventouse delivery, cranial osteopathy treatment should be automatic. I am seeing so many babies like this' (whose skulls have been temporarily shaped by mechanical delivery methods, affecting the pressure of the cerebrospinal fluid surrounding the brain, and therefore the pressure on the brain itself) 'who after two or three treatments, their mothers say, 'Thank you for giving me back a normal baby.' No one is sure how this altered pressure would make a newborn baby feel but possibilities include a throbbing, constant headache. Cranial osteopathy is very gentle and subtle and will not hurt your baby. If anything it is very soothing and relaxing. Contact the General Council and Register of Osteopaths or one of the schools for a fully trained cranial practitioner near you (see Useful Addresses page 412.) If you are on a low income or unemployed, some practitioners do offer a fees-based-on-ability-to-pay scale – especially for babies and young children. Ask them about it before you go for the appointment if money is tight.

Usually by the time the babies can move themselves about in bouncing swings at about 4 months, or baby walkers, from six months, they will be so happy with their own new mobility that they will no longer insist you carry them about all day. By this time too, most slight skull 'remodelling' which may have happened during the birth or delivery process should have resolved itself, which is another reason for formerly constantly crying babies becoming more contented.

If your baby has suffered from colic, which usually comes on in the evenings for a few hours but may last on and off all day, 80 per cent will have grown out of this within 3 months, the remainder by 4 months. If your baby cries excessively, try contacting CRY-SIS, an organization which supports and counsels mothers whose babies cry a great deal and can offer many practical and helpful suggestions (see Useful Addresses, page 412). Please also see Calming the Crying (page 86) and Banishing Colic (page 102) for some comforting strategies and options which work well and may alleviate the problem altogether. Again, cranial osteopathy has a good rate of success with both.

Standing comfortably
Have as good a standing posture as possible to help protect your back.
   How to stand tall:

1. Stand in front of a long mirror and look at yourself sideways. Drop and relax your shoulders, so your arms are hanging loosely and comfortably.
2. Stand up as tall as you can. Imagine a fine golden cord running through the middle of your body and out of the top of your head, pulling you upwards.
3. Tuck your buttocks in, then pull in your abdominals (your pubic bone should move forwards and upwards).
4. Move your feet to hip width.
5. Breathe slowly and deeply. Imagine as you are breathing out that you are sending energy down your legs, through your feet and into the floor.

Feel your way mentally around the new way you're standing, notice how all the different muscles are working to hold you in this position, and how comfortable it feels.
   Deliberately stand tall and walk at every possible opportunity. Keep reminding yourself, as it is easy to forget to do it.

Feeding easy
1. Put a stool, pile of phone directories, even the rung of a chair under your feet.
2. Place your baby on a pillow on your lap so they are raised up.
3. Draw your baby in towards you, whether you are feeding them from your breast or bottle, rather than leaning over to reach them. Sit well back in your chair, lower back well supported, perhaps by a soft pillow in its hollow. Start feeding, and enjoying the closeness and peace it can bring.

Housework made easier
- *The leg up*. Put one foot up on the bottom shelf of an open cupboard just below where you are working, e.g. the cupboard under the sink when you are washing up, or on a pile of two or three phone directories kept in the kitchen for this purpose.
- *Easy bending and hoovering*. Squat down with a straight back, rather than bend down when doing low-level jobs like making the bed, changing and dressing a toddler, sweeping something up with a dustpan and brush.
- *Hoovering*. This can be a major strain on a sore back. Get someone else, such as your partner, to do it for the first few weeks if at all possible. Be prepared to let floors get dirtier than usual for a while. Or if you cannot avoid it, move your weight to and fro over your front leg keeping your back straight and avoiding making any twisting movements when you are bending forwards.

Babychanging

Have a changing mat either:

— High enough so you do not have to bend over it. A level that raises your baby so they are lying level with the underneath of your breasts is ideal for the first few months, until your baby learns to roll over.

— Low down at kneeling height, so you can change and wash them on your knees. In hospital, the only place is the bed – but this raises up and down so put it at a comfortable height (or get someone else to do it).

When you kneel, do not do so on both knees, as this is bad for your back too. Instead, sit back on either heel with the other knee bent forwards and the foot flat on the floor, pulling your baby as close to you as possible between your legs.

Carrying your baby, and/or toddler

'Mothers looking after a new baby can be at risk of back problems but mothers with a new baby and a toddler are probably at the greatest risk of all,' says Stephen Sandler.

- Lifting toddlers. 'Your toddler needs your love and affection very much at this time, but you should always go down to their level and kneel before you attempt to pick them up, never bend from the waist. Once you are down, hug them close with their arms around your neck and then hold them tight with one hand under them, while you use the other hand to lever yourself up holding on to a table or chair for added support.'
- Be very careful when lifting your new baby in and out of the car. The leaning forward, lifting the child's weight (plus carrycot, or car cradle) and then twist and lift to bring them out of the car is a classic way for new mothers to injure their backs.

If someone else is around, ask them to do it. If not, squat down slightly to lift a toddler. For a baby in a car cradle with a handle, a carrycot or Moses basket, the easiest way to protect your back is Sit, Swing, Hold, and Rise . . .

Sit – sideways next to the carrycot with the car door open and slide it on to your lap.

Swing – both legs out of the car together.

Hold – on to the carrycot with one hand, using the free hand to hold on to the car door and help raise you slightly off the seat.

Rise – Now at the same time, replace the car-holding hand back around the baby's carrier and carry on rising up off the seat using buttock/thigh/leg muscles, rather than back muscles, and keeping your back straight.

This is not nearly as complicated as it sounds. Try it out just once with

---

Avoid wearing high heels. Go for trainers or shoes with medium-height heels which will not put a strain on your back.

Sling Tips
- Carrying a baby in a sling on your front or back strains your back less than carrying them on your hip. However, when younger people fall they tend to do so forwards (old people tend to fall backwards) so perhaps carrying a baby on your back might be safest for them as well as more comfortable for you.
- Back slings are fine when they are on, but it can be a bit difficult to put a very young, floppy baby in by yourself. It becomes easier as they gain more control over the necks and upper backs, at the age of three to four months.
- If you are later using a hip sling, alternate the side it is on, so both spend equal amounts of time bearing the baby's weight. Try to carry your baby on your back in a sling or African-style broad fabric sash after your baby is about six months old, as by then they will have become too heavy to carry for long on your hip without putting potentially back-damaging strain on your back.
- Place pads of material – rolled up soft tea towels, T-shirts or a towelling nappy folded into a protective pad will do fine – under each of the sling straps as they press into your shoulders or you may develop very sore shoulder muscles, which can soon translate into generalized acute, painful neck, and upper back tension.
- If you do develop soft tissue spasm in your shoulders from this, it can be severe enough to make your shoulder muscles, running from top of the arm to the neck, feel as hard as blocks of wood. Stop using the sling for a while. If the tension and pain remains entrenched, acupuncture or acupressure with massage beforehand is a good way of dispersing it rapidly. (See Useful Addresses.)

---

an empty carrycot or baby basket, and you will find it is just three smooth movements.
- When lifting a toddler or heavy bucket of soggy nappies pull your stomach muscles IN, tuck your buttocks UNDER and clench your pelvic floor muscles. Then keeping your spine straight, bend at the knees (squat right down if you need to), bring the weight close in to your body and using your thigh muscles slowly stand up.
- If you are carrying a baby along in a carrycot or basket have their head, which is the heaviest part of their body, nearest to you.
- *Never* bend and lift from the waist.

Back-friendly ways to bath your baby
Even if you use a surface high enough for you not to need to bend over, you still have to pick up the bath and carry it to a sink or bath to empty the water out of it afterwards. This can be both heavy and awkward, and it is difficult not to spill water on the floor however careful you are.

Instead, consider choosing a baby bath with a drainage plug in it, put it in the bath and fill it from the shower. To bath your baby in it, kneel next to it on one knee, keeping the other bent to maintain a straight back. Then just let the water drain out through its plug afterwards. If you kneel on two knees it will still hurt your back. Another good, safe, non-slip way of bathing your baby in an adult bath is to buy a large sponge which has a cut-out baby shape in the middle, and lay the baby on this in a warm adult bath whose water comes part of the way up their body. Then kneel by the side of the bath as described above, and gently squeeze water from a flannel over them or splash the warm water softly over their bodies. These sponges only cost about £5 and are sold in all good baby equipment shops and relevant areas of department stores.

Some parents get around the bathing question by using a very clean, large washing-up bowl which fits into the (clean) sink in their (warm, draught-free) kitchen. As long as the sink is at the right height, this puts the bathing baby at a good height too for your back. It also means you do not have to lift and carry a small but heavy bath of water anywhere afterwards to empty it.

Or use an adult bath. Get a rubber bath mat so you do not slip, run a warm (slightly above tepid) bath that is deep enough for both you and your baby and get in with them, letting them lie back, head slightly up, feet pointing downwards, floating lightly on your breasts and stomach. Or lay them in the same place on their fronts, head to one side. Many babies enjoy this enormously and it is one of the least troublesome ways to give them a bath, especially if they seem rather nervous of water or dislike their own small bath.

Note: Be especially careful not to slip getting in and out. Hold your baby close against you as you do so, and move slowly. It may be a good idea to have your partner or another helper in the room the first few times if you can, until you become used to doing this. Have the towel to wrap you both in hanging ready next to the tub.

Lying down

This should be very comfortable for aching backs, but if the bed is not supportive enough, or you are lying in the wrong position, it makes things worse.

Suggestions:

- If your bed is very soft, slide a board under the mattress. Or put the mattress on the floor.
- Avoid very hard beds. They are meant to be good for backs but in reality if you lie on a rock-hard mattress the curve of your lower back lies like a strained suspension bridge between the two areas where it touches that mattress. Get another, suitably comfortable mattress if you can possibly afford it. They last for years and so will be a very good investment.
- If your back is aching, lie on your front, as this can be an excellent reliever. Put one or two pillows under your waist as this raises your pelvis and flattens your back. Place another one or two under your head and shoulders if you have swollen tender breasts.

- If you like lying on your back, it may be comfortable to put a pillow under your knees or thighs.
- If you like to lie on your side, put a pillow against the small of your back and another between your knees.
- When you get out of bed, do not twist or turn with your knees apart. Instead,
  1. Tighten your abdominal muscles.
  2. Bend your knees.
  3. Roll onto your side.
  4. Push yourself up into a sitting position with your arms.
  5. Keeping your knees together, swing both legs off the edge of the bed.
     Do the reverse when getting back into bed.

Back Backup

Additional support is unlikely to weaken your back as long as you are doing back-strengthening exercises, and it can make you feel far more comfortable in the first few weeks after birth. Try:

- A pantigirdle. Old-fashioned they may be, but they provide gentle back and abdominal support. They also have the added advantage of making you look deceptively flatter and firmer in front as if you have suddenly regained your figure.

  Get your partner or a friend to drive you to a good local department store where there are trained underwear fitters (such as the bra department of a John Lewis store) where there is professional help available to choose the best type and size for you.

- A home-made binder sash. In the past, and still in traditional cultures all over the world, most new mothers wear these. They may be made of leather, woven grass, or material; some are wide, others simply consist of a piece of cord which is tightened a little every day. The binders may be used for a few days or in some cases three or four months after the birth. In many cultures they are worn with pride as an honourable sign that the woman is a new mother. Modern Japanese women still use one, called a hara-obi, from the middle of their pregnancies to about three weeks after they have had their babies. Those who wear them say it makes them feel more comfortable, especially if they are walking out and about or have to stand for long periods.

  Birth educator and anthropologist Sheila Kitzinger suggests you can make your own using a long crepe bandage or piece of material 15–20 cm (6–8 inches) wide, and 4.5 m (14 feet) long. It needs to go around you three times, and you can make two or three binders out of this one piece of cloth. Wind it around your lower abdomen and small of your back either under or over your clothes so it supports you firmly, but not so tightly it interrupts circulation. The idea is to feel 'neatly packaged but not constricted', and to lift and support the uterus, rather than squash it.

Exercising low backache away
The Cat Stretch
1. Kneel on all fours with your arms and thighs pointing straight down.
2. Blow all the air in your lungs out slowly, and arch your back like a cat's by tucking in your buttock and abdominal muscles and lowering your head.
3. Hold for four counts and let your back go flat again. Repeat 10 times, increasing to 20 times. This exercise not only helps aching backs but strengthens your buttock and abdominal muscles.

The Frog Stretch
This is very helpful if you have backache while you are pregnant, or at any stage after you have had your baby.

1. Kneel on the floor, resting on your elbows, and spread your knees as wide as is comfortable for you.
2. Stretch your arms gently upwards, reaching up as far as you can.
3. Lower your arms together in front of you keeping them straight, stretching them right out in front of you as they come down towards the floor.
4. Keeping your back straight, push the palms flat against the floor and slide

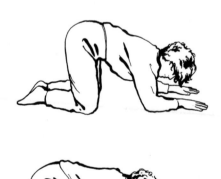

them slowly and steadily along in front of you until you are reaching forwards as far as you can comfortably go. Be careful not to arch your back.

5. It may be comfortable just to rest your forearms on the floor, or you may be able to stretch right out. Rest in whichever position you can reach for a minute or two, then come back up slowly.

The Knee Hug

This one is very comforting if you have had a fraught day (curling up and cuddling yourself can be immensely soothing, as if you too are reverting for a few moments to being a baby). It is also helpful for relieving both back and shoulder ache.

1. Lie on your back, and bring your knees gently up to your chest. Cross your ankles lightly if this feels right for you.
2. Hug your knees comfortably with your arms.
3. Rock gently from side to side.

Rock-and-roll Twists

1. Lie on your back on the floor.
2. Bend your left leg, and hook your toes under the right side of your right calf, rolling your knee towards the right.

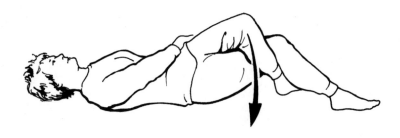

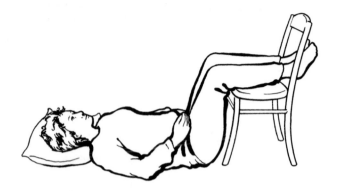

3. Place your right arm right across your body, so that the hand holds your left hip.
4. Rock from side to side gently, then roll back to the starting position again and repeat on the other side.

What else helps

- *Swimming* may well help considerably too, if you can get a chance to do it once or twice a week.
- *A hot-water bottle* left on the aching area for no more than 10 minutes (lest it inflame any nerves and nerve endings threading through the area and make it hurt even more) *alternating with cool packs* (again, no more than 10 minutes at a time) can be very useful if the problem is becoming acute. But only use these as a stopgap while waiting for an appointment with a back specialist, not instead of treatment, because if your back is hurting a good deal the pain is unlikely to go away on its own.
- *Hot baths* can help too, because as with hot-water bottles, the warmth has a relaxing effect on the muscles and ligaments in the area, which can reduce any pain if it is being caused by soft tissue spasm.
- *Lying on the floor*, legs up over a chair at roughly right angles (see diagram above) can be a good way to relieve back pain, both while you are pregnant and after you have had your baby.

HOW TO GET RID OF PERSISTENT BACK TROUBLE

If your back pain persists for more than a few weeks, is getting worse, or if neither gentle stretching nor exercises seem to help, go and see a registered osteopath or chiropractor who has a special interest in helping women with postnatal back problems. Many do, and some also offer pregnancy checks of women's backs and general posture, plus a standard postnatal back MOT as a preventative measure to help prevent new mothers' back problems occurring in the first place. See Useful Addresses page 411 for how to find one, and for details of those clinics offering treatment for reduced fees.

You may well start to feel relief from the first session. Unless there is a serious problem, you should not need more than about six altogether.

Both chiropractors and osteopaths work using slightly different techniques, but both use gentle manipulation of the spine, and sometimes adjoining limbs, to realign any joints or bones which have become badly positioned.

They may do this with gentle pressure, small pushes and controlled gentle twists, or they may occasionally use more leverage and strength. The latter is seldom necessary for women who have just had babies, as their ligaments are very soft and need little persuasion to adopt different positions.

DSP – THE BACK PAIN NO ONE SEEMS TO MENTION

What is it?
Diastasis symphysis pubis means the separation of the joint at the front of the pelvis, right in the middle of the pelvic girdle. It is not common, but it can happen and it is probably underdiagnosed.

The ligaments of this symphysis pubis bone (SP) are connected to the sacroiliac joint at the bottom of the spine round at the back. It is the job of these ligaments to help steady your pelvis when you move.

If these ligaments relax too far or are stretched too much, the joint pulls 'open' and there is a gap in the middle of what before felt like a single bone. The pain this causes can range from merely nagging to agonizing. It may begin in pregnancy from the twelfth week, but it is more usual for it to occur during a long or difficult labour. Most women find that the pain goes when their baby arrives. However, for some it can persist for weeks or months afterwards. DSP may, or may not, happen again with future pregnancies and childbirths, the experiences of different women vary hugely. Though postnatal backache is a subject women often hear about and receive advice about before it happens, DSP is rarely mentioned until it happens to you.

What causes it?
It is thought that the softening hormones of pregnancy might cause this condition. Most women do in fact go through their pregnancies without any problems with this joint, though some may find the joint gapes open a little when they walk or climb stairs, and that this hurts. However, a few women find the joint separates during labour. Many cases have been associated with the mother having had her legs up in stirrups on the delivery bed and having had to push in this position for at least an hour. Having had an epidural appears to be another contributing factor, as is having a large baby if you have a small pelvis.

DSP can be diagnosed by a straightforward X-ray after pregnancy, or by ultrasound.

Treatment
Self-help
Try ice packs, heat pads and hot-water bottles applied to the area alternately; hot baths, with aromatherapy oils which have a pain-soothing effect such as lavender; contacting a self-help group for support, a befriending ear and practical advice (see Useful Addresses page 412).

What helps
- Rest is immensely important, if you experience DSP after your baby's birth.
- Listen to your body too. If you know a specific activity, such as hoovering, causes discomfort, try to avoid it.
- Sit down for tasks you would normally stand for, such as food preparation, ironing.
- Only do lifting if it is absolutely essential. If your toddler wants to be picked up, for instance, get down to their levels and cuddle them, or help them climb up to your level instead. The more you carry, the more strain is on your pelvis.
- Be ladylike – avoid straddle movements, especially if lifting; and keep your legs together for movements like getting in and out of bed, the car or your bath.
- Swimming can help, as can exercising in water gently supported (remember to let your teacher know about your DSP) but avoid breaststroke.
- Avoid twisting movements of the body. Always face what you are doing.
- If pain is severe, use elbow crutches to take the weight off your pelvis and help you retain some vital mobility.

Complementary therapy
Certain therapies may be prescribed by your own GP. Osteopathy, chiropractic or acupuncture could be especially useful for DSP, but it would be best to find a practitioner with a specific interest in women's health, pregnancy and related issues. It is also essential that the practitioner is fully qualified and experienced or they might do more harm than good. If your GP does not know of one, contact the relevant professional associations (see Aromatherapy Organizations Council, the Council of Acupuncture, the General Council and Register of Osteopaths and the British Chiropractic Association, in Useful Addresses page 411–12).

What else helps
- Your GP can prescribe painkilling and anti-inflammatory drugs.
- A physiotherapist can offer several different treatments such as a support belt to hold the joint together until the ligaments firm and shorten sufficiently to hold it comfortably in place once again. As an alternative to this, a big Tubigrip bandage size K or L, cut long and worn tripled over around the hips can be very comforting and supporting for the area. Other options include shortwave diathermy, TENS, laser treatments, hydrotherapy (exercising gently, supported in water) and traction.
- Surgery. As a very last resort, the SP bone can be fused back together by

an orthopaedic surgeon. There is little research available on this method, but what there is suggests this is not a very successful option.

- Pain clinic. Your local hospital may have one of these departments, which specialize in the control and management of pain of all types, from arthritis to DSP pain, though they are usually of especial help to someone who is suffering pain long term, and there is usually a waiting list. Treatment options include nerve blocks, acupuncture, sclerosing injections which strengthen the ligaments, hypnotherapy and steroid injections to help control the pain.

USEFUL ADDRESSES

The Aromatherapy Organizations Council, 3 Latymer Close, Baybrook, Market Harborough, Leicester. Tel: 01858 434242.

Back in Action. Tel: 01628 527659.

A wide range of products by mail order for back comfort (chairs, bed accessories, back supports, to use while sitting/driving etc). Also a large shop at the BSO, see below. Tel: 0171 930 8309.

British Chiropractic Association, Equity House, 29 Whitley Street, Reading, Berkshire RG2 0EG. Tel: 01734 757557.

Can put you in touch with a professionally qualified chiropractor in your area who specializes in postnatal back problems.

The British Acupuncture Council, Park House, 206 Latimer Road, London W10 6RE Tel: 0181 964 0222.

British School of Osteopathy (BSO), 1–4 Suffolk Street, London SW1Y 4HG. Tel: 0171 930 9254.

Holds twice weekly expectant and postnatal mums' back clinics. You can have treatment here at much reduced fee levels (about £15 for a first visit, £11 for later ones) as you would be seen by a senior student under the direct supervision of an experienced osteopath tutor.

British Wheel of Yoga, 1 Hamilton Place, Boston Road, Sleaford, Lincs NG34 7ES. Tel: 01529 306851.

This organization can put you in touch with a professionally qualified teacher near you, who may be able to help your back problems by teaching some safe gentle stretches either one to one, or in the context of a regular group yoga class. If you have time and are able to get out to a class even once a week, it can be enormously de-stressing both physically and mentally for new mothers who suddenly find they do not seem to have any time for themselves any more.

Chartered Society of Physiotherapy, 14 Bedford Row, London WC1R 4ED. Tel: 0171 242 1941.

Can offer advice and information on exercises to correct postural and pelvic problems, especially back pain, which women may experience after having had a baby. Many helpful leaflets.

CRY-SIS, 27 Old Gloucester Street, London WC1N 3XX. Tel: 0171 404 5011.

The DSP Support Group, (HQ) 17 Muir Road, Dumpton, Ramsgate, Kent CT11 8AX. Tel: 01843 587356.

A support group for women who have experienced structural pelvic disorders as a result of childbearing.

General Council and Register of Osteopaths, 56 London Road, Reading, Berkshire RG1 4SQ. Tel: 01734 576585.

Can put you in touch with a registered osteopath near to you, and may be able to suggest someone who has a special interest and experience in women's postnatal back problems.

Hydrotherapy Association of Chartered Physiotherapists, 356 Dover House Road, London SW15 5BL. Tel: 0181 788 2471.

National Backpain Association, 16 Elmtree Road, Teddington, Middlesex TW11 8ST. Tel: 0181 977 5474.

Finding the best baby sling

Your choice of babysling is a very important factor in helping avoid back and shoulder or neck pain developing. It's worth investing in a really comfortable one, and that is often not going to be an ordinary standard 'straps over both shoulders and carrying pouch/seat in front' type that you would find in a high-street chain store. A more likely source is one of the many small independent babysling companies' models. Their slings will usually have been designed by mothers of young babies who made their own and found they worked.

It is worth shopping around a bit and investing, as you will probably be using a sling if you have one, for several hours a day every day – and anything which makes baby carrying easier helps protect your vulnerable back.

There are several small independent companies making wide-strapped, soft babyslings that use traditional cloth designs to help avoid back/shoulder strain and pain. Costs are from around £20. Ask for a design brochure from companies such as:

The Better Sling Company, 60 Sumatra Road, London NW6 1PR. Tel: 0171 433 3727.

Huggababy, 33 Dean Swift Close, Goodrich, Ross-on-Wye, Herefordshire HR9 6HQ. Tel: 01600 890569.

Wilkinett, PO Box 20, Cardigan, Wales SA43 1JB.

If you are not sure about the design having seen a picture of them, ring up and ask if you can have one to try for a few days, with the option to return it if you and your baby do not find it comfortable after all.

Postnatal Depression – Breaking Through

Feeling miserable, anxious, emotionally numb, or as if you are somehow out of contact with reality – after childbirth? Depending on how relatively mild or powerful these feelings are, doctors and midwives classify them as:

- The Baby Blues. These only last a few days and do not need treatment as such, but as much gentle support as you feel you would like.
- Postnatal Depression (PND). This can be cured in as little as three months, but if it goes unrecognized it may last for anything from several months to a couple of years.
- Postnatal Psychosis. This is quite rare, but when it does occur it is severe enough to mean you need to be cared for in hospital.

'It's NOT postnatal depression'

All of the above come under the medical umbrella term postnatal illness (PNI).

How common is PNI?

Very. Estimates vary as to just how common. But it is thought that between 50 and 80 per cent of women develop some degree of the blues, which fortunately only last for anything between a few hours and few days after the birth of their baby. Estimates for PND are between 10 and 15 per cent. Between 0.1 and 0.3 of 1 per cent – between one and three in every 1,000 – new mothers will experience postnatal psychosis (PNP).

The good news is that spotted early and treated properly, PND can be banished completely in as little as three months. And with proper treatment, nearly every single woman who develops the more serious postnatal psychosis will recover completely.

The period immediately after childbirth can be a high-risk time for women and depressive illnesses – your likelihood is about four times greater now than at any other time in your life. Yet it is a testament to the way in which women tend to manage any major life change, heavy physical or emotional demand, not that so many (about 70,000 a year) *do* develop a measure of PND – but that so many more of them don't.

Causes

Postnatal illness of any type is not a nebulous problem that appears for no good reason and is all in the mind. If you develop it, it does not mean that you are somehow less mentally well balanced than those who don't, that you are weak, neurotic, in any way inadequate, or going mad.

PNI can, and does, happen to anyone including the most psychologically robust, capable and down-to-earth of women. As the Association for Post-Natal Illness, a counselling and help organization, puts it: 'This is a *physical* illness, just like any other, not a mental weakness. And like any other illness it has physical, social and psychological causes.'

If PNI affects you, don't panic because there is help available to get you through it, and many useful medical treatments. Please do not feel you are on your own – you aren't. There are 70,000 to 100,000 other women out there this year feeling much the same as you are. Further, the problem has become increasingly well recognized over the last five years so public understanding of the area is far better than it used to be. *Any* good medical professional, whether they are a health visitor or a GP, should be on the lookout for PNI, and eager to help you.

And please do not feel you will never get better. Though it can be very hard to imagine at the time ever feeling your old self again, you will. Try calling the APNI and talking to some of their volunteer helpers, all of whom have had PND themselves and recovered fully. They will be able both to listen to you for as long as you need to talk, and to reassure you that you will recover (possibly far quicker than you think).

Risk Factors

Medical consensus about the risk factors and causes of PNI is that generally, as with other disorders which have a wide variety of symptoms such as PMS, there isn't one single reason for it. Rather that there are several contributing factors, some physical, some social. However, most experts also feel that the two biggest culprits are:

Hormones

In the days and weeks after childbirth, your body is having to adjust to a sudden rapid nose-dive in its levels of pregnancy and labour hormones, and a rapid increase in others such as prolactin, which encourages your breasts to make milk. The amount of hormones you have in your bloodstream are so tiny that they are measured in nanograms per millilitre or ng/ml – representing a tiny 1,000 millionth of a gramme per millilitre of your blood. The different ones whose levels are either rocketing or plummeting just after you have delivered your baby include:

- Oestrogens, dropping from 2,000 ng/ml in late pregnancy to 20 ng/ml by the third day of birth and zero by the seventh day.
- Progesterone, which sustained your pregnancy for the last 10 months, now dropping from 150 ng/ml at the end of your pregnancy to less than 7 ng/ml now.
- Prostaglandins, catecholamines and oxytocin, which encouraged your womb to contract powerfully during labour. The first two are dropping, the third is still produced, though in far smaller amounts, if you are breastfeeding.
- Prolactin, the milk-making hormone which is rising.

Tiredness and stress

A measure of both generally accompanies childbirth, and the first few months of caring for a new baby, especially if you have other small children as well. High levels of stress during your pregnancy are also thought to contribute substantially.

Symptoms

How can you look out for signs of developing postnatal illness in yourself, or perhaps see when a friend, relative or partner might need some help? You generally need to know someone pretty well to see its early signs, and different women show it in different ways.

There may be very little to notice at all, especially if the new mother is trying (consciously or unconsciously) to present a capable, cheerful front so she can still be seen by others to be 'coping beautifully' – and behaving like the prescribed sort of good, highly competent mother. Few women want to admit that they just do not feel they can handle their own baby, or that the child that everyone expects should have made them so happy is in fact making them miserable.

However: the following can be useful symptom guidelines.

When to start looking for help

- If you are feeling progressively less able, rather than more able, to cope as the weeks progress.
- If any problems such as weepiness and irritability are still there after three weeks, says PND expert Professor Channi Kumar of the Institute of Psychiatry in London, that is a major warning bell. Many women describe it as feeling 'as if I've got permanent, raging PMS'. Go to your GP, health visitor or midwife and tell them how you are feeling. Take a friend, relative or partner with you for moral support, to help put your case across if you suspect you may be feeling too fazed to be sufficiently forceful or articulate. Or call the APNI for advice.

It is vital to get help early, both from the point of view of being treated quickly and effectively so you are back to your old self as soon as possible – and from the point of view, psychiatrists now realize, of your baby too.

Research carried out at Cambridge University in 1994 by Dr Lynne Murrey suggested that if PND mothers did not receive prompt help, their babies' psychological and physical development was likely to be affected. She found mother/baby attachments were less secure, the infants whose mothers had had PND had more mild behaviour problems such as tantrums and sleep difficulties, poorer cognitive development and in baby boys, their general development was poorer long term. Any emotional or behavioural problems were found to persist past the children's fifth birthday.

It also suggested that the first four to five months was the most critical time for this, and that damage could be done, if a mother was postnatally depressed and finding it increasingly hard to relate to and bond with her baby, as early on as the first eight weeks of its life.

BABY BLUES

The baby blues can take many forms:

- Weepiness, feeling easily upset both by events and by other people behaving in a less-than-sensitive manner. They often take the form of what nineteenth-century novels refer to as a passionate storm of weeping. In the old days, this used to be called milk fever, as it tended to happen at around the same time as milk came into your breasts.
- Irritability.
- Mild depression or anxiety. The feelings may be generalized and unfocused (feeling, for instance, either permanently anxious or that everything is horrible). Or they may be specific anxieties about not being able to manage when you go home, wondering what you have let yourself in for, panicking about feeding your baby (any initial difficulties with breastfeeding can add to this) and extreme nervousness about handling them physically. All these are normal worries that most mothers have,

especially if the baby is your first, but if they become really extreme they can be warning signals of developing PNI.

- Feeling very vulnerable. The blues generally occur on the third or fourth day after your baby is born, coinciding with the uncomfortable engorgement of your breasts, then milk coming into your breasts, and potential discomfort from any perineal stitches setting in with a vengeance. Luckily these problems are all transient, but added together – and at the time – they can be enough to make even the most pro-motherhood of women feel dreadful.

As one new mother put it recently: 'I felt I was leaking from every possible orifice. I had breasts like volcanos – hot and liable to erupt at any time. I couldn't sit down comfortably. I had not yet got the hang of breastfeeding my baby so my nipples were getting sore, and Katy cried a lot. I was really tired, being woken up all the time either by other people's babies on the ward, or my own. I just wanted to go home. And you're asking me why I was feeling fed up?'

However, according to Professor Brian Harris of the University Hospital in Cardiff, 'The more severe end of the blues can slide into postnatal depression. So keep an eye on these feelings.'

The blues needs no medical treatment as such, and along with time, the following can all help the feeling to dispel as quickly as possible:

- The peace and quiet you need to bond with your baby.
- Some help if you need it to establish your baby's feeding, whether it's by breast or bottle.
- Soothing measures for any postnatal discomfort or pain, whether it be an aching back following an epidural or sore stitches (see page 366).
- Practical household help at home for several weeks with things like cleaning, cooking, and caring for any other children you may have so you can concentrate on looking after your baby and yourself.
- Loving emotional support from those around you.

The blues may just last a few hours, or continue for a few days. They are usually over by Day 10.

POSTNATAL DEPRESSION

Postnatal depression can apply to a wide range of emotional and mental difficulties experienced by women who have recently had a baby. It's also worth knowing that a PND reaction following a miscarriage or abortion can often be as strong as after a live birth.

Only about half of all the mothers who need help or treatment are actually getting any, and despite a greater awareness of PND, both in the primary healthcare medical profession and general public, it still can go unrecognized. ('She's just rather pulled down after the baby – it'll pass.')

PND usually begins to make itself felt in the first few weeks after a baby's birth, but for some women it will not do so for up to a year. Research carried out by a British PND specialist Dr Peter Cooper in fact suggests that of the new mothers who do develop PND, 27 per cent will do so within the first month after childbirth, 40 per cent within three months and 27 per cent during the last six months of the baby's first year.

As to how long it may last, Professor Kumar estimates that with appropriate treatment it can be anything from three months to a year. Without treatment however, it may persist for up to several years, and if the woman does not receive the help she needs this may even produce a permanent personality change for some. Without being able to be very specific about the problem, friends and family may find they are saying: 'She just hasn't been the same since the baby was born.' Or, as one woman's partner said sadly: 'I just want my wife back again.'

How does it feel?

One woman expressed it as, 'I was angry, miserable, insecure – you name it.' And another: 'I felt like I was in a sort of permanent fog. Nothing was really reaching me, or making me happy. It was all one long uphill trek to keep going.' 'I was detached, distanced from everything, functioning automatically.' 'It was like living in a bubble.' This last sensation is especially common for people experiencing all types of depression and stress.

If there can be said to be a checklist for anything as variable as PND, the major indicators would include:

- constant weepiness
- recurrent anxiety, nervousness, depression
- feeling guilty all the time, about just about everything
- feeling inadequate (ditto)
- loss of interest in sex
- loss of sense of humour, loss of enjoyment in life generally
- worrying obsessively about your baby – often coupled with resenting your baby
- feeling permanently exhausted
- temper on the shortest of fuses
- unwilling to accept help
- growing feelings of isolation
- increasing difficulty in communicating with other people.

Recurrence

If you experienced PND after a previous pregnancy your chances of experiencing it again are roughly doubled, to between 20 and 30 per cent.

It may be possible in many cases to prevent postnatal depression recurring at all. Removing areas of stress in your life and in your relationship with your partner before the birth (see Risk factors, page 415) can go a long way towards this. Different hospitals are currently trying different types of preventative medical treatments, including, for high risk women, antidepressants (which do not affect the baby if you breastfeed) being given within hours of the birth. One small American study of 23 women carried out in 1995 at the Western Psychiatric Institute in Pittsburgh suggests that giving antidepressants could more than halve the risk of postnatal depression for mothers who have experienced it before.

If you developed PND after your last baby was born and are now pregnant once more, discuss preventative options with your obstetrician. If they are unhelpful or unsympathetic, ring APNI for advice.

Men and Postnatal Depression

It is thought that one in 10 fathers will have developed clinical depression six weeks after the birth of their baby, almost the same proportion as new mothers. According to a report in the *British Journal of Psychiatry* in 1994, this falls to nearer one in 20 by six months after the birth. Unsurprisingly, this is far more likely to happen if their partner has postnatal depression herself.

Though men's depression is not likely to be hormonally-based, the psychological and social issues of having a child combined with the uncertainties that the birth may bring, together with:

- tiredness from disturbed nights
- taking on more household tasks
- the stress of coping with a partner who develops PND herself
– are probably the reasons for male PND.

According to Dr David Haslam, Head of the Examining Board for the Royal College of General Practitioners: 'Sometimes this manifests itself [in men] as tearfulness and taking to bed. Sometimes it may result in violence. Sometimes an apparently happily married man goes off to have an affair. It is an area where healthcare professionals may lose their sense of objectivity. How often have we seen a man behave curiously at this time and had the reaction: "He's just being a bastard"? He may just be severely depressed.

'It seems that a lot of issues come crowding in on a man when a baby arrives. Anxieties about employment, being burdened and tied down, about responsibility and the financial and emotional ties this creates. As one father said: 'When the baby arrives you cannot fantasize any longer about parenthood. Reality begins with the very first cry.'

If a man's partner is herself experiencing postnatal depression, he is likely to be confused and also depressed by her behaviour. He does not usually really understand what is happening, and feels his partner should be happy not miserable – after all, she really wanted the baby, didn't she? And if he is very pleased with his son/daughter, why isn't she? His sleep is likely to be disturbed even if he is not actually the one getting up to feed the baby at night, and even more if he is. His work and concentration may suffer because of this. He is also probably having to do more around the house, and may be unused to this and unsure about how best to do the chores himself.

He may also feel guilty because he may fear his wife's illness is somehow his own fault – he got her pregnant, after all. Sexually, he will probably be frustrated, as his wife seems to have no interest in him physically. He may also feel, because of her increasing self-absorption and isolation, that he has somehow lost a best friend and companion.

'There is also the stigma (fading, but still around) that even if the man recognizes his partner is suffering from a clinical depression, that this is *a mental illness*, an embarrassing, slightly shameful condition that *normal people simply don't get*.

'This can mean that the new mother's partner may feel, against his will, rather ashamed of her, or because of her, and also guilty about that as well. To add to his difficulties, his own relatives and friends and his wife's may be proving quite intrusive at this time, wanting explanations that he cannot give, reassurances of when she's going to be better that he cannot offer. Some may even appear not to believe that she is not well, and might insinuate instead that she is lazy, self-indulgent or just needs to pull herself together.'

However, telling someone who is clinically depressed to pull themselves together is about as sensitive and helpful as telling an asthmatic having an attack to 'breathe *properly*'. You would if you could, but you can't.

The positive side of postnatal depression for couples is that having helped each other through the difficulties it presented, by supporting and backing each other up the best way they could, a relationship can seem doubly precious afterwards and become stronger than ever.

POSTNATAL PSYCHOSIS

Sometimes called puerperal psychosis, this is a severe mental illness – a full-blown psychotic breakdown. With the right treatment women almost always recover fully from it, but it usually means a stay in hospital.

There are six or seven specialist units in the UK called Mother & Baby units where women experiencing postnatal psychosis can be cared for along with their babies, so they need not be separated from them. Unfortunately, most of these are under threat of closure due to shortage of NHS funds and it is more usual to be looked after in a psychiatric ward of a big general hospital, or a specialist hospital. This means your baby needs to be cared for separately at home, and brought to visit you as often as possible.

The latter is not ideal. Apart from the fact that you might miss your baby very much indeed, and feel guilty about having to be apart from them, it may even damage the bonding between you, temporarily or perhaps permanently affecting the baby's future development and perhaps even their later ability to form their own relationships. However, even if you both do have to be in different places for parts of each day, you can also be together for parts of it too, with any separation usually being relatively short term. And if you are very unwell, at least a hospital stay means you will have the right support and treatment to help you get well again as fast as possible.

Postnatal psychosis is rare, and very different from PND. The mother's reaction to the illness may include any or a mixture of the following, and it may indeed seem that she has gone mad:

- Manic behaviour. A mother experiencing manic mood swings during puerperal psychosis may seem very high, hyperactive, unnaturally euphoric, uncontrollable. She may be excited and exhilarated one minute, deeply depressed the next. She may lose her sexual inhibitions totally and proposition unlikely people; spend money like water, or drive her car at 120 m.p.h. because it's *fun*.
- Severely depressive. Feeling totally unhappy and dejected, even suicidal; with fits of panic and feelings of total inadequacy. Sleep, appetite and energy levels may well be severely affected too.
- Hallucinations and delusions. The mother may become so unwell that she withdraws from reality and can no longer distinguish between what is real and what isn't. She may see things which aren't there, hear the voices of invisible beings telling her what to do, believe she has given birth to Jesus Christ or a demonic being; imagine that her husband is trying to kill her. The delusions may even make her try to kill or harm her baby.

PNP usually begins, if it is going to, about a month after childbirth and may last several months. The good news is that with the right sort of prompt treatment and support, the mother may begin feeling considerably better within a few short weeks.

Men and postnatal psychosis
The illness can cause severe disturbance within families, for any other children the couple may have and for the father himself. Many men report they are totally devastated by what has happened, feel very guilty, worried they may somehow have been the cause of the problem in the first place, and be very distressed at the idea that they have 'sent' their wife to a psychiatric hospital.

They may also be deeply anxious about the outcome, perhaps fearing their wife may try and take her own life, that she may always be mad, that things may never be back to normal. Fathers whose partners are ill with PNP also have the burden of the entire household plus their job if they have one, on top of responsibility for the baby and/or other children and be afraid they cannot possibly cope with it all.

Fathers need as much support as mothers when this happens. In fact, the family needs to be helped as much as possible as a whole, though some health professionals seem to approach this from the point of view of splitting them up into labelled individuals with problems (the 'psychotic mother', 'abandoned boy', 'distressed older children', or 'stressed and depressed partner') rather than trying to help them all together, as a many-sided but close-knit unit.

RISK FACTORS AND SELF-HELP

There is a good deal of argument about some of the possible contributing factors which make any one woman more likely to develop postnatal illness than others. But, encouragingly, many are within your own control.

Help avoid PND by:

- Getting some practical help organized for when you bring your new baby back home. It can be the single most effective thing you can do to alleviate *and* avoid PND.

  If you have a relative you get on well with, such as your mother or sister, who can either come and stay for a few weeks or pop in at regular times each day to help, this is ideal. However, not everyone does get on well with their female relatives for periods of more than a few hours at a time, and not all of them (especially younger, single, childless ones) know enough about helping care for young babies and households to be much help.

  If you do feel comfortable with them, they can be the best possible person to have around as they also offer much-needed emotional support. If your relationship is anything less than good, consider alternatives – a mother/mother-in-law/sister you don't get on with can be the worst possible person to be with you when you have just had a baby and are feeling especially sensitive.

  An alternative, if you can afford it, is to get a mother's help who can do some cooking and cleaning, and, if you would like, some babyminding, for the first three months. Even a couple of times a week for 2 to 3 hours at a time can make all the difference.
- Sorting out breastfeeding problems (See breastfeeding difficulties and how to overcome them, page 23.) Breastfeeding may be natural, but it can take a little practice for both a new mother and her new-born baby to get the exact hang of it. Usually, if you are in hospital after the birth of your baby there should be experienced midwives and postnatal ward nursing staff to help you, though this is becoming less likely as the trend towards discharging even first-time mothers within 24 hours grows. At home, your community midwife should visit you daily for the first 10 days. However, her visits will not necessarily coincide with the times you need breastfeeding advice.

  In case you need someone to talk things over with, track down your local NCT, La Leche or Association of Breastfeeding Mothers advisor's number (see Useful Addresses) before you have your baby so you've got it to hand if you find you need it. Often, volunteers from these organizations will visit you to see how they can help (distance permitting) and all will advise you and listen to you over the phone. Friends who are breastfeeding, or who have breastfed, their babies may have helpful support and advice too. A little help exactly when you need it can make all the difference in the world, and often a very small adjustment in the way you and your baby are feeding together can do the trick.

- Breaking isolation. Finding yourself at home alone with even the most adorable of babies all day long can be a major culture shock, especially if you are used to having a full social life and being out at work every day amongst other adults. The company and support of other mothers can be immensely comforting, helpful – and fun. So again, try to track down your local mother and baby groups *before* you have your baby so you have all the numbers, times and addresses when you need them. It's easier to find the time and energy to do this without a new-born baby and possibly little sleep, than with one.

  There are many different types of groups, some run by the community, others by the NCT, or MAMA, the Meet-A-Mum support network, and you may find you like one better than the others so it can pay to shop around a little. (See Useful Addresses, and also check with your community midwife, GP practice or Social Services for contacts.)

  And let selected friends know that you'd be very glad to see them (if you would) if they come round to your place and bring their own biscuits and make their own cups of tea and ignore any mess. Or suggest they might like to arrive in a car to take both you and your baby out on a short but welcome jaunt for a change of scenery. These include parks, tea shops, even an art gallery for a short while with your baby in a sling, whatever you like the idea of best.

  But also let your friends know that they will have to forget about you doing some of the things you used to with them, like lengthy shopping trips, long evenings down the wine bar or being an attentive or energetic hostess, until further notice. Friends often welcome this sort of honesty. Not only does it help them relate to you in your new situation, but many (especially childless ones), after coming to see the baby once, do not know quite how to handle a new mother and child team as so many of the things you used to enjoy doing together as friends are now not practical. Or they assume you'd rather be left alone to get on with it as you seem so busy – when actually what you wouldn't mind is a bit of civilized company for an hour, and reassurance you are still you (and interesting) as well as someone's new mother.

- Trying to make sure you don't get too tired. Having your sleep patterns disturbed, no longer getting enough sleep, taking too long to get back to sleep after your baby has woken, having too much to do during the day (new babies can create a remarkable amount of work) – all this mounts up until you feel exhausted.

  Try to pre-arrange help in the house, even for a few weeks. Ask for and accept any help offered. Try to cat nap whenever your baby is asleep during the day too, as even half an hour here or there can really help to keep you going – bother the house for a while. Get your partner to do one of the night feeds. Even if you are breastfeeding they can do this with your expressed milk in a bottle (see Beating Exhaustion page 311).

- Eating properly. Clinical nutritionist Dr Stephen Davies suggests that there may be a connection between PNI and lack of the B group of vitamins, calcium and magnesium.

424 *What They Don't Tell You About Being a Mother and Looking After Babies*

- Choosing contraception carefully. Some women choose the combined Pill as contraception (or the progesterone only 'mini pill' if they are breastfeeding). However, some doctors suggest the artificial hormones in the Pill may depress the woman's own natural production of progesterone, thus making her more vulnerable to PND.
- Eating the placenta.

A few women believe very strongly that eating the placenta may help prevent PNI.

Though there has never been a clinical study to back this up there are certainly several anecdotal accounts from the women who have tried it which suggest it did indeed help them. The rationale behind this is that the placenta is very rich in hormones which you would otherwise lose suddenly, and also in minerals such as zinc. Shortage of zinc has been linked with depression for some time.

If you wanted to try eating your placenta yourself, discuss the idea first with your obstetrician or midwife, so it can be kept clean and stored safely rather than being disposed of in the usual way. It is possible either to eat it in raw chunks a little at a time, perhaps over a couple of days (keeping it refrigerated in between), or to cook it. Some women flavour it with garlic and onions.

Medical experts say they doubt that the hormones in the placenta would be much use if you ate them, as they were likely to be broken down by the digestive system. They also suggest that the body might not be able to absorb large quantities of minerals and hormones all at once because it tends to excrete any excess it cannot use.

If you are interested in the possible connection between zinc/PND, perhaps an easier option would be to consider taking some gentle zinc supplementation during late pregnancy and for two or three months after your baby's birth. Between 25 mg and 40 mg a day is recommended for anyone who is not found to be clinically deficient in this mineral. White spots on your nails are considered to be a sign of zinc shortage.

NEXT TIME?

Preventing PNI medically

In clinical studies, both large amounts of antidepressants given either before or a few hours after the birth, and progestogen given by suppository or injection, have been found to help. Some women have also been given progesterone during the actual labours.

It is not known what the long-term effect on the baby may be if its mother takes antidepressants for several weeks or months while pregnant. Some doctors feel the possible risks are outweighed by the benefits if it can avoid the mother experiencing several months of depression postnatally.

Natural progesterone has been pioneered and used by Dr Katharina Dalton who has a clinic at University College/Middlesex Hospital, London and a private practice. Her methods have not been proven in strict medical trials, but in her study of 94 women in 1985, all of whom had previously had PND, the recurrence rate was 10 per cent – compared with the expected rate of 20 to 30 per cent. Psychiatrist Dr Brian Harris of the University of Wales College of Medicine is doing a similar trial, but a carefully medically controlled one of the type which the medical establishment expects to see before it accepts or rejects a particular sort of treatment, so by the time this book is printed the situation may be clearer.

Dalton and her followers insist however that the progesterone used is in its natural form (which cannot be taken in pill form) and that the synthetic type that you can take by mouth is of no use.

If you are interested in preventative progesterone treatment, contact the National Association for Premenstrual Syndrome (see Useful Addresses page 429) (a disorder for which progesterone is also used) for how to find a doctor offering this treatment if your own GP or doctor is unwilling.

TREATING PND

Counselling and Support
It can be very helpful to talk to an experienced and sympathetic person (whether they be a wise friend, volunteer worker on a support-line or health professional) about your feelings, in a safe space. Good counsellors are not likely to 'tell you' what to do, rather to guide you a little – and listen – as you yourself work through what you are feeling. Counselling should ideally always be offered to mothers with PND either before, or as well as, any medical treatment. And it may be all that is needed.

Proper support and both emotional and practical backup helps enormously. Contact MAMA or the APNI (see Useful Addresses) who can keep in very regular contact with you, and distance permitting, come to visit you. It is very comforting and encouraging to be able to talk to other women who have experienced what is now happening to you and come through it. They know exactly how you feel, and can often offer very good practical advice as well as a sympathetic listening ear.

Thyroid hormones
These are shown to be associated with non-PND depression in both men and women. The thyroid produces a hormone which affects the speed at which your body works. If it is not producing enough the results can include extreme tiredness, and depression. Your doctor can check for thyroid deficiency by taking your pulse rate, and also by a blood test.

It is thought that some 5 per cent of women are not producing enough thyroid hormone postnatally, and about one in 10 of all women with PND have a thyroid problem. For most, this is easily corrected with a course of medication. You need not take this permanently as your body usually adjusts back in time.

Progesterone

Most doctors feel there is no good clinical evidence that progesterone treatment definitely helps PND, i.e., in the sort of clinical trials that include comparing the hormone treatment with placebo, or dummy, treatment, which the medical establishment usually insists on to validate any treatment. However it has been much used by Dr Katharina Dalton and her followers for the last 30 years, reportedly to very good effect.

If it does work it may be because:

- There is a very dramatic drop in the amount of progesterone in your system in the first few days after childbirth, so your body has suddenly to adjust to far lower levels. And there is a definite connection between this and the blues. According to Dr Brian Harris, the bigger the drop the more severe the blues effect.
- Progesterone has a calming and sedative effect upon the neurological system. At McGill University in Montreal scientists fed large doses to rats and they fell asleep. It was also found that it is very difficult to produce an overdose effect. The hormone affects mood by attaching itself to the same receptor sites as benzodiazepine tranquillizers do.

You cannot take progesterone in the form of a pill by mouth because it gets broken down by your liver. The progesterone in the contraceptive Pill is a synthetic version called progesto*gen*, and you can take this by mouth because the liver cannot break it down in this form. This means that you must take natural progesterone in suppository form, or by injection.

Oestrogen

Again there is no good evidence of a connection with PND and your level of oestrogen. However a recent study at King's College Hospital in London in about 60 women (using the requisite dummy treatments too as a comparison) found it did indeed help over a period of six months. This oestrogen was used in the form of a hormone-impregnated patch stuck to the skin, as is used for HRT.

Now, because of the potential risks of giving oestrogen without progesterone to balance it (increased risk of breast and womb lining cancer, for instance, as well as blood clotting) work is being carried out to see if lower doses, used only in the first month after childbirth, will have the same effect.

The Pill

There is anecdotal evidence that being on the Pill after delivery can aggravate existing PND or maybe even make developing PND in the first place more likely.

It is thought possible that the artificial form of progesterone in the Pill reduces the body's output of its own natural progesterone, and so increases the chance of depression.

Antidepressants

These are used to lift depression and calm feelings of anxiety and distress. They can be especially helpful if your depression has what specialists call 'biological features' too – by which they mean that it is making you feel very agitated, or you're unable to sleep. Antidepressants are also suggested if you have been having counselling and it does not seem to be helping you sufficiently.

They are often given to women with PND to tide them over their period of depression by giving them a breathing space from its symptoms. This can give their bodies the chance to adjust to the new demands being made on it and, it is hoped, for any hormonal disturbances to settle down naturally in their own time.

Antidepressants should be used together with, *not* instead of, good counselling and support. Unfortunately, where resources are scarce (it is cheaper for a health authority to offer a drug prescription than pay for several hours of one-to-one counselling time) or GPs less than helpful or knowledgeable about PND, the drugs are frequently used alone.

Antidepressants do not work straight away and it will be two to four weeks before you would begin to feel better. If there is no improvement after six weeks, go back to your doctor and ask for a different variety. Take a friend or partner with you if necessary to help back you up, or write down the points you wish to make. Not all anti-depressants are helpful or suitable for everyone and it may be a case of finding one that suits you personally the best.

You would need to continue taking the antidepressants for about six months after you started to feel well again. If you cease after three months (which used to be advised) there is a likelihood that the depression could return.

Many of these types of drug have side-effects such as a dry mouth and sleepiness, but different ones have different effects so it is possible to modify this. Ask your doctor about any side-effects, so you will be better equipped to deal with them.

Also – make sure you are being put on the full dosage. Some doctors, in a well-meaning effort to try to minimize the side effects, will try a half-dose at first. Unfortunately, instead of having half the side-effects, this tends to have no therapeutic effect whatsoever.

It is thought that there are many antidepressants you can take while breastfeeding, but no firm evidence of this. To be on the safe side, keep a diary of your baby's behaviour and mood over the weeks when you are taking medication. If there are any adverse changes such as lethargy or irritability, report them to the prescribing doctor and suggest a change of medication. If the latter is not possible, it may be wise to consider changing to bottle-feeding instead if you are not yet well enough to discontinue the drugs.

Mild antidepressants are not addictive.

All forms of postnatal illness are curable, sometimes in a matter of weeks. Do not simply put up with any type of PNI, suffering in silence. There is a lot of effective, sympathetic help out there and you are entitled to as much of it as you need.

Tranquillizers

These include drugs like Valium and Librium. Unless you are in hospital, your doctor should only offer you these for PNI if you have severe insomnia or considerable anxiety and this is exhausting you and exacerbating your postnatal illness. They may do so on the basis that getting some proper sleep can be a huge help in itself.

However these drugs should only be used as emergency measures and ought not to be taken for longer than four weeks because they are highly addictive.

The same goes for very strong tranquillizers like chlorpromazine, though again these can be very helpful, especially if a woman has developed severe psychosis. They should only be given under careful supervision, in a hospital.

ECT

This stands for electroconvulsive therapy. It has acquired a bad name as in the past it has been much overused, and misused. But if used carefully and properly with the woman and her family's informed consent it can, says Professor Kumar, turn around a really serious postnatal psychiatric illness within a few weeks. It might be used for puerperal psychosis but should never, ever be given for postnatal depression.

If your doctors feel your illness is sufficiently severe to warrant ECT but you are very concerned about it, ask, or get your partner to suggest, that you should be put in touch with one or two other mothers who have been treated with it for puerperal psychosis. The doctor ought to be willing, and able, to put you in touch with them promptly so that both you and your family can ask questions of someone who has had a personal experience of the therapy.

However, if you feel that the ECT is not necessary, ask for a second opinion. If you have a problem getting one, contact the APNI for advice.

USEFUL ADDRESSES

Association of Breastfeeding Mothers, PO Box 441, St Albans, Herts AL4 0AF. Tel: 0181 778 4769.

The Association for Post-Natal Illness, 25 Jerdan Place, London SW6 1BE. Tel: 0171 386 0868.

Holds a register of women who have recovered from all types of PNI, and who can stay in supportive telephone contact with mothers who are currently depressed. Some may be able to visit you regularly at home, distance permitting. The association also answers letters on getting treatment, backed up by an eminent board of obstetricians and psychiatrists, and has a useful selection of literature. Besides providing non-professional support, the association can also advise on where to get good counselling, and treatment.

MAMA (Meet-A-Mum Association), Cornerstone House, 14 Willis Road, Croydon CR0 2XX. Tel: 0181 665 0357.

Network of self-help, social and support groups which meet regularly for new mothers, to make contact with others in their area. Special interest in PNI.

The Maternity Alliance, 45 Beech Street, London EC2P 2LX.
Tel: 0171 588 8582.

Advice and useful literature about all aspects of your rights concerning work and pregnancy and parenthood.

The National Association for Premenstrual Syndrome (NAPS), PO Box 72, Sevenoaks, Kent TN13 1XQ. Tel: Helpline 01732 741 709.

National Childbirth Trust, Alexandra House, Oldham Terrace,
London W3 6NH. Tel: 0181 992 8637.

Support, education and advice on all aspects of maternity and childbirth, including PNI.

Banishing Postnatal PMS

Premenstrual syndrome (PMS) is not something most women would associate with recent childbirth. In fact, it's probably just about the last thing on your mind if you've just had a baby. However, research suggests that:

- The commonest time for a woman to develop PMS is soon after she has had a child – usually her second.
- Many women also report existing PMS becoming more noticeable after the birth of their babies. This may be partly linked to the fact that the condition tends to worsen anyway as you become older.

If you either had PMS already or developed it after you had your baby, the good news is that there have never been so many different options available, many of which are natural methods without problematic side effects. With a bit of prior information, you can act quickly and positively to squash PMS before it begins to disrupt your life.

WHAT IS PMS?

PMS is a blanket term covering more than 150 emotional, physical and behavioural symptoms which occur singly or in combination, every single month – *in the last half of your menstrual cycle, the time between ovulation and the*

A survey of 324 women with PMS at the specialist clinic at St Thomas's Hospital Medical School in London, 1985 showed:

- 142 developed their PMS after the birth of one of their babies (73 said after their second, 47 said after their first and 22 did not specify).
- 100 did so after starting their periods for the first time.
- 12 after stopping taking the Pill.
- 6 after having a sterilization operation as a permanent form of contraception.

(The other 64 came under the headings of 'no identifiable event/miscellaneous') *first day of your period.* If they occur during the *first* part of your menstrual cycle (between the day after your period stops and ovulation time) the cause isn't PMS.

If you do have PMS you are certainly not alone. It's thought that up to 80 (some estimates suggest 90) per cent of women who have periods experience some premenstrual symptoms, that between 20 and 40 per cent do so sufficiently badly to seek help from their doctor, and that 2 to 6 per cent of them find these symptoms incapacitating. And the good news is that the problem is now generally well recognized, and that there is a wide range of treatments to combat it successfully.

Even though PMS is far better understood than it used to be, there are still a few ill-informed doctors who believe it's either all in the mind, or a woman's lot to be put up with stoically. This is fortunately now uncommon, but what you may still come up against is the over-busy or brusque GP who, having tried one standard treatment and found it doesn't help, seems to lose interest. In fact, a recent study of 100 women at a specialist PMS clinic in Holland found that 40 per cent of them had had either to refer themselves there or ask a well woman clinic to do it for them because they had got nowhere with their GPs.

However, if you do have a GP who seems unsympathetic when you ask for help, not especially interested or even appears unsure of what to do to help you, either ask to see another GP if it's a multi-partner practice (it is your right to do this, and you do not have to give the receptionist a reason when you ring up for an appointment) or call up one of the helplines listed at the end of this chapter. They will be able to advise you about whether there are any suitable well women clinics in your area which can help, a more helpful GP, or even if there are one of the few PMS specialist clinics within a reasonable distance, to which you can request referral.

Note: When you see your GP about PMS, take the symptoms chart you have been filling in along too to show them, otherwise they will probably just tell you to go away and fill one in over the next few weeks. Seeing the chart will help them greatly in their diagnosis.

SYMPTOMS

Have I got PMS?

The acid test of whether or not the symptoms you are getting are PMS is when they occur. Keep a chart for at least two, preferably three, months, marking PMS-free and PMS-prone days as you experience them. Also write down the exact symptoms you are getting such as irritability, and tiredness.

Symptoms checklist
The most usual ones include:

Physical symptoms
• Breast swelling and tenderness.
• Abdominal bloating, weight gain, swollen hands and feet.

- Headaches and migraines. However, menstrual or mid-cycle migraine can also be a separate problem, requiring different treatment.
- Pelvic discomfort – pain not associated with period pains themselves (see Pelvic Pain page 378). *Always* check any pelvic pain with your GP.
- Changes in your bowel habits: includes constipation, as well as a tendency towards looser motions.
- Food cravings, especially chocolate.
- Lank hair, greasy skin, spots.
- Increased appetite. PMS specialist and clinical nutritionist Dr Alan Stewart suggests that women's requirements for food can go up by as much as 20 per cent during this time.
- Tiredness.
- Reduced tolerance to alcohol, especially in the last four days before your period begins.

Behavioural symptoms
- Clumsiness, poor co-ordination and a greater likelihood of physical accidents.

According to Stephen Sandler, senior lecturer at the British School of Osteopathy and consultant osteopath at the Portland Hospital for Women & Children in London, it's been clinically confirmed that you are more likely to hurt yourself at this time than at any other during your cycle. He suggests that the number of women who injure their backs at this time rises noticeably (partly because of the accident-prone factor, and partly because your body is making more of the hormone relaxin in the latter half of your cycle).

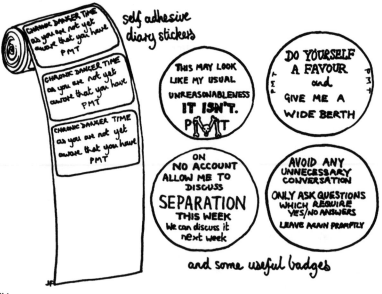

PMT IV

Relaxin is the substance which, along with progesterone, helps make your ligaments progressively soft and stretchy throughout pregnancy in preparation for childbirth. Its effects tend to last for many weeks, even months after your baby is born, which is one major reason why so many women find they hurt their backs when they have a new baby (see Backs, page 398).

- Women also report reduced ability to think clearly.
- More difficulty in making decisions.
- Altered enjoyment of sex (either less, or more – see The Up Side of PMS).

Psychological symptoms
- Anxiety and tension. This is one of the very commonest symptoms and 90 per cent of women with PMS say they experience it.
- Irritability, which can be extreme and lead to violent outbursts of ill temper or violent behaviour. If a woman has committed a crime such as a violent assault, and has a strong history of PMS, this has successfully been used in British courts as a valid reason for pleading diminished responsibility.
- Depression.
- Disturbed sleep.
- Suicidal thoughts.

The Up Side of PMS

Believe it or not, for many women there is one. Partly because once it has been recognized, PMS can be dealt with very effectively if you get the right treatment for you personally – see What helps, page 436. And partly because, according to one study carried out at Toronto University in Canada in 1989, many women are also actually having positive symptoms in their premenstrual phase. These included:

- 37 per cent reporting an increased libido.
- 29 per cent reporting that their additional aggressiveness at this time was channelled into 'more of a tendency to get things done'.
- 20 per cent said their breasts became rounder, fuller and 'more attractive' – for some however this may have been at the expense of breast tenderness.
- 18 per cent said they had more, not less, energy.
- 11 per cent that they seemed to come up with more creative ideas at work.

All in all, says the university's Associate Professor of Psychiatry Donna Stewart, seven out of 10 women said there was at least one good thing about their pre-menstrual phase.

When PMS gets confused with PND

Postnatal depression (PND) and PMS can occasionally be confused with each other. This occasionally happens when the PND (see previous chapter) has been slow to begin and has built up insidiously over weeks, or months. Its most common time of onset is all at once about six to eight weeks after you have your baby.

Further confusion can be caused because both share some major symptoms such as depression, irritability, tiredness and anxiety. It is also possible for postnatal PMS to slide into long-term PND. A mother may even experience both PMS and PND at the same time. If this is the case she would need help and treatment for both *separately* – perhaps good counselling and practical help for her PND, and possibly nutritional or hormonal treatment plus some sensible self-help measures such as eating every three hours, for her PMS.

However because the treatments for one are so very different from the treatments suitable for the other, it is vital that your doctor gets your diagnosis right. Again, the acid test is *when* your symptoms occur. Keep a diary of them for two months, with daily ratings of how mild or severe they are each day, on a scale of 0 for non-existent, to five. This will help your doctor enormously to identify the problem accurately.

Causes

Theories vary widely but the three main schools of thought are:

1. Hormonal imbalance

There is no PMS if your ovaries are not working – i.e., before your periods begin pre-puberty, or after your menopause is complete – so it is widely accepted by most doctors that PMS is due to an imbalance between the two ovarian hormones oestrogen and progesterone. The problem is that there are so many things which can affect this balance (including stress, smoking, what you eat and drink) that there is still considerable argument over the best ways to treat the condition. Women therefore find that their treatment will vary for exactly the same symptoms depending on which doctor or gynaecologist they see. Their medications may include both natural oestrogens and artificial progestogens – whose effects are completely different from each other – mood-altering drugs, dietary manipulation and stress control.

A hormonal imbalance can be produced by anything from gynaecological disorders (such as polycystic ovaries); to childbirth, after which your body's complex hormonal orchestra may not quite manage to click back into its former perfect synchronicity again. According to Dr Michael Brush, honorary consultant biochemist at St Thomas's Hospital in London and advisor to the PMS help association PREMSOC, this failure to precisely 'resynch' may become more pronounced after each pregnancy and birth, which could be one reason why PMS tends to worsen with the number of babies you have had.

2. Shortage of certain vital nutrients

These would usually only be very slight shortages, which doctors refer to as a 'subclinical nutritional deficiency', as opposed to a major one such as the extreme lack of vitamin C producing scurvy. Marginal shortages of certain substances obtained from food – notably minerals and vitamins like B6, magnesium and zinc, or essential fatty acids, can:

- Affect your hormone balance, which in turn affects your chances of developing PMS.
- Alter the production of certain mood-controlling substances produced in the brain.

Thrush and PMS

If you tend to get thrush (*Candida albicans*) infections frequently, your PMS symptoms may be worse. No one is sure why this should be, but from anecdotal evidence offered by nutritionists, and many ex-PMS sufferers as well, it appears that many women do find that once their thrush is under control, their PMS becomes less severe.

Candida albicans is a yeast organism which causes thrush and it is naturally present in small amounts in our bowel where it is kept under control by competing bacteria. If the balance between the two is destroyed and the candida multiplies out of control – this is quite common when you are pregnant, taking long-term doses of antibiotics or on the Pill – you tend to develop thrush infection.

Genital symptoms of a candida infection include a redness, itching and white curdy discharge from your vagina, which may end up on your pants. General bodily symptoms include bloating, wind, constipation, diarrhoea, general lack of energy, craving for sweet or yeasty foods – and disturbances in the menstrual cycle.

Treatment: Try to avoid sweet, sugary foods; or yeast-containing foods like bread (go for crispbreads, unleavened bread, rice cakes instead). The same goes for wine, beer, cider, vinegar, cheese (unless it's curd/cottage cheese) and mushrooms. And ask your GP about oral treatment such as Nystatin pills – which kills thrush throughout the body – to get rid of any generalized infection, plus some cream and vaginal pessaries like Canesten for the genital infection.

Note: Some really stubborn cases of thrush in the bowel have been successfully treated with colonic irrigation, a type of very thorough plain water enema which helps flush out all old bowel waste, including lurking *Candida albicans* deposits. This complementary health treatment is only available privately (cost from around £50) – see Useful Addresses page 447.

3. Sensitivity to hormone levels

PMS women may simply be more sensitive than others to the monthly changes in their hormone levels.

Two possible explanations for this are that *either* the chemical transmitters in their nervous system are just extra reactive to the standard level of stimulation from sex hormones – *or* that their bodies are making too many/too few mood-mediating neurochemicals. Those neurochemicals include dopamine, noradrenaline (one of the fight or flight hormones), serotonin (which has a calming and antidepressive effect) and acetylcholine (which is involved in the transmission of nerve impulses). The nicotine in cigarettes can reduce the amounts of acetylcholine which are made, which is why someone smoking a cigarette will find they are temporarily calmer.

4. Low blood sugar

When you haven't eaten for some time, your blood sugar – with which all the cells in your body, including those of the brain, are fed – drops. This can produce a physical state called hypoglycaemia, which can make you feel tired, shaky, a bit sick, irritable and even faint. Some doctors such as long-term PMS campaigner Dr Katharina Dalton suggest low blood sugar also causes the release of a rush of adrenaline. She suggests that this in turn inhibits the action of progesterones, and that snacking on complex carbohydrates (see The Carbo Cure page 438) every three waking hours can stop this happening, and prevent your PMS.

What helps
Self-help

If your PMS is causing you a mild-to-moderate amount of trouble rather than a great deal of trouble (in which case ask for medical treatment for it at once) there are several self-help first-line approaches you can try before visiting your doctor which can be very helpful. In fact, some women find that these DIY modifications are all they need. These include:

1. Taking additional vitamins and minerals

Note: With vitamins, minerals or fatty acids the effect will be slow and steady. You need to take them for at least six to eight weeks *before* you notice any improvement. It will probably be nearer three months before you feel their fuller effects.

- Vitamin B6. In each menstrual cycle, take vitamin B6 from two days before your symptoms usually begin to two days after your period has started, then stop.

    Begin with 50 mg twice a day for six weeks, increasing the dose to up to 100 mg twice a day if there is only a little improvement. Beware of taking more without consulting a clinical nutritionist (medical doctor with special training in nutrition (see Useful Addresses page 477)) because higher doses of vitamin B6 carry the risk of nervous problems.

    It is thought that B6 may help because it is needed for making the

body's calming neurochemicals, such as serotonin and dopamine.
- Multivitamin tablets (nutritional supplements) specially formulated for PMS. Independent clinical trials suggest Optivite and Magnesium-OK are likely to be the most helpful of these, though there are several others for sale on any chemist's or health food shop's shelves. Most anti-PMS pills will probably contain, amongst other ingredients:
— Vitamin C, because it is thought to slow the clearance rate of oestrogen, so there is more of it around for longer right into the latter half of your cycle to help balance the 'PMS-causing' hormone progesterone.
— Magnesium, because in PMS patients who have had blood tests, almost all are found to be short of magnesium.
— Zinc, as some trials have found PMS women are short of this too.
— Vitamins A and E. A is supposed to be useful for symptoms like bloating, breast pain and tenderness and weight gain (100,000 to 300,000 UI daily) in the latter part of the menstrual cycle. Some women may experience yellowing/tanning of the skin and bright orange urine if certain forms of vitamin A, like beta carotene and retinol, are used in high doses, together. Vitamin E is thought to be helpful for anxiety and irritability.

2. Taking substances high in essential fatty acids, such as evening primrose oil
Oils such as evening primrose oil (EPO), starflower (borage) oil, blackcurrant seed oil – all contain gamma-linolenic acid (GLA) which the body needs to make E-prostaglandins. It is thought that if you are short of the latter, your body becomes oversensitive to the action of oestrogen and progesterone. In clinical trials EPO supplements have been shown to be especially helpful for many PMS symptoms but especially breast tenderness.

One type of EPO capsules is now licensed and available on prescription for premenstrually painful breasts – though not for other PMS problems. If women want EPO on prescription (as it can work out quite expensive to buy the supplements in large enough quantities each month) to see if it will help their other PMS symptoms, they are advised to say that they would like it to help with PMS-related breast pain rather than other PMS related problems such as anxiety, food cravings or irritability. If you do have to buy it for yourself without prescription, the less costly form is starflower oil, though it is just as high as EPO in GLA.

The usual dosage is four to six 500 mg capsules twice daily after food, beginning two days *before* your symptoms usually start and finishing two days after your period has begun. A few women find they experience mild diarrhoea and gastric upset with EPO – and you should not use it if you have temporal lobe epilepsy. In more severe cases of PMS it may be worth taking this all month without a break, and many women find a 'holding' dose of 500 to 1,000 mg a day helpful after their PMS has stabilized.

EPO used to be very popular, but since a short Swedish trial in 1994 (which only lasted three months, though the treatment regimes recommended are three to six, and used rather lower doses than the ones usually recommended) found it of little use, it has become less so. EPO enthusiasts argue that the trial, which received considerable publicity in the press, got the results it did because it did not use enough EPO for long enough.

B6 and GLA are often used together.

3. The Carbo Cure

This is simply eating small carbohydrate-rich meals or snacks every three hours. It can be remarkably effective.

Eat unrefined carbohydrate foods such as:

- brown bread
- potatoes
- fruit, such as bananas
- wholemeal pasta
- cereals
- oatcakes
- rice cakes from the health food shop
- Crispbreads.

All help prevent PMS when eaten three-hourly as they assist the body in producing the neurochemical serotonin. Serotonin helps regulate your mood and has a calming effect. Women who are depressed either because of conditions like Seasonal Affective Disorder – a now-recognized condition often called the 'winter blues' which can debilitate some people completely – or straightforward clinical depression, respond well to pro-serotonin drugs and so do women whose PMS produces depression.

PMS sufferers often find this is all that's needed as regular amounts of these foods give a steady level of blood sugar, which helps control not only mood but food cravings for things like chocolate and sweets too.

4. General diet – eating to beat PMS

Eating a generally healthier diet with more unrefined foods and fewer stimulants can often help too. Follow the well-known (many would say boring but Tried & Tested) rules about eating:

- *Less fat.* Go for reduced-fat versions of milk, cheese, yoghurts and low-fat meats such as chicken, fish and meat substitutes.
- *Less sugar.* Avoid sweet 'health bars', cakes, biscuits, sweets.
- *Fewer stimulants*, like tobacco, tea, coffee, alcohol or colas.
- *More fibre.* Go for whole, i.e. unrefined, cereals like porridge and muesli, brown wholemeal pastas, bread and rice, fresh fruit and vegetables.

The WNAS can advise you on the type of an eating plan to help control PMS in detail depending on what your particular symptoms are.

5. Talking about it, and counselling

Tell your family about it, especially your children. If necessary, show them some books, articles, even cartoons on the subject; perhaps your diary. It may also

Anti-PMS pocket snacks

For those in a hurry, women who are constantly on the move or who find it hard to get the time for small regular meals – like mothers with new babies – it will be useful to carry around:

- bananas (which come in their own packaging and are very quick to eat)
- a packet of unsalted nuts
- small lidded pots of pasta with topping
- wholemeal buns with honey or peanut butter in them, wrapped in cling film.

All fit into a pocket, bag or briefcase without making a mess, and can prove invaluable.

Fast Snacks

- Rice cakes, slice of wholemeal bread and butter or a couple of crispbreads
- portion of cooked brown rice
- small tin of baked beans on toast
- bowl of breakfast cereal, especially muesli or porridge. Add bananas if possible
- jacket potato with any filling, or just butter.

Night food

Try a banana sandwich of brown bread, crispbreads with peanut butter on them, a small dish of pasta or small bowl of muesli *last thing at night too*. Otherwise you will probably find that your PMS symptoms make themselves felt first thing in the morning, only starting to recede about half an hour after you have had your breakfast.

be helpful to get your GP to back you up on this, especially if you are trying to explain things to a dubious partner. Try to put over the way you feel to them – especially any psychological symptoms like that sudden blazing irritability, which to someone on the receiving end appears to blow up from nowhere, and may be upsetting or very disconcerting for them. Ask for their understanding and patience on bad days and reassure them that it's nothing they said or did.

Even quite small children will understand that you have 'off days' occasionally which are no reflection on them or how much you love them – tell them in advance that it might help today if they are extra nice to you.

Support and advisory groups, such as the National Association for Premenstrual Syndrome, or the Women's Nutritional Advisory Service, PREMSOC or Women's Health Concern, can be very helpful too. Not only can they provide a sympathetic listening ear but many have trained counsellors who can offer suggestions and advice, can send you useful reading material, help you find a GP or gynaecologist sympathetic to PMS or a specialist clinic. Many also have a befriending system, where you can talk to other women who live near you who have successfully dealt with their own PMS, but know only too well how you feel.

Finding the right doctor: PMS is not an especially popular area with most doctors as it can be time-consuming to diagnose (often requiring an extensive medical history and interview with you that the average six-minute GP consultation cannot stretch to) and take persistence and patience to find the right treatment. There are only about half a dozen specialist clinics countrywide attached to NHS hospitals (to which you can ask your GP to refer you, probably on an extracontractual basis). However, some family planning clinics offer some general well woman facilities such as PMS sessions perhaps one afternoon a week (ring the Family Planning Association – see Useful Addresses – and ask if they know of any in your area) as do charitable but fee-paying clinics like Marie Stopes.

Always take your chart with you when you go and see them.

6. Relaxation and exercise

Anything at all which reduces stress can help reduce PMS.

There are many reports of the mood-enhancing effect of exercise including one study of 748 female university students in 1971 which found that those following physical education programmes had fewer menstrual headaches, less anxiety and depression than non-exercisers. Bafflingly, they still had PMS-related swollen stomachs and extremities and breast tenderness. The key might be that endorphin (mood-enhancing neurochemicals) levels rise when you exercise, and remain raised for a while afterwards. In fact, the feel-calm factor can last for two to four hours after as little as 20 minutes of aerobic exercise, say researchers of Kinesiology.

For mothers with small babies and toddlers, or both, the type of exercise or relaxation method you choose will depend partially on what you can fit in to a probably very full day. It is your baby-tight schedule which may make options such as regular meditation for an hour at a time, or daily exercise in the swimming pool, impractical. But you might find any of these beneficial.

- Yoga. This has been used successfully in children and adolescents with depression (studies such as those carried out in Italy by Plantania-Solazzo in 1992 bear this out) and it's well known for its mood-improving effects.
- Swimming. Both swimming and yoga have been found to be equally helpful in terms of reducing tension, fatigue and anger, writes consultant gynaecologist John Studd, a great advocate of hormonal treatments for PMS.
- Jogging.
- Fast walking.
- Transcendental meditation, or even if you have no time for this, as little as a couple of minutes slow deep breathing can make a real difference. Try inhaling for a count of eight, holding for eight and exhaling for eight.

    The reason this helps is that if you can bring your breathing under control it also regulates the other sympathetic body functions (such as heart rate and blood pressure) very quickly, says the Yoga Biomedical

Trust in Cambridge, an organization which researches the clinical effects of yoga – which is based on breathing control.

- Self-hypnosis (taught in one or two sessions by a properly qualified hypno-therapist).
- Aerobic exercise to music – whether dance, or water aerobics in the local pool.
- Cycling.
- Autogenic Training.
- Hot baths can have a similar effect to exercise from a calming and relaxing point of view. The heat of the water encourages the release of opiate-like, mood-enhancing chemicals called endorphins.
- Hard physical work like gardening or scrubbing a floor. Again, this encourages the release of endorphins, and if you are feeling really aggressive you can take it out on weeds, grubby floors and inanimate, hittable objects like pillows.

COMPLEMENTARY THERAPIES

These can be very successful in combating PMS and removing the root cause of it as well as treating the symptoms. Practitioners say the therapies can be used to help redress any hormonal imbalances within the body. (See Useful Addresses for how to find a professionally qualified therapist in your area.) The therapies which are the most helpful for PMS are:

Aromatherapy
According to medical aromatherapist and former head of the Aromatherapy Organizations Council (umbrella body for all the different associations) Dr Vivienne Lunny, if your breasts are swollen and painful to touch premenstrually, cold lavender compresses are therapeutic. Add 10 drops of lavender to a bowl of water, dip in two clean flannels, wring out slightly and place over the breasts for 10 minutes to reduce pain. For tiredness and lethargy she suggests blends of geranium, bergamot and rosemary; for headaches a head, neck and shoulder massage with lavender, sandalwood and chamomile oils.

Homeopathy
According to one top UK practitioner, medical homeopath Dr Andrew Lockie, the best way to treat PMS is usually with a constitutional remedy, i.e. one which takes into account the whole picture of a woman's health, her habits, personality and medical history. However he adds that there are several remedies which may help specific symptoms, such as Sepia for screaming PMS irritability, which feels worse when you are under stress, and if you feel you just want to get away from everything. Nat mur may be helpful if your symptoms are lack of confidence, depression, anxiety and a detached feeling, or if you also suffer from headaches before your periods;

Kali carb if your PMS package is irritability, panic attacks, anger, tension, a desire for sweet things and sugar and a lowered sex drive.

Bach Flower Remedies

Very useful for treating emotional states, aspen may help those who are feeling anxiety with their PMS, gorse if you are depressed and despondent; crab apple if you have an 'ugly' feeling or find menstruation disgusting and messy; cherry plum if you suffer major mood swings when your irritability overwhelms you (the remedy's makers say this is the one for 'desperate fear of the mind giving way, of insanity and the impulse to do harm to other people'). Scleranthus may be helpful for other types of mood swing – say from slightly cheerfully manic to miserable; olive and hornbeam if you find a major part of your PMS seems to be exhaustion. Rescue Remedy, a composite of several of the other remedies, can be very effective in emergency situations when you feel you are about to blow your top or have a crying fit. Its effects are rapidly apparent and it can be a very useful standby to have while the causes of your PMS are being investigated.

For the following information, our especial thanks to Dr Peter Lewis, a practitioner and researcher who is also co-founder of the Centre for the Study for Complementary Medicine at Southampton University. (The *International Journal of Alternative & Complementary Medicine*, January 1996.)

Herbal medicine

Herbalists' treatments might include milk thistle which is a stimulant for the liver and may reduce excess oestrogen levels. Also try Chinese angelica, as it contains phyto-oestrogens (vegetable oestrogens) which can have a balancing effect on hormonal levels by occupying oestrogen receptor sites even though plant oestrogens are far weaker than the human equivalent. Another useful anti-PMS substance is Ginkgo biloba which affects the neurotransmitters to help relieve depression; and Agnus castus which can increase the body's output of luteinizing hormone. This results in a shift in the ratio of oestrogen and progesterone. In fact one survey of 1,542 women (by two doctors called Dittmar and Bohnert, published in *TW Gynakol* in 1992) found that in 90 per cent of cases that treatment with Agnus castus brought relief from PMS when it was used over several months. There was a minor side effect of a skin rash for some of the women, but that was all.

Traditional Chinese herbal medicine

The ancient philosophy of this therapy suggests that PMS is often associated with Liver Chi (energy) stagnation and Spleen deficiency. Between five and 20 herbs and roots and barks are generally used to address this, but the exact mixture depends on your exact constitution and symptoms. One which is widely used is a powder they have named Xiao Yao San or Free & Easy Wanderer Powder.

What else helps?
- Massage, as it has such a calming and relaxing effect.
- Cognitive therapy, a behavioural therapy used to treat many psychiatric conditions such as depression, anxiety, and phobias (see Useful Addresses for how to find a professionally qualified therapist).
- Autogenic training. This is a form of deep relaxation which can be learnt in groups, within about eight to 10 sessions. When you become practised at it, as little as 10 minutes can be beneficial. It has been used successfully in NHS clinics to combat heart disease, chronic insomnia, irritable bowel syndrome and asthma – and, in other countries, even to reduce the pain of childbirth. Studies in the latter area were begun by a Professor Prill, Head of the Obstetrics Department at Würzburg University, and his results confirmed by other research at Kyoto in Japan (1961) and in Italy in 1966.

    The technique lends itself well to helping deal with PMS symptoms, especially the psychological ones such as anxiety and depression. It can also be adapted for uncomfortable/painful gynaecological problems which may appear after childbirth such as painful periods and unexplained pelvic pain.
- Regular exercise. If you are interested in doing some regular exercise – and that means two or three times a week if you are going to get any benefit – but are not quite sure where to start, the Exercise Association of England or The Sports Council (see Useful Addresses) or your local council can give you advice, and details of facilities available locally. For local exercise classes, perhaps in the evenings when a friend or partner could care for your baby for an hour or two, check out noticeboards in GP surgeries, community centres and local leisure pools and complexes.

Medical treatments without hormones
These are usually the next step if self-help techniques either did not help, or did not help you sufficiently. **Diuretics**, to control water retention and bloating, and **tranquillizers and beta blockers**, to soothe the symptoms of anxiety, treat PMS symptoms. They do not tackle their cause, so they may be useful purely as a holding measure while you and your doctor try to find, and treat, the root of the matter.

Tranquillizers can be highly addictive and should only be used as a short-term (up to four weeks) holding measure. The other mood-mediating drug, which has only fairly recently been tried for PMS, is fluoxetine (Prozac).

This drug enhances the level of serotonin in the brain, so regulating your mood. In the UK a few gynaecologists have found it can be helpful for women with severe PMS, with, according to a 1993 study done at the Otago Medical School in New Zealand, the improvements showing after two to eight weeks. The symptoms return fairly smartly – within 18 to 25 days – after the patients stop taking it. It is important, says Dr Mary Jones, formerly head of one of the very few PMS clinics in Britain (the unit at Leeds) that *only the minimum dose of 20 mg daily* – should be used by women to treat PMS and that this dose should be taken in the morning. It ought not to be taken by women who have a history of epilepsy nor by women on certain types of antidepressant (the MAOI variety).

When it was first launched in America, Prozac became very popular for certain types of depression and was hyped as being a genuine wonder drug – a mood-enhancer which appeared to create no dependency problems, and have no troublesome side-effects. A backlash has since followed as some instances of aggression (both thoughts and actions – and in a few cases some major outbursts of violence) were also linked with it. Prozac's manufacturer, Eli Lilly, is currently facing several lawsuits in the US because of these.

Other side-effects reported include certain disorders of the nervous system such as tardive dyskinesia (where muscles spasm and twitch voluntarily), nervousness, insomnia, skin rashes and inflammation of the blood vessels. Oh, and sexual difficulties. According to Richard Balon of the Wayne State University School of Medicine in Detroit, Michigan, any doctor thinking of prescribing Prozac needs to keep in mind that two papers appearing in the *Journal of Clinical Psychiatry* in 1992 and 1993 found it could cause sexual dysfunction in respectively up to 34 per cent and 75 per cent of all cases. The American drugs reference bible, which most doctors would use there (the *Physicians Desk Reference*) puts it at 1.9 per cent and this is also the level being quoted by the British psychiatrists we spoke to.

Prostaglandin synthetase inhibitors such as mefenamic acid (also prescribed for painful periods) may be appropriate if the PMS symptoms troubling you are headaches, tiredness, and mood swings. However, they are not much help for others such as tension, bloating, breast tenderness, poor concentration and insomnia.

Hormonal treatments
The ones your GP can give you are:

The Pill
Because the combined oral contraceptive pill (containing both oestrogen and progestogen) prevents ovulation, it should, in theory, be able to treat PMS. Large surveys by women on the combined Pill suggest that there was less PMS overall. However individual women may get PMS-like symptoms all the way through the month if their Pill disagrees with them, and may have to try one – or several – other varieties until they find one which suits them. Also the Pill's artificial oestrogens can have side-effects of their own. Giving progestogen-only pills (known as the POP or mini Pill) cyclically can also reproduce your original PMS symptoms, so you are back where you started. However as a general rule, for those women who find the Pill helps, they tend to see more improvements with the higher progestogen pills, and fewer improvements (or indeed worsening symptoms) with the higher oestrogen pills. There are few of the latter prescribed anyway these days because of fears of long-term use potentially encouraging pre-existing breast cancer later in life.

Progesterone (the natural form of the hormone) and progestogens (the artificial form)
If your doctor feels that your PMS might be due to low levels of the 'calming' hormone progesterone, they might prescribe this rectally or vaginally in

suppository form for you. You cannot swallow it as a tablet because it would be broken down by your liver, and rendered useless. You can however take the artificial variety called proges*togen* as a pill.

Charting the days when your symptoms usually begin is very important as you need to insert these progesterone suppositories yourself, up to two or three times a day in the few days *before* symptoms appear until your period begins. If you were having progesterone in the form of injections, they would need to be given by a doctor every other day, which could be both tedious and unpleasant, so they are reserved for especially difficult cases, or after a woman has recently had a baby, to help prevent postnatal depression if she is felt to be at risk of it. It is important to use high enough doses with natural progesterone starting with 400 mg daily and going up to 400 mg four times a day if necessary.

Some PMS experts, including Dr Katharina Dalton whose pioneering work has done a great deal to get PMS recognized and taken seriously in the UK, and who developed this treatment, also feel natural progesterone (not the artificial progestogens) is by far the best option. It has to be said that most other doctors are sceptical of this treatment, pointing out that Dr Dalton's treatment has never been medically proven because it has never, in all the years she and those who agree with her have been using it, been subjected it to the traditional type of clinical trials which the medical establishment requires before it will accept that a particular medication really works. However, the fact remains that both Dr Dalton, and several other doctors who agree with her methods, have between them treated several thousands of women over the last 30 years, many of whom feel it has helped them considerably.

Artificial or synthetic progesterone, progestogen, can be taken in pill form by mouth, but its success in treating PMS varies widely. The two commonest types which you may be offered are dydrogesterone and norethisterone.

Danazol

This is a powerful drug which is not in itself a hormone, but it is classed as a hormonal treatment. This is because it acts upon your pituitary gland, ensuring it cuts down your ovaries' production of sex hormones. The effect is similar to that of the Pill, i.e. suppressing your natural hormonal highs and lows whose side-effects you might otherwise experience as PMS.

Its side-effects can be unpleasant – they include acne, hairiness, weight gain, a drier vagina, smaller breasts, skin oiliness and occasionally deepening of the voice. It is unpopular with many women because of these (though the side-effects may be very mild and, some women feel, decidedly preferable to the 10 days of PMS they used to have instead) and so is now seldom prescribed by well-informed doctors. As Dr Michael Brush puts it: 'Danazol is an unpleasant drug to be on.'

Bromocriptine (Parlodel)

This works by making the body reduce its production of a hormone called prolactin. All women produce this naturally, especially if they are breastfeeding, as it is involved in milk-making. However, too much prolactin at other times can produce symptoms such as headaches, mood changes and breast discomfort. Parlodel may be useful for purely symptomatic relief but it will not do anything to tackle the cause of your PMS. It is clearly not much help if your symptoms include, for example, anxiety and irritability. Also, it frequently causes nausea, and may also produce some dizziness and low blood pressure. Take the drug with meals, or with a snack at bedtime, to help reduce the sickness.

Oestrogen therapy

The idea that lower oestrogen levels cause PMS has been pioneered for many years by John Studd, a top gynaecologist from King's College Hospital in London. His specialist PMS research clinic was one of the first in the UK and initially he used to treat PMS women with high doses of natural oestrogen in implant or skin patch form, but his current research (1995) shows that smaller doses are equally effective in relieving PMS symptoms.

. . . **as skin patches:** A popular way to give these smaller doses of oestrogen is via skin patches. These are small transparent plasters of the sort used to give HRT to menopausal women, or nicotine for smokers trying to kick the habit, via the skin. According to Dr Nick Panay, research fellow in gynaeco-logical endocrinology at the Psycho-Endocrine Clinic at the Chelsea & Westminster Hospital in London, the patches:

* are suitable for women with severe rather than mild-to-moderate, PMS
* last for three to four days each before they need renewing
* are given throughout the entire cycle
* can produce some substantial improvements in PMS symptoms of all types
* are only at present used by a handful of gynaecologists with a special interest in premenstrual problems.

The patches also need to be taken with progestogens in pill form for seven to 10 days at a time – which can sometimes bring back the very symptoms you were hoping to be rid of in the first place. Other side-effects can include weight gain and nausea, though Panay says these are usually milder than the ones the woman was experiencing with PMS. Clinicians are currently experimenting with a progestogen-impregnated coil called Morena as a way of reducing side-effects, as this acts directly via the womb lining.

Lower dose patches may be helpful for women with milder PMS but more research needs to be done on this area to confirm this.

. . . **as implants** under the skin. Generally used if the oestrogen patches were helping, but not enough. These are only really suitable for more severe cases of PMS. The problem with these is that if they do not suit you, they will have to be surgically removed, which can occasionally cause problems.

> **Feeling Sick?**
> If you are using these patches and they are helping your PMS but making you feel sick, ask whether antinausea drugs, either on prescription or whether those sold over the counter in the local pharmacy for seasickness (such as Sea Legs) might help.
>
> Try also the elasticated wristbands that have a small plastic stud on them, which are worn to stimulate the Nei Kwan acupressure point. According to traditional Chinese medicine practitioners, these can often help control nausea. The wristlets have been shown to help reduce both seasickness and the morning sickness of early pregnancy in up to 80 per cent of cases, and are even suggested by some radiologists in NHS cancer units when patients are receiving chemotherapy. (Available in major chemists, approximately £7.50 a pair.)

USEFUL ADDRESSES

Aromatherapy Organizations Council, 3 Latymer Close, Braybrooke, Market Harborough, Leicestershire LE16 8LN. Tel: 01858 434242.

The Bach Centre, Mount Vernon, Bakers Lane, Sotwell, Wallingford, Oxon OX10 0PZ. Tel: 01491 834678.

British Homeopathic Association, 27a Devonshire Street, London W1N 1RJ. Tel: 0171 935 2163.

The Family Planning Association, 2–12 Pentonville Road, London N1 9FP. Tel: 0171 837 5432.

The Institute of Complementary Medicine, PO Box 194, London SE16 1QZ. Tel: 0171 237 5165

Information on all aspects of complementary therapy.

National Association for Pre-Menstrual Syndrome (NAPS), PO Box 72, Sevenoaks, Kent TN13 1XQ. Tel: helpline 01732 741709.

Strong believers in regular carbohydrate snacks and progesterone therapy. Offer helpline, support and campaign group.

The National Institute of Medical Herbalists, 56 Longbrook Street, Exeter, Devon EX4 6AH. Tel: 01392 426022.

The Sports Council, 16 Upper Woburn Place, London WC1H 0QW. Tel: 0171 388 1277.

The Women's Health Concern. Tel: 0181 780 3007.

Registered charity which gives women advice and support on a whole range of gynaecological problems, including PMS and the menopause. Has several trained nurse counsellors who are available for telephone consultation, and a wide range of useful leaflets and booklets.

The Women's Nutritional Advisory Service, PO Box 268, Lewes, East Sussex BN7 2QN. Tel: 01273 487366.

Takes the clinical nutrition approach, using of minerals and vitamins to combat or eradicate any shortages or nutritional imbalances within the body which may be responsible for the PMS. Can do an individual postal and telephone advisory programme for you (from £35). Also has three clinics at Hove, Lewes and in London, charges from £55 for a first consultation and from £25 for follow-ups.

Hair Loss? Growing it Back

If you were one of the lucky women whose hair looked and felt wonderful while you were pregnant – glossy, thick and full of bounce – finding handfuls of it in the bathroom sink in the weeks after your baby is born is both alarming and upsetting. Nearly all women experience hair loss after childbirth. It may begin at any time from one to four months after delivery and can continue for as much as six months or longer. If you're breastfeeding, it may be delayed until after you've stopped feeding.

The good news is that hair lost after childbirth is not gone permanently. It does grow back. When is rather an individual matter, but your hair should be fully recovered within a year. Losing hair after your baby's born isn't a sign that something awful is happening to it, quite the reverse in fact. It shows that your hair's growth pattern is readjusting itself to return to normal.

How pregnancy affects your hair

Much has been made of the benefits of pregnancy for the hair and skin. Increased hormone levels are said to give a radiant complexion and promote thick glossy hair. One of the most major effects of pregnancy is the dramatic

'Hey ho'

'The main reason that some women lose hair excessively after childbirth is that they become iron deficient, and in some cases severely iron deficient, during pregnancy,' says Dr David Fenton, Consultant Dermatologist at St Thomas's Hospital in London.

increase in the levels of the female hormones oestrogen and progesterone circulating in the bloodstream to amounts several hundred times greater than normal. After childbirth these hormone levels plunge dramatically, dropping as much as a hundred-fold in the hours immediately after delivery, and returning to almost normal levels within days. This accounts for the very common transient 'baby blues' many women experience about four or five days after the birth, and is an important factor in postnatal depression. This same dramatic drop in hormone levels is also responsible for post-pregnancy hair loss.

Hair needs iron

Although hair loss after childbirth affects nearly everyone, for some women it's slight and scarcely noticeable, while for others it can be considerable with as much as 30% to 50% of the hair falling out. The difference is due to how well nourished you were before, and during pregnancy. If your iron stores were drained during pregnancy you're likely to lose more hair after childbirth, and if they remain low your hair may not grow back as well as it should.

Iron is obtained from food, and any extra is stored as ferritin, mainly in the liver and in the spleen and bone marrow. Iron stores are built up over a long period of time. When your body's demand for iron is more than the amount absorbed from food, such as during pregnancy, iron stores are mobilized and can become depleted. And if iron stores are low to begin – which is often the case with women who have had heavy periods before pregnancy and those on vegetarian and vegan diets, then pregnancy wipes out the small reserves. Hair loss can be one quite visible result.

Women who become pregnant for a second or subsequent time without replenishing iron stores between pregnancies are especially at risk of hair loss, since their iron levels become lower and lower and hair loss greater with each pregnancy.

Are you low on iron?

Anaemia may develop after childbirth (see page 337 for symptoms of this). However, it's quite possible to have low iron stores and be iron deficient without being anaemic and this is probably more common than doctors realize. One study in Canada showed that 19 per cent of the population studied had evidence of iron deficiency but only 2 per cent were anaemic.

You can help replenish iron stores by eating plenty of iron-rich foods (see page 338) and/or taking an iron supplement. If you do decide on an iron supplement bear these points in mind:

- Iron can be taken in the form of iron gluconate or iron fumarate. Preparations containing between 50 mg and 100 mg of iron can cause gut pain, black stools and constipation. Floradix and Floravital are two liquid supplements which claim to be gentle on the stomach (made from vegetable sources of iron, available from health food shops). In severe cases of anaemia, iron injections can be used.
- Don't take more than the recommended dose. Iron is toxic, and can be fatal in overdose. Small children can be poisoned by as little as 20 mg, so store tablets safely.
- Vitamin B12, zinc, folic acid, magnesium and chromium are also all important for healthy hair growth. A good multivitamin and mineral supplement should contain these.

Other reasons for post-baby hair loss

However alarming hair loss after the birth of your baby may seem, remember that your hair will normally grow back given time. 'Usually hair lost after pregnancy should be completely recovered,' says Dr Fenton, 'unless there's some background medical reason.'

The most common reason for continued loss or poor regrowth is iron deficiency but other factors that can affect your hair include:

- A tendency to male pattern baldness. Most of us don't realize that women do go bald in the same ways as men as they age – not as much, or as early, but hair thins and is lost with age in both sexes. Male pattern baldness in women seems to be on the increase and trichologists speculate that it may be associated with many women's increasingly stressful lifestyle. For some women pregnancy and childbirth can uncover this tendency for the first time and hair may not recover fully. Treatment by a dermatologist can help.
- The contraceptive pill. Going on the Pill straight after you have your baby can in itself cause a 'moult' because of the Pill's effect on hormones. Progestogen, the synthetic hormone in the Pill has a male hormone, or androgen component, which affects hair growth in some women. This can be especially true of women who've inherited a male pattern baldness tendency and may be especially sensitive to the male hormone. Some types of pill have higher levels of progestogen than others. Changing your type of pill, or choosing an alternative method of birth control might help if you feel it is affecting your hair.
- In around 10 per cent of women the thyroid gland is temporarily unbalanced after childbirth. It may underproduce, then overproduce the hormone thyroxine before returning to normal, usually within six months of delivery. Lack of thyroid hormone commonly causes hair loss. A blood test can check your thyroxine levels.
- Sudden weight loss can cause hair loss within one to six months of starting a diet. Crash dieting can cause a drop in metabolic rate which in turn reduces the production of thyroid hormone. A slow, steady weight loss is better.

- Antidepressants can cause hair loss, particularly if you are prone to the problem as an inherited trait. Prozac is one medication which lists hair loss as a side effect.

If your hair loss continues for more than four months after your baby is born and you're worried about it, see your GP and ask them to run some blood tests or refer you to a consultant dermatologist, advises Dr Fenton.

How to help get your hair back
The most important thing you can do to help your hair recover is to eat well and pay attention to improving your overall health with plenty of rest, relaxation and moderate exercise – all far easier said than done with a baby or small child. Hair is a sensitive barometer of your general health and illness, shock, stress, surgery, the eating disorder anorexia, pregnancy and childbirth all have an effect on its condition. The hair follicle takes two or three months to respond to changes in diet but because hair cells are so quickly manufactured visible results can be seen quite soon after that.

- Aim to eat at least *one* good, well-balanced meal a day which includes some protein, carbohydrate and fresh fruit or vegetables. Make sure you can sit down to eat in a relaxed and unhurried way.
- Try to eat regularly and not to skip meals.
- Watch your tea and coffee intake. It's easy to clock up an alarming number of cups (and packets of biscuits) if you're at home with a small child. Try fruit juice, herb tea or water instead.
- Make sure you get enough protein from meat, or a variety of vegetable sources (including pulses, legumes and cereals). Protein is important for hair health and vegetarians and vegans are especially vulnerable to hair loss.
- Eat as much fresh food, especially fruit and vegetables, as you can to boost your intake of vitamins, minerals and micronutrients. Try not to rely on heavily processed or ready-made meals.
- A good well-balanced multivitamin and mineral supplement containing iron, B vitamins, selenium, magnesium, chromium and zinc, taken regularly for several months will ensure you're getting all the nutrients you need. Ensuring enough B vitamins is especially important if you are a vegetarian or vegan. Your GP can prescribe an appropriate supplement on the NHS if they feel you could be at risk of vitamin deficiency.
- Regular exercise – even just a brisk daily walk, improves circulation and overall health. The benefits are seen in skin, hair and general wellbeing.
- Scalp massage (see how below) is recommended by trichologists as an important way of improving circulation and supply of nutrients to hair follicles of scalp.
- Don't panic about post-pregnancy hair loss. It's quite normal and hair will, in nearly all cases, grow back. Extra worry won't help your hair.
- Treat hair gently. Don't tug when you brush or comb, avoid tight elastic bands that can tear or break the hair shaft.

How to make the most of what is there

It will take time for your hair to recover from the upheaval of pregnancy and childbirth, in the meantime there are several strategies for making the most of however much of it you have, while you wait.

Usually hair is lost mostly from the front and sides of the hairline. Some women also notice thinning on top, especially if there's any inherited tendency to male pattern baldness. You may find your hairline receding slightly or your fringe getting thinner and finer. As new hair begins to regrow you'll start to notice lots of very short, tapered hairs sticking up in the thinned areas. At first you may not be madly grateful for this new growth because in its early stages it looks untidy. The problem is usually very short-lived and in another month the hair will be long enough to lie flatter.

Ringing the changes with a new cut, colour or perm is a common morale booster after having a baby, but if you do decide on a new look, think twice before having any potentially damaging treatments such as perming, bleaching or straightening. If your hair is already fine or fragile, any further breaking or splitting may make it look worse, not better. A good cut may be the best bet while hair recovers.

HAIR CARE

Wash and . . .

If you're shedding hair you may feel frequent washing is going to make matters worse. It won't. Trichologists are adamant that daily washing is good for hair, and does not 'dry it out'. On the contrary a good shampoo and conditioning produce will remoisturize and improve it. Philip Kingsley, trichologist to many celebrities in London and New York, says it's the single most important aspect of hair health. 'Everyone's hair looks its best after shampooing. If it doesn't, you are either using the wrong products or not shampooing correctly. Overall, shampooing helps overcome hair problems, rather than adding to them,' he says. Now may be the time for a simple, short cut which can be washed often and left to dry alone without the need for too much styling.

. . . dry

- More damage is done to hair during drying than at any other time, according to Kingsley. The ideal way to dry hair is to pat it with a towel and leave it alone. However, using a dryer isn't damaging if done carefully.
- Comb gently. It's more easy to damage hair when wet. Hold the dryer six inches away from your hair. Dry the back and sides first, working towards the crown and front.
- Start on high speed and temperature, and as hair dries, reduce both.
- Ideally, hair should be left slightly damp. It's the last stages of drying that damage hair.
- For the last minute of drying, hang your head down towards the floor. Gently brush hair in this direction to give added bounce.

- Use heated rollers, curlers and tongs with care. They can dry and damage hair.

Hair thickening recipes

An infallible, inexpensive protein conditioner to give fuller, bushier hair instantly:

1. Pour your normal amount of shampoo into a bowl. Add a single sachet of powdered gelatine. You can also optionally add one beaten egg.
2. Shampoo as usual and leave on for 5–10 minutes.
3. Wash well in cool water. Don't use hot or you'll end up with scrambled egg on your head.
4. Blow dry on a cool setting.

Non-detergent shampoo

All shampoos are basically detergents, and there's no harm in this, but if your hair's feeling really 'stripped' you could try this alternative from Mark Constantin, product development advisor to The Body Shop.

1. Take a bowlful of cooled lentils that have been cooked ready to eat.
2. Massage a handful into dry hair to absorb dirt and grease.
3. Rinse well for five minutes in cool water.

Home-made shampoo moisturizing treatment

For a weekly treatment to improve condition and shine, whisk in a blender: 2 eggs, 1 oz (25 g) castor oil, ½ oz (13 g) olive oil, 1 oz (25 g) unsalted butter, 2 oz (50 g) plain yoghurt, 2 oz (50 g) double cream, 1 banana, juice of 1 lemon.

Refrigerate overnight. Apply mixture to whole length of hair by parting in sections then combing through with a wide comb. Apply extra mixture to the ends and press in with the fingers. Knead the scalp for 10 minutes and press the cream into the ends again. Leave for a further 10 minutes, or overnight by covering with a plastic cap. Shampoo and condition as normal using moisturizing products. (Suggested by Philip Kingsley.)

Lotions, potions and pills

There really is no need to treat post-pregnancy hair loss because it's a condition which will right itself in time provided you eat well and take reasonable care of your hair. The exception to this is if there's an underlying medical disorder, (see page 451) in which case you'll need specialist medical help.

Products to treat this type of hair loss come in two main forms.

- Topical lotions, which are applied to the scalp, e.g., Regaine, which contains the drug minoxidil; and Silicium 44, which contains the mineral silicium. These are for the treatment of premature male pattern baldness and are inappropriate for hair loss after childbirth. Kevis is one product, containing hyaluronic acid, which does shorten the amount of hair shed after childbirth.

- Food supplements and vitamin pills. A wide range of products containing vitamins, minerals, trace elements and amino acids claim to help promote healthy hair growth. Kervans Silicia (containing silicia), Pil-food (contains millet and several amino acids), Nourkrin, which comes in tablet, lotion and shampoo form (containing vitamins) are just a few. There are also many 'hair and nail' formula vitamin supplements available which often contain a combination of iron, B vitamins, sometimes zinc, selenium and other ingredients. None of these is harmful (unless taken to excess) but there is no good scientific evidence that they are beneficial and some are extremely expensive.

USEFUL ADDRESSES

Hairline International, 39 St John's Close, Solihull, West Midlands B93 0NN. Tel: 01564 775281.

A society offering support and help for patients suffering balding or alopecia areata.

The Institute of Trichologists, 20–22 Queensberry Place, London SW7 2DZ. Tel: 01625 862679.

Can refer you to a properly qualified trichologist in your area.

USEFUL READING

Coping with Sudden Hair Loss, Elizabeth Steele, Thorsons.
Hair – An Owner's Handbook, Philip Kingsley, Aurum Press.
Super Healthy Hair, Skin and Nails, Stella Weller, Thorsons.

How to Get Your Body Back

Taking a good long look at yourself naked in the mirror for the first time after your baby's been born is usually a little depressing. Now that the bump has disappeared, larger hips and thighs seem especially conspicuous. You wonder if you'll ever get your pre-pregnant shape back. Even if it wasn't that great, it was still better than this.

These sorts of feelings aren't the least bit unusual. While you may have been quite happy with your pregnant shape, enjoyed having fuller breasts for the first time in your life or felt proud of your growing bump, your postnatal body can come as quite a shock. One study of body attitudes during pregnancy and the postpartum period published in 1985 in the *Journal of Obstetrics and Gynaecology and Neonatal Nursing* found that women felt far more negative about their bodies during the last three months of pregnancy and after childbirth than they had before pregnancy.

In time you *can* recover your figure, regain your former energy and your

'I love my body just the way it is, I love my bulgy belly, I love my . . . oh forget it'

sense of wellbeing, although this can take a bit longer than you anticipated. However, it has to be said that your body's 'normal' after your first baby will not be exactly the same as it was previously. Your waist may remain slightly thicker, your breasts may not be as freestanding as before, your stomach never as completely flat again. Orgasms might not be as intense if your pelvic floor muscles have been overstretched – although many women report they're actually more powerful after childbirth. (See Sex After Childbirth page 478.) But who says becoming a mother does not mean you cannot also be a physically attractive and desirable woman? Many women say that they both feel and are regarded by their partners as even sexier and more womanly after having had a baby. Others report that they now feel genuinely comfortable in their own bodies for the first time in their lives – the French have a phrase for it: *'Je suis bien dans ma peau'* ('I'm happy in my skin' – and far more assured and conscious of their sexuality. But the physical changes of pregnancy and the postnatal period can also knock your former sense of physical and emotional self.

Getting comfortable with yourself again

As far as getting back to normal as fast as possible goes, try not to be so hard on yourself, and give it time. The last thing you need in the first year is worries about your weight and shape to add to the stresses of managing a new baby, your new role of motherhood, so little time and so much responsibility.

Get it in perspective a bit if you can – think about what your body has been doing for the past 9 months, the enormous achievement it has made – growing your baby inside it, expanding remarkably both inside and out to accommodate this *and then* giving birth as well. It is greatly to the credit of women's powers of recovery that your body is not looking even more altered than it is. Childbirth may be normal, but that doesn't mean it's not a major physical undertaking which puts considerable gravitational and mechanical stress on your skin, muscles, ligaments and internal organs. No wonder they do not look as they did before from the outside. But give it time and they will, give or take an inch or two. It is also well worth remembering that:

- Your changed body shape is a temporary, limited stage of your life. Try to keep a sense of perspective on it time-wise, because it really will pass even if it seems permanent now. Relax and enjoy nursing and caring for your new baby while it lasts. Don't make yourself miserable about your weight. (As one new mother put it: 'Those beautiful statues of breastfeeding fertility goddesses are at least size 16, aren't they? Different stage in life, different shape. It feels right to me for the moment.')
- Different women recover at different rates from pregnancy and childbirth – it is as individual as the mothers themselves and the babies they have. It also depends whether you have had babies before. If your abdominals have been stretched once or twice before, your pregnancy may be very noticeable say at month four rather than month six as it was first time around and it may well take longer to get back into shape again afterwards too.

- If you can possibly afford it, buy some new clothes that fit you now. You'll probably be sick of your maternity clothes, which may be the only things that fit you for a few weeks or even months after delivery. Don't buy new clothes exactly the size you were before the baby and then feel fed up because they're too tight.
- Weight gain is often associated with depression. If you find yourself comfort eating it may be worth while examining your motives for diving into the biscuit tin. It can also be associated with chronic tiredness, as most of us will go for a quick fix energy source (like sweet snacks, biscuits or crisps) if we are short of time – which new mothers generally are – and feeling low in energy, in need of a lift to keep going. Unfortunately it's the junk and fattening foods that tend to be the quickest. There are some healthy instant/four-minute options though which you might like to try instead, see page 314.
- Life may be too full and chaotic to pay much attention to what you eat or to make time for exercise. It may take you several months to work out a routine that allows you to look after the baby, cope with the domestic routine and pay attention to your own eating and exercise. Don't abandon all hope if you don't manage what you'd like to do in the early months.
- Consider your needs for energy and what you have to do to take care of your baby and yourself. It's more important to keep up your energy levels than to diet in the early months.
- Most women who are eating normally continue to lose weight up until six months after delivery. Therefore when your baby is six months old is probably the time to take stock because any excess weight you're left with then is likely to become permanent, unless you take action to lose it.

Be patient

After you've had your baby, official postnatal care finishes at six weeks with a health check from your GP or obstetrician. At six weeks your uterus should have shrunk back to its pre-pregnant size and discharge (lochia) stopped. The assumption is that because your reproductive system is now back to normal you too are recovered from every possible health problem associated with pregnancy and childbirth. The truth is that most women feel anything but back to normal.

A survey conducted in Grampian region in 1991 by Dr Cathryn Glazener of the Health Services Research Unit at the University of Aberdeen questioned 1249 women at five days and eight weeks after delivery, and half of them again when their babies were aged between 12 and 18 months. At eight weeks 89 per cent had one health problem, and at 12 to 18 months 73 per cent still had one problem. This highlights the fact that complete recovery from childbirth and getting back to normal physically takes not a few weeks or months but at least a year for the majority of women, and perhaps longer.

Be patient with yourself and don't get depressed if it takes much longer than you'd expected to feel comfortable with your body again after you've had a baby. It is not at all unusual.

What shape are you in? And why?

Body shape is not just a matter of size, but of muscle and skin tone too. A new mother's is temporarily stretched in several different areas, because of the elastic effect and the effects of hormones on ligaments and muscles. During pregnancy the hormones relaxin and progesterone produced by the placenta soften ligaments and allow them to stretch.

- It takes around 12 weeks for most ligaments and muscles to return to their normal length and strength. Some ligaments around the pelvis may not return fully to their pre-pregnant state.
- The effects of hormonal changes may last for three to five months after childbirth and your joints may ache, especially those of the pelvic girdle, the lower back behind, and symphysis pubis in front. Your joints are also still vulnerable to damage during this time.

Abdominal muscles – mind the gap

During pregnancy the abdominal muscles stretch and elongate to as much as twice their original size. In particular the two bands of muscle which run down the abdomen from the rib cage to the pubic bone (the recti abdominis) part company down the midline rather like a zipper coming apart, to allow for the size of the expanding uterus. This condition, known as diastasis recti, isn't painful and you won't even know it's happened. The resulting gap can be anything from a short opening 2–3 cm wide just around the navel, to 12–15 cm parting almost the whole length of the muscles.

After delivery you'll probably find your abdominal muscles are extremely feeble and have little control over anything. One of the main functions of the abdominals is to support the lower back. While they remain weak and separated your back will be especially at risk of injury and if they are not restrengthened it could leave you with a chronic back problem.

During pregnancy the lower three ribs flare out to make room for the growing baby. After you deliver they'll remain flared out unless pulled back in. Restrengthening the abdominals to which they're attached will help do this job. However your rib cage will have expanded and may not return to its pre-pregnancy size and your waist size will probably remain larger than before.

The pelvic girdle and pelvic floor

The pelvic girdle is the bony framework comprising your hip bones, which curve from back to front where they join at the symphysis pubis, the base of the spine (sacrum) and the coccyx (all that remains of our tail). Normally these joints don't move at all, but during pregnancy the ligaments soften to allow for expansion of the pelvis as the baby's head passes through during labour.

Your pelvic floor, the hammock of muscles which supports the bladder, bowel and uterus, will almost certainly be weaker than it was before childbirth. It will have softened to allow for the growing baby and, if you've had a vaginal delivery the perineum will have been stretched and extended further during labour and may also have been torn, or cut and stitched.

The back

During pregnancy the extra weight of the growing baby alters your centre of gravity so that you may lean slightly backwards to compensate. This altered posture is the beginning of backache for many women. It can cause an increase in the hollow in the lower spine and compensation adjustments in the abdominal muscles.

GETTING YOUR BODY BACK – HOW TO RECOVER YOUR BODY INSIDE AND OUT

If you have your baby in hospital you'll probably have a visit from an obstetric physiotherapist in the days immediately after birth. Current thinking is that even a few very gentle movements such as drawing in your abdominal muscles and trying a few gentle pelvic floor exercises can help speed recovery. Do try to give them a go if you possibly can, even if it's a very feeble go at first. Don't dump the exercise sheets you're given, even if you can't face them right now, they may prove helpful later. It's never too late to begin pelvic floor exercises, for example.

Many women don't even want to think about exercise until at least six weeks after childbirth and six months is too soon for some. However, at whatever point you decide to start, the principles are still the same: firming up the flab and losing the extra padding that's gone on during pregnancy are priorities for most women. Improving cardiovascular fitness by exercising your heart and lungs is also important, this type of exercise will improve energy levels, help with tiredness and speed up weight loss.

The exercises described below will help firm and strengthen. They can also help mobility and ease joint aches and pain, especially backache.

The first few days

These exercises can all be done lying down in bed:

- *Breathing exercises* – they may not sound like much but they will improve circulation, strengthen abdominals, help relaxation.
    Lie comfortably on your back, bend knees up. Resting your hand on your abdomen take a slow, deep breath in through your nose, breathe out gently through your mouth and draw in your abdominal muscles at the end of the outward breath. Repeat four times every few hours.
- *Foot exercises* – to improve leg circulation, help reduce swelling.
    Lie comfortably with straight legs and feet about 30 cm (12 inches) apart. Bend and stretch your feet up and down briskly for about 30 seconds each. Circle feet eight times in each direction. Repeat every few hours.
- *Pelvic rocking* – to firm abdominals, helps ease backache and constipation.
    Lie comfortably on your back with knees bent together. Blow out, draw in abdominal muscles, squeeze buttock muscles together, tilting bottom

up and pressing back firmly against the bed. Hold for four counts. Try 10–20 rocks a day.

- *Curl-ups* – to strengthen abdominals and close the gap between them, helps back pain.

  Lie on your back, bending knees up high so your feet are flat on the bed. Pull in abdominals and draw buttocks together. Tuck chin to chest and lift head and shoulders, stretching hands towards your feet. Hold for four counts then lower slowly. Begin with six, increase to 20 per day.

- *Pelvic floor exercise.* This is perhaps the most important exercise of all and you can try it, carefully in the first few days after delivery (see page 350 for full instructions). Don't be dismayed if you can only do a few at a time, you can build up gradually. (See page 352 for the most effective and easiest way to do these.)

If you've had a Caesarean delivery it will be hard for you to move because of postoperative pain for the first few days. As soon as you feel ready you could try:

- foot exercises
- drawing buttocks together tightly and relaxing
- bending and stretching knees
- deep breathing

For further detailed information about getting comfortable after a Caesarean, please see page 385.

The first six weeks

Exercising every day, even if only a little, will help speed recovery and improve muscle tone. Build on the exercises above by adding the following.

• *Waist bends* – work the muscles at the sides and front of your waist.

  Sit on a chair with knees and feet apart. Hold your abdomen in firmly. Bend sideways and stretch your hand towards the floor. Make sure you keep your tummy flat and don't lean forward or back. Repeat on the other side. Begin with four times each side, working up to 12.

• *Waist twister* – uses abdominal muscles.

  Sit upright on a chair, knees and feet apart, arms lifted and bent in front. Pull your abdomen in hard, twist to right as far as you can, count four, twist to left, count four. Return to the middle and relax. Repeat six times each side, increasing to 12.

- *Buttock toner* – firms bottom, strengthens lower back, helps backache.

   Lie flat on the floor on your front, rest your head on hands. Keeping knee straight, lift each leg in turn. Don't allow your pelvis to twist sideways while you lift the leg. Lift each leg alternately 10 times, increasing to 12.

- *Standing pelvic rocks* – to strengthen abdominals and ease backache.

   Stand with your feet apart, bend knees slightly. Breathe out and draw abdominal muscles in hard, relax and arch your lower spine by sticking your bottom out, breathe in. Repeat rhythmically, breathing in as you draw in abdominals and out as you arch spine. Begin with six and increase to 12.

After six weeks

How you feel at this stage is a very individual matter. Women who have been following an exercise programme will probably find muscles have regained some of their strength. Others, especially those with their first baby, may still feel pretty wobbly and a long way off wanting to exercise regularly. Your ligaments should be firmer and stronger, but are by no means back to normal and are still at risk of damage.

   Continue to exercise to improve muscle strength (or begin with those given first if you haven't started yet). Plan an exercise routine that includes work to strengthen abdominals, back, buttock and legs, chest and arm muscles. You can add the following exercises to those already outlined above:

- *Curl-ups and curl-downs* – works abdominals hard.

   For curl-ups see page 461, but step up the pace by folding your arms across your chest or putting them behind your head while you do them.

Curl-downs – sit up straight with knees bent and both hands stretched out in front. Keeping back rounded, curl your body slowly downwards towards the floor. Start with six, increase to 12.

- *Bottom walking* – strengthens back, abdominals and thighs.

  Sit on the floor with your back straight and arms stretched out in front. 'Walk' eight steps forward and eight back. Start with six sequences and increase to 12.

- *Side bends* – to trim waistline.

  Stand with feet hip-width apart. Tuck pelvis in, put hands on hips and stand straight – don't lean forward or back. Bend sideways towards the left, return to the centre, then to the right. Repeat four times, working up to 12.

- *Thigh and hip firmer* – to tone and trim these areas.

  Lie on your right side, supporting head on right hand. Put your left hand on the floor in front of you. Keep your left leg straight and lift it up as high as you can and hold for four. Lower gently and steadily. Keep your body from head to foot in a straight line while you do this exercise. Repeat on left side. Begin with six times each side, increasing to 12.

Also, if you possibly can, add some aerobic exercise to increase fitness and stamina and speed weight loss. Walking and swimming are ideal. For cardiovascular fitness, aim for three 20-minute exercise sessions a week if you can.

If you are very housebound and find it difficult to get out, you can still give your heart and lungs a workout without going outside. Put on some favourite music and try gentle dancing on the spot, use the bottom stair as a step aerobics alternative and try a few minutes of stepping on and off with

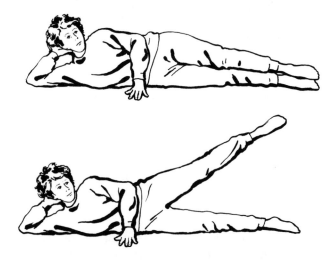

Saffie: Mum, all you've got to do if you want to lose weight is eat less and take a lot of exercise.

Edwina: Sweetie, if it was that easy everyone would be doing it.

From Absolutely Fabulous'.

alternate feet to raise pulse and heart beat. Take it easy, warm up first and never exercise until you feel sick or dizzy.

FIRMING UP

A toned size 14 looks far more touchable and physically attractive than a skinny, but flabby size 10. So what if you are bigger than you were – either temporarily or permanently? Tone up a little and you will be just as physically and sexually attractive as before, if not more so.

Classes and courses

You may be happy following an exercise programme on your own at home, but embarking on a class or course can be an incentive to keep it up, and there's the added plus of meeting people, getting out of the house or having an hour to yourself if you can find someone to take the baby or there's a crèche at the class of course. Check out your local leisure or fitness centre for what's on offer. Many have a crèche facility at least once or twice a week.

When can I begin exercise?
Anytime after six weeks, provided your six-week check was fine. For women who've had a Caesarean, eight to 10 weeks after delivery, provided your GP has said all is well.

What sort of exercise is safe?
Because of the influence of the hormone relaxin, your joints are still vulnerable until three to five months after delivery. Avoid high impact aerobics that can jar the spine, treat your joints with respect, especially your back. Inform the teacher before you begin a class that you've recently had a baby and ask their advice about avoiding certain exercises or routines if necessary. Stop if anything hurts. You need to be completely fit before you begin competitive sports such as tennis and squash again and this may take longer.

What's on offer?
- The NCT have postnatal exercise classes taught by specially trained and qualified NCT teachers at many branches around the country. These classes include a discussion time at the end of the class which deals with problems and issues of concern to women in the postnatal period. You don't need to be an NCT member to join a class. Prices vary but are around £26 for six classes.
- The YMCA have specialist postnatal exercise teachers around the country. The Exercise Association (see Useful Addresses) can put you in touch with qualified teachers.
- Yoga is excellent for strengthening the back and tummy muscles. It can also promote relaxation and help relieve stress. There are several forms of yoga, the one most commonly taught in this country is Hatha yoga. Classes are widely available at adult education institutes, leisure centres and private schools. Before beginning a class you should inform the teacher that you have recently had a baby and avoid doing exercises that could possibly strain joints. It's important to avoid overstretching, even though it may feel good to be more flexible than usual.
- Aqua-cise classes. Exercise in water is gaining in popularity. Aquanatal classes are available for shaping up before childbirth and the benefits are just as good postnatally. Exercise in water puts less stress on joints since body weight is supported, the resistance of the water makes exercises more effective and backache is often relieved. Check with your local leisure centre.
- Swimming is the ideal postnatal exercise for the reasons outlined above and a great way of getting fit safely. Swimming lengths can improve cardiovascular fitness, muscle tone and stamina. Many pools have special women's only sessions and a crèche facility at least once a week. It's well worth making the effort to swim.

Two not to do

These are two exercises you should never try during the first weeks after delivery. They are:

* Lying flat on your back with both legs straight on the floor and then trying to lift them together.
* Lying flat on your back with both legs straight and trying to sit up.

Both these exercises can easily damage fragile abdominal muscles and back ligaments.

How to exercise without exercising

If formal exercises aren't your style, there are plenty of opportunities to shed unwanted weight and get fit again without them.

* Walking is the ultimate weight-loss weapon. It is also a wonderful way to release stress. Walk as fast as you comfortably can whenever you can with the baby in the buggy, to the shops, to visit friends, to the bank, the clinic or doctor. When you get fitter and stronger try to include a route that takes you uphill, walk more quickly with longer, stronger strides. Make sure the buggy handles are at the right height and you're not stooping to reach them.
* Run upstairs – you probably go up and down hundreds of times a day anyway. Use the stairs instead of escalators when you go out if you've got the baby in a backpack.
* Improve your thigh muscles (and save your back) by squatting to pick things up, not bending over. Bend your knees and keep your back straight.
* Cycling is good for fitness, improves your stamina and is good for leg muscles. If you have someone to take care of your baby it's a good way of getting about or doing small shopping errands. You can carry a fair amount of baggage in panniers.
* Exercise in the bath – the water supports your weight and you'll feel more relaxed doing pelvic exercises if you're tense or tight in this area.
* Gardening is good exercise and relaxing therapy. Avoid heavy lifting and take care with awkward bending or twisting movements, be aware of potential damage to your back, but otherwise enjoy the varied activity it offers and the chance to be outside.

Thinner thighs

Thighs, hips and buttocks all gain extra padding during pregnancy, which can be hard to shift. Women are prone to heavier thighs normally because the female hormone oestrogen directs our bodies to store fat here and extra oestrogen during pregnancy boosts the process. Add the effect of weakened muscles and this area generally looks rather lumpy and flabby post-pregnancy.

Fat cells in this area tend not to be very metabolically active and are hard

How to lose four inches from your waist – instantly

During pregnancy the growing weight of the baby alters your centre of gravity and most women develop a backward lean to compensate for the weight of the bump sticking out in front. This can cause the curve in the lower spine to increase and contribute to backache. After your baby's birth you need consciously to readjust your posture and learn to stand straight and tall again. Here's how:

- Look at yourself sideways in a full-length mirror or ask a friend to help check your posture.
- Stand as tall as you can, imagine someone is lifting you gently up by your hair. Relax your shoulders down and back, lift your breastbone and rib cage upwards.
- Draw in your abdominal muscles, tighten buttocks and tip them under.
- Then tilt your pelvic girdle down at the back, tucking your tail bone in, and up at the front pushing your pubic bone up and out.
- Stand as tall as you can.
- Relax and sag back. Measure your waist. Adjust your posture and stand tall again. You'll find your waist measurement is between two and four ins less. Remind yourself to stand tall and not to sag whenever you think of it during the day.

to shift at the best of times. Even during heavy exercise fat is more likely to be lost from the abdomen than the thighs. Improving muscle tone is a better bet than dieting. When muscles become larger the layer of fat covering them is spread over a larger area, resulting in a firmer and more slender look. Here are some suggestions:

- Strengthening your buttock muscles can help minimize saddlebags at the top of the thighs.
- Climb stairs whenever you can. It's a great way of improving thigh muscle tone.
- Swimming regularly will help get thighs back in shape. The kicking motion develops muscles and cool water helps redistribute fat over a wider area for insulation purposes, rather than being clumped just in the thigh area.

Will I stay fatter for good, now?

What happens to your weight after you've had your baby is a very individual matter and depends on many things such as how much you eat, how active you are, changes to your lifestyle and how much weight you put on during pregnancy. The average woman loses *most* of the weight she puts on during pregnancy but we all tend to gain weight as we age because our energy needs become less and we tend to eat as much. Weight gain due to normal ageing is often blamed on pregnancy.

This aspect of postnatal care hasn't received much research attention, studies tend to be old, and often contradictory. However, a major 1988

American study of 7,111 women who had two pregnancies within six years, conducted by The Nutrition Program of Penn State University, Pennsylvania found that:

- 73% of women gained 2–5 lbs permanently due to pregnancy, after adjustment for the normal trend of weight gain over time.
- At least one in 10 women gained over 15 lbs and stayed substantially heavier after pregnancy than before.
- Women who gained over 20 lbs during pregnancy were most likely to keep on extra weight and be 5.7–10.2 lbs heavier at the start of their second pregnancy.
- Normal weight or overweight women who gained less than 20 lbs during pregnancy managed some weight loss due to pregnancy. 12% of women lost more than 5 lbs between pregnancies.

The amount of weight you gain during pregnancy is a major factor that determines how much you will keep on afterwards. Pregnancy is a risk factor for the development of obesity and in some overweight women a significant weight gain due to pregnancy can push them up to the limit of normal weight for their height. On the other hand, if your weight was average before pregnancy, a gain of 2–5 lbs (1–2.5 kg) may not bother you too much.

If you were overweight before you became pregnant and gained quite a lot of weight, you may feel the need to get serious about shedding unwanted pounds afterwards.

Will breastfeeding help me lose weight?
The short answer is no, not in the short term but there are some small weight-loss benefits for mothers who breastfeed long term. (See Happy, Successful Breastfeeding page 15.)

Some women find, much to their surprise that they actually gain, not lose weight while they're feeding and it's possible that breastfeeding mothers are being advised to eat extra calories unnecessarily. Current advice from the Department of Health's COMA Committee in 1991 is for an additional 450–570 calories daily for breastfeeding women with babies under three months and 570 calories for those feeding exclusively breastfed babies up to six months.

However, if you're already eating a good diet it's possible that you might not need this extra fuel to supply enough milk for your baby. One small study at the University of California's Department of Nutrition found that well-nourished breastfeeding women were able to reduce their calorie intake (to no less than 1500 calories a day) without it affecting their supply of milk, although the study lasted only for one week because the researchers didn't want to run the risk of reducing the mothers' milk supply. The researchers suggested that current recommendations for eating for extra energy during breastfeeding are too high. In their study group women eating an average of 2215 calories a day were producing enough milk and gradually losing weight. At present women are cautioned against weight loss until after they've finished weaning. These researchers found a loss of 0.5 kg (1 lb) a week didn't adversely affect milk supply. Those who ate approximately 2,600 calories daily didn't lose weight.

Current advice to eat extra and to relax and rest to safeguard your milk supply during the period you are breastfeeding could in fact prevent weight loss, and may even contribute to an overall weight gain.

If your weight is within normal range but you still feel you'd like to lose a few pounds, consider whether what you're really unhappy about is your shape, or your self-image, rather than weight. In this case exercise might be a better option than dieting.

How to lose weight without dieting

Pregnancy is a major risk factor for gaining weight *not* associated with your baby's placenta and amniotic fluid, and keeping it.

Most women lose around half the weight they've gained – between 12 and 17 lbs (5–8 kg) – immediately after childbirth, and another 7–14 lbs (3–6 kg) in the next three months, however, a stubborn half a stone in place on the hips and thighs can hang on for much longer. Although you may be longing to fit into prepregnancy clothes, don't even think about dieting until your baby is six months old. Provided you're not eating much more

---

Are you really overweight?

Do you just feel fat, or are you really overweight? Obesity is on the increase, with 16% of British women and 13% of men clinically obese according to government figures, that is more than 20% over their maximum desirable weight. A good starting point is to determine if your weight is within the normal range for your height. You can do this by asking to be weighed accurately next time you go to the baby clinic or your GP. Alternatively you can calculate your Body Mass Index (BMI). This is the measure doctors and nutritionists use to determine if a person is a healthy weight for their height. Find your BMI by dividing your weight (in kilograms) by your height in metres, squared, i.e.:

$$BMI = \frac{\text{weight in kg}}{\text{height in metres} \times \text{height in metres}}$$

A BMI of 30 or above is defined as obese; 20–25 is a healthy normal weight; 26–29 is overweight.

If your BMI is not within the normal range, you probably need to tackle your weight for health reasons since obesity does increase your risk of serious illness such as high blood pressure, heart disease and diabetes in later life and you should ask for your GP's help with this. You can be referred to an NHS dietician for dietary advice and support if you have a lot of weight to lose. You'll probably be advised to aim for a weight loss of around 2 lbs (1 kg) per week. Eating 500–750 fewer calories a day should do this.

than you need, it's likely your body will still be shedding the excess fat stores it's laid down. Also you'll be too busy, too tired and have enough to worry about without thinking about making food changes of fiddly calorie counting before then.

At six months if you feel unhappy with your weight it might be time to take stock and decide if you really do need to lose a few pounds and how best to do this. An enormous amount of myth and mythology surrounds the subject of diets and dieting. In fact losing and gaining weight is a pretty simple energy equation. If you eat more than your body needs to fuel normal body processes such as breathing, digestion, elimination, circulation and your physical activity, you will gain weight. If you eat less than you need you will lose weight.

The idea that some people have a slower metabolic rate than others, and so are more at risk of putting on weight, is not true. Studies from the MRC Dunn Nutritional Centre in Cambridge have shown that very overweight people have a higher metabolic rate because they need more energy to fuel their larger frames. Although some people do inherit a family tendency to pile on the pounds, the real reason that most of us gain weight is that we eat too much for our physical needs.

This said, pregnancy and the postnatal period do bend the normal rules of weight gain and loss. In pregnancy hormonal changes direct the body to provide fat stores as protection for the growing baby towards the end of pregnancy and for breastfeeding fuel afterwards. Then in the postnatal period at around two months after birth, your fat cells actually 'want' to shed the extra fat they've acquired and the enzymes within them are more active. The body doesn't need the extra protective fat any more, so it is easily lost. However, by six months after childbirth most of the effect of these exceptional weight changes should have stopped and the normal rules of weight loss and gain will apply again.

If you need to lose weight, don't attempt to do it by putting yourself on a calorie-controlled 'crash' diet. It's miserable, and it doesn't work long term. Instead, take the following steps:

- Set yourself a steady, realistic goal for weight loss. Aim to lose around 2–3 lbs (1–1½ kg) a month. Be generous and give yourself six months to lose half a stone.
- Weigh yourself and chart your progress regularly, but not too often, about once a month is right.
- Think about your energy equation, are you more/less active than you were before you had your baby? Are you eating more/less than previously? Have your eating patterns changed? Are you resting more? The average energy requirement for a moderately active woman is around 2,000 calories per day.
- If you are less active than you were before you had your baby, try to work some more activity into your daily routine. Walking is ideal.
- Do you need to lose weight or just tone up? Exercise that tones and trims

muscles will make you look, and feel better by increasing energy levels and improving mood. It will also help burn extra calories.

EATING FOR WEIGHT LOSS

Making changes to your diet is very difficult but following a few simple principles can help. Although you may be very busy with a new baby, it's likely that more of your time is spent at home and centres around food and the kitchen. Use this time positively to feed yourself well and improve your eating habits.

- *Reduce the amount of fat you eat.* Fat is readily stored as body fat. It does not suppress appetite as carbohydrates and protein do so it is easier to overeat on a high-fat diet.
- *Increase your intake of complex carbohydrates.* Starchy foods like bread, pasta, potatoes do not make you fat. The body uses more energy to convert and store carbohydrates as body fat than it does to store fat. Carbohydrates are very filling and reduce appetite, so they lower the risk of overeating.
- *Eat only when you're hungry*, but not starving because then you'll be tempted to stuff yourself uncomfortably full. Smaller, easier meals more often are better to keep energy levels up.
- *Learn to love vegetables.* Many are quick and easy to prepare – celery, cucumber or carrot sticks, tomatoes or slices of red or green pepper, for example. They are nutritious and non-fattening, they can make a good sustaining small meal with a humus or yoghurt dip and some pitta bread.
- *Drink plenty of fluids.* You may be extra thirsty if you breastfeed. Plain water and herbal teas are the only ones that won't be giving you extra calories as well as quenching your thirst. Fizzy drinks, fruit juice and milk drinks are all high in calories. Coffee, colas and strong tea all contain substantial amounts of caffeine; weak tea is the best choice if you're concerned about your caffeine intake.
- *Eat as much simple, unprocessed food as you can.* This can be difficult since convenience foods can be a real boon with a small baby, but bear in mind pre-prepared foods are often high in fat and sugars so don't rely on them the whole time.
- *Beware empty calories* – chocolate, crisps, biscuits, sweets – just the type of comfort foods you reach for when you need a quick lift and are too stressed or exhausted to make a proper meal. They may give you an energy boost but may leave you famished in an hour or so. These also tend to be high-fat, high-sugar snacks, which are calorie-loaded but don't provide much in the way of nutrients like vitamins or minerals. Try a banana, a handful of raisins or some dried apricots instead.
- *Eating regularly.* Don't skip meals, especially breakfast, which sets you up for the day.
- *Make small changes to your diet* that you can live with – swop butter for low-calorie spread; substitute semi-skimmed milk for full fat; trim all the

fat from meat; grill, steam or bake food instead of frying. Small calorie savings add up.
- *Put less on your plate.* This sounds too simple to be effective, but it works – put a third less of everything on there than usual.

Why dieting is not a good idea
It is possible to eat well and lose weight by eating more of the right things and less of the wrong ones. An average woman needs around 2,000 calories a day. Low-calorie dieting that aims for a much lower intake than this is not a good idea because:

- It doesn't work. An estimated 90% of dieters regain all the weight they've lost (and often add some more) within one year.
- Crash diets cause the body to become very energy efficient with the fuel it's given. The body reacts as if it's being starved and learns to get by on very little, by lowering the body's metabolic rate. In this way it's possible to eat less and still not lose weight.
- It can rob you of essential nutrients such as calcium, magnesium and iron because you are eating less, and possibly less of certain foods, such as meat or dairy produce. These nutrients are especially important when you are recovering from childbirth since your reserves may already be low.
- It can make you feel tired, moody, stressed and irritable, not a good idea when you have a baby to cope with and need all the energy you can get.
- Following fiddly calorie-controlled diets is impractical when you're busy with a new baby and/or stressed.

Why healthy eating is a good idea
- It will give you more energy. If you are well nourished your body will be obtaining the nutrients if needs to function at its best. Eating regular sustaining meals avoids the peaks and troughs associated with low blood-sugar levels which cause fatigue, lack of concentration and irritability (see Beating Exhaustion, page 311).
- It will help you lose weight. You are less likely to raid the fridge or pig out on junk food because you're starving hungry.
- It will promote better health. A diet rich in fresh foods and fruit and vegetables will provide the antioxidant nutrients that may protect against illnesses such as heart disease and certain cancers like bowel cancer.
- It will make you feel you are doing something right – i.e., eating well – rather than something wrong – failing to lose weight on a diet.
- It will set up good eating habits for the whole family and encourage your child to make good food choices when they are old enough.

Four principles of weight loss
- Decrease the amount of fat in your diet.
- Increase the amount of carbohydrates you eat.
- Eat only when you're hungry, don't constantly pick and nibble.
- Keep active, take some exercise.

> ### Healthy eating on a plate
>
> The Government's National Food Guide, published in 1994, outlined the basis of a healthy diet as follows:
>
> We should choose our foods from the four main food groups in these proportions:
>
> Bread, potatoes, pasta, cereals – 34%
> Vegetables and fruit – 33%
> Milk, cheese, yoghurt – 15%
> Meat, fish, and alternatives – 12%
>
> Fatty and sugary foods should make up only 7% of our food intake.
>   More simply put the healthiest way is to:
>
> * Eat two-thirds of your food from starchy foods – bread, pasta, potatoes, cereals, vegetables and fruits.
> * Eat one-third of your foods from lean meats, low-fat dairy produce.
> * Keep sugary and fatty foods as 'extras' to the diet.

Small changes . . . big difference

Lowering the fat content of your diet is one of the best and easiest ways to starve fat cells. Try these fat-reducing tips.

* Keep the butter out of the fridge in a covered dish, so you can spread it very sparingly if you use it.
* Change over to semi-skimmed milk, lower fat cheeses and yoghurts.
* Steam, boil or grill foods in preference to frying or roasting.
* Go easy on the cream sauces, mayonnaise, peanut butter.
* Avoid crisps, peanuts, biscuits and cakes if you can. Be strong and choose a piece of fruit instead, or a high-energy snack like a handful of nuts and raisins, a crispbread or slice of good bread with a thin slice of low-fat cheese or ham.

Habitwatch

Having a baby, especially your first one, is a major upheaval and lifestyle change. You may be at home all day with a small baby instead of at work, your normal routine is likely to be completely disrupted and it may take some months to establish a new one. During this transition period it's likely your eating habits will be erratic. Watch out for the following pitfalls:

* *Comfort foods.* Most of us tend to eat more when we feel stressed or under pressure. Be aware if you're looking for comfort in the biscuit tin or using eating to soothe anger or resentment. If what you really need is more emotional support/understanding/help around the house/someone to take the baby while you have an hour's peace, try to find a way of getting this.

- *Beware, quick fixes.* It's so tempting when you're exhausted and never seem to have a moment, just to eat a quick packet of crisps or bar of chocolate to keep you going. It will, but only for a short while, and blood sugar levels that rise and fall rapidly can leave you irritable and tired, needing another quick fix. This is an easy way to increase your calorie count.
- *Don't skip meals.* It's easy to convince yourself that it's not worth making a meal just for yourself. It is. Skipping breakfast or lunch will make you feel weak and hungry later on, leaving you prey to yet another snack attack.
- *Food as a reward.* Being a mother is extremely hard work and most of us rightly feel we deserve a treat or two, especially at the end of a long, hard day. If you're trying to lose weight, avoid the treat being a chocolate bar, packet of peanuts or bag of crisps. Would a long hot bath, half an hour with a book, magazine or newspaper, your favourite television programme or a phone call to a friend do instead?

USEFUL ADDRESSES

Active Birth Centre, 25 Bickerton Road, London N19 5JT. Tel: 0171 561 9006.

Postnatal yoga, baby massage and gymnastics, mothers' talking groups. London-based but do have some groups in other areas.

British Wheel of Yoga, 1 Hamilton Place, Boston Road, Sleaford, Lincolnshire NG34 7ES. Tel: 01529 306851.

For information about yoga classes and courses. Also see your local education institute prospectus.

The Exercise Association. Write with s.a.e. to Unit 4, Angel Gate, City Road, London EC1V 2PT. Tel: 0171 278 0811.

A professional association of fitness instructors. Can give details of regional instructors who've trained specifically in postnatal exercise teaching.

National Childbirth Trust, Alexandra House, Oldham Terrace, London W3 6NH. Tel: 0181 992 8637.

Can give information about which of the 350 nationwide local groups offer postnatal exercise classes.

USEFUL PUBLICATIONS

Get into Shape after Childbirth, Gillian Fletcher, Ebury Press/National Childbirth Trust, £9.99.
A fully illustrated guide to postnatal exercise from the early weeks onward.

Get into Shape after Childbirth, Gillian Fletcher. Two audio cassettes plus illustrated poster, £7.99.

Both these items can be ordered from NCT Maternity Sales Ltd, 239 Shawbridge Street, Glasgow G43 1QN. Credit card sales: 0141 636 0600. Add 80 pence p. and p. for tape cassette, £1 for book.

Healthy Eating on a Plate, Janette Marshall, Vermilion.

The Postnatal Exercise Book, Margie Polden and Barbara Whiteford, Frances Lincoln.

The Y Plan for Before and After Pregnancy, a complete video cassette exercise programme. £10.99 at video stores or by mail order from Training and Development, London Central YMCA, 112 Great Russell Street, London WC1B 3NQ. Add £2 for p. and p.

Your Sex Life After Childbirth

When can you have sex after childbirth – and are there any best ways to do it? There is a huge range of what's 'normal'. Basically, it's whatever both you and your partner feel comfortable with. A recent straw poll at a mothers' and toddlers' playgroup in Manchester found one woman out of the 20 whose partner had insisted on intercourse two days after she gave birth (and she said 'it wasn't so bad', either) but another who still hadn't felt ready to make love after 12 months, but had plenty of cuddles with her partner instead. Although she felt they were getting out of the habit rather, that was all that she could handle at the moment.

There are no rules, providing any postnatal bleeding has ceased. Just do what you both want, when you *both* feel like it again. It is natural to want sex as soon as possible after childbirth. It is also natural not to want it for many months. If new parents knew this – and many instinctively do, but fear they may be a bit unusual in their beliefs – it would take a lot of stress and guilt away. They have enough going on already because they are caring for, getting to know and falling in love with their (probably) exhausting new baby.

And falling in love is precisely how many parents describe it: or as Brigid McConville, in *Mad to be a Mother*, puts it, new mothers especially may find 'they are totally, painfully, vulnerably, ecstatically infatuated'. Often the intense feelings mothers have for their newborn babies are so powerful they take most of their emotional energy (which may be running low after the intense experience of childbirth anyway). It can be like the passion during the early part of a love affair that is so all-consuming and emotionally satisfying that it excludes everyone else. Two adults who have just fallen very much in love can appear to others to be inhabiting a private world of their own. They shut everyone else out. This can be just as true – for a while – of a mother with a newborn baby. However, both tend to calm down into a love that is just as deep, but which allows them the freedom to turn outwards to include others again.

Just as it is true that this stage of total mutual absorption passes, it is also true that it need not exclude fathers, who have some falling in love to do, and new-baby discoveries to make, of their own. However, they may equally be feeling hurt, puzzled and left out. There is an enormous amount that fathers can do to feel part of what is happening in their new family, which will not only bring them great joy and delight, and closer to their child, but

Sex after childbirth

Just for the record, there can be plenty of sex after childbirth. About half all new mothers report that their sex lives had stayed just the same or even positively improved, according to an NCT survey in 1994, though the other half have said theirs had gone downhill for the moment, listing extreme tiredness as the main reason. Some of the women who replied to the survey added that although sex might be less frequent, it was better quality when they and their partner did manage to find a quiet, mutually compatible moment. Or as one interviewee said: 'Quantity down, quality up.'

will bring them far closer to their partner too. Because they will no longer be, as some men have described it, on the outside looking in. This is important not just for general new-family dynamics but also for creating an emotional environment where a new father and mother can feel close and loving *with each other*. Feelings of all three of you belonging to each other, and of loving involvement, also lay the foundations for the sexual relationship between the two adult partners to begin again – if indeed, they stopped in the first place for a while. However, an atmosphere of resentment and isolation on a new father's part can put up barriers which prevent a loving physical relationship with his partner from easily beginning again.

What's normal?

No one usually gets around to telling expectant parents much about what they might be able to expect sexually after the birth. As midwife Vicky Bailey puts it: 'I am often so busy considering the physical needs of women in my care that it is easy to ignore their emotional and sexual needs . . . although I have given much advice on antenatal care, labour and postnatal care, I have never considered the woman's sexual feelings about herself.'

Part of the problem is that antenatal classes just cannot fit in to the standard 6 sessions everything a new mother might eventually need to know. And even if they did, no one can cope with that much new information packed into so short a space – new mothers have to find out most of it on the job. Something as potentially important as postnatal sexuality barely gets even a passing mention – because most antenatal education focuses, by necessity, on the event in hand – childbirth itself. However, though sex is not really an issue for most couples in the last few weeks of pregnancy and the first few after their baby is born, it may become quite a major one later on. But does any one mention it? In the NCT's survey only a quarter of women got any chance to talk about sex after childbirth while they were pregnant. Much of the advice they do get comes from friends, their own mothers perhaps, and from the media.

The latter have a lot to answer for. Many women's magazine articles recommend a woman struggles back into a tight little black dress as soon as possible after the six weeks postnatal period is up, cooks her partner a cunning candlelit dinner (when, if the baby seldom sleeps? Most mothers find they are so busy they are living off breakfast cereal) and woos him all over again. Generally, the standard parenting books aren't much more help either. They place the onus squarely on a new mother to shape up and get back to normal as fast as she can in order to become desirable again to her man. Her mâle partner is advised to be patient, understanding and help out a bit with the baby. Even the usually sensible breastfeeding bible *Breast is Best* by Dr Andrew and Penny Stanway recommends: 'Make sure your husband doesn't feel left out. You've got a baby to cuddle, who's he got?' Fair enough, but unfortunately they continue: 'Keep up your previous mistress image as much as possible.' It may well be true that if you look good you will feel sexually attractive, but does it really all need to fall into place quite so fast?

It is not easy reconciling this sort of advice, especially if, like three-quarters of all women, it's all you are getting, when you also have leaking breasts, still-sore genitals and a powerful preference for sleep over sex. Part of the trouble is that postnatal care for a new mother is usually limited to home visits from a midwife until your baby is just 10 days old (three weeks on specific request) when sex is probably the very last thing on her mind. After that, care tends to centre solely around the new baby's welfare, unless you have a good, regular local mother and baby clinic with sympathetic health visitors as well as doctors there to answer new mothers' own questions about themselves as well as their babies. Usually, however, as their new baby is the number one priority, they rarely get around to talking about their own wellbeing unless it is purely physical (stitches still causing trouble, feeding problems). The only other time new mothers might have a specific opportunity to bring up the subject of their emotions and sexuality is at their six-week postnatal check.

'This is a pretty arbitrary date for a checkup,' says Professor Mike Chapman, head of Obstetrics & Gynaecology at St George's Hospital, Sydney. 'It is carried out at this stage because by now, any lochia discharge will have stopped, perineal stitches should have healed up and the womb should have shrunk back to its pre-pregnant stage. One of the reasons women are "meant" to have at least tried to resume sexual relations with their partners is that if there are any major problems they can tell their doctor about them. In reality, most will probably be feeling far from normal and not want sex – I suspect many have tried it because they think they should, rather than really wanting to. There's a lot of pressure on women to be back to normal within six weeks, which is unrealistic.'

Some of this pressure comes from the existing statistical norms much quoted by professionals, especially the University of Maryland School of Nursing's famous study in 1984, which found that '43 per cent of mothers had resumed sexual intercourse before their sixth week.' This sounds as if

---

'It's much like trying to climb Mount Everest in a cocktail dress. One wants to make it look simple and effortless, but those tell-tale beads of sweat keep forming on the upper lip.'

Sex Tips for Girls, Cynthia Heimel

nearly half all couples are back to normal sexually within the magic six week-time limit. They're not.

The phrase 'resumed sexual relations' only means that they tried having sex at least once, not that they are now doing so regularly and liking it. Researchers do not bother to find out how *often* new parents are having intercourse, or whether they tried it once and then left it, as many do, for the time being and found other ways of expressing their love. The studies also seem to assume sex has to mean penis-in-vagina sex. It doesn't. Gentle oral sex, a little mutual or solo masturbation and some erotic kissing, or caressing and massaging of areas other than the breasts and genitals are sex too – and are probably much more the sort of thing that new mothers feel like at first. Hugs, cuddles and sleeping curled into each other or snuggling up together on the sofa may not give you an orgasm but they are as good a way of showing you love and appreciate each other as intercourse is.

When you both do feel ready for penetrative sex after childbirth, it needs to go very gently for the women for the first few weeks or even months, as their genital area may well be sore from the stretching, from repair stitches, or both. A telling figure (again from the Maryland study) found that initial sex after childbirth was rated as 'unsatisfying' by 34 per cent of women – but only 4 per cent of their male partners said they had not enjoyed it. New mothers may be happy to have had intercourse again, but that does not necessarily mean they actually enjoyed it, felt aroused or had an orgasm, nor that they want to do so again regularly yet. They may have been pleased about it because:

- The fact that they have tried sex once again suggests things might be getting back to normal at last.
- They felt unkind saying no yet again to a partner whom they felt had been very patient for a long time.
- They thought all the other new mothers they knew must be already doing it again and they would be abnormal if they didn't too.

In fact, you do not need to feel that everyone else is having more sex than you, because they aren't. More than half all *childless* couples and those with older children are not even having sex the supposedly national average 2 to 3 times a week. According to a survey in *Esquire* UK with MORI Poll in 1992, only 46 per cent of all 18- to 45-year-old men manage the traditional 2.5 times a week. The rest range from a more sedate once a fortnight to 'never at the moment'.

But wanting to want sex is not quite the same as wanting sex itself. As one woman 34-year-old new mother from Criccieth in Wales put it: 'In my mind, I wanted sex with Phil. Physically – I just could not face it.' Another said feeling that she 'owed' her partner sex 'on top of everything else I was now having to cope with it just felt like I'd been given one more flaming thing to do before I could finally go to sleep at night. Even then I knew I was going to get woken up in three hours at best to do another feed.'

Taking a break

Many monogamous traditional societies have a temporary postchildbirth sex ban. New parents belonging to the Abelam society of Papua New Guinea have to avoid intercourse until their baby is old enough to walk. The Alorese of Oceania are told to wait until their child can sit up alone. Mexican women are not supposed to until they have menstruated following a 41-day break after the birth. The Masai are forbidden sex until their child has cut its teeth; and the Murai (a central Indian tribe) are not meant to make love for the first six to 12 months of breastfeeding. But a Murai father is lucky in that he has a get-out clause. Their law states that if he has seen a smile on his new child's face, he is then allowed to sleep with his wife again.

There are some good, purely practical reasons for traditional society's temporary 'no sex' taboo. It helps protect the new mother's health when resources are scarce and contraception unreliable. But there are major emotional benefits too. If new mothers, whether they are from the Masai or Manchester, want to spend a lazy, relaxed, disorganized few months just getting to know and learning how to handle their baby without any pressures to do anything further – is that so bad? If your emotional energy is sapped from the birth and the unique, stunned, all-absorbing delight which many mothers find is triggered by the arrival of their new baby, and you do not have much left over to channel into sexuality, maybe this can even give a woman and her partner time to get to know each other better in non-sexual ways. Many heterosexual relationships depend heavily on sex as a method of deep communication and sharing emotions; might the first few postnatal months offer couples the chance to find some others?

Sex? how do you spell that?

WHY WOMEN MAY WANT SOME TIME OUT

1. Tiredness

Rated the number one reason for not wanting sex in the NCT's survey. Looking after a demanding new baby is, unless you are very lucky, extremely tiring, and it does not stop during the night. The good news is that this does get better, but until it does, managing on three hours uninterrupted sleep when you are used to eight forces every new mother to prioritize her energy. Care of a small baby's needs come first, second and, it seems, third. Care of your own or your partner's tends to be fitted in if there is time or the energy, which there often isn't. And the bottom line is that you can survive without sex, but not without sleep.

From a purely clinical point of view, the first thing to go if you experience sleep deprivation is your libido. The hormone regulating your libido, testosterone, drops when you are tired. Also, constant fatigue makes you more irritable, more liable to anxiety/depression/mood swings; and feel (and possibly look) less attractive. None of these effects is conducive to sex. Men, even if they are tired from helping to look after their new baby, tend not to get so tired as women because they are not usually quite so involved. Further, according to the Co-President of the British Sleep Society, Dr Chris Idzikowski, their hearing is less acute than women's so they sleep more soundly when they have a new baby than women do, and wake up less easily at night. Men also tend to be out at work during the day while their wife or girlfriend remains behind looking after the new baby, at least at first.

Any woman who has tried both options, and an increasing number of mothers have as they have had to return to work when their baby was a few months old, can confirm which is the most tiring. It is therefore not surprising that the Maryland survey found that a year after the baby's birth, 60 per cent of fathers felt their sexual desire levels had not changed but only 37 per cent of mothers could say the same.

2. Practical reasons

Mothers and their new babies are usually so emotionally and physically close that they are also spiritually fine-tuned to each other. This explains a good deal, such as why mothers find they repeatedly wake up at night a minute or two before their babies do, how they know their child is crying upstairs in their cot even if no one else in the house can hear them, how they are certain that their child is really ill when no one else is quite sure. It also explains what parents, laughing hollowly, refer to the infant sex police effect – many babies having an uncanny knack of waking up and crying whenever their parents begin to try to make love. The babies probably just sense a change in atmosphere, one they do not recognize but which they feel excludes them, and they understandably do not like it. It can be immensely off-putting having every (rare) lovemaking session rudely interrupted like this, especially if you have had to make a major effort to get round to it in the first place. Nothing makes you feel non-sexual as fast as your baby crying loudly throughout. Except . . .

> **Working mothers do not necessarily get tireder**
> If you have chosen to go back to work full or part time when your baby is still young, and friends (or especially older female relatives) are suggesting that you would not be so tired if you stayed at home as a full-time mother, ignore them.
>
> Whether Maryland mothers were working full time or part time outside their home, or caring for their baby full time, it seemed to make no difference to how tired they got. Though many women much prefer to look after their own babies full time, others report that they need a mixture of paid work and childcare for their sanity, as each uses up their energy in different ways – one demanding constant emotional and physical output and the other needing intellectual/organizational energy.
>
> Varying the two types of demands can be one way of keeping some emotional energy in the bank that could go into other areas which are temporarily having to take a back seat, such as your sexual relationship with your partner.

3. Soreness and pain

Rated roughly equal third with lack of libido by the NCT research. The good news is that almost half all new mothers have no particular pain or discomfort *of any sort* after childbirth, according to the ongoing Avon Longitudinal Study. However, of those who do experience discomfort, a sore stitches site is the commonest problem producing pain during intercourse.

The medical term for this is dyspareunia, and it may be superficial, meaning it is on the outside, around your perineum and the vagina's entrance; or deep, meaning right up inside.

Superficial pain may be due to:

- The way in which a tear or episiotomy site stitches have healed.
- Deep bruising of the area which may take some time to emerge and wear off.
- A small tar of scar tissue which is pulling and catching during intercourse.
- A poorly healed, lumpy scar which is tender when pressed.
- A scar that puckers or pulls to one side.
- A skin bridge, which is a loop or thin area of skin, often at the back of the vagina where the protective lips which fold over it meet.
- A trapped nerve ending (neuroma) in the scar tissue. The telltale sign of this is that there will be one tiny spot on the scar which is very painful when touched.
- A granuloma, a little area of scar that has not healed fully, showing itself as a small red patch.
- Stitching too tight. There is usually a good deal of local swelling in the area just after childbirth and though this subsides quickly, whoever is stitching up a tear or episiotomy needs to take that into account. If the stitches are too tight this is usually apparent a couple of days afterwards

at the latest, and they can usually be loosened without needing to be removed and redone. However, if they are not loosened, it can produce an uncomfortable scar site.

- A smaller vaginal opening as a result of the stitching taking in too much vaginal tissue, like putting too large a tuck in a waistband you are repairing on a skirt.

Deep pain, which is far less usual, may be because the cervical ligaments have been torn, or a laceration extends up inside the vagina. This heals in time but until it does it makes deep penetration extremely painful.

Scar problems also tend to settle down with time, and usually the area does heal well and quickly as it has such a rich blood supply. But it rather depends how much it is hurting and how much time you are prepared to give it. If things are still as sore as ever after three months, go and see your GP. If they are not helpful, insist on a referral to a good consultant gynaecologist.

What a specialist doctor can do
A persistently sore perineum may be treated with ultrasound; poorly healed or lumpy scars recut and resewn carefully. A neuroma should be removed, though some hospital physiotherapists might try to desensitize it using ultrasound. A granuloma can be cauterized, though it will often heal up on its own within a year or so.

What you can do
According to birth educator Sheila Kitzinger in *The Year After Birth*, 'Most women for whom the idea of intercourse is painful say that it is pain *on entry* that puts them off the whole idea. If penetration is gentle with extra lubrication, they feel much more comfortable beyond that point unless they are being rushed. Ask your lover to slide in gently . . . It is often surprising how, once your lover's finger or penis is inside, and you feel safe, pain disappears and you begin to enjoy lovemaking.'

Making love gently does not have to mean the missionary position, usually felt to be the gentlest as it is seen to be the least adventurous. It's not necessarily the best option for women who have recently had a baby though, because it places weight on the woman's abdomen and breasts, and puts quite a lot of abrasive pressure on her perineum too. As all these areas

---

'We cannot find anything wrong'
This is not what you want to hear when you have finally plucked up courage – and got an appointment – with a good gynaecologist. Unfortunately, it is often what women are initially told, as the reason for the pain is not always easy to see. Finding small bits of scar tissue in the wrong place can be made easier if you are examined standing up rather than lying down.

may be sore, you might find other positions such as the following far more comfortable and therefore more erotic.

Woman astride. For instance, if you sit astride your partner this keeps his weight off your body, you have far more control over how much he moves, how far his penis enters into you, how fast or how slow his lovemaking movements are, and also control over the angle of penetration and which parts of the vagina his penis is pressing against the most. He can also reach your clitoris and breasts easily to stimulate them for you.

Back entry. If you are on all fours and he enters you kneeling behind you, this puts far less pressure on the perineum, which may still be sore from healed stitches, than the traditional missionary position. Variations include you on his lap with your back against his chest as he sits either on a chair, or on the bed so his legs are stretched out in front of him. Less strain is put on his back if it is supported by pillows against the wall or bedhead above the bed. Or try this as your curl together lying down sideways in the spoons position.

Edge of the bed. If you sit on the edge of the bed or lie on your back with your legs over the edge, and your partner enters you by kneeling on the floor between your legs. This helps keep weight off you, and is also a good position for keeping much of the pressure off the front part of your vagina, if that is where it is sore.

It also helps to use plenty of additional lubrication at first too: try saliva (either your own or your partner's) or KY gel from the chemist.

4. Breastfeeding
Breastfeeding can:

- Enhance and heighten your sexuality,
- Provide sensual and sexual stimulation in its own right, or
- it may completely obliterate your interest in sex.

All three reactions are completely normal.

According to sex research pioneers Masters and Johnson, breastfeeding mothers are more comfortable with their own sexuality and therefore more interested in renewing their sexual relationship with their partner than mothers who are bottle-feeding their babies. Many mothers say how deeply satisfying and fulfilling breastfeeding was for them both emotionally and physically, how fertile and female it made them feel and how this new sense

Warning
If you are not breastfeeding fully and exclusively you will also need to use contraception every time you have intercourse because you can conceive three weeks after you have just had a baby. According to the Birth Control Trust, the months after childbirth are a common time to become accidentally pregnant (see Which Contraceptive, page 499).

of themselves as women coloured their attitude towards their partners too. ('I felt really womanly and sexy – much more so than ever before when I found I could breastfeed,' remembers one woman responding to the NCT's survey.) Others remember that the tenderness and sense of deep inner peace which they had while they were feeding their baby flowed over into their feelings towards their whole family, including their partners. 'I had this lovely all's-right-with-the-world feeling, and felt really loving towards my whole family so it seemed very natural and right to show this by making love as often as possible,' reported one mother.

The sexual side of breastfeeding

It is not only the feeding and nurturing side of breastfeeding that affects many women profoundly. Others also find, often to their surprise, that it is physically enjoyable, even erotic. They may feel sexually aroused as their baby tugs and sucks rhythmically against their nipples, and occasionally even have an orgasm as a result. A few mothers are relaxed enough about their own sexuality to find this experience elating and welcome, if unexpected. Others feel it is deeply inappropriate, even incestuous (especially if the baby is a boy) and it makes them both embarrassed and ashamed.

Yet feeling sexually aroused by breastfeeding is completely physically normal. It definitely does not mean that you are somehow perverted. It is simply a common and straightforward physical response to nipple stimulation, which a breastfeeding mother can hardly avoid (how else are you supposed to give them a drink?) and there are some very ordinary physiological reasons for it. According to Swedish psychiatrist Dr Tore Hakansson who practises in Stockholm, these are:

- Stimulation of the nipples produces the release of two hormones called prolactin and oxytocin. Prolactin stimulates milk-making, while oxytocin stimulates the milk let-down reflex. The latter also stimulates contractions of the womb (the sort created by orgasm itself, and the contractions of childbirth). This is the reason why breastfeeding women's milk tends to flow when they are sexually aroused – so it is logical that the reverse can also happen – that as their milk flows, this can trigger sexual feeling. Studies show that high levels of oxytocin also decrease anxiety, and lift the mood. 'Lactation is a sexual experience and so is birth,' writes psychologist Alayne Yates, 'yet few mothers breastfeed and even fewer permit themselves to savour the experience.'
- Skin contact (its warmth, texture and special scent).

Yet breastfeeding also reduces your testosterone output – it is possible that the increased production of oxytocin interferes with it, explains Doria Schmidt, lecturer in Sexual Therapy at London University's Birkbeck College. 'As testosterone is the hormone driving sexual desire, this can cause decreased or zero libido. Many women report that while they were breastfeeding they were simply not the least bit interested in sex, but that their libido returned dramatically as soon as they ceased feeding their baby themselves.

This reduced level of oestrogen also affects your natural vaginal lubrication, and leaves the area far drier than usual. Sometimes the tissues of the labia and vagina can become quite fragile, and if they do, applying oestrogen cream prescribed by your GP is highly effective. Usually however, a natural lubricant such as saliva, or a water soluble commercial lubricant like KY gel (far more effective than Vaseline, which also destroys condoms if you are needing to use one) is enough. The dryness ceases as soon as you stop breastfeeding.

Women who are feeding their babies themselves may also feel that their breasts belong – for the moment, at least – to their baby and do not want their partners to fondle them or even admire them. This is perfectly normal too, as the breasts' twin roles of nurturing feeders and erotic playzones are a long way apart in most people's minds and it can be hard to keep switching from one to the other (which is partly why mothers can feel so uncomfortable about feeling sexual pleasure from breastfeeding). If you feel this way about your breasts at the moment but would enjoy the rest of your body being touched, let your partner know that he can look for the moment but not touch them – which he may find very arousing anyway, as men react powerfully to just looking – but that anywhere else is fine.

5. Wanting the privacy of your own body back
Every woman's experience of labour is different, as different as the women and babies themselves. Some have a terrific experience of childbirth, which they remember as hard work but an exhilarating time that was also the most satisfying, exciting and life-enhancing event that they had ever been part of, and which has left them feeling powerful and complete.

If women have not really enjoyed lovemaking before they had a baby they may well become more sexually aware after a birth experience which was a good one – it is as if they have suddenly discovered just what their bodies can really do and so feel even more confident inhabiting them.

For others the experience was mixed. 'I positively enjoyed some parts of Molly's labour and birth, was totally fascinated by others, could put up with some because I had to – but there were a couple of bits I just wanted over and done with,' as one woman put it after her first baby. Whether the birth was great, or variable, some new mothers report more powerful orgasm, and multiple orgasms, which they never had before – which may be due to slight changes in the blood flow to the pelvis which labour contractions can produce or to a permanent change in the diameter of the pelvic blood vessels following 9 months of high progesterone levels.

Flashbacks and birth trauma
But for a third group of women, childbirth can be immensely distressing. This may be because for them, labour went very differently from the way they had hoped. Perhaps they had very much wanted and carefully planned for a natural childbirth and ended up needing every other intervention in the book. They may have been insensitively or incompetently treated by desperately busy, inexperienced or rude hospital staff. They may have been

frightened; in exceptional pain for long periods; traumatized by a rough forceps delivery or emergency Caesarean. A few even say it was like being physically violated, and use the language of rape and sexual assault to explain how they still feel about it. Like many experiences of sexual violence, the memory can remain for a long time, and be brought flooding back by any attempts at lovemaking, partly because many of the positions in which couples usually have intercourse are similar to those of labour and delivery and vaginal penetration may violently recall medical intervention in the area.

These memories are called flashbacks and they are more than just mental recall – they are intense re-enactments of what happened to you and they may even produce physical distress responses such as breaking out in a cold sweat, a pounding heart, soaring blood pressure or rapid, frightened breathing. You may feel that as your partner tries gently to touch your genitals or enter you, you suddenly feel as if you are back on the delivery table being prodded painfully by a doctor, find yourself crying helplessly and pushing your partner away. Some women also say that they were disappointed by their partner's behaviour during labour – perhaps also blaming them consciously or unconsciously for not managing to save them from painful or undignified interventions. This resentment can also be saved up, and act as a barrier between you when you try to make love.

If you realize that this is what is happening to you, tell your partner and think about talking to a sympathetic professional counsellor (perhaps from an organization like Birth Crisis, or the Relate network, see Useful Addresses) about the way you are feeling. This, plus sensitive, gentle help from your partner, can help you heal emotionally and stop the flashback associations recurring. Or you may just want to be left alone for a while to get back a sense of ownership of your own body. Regaining this may also be important for a woman who has needed 'repair' treatment after childbirth – perhaps involving the repeated examination, poking and prodding of a poorly healed episiotomy site, which then needed recutting and sewing.

Even some women who had had 'good' births want this space and time to recharge their sense of physical privacy after so many requests over so many months to 'Lie down. Let me feel your tummy. Open your legs please.' 'Let's feel how far you have dilated [again].' 'Let us strap you up or unstrap you to the fetal monitor.' 'This little hook is just going to break your waters for you.' 'We'll just use these forceps to help your baby out.' 'Feet up in stirrups, we need to sew you up . . .'

To someone with a strong sense of physical privacy, this is a cumulation of what one woman described as, 'my body going public for months. I seem to have been forever lining up to have my bump felt, breasts looked at, blood tested, cervix checked and tummy prodded – and that was even before I went into labour. I wasn't me any more, I was this walking womb which everyone wanted to keep tabs on and I'm fed up with it. I want to be left alone. I just want my body to myself for a bit with no one else poking it about . . . and that includes, I'm sorry to say, my husband.'

This phase is sensible self-protection, and it generally lasts for as long as a new mother feels it needs to. However, if she still feels she does not want to be touched *at all* after three or four months and there is nothing causing physical problems such as a sore Caesarean site or a damaged perineum, it may be an idea to try to talk about your feelings a little, perhaps initially by calling up a sympathetic, anonymous professional helpline (see Useful Addresses). Or have a word with your health visitor, GP or midwife, especially if your partner says he is feeling very rejected and excluded. Rejection of sex is not the same as rejection of love, and many men do understand this well; but rejection of touch and affection must seem very close to it if it has been going on a long time.

6. Postnatal depression
Around one in 10 new mothers experiences some degree of postnatal depression after their baby is born (see Postnatal Depression: Breaking Through, page 413) – and so do 50 per cent of the partners of PND mothers, according to Dr Simon Lovestone at the Maudsley Institute of Psychiatry. With sympathetic help, the right treatment and practical backup, the problem can be gone within as little as three months but until this happens, one of the first symptoms of clinical depression is loss of libido.

7. Birth by Caesarean section
It is now very common to have your baby by Caesarean. Rates are at an all-time high (15 per cent) in the UK though the World Health Organization sets the maximum necessary as nearer 10 per cent. Although it is done so often and is very safe it is still a major operation in which both your womb and abdominal wall need to be cut open and carefully restitched, so any insensitive person who suggests you had your baby the easy way does not know what they are talking about.

An elective Caesarean planned well in advance with your full co-operation, for which you have a powerful epidural so you can remain awake and see/hold your baby right away if you want to, with the operation handled sensitively and well by medical staff, can be satisfying and exhilarating. However, an emergency Caesarean perhaps carried out after a painful or tiring trial of labour is not – it can be both pretty alarming and a shock. And while some mothers cope with this pragmatically and calmly as one of those things, it may leave others with many negative feelings to sort through. These can range from acute disappointment, distress, feeling inadequate because they could not give birth to their baby vaginally; anger, denial or a sense of physical and psychological violation. The sense of wanting to keep your body to yourself for a while which many women mention after they have had a baby, may be especially strong for some mothers who gave birth via Caesarean.

These feelings can affect a woman's sexual recovery postpartum just as profoundly as the physical healing of the stitches sites. Loving support and understanding from her partner and friends will help greatly, as may talking through and discussing the delivery itself and the reasons for it. For sympathetic and sensible backup, befriending and advice, you might want to think about contacting the Caesarean Support Network (see Useful Addresses, page 497), or even, if you feel very distressed about the way you had your baby, Birth Crises. If the memory of it continues to cause you sexual difficulties for a long time, a counselling service, such as Relate, may well be able to help you.

One good thing about Caesareans from a sexual point of view is that if you have one planned in advance they do, as one Florida clinic's promotional literature heartily points out, 'keep your tubes honeymoon fresh'. And if you feel like having gentle penetrative sex a few days after the operation, scar discomfort permitting, you can do so without any of the pain around the vagina or perineum which women who gave birth vaginally may feel for a while. However, you will probably still be rather sore and bruised in the area if you had a prolonged trial of ordinary labour.

MEN, BIRTH AND SEX

New fathers' attitudes to sex after the birth of their baby vary enormously. Some demand that they get paid the attention they are used to (whether their partner feels capable of sex or not) as soon as possible, especially if their partner did not want to make love much during her pregnancy or not at all for the last weeks/months. Others find they were so profoundly moved by the birth that they feel closer to their partners and more passionately in love with them than ever, and that they regard the baby as a part of it all. However, talking to a group of men in Camden, London in 1996 whose first baby had been born during the previous three to eight weeks, their reactions were hugely varied, and sounded as if they were going to colour their relationship with their partners for at least a while afterwards, in the same way as their partner's birth experiences were going to affect their relationship with their men.

Some were at the birth fully intending to help, but found they were deeply distressed by it. 'She was in such pain and I could not help her, so I was crying my eyes out,' remembers one. 'I cannot forget the sight of the doctor's hand *up my wife* pulling our baby's head down. I now feel completely different about entering her myself. I can't explain it but it all seems spoilt somehow. I just have to try and forget it but I keep seeing this image in my mind's eye.' 'I couldn't stay – my wife was howling like an animal and there was blood all over the sheets,' remembers another. 'I have never seen anything so amazing in the whole of my life. I even got to cut the cord. It felt like that was what made our baby a separate being from Julie – and that I could reclaim her again. The baby is part of us but I feel Julie and I are truly together again,' says another.

According to natural and water birth pioneer Dr Michel Odent, the belief that men being present at the birth of their baby will make the bonds between them and their partner stronger is nothing but doctrine and theory. 'In practice men find it traumatic, and there is nowhere for their emotions to go.' If men are upset by seeing their wife give birth, and if it does mean problems for them later, they are often made to carry an unfairly heavy burden: 'nowhere to go' is right. Feeling this way is hard enough, but having no one to talk to about it – and they may not want to talk to their partner for fear of upsetting or offending her – is worse.

Part of the trouble is that unlike women, men do not have any informal networks like the ones women form via the National Childbirth Trust or local mothers' and toddlers' group. Nor do they tend to talk to other new fathers about it all, except to joke wryly about the baby having colonized their entire house, sleepless nights and it all costing them a fortune now their partner's not working. They tend not to discuss the completely natural alarm they may feel at the huge responsibility for another human being; their financial worries, about their altered relationship with their partner; or mention it if they feel trapped, though subsequent behaviour ('He's being a right bastard to her') might make the latter obvious. If they are in difficulties they think either it's just them – a fear that a group could have put to rest, and this is one of the biggest pluses of women's support groups – or that it is admitting they cannot cope and are therefore not a proper man, if they try to discuss it.

Fathers and babies
If fathers are also able to be close to their babies and enjoy them, they might not feel nearly so pushed aside because they can be secure in the knowledge that they too have a proper role, a place, they are needed, loved, and involved. Having their own special relationship with their new son or daughter also helps fathers to feel far more relaxed about their partner's very close, sometimes excluding maternal bonding.

New fathers say that these are some of the things which helped them create their own special relationship with their baby:

- Carrying the baby about in a sling, around the house. Or in a front or back pack when going for walks. Babies love the closeness to a calming male presence, and the swaying movement of walking. Sit them right next to you in a buggy or bouncy chair if you are reading, watching TV (without the sound too loud) as they will like being close by you.
- Singing to them. Even if you think your voice is bad, they won't. They will like it because it is yours and you are paying special attention to them. Try nursery rhymes, nonsense songs, humming, bits of rock songs, tell them any poetry you can remember – anything.
- Getting up at least once a night if your baby needs lots of attention then (even if you are working during the day – so's your partner) and give one night feed. Often the last one before adult bedtime may be 11 p.m., and many fathers often like to make that one theirs if they stayed up to work or watch TV or were out earlier with a friend. Cuddle your baby up with you in a shawl close to your own body; sit in a comfortable chair or on the sofa, turn the lights down low, maybe put on some quiet gentle music, and be with your baby while you feed them. There is often a peaceful magic when there are just the two of you in a quiet house or flat, no one around to tell you you are holding the baby wrong or feeding them too

fast, just you and your (hopefully) contented, warm, sleepy baby. Enjoy your private time together.

- 'It's usually still men who make the greater percentage of sexual advances in relationships' says Doria Schmidt, 'and the trouble is that if they stop for a while – perhaps you have a gap for the last few weeks of pregnancy when you felt too cumbersome, and for two or three months after the birth itself – you stop wanting sex. If a man has no desire, his partner usually loses hers too. Couples can literally get out of the habit. If in addition to this the woman is worried about her body after childbirth – Is my vagina larger? Am I still half a stone or more heavier than usual? Does he think I'm fat? What about those stretch marks on my breasts and belly? What about the fact that my breasts, well used for feeding, seem to be drooping? – she thinks her partner will no longer find her sexually attractive, and this in itself is inhibiting. It discourages her from making any sexual advances herself for fear she may be rejected, and if she does not feel attractive, she will not be feeling sexual either.'

The new roles of father and mother
Parenthood can be at odds with your feeling as a sexual person, a lover, not only as a mother. The same can be true for men, what psychologists call the Madonna/Whore syndrome. Sometimes the instinctive reasoning process may be: How can someone want to be a sexual partner (whore) yet be fit to be a mother? If the answer each partner finds is 'You can't', again this causes difficulties. It takes practice to be comfortable in slipping in and out of multiple (often conflicting) roles. Yet this is exactly what women learn to do. They have many roles to fulfil, that of friend, playmate, mother, lover, money-earner, cook, housekeeper, child psychologist, hostess . . . You often dress differently for each one, and behave differently for each one too. Multiple-role assumption is perfectly possible, it can even be stimulating and fun, but it takes time to make the different components all work as a comfortable whole.

What helps couples to get close again?
Most couples will find what works best for them as they go along, but here are some of the options and ideas that new fathers and mothers say they liked best.

- *Talking.*
  Both of you, keep talking as much as you can, whenever you can, about life in general, about what happened to you today, about sex – what it has meant to you up until now, what it feels like for you now, what you are hoping for and what you are worrying about. Talking and sex are both the ultimate forms of communication and if you are sharing one it makes the other, or the possibility of it, easier.

  New mothers need to let their partners know what they feel they can handle, what feels good, what does not and where. Often the first few months after childbirth is one of the few periods that normally reserved women feel they can legitimately use for letting their partners know what they need, because they are actually being asked (possibly for the first time). And if a partner's technique has not been satisfying or what you had really wanted up until now, but you never felt able to tell him for fear of embarrassment or hurting his feelings, you can use the excuse: 'What you were doing before was great, but now because I am still sore/ am taking longer to become aroused/I am a bit nervous/the erogenous zones I get most pleasure from have changed, I think I would like to try such and such instead and see if it helps.'

- *Touching.*
Having children can often show adults that a good deal of the sexual need is a longing to touch lovingly, and to be touched. The first few months after childbirth is a good time to rediscover kissing, stroking, holding, feeling (foreplay – or good old-fashioned snogging) rather than going straight to first base, which may in the past have become a bit of a restrictive habit. If full sexual intercourse is not possible for a while, tenderness and physical intimacy which do not involve genital contact offer a chance to break out of old patterns, which may have become a bit predictable without your realizing it. Try not to compare how often you have ordinary sexual intercourse now with how often you used to before pregnancy – it's not a fair comparison and it's not a very good gauge of emotional closeness either.

    The trouble can be that having a baby around means lovemaking is done with one ear open for crying, with less concentration and more hurriedly because of fear of interruption at any moment. If your baby is rooming in with you, loss of privacy also inhibits desire – yet there are other rooms you can make love in if you wish to.

- *Oral sex.*
This can be intensely erotic, and is far gentler than penetrative sex. If as a new mother you are worried that stitches may have made you appear ugly down there, take a mirror and have a quick look in private. What you will probably see is a healed area, smaller than you'd imagined, barely distinguishable if at all from its surroundings, the usual pink, labia lips folded protectively around the bud of the clitoris and the vagina's entrance. A man giving a woman oral sex is usually tender, and it can be very healing emotionally, as if you are simultaneously stimulating the area sexually – and 'licking it better', as a female animal's mate would with an area that had been hurt. A woman giving her partner fellatio – if she feels she wants to – is something most men love and does not in any way threaten the woman's own still sore genital area, though it can be satisfying for her partner.

- *Manual sex.*
You have far more control over a gently questing finger than over an enthusiastic penis (however careful its owner is trying to be) and because it is also smaller, it is potentially less threatening. If you are worried about having anything inserted into your vagina, let your partner finger the entrance gently until you want him to go further – if you do want this.

If not, do not be afraid to say so, because you have every right – and need – to be calling the shots for a while. You will probably begin to feel both aroused yet increasingly safe as you realize it is not going to hurt you after all. You can also use your own fingers and hands to stimulate your partner's penis as you kiss and caress. Or caress yourself with one hand and your partner with the other. If you feel very nervous of your partner touching you there, ask him just to cup his hands warmly and protectively over the area as this in itself can feel loving, soothing and reassuring – for both of you.

- *Masturbation.*
  Some couples find the idea of masturbation a bit difficult to deal with, feeling that it is traditionally a slightly furtive solo act when you cannot have the real thing. But if you can't have 'the real thing' at the moment, or don't feel ready for it physically or emotionally – why not? Masturbating on your own is, for a woman who has just had a baby and is trying to pluck up the courage to start exploring her own body again, a gentle, arousing way of rediscovering her own sexuality in her own time at very much her own pace, without the additional pressure or downright embarrassment of her partner's presence. It can help you build up your confidence again that you are still a sexual being.

  'Playing with myself reassured me that I could still feel sexual pleasure. Feeling tentatively around down there showed me I had not been mutilated by the birth – like it felt like I had for a while – and that everything was in fact more or less in working order,' remembers one mother whose son is now 11 months old. 'I just didn't feel I could do it with Robert watching, that was all. I was too unsure of what I might find, and it was a sexual self-checkup, an exploration – not an exhibition to turn him on.'

- *Massaging.*
  You do not need to do this any special way, just ask your partner and let him ask you what feels good and where. Just massaging hands, feet and lightly stroking the face feel wonderful and very intimate in a non-confronting way as there are so many nerve endings there, but these areas seldom get paid much attention. Massage provides contact, physical touch and pleasure, and also encourages deep trust and new bonds between new parents. It can be as sexual or non-sexual as you like. Babies love massage too.

- *Three in a bed (one's your baby).*
  Snuggling up in a spoon-shaped heap together or taking a bath all together is a powerful way for fathers, mothers and babies to bond together and feel a part of each other. If you are feeding your baby in bed either by breast or bottle, your partner can snuggle into your back and cuddle both of you gently while this is happening, or he can feed the baby by bottle, tucked in to bed instead of you, or with you there too. Some men want to try the taste of breastmilk out of curiosity, or because they find the idea of suckling on their wife's breasts very arousing. This can be enormously pleasurable for both, but equally one or both parents might be shocked or disgusted by the idea, as it seems very inappropriate to them, or one/

both feel that the breasts of nursing mothers are for babies, not for an adult male partner. Just do whatever feels right to you personally.

- *Talking to other new parents.*

Casual discussions with friends and neighbours about how they survived new parenthood can really take the edge off any needs that are being met at the moment. It also helps take away the 'it's just us' feeling. Other couples also may have some good practical tips and suggestions.

- *Cracking jokes, sharing humour.*

Couples who've developed a strong sense of humour about how the baby seems to be running their lives or how they have little/no time or energy for sex are keeping their lines of communication open and expanding upon them. Making someone laugh can be oddly sexually attractive (several magazine surveys show women especially rating a good sense of humour above sexual athletics and earning power in a man) and it bonds you together – 'us against the rest of the world' – and so helps deepen intimacy at all levels. Sometimes too a sense of humour which is being preserved against all comers is all that stands between you, your partner and either a screaming session or a crying jag. But humour must be gentle, and kindly meant. Barbed remarks that are funny only at someone else's expense, or which are bitter reminders of unmet needs, do not qualify.

- *Ego-boosting.*

New mothers and fathers need their egos stroked as much as, if not more than, their bodily parts,' says William Van Vert (author of *Tales for Expectant Fathers*, Dail Press, 1982). 'A man wants to know he is still virile . . . a woman wants to know she is still seductive, even though she may not think she is or may not choose to act on it. Talking, looking and stroking apply here too.' Both partners need to be appreciated for any efforts they are making in other directions too, whether it's the mother of a seven-week-old baby having somehow cooked a decent meal amidst all the baby chaos for a partner coming home from work; or the new father who just did all the Tesco shopping on the way home from a late evening at the office, or who now makes breakfast in bed for them both every morning. 'You are fabulous' delivered with a large hug, makes up for a lot. Nothing makes you go off your partner faster than feeling unappreciated.

- *Getting time off together.*

Try if you possibly can to make one regular evening – even if it is only every 10 days or two weeks, where you and your partner can *go out somewhere on your own*. Even if all you can afford or have the energy for is a drink in the local pub, or falling asleep together in the cinema because you've had too many broken nights to stay awake. If you can put on a clean shirt, or a spot of make-up and decent outfit respectively, so much the better because it can make you feel more positive about yourself. If not, just drag a brush through your hair, spray on a quick bit of perfume and go out anyway.

Time to be together, not as parents but as people, and as lovers, is vital to any relationship. New parents have multiple roles they may need to be able to play – mother/father/worker/careerperson/mopper-up and nurturer/lover/housekeeper/friend/partner/humorist/date/night nurse/breastfeeder. You can, however, keep most or all of them going if you can just change environments for a little while, now and then. When you are trying to arrange everything to get away it seems like just too much trouble – but when you finally manage it, you realize how good it is to be out on what might legitimately be called a date, again.

Even if you are breastfeeding on demand, you can still get out for an hour or two at a time if you wait as long as you can before the last feed, then encourage your baby to drink as much as possible because they will by now be properly hungry. If you can persuade your baby from an early age to accept perhaps a bottle a day from you or another carer, so much the better as you can put some expressed milk in it or even give a single formula one a day. Breastfeeding purists claim this can produce nipple confusion, when the two different teat shapes so puzzle the baby that it will refuse to feed at all, or affect your milk supply, but once breastfeeding is properly established, in practice this is unusual.

Do you have a mother, sister, good friend or know another mother with a small baby who can help baby-sit just for a couple of hours at a time? If you have a nanny or mother's help already there is no problem (except extra baby-sitting money). Another option is to ask them to come over to the house and look after your baby for a couple of hours either in the house or taking them for a long pram walk if the weather is reasonable, while you and your partner retire for an uninterrupted two hours in bed.

You may well just want to go to sleep sometimes, but knowing you have some guaranteed uninterrupted time ahead may mean you can spend some time making love too if you feel like it. 'It was great – sloping off to bed together in the middle of a Saturday afternoon,' remembers one new mother. 'Sometimes we were so tired we did just cuddle and fall asleep – but not always. It felt naughty, adolescent and indulgent – a bunk-up, in fact – it was a real treat.' If you are worried that this might look bad, just explain to the sitter that you both have had so many interrupted nights that you badly need some sleep, thank her profusely and disappear.

When it's new fathers who don't feel ready

New fathers may have unsortably mixed emotions after the birth of their baby. And while some feel no different at all towards their wives, others may have found that watching the birth was a major shock, or as an article in *Parents* magazine recently put it: 'feel a mixture of awe, disgust – and guilt at having caused this appallingly painful process in the first place; closely followed by a deep secret shame for possessing such parentally incorrect emotions.'

Many men will have felt very distressed to see the woman they love in so much pain yet being powerless to help her, and this can stay with them. According to Zelda West-Meads, formerly of Relate, you can help perhaps not by objecting that they never touch you any more, but try to have a discussion based around feelings rather than sex itself. Something along the lines of, 'The baby and I seem to be getting all the attention at the moment – how are you feeling about everything?' perhaps later moving along to, 'We don't seem to have really made love for a while. That's all right if you don't want to at the moment, but I really miss your hugs,' and take it along from there. Sometimes couples may find it easier to talk things through with a neutral third party there to act as a mediator if things start getting heated. Relate has a UK wide network of counsellors, with fees on a sliding scale based on ability to pay (see Useful Addresses).

USEFUL ADDRESSES

Association for Post-Natal Illness, 25 Jerdan Place, Fulham, London SW16 1BE. Tel: 0171 386 0868.

Information and support network for mothers suffering postnatal illness of any type, and their partners.

The Avon Episiotomy Support Group (now national), c/o Lilah Beecham, PO Box 130, Weston-Super-Mare, Avon BS23 4RH. London organizer: Sally Barrett, Tel: 0181 482 1453.

A support network with newsletter for women who have had problems with episiotomies and tear sites.

Birth Crisis.

A countrywide befriending and counselling network of mothers trained by birth educator Sheila Kitzinger, which helps women who have had distressing experiences of childbirth (no matter how long ago this may have been). Contact is usually by phone, but face-to-face counselling is available too, distance permitting. Contact Sheila Kitzinger, The Manor, Standlake, Witney, Oxford OX8 7RH. Tel: 01865 300266 for a counsellor in your area.

Caesarean Support Network, Yvonne Williams, 55 Cooil Drive, Douglas, Isle of Man. Tel: 01624 661269.

Leaflets, information and support on all aspects of Caesarean delivery, including sexuality.

CRY-SIS, 27 Old Gloucester Street, London WC1N 3XX. Tel: 0171 404 5011.

Tiredness is the factor most often mentioned when new parents are asked what is currently interfering most with their sex life. A high-need, difficult, constantly crying baby is another very common problem. CRY-SIS is a national help and support/advice line for mothers and fathers whose babies cry excessively or sleep very little and who are coming to the end of their tether.

Exploring Parenthood, 4 Ivory Place, 20a Treadgold Street, London W11 4BP. Adviceline: 0171 221 6681.

Advice, education, counselling and a sympathetic listening ear for mothers and fathers on all aspects of parenthood.

The Family Planning Association (FPA), 2–12 Pentonville Road, London N1 9FP. Tel: 0171 837 5432.

La Leche League, BM Box 3424, London WC1N 3XX. Tel: 0171 242 1278.

Advice on all aspects of breastfeeding, including its effects on women's sexuality, and its use as a method of contraception.

The National Childbirth Trust, Alexandra House, Oldham Terrace, London W3 6NH. Tel: 0181 992 8637.

Advice, information and support on all aspects of pregnancy, childbirth and breastfeeding – include postnatal sexuality, and breastfeeding as a method of contraception.

Parents Anonymous. Tel: 0171 268 8918.

Helpline you can call in total confidence for parents with children of all ages, from newborn babies upwards, on any problems involving *any* aspect of parenthood, including sexuality.

Postnatal Contraception – Your Chance to Choose

WHICH CONTRACEPTIVE

You may well be asked about your next choice of contraception a day or so after the birth of your baby, which can seem the height of insensitivity.

The reason for this eagerness on the part of the medical profession to ensure you have a method is that it is possible to become pregnant before your periods resume, and if you are not breastfeeding on demand it is possible (though not usual) to ovulate within a week or two of the birth and conceive within a mere three weeks of delivery. The next time a health professional will have contact with you routinely (apart from the midwife up until your baby is 10 days old, at home) is at your six-week postnatal checkup, and technically you may have become pregnant by then already. The first six to nine months after childbirth is one of the peak times for accidental pregnancies, says Ann Furedi, Director of the Birth Control Trust. 'Many women are unsure about how long it takes their fertility to return, others may be using a new method of contraception (which always takes some time to get used to, especially if it is a barrier method like the diaphragm). And the mere fact of not having had to worry about contraception for at least the past year may mean, for some women, that it is not easy to get back into the habit of it again.'

The following is a brief summary of the contraceptive methods and any special points relevant to new mothers. For fuller information, speak to your local family planning clinics (call up the FPA HQ in London to find your nearest one and its opening times, as clinic times have been cut back savagely over the last few years). Or if your GP has a special certificate in family

---

A chubby woman in perky leisurewear bounced into the ward. 'Hi. My name's Pam. I'm your birth-control adviser. Basically there are three methods I would advise at this stage. The pill, the cap, the –' 'Wait!' I put my hand up like a traffic warden. 'I've just given birth. Do you really think I intend having sex *ever again*?'

Foetal Attraction, Kathy Lette.

planning, which means they have had a certain amount of specialist training in the area, you may like to see them instead, especially if you know and trust them already.

The male condom
Works by acting as a barrier to stop sperm getting into the vagina at all.

Effectiveness: failure rate 2 per cent only with very careful use, but can be as high as 15 per cent. The more practised you and your partner are at using them, the more effective they are at preventing unwanted pregnancy.

User details, such as remembering to squeeze the air from the teat at the end when you put it on, and occasionally checking to see if it is still reaching down to or near to the base of your partner's penis during prolonged or vigorous sex so it does not work its way down and come off inside the vagina, and holding it at the base firmly when withdrawing, are all important to its success.

If you are breastfeeding, but not wishing to rely on this as a means of contraception (perhaps you are also supplementing with bottles), and this has caused temporary dryness in the vaginal and labial tissues, you may have been prescribed some oestrogen cream to rub on the area. This is wonderfully effective for the dryness problem but oestrogen creams destroy the latex rubber condoms are made of, putting you at risk of unwanted pregnancy. You could use KY jelly for temporary lubrication.

Women who have just had a baby may like the idea of using a condom as an interim measure if they feel their hormone levels have still not settled down fully after pregnancy and birth, or that they have but they still feel that it wouldn't take much to destabilize them again. Others feel that after all the medical care, tests, and discomforts of the last few months which arose from becoming pregnant in the first place no matter how welcome this was, that it is their partner's turn to take some responsibility for their sexuality as a couple for a while.

Postnatally some women may take longer to become sexually aroused and to reach orgasm, so the slight desensitizing effect the condom has for the men may be useful. If this is an issue for a couple, the other effective condom-related option is for the man to put some mild anaesthetic 'delay' spray such as Stud (available at chemists next to the condoms) on his penis, slip over a condom to avoid desensitizing his partner, and then be able to make love for longer. As 60 per cent of men climax within two minutes of penetration, this may be a very welcome new initiative for many women.

Family planning clinics supply condoms for free. They have no side effects for a new mother, or her baby if she is breastfeeding.

The combined pill ('The Pill')
Contains both oestrogen and progestogen (artificial progesterone). Works by flattening out the usual regular rises and falls of oestrogen and progesterone in the woman's body, and thus preventing ovulation.

Effectiveness: 98–99 per cent.

The Pill is not recommended if you are worried that you may be developing a measure of postnatal depression or if this happened to you when you last had a baby. Contraception experts have always up until now maintained that the CP is not suitable for breastfeeding mothers either, as it would reduce the supply of milk. However, Ann Furedi suggests that this advice is starting to change, and that as long as breastfeeding is really well established and the baby is suckling strongly and regularly, if a woman would like to use the CP she probably can do without risking her milk supply diminishing.

When to begin taking the CP after childbirth? Technically it's after 21 days. However, if you have always found that you are very susceptible to any hormonal change, had problems for several months when you last went on the Pill, or if you feel that you are only just beginning to get back to near normal after many months of hormonal upheaval (pregnancy, childbirth, perhaps a period of breastfeeding too), perhaps it would be a good idea to wait a few months before starting. Likewise, if you are getting back to normal well, you might also think that you do not really want to tamper with your body's hormonal balance any further until it has completely settled.

If none of the above rings a bell with you, you can begin to take the Pill 21 days after your baby was born.

Note: If you were taking the Pill before you became pregnant, you may find that your old one no longer suits you quite as well as it did, as your hormonal balance and makeup might have changed subtly. See your family planning doctor or clinic to discuss this fully, as you may find that a different type will now suit you better.

The female condom (Femidom)
This acts as a barrier to sperm, like a male condom.

Like a combined loose condom with a flexible ring like diaphragm at the closed upper end, the woman inserts Femidom internally so it lines the vagina, also covering her outer genitalia loosely and protecting her labia. Femidoms are used once and then discarded. They may offer a useful option if the outer labia area is still a bit sore. A Femidom may also be useful if you seem to be prone to infections such as thrush postnatally, which can be encouraged by abrasion, and any semen left in the vagina provides a rich source of nutrients for the fungal infection. However, you may be feeling a bit bruised and sore internally for a while so until this settles down, a Femidom may not be comfortable because of the sizeable flexible ring at its upper end.

Effectiveness: a relatively small British study found the failure rate similar to a male condom. The method needs a bit of practice to get used to, so learning how to put it in correctly (even the manufacturers recommend at least three attempts), avoiding common user pitfalls such as the penis managing to enter the vagina down the side of the condom, and getting used to the slight rustling noise it may make during intercourse, may be the last straw if sex is not easy at the moment and there seems to be little time for it anyway.

Cap or diaphragm, with spermicide

Devices act as a partial physical barrier to sperm and hold the spermicide exactly where it is needed to kill them before they pass through the passage in the cervix and up into the womb.

The two terms are often used interchangeably but strictly speaking caps mean cervical caps, which are small, cannot be felt during sex, and may be left in place for up to 24 hours. They can also be used by women who have weakened vaginal muscles and cannot keep a diaphragm in place. Diaphragms are larger, usually with a springy rim. This can be felt by a male partner during intercourse.

Effectiveness: it depends on how practised you are at using it. It used to be estimated at 2 to 4 per cent, however the most recent review research, carried out in 1994, has put the failure rate up somewhat. Apparently, careful, experienced users can expect between 4 and 8 per cent failure, and 10 to 18 per cent for less careful or experienced users. So if it is very important for you that you have a gap of a year or more to allow you to get your breath back between the recent birth of your baby and the conception of the next, perhaps a diaphragm would not be the best choice.

If you had been using a diaphragm before you became pregnant and wanted to go back to the same method again, it is vital that a family planning expert checks the size which you will now need as after the birth of your child you will probably need a larger size than the one you had before. You need to wait at least six weeks after the birth before having a new fitting as this is the time it generally takes for the area to regain most of its muscle tone. However, because your body's internal contours are still changing slightly even after six weeks, and because you may be continuing to lose weight – and this too affects cap dimensions – it is also important to be rechecked for sizing once again when your baby is about six months old.

If you are not feeling very interested in sex for many months after you have had your baby, again a cap or diaphragm may not be an ideal choice for you as it involves a certain amount of planning ahead to preinsert it, appropriately covered in spermicide gel, just in case you feel like (and find the time to) have intercourse. As one woman put it, 'It was yet another thing I had to do, just in case we might feel like or have the energy to make love. Then I would feel cheated when we didn't.'

The other point to consider is that learning the easiest way for you personally to put in a diaphragm can take practice – some women find they can do it in half a minute or less, for others it may take 20 minutes and several increasingly frustrating attempts. Sometimes this is an additional minus point if you are having to find ways around one or two temporary postnatal sexual difficulties as well. If this is the case, you might want to try an easier method (say, a condom if you and your partner are used to these) until things settle down a bit, then try the diaphragm when you are under less pressure.

Neither the cap nor the diaphragm have any effect on a baby if you are breastfeeding.

One thing that often puts women off using a diaphragm is the traditional advice that you have to put spermicide gel around the rim, inside and out. You don't. Two small strips of spermicide gel on the side facing the cervix should do the trick, or alternatively a piece of spermicide film called C-Film which avoids the mess altogether as it melts later with the heat of your body.

The Progestogen-only pill (Mini Pill)
This stops ovulation for some women, makes it very erratic for others, and also thickens the cervical mucus so sperm cannot get past.

Effectiveness: It has a 0.5 to 4 per cent failure rate.

Breastfeeding women can take this Pill without their milk being affected, and it can be started from 21 days after their baby's birth, though beginning it later at 5 weeks does mean that you may experience less irregular bleeding (one of its usual side effects).

The POP needs to be taken at the same time each day (or at most, within three hours of that time) and this is more difficult if you do not have a fairly organized daytime routine. Usually, though, new mothers are not organized like clockwork as they have, at first at least, to plan their lives around a young baby whose erratic feeding and sleeping habits might make instilling a strict routine difficult, if not downright impossible. Though the POP is a very effective, easy-to-use method you might want to think about waiting until life has settled down a bit before trying it, especially if you are not having intercourse that often anyway for the first three or four months. On the other hand, some new mothers find, because their baby has especially regular, strict feeding patterns they virtually go through each day and night clockwatching, and that because they are so very aware of what time it is at any given moment, it is easy to ensure that their POP is taken, e.g. when their baby has their 9 a.m. feed.

The FPA also warns that the POP may be less effective in women weighing over 11 stone (70 kg). Even if you are not usually this weight you may be for a while if you still have, as many women do for a while, 1 to 1½ stone (6.5–9.5 kg) or so left after pregnancy. It does not help that weight gain can be another of this type of Pill's side effects, as can loss of sex drive.

This Pill is rather under-used, as doctors often forget that it is there, so if you are told 'you can't go on the Pill, you are breastfeeding' ask about the POP.

An ordinary IUD
There is some discussion over how this works. It may act as a foreign body, setting up an inflammatory response from white defence cells in the womb meant to attack the IUD, but which then also target other 'foreign matter' in the area including sperm and egg. Or it may affect the womb lining so that it does not allow implantation of a fertilized egg.

Effectiveness: Ordinary IUDs are pretty effective as they have only a 0.5 per cent to 2 per cent failure rate, dropping even further to 0 to 0.3 per cent after four years of use. Copper wire IUDs last between 5 and 8 years, depending on the make.

If it is especially important for you to be able to have a good space between your new baby and your next pregnancy and you do not want to have to worry about your contraception (if you are planning on having another, that is) IUDs can be a good choice. Though, for many women, IUDs can be uncomfortable to have fitted, but women who have had a baby have less trouble than women who have not.

The new IUD (the Mirena IUS or intrauterine system)

This releases a form of progestogen called levonorgestrel.

How it works: it sets up inflammatory response in the womb lining (see above); thickens the cervical mucus to help stop sperm getting through; makes the womb lining thinner so it's less receptive to a fertilized egg implanting; and prevents ovulation too for a quarter of all women.

Effectiveness: There is a very low failure rate of 0.1 per cent, and the IUD can be left in place for up to seven years. A major improvement over other IUDs which have to be changed more often, tend to make periods heavier and more painful, and carry a small risk of infection, this one actually offers protection against pelvic infection. It also makes periods lighter and less painful, so much so that it has been suggested as a device for women who usually have heavy, painful menstruation.

As many women's periods tend to become heavier/more uncomfortable after their first or second baby, this type of IUD may offer real benefits to new mothers who find they experience these problems. If it is very important to you that you should not become pregnant again for a couple of years or more, this method may also offer especial reassurance.

IUD Note: You will:

- Need to wait about six weeks after the birth before having any type of IUD fitted, as the earlier after the birth it is done, the more chance there is of your womb pushing it back out again. If you are still sore, wait a few more weeks until this has completely settled down. This is because it can be uncomfortable having an IUD inserted at the best of times – but also the newer form of IUD is thicker than the other types which means it can be even less comfortable to have put in. If you have had a Caesarean delivery, it is best to wait three or four months before having an IUD inserted, to make quite sure the incision which was made in your womb has healed completely first.
- If you are breastfeeding, try not to do so for at least three hours before IUD insertion. Breastfeeding makes your womb contract slightly and a smaller uterus is slightly more likely to be damaged when an IUD is inserted. The risk of this is very small, but anything which weights the safety and comfort factors more in your favour is worth doing. If it is possible to give your breastfed baby a bottle for their next feed too (of either expressed or formula milk) this is also a good idea, it stops your womb contracting – something you could do without if an IUD has just been put in an hour or two before, as this might cause you considerable discomfort.

Breastfeeding as contraception

Breastfeeding itself has a contraceptive effect because the milk-stimulating hormone prolactin suppresses your production of oestrogen. Without oestrogen, no egg will ripen and be released for potential fertilization by your ovaries. No egg, no pregnancy.

If you are feeding your baby yourself *on demand or every three to four hours during both day and night* (as many breastfeeding new mothers are) this can prevent unwanted pregnancy for 98 per cent of women. Unfortunately if your baby begins to go longer without needing feeds, or sleep for longer intervals at night, take solids or formula bottles which reduce their demand for breastmilk, the contraceptive effect of breastfeeding starts to drop.

In practice, what many women do is breastfeed fully perhaps for the first two or three months and use this as their contraception too. Then as weaning begins, they choose an additional method of contraception, often a barrier method like a sheath or cap.

Contact The National Childbirth Trust, or La Leche League (see Useful Addresses) for further detailed information and advice about using breastfeeding as an effective contraceptive method.

Implants

They work by thickening the cervical mucus so sperm find it difficult to get past; and by making the womb lining less receptive to a fertilized egg. They may also stop ovulation for some women.

Effectiveness: Failure rate is low (0.2 to 1.6 per cent) but it is not licensed for use for mothers who are breastfeeding.

The only implant available at the moment in the UK is called Norplant. It consists of six small soft tubes of synthetic progestogen inserted in a fan shape under the skin of your inside upper arm. This form of contraception lasts for five years. Technically the implants can be removed at any time but in practice there have been a few problems with this, which could cause difficulties if you only wanted to use the method for a year or two. And many women do want them removed before their 'sell by' date is up. According to the doctors drugs information magazine *Drug & Therapeutics Bulletin* (1994) 10 to 15 per cent of women have Norplant removed after their first year of use and up to half will have had them taken out by the end of five years.

The commonest side effects are irregular bleeding for several months, closely followed by headaches, weight gain and mood swings, which for some women have proved extremely troublesome. The pros of the method for new mothers are that it is very effective and once in place, you do not have to remember to do or take anything else. The cons centre around the occasional problems locating and taking out the hormone-releasing tubes (perhaps one cannot be found, or another will break up) in case you want another baby sooner than you had originally planned – or if Norplant's side effects are causing you problems.

Contraceptive injection

The injection stops ovulation (no egg, no pregnancy) and thickens the mucus which forms a protective barrier across the cervix to help stop sperm getting past.

Injections contain progestogen. The most common type is called Depo-Provera and it lasts for 12 weeks; the other type used is called Noristerat and lasts for eight weeks.

Effectiveness: Their failure rate is very low – 0.1 per cent. Depo-Provera is licensed for use by breastfeeding mothers, but it is suggested that women who are feeding their babies themselves should wait between four and six weeks after their baby's birth to begin with these injections, because bleeding irregularities appear to be more common if you begin sooner. However, it is highly likely that tiny amounts of the artificial progestogen are passing through to the baby via breast milk. And though there is no evidence to suggest this may do any harm, there is none to suggest it has no effect on the baby either. So many mothers choose not to use Depo-Provera while feeding their baby themselves.

The disadvantage of the injections is that if you find you suffer from their side effects (which can include heavy menstrual bleeding, mood swings and weight gain) you have to put up with them for two or three months until the injection has worn off. The other is perhaps that if your body has only just started to settle down hormonally from pregnancy, birth and perhaps a few weeks or months of breastfeeding, you might find even tiny amounts of artificial hormones, such as are in the Pill, POP, injections and implants destabilize your still precariously balanced system again – which some women describe as 'feeling like I have PMS, only all the time.' Some new mothers are more sensitive to hormonal change than others, though, so this may not affect you at all.

Another point which may be especially relevant for women who are establishing their families is that it tends to take about six to 12 months for your fertility to fully return after the last contraceptive injection has worn off, whether you had two or 20; sometimes far longer. So it would not really be suitable for mothers who especially wanted a year or two's spacing between their present baby and their next.

Natural family planning methods

These mean avoiding sex during/around ovulation time.

Effectiveness: Done properly and carefully with no cheating or risk-taking, this can be 97.5 per cent effective.

You need to predict when you are ovulating and avoid unprotected intercourse around that time of the month. Checks include:

- Charting at least six months' worth of your menstrual cycles to see what pattern it formed.
- Temperature-taking as your temperature drops slightly when an egg is released, then becomes higher and stays higher for the rest of the cycle.

- Checking your cervical mucus, which becomes stretchy and clear like egg white around ovulation time.
- About one-third of women experience a mid-cycle ovulation pain on one or other side of their abdomen.

However it is very much a method that a couple does together because you need your partner's full co-operation. Many couples who use this method, and find the eight to 10 days of 'no penetrative sex' – because while eggs live for 24 hours, sperm can live for five or six days – very frustrating and restrictive, opt for using a barrier method such as a condom during these days instead. It is not really suitable for women who have irregular or unpredictable menstrual cycles, so new mothers may have to wait until their menstrual cycle is back to normal after their baby's birth before trying it. It's a method for the well-organized, something which mothers of young babies may not be able to be for a while.

It is not possible for learn natural family planning from a book, though you can find out far more about it from one. Try *Natural Birth Control* by J. and K. Drake, published by Thorsons, or *Natural Family Planning* by Dr Anna Flynn and Melissa Brooks, published by Unwin Hyman. However, if you would like to learn how to use it in detail, it is best to have some training sessions from a specialist counsellor in natural family planning such as at the Natural Family Planning Service. The new Persona kit (£50 from chemists) simplifies the identification of 'safe' and 'no sex' days.

Sterilization
The tubes which carry a fertilized egg to the womb, or those which carry sperm from the testes, are severed or blocked.

Because this is meant to be a permanent method, couples are not encouraged to have it done (either the male or female version) until their last child is about a year old. The reason for this is that though many couples may feel, while struggling to bring up a high-need baby or a baby who doesn't seem to need much sleep, that there is no way they could ever possibly want another child, as things get easier they might feel rather differently. Also, the uncommon but tragic possibility of cot death is another factor against prompt and permanent contraception.

A sterilization carried out on a new mother soon after the birth is also more likely to fail than one which is done a year or so later, because the blood supply to the Fallopian tubes is far greater soon after delivery so there is more of a chance that if severed – which is what is done to them during the operation – they might possibly be able to join up again, rendering you fertile once more. If it is very important, perhaps to protect a woman's health, that a sterilization be performed, it would be safer for her male partner to have one (a vasectomy) as this carries a failure rate of only 0.1 per cent and it is a more minor procedure than for a woman, requiring only local anaesthetics.

Though family planning organizations and surgeons do not usually mention the fact, should circumstances ever change radically, it is often possible

Emergency contraception

If you think that you might be at risk of an unplanned pregnancy because there was a problem with the method of contraception you were using (perhaps a condom slipped off during intercourse) or you forgot to take precautions, contact your GP, local casualty department or family planning clinic as there are two possible ways to prevent a pregnancy occurring:

- Two special high doses of contraceptive hormones (often referred to as the Morning After Pill), taken 12 hours apart, which can be used up to 72 hours after unprotected sex took place. The pills can also make you feel very sick, so take them with some food each time, or with some travel sickness tablets such as Sea Legs. 95 per cent of women who use them avoid pregnancy.
- Fitting an IUD within five days of anticipated ovulation date.

to have a vasectomy reversed successfully. Chances are best up until five years after the original operation, becoming steadily lower as time passes. It is more difficult to reverse a female sterilization, but around one in 30 vasectomies is now undone on request. If an experienced urologist uses microsurgical techniques there is a 40–45 per cent chance of ensuring live sperm return to the male reproductive tubes, but actual pregnancy rates are lower – about 50 to 60 per cent.

Getting the best possible advice

If your family planning advice is being handled at home by your own GP, politely check whether they have the necessary training. Family planning is a specialized area. It is not merely a matter of offering a woman a choice of the three most popular Pills, or an IUD/diaphragm when that particular GP only does a few fittings a year and may not be very practised at it. The more skilled the doctor or nurse, the better your method of contraception is likely to suit you, because any new method you use tends to need some fine-tuning at first.

Special training in the area includes either a Joint Committee on Contraception Certificate, an FPA Certificate, or a Diploma from the Faculty of Family Planning from the Royal College of Obstetricians and Gynaecologists.

If your GP has none of the above, or if they do but you find them rather unhelpful or unsympathetic, ring the FPA (see Useful Addresses) and find the nearest family planning clinic in your area. You can go to them for contraceptive advice, treatment and supplies while continuing to have your own GP care for other aspects of your health.

USEFUL ADDRESSES

Birth Control Trust, 16 Mortimer Street, London W1N 7RD.
Tel: 0171 580 9360.

Provides information on unplanned pregnancy and abortion. Has an advice line (10 a.m. to 3 p.m. weekdays) answering queries on all aspects of contraception; literature on the different methods, a list of the GPs with specialist FP training and family planning clinics countrywide.

La Leche League, BM Box 3424, London WC1N 3XX. Tel: 0171 242 1278.

Advice on all aspects of breastfeeding, including its effects on women's sexuality, and its use as a method of contraception.

National Childbirth Trust, Alexandra House, Oldham Terrace,
London W3 6NH. Tel: 0181 992 8637.

The Natural Family Planning Service, Clitherow House, 1 Blythe Mews,
Blythe Road, London W14 0NW. Tel: 0171 371 1341.

Index